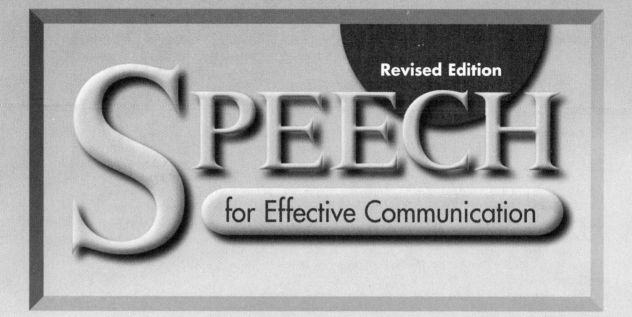

# Revised Edition

# SPEECH

## for Effective Comunication

**Rudolph F. Verderber**

**HOLT, RINEHART AND WINSTON**
*Harcourt Brace & Company*

**Austin** • New York • Orlando • Atlanta • San Francisco • Boston • Dallas • Toronto • London

**Rudolph F. Verderber** (Ph.D., University of Missouri) is a professor and former Head of the Department of Communication at the University of Cincinnati. During his career he has taught speech courses at both the college and high school levels. In addition, he consults with high school teachers and gives workshops for teachers and private organizations. He has served as parliamentarian for state and regional meetings of several national organizations and as Director of Forensics at the University of Cincinnati. His publications include numerous articles; a manual on debate for high school and college courses; and three best-selling college texts covering public speaking, interpersonal communication, and general speech communication skills.

## STAFF CREDITS

*Associate Director:* Mescal Evler

*Editorial Staff: Managing Editor,* Steve Welch; *Assistant Managing Editor,* Amanda F. Beard; *Project Director,* Lynda Abbott; *Project Editor,* Susan Sims Britt; *Editor,* Ed Combs; *Copyediting Supervisor,* Michael Neibergall; *Copyeditors,* Joel Bourgeois, Roger Boylan, Kathy Hoyt, Mary Malone, Barbara Sutherland; *Senior Editorial Coordinator,* Marie Hoffman Price; *Editorial Coordinators,* Susan G. Alexander, Rebecca Bennett; *Support,* Ruth Hooker, Margaret Sanchez, Kelly Keeley, Pat Stover

*Editorial Permissions:* Janet Harrington

*Production: Pre-press,* Beth Prevelige, Simira Davis; *Manufacturing,* Michael Roche

*Book and Media Design: Art Director,* Diane Motz; *Design Manager,* Joe Melomo; *Designer,* Rhonda Holcomb

*Photo Research: Photo Research Manager,* Peggy Cooper; *Assistant Photo Researcher,* Mike Gobbi

## CRITICAL READERS

Grateful acknowledgment is made to the following critical readers who have reviewed materials for this book:

**Suzanne Byrom**
Barboursville High School
Barboursville, West Virginia

**Kathleen L. Kinney**
West High School
Salt Lake City, Utah

**Susan Pundzak**
North High School
Des Moines, Iowa

**Nancy Sprowls**
Brunswick High School
Brunswick, Ohio

**Pamela Cockcroft**
Paris High School
Paris, Illinois

**Sandra Linn**
Huntington East High School
Huntington, West Virginia

**Debarah K. Shoultz**
Columbus High School
Columbus, Indiana

**Craig R. Streff**
Wauwatosa East High School
Wauwatosa, Wisconsin

**Willie Mae Crews**
Birmingham Public Schools
Birmingham, Alabama

**Gretchen Polnac**
Reagan High School
Austin, Texas

**Alease Sims**
Jefferson County School District
Birmingham, Alabama

16   043   09   08                    2008 Printing

# CONTENTS IN BRIEF

# CONTENTS

## UNIT 1:
## The Communication Process

# UNIT 2:
# Interpersonal Relationships

---

# UNIT 3:
# Public Speaking

**CHAPTER 9** **Getting Ready** 215

# UNIT 4:
# Speaking for a Purpose

CHAPTER 14 | Speaking to Inform 355

**CHAPTER 15**  Speaking to Persuade  383

**CHAPTER 16  Speaking for a Special Occasion  417**

# UNIT 5:
# Democratic Processes

# Unit 6:
# Performing Arts

Forward, the Light Brigade!

RESERVED
SEC ROW SEAT
CTR D 21
ADMIT ONE
COMMUNITY
THEATER
PRESENTS

UR TOWN
RDAY
ER 19
.M.

.00
SERVED

CTR
RESERVED
SEC ROW SEAT
D 20
ADMIT ONE
COMMUNITY
THEATER
PRESENTS
OUR TOWN
SATURDAY
DECEMBER 19
8:00 P.M.
$10.00
RESERVED

# Appendix of Speeches

Unit 1

# The Communication Process

Hello

Verbal
MESSAGE
Nonverbal

Sender
Receiver

Receiver
Sender

Verbal
FEEDBACK
Nonverbal

# Understanding Communication

**After studying this chapter, you should be able to**

1. Identify and define the elements of communication.
2. Identify how and why communication skills are important in your own life.
3. Tell the difference between verbal communication and nonverbal communication.
4. Identify and describe various kinds of formal and informal communication settings.
5. List and explain the interrelated steps of the communication process.
6. Explain the qualities that make someone an effective communicator.

## What Is Communication?

You communicate every day, and if you are like most people, you take the process of communication for granted. However, to communicate more effectively, you need to take a closer look at how the communication process works.

**Communication** is the process of sharing information by using symbols to send and receive messages. You communicate when you share thoughts, ideas, and feelings with others. Using a variety of symbols, you probably send messages and receive messages from others, beginning the moment you wake up in the morning and continuing until the moment you fall asleep at night.

Although it is possible to communicate with yourself (see intrapersonal communication, Chapter 5), the type of communication you will primarily study in this book is **interpersonal communication**—communication between two or more people.

# Sending and Receiving Messages

Communication between people always involves sending and receiving a message. A **message** consists of the ideas and the feelings that make up the content of communication. The person who sends the message is called the **sender.** The person who receives the message is called the **receiver.**

To be effective, communication must also include **feedback**— a return message. Notice in the diagram below that the sender and receiver exchange roles, depending on whether the message is being transmitted or feedback is being returned.

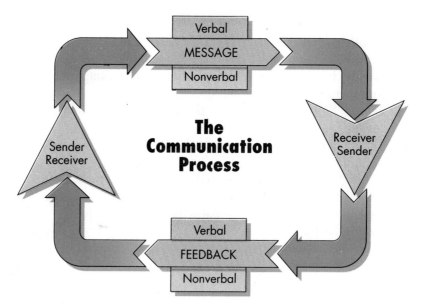

Messages are carried by verbal and nonverbal symbols. **Verbal symbols** are words; **nonverbal symbols** include gestures, facial expressions, and sounds such as laughter, clapping, hissing, and whistling.

All messages are transmitted through **channels,** the means for sending communication. If you use verbal symbols to send a spoken message, the channel is sound waves. If you use nonverbal symbols to send a message, the channel can be sound waves, light waves, or the sense of touch.

To gain a better understanding of the communication process, read the following conversation between Rosalie and her friend Juan about their math assignment. Pay close attention to the verbal as well as the nonverbal portions of the conversation. You will see how the elements of the process work together to create effective communication.

Wrinkling his forehead, Juan worriedly asks, "Rosalie, are we supposed to do *all* of the problems in Part A in the math chapter?"

Calmly placing her hand on Juan's shoulder, Rosalie replies, "No, just the odd-numbered ones." Juan shoots his fist into the air, smiles, and walks toward the bus stop.

The short exchange between Rosalie and Juan shows how the communication process works. First, as the *sender,* Juan uses *verbal and nonverbal symbols* to send his *message* to Rosalie, the *receiver.* The symbols Juan uses are words, facial expressions, and tone of voice. With these symbols, he communicates his message of nervous uncertainty to Rosalie. Because Juan uses both verbal and nonverbal symbols, the message travels through two *channels:* sound waves that can be heard and light waves that can be seen. After Rosalie receives Juan's message, she gives him her response, or *feedback.* To do so, she must exchange communication roles with Juan.

In the second phase, Rosalie becomes the sender. Like Juan, Rosalie uses both verbal and nonverbal symbols to send her message. The symbols she uses are words, tone of voice, and touch. With these symbols, she communicates her message of calm reassurance to Juan. Her symbols also travel through channels: sound waves and the sense of touch. After Juan receives Rosalie's message, he gives her nonverbal feedback in the form of a gesture and a facial expression.

The chart on the following page summarizes the key elements in the communication process.

## The Elements of Communication

| Elements | Definitions | Examples |
|---|---|---|
| **Senders and Receivers** | A person who sends a message is called the sender. A person who receives a message is called the receiver. | When Juan asked Rosalie about the assignment, he *sent* a message. Rosalie *received* the message and *sent* another message (*feedback*) to Juan. They alternated roles as sender and receiver. |
| **Messages** | Messages are the ideas and feelings that make up the content of communication. | Juan sent a message to Rosalie, which expressed his feeling of concern about the math assignment. |
| **Verbal and Nonverbal Symbols** | Verbal symbols are words. Nonverbal symbols (such as gestures, tone of voice, and facial expressions) are messages sent without words. | Rosalie used verbal symbols when she told Juan the correct assignment. She used a nonverbal symbol when she placed her hand on his shoulder. |
| **Channels** | Channels are the sound waves, light waves, and sense of touch by which messages are sent. | Juan's words and tone of voice traveled by means of sound waves. His gestures traveled by means of light waves. Rosalie's feeling of reassurance traveled by means of sense of touch. |
| **Feedback** | Feedback consists of the verbal and nonverbal responses to messages. | After Rosalie received Juan's message, she gave him both verbal and nonverbal feedback. After Rosalie told Juan the correct assignment, he sent feedback that showed his relief; he shot his fist into the air and smiled. |

## Sending Nonverbal Messages

**W**ork with a partner to determine a situation in which you must communicate nonverbally. For example, imagine that you and your partner work part-time in a convenience store. Unknown to your co-worker, your boss has confided in you that she has grown tired of granting favors to her employees. Just as your boss joins you and your co-worker behind the counter, your co-worker whispers to you that he plans to ask for the afternoon off. How would you communicate to him non-verbally that his request is not a good idea? With your partner, make a list of the different ways that you could convey the message. Choose the method that seems the most effective, and practice the scene. Then present it to other members of the class.

# Using Communication

Whether you are passing time with friends, participating in class, helping your brother make dinner, or applying for a job, nearly everything you do involves communication. Communicating with others helps you to satisfy your social needs and to make decisions.

## Meeting Social Needs

All human beings have social needs. We need to love and to be loved, to show feelings, and to interact with others. Through communication, we fulfill these needs.

Communicating helps people to feel good about themselves and about their world. Even greeting strangers on the street can give you pleasure and make you feel like you are a part of the world around you. Communication promotes social cohesion and bonding.

Through words and gestures people communicate that they care about each other. A simple "hello" or "what's happening?" can improve your spirits and give your day a cheerful lift.

Communicating also helps people build and maintain satisfying relationships. When you first meet people, you communicate to find out whether you like the same food, listen to the same music, share political beliefs, and have similar hobbies. If you find that you have much in common and that you enjoy each other's company, you become friends. As you continue to communicate, you deepen or maintain your relationships and often establish lasting friendships.

## Making Decisions

Every day you must make personal decisions. Making many of these decisions involves communicating with others. By talking with other people, you can get information, exchange ideas and feelings, and ultimately decide what actions to take. For example, you might talk with your next-door neighbor about her college experience when you make decisions about your future education. In this conversation you would use communication to help you make a thoughtful and informed decision.

Communicating with others often involves influencing the decisions they make. For example, you might talk to your supervisor about rescheduling your weekend shift because you have tickets to a concert on Saturday night. In this conversation, you would use communication to help you influence the decision making of another person.

**FUNKY WINKERBEAN**                                    **BY TOM BATIUK**

SPEECH I –

THIS COURSE IS OFFERED FOR THOSE STUDENTS WHO PLAN PROFESSIONS REQUIRING GOOD COMMUNICATION SKILLS SUCH AS RADIO, TELEVISION, TEACHING, AND WORKING AT A FAST FOOD DRIVE-THRU WINDOW!

2-14

# Considering Different Settings

A large percentage of your waking hours is spent communicating. This communication takes place in both formal settings and informal settings.

## Communicating in Informal Settings

Most of your communication occurs in **informal settings,** which are casual, unstructured situations. [Informal communication is explored in detail in Chapter 7.] In informal settings, communication is usually spontaneous: You think about what to say as you go along, and then you say it. For example, every day you probably take part in informal communication situations, such as

- talking with family and friends
- introducing people
- giving instructions
- talking on the telephone
- giving and receiving information in class
- asking for directions

*I*n your speech class, one of your goals will be to become aware of yourself as a communicator. One way to do this is to keep a communication journal. Start by recording some instances in which you used communication skills in the ordinary, informal settings that you find in daily life—visiting friends, attending classes, shopping, spending time with your family, walking through your neighborhood. Also record instances in which your communication skills helped you to successfully convey messages. As you jot down these experiences, list one or two reasons why you know that you communicated successfully.

## Communicating in Formal Settings

**Formal settings** are situations that you can prepare for ahead of time. Although much less of your everyday communication may take place in formal settings, these situations allow you to affect the ideas and feelings of people in important positions. The situations described on the following pages are examples of formal settings for speech communication.

**Job and College Interviews.**   An **interview** is a form of communication in which people ask and answer questions. Interviewing is usually a one-on-one form of communication. In a job interview, you may sit with a potential employer and ask and answer questions about your work skills, your ability to get along with others, the responsibilities of the job, and the salary. In a college interview, you may sit with the dean of admissions, who tells you about the college, asks you about your goals and interests, and answers questions about the school's facilities and requirements.

**Group Discussions.**   A **group discussion** is a face-to-face meeting among a small number of people who convey information, express their views, and reach conclusions about particular issues. The more effectively you and the other group members communicate with each other, the more informed your decisions will be. [See Chapter 17 for more about formal methods of problem solving and decision making.]

**Public Speaking.** In **public speaking,** one person addresses an **audience**— the listeners or spectators attending a presentation or a performance—to inform, persuade, or entertain them. In this book, you will learn how to prepare and deliver effective speeches. Most people find speaking in public more difficult than speaking in informal situations or in small groups. Yet public speaking is very important. Many key decisions in our society are made on the basis of what we learn from, and how we are influenced by, public speakers.

**Debate and Parliamentary Procedure.** **Debate** is a formal communication situation in which speakers take opposing sides on an issue and try to prove or disprove a statement about that issue. **Parliamentary procedure** is a set of rules used to conduct orderly meetings. Precise and convincing communication is essential in debating and in conducting meetings that follow parliamentary procedure.

**Interpretive Situations.** **Oral reading** is a performing art in which literature is read aloud and interpreted for an audience. **Drama** is a performing art in which the characters in a play are interpreted and presented by actors on a stage. To present a powerful oral reading or a dramatic performance, you need to give clear and effective verbal and nonverbal messages to your audience.

**Electronic Communication.** **Electronic communication** includes radio, television, and video, three of the most common and influential means of mass communication. [Some of the skills specifically related to radio and television performance are covered in Chapter 22.] Electronic communication provides opportunities for reaching an audience of thousands or even millions at one time.

## Analyzing Formal Communication Situations

Identify two formal communication situations that you take part in during an average week. Remember that you can participate in these situations as a listener or as a speaker. For each situation, identify the elements of communication that seem most important when sending and receiving information. [Review the chart on page 6.] Share your findings with your classmates.

# Developing the Communication Process

The communication process consists of a series of several inter-related steps:

- You find ideas to speak about.
- You adapt your message to the needs of your audience.
- You determine how to present your ideas in the most effective way.
- You interpret audience feedback.
- You deal with verbal and nonverbal interference.

The progression of these steps can vary according to the people involved, the setting, and other circumstances. To some extent, these steps come into play in all communication situations, whether you are talking with one person, participating in a group discussion, or speaking before a large audience.

## Finding Ideas

Finding good ideas to talk about is one key to effective speaking. This step is especially important for occasions such as group discussions and public speaking. When you choose ideas, you will need to consider factors such as your audience, the setting, and the time allotted for your presentation.

You can find many interesting ideas for formal and informal speaking situations by

- examining your own experience
- looking at the lives of the people around you
- watching television shows or movies
- reading newspaper or magazine articles

You can find ideas anywhere, any time. Always be open to new ideas. Jot them down in your journal or make notes on scratch paper.

## Adapting to Your Audience

To communicate effectively, you must adapt to the needs of your audience. Adapting to your audience involves learning something about the people you address. In some formal situations you can learn about your audience before you prepare your speech. However, in many formal and informal settings, you learn about your audience while you communicate with them.

Being aware of cultural, sociological, and individual information about your audience will help you to present thoughts and ideas effectively. These factors will help you to anticipate your audience's response, interpret feedback, and respond to your audience appropriately.

**Individual Characteristics.** When you examine your audience's **individual characteristics,** you look at such things as a person's personality, interests, and aspirations. These items help you to predict how an individual will respond to certain information. The individual level is particularly important to consider in everyday conversation.

EXAMPLE: If you are speaking to a classmate who is the photographer for the school newspaper, you can assume that she'll understand an anecdote about a single-lens reflex. However, if you want to tell the same story to someone who knows nothing about photography, you may have to begin by explaining that a single-lens reflex is a type of camera.

**Cultural Characteristics.** When you examine your audience's **cultural characteristics,** you look at such things as age, religion, and national and ethnic background. This helps you to focus your presentation in such a way that your audience will understand and respond favorably to your message.

EXAMPLE: When Robin presented a speech to the prom committee, she knew that several members in the group had recently immigrated from Korea and the Philippines, where proms are not a part of high school culture. Before she discussed the prom theme, she explained its importance and gave examples of prom themes used in previous years.

**Sociological Characteristics.** When you examine your audience's **sociological characteristics,** you look at elements such as their affiliations, their educational backgrounds, and their occupations. Based on what you discover, you can formulate some general ideas about your listeners.

EXAMPLE: When Tony prepared a speech about the powwow at the Taos Pueblo, he knew he would be addressing a group of craftspeople. For this reason he focused his presentation on the dancers' elaborate costumes. Last year, when he was asked to speak to a group of third-graders, he discussed the dances that the children perform during the pow-wow competitions. By adapting his speeches to his audiences' professions and ages, he selected topics that would attract their attention and hold their interest.

## Encoding and Decoding Information

To communicate successfully, you must decide how to send and interpret messages. This process involves encoding and decoding information.

**Encoding.** The process of turning ideas and feelings into verbal and nonverbal symbols is called **encoding.** In a formal situation, you take time to plan how you want to state a certain idea. For a speech, you may even try two or three ways of stating an idea before you select the best way to present it to a particular audience. Informal speaking is quite different. In informal conversations, the encoding process is nearly instantaneous.

**EXAMPLE:** If you want salt on your tomatoes, you ask the person next to you to pass the saltshaker. You don't stop and think, "How can I get someone to move the salt closer to me?" You automatically encode your needs into words.

Encoding is not just a matter of verbal communication. At the same time that you verbalize, you almost always send nonverbal messages that affect the receiver's response. The various ways that are possible to combine verbal and nonverbal symbols are almost limitless.

**Decoding.** For communication to be complete, a receiver must decode a message. **Decoding** is finding the meaning of verbal and nonverbal symbols.

In conversation, the decoding process is usually instantaneous. A split second after you ask for the salt, someone is likely to pass it to you. However, in formal and some informal situations, the receiver may need to translate messages into meanings that make sense in their given context.

**EXAMPLE:** If you just left a chemistry lab, you may decide to say, "Sylvia, please pass the sodium chloride." Upon receiving this message, your classmate may look at you with a puzzled expression and say, "The *what?*" A few seconds later, she may answer, "Oh, the sodium chloride—the salt—sure." Sylvia, your receiver, would have completed the decoding process, having translated the chemical name for salt from a meaning that made sense in the chemistry lab into a meaning that made sense in the lunchroom.

To a large extent, the words and nonverbal symbols you use in communication depend on your understanding of the needs and abilities of your audience. To encode and decode messages clearly, you will want to consider the individual, cultural, and sociological characteristics of your receiver or sender.

## Interpreting Feedback

In conversation we expect others to talk with us. In other words, we expect people to respond to our messages with feedback that expresses what they think, feel, and observe. In public situations, audience responses are generally nonverbal. People clap to show approval, yawn to show boredom, and sometimes actually stand up and leave the room to show disapproval.

In both formal and informal settings, the more you know about your audience, the better able you will be to recognize and interpret the verbal or nonverbal feedback you receive.

## ACTIVITY 3

### Analyzing Nonverbal Feedback

Think of three nonverbal messages that you received today. Then draw cartoons that illustrate each one. Beneath each cartoon, jot down a caption that explains the nonverbal message. For example, you might draw a shopper waving at you as he scurries in front of your car to get to the store. Beneath the drawing, you could write, "A shopper waves to tell me that he appreciates my stopping to let him cross the street." When you complete your cartoons, share them with your classmates.

## Dealing with Interference

**Interference** is anything that gets in the way of clear communication. In formal and informal situations, three common types of interference are *physical noise, psychological noise,* and *semantic noise.*

**Physical Noise.** **Physical noise** consists of any sound that prevents a person from being heard. Physical noise interferes with a speaker's ability to send messages and with an audience's ability to receive them.

> **EXAMPLE:** When you are giving a speech or acting in a play, people in the audience might interfere with whispers or cheers. Or you could be in the midst of a conversation on a crowded street, and passing cars might make it difficult for you to hear your friend's comments.

**Psychological Noise.** The thoughts and feelings that distract people from listening to what is said are called **psychological noise.** Psychological noise interferes with the audience's concentration and ability to hear a speaker's presentation.

**EXAMPLE:** Members of an audience may not pay attention to a speaker because they are absorbed in their own thoughts. One person may be thinking about an idea for a poem, while another is worried about how much homework she has to do, and a third is dreaming of his date for Friday night.

**Semantic Noise.** The interference caused by words that trigger strong negative feelings against the speaker or the content of the speech is called **semantic noise.** Semantic noise leads to misunderstanding, as well as unpleasant and distracting nonverbal feedback from the audience.

**EXAMPLE:** An audience of classmates might agree with you if you called your town "a dreary place." However, they might stop listening to you if you began calling the town "a dump."

# ACTIVITY 4

## Dealing with Interference

With three or four classmates, read the following situations and identify the type of interference represented. Decide how you would deal with the interference if you were the speaker. Then take turns being the speaker, and act out each situation. After the performances, discuss whether your attempts to deal with the interference were successful.

1. You and a friend are discussing a problem. Three people at the other side of the room begin to talk so loudly that you cannot concentrate on what your friend is saying.
2. You are leading a group discussion. One of your group members is staring out the window, and another is doodling.
3. You are giving a report to your history class. The lights are making a very loud buzzing noise.
4. You are acting in a play. Suddenly a storm strikes, and thunder drowns out your words.
5. You are giving a speech to an audience of city council members. You mention the recreation center's "stupid, boring weekend dances," and a buzz goes up from the audience.

# Communicating Effectively

In this chapter you have looked at the key elements, functions, and steps of the communication process. The guidelines on the next page provide suggestions that will help you to become a more effective communicator.

1. **Care about your communication success.** Most of your communication has a purpose or goal. Whether that purpose is to transmit information, to change people's minds, or to greet a friend, your effectiveness will depend on others' believing that you really care about them and that you care about what you are saying to them.

2. **Know what you are talking about.** People are likely to pay attention to someone who has the facts, who is knowledgeable about the given subject, and who clearly understands the situation. To grab your audience's attention and to convey the importance of your topic and your opinions, express your ideas and opinions with wisdom and authority.

3. **Be organized.** When people cannot follow what a speaker says, they lose interest and patience quickly. By organizing your ideas, you allow your audience to understand, quickly and easily, the information that you communicate.

4. **Use language well.** People enjoy listening to a speaker who has a skillful command of language. To communicate effectively, choose your words carefully and put them together in a lively and powerful manner.

5. **Use effective nonverbal signals.** The more effectively you use nonverbal behavior, the more powerful your presentation will be. Your use of gestures, facial expressions, body movement, and tone of voice will reinforce your communications.

6. **Listen carefully.** Sometimes the best communicators are those who are good listeners. By listening carefully, you can learn more and therefore respond appropriately to your audience. Effective listening will enable you to identify when your audience is not receiving your message. It will also help you to determine better ways to communicate your message to your audience.

## GUIDELINES

### for Effective Communicating

- Do I care about the success of my communication?
- Do I know what I am talking about?
- Are my thoughts well organized?
- Have I selected my words carefully?
- Do I use effective nonverbal signals?
- Do I listen carefully to others?

# PROVIDING INFORMATION

### Serving the Public

Travel counselors constantly rely on their communication skills. They speak to others almost nonstop—on the telephone, across their desks, around the conference table, and from the podium.

### Characteristics of a Travel Counselor

A travel counselor is responsible for providing the general public with accurate and helpful information on a variety of general or specific topics. A travel counselor

**1** helps members of the public to identify the information they want or need to know

**2** provides, if possible, the information requested

**3** informs the person requesting information if it is unavailable or if access to it is restricted

**M**eet the Travel Counselor

Mary Jackson is a travel counselor at a State Department of Transportation. Her job involves giving people information about restaurants, lodgings, tourist attractions, and parks throughout the state. "I enjoy helping people," says Ms. Jackson, "and it makes me feel good to know that they'll enjoy discovering many of our state's wonderful attractions."

*Mary Jackson*

## ACTIVITY

### Situation

You have a summer job at a travel information center. A family, exhausted from driving all day, asks you for a restaurant recommendation.

### Preparation

Consider what questions you could ask the family to identify specific types of food they would like to eat, a price range, and so on. If you are not already familiar with restaurants in your area, check the Yellow Pages for names of restaurants and the types of food they serve.

### Analysis and Assessment

Write a dialogue in script form showing how you will respond to the family's request. With a classmate or two, perform your scene in class. Remember that your main purpose is to be a helpful and friendly communicator. Ask your classmates to critique your effectiveness.

# S•U•M•M•A•R•Y

**UNDERSTANDING COMMUNICATION** means being aware of elements in the process by which you share thoughts, ideas, and feelings with others.

- **Send and receive messages** by using symbols to create messages. Messages, which may be made up of verbal or nonverbal symbols, are transmitted through channels. The communication process involves continuous interchange, starting with a sender who communicates a message to a receiver. The receiver responds by sending feedback.

- **Use communication** as an important part of almost every activity of your daily life. Communication is used by most people to help them meet social needs and to help them make decisions.

- **Consider different settings** that may affect the process of communicating. Communication in informal settings is usually casual and unstructured; communication in formal settings is usually planned in advance.

- **Develop the communication process** in your own speaking as you increase your speaking skills. Begin with an idea; adapt your idea to suit the characteristics of your audience; communicate your idea to others by encoding and decoding information; then interpret and respond to your audience's feedback. Deal appropriately with interference.

- **Communicate effectively** by caring about how well you communicate to others, and by knowing your subject, organizing your ideas, using language well, using effective nonverbal behavior, and being a good listener.

## Vocabulary

Look through this chapter to find the meaning of each of the following words. Write each term and its meaning in your communication journal.

audience, *p. 11*
channels, *p. 4*
communication, *p. 3*
cultural
 characteristics, *p. 14*
debate, *p. 11*
decoding, *p. 16*
drama, *p. 11*
electronic
 communication, *p. 12*
encoding, *p. 15*
feedback, *p. 4*
formal settings, *p. 9*
group discussion, *p. 10*
individual
 characteristics, *p. 14*
informal settings, *p. 9*
interference, *p. 17*
interpersonal
 communication, *p. 3*
interview, *p. 10*
message, *p. 4*
nonverbal symbols, *p. 4*
oral reading, *p. 11*
parliamentary
 procedure, *p. 11*
physical noise, *p. 17*
psychological noise,
 *p. 17*
public speaking, *p. 11*
receiver, *p. 4*
semantic noise, *p. 18*
sender, *p. 4*
sociological
 characteristics, *p. 14*
verbal symbols, *p. 4*

# Review Questions

1. What is meant by the term *communication*?
2. The communication process involves six key elements. One of these is the *message*. What are the other five?
3. How does nonverbal communication differ from verbal communication?
4. To a large extent, verbal messages are sent through the air by sound waves. What channel or channels are used to send nonverbal messages?
5. Imagine that two people are having a conversation. What role does *feedback* play in ensuring that effective communication takes place?
6. What are some of the settings in which formal communication takes place?
7. Regardless of the type of communication, a speaker must always *find ideas* to communicate. What are the other steps of the communication process?
8. Why is it important to have information about an audience? What three kinds of information is it important to have?
9. What is interference? What are the three types of interference?
10. What are the six characteristics of an effective communicator?

# Discussion Questions

1. Your friend Jan says, "Getting that grade on my project really made my day!" What she means depends not only on her words but also on the way she says those words. Discuss how a listener could interpret Jan's words depending on *how* Jan says them.
2. Discuss the meaning of the following statement: Human beings are always communicating, whether they are conscious of it or not. Do you agree or disagree with this statement?
3. You are to give a speech in support of a political candidate. Discuss the ways in which your knowledge of your audience would affect what you would say and how you would say it. For example, how would a speech given to a group belonging to the same political party as your candidate differ from a speech given to a group that belongs to another political party?
4. Ralph Waldo Emerson once wrote: "All persons are puzzles until at last we find in some word or act the key to the man, to the woman; straightway all their past words and actions lie in light before us." First, discuss the meaning of this quotation. Then, discuss how this quotation relates to the encoding-decoding process.
5. Many wonderful opportunities await you in the near future. You are likely to play the role of college student, employee, boss, and possibly mother or father. Discuss how communication skills will help you to make the most of these roles.

# ACTIVITIES

1. **Identifying Occupational Uses of Communication Skills.** Conduct a survey to find out your classmates' future plans. Then list the occupations that they intend to pursue. Under each occupation, jot down how communication skills will be an effective tool for advancement. For example, a nurse would need good communication skills to understand patients' needs and to tell them about proposed methods of treatment. When you complete your list, share it with your classmates.

2. **Interpreting Nonverbal Communication in Television Programs.**
   A. Watch a television interview show. Make a list of the ways in which people communicate nonverbally during one conversation. Share your list with your classmates.
   B. Watch a television program with the sound off. How much of the story are you able to follow? What nonverbal symbols help you to follow this much of the story? Share your findings with your classmates.
   C. A television advertiser has only fifteen to thirty seconds to communicate a message. Therefore, every second has to count. Watch several television advertisements. How does the level of nonverbal communication in the advertisements compare with that in regular programming? Are there more or fewer gestures and facial expressions? How forceful or dramatic are these gestures and expressions? Share your comparison with your classmates.

3. **Analyzing an Audience.** In the following photographs, identify specific interests or experiences a speaker could assume audience members might have in common. What visual clues give you this impression?

How serious is each audience? List ways that a speaker might adapt a message to each of these audiences.

# CHAPTER 1

**4. Creating and Analyzing a Dialogue.** Working with a partner, write a brief dialogue. Your dialogue might be humorous or serious, informative or persuasive. Using a chart like the one on page 6, analyze the key elements of your dialogue. Examine the changing roles of the sender and the receiver, and practice encoding and decoding nonverbal symbols.

**5. Learning About Manual Communication.** Interview, or if possible invite to your class, a person skilled in sign language. A speech pathologist or a sign language instructor from a local university or community college would likely be willing to demonstrate and explain sign language and to teach you some common signs.

**6. Identifying Learning Goals in a Speech Class.** With a group of four or five classmates, develop a list of goals that you hope to achieve this year. Then discuss what you expect to learn from pursuing these goals. After fifteen minutes, share your list with the class.

**7. Diagraming Messages.** Review the diagram of the communication process on page 4. Then, using this format, diagram four messages that you sent or received today. In the diagrams, identify the sender and the receiver. Write brief summaries of the messages and feedback.

**8. Analyzing Feedback.**
  **A.** Prepare a short message. Deliver exactly the same message to five different people. Then tell your class how the feedback you received differed from person to person.
  **B.** In addition to acting as a sender of messages, you also act as a receiver. Report to your class on the feedback you gave to five different messages today.

**9. Inventing Nonverbal Symbols.** The following illustrations show some common nonverbal symbols. Do you know what each of these symbols means?

Now, invent five nonverbal symbols of your own. These symbols can include gestures, pictures, and colors. When you have finished, take turns showing or demonstrating your symbols to a partner. How effective are your symbols? Is your partner able to decode them correctly?

# EVERYDAY COMMUNICATION

### Situation

You have just won an important prize. The prize could be first place in a writing contest, a blue ribbon in photography, a sports trophy, or any other prize you can think of.

### Problem

You have been asked to give an acceptance speech in which you describe the prize, the events that led to your winning it, and how it felt to win.

### Assessing Your Skill

Write a one- or two-page acceptance speech. Be sure your speech includes what you won, how you won it, and what you thought when you won. When you finish, practice reading your speech out loud. Then read the speech to your classmates and ask for feedback about how effectively you expressed these ideas.

# COMMUNICATION IN THE WORKPLACE

### Background

Police officers call on their public-speaking skills many times a day. However, what they say and how they say it are likely to be different when they are issuing a speeding ticket than when they are making a public-service announcement on television.

### Preparing to Do the Job

You are a police officer. In one or two pages, write a description of what you might say in two different public-speaking situations, such as addressing a middle school assembly or comforting an elderly person who has broken an ankle in a fall from a sidewalk.

### Testing Your Skill

Each of your two descriptions should reflect the audience addressed. Read both descriptions to your classmates and ask what differences they noticed in your word choice, tone, and nonverbal behavior.

A

B

C

**pitch**

**pitch** (pich) *v.* **1.** to throw or toss **2.** to set up or erect [*pitch* camp]
**3.** to fall, plunge, or lurch forward **4.** *slang* to sell, promote, or
advertise [*pitch* a product] **5.** *Baseball* (*a*) to throw the ball to the
batter (*b*) to serve as pitcher for a game **6.** *Music* to assign the
pitch or key of a musical work or instrument
**pitch·er** (pich´ər) *n.* **1.** a container (usually with a handle and lip)
for holding and pouring liquids **2.** a person who pitches;
a pitches the ball to the opposing batters

# 2

# Sending Verbal and Nonverbal Messages

**OBJECTIVES**

**After studying this chapter, you should be able to**

1. Explain the differences between verbal and nonverbal language.
2. Identify and explain five characteristics of verbal language.
3. Define *denotation* and *connotation* and explain how they affect communication.
4. Explain the appropriate use of standard American English, jargon, slang, and dialect.
5. Explain how body language, appearance, paralanguage, and environment affect communication.

## What Are Messages?

**Messages** are ideas and feelings that people send or receive when they communicate. People use words to send messages back and forth, but verbal language is not the only way to communicate. When you speak, for example, your listener gets messages not only from what you say but also from how you look and act.

How important is this nonverbal language? In your everyday communication, 50 to 90 percent of the messages you send are nonverbal. Sometimes, however, the verbal and nonverbal messages contradict each other and create confusion.

In this chapter, you will study the relationship between verbal and nonverbal messages and will explore some of the ways that this relationship affects communication.

# Comparing Verbal Language and Nonverbal Language

People send and receive messages by using verbal and nonverbal language. **Verbal language** is a system of spoken and written words. **Nonverbal language** is communication without words. Body language, appearance, and the sound of the voice are the **cues,** or signals, of nonverbal communication. Nonverbal language serves four functions:

- to complement (agree with) verbal messages
- to emphasize verbal messages
- to replace verbal messages
- to contradict verbal messages

## Interaction of Verbal and Nonverbal Language

| Verbal Message | Nonverbal Cues | Function |
|---|---|---|
| "That's hilarious." | smiling, laughing | complements verbal message |
| "Do it now!" | pounding on desk | emphasizes verbal message |
| No verbal answer (in response to the question "Did you get tickets?") | nodding or shaking your head | replaces verbal message |
| "Great haircut you got there." | spoken in an unfriendly tone of voice | contradicts verbal message |

ACTIVITY 1

## Exploring the Effects of Verbal and Nonverbal Messages

Think of a short verbal message to send to a partner. For example, "I've got to leave now," "Where did you get that sweater?" or "Please don't say that." Express the same message verbally three times. However, each time you repeat the words, change your nonverbal cues to convey a different function or meaning.

# Understanding Verbal Language

## Analyzing Language

Verbal language is a system of sounds and symbols used to communicate ideas and feelings. Verbal language has five important features:

1. **Language Is a System.** A **system** is a group of elements that work together. A language system consists of three subsystems—sounds, words, and the way these sounds and words are arranged. All three must be blended together to make a language.

The chart above shows symbols from several language systems:
  I. Clog Almanac
 II. Egyptian Hieroglyphic Letters
III. Phonetic Languages of Asia
   a. Sanskrit
   b. Hebrew
   c. Samaritan
   d. Syriac
   e. Syrio-Chaldaic
   f. Arabic
IV. Phoenician and Egyptian Writing
   g. Moabite Stone
   h. Rosetta Stone
 V. Chinese Ideographic Writing

2. **Language Is Symbolic.** A **symbol** is something that stands for something else. Words are symbols for ideas, actions, objects, and feelings. For example, *car* is a word that stands for something you drive. The word *car,* of course, is not the object. It represents the object.

3. **Language Is Conventional.** **Conventional** means "accepted by a large number of people." Speakers of English have accepted the word *pen* or *pencil* to stand for a particular object that you write with. If you call a pen a *gork,* other people will not know what you are talking about. Words in a language communicate meaning because the large numbers of people who use that language recognize specific meanings for specific words.

4. **Language Is Learned.** Children learn the language of their culture. The process of learning language follows general principles.

- Children learn symbolic meanings first. For example, children quickly learn short words like *yes* and *no*. In addition, children learn specific words like *mama*, *daddy*, and *milk* before learning general words like *parents* and *food* or abstract words like *love* and *hunger*.
- Once children learn a rule of language, they often **generalize** that rule, applying it to all cases, including some to which the rule does not apply. For example, after learning to form the past tense by adding *–ed* to verbs, children often add *–ed* to all verbs. They will say, "She drinked her milk."
- Children understand more symbols than they use. For example, hearing the sentence "Paul was *imbued* with the qualities of goodness and kindness," a child might know that *imbued* means "filled." However, the child might not feel comfortable using the word *imbued*.

5. **Language Changes.** The English language is constantly changing. The meanings of words change, new meanings are given to words, and new words are added. However, these changes usually occur slowly enough so that most speakers of the language can adapt to the changes as they occur. Building a broad, effective vocabulary is important, because the more words you know and use, the better you will be at communicating both spoken and written messages.

## Common Ways That Language Changes

| Sources of Change | Examples |
|---|---|
| Words come from other languages. | Spanish: *canyon, tornado*<br>Native American: *raccoon, persimmon*<br>Chinese: *typhoon, ketchup* |
| Whole words are put together to create new meanings. | *busybody, downfall, lifesaving, videotape, skateboard* |
| Words are blended to create new meanings. | *smoke + fog = smog*<br>*motor + hotel = motel* |
| New words are needed for new objects and ideas. | *microchip, artificial intelligence, ethanol, laser, killer bees* |
| Meanings of words change. | meanings of *nice* over six hundred years: "foolish," "strange," "lazy," "modest," "precise," "dainty," and "pleasant" |

**Computer** (kǒmpiū'təɹ). Also **-or**. [f. COM-
PUTE *v.* + -ER¹.] One who computes; a calcu-
lator, reckoner; *spec.* a person employed to make
calculations in an observatory, in surveying, etc.
**1646** SIR T. BROWNE *Pseud. Ep.* VI. vi. 289 The Calenders
of these computers. **1704** SWIFT *T. Tub* vii, A very skilful
computer. **1744** WALPOLE *Lett. H. Mann* 18 June, Told by
some nice computors of national glory. **1855** BREWSTER
*Newton* II. xviii. 162 To pay the expenses of a computer
for reducing his observations.

*The Oxford English Dictionary* identifies the
approximate date of a word's first
appearance in English and shows, in
a quotation, the way the word was
spelled and used at that time.

# A·C·T·I·V·I·TY
## 2  Exploring the Meanings of Words

**I**n a group with two or three other students, choose one of the following words.
Discuss what you think the word means until your group can agree on a definition. Then check a dictionary with etymologies and identify the meaning of the
original root words. Describe briefly how the meaning of the word has changed
over time. Share your group's findings with the rest of the class.

| | | | | |
|---|---|---|---|---|
| amuse | fond | hobby | October | stew |
| bread | forlorn | nice | silly | temper |

## Understanding Shades of Meaning

To communicate well, you need to keep in mind that words may
have a variety of meanings, some of which are not immediately
apparent. These hidden meanings of words may have a great effect
on your ability to convey the message you intend. Meaning is communicated through both a word's denotation and its connotation.

**Denotation.**   The **denotation** of a word is its dictionary meaning.
The same word may have several different denotations.

> **EXAMPLE:** One denotation for the word *quarter* is "one fourth
> of a unit of measure, such as a dollar." Another denotation for
> *quarter* is "an area or section of a city." Still another denotation
> of *quarter* is "the compassionate treatment given to an enemy
> who surrenders."

**Connotation.**   The **connotation** of a word is its hidden meaning, the often powerful feelings and associations that the word arouses. The feelings that you have about a word may depend on the experiences you have had.

EXAMPLE: If you have had pleasant experiences with dogs, the word *dog* may give you feelings of love, warmth, and security. If a dog has chased you or bitten you, however, the word *dog* might give you feelings of fear and hostility.

Good communicators choose words that lead an audience to make certain associations. Advertisers, for instance, sell their products with words that are likely to have positive connotations. You can make the connotations of words work for you by becoming sensitive to the reactions words arouse.

EXAMPLES:
1. Positive connotation: handsome, natural, healthy
2. Negative connotation: rat, pain, decay, foul
3. Neutral connotation: table, number, paragraph, exterior

PEANUTS reprinted by permission of UFS, Inc.

# A·C·T·I·V·ITY 3

## Identifying Positive and Negative Connotations in Advertising

Tape-record and listen to three different commercials from television or from the radio. On a sheet of paper, make two lists for each commercial. In one list, write the words that the advertisers have used to arouse the audience's positive feelings toward the products or services. In the other list, note any words the advertisers have used to arouse their listeners' negative feelings toward competitors' products or services or toward consequences that may follow from a listener's failure to use whatever the advertisers are promoting. Share your findings with your classmates.

## Adapting Language to Specific Situations

Speakers adapt their language to fit the situation, or setting. You probably would speak one way to the person who interviews you for a job, and another way to your friends at a basketball game. In formal situations you would use standard American English. However, in informal situations, you might relax the rules and conventions.

**Standard American English.**   **Standard American English** is language that follows the rules and guidelines found in grammar and composition books. These rules and guidelines cover topics such as agreement of subject and verb, correct use of tenses, and avoidance of double negatives. Because standard American English is widely used and accepted, it allows people from many different regions and cultures to communicate clearly with one another. [For more about the use of standard American English, see pages 289–299.]

**Jargon, Slang, and Dialect.**   Jargon, slang, and dialect are all sublanguages. A **sublanguage** is a subsystem of an established language. **Jargon** is the specialized vocabulary that is understood by people in a particular group or field. **Slang** consists of recently coined words or old words used in new ways. As a sublanguage that is usually limited to a particular time period, slang starts within a group—such as teenagers or rock musicians. It often spreads quickly to the general population and just as quickly begins to sound old and dated. A **dialect** is a regional or cultural variety of language differing from standard American English in pronunciation, grammar, or word choice.

| Sublanguages | | | |
|---|---|---|---|
| **Type** | **Examples** | **Appropriate Use** | **Inappropriate Use** |
| **Jargon** | • television: *sound-bite, anchor, talking head*<br>• football: *punt, nose guard, goal* | when speaking to people in a particular group or field that uses that jargon | when speaking outside the particular group that uses that jargon |
| **Slang** | • newly coined words: *nerd, hassle, bummer*<br>• old words used in new ways: *awesome, hot, cool, dude* | when speaking in informal situations | when speaking for formal occasions |
| **Dialect** | • pronunciation: *greassy/greazy* or *hog/hawg*<br>• grammar: *you/youse/ you'uns/y'all* or "He don't care."<br>• word choice: *pail/bucket* or *flapjack/pancake* | when communicating with others who use that dialect | when speaking for formal occasions |

# A·C·T·I·V·I·T·Y
## 4    Analyzing Slang

**W**orking in a small group, draw up a list of ten slang expressions that you hear at your school. Then ask your parents or grandparents for five slang expressions that they used when they were in school. Share your group's findings with the class. Then, working with the whole class, compile two new lists, one of common slang expressions popular today and one of common slang expressions from the past. What expressions appear on both lists? What conclusions about the times can you draw from these lists?

**Sharing Language with Your Audience.**   Language is a powerful tool. In choosing what to say and how to say it, concentrate on the expectations and limitations of your audience. The less well you know people, the more important your words become in establishing shared meanings and understanding. Learn to use language carefully to improve your effectiveness as a speaker.

# HOW TO > Use Language to Present the Best Possible You

1. **Use words carefully.** If you are not sure of the meaning of a word, look it up in a dictionary before you use the word in speaking or writing.

2. **Understand the connotations of words.** Know not only what a word means, but also what it suggests—the feelings and associations it arouses. Use words that will get the reactions you want from your listeners.

3. **Use language that is appropriate to the communication setting.** Know and respond to the expectations of your audience. In formal settings, use standard American English. In professional or occupational settings, you may use jargon when your listeners understand it. In informal settings, slang and dialect may be more appropriate than standard American English.

4. **Improve your language.** Use your ears and eyes to study the way effective speakers and writers communicate. Listen carefully, read as much as you can, and write!

𝒮et aside several pages in your journal to take notes about the methods effective speakers use. Whenever a guest speaker, a newscaster on television, a teacher, or a friend impresses you with his or her speaking ability, try to determine why the speech is effective. Is it the speaker's delivery? the choice of words? the body language?

𝒞OMMUNICATION JOURNAL

# Understanding Nonverbal Language

Nonverbal language uses all the elements of communication except words. Instead, a person using nonverbal language conveys messages through signals called cues—body language, appearance, and vocal sounds. Other people interpret these signals as indicating particular meanings. Since nonverbal messages often accompany verbal messages, they tend to have one of the following effects on the verbal message: They may complement or reinforce the verbal message, they may emphasize it, they may contradict it, or they may completely replace a verbal message.

**EXAMPLE:** You are reading and your brother leans over, pulls down the book and asks, "Did you get the tickets yet?" In response, you slowly squint one eye at him, then nod your head and raise your book to continue reading. Your brother could probably interpret the meaning of your nonverbal message: "Of course, I got the tickets. Don't bother me with silly questions while I'm busy reading."

If a nonverbal message is interpreted incorrectly, however, an inappropriate response may result. For this reason, people often do a **perception check,** a verbal response stating one person's understanding of someone else's nonverbal behavior.

**EXAMPLE:** Lucia asks Tyrone if he liked the game. Tyrone looks upward briefly, then glances at Lucia and says, "Right." Lucia does a perception check. She says, "It looks as though you really mean that the game was awful. What happened?"

## Analyzing Body Language

**Body language** is the use of facial expressions, eye contact, gestures, posture, and movement to communicate.

- **Facial expressions.** People are capable of making many facial expressions that can have a variety of meanings. People also use **masking** (adopting facial expressions normally associated with one feeling to disguise other, true feelings—smiling to hide pain, for example).
- **Eye contact.** In American society, a speaker and a listener generally look each other in the eye during much of a conversation. Eye contact is usually interpreted as a sign of honesty and straightforwardness. However, staring directly at a person too long is considered impolite.
- **Gestures.** Gestures are the movements people make with their arms, hands, and fingers.

- **Posture.** Posture is body position. The way you hold your body when you walk and the way you sit on a chair tell others a great deal about you.
- **Movement.** Movement is simply the way a person moves. The way you walk, stand, sit, and perform other actions creates an impression on others and is interpreted as having meaning.

Body language can sometimes express a message clearly without the need for words.

| Communicating with Body Language | | |
|---|---|---|
| **Type** | **Examples or Meanings** | **Functions** |
| **Facial expression** | winking; making eye contact; raising an eyebrow; smiling; frowning; sneering | • can help to show a person's feelings, either as a substitute for or as a reinforcement of a verbal message<br>• can emphasize or contradict verbal language |
| **Eye contact** | looking the other person in the eye while speaking or listening | • can indicate honesty, sincerity<br>• can demonstrate the intensity of interest that the speaker or listener feels about the communication between them |
| **Gestures** | nodding for "yes"; shrugging the shoulders for "I don't know"; pointing with index finger; gesturing to show size, shape, or length | • can replace words in certain messages<br>• can emphasize meaning of verbal language<br>• can add to meaning when a speaker gives descriptions |
| **Posture** | standing tall and sure; slumping in a chair | • can convey attitude, such as confidence and poise or dejection and weariness |
| **Movement** | walking with a quick, lively step; dragging feet reluctantly | • can enhance the impression you want to make or the message you intend to convey |

# ACTIVITY 5

## Using Body Language to Express Emotion

**W**ork in a group of five or six students. Have each person act out a situation in which he or she uses body language to express a strong emotion. The situation could be stubbing a toe, dropping car keys into a sewer, finding a dollar on the ground, bringing home good (or bad) grades, or winning a prize. Write down the body language that each student uses to present the situation and to show emotions. After everyone has had a turn, discuss the different types of body language each group member used.

## Evaluating the Message Your Appearance Sends

As you get to know people better and they get to know you, appearance becomes less important in making judgments. Nevertheless, first impressions count. A major part of a first impression is created by appearance.

**1.** Appearance can be interpreted by others as a clue to your interests.

**EXAMPLES:** If you wear a business suit and carry a briefcase, people will assume you spend time in a business environment. If you wear jogging shorts and running shoes, people will assume you are interested in running.

**2.** Appearance can be interpreted as expressing a person's attitude toward another person, especially when a specific kind of attire is expected.

**EXAMPLE:** Juliana asks her friend Dan to join her family for dinner at one of the town's better restaurants. Although Juliana does not say anything to Dan, she expects him to dress formally.

If Dan shows up in cutoffs and a T-shirt, she may feel hurt, assuming from his informal attire that he thinks meeting her family is unimportant.

**3.** Appearance can be interpreted as a sign of a person's self-regard.

**EXAMPLE:** If your clothing consistently looks messy, wrinkled, or soiled, people may interpret your lack of grooming as a sign that you do not think very highly of yourself. If you are well groomed, people may assume you have a good opinion of yourself.

In deciding how you want to look, first consider the impression you want to make, the image you want to project. Second, consider the expectations of others. Then groom yourself and select clothing that projects the image you want to convey to others.

# ACTIVITY
## 6    Analyzing Pictures for Nonverbal Cues

Find a magazine article or an advertisement that features a photograph of one person, and bring it to class. Work with a group of five or six classmates, studying— without discussing—the photographs that everyone in the group brought. Silently, jot down three to five adjectives for each photograph, such as *lively, warm,* and *sympathetic,* that you associate with the person in each photograph. Then compare your lists of adjectives with those compiled by other members of the group. Discuss why each of you selected your particular adjectives. Are there any major differences among the descriptions?

## Analyzing Paralanguage

**Paralanguage** is a type of nonverbal communication that involves using voice variation and extraneous words and sounds to communicate. Although paralanguage may involve making sounds, these sounds are simply used to fill a pause. The three types of paralanguage are shown in the sound of a speaker's voice, the speaker's use of pauses, and the speaker's use of extraneous sounds.

The sound of a person's voice is one aspect of paralanguage. Your voice can be as flexible as any musical instrument. Your voice can

- go up and down in scale (pitch)
- be loud or soft (volume)
- say words quickly or slowly (rate)
- take on different tones or qualities to express various emotions (quality or tone of voice)

A second aspect of paralanguage is a speaker's use of pauses. You can use pauses to indicate uncertainty or to create suspense, or you can pause to add emphasis. For example, a speaker might use a pause to add emphasis or create suspense in saying, "The winner of the scholarship is (pause) Vincente Martinez."

A third aspect of paralanguage is the use of extraneous words and sounds in spoken communication. Some of the words and sounds most commonly used are "uh," "well uh," "um," and "you know." Even though some of these are words, they are considered to be vocalized pauses because they contribute no information to the verbal message into which they are inserted by a speaker. For example, if you say, "Well uh, I think I'm unhappy about my term paper grade," you are using *well* simply to introduce what you are going to say.

# ACTIVITY 7

**D**ramatize the following brief dialogue in three ways. First, add paralanguage cues to the dialogue to show that the two people speaking really like each other. Second, use another set of paralanguage cues to indicate that the two people are not particularly interested in each other but are just being polite. Finally, use paralanguage cues to show that the two people do not like each other at all. After the dramatizations are completed, discuss how paralanguage affected the message in each situation.

> "How are you?"
> "Great. How about yourself?"
> "Just fine."
> "I've got to be going now."
> "I'll catch you later."

## Identifying How Environment Affects Communication

Your **environment** includes all features of the immediate surroundings. Features of the environment are counted as nonverbal communication because they can affect your behavior and mood as well as that of your audience.

When you think of nonverbal communication, you may not think immediately about the effect of the environment, but features of the environment can send important messages. These features may include

- color
- lighting
- sound
- space

**Color.** People often respond to the subtle effects of color in their surroundings. Some colors, such as reds, yellows, and oranges, have a stimulating effect. To many people, these colors seem warm, full of vitality, and exciting. Other people see blues, greens, and beiges as cool, peaceful, or neutral. In general, black and brown seem mysterious and sophisticated, while white seems innocent and childlike.

**Lighting.** Lighting can affect an audience's behavior and mood in various ways. Low lighting tends to create a relaxed, quiet atmosphere in which people want to linger. Bright lighting stimulates conversation and interaction, while extremely bright lighting may cause fatigue.

**Sound.** Sound often complements lighting. In a dimly lit restaurant, you expect soft music. In a brightly lit restaurant, you expect somewhat louder music. However, loud or continuous noises are almost always distracting. A lawn mower outside, a jet overhead, a noisy air conditioner, or a faulty fluorescent light buzzing makes communication difficult.

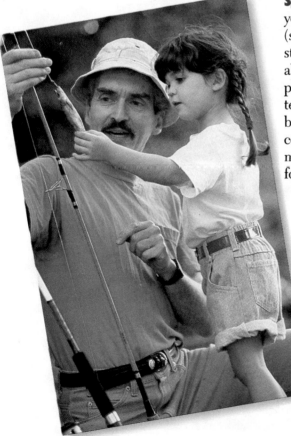

**Space.** Strictly defined, the space around you may include large, permanent elements (such as various kinds of buildings), smaller structures (such as rooms and walls), movable elements (such as furniture), and the personal spaces that people regard as their territory. Generally, the amount of space between you and your audience affects your communication. Researchers have determined that most people function with at least four different distances.

1. Your **intimate space** consists of up to eighteen inches between you and other people. It is the distance at which you feel comfortable communicating with family members and close friends. Violation of intimate space by strangers causes friction. Most people will back away from others who get within the eighteen-inch range if they are not close friends or relatives. To some extent, the boundary of intimate space is dictated by custom. In other countries it may be less or more than it is in the United States.

2. Your **personal space** consists of a distance ranging from eighteen inches to four feet between you and other people. It is the distance at which you conduct most conversations with acquaintances. You want people to be close enough so that you can hear and see each other easily, but not so close that either of you feels uncomfortable.

3. Your **social space** consists of a distance from four to twelve feet between you and other people. It is the distance at which you carry on interviews and other formal kinds of conversations.

**4.** Your **public space** consists of the area beyond twelve feet between you and others. It is the distance at which you expect such types of communication as public speeches and oral readings to take place.

# ACTIVITY 8

## Analyzing an Environment

Select three communication environments—for example, a classroom, a sitting area in your home, and a public meeting room. Describe the color, lighting, sound, and space in each environment. How do these features contribute to or detract from the communication setting? How do these features differ from one environment to another? Compare your findings with those of your classmates.

# HOW TO Use Nonverbal Communication Effectively

1. **Use body language that supplements what you want to say.** Consider your facial expressions, eye contact, gestures, posture, and movements. Change any that contradict your verbal message.
2. **Make sure your appearance is in keeping with what you want to accomplish.** Consider the image you wish to project. How does it relate to your listeners' expectations and to the demands of the situation?
3. **Make sure that the sound of your voice is in keeping with your message.** Learn to control the pitch, volume, rate, and quality of your voice. Pay attention to your use of pauses and extraneous sounds and words.
4. **If possible, create an environment that is suitable for the kind of communication you want.** Use color, lighting, sound, and space to accomplish your purpose.

Think of situations in which people gather together to talk. Describe briefly a situation in which people would feel comfortable talking at an intimate distance. Then briefly describe a situation in which the participants would feel more comfortable conversing at a personal distance.

COMMUNICATION JOURNAL

## for Effective Verbal and Nonverbal Communication

- Do I understand the denotations and connotations of the words I use?
- Do I use standard American English when appropriate?
- Do I use jargon, slang, and dialect only in appropriate settings?
- Does my body language complement my verbal message?
- Does my appearance project the image I wish to create?
- Is the sound of my voice in keeping with my verbal message?
- Do I consider how my environment affects my communication?
- Am I aware of what my verbal language and nonverbal language tell others about me?
- Am I working to improve my verbal and nonverbal messages?

# USING HAND SIGNALS

### Helping Hands

Baseball coaches employ a system of hand signals and gestures to relay information to players during games. These signals are particularly important in instances where noise makes it difficult for players to hear a coach's nonverbal instructions. They also prevent the opposing team from learning the team's plans in advance.

### Characteristics of an Effective Coach

An effective coach

1. uses simple, clearly visible gestures

2. may pause briefly between each gesture to prevent individual movements from being confused with one another

3. uses effective body language as needed to make the meaning of the signal clear

### Meet the Coach

As a baseball coach at Huston-Tillotson College, Alvin Moore works with students who want to bring glory to their school as well as excel academically. "The most rewarding aspect of my job," he says, "is watching dedicated athletes develop a well-earned sense of pride in their abilities, both on the field and off."

*Alvin Moore*

## ACTIVITY

### Situation

The traffic signals have malfunctioned at a busy, three-way T-stop intersection. You are the police officer called to the scene to direct traffic. To do your job, you need to use nonverbal communication effectively.

### Preparation

Take turns serving as the traffic officer who is using nonverbal signals to direct traffic. While you direct traffic, some students can be the "cars" and others can observe and evaluate the effectiveness of your signals. The guidelines for effective nonverbal communication on page 45 can be the basis for the observers' evaluations.

### Analysis and Assessment

Discuss and compare the observers' evaluations of the various traffic officers' performance. Which signals and body language seemed to work more effectively? Which signals were less effective?

# S•U•M•M•A•R•Y

**SENDING VERBAL AND NONVERBAL MESSAGES** involves both verbal and nonverbal language. Verbal language uses spoken and written words; nonverbal language uses cues that communicate ideas and feelings without using words. When you communicate, your verbal language and your nonverbal language work together to reveal a great deal about you.

- **Understand verbal language** as a system of sounds and symbols. Verbal language relies on learned conventions that are slowly, but constantly, changing.

- **Understand shades of meaning** of words. A word's meanings may include a variety of denotations or connotations. Denotations are the dictionary definitions of a word, and connotations are the positive, negative, or neutral associations and feelings the word arouses. Verbal language adapts to suit the communication situation. Depending on the circumstances, a speaker can usually use standard American English. In specific instances, a speaker may use jargon, slang, or dialect to communicate.

- **Understand nonverbal language** as a system that uses all the elements of communication except words. Nonverbal communication serves four main functions: to complement, to emphasize, to contradict, and to replace verbal messages. Nonverbal communication involves body language, appearance, the sound of the speaker's voice, and environmental features.

## Vocabulary

Look back through this chapter to find the meaning of each of the following terms. Write each term and its meaning in your communication journal.

body language, p. 36
connotation, p. 32
conventional, p. 29
cues, p. 28
denotation, p. 31
dialect, p. 33
environment, p. 41
generalize, p. 30
intimate space, p. 42
jargon, p. 33
masking, p. 36
messages, p. 27
nonverbal language,
   p. 28
paralanguage, p. 40
perception check, p. 36
personal space, p. 43
public space, p. 44
slang, p. 33
social space, p. 43
standard American
   English, p. 33
sublanguage, p. 33
symbol, p. 29
system, p. 29
verbal language, p. 28

## Review Questions

1. What are the functions of nonverbal communication?
2. Define *verbal language* and list five important features of it.
3. One principle of language learning is that such learning proceeds from simple to complex. What are two other principles of learning language?
4. List four ways in which the English language changes.
5. What is the difference between the denotation and the connotation of a word?
6. Why is it important to communication to establish a common language such as standard American English? When is it appropriate to use nonstandard English?
7. How can you improve your use of language?
8. One way that body language communicates is through gestures. What are four other ways that body language communicates messages?
9. What is paralanguage?
10. Social space is one type of distance between people who are talking to each other. What are three other types of space, or distance, that affect communication?

## Discussion Questions

1. You have discovered an object for which there is no name. What will you call it? Will the name you choose describe what the object does, tell what it is made of or perhaps show the object's similarity to something else? Discuss how the name you give the object would become part of the language.
2. In a *New York Times* interview, Carl Sandburg once called slang "language that rolls up its sleeves, spits on its hands, and goes to work." What do you think Sandburg meant by this description? Do you agree or disagree with Sandburg's statement? Discuss your reactions to slang.
3. Eye contact is an important part of conversation. Discuss how you can use eye contact to (a) encourage people to talk, (b) show that you are listening, and (c) show that you would like the conversation to end.
4. Roderick Nordell once wrote, "If only everyone talked the way we do in my household. I mean . . . if only everyone . . . like . . . talked . . . you know . . . the way we do . . . right? It would be so much . . . like . . . easier to . . . you know . . . understand . . . right?" What characteristic of modern speech is Nordell making fun of? How does this characteristic of modern speech affect our communication?
5. Discuss the kinds of nonverbal communication you would use to show each of the following emotions: anger, interest, surprise, self-confidence, happiness, and boredom. Then discuss whether you think people from different cultures use basically the same nonverbal cues to express these feelings.

# ACTI V ITIES

1. **Analyzing the Meanings of Words.** List the five words you use most frequently to show your approval of something or someone. First, write the meanings you intend the words to have. Then look up the meaning of each word in a dictionary. Do the words mean what you thought they meant? How many of the words are dialect or slang? Share your findings with your classmates.

2. **Defining Language.** Many writers have tried to define *language*. Use quotation books such as Bartlett's *Familiar Quotations* to compile a list of five quotations about language that you especially like. Share your list with your classmates.

3. **Using Pantomime to Communicate Nonverbal Messages.** Pantomime is a way of sending messages nonverbally. Use pantomime to convey one of the following messages or another message that you choose.
   a. I'm really glad to see you.
   b. Which way should we go?
   c. Don't tell me any more!
   d. What did he say?
   e. That's a great idea!

4. **Adjusting Language to Suit Different Audiences.** Identify two different communication settings, such as talking with your friends and visiting with your grandparents. Plan to present the same information in each setting: that you have been offered a scholarship to your first-choice college or university. How do you alter your verbal and nonverbal language from one communication setting to the next?

5. **Analyzing Problems in Communication.** Being in certain situations can make it difficult for you to communicate clearly. Look at each of the situations shown in the photos on this page. What elements of the situation would likely interfere with

communication? What could a speaker do to compensate for such interference? What could a listener do?

6. **Analyzing Nonverbal Communication in Silent Movies.** Watch a silent movie such as Charlie Chaplin's *The Gold Rush* or Mel Brooks's *Silent Movie*. Or, simply

turn down the volume on a regular movie. How do performers in the movie communicate? Which gestures seem to be more effective? Present five of these gestures to your class and describe how the gestures were used in the movie. Discuss how such gestures are used in normal speech.

7. **Giving an Oral Report on Nonverbal Factors Affecting Communication.** Many self-help books tell people how to dress, use body language, or design an environment to achieve power or success. Read one of these books, such as John T. Molloy's *Dress for Success* or Jill Briscoe's *Body Language*, and present an oral report about it.

8. **Communicating by Using Paralanguage.** Working with a partner, choose an animal whose sounds you will use to communicate. For example, you might decide to meow, hiss, and purr like a cat. Make up a brief message; then try to communicate this message using only paralanguage and the animal sounds you chose. Wherever appropriate, use animal gestures to reinforce the message. See if your classmates can guess what message you and your partner are expressing.

9. **Analyzing Verbal and Nonverbal Language.** Record a conversation between yourself and a partner. (Ask a classmate to make a videotape of the conversation if you have access to a video camera.) The conversation may be about a subject such as sports, music, movies, food, computers, or cars— any subject that interests both of you. After you've recorded the conversation, play it back. Analyze and evaluate the verbal and nonverbal language you hear and see on the tape.

10. **Using Nonverbal Communication in Drama.** Examine the three photographs of Edward James Olmos shown on this page. The first picture shows Olmos in everyday life. The second shows him portraying a role in the movie *Blade Runner*. The third shows Olmos as he appeared in the movie *Stand and Deliver*. Discuss the ways in which Olmos "creates new characters" by changing his appearance and body language.

# COMMUNICATION IN THE WORKPLACE

### Background

After working at your job for one year, you have decided that it is time to ask for a raise.

### Preparing to Do the Job

You should use effective verbal skills to explain clearly and convincingly why you deserve a raise. Your request should be brief, positive in tone, and tailored to suit your audience.

### Testing Your Skill

Work with a partner to devise an approach to asking your supervisor for a pay raise. Take turns playing the roles of the supervisor and the employee asking for the raise. Present your scene in class. Afterward, ask your classmates to explain why they would or wouldn't give you the raise if they were the supervisor.

# EVERYDAY COMMUNICATION

### Situation

In certain situations, verbal communication can be less effective than nonverbal. When giving directions, for example, your meaning may be more clear if you point or draw a map than if you use abstract words like *north*, *left*, or *block*.

### Problem

Identify two situations in which nonverbal communication helps clarify a situation more than verbal details do. Then prepare a short speech explaining how nonverbal cues improve understanding in both situations. Include specific examples to demonstrate your point.

### Assessing Your Skill

Present your speech to the class, acting out the nonverbal cues. Then discuss your presentation with your classmates to see whether they think the nonverbal cues in the examples you presented helped make your message clearer.

mek ʌ nɔɪz.

Make a noise.

[m]    map
[e]    bake
[k]    cat
[ʌ]    hut
[n]    nut
[ɔɪ]   toy
[z]    zip

# CHAPTER 3

# Using Your Voice

**OBJECTIVES**

**After studying this chapter, you should be able to**

1. Explain how sound is generated.
2. Define *resonance* and identify each of the major resonators of voice.
3. Define *articulation* and identify each of the major articulators of sound.
4. Identify and define each of the key characteristics of vocalization.
5. List the four major aspects of vocalization that affect how you sound to others.
6. List four common articulation problems.

## How Your Voice Is Produced

Speaking is our ability to form sounds and to use them to communicate abstract ideas and feelings. We do not have a specialized speech system in the same way that we have a digestive system or a respiratory system. The human voice is generated and shaped by parts of the body that have primary functions other than producing speech. The lungs are primarily for breathing, while the various parts of the mouth and throat are primarily for chewing and swallowing food.

To produce speech, the lungs, the mouth, and the throat and other parts of the body coordinate to

- *generate* sound
- *resonate* sound
- *articulate* sound

In this chapter you will learn how your voice is produced and how to best use your voice.

# Identifying the Generators of Sound

Respiration is the main function of the breathing structure, but it is not the only function. This structure also helps you generate, or produce, sounds for speech.

The primary generators of sound are the **vocal folds** (commonly known as the **vocal cords**), which are the muscles that make up the larynx. Sound is generated by pushing out air in such a way that the vocal folds vibrate. To understand this process better, look at the following illustration. Notice that many body parts must coordinate, or work together, to produce sound.

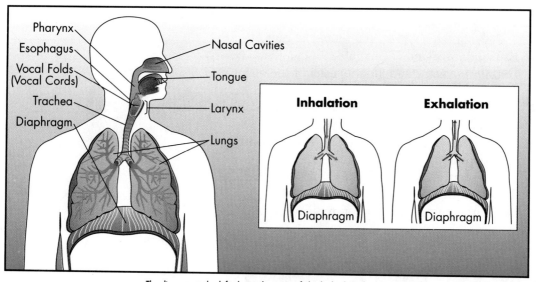

The diagram at the left shows the parts of the body that play a part in generating speech. The diagram at the right illustrates how the diaphragm contracts for inhalation and relaxes for exhalation.

## The Respiration Cycle

The respiration cycle consists of inhalation and exhalation, the drawing in and breathing out of air from the lungs. This cycle begins with contraction of the **diaphragm,** a dome-shaped muscle at the base of the lungs. The cycle ends when the diaphragm relaxes. Another cycle begins again almost immediately with the next contraction, and thus the cycles continue. [See the illustration above.]

**Inhalation.**   As the diaphragm contracts, air is drawn in through the mouth or nose and down the throat. In the throat, the air passes through the **larynx** (what most people call the voice box) and the **trachea** (what most people call the windpipe), and then is drawn into the lungs.

**Exhalation.**  As the diaphragm relaxes, the air in the lungs is pushed back up through the trachea and larynx, through the throat, and out through the mouth or nose. Since the same upper passageway is used for air, food, and drink, a valve in the larynx must open and close to make sure that food and drink go one way while air goes another.

During quiet breathing, the vocal folds remain open so that air can move freely in and out of the lungs. When you eat or drink, the vocal folds protect you from choking by closing off the trachea.

## Using Respiration for Speaking

When you speak, you make slight changes in regular breathing to generate sound.

1. You send a burst of air from the lungs up to the larynx to set the vocal folds into vibration. You can feel this vibration if you place your hand lightly on your throat while saying "ah." Because you must be able to sustain this vibration in the larynx to speak clearly and completely, you make two adaptations to your normal breathing pattern:

   - You inhale more swiftly and more deeply than you do during normal breathing.
   - You prolong the airflow as you exhale.

2. Muscles in the chest wall contract to counteract the force of the relaxing diaphragm as you exhale so that all your air does not escape at once. When you are about to run out of air, another set of muscles begins to contract, forcing a bit more air from your lungs and allowing you to sustain speech. When speaking, you learn to control the amount of air you take in, or else you find yourself "gulping air," or taking in large quantities of air quickly, in order to finish sentences.

# ACTI**V**ITY 1

## Practicing Proper Breathing

**F**or speaking, you need to regulate your airflow so that you do not run out of air in the middle of a sentence. Practice proper breathing by placing the open palms of your hands tightly against your lower front ribs. Inhale slowly and deeply through your mouth and your nose. Notice how your lower ribs push against your hands as you inhale. Hold your breath for the count of five and then say a long, continuous "oooh" as you exhale slowly. Practice this procedure until you are able to control the rate at which you exhale.

# Understanding the Resonators

Before sound produced by exhaling air can be speech, it must be given **resonance,** or reinforcement produced by vibration. The **resonators** of sound for speech are

- the bones in the chest, neck, and head
- the cavities of the throat, nose, and mouth

These two groups of resonators amplify sound in different ways.

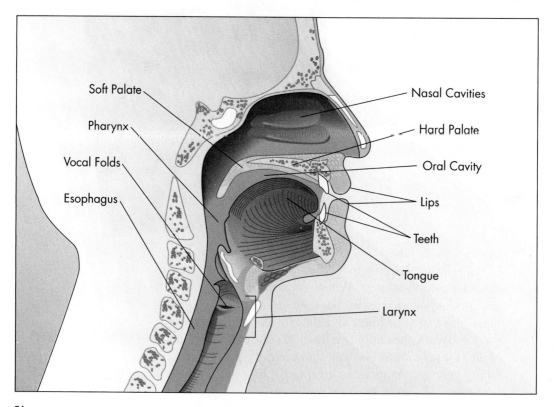

Soft Palate

Pharynx

Vocal Folds

Esophagus

Nasal Cavities

Hard Palate

Oral Cavity

Lips

Teeth

Tongue

Larynx

Bones resonate by picking up vibrations of sound. To discover how bone resonance works, try a few simple experiments. As you follow these instructions, remember to keep your throat, jaws, lips, and tongue relaxed.

1. With your lips barely touching, hum *m-m-m-m-m-m-m-m*. Feel how this sound vibrates in the bones of your head.

2. Touching the bridge of your nose, hum *ng-ng-ng-ng-ng*. You can feel the resonance of these sounds as you pronounce them.

Most resonance occurs in the cavities of the throat, nose, and mouth. A **cavity** is a partially enclosed area. Every cavity has a natural range of sounds it reinforces, depending on

- the cavity's size
- the cavity's shape
- the texture of the material forming the cavity
- the size of the opening into the cavity

Ordinarily, the larger the cavity, the lower the sounds that it resonates; similarly, the smaller the cavity, the higher the sounds it resonates. To remember this, think of cavity resonance in terms of musical instruments. The tuba—a wind instrument with a large cavity and opening—resonates the deepest sounds. In contrast, the piccolo—one of the smallest of the wind instruments—resonates the highest sounds. Remember that the texture of the walls of the cavity also affects sound. For example, the sound of a metal clarinet differs from that of a wooden clarinet.

## The Throat

Resonance begins in the throat, or **pharyngeal cavity.** Because this cavity is very flexible and differs in size and wall thickness from person to person, each individual has a distinct resonance or vocal quality. In addition, you have a great amount of control over how you use your throat to create sound.

> **EXAMPLE:** When your throat is tense, it resonates high pitches, and your voice is likely to sound harsh. When your throat is relaxed, it resonates lower pitches, and your voice will usually sound mellow. When you tense your throat, it resonates high pitches—metallic sounds. However, when you relax your throat, it resonates lower pitches—deep, rich, mellow sounds.

## The Nose

The nose, or **nasal cavity,** has a direct effect on the three nasal sounds that you make:

- the [m] as in *make*
- the [n] as in *now*
- the [ŋ] as in *sing*

When you produce each of these sounds, your teeth and tongue block the passage of air, forcing the sound to come out of your nose. To some extent, the nasal cavity affects the sound of all speech.

> **EXAMPLE:** When people talk with their mouths partly closed, the nose resonates all their vowel sounds, and their speech has a twangy quality. In contrast, when someone has a cold, the nasal passages get blocked and the nose gives little resonance, even to the [m], [n], and [ŋ] sounds. As a result, that person's speech has a dull or muffled quality.

## The Mouth

Of all the resonators, the mouth, or **oral cavity,** is the easiest to alter. You can change the size of the cavity and the shape of its opening by moving your tongue, lips, and jaw.

> **EXAMPLE:** You form various vowel sounds by changing the size of your oral cavity. You keep your tongue back and your mouth open wide to form the *o* in *hot,* while your tongue is forward and your mouth is more nearly closed to form the *ee* in *meet.*

[For more on the function of the throat, the nose, and the mouth, see the discussion of vocal quality on pages 67–69.]

# ACTIVITY 2

To experiment with sound production, take a large rubber band (the kind sometimes used to bind daily newspapers or bundles of papers). Loop the band over your hands and stretch it as far as it will go without danger of breaking. While it is stretched tight, pluck the band with your thumb. Describe the sound.

Now move your hands closer together to loosen the band. Pluck it again. Compare the sound of the tightly stretched band to that of the looser band. What does this experiment show you about sound production? How do your findings relate to the process of producing human speech?

# Identifying the Articulators of Sound

**Articulation** is the shaping of speech sounds into recognizable oral symbols that go together to make up a word. Many communication problems are caused by poor articulation.

The major articulators of sound are in the mouth:

- the tongue
- the hard and soft palates
- the teeth
- the lips

Vowel sounds are formed by changing the size of the oral cavity and the shape of the opening. Consonant sounds are formed in three ways: by moving the tongue to various parts of the mouth; by pointing, arching, or flattening the tongue; and by moving and shaping the lips.

EXAMPLE: While saying "ah," raise the tip of your tongue so that it touches the edge of the gum behind the two upper-front teeth. Notice that the sound changes from "ah" to [l]. Now while saying "ah," bring your upper and lower lips together. Notice that the sound changes from "ah" to [m].

## The Sounds of English

A speaker who produces clear consonants and distinct vowels is said to have good articulation. If the speaker combines precisely articulated sounds into distinct words, then the speaker is said to have good **pronunciation.** If you have ever had difficulty understanding the speech of someone from another region of America or from another English-speaking country, you are already aware of the importance of clear pronunciation.

While the English alphabet has only twenty-six letters, the English language uses forty-five different sounds: twenty-five consonant sounds and twenty vowel sounds. Frequently, the same letter is used to represent different sounds. For instance, *c* is pronounced [k] in *cattle* and [s] in *exercise.*

A more effective system for symbolizing sound is the International Phonetic Alphabet (IPA). In this system, each of the forty-five sounds in English has its own individual symbol. Familiarity with this system, shown in the chart, is important for anyone trying to talk about or write about sound.

As you review this chart, keep in mind the following points.

1. Each IPA symbol represents only one unit of sound.
2. When a sound is shown in a sentence, it is placed within brackets. For instance, the sound [d] is one sound.
3. A consonant sound is pronounced by itself, without an accompanying vowel sound. For instance, usually when you are asked to give the sound for the letter *d,* you say "dee." However, "dee" is two sounds—a [d] and an [i]. (The IPA symbol [i] is the same sound that is represented by the letters *ee.*) The actual pronunciation of the sound produced by the letter *d* is simply [d].

## International Phonetic Alphabet (IPA) Symbols Frequently Used in Speech

**CONSONANTS**

| | | | | | | | |
|---|---|---|---|---|---|---|---|
| [b] | *boy* | [p] | *pie* | [d] | *dot* | [t] | *tap* |
| [g] | *got* | [k] | *cat* | [v] | *vain* | [f] | *far* |
| [ð] | *then* | [θ] | *thin* | [z] | *zip* | [s] | *sat* |
| [ʒ] | *leisure* | [ʃ] | *show* | [dʒ] | *jet* | [tʃ] | *chin* |
| [h] | *hot* | [m] | *map* | [n] | *now* | [ŋ] | *ring* |
| [l] | *lit* | [r] | *rid* | [j] | *yet* | [hw] | *why* |
| | | | | | | [w] | *wit* |

**VOWELS**

| | | | | | | | |
|---|---|---|---|---|---|---|---|
| [i] | *me* | [ɪ] | *it* | [e] | *bake* | [ɛ] | *pet* |
| [æ] | *back* | [a] | *bother* | [ɔ] | *caught* | [o] | *go* |
| [ʊ] | *took* | [u] | *soon* | [ʌ] | *hut* | [ə] | *above* |
| [ɝ] | *bird* | [ɚ] | *never* | | | | |

**DIPHTHONGS**

| | | | | | | | |
|---|---|---|---|---|---|---|---|
| [aɪ] | *ride* | [aʊ] | *cow* | [ɔɪ] | *toy* | [ju] | *cute* |
| [eɪ] | *may* | [oʊ] | *hoe* | | | | |

FRANK AND ERNEST reprinted by permission of NEA, Inc.

F W WNT T TLK RLLY GD, W'LL HV T NVNT VWLS.

THAVES 10-16

The caveman's statement is humorously ungrammatical: "If we want to talk really good, we'll have to invent vowels." The caveman's point, however, is a good one. The consonant sounds of English are fairly predictable, while the vowel sounds differ widely, depending on how they are combined in a word, how stress is placed on various syllables of the word, and how individual speakers pronounce certain sounds.

## Classification of Sounds

Sounds are either voiced or voiceless. **Voiced** means that the vocal folds are vibrating when the sound is being made. **Voiceless** means that the vocal folds are held open so that air breathed out does not vibrate them.

> **EXAMPLE:** First, say the word *view*. Notice that [v] is made by placing the lower lip against the inside of the upper front teeth. Now say the word *few*. Notice that the placement of your lip and teeth for [f] is exactly the same as for [v]. The difference is that the [v] sound is voiced, while the [f] sound is voiceless. (Place two fingers on your Adam's apple, and alternate saying *view* and *few*. When you say the [v] sound, you should feel a vibration. However, when you say the [f] sound, you should not feel any vibration.)

Consonant sounds can be further divided into four separate sound groups.

1. The **plosives** form a small explosion when you say them. The sounds [p] and [b], [t] and [d], and [k] and [g] are all plosives.
2. The **fricatives** make a frictionlike noise as they are spoken. The fricatives are [f] and [v], [θ] and [ð], [s] and [z], [ʃ] and [ʒ], and [j].
3. The **nasals** are sounds that are resonated in the nasal cavity. The nasals are: [m], [n], and [ŋ].
4. The **glides** are sounds that result from the gliding movement of the articulators. The sounds [l], [r], [w], [hw] and [j] are glides.

Using the International Phonetic Alphabet (IPA) shown on page 60, decipher each of the following statements.

1. hwaɪ mi?
2. hu tʊk ðə bɔl?
3. aɪ lʌv pitsə.
4. gɪv mi ə tʃæns.
5. aɪ dʒʌst eɪt.

## Improving Vocalization

There are four aspects, or characteristics, of vocalization that affect how you sound to others: pitch, volume, rate, and quality. In this section, you will look at these aspects and at some of the problems that speakers have with them. Fortunately, there are ways to correct these problems.

### Pitch

**Pitch** is the highness or lowness of the sound you make. Vocal pitch varies from person to person, depending on individual differences in vocal structure. To understand pitch, think of the strings of a guitar or a violin. The longer, thicker, or looser the string, the lower the pitch. The shorter, thinner, or tighter the string, the higher the pitch. Several factors are included in evaluating pitch: key, melody, range, and inflection.

**Key** is the average pitch at which you speak.

**COMMON PROBLEM:** Speaking in too high or too low a key can be a problem because it can strain your voice or cause it to sound unpleasant.

**SOLUTION:** Find your **optimum pitch**—the pitch at which you speak with the least strain and with the very best resonance. Your optimum pitch will probably be about four notes above the lowest note at which you can speak comfortably.

**Melody** refers to the variations in pitch that help to give expression to a person's voice.

**COMMON PROBLEM:** A **monotone** is a melody pattern that consists of only one tone. No one actually talks in a true monotone, with every word spoken at exactly the same pitch. However, many people approach a monotone when they are giving a speech or reading out loud.

**SOLUTION:** When you speak, you should try to vary your melody to help give meaning to what you are saying—to make your voice expressive.

**Range** is the spread between the lowest and the highest notes you can speak comfortably. The greater your range, the more flexible your voice.

**COMMON PROBLEM:** If your voice is limited to a range of three notes or fewer, it will sound monotonous.

**SOLUTION:** Practice extending your vocal range until you can cover ten tones. Having a greater vocal range will allow you more room for variation in your pitch and will therefore enable your voice to be more expressive.

**Inflection** is the upward or downward glide of your pitch as you speak. By altering your voice upward or downward, you express shades of meaning.

1. Rising inflections are generally used in communicating doubt, uncertainty, indecision, questioning, surprise, or an unfinished thought.

   **EXAMPLE:** If you glide your voice upward on the word *home* in the following sentence, the upward glide indicates uncertainty: *Are you going home?*

2. Falling inflections are generally used in communicating certainty, finality, or a completed thought.

   **EXAMPLE:** If you glide your voice downward on the word *home* in the next sentence, the downward glide indicates certainty: *I'm going home.*

3. A **circumflex** is an up-and-down inflection.

   **EXAMPLE:** Suppose someone asks you what you are doing tomorrow, and you respond, "Tomorrow? Hmm, I'm not sure." As you say the word *tomorrow,* it is likely that your voice will glide up and down the scale.

4. While inflections are gradual upward or downward glides, a **step** is an abrupt change in pitch. By abruptly changing your pitch, you emphasize a word in a sentence.

   **EXAMPLE:** Suppose a friend demands that you drop what you are doing and go with him. If you reply "I can't go," most likely you will abruptly change your pitch to emphasize the word *can't:*

Hi & Lois by Dik Browne. Reprinted with special permission of King Features Syndicate, Inc.

# ACTIVITY 4

## Evaluating Vocal Pitch

Experiment with two classmates to demonstrate how pitch affects meaning. Use the sentence *Tom is the one who took the book.* Have every speaker read the sentence, changing pitch to give the sentence a different sound and meaning.

Begin by having the first speaker say the sentence in a monotone, expressing every word on the same pitch. Have the second speaker say the sentence in a way that emphasizes that it was Tom, not someone else, who took the book. Have a third speaker say the same sentence, this time emphasizing that it was the book Tom took, not a pencil.

Discuss in the group how each speaker used pitch to change the meaning of the sentence. You might experiment further to see how many other ways you could change pitch to give this sentence other meanings.

# Volume

**Volume,** or loudness, is the intensity of sound. Volume depends on the force exerted to produce the speech tone. To increase loudness, you have to increase the pressure behind the column of air being forced up from the lungs through the vocal folds. The louder you want to talk, the more pressure you need.

**COMMON PROBLEM:** Some people talk too loudly or too softly and do not realize that their volume is a problem. They have become so used to the way they talk that it sounds just right to them.

**SOLUTION:** To identify this problem in your own speech, ask a friend to alert you whenever you speak too loudly or too softly.

A *spectrogram* makes speech visible. This one shows the sound waves produced when a person says, "It's not easy to recognize speech."

To talk loudly, you must exert pressure. This pressure should come from muscles in the stomach area or the lower chest, not from the neck or upper chest. If that pressure comes from muscles in your neck or upper chest, you will sound louder, but your voice will have an unpleasant, harsh, metallic sound.

By getting pressure from the right place—the stomach and lower chest—you can talk loud for quite a while without getting tired or hoarse. However, if you get pressure from the wrong place—the neck and upper chest—your throat will soon hurt, you will grow tired, and you will probably become hoarse.

## Experimenting with Loudness

You will be able to speak more effectively and efficiently if you learn to use the correct muscles to increase volume. Place your hands around your waist like a belt. In a normal voice say, "Get over here as fast as you can." You will probably feel light pressure at your waist. Now say the same sentence very loudly. On at least three of the words, you should feel a sharp tensing of the stomach muscles. If you do, you are getting pressure from the right place. To identify power from the wrong source, again say the sentence very loudly. This time, though, wrap your arms tightly around your waist to prevent use of your stomach muscles. You should feel tension in your throat and should notice that your voice takes on an unpleasant, harsh quality.

## Rate

**Rate** is the speed at which you talk. Normal speed is from about 120 to about 160 words per minute. Rate is influenced by a number of factors, including the emotional content of the message.

EXAMPLE: When you read aloud, you are likely to go much faster than when you talk with a friend. If what you read is simple material, your speech may get to a rate of 180 words per minute. Also, your rate of speech will be affected by the emotion or mood of the passage you are reading.

Changes in rate are normal—in fact, they are necessary. Like changes in pitch, they help communicate the shades of meaning that you wish to convey to your listeners.

# ACTIVITY 6

## Timing Your Rate of Speech

**M**easure and compare your speaking rates in conversation and in reading aloud. (You need to measure both because these rates differ.) First, with the permission of the person you are speaking to, tape-record a conversation. Next, record a few minutes of oral reading—perhaps an article in the newspaper or a passage of average difficulty from a book. Then, using a timer or a watch, listen to the tape and count the number of words you spoke or read in one minute. If your average rate of conversational speech is outside the normal range (120 to 160 words per minute), you can make a conscious effort to slow down or to speed up.

## Quality

**Quality** is the tone of your voice. Your personal vocal quality is the tone that makes your voice identifiable as yours. Sometimes, a speaker's unpleasant vocal quality is caused by a physical problem or impairment. However, some people develop unpleasant qualities that can and should be changed. The most common quality problems are nasality, breathiness, hoarseness, and harshness.

**1. Nasality** is characterized by too much nasal resonance of all vocal sounds. It is caused by incomplete closure of the passage between the oral cavity and the nasal cavity. Nasal resonance itself is not wrong. The three sounds [m], [n], and [ŋ] are supposed to be nasal. In addition, most people have a touch of nasal resonance in normal conversation. The problem arises when the nasal resonance is so pronounced that the voice sounds whiny or tinny.

**EXAMPLE:** To hear how a truly nasal voice sounds, try talking "through your nose." Raise the back of your tongue toward the roof of your mouth so that the mouth is blocked and that sound is directed into the nasal cavity. Now speak. Notice how unpleasant the sound is. While you are speaking, lower the back of your tongue so that sound is sent to the mouth. Notice how your voice changes.

**2. Breathiness** results from too much unvoiced air escaping through the vocal folds as a person is speaking. It is caused by failure to bring the vocal folds close enough together. One cause of breathiness is habit: People may prefer breathy speaking because it takes less energy. Another is the development of growths on the vocal folds themselves. These growths prevent the folds from coming together smoothly.

A breathy quality may be fine if you wish to sound that way. Some people even associate breathiness with softness or warmth. However, if your voice is too breathy, your listeners may be distracted by the quality of your voice and not be attentive to your message. If you have a problem with breathiness, you may want to consult a speech therapist to find out its cause. If the cause is simple laziness, you can correct it by doing vocal exercises.

**3. Harshness** is characterized by an unpleasant, grating sound that may also be hard or metallic. Harshness is caused by speaking with too much tension in the larynx area. People who wrestle, play football, or engage in other activities that demand strong neck muscles may tend to keep their neck muscles tense all the time. A harsh voice is sometimes caused by a speaker's attempt to talk at a pitch that is too high or too low. The cure for harshness is to relax the neck muscles.

Film actress Marilyn Monroe was famous for the breathiness of her voice.

**EXAMPLE:** To hear what harshness sounds like, tense your neck muscles as much as you can. Then try to talk for two minutes. Notice what happens to the sound of your voice after just two minutes.

**4. Hoarseness** is characterized by a thickness of sound or a muffled or rasping sound. Like harshness, hoarseness is caused by speaking with excessive tension in the larynx area. Although a physical problem may lead to hoarseness, in many cases hoarseness is brought on by poor speech habits.

**EXAMPLE:** People often abuse their voices by yelling at athletic events or by screaming at rock concerts. The kind of hoarseness that results from this abuse is usually temporary and can be cured by resting the vocal folds.

*A*s you go about your daily routine, make notes in your communication journal about speakers you encounter who have especially good voices to listen to and those whose voices are somehow unpleasant to listen to. Write down your ideas about what makes one speaker's voice pleasing and another's irritating.

# Correcting Articulation Problems

To communicate effectively, you must speak so that people in your audience can understand your message clearly and easily. Once a speaker has discovered one of the common articulation problems, he or she can usually remedy the difficulty with practice.

Permission by Archie Comic Publications, Inc., and Creators Syndicate.

## Substituting One Sound for Another

Substituting some sounds for others may not prevent your speech from being understood, particularly among family, friends, and neighbors. These sound substitutions may, however, diminish your effectiveness when you are communicating to some listeners.

| Common Substitution Problems | |
| --- | --- |
| **Substitutions** | **Examples** |
| [d] for [ð] | **da** for **the, radder** for **rather, dose** for **those** |
| [t] for [θ] | **tink** for **think, anyting** for **anything, bot** for **both** |
| [ks] for [s] | **excape** for **escape, expecially** for **especially** |
| [f] for [θ] | **bref** for **breath, bof** for **both, arifmatic** for **arithmetic** |
| [n] for [ŋ] | **doin** for **doing, growin** for **growing, bein** for **being** |
| [t] for [d] | **coutn't** for **couldn't, woutn't** for **wouldn't** |
| [ɪ] for [ʌ] | **jist** for **just** |
| [ɪ] for [ɛ] | **git** for **get, pin** for **pen** |

## Leaving Out a Sound (Omission)

Leaving out, or omitting, sounds is a kind of shortcutting. Although some shortcutting is normal when speaking, excessive shortcutting is considered an articulation problem.

| Common Omission Problems | |
|---|---|
| **Omissions** | **Examples** |
| dropping [d] | **wount** for **wouldn't, frien** for **friend, gole** for **gold** |
| dropping [t] | **mos** for **most, jus** for **just, kep** for **kept, bes** for **best** |
| dropping [l] | **hep** for **help, sef** for **self, woff** for **wolf, sauve** for **solve** |
| dropping initial [h] after other words | **see'um** for **see him, gave'er** for **gave her** |
| dropping [ə] along with a consonant sound | **probly** for **probably, member** for **remember, awmobile** for **automobile** |

## Adding an Extra Sound

Sometimes the problem of adding a sound stems from pronouncing a letter that should be silent. Sometimes it is the result of adding a sound to make a word easier to say.

| Common Problems with Adding Sounds | |
|---|---|
| **Additions** | **Examples** |
| adding [t] in words where *t* is silent | **soften** for **sofen, hasten** for **hasen** |
| adding [ə] | **filum** for **film, athaletic** for **athletic, childaren** for **children** |
| adding [r] to ends of words | **idear** for **idea, drawr** for **draw** |
| adding a sound to the beginning of a word | **ahold** for **hold, especial** for **special, ascared** for **scared** |

## Transposing Sounds

Transposing sounds refers to the switching, or reversing, of the order in which sounds are spoken.

| Common Problems with Transposing Sounds | |
|---|---|
| **Transpositions** | **Examples** |
| [ks] for [sk] | **aks** for **ask** |
| [ɚd] for [rɛd] | **hunderd** for **hundred** |
| [pɚ] for [pri] | **perscribe** for **prescribe, perfer** for **prefer** |
| [ɚn] for [rɛn ] or [rɛn] for [ɚn] | **childern** for **children, modren** for **modern** |

# ACTIVITY 7

## Correcting Articulation Problems

Identify any problems you have with substituting, omitting, adding, or transposing sounds. To do this, read aloud the words used as examples in the four parts of this section. Practice the correct pronunciations. After you have pronounced the sounds correctly for a while, they will become a natural part of your speech.

# Sending Effective Vocal Messages

**1. Breathe properly.**   Proper breathing gives you the air necessary to generate speech: It also allows you to talk without excessive strain on your neck and chest muscles.

**2. Resonate sounds effectively.**   Proper use of the throat, the nose, and the mouth helps you to shape the vowel sounds necessary for clear speech. It also produces a strong, rich vocal tone free of excessive breathiness, nasality, harshness, or hoarseness.

**3. Articulate clearly.**   Good articulation enables you to deliver your words clearly so that your listeners can understand you.

**4. Use vocal variety and appropriate emphasis.**   Vocal variation and emphasis allows you to give the precise meaning you intend to your words and sentences. Moreover, your use of proper pitch, loudness, and rate makes your voice expressive and pleasant.

## for Vocalizing

- Do I breathe properly?

- Do I get power for speech from the proper sources?

- Do I resonate my sounds effectively; in other words, are the sounds I produce loud and full?

- Do I speak in a key that is at my optimum pitch?

- Do I use inflections and steps to produce vocal variation and emphasis?

- Do I speak slowly enough to be understood yet fast enough to be interesting?

- Is my voice free of breathiness, nasality, harshness, and hoarseness?

- Is my speech free of substitutions, omissions, extra sounds, and transpositions?

# USING VOCAL SKILLS EFFECTIVELY

### Reading for Those Who Can't

An audiotape narrator preserves books and periodicals on audiotape for persons who are unable to read printed text— people who perhaps have visual or physical impairments.

### Characteristics of an Effective Narrator

An effective audiobook narrator

1 articulates carefully

2 speaks at an optimum pitch, avoiding breathiness, harshness or other distracting vocal manifestations

3 speaks slowly enough to be understood yet fast enough to be interesting

## ACTIVITY

### Situation

You want to be a narrator for an audiobook program for the blind. You have to audition to demonstrate your ability to use effective vocalization.

### Preparation

First, review the guidelines for good vocalization on page 73, and then select a narrative passage to read. Record yourself reading the passage, exchange tapes with a partner, and listen to your partner's tape. If recording equipment is not available, you can read aloud to a partner who will evaluate your delivery.

### Analysis and Assessment

Write a one- or two-page evaluation of your partner's reading using the guidelines for good vocalization on page 73. Share and discuss evaluations with your partner.

## Meet the Narrator

As a narrator for the Texas State Library Talking Book Program, Thérèse East enjoys bringing the joy of reading to people with visual limitations or physical disabilities. She says, "Although the process of recording books can be long, complicated, or even tedious—depending on the subject matter—the satisfaction of making audiobooks available for those who need them makes the task extremely rewarding."

*Thérèse D. East*

# S☆U☆M☆M☆A☆R☆Y

**USING YOUR VOICE** means that you must coordinate parts of your body to generate sound, to resonate sound, and to articulate sound.

- **Generating sound** is primarily a function of the vocal folds (vocal cords)—the muscles of the larynx that vibrate when they are drawn close together.
- **Resonating sound** is effected by the bones in the chest, neck, and head and the cavities of the throat, the nose, and the mouth. These groups of resonators amplify sound.
- **Articulation** is the shaping of the speech sounds into recognizable oral symbols that go together to make a word.
- **Vocalization** has many characteristics: *pitch* (the highness or lowness of sound), *volume* (the force exerted to produce speech tones), *rate* (the speed at which a person speaks—normally from 120 to 160 words per minute), and *quality* (the tone of voice).
- **Articulation problems** make it difficult for a speaker to be understood clearly and easily. The four most common articulation problems are sound substitutions, omissions, additions, and transpositions.
- **Vocalizing effectively** requires breathing properly, using resonators effectively, articulating clearly, and using variety and emphasis.

Look back through this chapter and find the meaning for each of the following terms. Write each term and its meaning in your communication journal.

articulation, p. 59
breathiness, p. 68
cavity, p. 57
circumflex, p. 64
diaphragm, p. 54
fricatives, p. 61
glides, p. 61
harshness, p. 68
hoarseness, p. 69
inflection, p. 63
key, p. 62
larynx, p. 54
melody, p. 63
monotone, p. 63
nasal cavity, p. 58
nasality, p. 67
nasals, p. 61
optimum pitch, p. 62
oral cavity, p. 58
pharyngeal cavity, p. 58
pitch, p. 62
plosives, p. 61
pronunciation, p. 59
quality, p. 67
range, p. 63
rate, p. 66
resonance, p. 56
resonators, p. 56
step, p. 64
trachea, p. 54
vocal folds (vocal cords), p. 54
voiced, p. 61
voiceless, p. 61
volume (loudness), p. 65

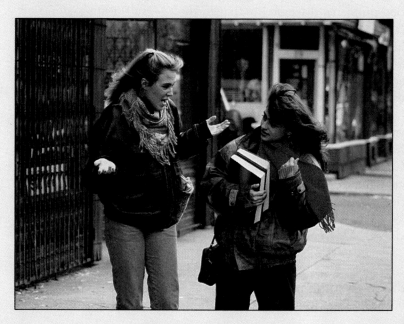

# Review Questions

1. What is the basic difference between the breathing process used in regular breathing and the breathing process used by a person who is speaking?
2. Define *resonance* and explain how bone resonance differs from cavity resonance.
3. Identify the three major cavity resonators and explain how each one affects the sound of the voice.
4. What are the major articulators of sound that are located in the mouth?
5. Why is the International Phonetic Alphabet more effective in symbolizing sound and in studying speech and speech problems than the regular alphabet?
6. What is the difference between pitch and volume as aspects of vocalization?
7. What common problems do speakers have in controlling volume, or loudness?
8. What are the four major vocalization problems that relate to the quality, or tone, of the voice?
9. What are the four major articulation problems that can be remedied with practice?
10. What is the difference between nasal resonance and nasality?

# Discussion Questions

1. Discuss how learning to control pitch, rate, and volume can contribute to the expressiveness of your voice. How can these aspects of your voice be used to emphasize key ideas?
2. Identify ways that a speaker might remedy any of the four articulation problems discussed on pages 70–72—substituting, omitting, adding, or transposing sounds. What particular methods might help to correct these problems?
3. Suppose you are giving a speech in a large room with no public address system. To be heard by everyone in the room, you have to use a loud voice to deliver the speech. Discuss the specific vocalization problems this situation presents. Then discuss the ways in which you can assure yourself that you are generating loudness from the proper source.
4. Consider a wide range of people in the public eye—such as politicians, performers, and newscasters. Do you think that having effective voices is particularly useful for these people? Why or why not? Which of these people in the public eye have particularly effective voices? What makes their voices so effective?
5. The movie *My Fair Lady* is based on Bernard Shaw's play *Pygmalion*. In the play, Professor Higgins claims that he can pass off a flower peddler as a cultured person simply by teaching her how to speak properly. Discuss with your class whether or not such a feat is possible.

# ACTIVITIES

1. **Practicing Breath Control.** Refer to the picture below as you practice the following breath control technique.

   a. With your open palms against your ribs, inhale quickly through your mouth, purse your lips, and blow a steady, forceful stream of air, as if you were trying to blow out a candle some distance from you.

   b. Continue blowing until most of your breath is exhausted.

   c. Feel the inward movement of the abdominal wall and the gradual lowering of the ribs.

   d. Try this also with an actual candle in front of you, this time blowing evenly, with little force, so that the flame merely bends steadily away from you but does not go out and does not waver.

2. **Practicing Vowel Sounds.** The formation of vowel sounds is dependent on how the mouth opening is formed. Say "ah," "aw," "o," "oo," and "ee." Note how your mouth moves from open to closed. Now say the following words separately: *cow, taught, nose, who,* and *me.* Note the opening of your mouth and the changes in that opening as you go through all the words.

3. **Experimenting with Resonance.**

   **A.** Look at the following illustration of bottles filled with liquid. Describe what you think would be the differences in the sound each bottle would make if you blew into each of the bottles in turn to make a musical sound.

   **B.** To perform an actual experiment with cavity resonance, find four 12- or 16-ounce glass bottles similar to the ones shown. Fill each with a different amount of water. Now stretch a thick rubber band between your two hands until it is tight. Hold the rubber band about one inch above one of the bottle openings and then pluck it with your thumb. Repeat this procedure for each of the bottles. In which case was the sound the loudest or fullest? In which case was it the weakest?

   **C.** Next, experiment with different degrees of tightness. While plucking the rubber band, move your hands closer together and then farther apart. When you stretch the rubber band very tight, which bottle now resonates the sound—the one with the most or the one with the least water? Explain your observation about how cavity size affects sound production to your class.

**4. Relaxing the Throat to Gain Resonance.**
The throat works best as a resonator when it is open and relaxed. To open and relax your throat, begin by yawning. Feel the tongue as it is lowered in the back. Your throat is now open. With the aid of a mirror, explore as much as you can see of your mouth and throat during this exercise. Note the position of the tongue when the throat opens. Then with your throat open, read the following phrases aloud to hear how opening your throat affects the sound of your voice.

> Who are you?
> Over the rolling waters go
> Up, up, and away
> Our other operator

**5. Practicing Pronunciation and Articulation.**
Say each of the following lines aloud three times in succession. Try to pronounce each word as carefully as you can.

a. The sea ceaseth and it sufficeth us.
b. The sixth sheik's sixth sheep is sick.
c. She sells seashells by the seashore.
d. The pitcher chided the churlish catcher for changing his signals.
e. Ruby rented rubber baby-buggy bumpers.
f. Three sixths equals six twelfths.
g. Theosphilus Thistle, the successful thistle sifter, in shifting a sieve full of unsifted thistles, thrust three thousand thistles through the thick of his thumb.
h. A tree toad loved a she toad that lived up in a tree.
   He was a three-toed tree toad, but a two-toed toad was she.
   The three-toed tree toad tried to win the she toad's friendly nod,
   For the three-toed tree toad loved the ground
   That the two-toed tree toad trod.
i. How much wood could a woodchuck chuck if a woodchuck could chuck wood? A woodchuck couldn't chuck but a chopped-up chunk if a woodchuck could chuck wood.
j. Peter Piper picked a peck of pickled peppers. If Peter Piper picked a peck of pickled peppers, where is the peck of pickled peppers Peter Piper picked?

**6. Identifying Articulation Problems.** Read each of the following sentences aloud. Then identify each word or word part that contains an articulation problem. Label each problem as a substitution, an omission, an extra sound, or a transposed sound.

a. I think I'll order the roas beef sammich.
b. Janine got an athaletic scholarship to the state university.
c. I'm bout at the end of my rope.
d. Larry aksed her to dance.
e. A scale drawring of the project is available on request.
f. Grandpa jist planted dose rose bushes.
g. This book is due back in the liberry on November 12.
h. My dog Ruffles is ascared of thunder.
i. Bof of dese typewriters need fixin.
j. My favrite circus preformer is the fearless line tamer.

# COMMUNICATION IN THE WORKPLACE

### Background

Your company has assigned you to announce a new development or product in a short address to a local group and in a public address on television or radio.

### Preparing to Do the Job

First, identify a development or product in a field that you know something about. Next, prepare one announcement for a specific group and another for a specific television or radio station.

### Testing Your Skill

Tailor your announcements to suit each of the audiences you chose. Be prepared to present in class one or both of your announcements. Ask for feedback on the effectiveness and clarity of your presentation.

# EVERYDAY COMMUNICATION

### Situation

Your car has been rear-ended at a stoplight. As you climb out to check the damage, you see the other driver yelling angrily. A crowd of witnesses gathers. A few minutes later, a police officer arrives.

### Problem

How would you address the irate driver? the police officer? the witnesses? Write a short scenario showing how you would use communication skills to deal with these different people.

### Assessing Your Skill

This situation requires various methods of communication. You need to be able to change your manner of speaking to assume the roles of all the people in the scenario. Be prepared to present your scenario in class and to discuss how and why you varied your communication for each individual.

Active Listening

C H A P T E R 4

# Listening and Evaluating

**After studying this chapter, you should be able to**
1. Name and analyze factors that affect listening.
2. Identify skills for critical and active listening.
3. List and explain five types of faulty reasoning.
4. Explain what is meant by propaganda.
5. Identify the most commonly used propaganda techniques.
6. Evaluate a speech with an oral critique and a written critique.

## What Makes a Good Listener?

How often has a friend, a relative, or a teacher accused you of not listening? You were obviously within earshot, and you heard what had been said. But hearing and listening are different. **Hearing** means being able to detect sounds. **Listening** means getting meaning from sounds that are heard. Listening seems to be such an easy thing to do, but good listening can be one of the most difficult of all communication skills to master.

What does being a good listener mean? If you try to pinpoint examples of good listening or of people you admire as being good listeners, you begin to see that listening is a valuable skill. Good listeners are attentive and receptive. They actively seek out information, evaluate what they hear, and respond to it.

Effective listening requires concentration and effort. The rewards are worth the effort; as a good listener, you can

- develop your interpersonal skills
- discover unexpected insights
- increase your knowledge and your ability to evaluate
- improve your performance in school and at work

# Analyzing Factors That Affect Listening

Your ability to listen depends on many factors. Recognizing these factors, or conditions, is a first step toward becoming a good listener. Each factor is a potential obstacle to good listening. However, you can learn how to control each one and how to make it work to your advantage.

## Your Physical and Mental State

Attentive listening requires energy and focus. Your energy level can be affected if you are tired or hungry. For example, your ability to focus is lessened if you are distracted by thoughts about personal problems, your plans for the upcoming weekend, or other issues.

## The Speaker

Some people base their willingness to listen on how well they respond to the personality of the speaker. Personality involves a person's traits, attitudes, and habits. Some people attract us; some people annoy us. In listening, personal biases may apply not just to a topic but also to the person speaking. It is true that good listeners prefer to hear dynamic speakers. But you may miss some real enrichment or entertainment if you respond only to a speaker's personality and characteristics or to the manner of delivery.

## Your Prejudices

A **prejudice** is a "prejudgment," or bias: a belief you have already formed that may not be grounded in facts. It is natural to have opinions about ideas, events, and issues. Sometimes, though, you might block real listening by starting out with fixed ideas of what is right or wrong, interesting or boring. Recognizing the effects of your prejudices can help you become a better listener.

## The Environment

The physical setting affects how well you can listen. Are you at a cookout near a lake? Are you in an air-conditioned car on a freeway? Are you in a crowded and overheated auditorium? Are you in a telephone booth at a busy intersection on a cold and windy day?

Listeners constantly have to confront a number of environmental factors such as temperature, light, noise, space and seating, and other people. Good listeners try to overcome the effects of a poor listening environment. For example, despite irritating noise, a good listener may simply concentrate harder to tune out background distractions.

## HOW TO ▷ *Control Factors That Affect Listening*

1. **Be energetic and focused.** Whenever you must be prepared to listen well (for example, in an important review class or in an interview), eat and sleep well beforehand. As you listen, push aside distracting thoughts, plans, or worries.

2. **Focus on the message.** Listen to what is being said. Try to overlook distracting mannerisms that the speaker may have or annoying qualities of the speaker's voice.

3. **Keep an open mind.** Don't shut out any topic or viewpoint. Be ready to learn something new or to deepen your appreciation of your own position.

4. **Do what you can to adjust the physical environment.** When you can, choose your position in the room. Adjust the temperature and lighting, if this is possible. Block out noises or other interference as much as you can.

## Analyzing Your Listening Habits

Over the next two days, identify five listening situations and determine whether or not you listened attentively in each situation. If so, what factors helped you to listen so well? If you had trouble listening, what factors hindered you? Were you able to overcome these factors? How? Share your findings.

## Listening Critically

**Critical listening** means not only comprehending what is being said but also testing the strength of the ideas. Critical listeners are active, not passive.

### Identifying the Speaker's Goal

Good listeners are careful to identify a speaker's specific goal so that they can examine how effectively the speaker achieves that goal. A speaker's **goal** is the purpose he or she has for giving a speech. A speaker has both a general goal and a specific goal.

> **EXAMPLES:** A speaker whose general goal is to amuse an audience might have the specific goal of telling about being a department-store Santa Claus. A speaker whose general goal is to influence others' beliefs might have the specific goal of convincing listeners of the benefit of using solar energy. A speaker who wants to inform his or her audience might explain a geometry theorem.

Sometimes, you will hear the speaker state a goal at the very beginning of the speech. At other times, you will notice that a speaker builds toward the goal and states it only at the conclusion.

### Identifying Main Ideas

**Main ideas** are the speaker's most important points. When speakers imply their main ideas or refer to them vaguely, you will have to analyze the information to identify what you believe are the main ideas. However, some speakers state their main ideas quite clearly—often in the introduction or the conclusion.

> **EXAMPLE:** To conclude, the arguments for solar energy are irrefutable: It is clean, practical, inexpensive, and inexhaustible.

Listen for two techniques, or devices, that speakers use to alert their listeners to main ideas. A speaker may use **repetition,** or repeat a certain word, phrase, or sentence each time a new point is raised. Some speakers rely on **signal words,** words that indicate that a list, contrast, or connection is about to be made.

**EXAMPLES:**

**Repetition:** In this election, *we are fighting for* health care. *We are fighting for* new jobs. *We are fighting for* change.

**Signal words:** *Above all,* we want to vote for change.

## Identifying Supporting Details

**Supporting details** are the examples, facts, statistics, reasons, anecdotes, or expert testimony that a speaker uses to back up main ideas. Identifying supporting details helps you to evaluate whether or not the evidence sufficiently supports the speaker's ideas.

**EXAMPLE:** To support the main idea that solar energy is inexpensive, the speaker might use the following statistic: Out of a sample of 500 families living in Vermont, those who heated their houses with solar energy spent 50 percent less on heating during one winter than did those who heated their houses with oil.

## Using Context Clues

When using words or technical terms that are unfamiliar to an audience, speakers usually provide meaning clues for such terms in the **context,** the surrounding words and sentences. Listen for context clues that a speaker gives you through his or her use of synonyms, comparisons, contrasts, and examples.

**EXAMPLES:**

**Synonyms:** The immune system is vigilant in its search for viruses, always watchful for dangerous invaders. (The less familiar word *vigilant* is explained by the more familiar synonym, *watchful.*)

**Comparisons or contrasts:** Many invading agents are benign, but the body defends itself anyway. (The contrasting word *but* signals that the body does not need defense from something benign. Using this clue, you can guess that *benign* means "not harmful.")

**Examples:** Some people experience anaphylaxis from allergies and can break out in hives, go into shock, and stop breathing. (The examples—break out in hives, go into shock, and stop breathing—show that *anaphylaxis* is a technical term for a severe, life-threatening allergic reaction.)

## Taking Advantage of Nonverbal Clues

In Chapter 2 you learned the importance of **nonverbal clues** such as

- eye contact
- posture
- paralanguage (voice sound and variations)
- movement and gestures
- facial expression
- silence

Since nonverbal clues provide as much as 85 percent of the social meaning of communication, effective listeners carefully weigh speakers' behavior against their words. For many good listeners, paying attention to nonverbal clues—especially those that emphasize or contradict a speaker's words—is an unconscious part of their behavior. To avoid being misled, be alert to two basic effects of nonverbal clues.

**Emphasis.** Speakers can emphasize key meanings through changing volume, stressing certain words, and using gestures.

> **EXAMPLE:** Someone has placed a birthday gift on Maria's desk, and LuAnne is asked if she saw Greg and Xavier leave the gift. The suggested meaning of LuAnne's response will change depending on how she stresses different words.

> I didn't **see** Greg and Xavier put anything on your desk.
> I didn't see **Greg and Xavier** put anything on your desk.
> I didn't see Greg and Xavier put **anything** on your desk.

BLONDIE reprinted with special permission of King Features Syndicate, Inc.

**Contradiction.** By contradicting what a person says, nonverbal clues are like warning flags. However, contradiction does not always mean "This is a lie—beware!"; it may indicate the speaker's uncertainty, confusion, or hidden motive.

> **EXAMPLE:** A friend announces what would seem like good news by saying, "I finally got the letter. I've been accepted at Morganton." However, his low tone of voice and subdued manner indicate his uncertainty.

# A·C·T·I·V·I·T·Y
## 2   Using Critical-Listening Skills

Read an editorial or feature article in your local newspaper. Identify the writer's goal(s), main ideas, and supporting details. Use context clues to determine the meanings of unfamiliar words. Then read your article aloud to a partner while your partner uses critical-listening skills to identify the goal(s), main ideas, supporting details, and context clues. Compare your findings. Then have your partner read his or her article aloud while you practice your critical-listening skills.

# Listening Actively

Good listeners are active, not passive. They look for meaning, think about what they hear, and respond to it. The following chart lists a number of techniques that you can use to develop your ability to listen actively.

| Techniques for Active Listening | |
|---|---|
| **Strategy** | **Examples** |
| **Apply what you hear to yourself.** | • Relate the information to your personal experience.<br>• Use your own knowledge to understand new information.<br>• Imagine yourself using the information in the future. |
| **Think as you listen.** | • Summarize and review throughout the presentation.<br>• Start thinking of questions you want to ask the speaker later.<br>• Predict the speaker's direction, but do not jump to conclusions.<br>• If your prediction about the speaker's meaning is wrong, decide what misled you. |
| **Use associations and mnemonic devices to remember important details.** | • Make an **association**—a vivid mental image—that will help you remember. For example, picture the main factors in early U.S. economic development (cotton and transportation) as a locomotive pulling a canal boat carrying a cotton gin.<br>• Use a **mnemonic device**—a rhyme, acronym (word formed from initials), or other wordplay. For example, the acronym *PIE* might help you to remember three speaking purposes: persuade, inform, entertain. |
| **Take notes.** | • Do not write every detail or quotation verbatim. Use your own words (paraphrase), and focus on key phrases and topics.<br>• Develop a consistent method you can use every time you take notes. For example, write key ideas on the left and details on the right. |
| **Give the speaker— and yourself— feedback.** | • Use body language such as eye contact or a nod to show that you are listening.<br>• Courteously comment or ask questions when the speaker gives you the opportunity to do so.<br>• Always assess your response. Were you impressed, irritated, or neutral? Why? |

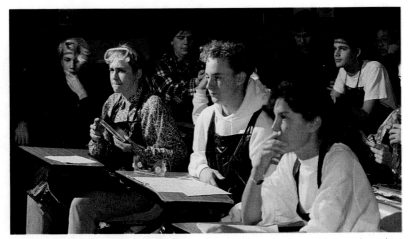

Listening attentively not only shows your regard for others but also improves your ability to understand and respond to the speaker's message.

# ACTIVITY

## 3 Analyzing Your Use of Active-Listening Techniques

Choose a situation in which you can practice active listening. You might choose a situation in the classroom, such as a teacher's lecture or a classmate's speech. Use the chart on page 88 to remind you of specific active-listening techniques that you can use to improve your ability to listen effectively. After the lecture or speech, write a brief summary of the techniques for active listening that you used. Were some of these techniques easier for you to use than others? If you neglected certain techniques, determine why. Then share your summary with a partner or with a small group.

SMALL SOCIETY reprinted with special permission of King Features Syndicate, Inc.

# Evaluating a Speaker's Reasoning

An important part of being an effective listener is evaluating a speaker's reasoning, or logical thinking. Ask yourself if the speaker is using faulty reasoning. **Faulty reasoning** may sound like a contradiction, but it is all too common. Statements that seem reasonable, even well reasoned, are very often based on mistakes in logic. Good listeners know that even when supporting details are precise and accurate, the conclusions drawn from them may be illogical. They can recognize several types of faulty reasoning.

## Hasty Generalizations

**Generalizations** are general conclusions or opinions drawn from particular observations. Valid generalizations are based on sufficient evidence and carry required qualifying words like *most, some,* and *generally.* **Hasty generalizations** are conclusions or opinions that are drawn from very few observations or that ignore exceptions.

> **EXAMPLE:** Seeing John turn his paper in late today, a classmate might make the hasty generalization that John never turns his work in on time.

> **ANALYSIS:** Today may be the only time John has turned in a paper late. Basing a conclusion on only one observation is faulty reasoning.

## Begging the Question

**Begging the question** means assuming the truth of a statement before it is proven. Listeners must be careful to see that speakers have actually proven what they claim as fact.

> **EXAMPLE:** A speaker says, "With my plan, this country's failed and ineffective health care system can be remedied within a decade."

> **ANALYSIS:** The speaker has given no proof that the country's health care system is an ineffective failure.

## False Premises

A **premise** is a stated or implied starting point for an argument: It is assumed to be true. A **false premise** is a premise that is untrue or distorted.

**EXAMPLE:** We're bound to have a winning team this year. Five of our starters are back.

**ANALYSIS:** This statement is built on the premise that experience ensures skill and success. This is not necessarily true (the five returning players may be mediocre), so you cannot conclude that the team will automatically have a winning season this year.

## False Analogies

**Analogy** is a form of reasoning by comparison. A good analogy draws valid conclusions from items that can be logically compared. A **false analogy** draws invalid conclusions from weak or often far-fetched comparisons.

**EXAMPLE:** A band member says to a friend, "I wish you'd learn to play the saxophone so you could join the marching band. Since you play the violin so well, I'm sure you could learn the sax easily."

**ANALYSIS:** The speaker's reasoning is based on a false analogy. Playing a violin well does not ensure that one can also play a saxophone well; both the instruments and the skills needed to play them are very different.

**HAY IS TO HORSES AS...**

**GAS IS TO CARS.**

In this illustration, the analogy is based on a comparison of energy sources, or fuels.

## Irrelevant Evidence

**Irrelevant evidence** is information that has nothing to do with the argument being made. The evidence may sound impressive, but unless it is related to the point at hand, you should ignore it.

> **EXAMPLE:** The merchandise at the Ultra Store is top quality. The manager has clothes shipped in from all over the world.

> **ANALYSIS:** The fact that the clothes come from all over the world is an irrelevant detail that does not support the conclusion that the merchandise is top quality. The manager could be searching worldwide for cheap goods.

# ACTIVITY 4

## Analyzing Faulty Reasoning

With a partner or small group, evaluate each of the following items. Identify the form of faulty reasoning in each one—hasty generalization, begging the question, irrelevant evidence, false premise, or false analogy—and write a brief logical analysis explaining your answer. Be prepared to discuss your answers with the rest of the class.

1. Jackson was the lowest scorer in the game last night. He's simply not a great player and not worth the big money they paid for him.
2. The people claiming doom from the greenhouse effect are like the little boy crying wolf. It hasn't happened, and we shouldn't respond.
3. The nation's food companies are cheating their consumers—every one of us—by raising prices this year. After all, farmers had perfect weather and no shortage of workers.
4. The saleswoman said I looked terrific in the jacket, so I bought it.
5. Look at the year's progress: five new downtown high-rises and not one new park. The manipulation of the city commissioners by real estate developers must be stopped.

# Examining Propaganda Techniques

**Persuasion** is the attempt to convince others to do something or to change a belief of their own free will. [For more information on persuasion and its purposes, see Chapter 15, pages 383–415.] **Propaganda** is persuasion that deliberately discourages people from thinking for themselves. Because its sole purpose is to spread information and claims that further—or destroy—a cause, idea, product, or person, propaganda at its worst relies on one-sided or distorted arguments.

Persuasion also relies heavily on emotional appeals, which attempt to sway people through feelings, not logic. Emotional appeals are perfectly acceptable in persuasion; in fact, they are very important. But when emotional appeals ignore logic or reason, they become a propaganda device. A good listener closely examines any persuasive statement to identify propaganda techniques.

## Transfer

**Transfer** is a method that builds a connection between things that are not logically connected. In advertising, this connection is built between a product and a positive value. Good listeners demand that the link between these things be supported by evidence.

> **EXAMPLE:** An advertisement might show a prosperous, happy, loving family drinking a certain brand of milk. The goal of the transfer technique is to get the viewer to associate the brand of milk with prosperity, happiness, and love.

ONE BIG HAPPY by Rick Detorie. By permission of Rick Detorie and Creators Syndicate.

## Bandwagon

The **bandwagon** technique encourages people to act because everyone else is doing it. Bandwagon attempts to substitute peer or crowd pressure for analysis of an issue or action. Good listeners insist that the speaker give support for the call to action.

**EXAMPLE:** Someone says that you should vote for a proposal because all your friends are voting for it; however, no one mentions why the proposal is worth supporting.

## Name-Calling

**Name-calling** is labeling intended to arouse powerful negative feelings. Its purpose is to represent a particular person or group as inferior or bad without providing evidence to support the claim. Good listeners look beyond labels and ask for evidence to back up the speaker's position.

**EXAMPLE:** A speaker might ask you to vote against a candidate because that candidate is "a warmonger," "a tree hugger," "a preppie," or "an egghead."

## Card-Stacking

**Card-stacking** is based on half-truths. It presents only partial information in order to leave an inaccurate impression. All effective speakers emphasize information that supports their viewpoint. Good listeners withhold judgment until they hear the supporting details or the case for the other side.

**EXAMPLE:** A speaker might refer to a person who has amassed a fortune through intimidation and illegal means as a "good breadwinner." This phrase tells only part of the story since it ignores the negative methods the person used to become a "good breadwinner."

## Stereotypes

A **stereotype** is a biased belief about a whole group of people based on insufficient or irrelevant evidence. A stereotype ignores the individual. Good listeners reject stereotypes and demand specific information.

**EXAMPLE:** A co-worker might say, "Surely you don't plan to discuss the issue with the president of the company! Presidents are too interested in profit and personal gain to care about the problems of a single employee."

## Loaded Words

**Loaded words** evoke, or draw out, very strong positive or negative attitudes toward a person, group, or idea. They can be powerful in their ability to create bias, a leaning toward a particular point of view. The "load" they carry is **connotation,** the feelings or associations a word evokes, in addition to its **denotation,** or specific meaning. Good listeners carefully evaluate the connotations and denotations of words. [See Chapter 2 for a detailed explanation of connotation and denotation.]

> **EXAMPLE:** In discussing assertive behavior, Nan describes herself as "confident," Chris as "pushy," and Rita as a "braggart." Although the behavior described is exactly the same, the use of loaded words makes Nan's behavior seem positive, Chris's behavior seem negative, and Rita's behavior seem worst.

## Emotional Appeals

**Emotional appeals,** or statements used to arouse emotional reactions, can be appropriately used in persuasion. However, when emotional appeals distort the truth or provoke irrational desires and fears, they become propaganda techniques. Good listeners respond to emotional appeals but demand support for any conclusion presented.

> **EXAMPLE:** To gain support for the local humane society, a speaker might tell moving stories about the disposal of animals because of limited resources. People who want to help animals would probably respond emotionally to these specific examples.

In this scene from Arthur Miller's play, *Death of a Salesman,* a son (played by Stephen Lang) makes an emotional appeal for understanding to his father, Willy Loman (played by Dustin Hoffman).

# A·CTI·V·ITY

Identify each of the following items as an example of one of the propaganda techniques discussed in this chapter. When you complete the items, work with a small group of your classmates to compare your answers. Do you disagree on any items? Be prepared to explain your answers.

1. Folks, the upcoming election is going to be a landslide. Garver is carrying the entire West Side. Here's your chance to support a winner the people really want!

2. Friends, my opponent is a fine woman, but she is over sixty. Can you afford a mayor without youth's vigor—who might tire under the pressure, long hours, and huge workload?

3. Only fashionable, good-looking people buy Goodlook clothing. It's the brand to buy.

4. Wilson must be a gangster; he comes from a family of gangsters. A vote for Wilson will put the criminals in control.

5. They're calling Wilson a mouthpiece of organized crime. But would a criminal treat his family in the loving way Wilson does? He is a devoted husband and father. Vote for Wilson.

6. At night, these refugees go to sleep with no food or shelter. In the morning, they wake up to face another day of hunger. Do not ignore the plight of these helpless people. Send money to feed them now.

7. I might be thin, but Kelly is skinny. And Yolanda looks practically emaciated!

8. I want to tell you what a vote for me means. My roots are in a small, rural town. There the sick were always cared for. There the police were always friends, not adversaries.

9. The whole student council and the Athletes' Forum are going to the school board meeting to protest the dress code. You'll be part of the group that stands up and fights!

10. The all-wheel-drive Lion doesn't just go up hills. It positively leaps. Stubborn and sure footed, it is king of the mountain. If your dream is to stand alone on the top, get one vehicle only: the Lion.

# Listening and Evaluating

As a critical, active listener you are always evaluating what a speaker says and how the speaker says it. After your classmates present speeches, you might be called upon to give an oral or written critique of the speaker's effectiveness. A **critique** is an analysis and evaluation.

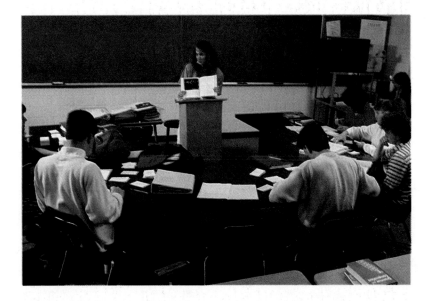

## The Oral Critique

Oral critiques—analyses and evaluations given out loud—provide a valuable learning tool because everyone in the class can profit from analyzing the successes and mistakes of others. Remember that the purpose of an oral critique is not to show how wonderful the critic is. It is to help the speaker understand what went right and what went wrong in the speech. In this way, the speaker can try to build on successes and make needed improvements in later speeches.

# HOW TO > *Give an Oral Critique*

1. **Give positive feedback.** Remember that everyone needs positive reinforcement. Praise one or two things that the speaker did well in the speech. This positive feedback gives the speaker something to build on in the next speech.

2. **When giving negative feedback, concentrate on only one or two criticisms.** Try to avoid overwhelming the speaker by identifying everything that you think the speaker did wrong.

3. **When making criticisms, mention what the speaker could do to improve.** The speaker will find it helpful to have a suggestion or two to think about.

4. **Be specific.** Mention something in particular that the speaker did well. Once again, the speaker will be able to use this information to make his or her next speech better.

## The Written Critique

A written critique usually takes a more complete and detailed look at a speech than an oral critique does. One good way to develop a written critique is to make a checklist of questions. Group these questions in four sections: organization, content, language, and delivery. The answers to your questions will provide you with specific details for your critique.

## HOW TO > *Develop a Written Critique*

1. **Think about the organization of the speech.** How well did all the parts of the speech work together? Did the introduction gain the audience's attention and present a clear statement of purpose? Were the key points of the speech well linked and easy to follow? How effective was the conclusion in summarizing the key points and closing the speech on a high point?

2. **Consider the content of the speech.** Think about how easy it was to understand the message of the speech. Was the topic well developed with sufficient details and examples? Was the message of the speech made clear to the specific audience? Do you think the audience will remember the key ideas of the speech? What did the speaker do to help the audience remember the key ideas?

3. **Analyze the language the speaker used.** Did the language help or hinder the audience's understanding of the speech? Did the speaker use words that the audience understood? Did the speaker define any unfamiliar words or technical vocabulary? Were the words of the speech concrete and vivid or vague and empty?

4. **Comment on the delivery the speaker used.** What do you remember about the speaker's appearance, voice, attitude, and mannerisms? How did each of these affect the success of the speech? What could the speaker do differently in his or her next speech?

*H*ow would you evaluate the speakers you hear on television programs, on the radio, and in your daily life? Make notes in your communication journal about speakers whom you found to be particularly effective. What did they do to make their speeches memorable? What could they have done differently?

# ACTIVITY 6

## Giving an Oral and a Written Critique

**L**ook at the speeches that are listed in the *Appendix of Speeches* [pages 658–683]. Choose one of the speeches listed in the *Appendix* and practice evaluations with a partner. Deliver the speech as if you were delivering a speech you had written. Have your partner use the guidelines discussed in this section to give you an oral critique. Practice to improve your delivery, and then give the speech again. Then, your partner should deliver the speech and you should prepare a written critique of the content and delivery.

# GUIDELINES

## *for Listening Effectively*

- Do I get enough rest and eat properly?

- Do I clear my mind of thoughts and worries that may distract me or affect my ability to concentrate?

- Am I able to overcome a poor listening environment by adjusting it or by ignoring distractions?

- Do I listen even when I am not particularly interested in the topic or disagree with the speaker's position?

- Do I listen to content—what the speaker is saying—rather than focus on a speaker's personality or delivery?

- Do I listen critically by identifying the speaker's goal, the main ideas, and the supporting details of the speech?

- Do I listen actively by thinking as I listen?

- Do I evaluate carefully, keeping alert to faulty reasoning and propaganda techniques?

# LISTENING ACTIVELY

### Listening as Good Medicine

The importance of good listening is emphasized throughout a medical doctor's training. Doctors learn to use the patient's words, tone of voice, facial expressions, posture, body movement, and gestures when they assess the patient's condition.

### Characteristics of a Good Physician

When talking with patients, a good doctor

1. sets aside distractions and listens actively to the speaker

2. responds to others with respect and understanding

3. understands the thoughts and feelings of others

4. asks questions to clarify points that are confusing or unstated

## ACTIVITY

### Situation

You are a volunteer for a group that matches students with appropriate tutors. It is your job to interview the students and determine which specific academic subjects are causing them trouble.

### Preparation

Your goal is to find out how you can best help the student. Make a list of questions that you could ask to determine what academic problems the student is having. You could start by asking which subject (such as math or English) is most difficult for the student, then you could narrow the area of difficulty down to a specific topic (such as fractions or spelling).

### Analysis and Assessment

Have a partner play the role of the student, and present the question-and-answer session in class. Ask for feedback about how actively and effectively you listened and responded to the student's difficulties.

### Meet the Physician

"Listening is an important skill for doctors," Dr. Ira Bell says. "Listening helps me evaluate a patient's condition accurately so I can recommend appropriate treatment. In addition, I sometimes have to evaluate and question what patients don't say just as carefully as what they do say."

*Ira Bell, III, MD*

# S ☆ U ☆ M ☆ M ☆ A ☆ R ☆ Y

**LISTENING AND EVALUATING** are essential skills for communication. An effective listener is attentive and receptive, actively seeks out meaning, evaluates what is said, and responds to it. Becoming an effective listener includes the following steps:

- **Analyze factors that affect listening.** These include your physical and mental state, your prejudices, the speaker's personality and delivery, and the general environment.
- **Recognize and learn to overcome obstacles** to listening.
- **Listen critically** by identifying the speaker's goal, main ideas, and supporting details; by using context clues; and by taking advantage of nonverbal clues.
- **Listen actively** by applying what you hear to yourself, by thinking ahead, by using associations and mnemonic devices to remember important details, by taking notes, and by giving the speaker and yourself feedback.
- **Recognize faulty reasoning,** including hasty generalizations, begging the question, using irrelevant evidence, reasoning from false premises, and using false analogies.
- **Identify propaganda techniques** such as transfer, bandwagon, name-calling, card-stacking, stereotypes, loaded words, and emotional appeals.
- **Give oral critiques and written critiques** of speeches by using guidelines.

## Vocabulary

Look back through this chapter to find the meaning of each of the following terms. Write each term and its meaning in your communication journal.

analogy, p. 91
association, p. 88
bandwagon, p. 94
begging the question, p. 90
card-stacking, p. 94
connotation, p. 95
context, p. 85
critical listening, p. 84
critique, p. 96
denotation, p. 95
emotional appeals, p. 95
false analogy, p. 91
false premise, p. 91
faulty reasoning, p. 90
generalizations, p. 90
goal, p. 84
hasty generalizations, p. 90
hearing, p. 81
irrelevant evidence, p. 92
listening, p. 81
loaded words, p. 95
main ideas, p. 84
mnemonic device, p. 88
name-calling, p. 94
nonverbal clues, p. 86
persuasion, p. 92
prejudice, p. 83
premise, p. 91
propaganda, p. 92
repetition, p. 84
signal words, p. 85
stereotype, p. 94
supporting details, p. 85
transfer, p. 93

# CHAPTER 4

## Review Questions

1. How is listening different from hearing?
2. What are four reasons for developing good listening skills?
3. There are four obstacles to effective listening. List all four obstacles and give one possible way to overcome each obstacle you named.
4. List and explain the five strategies that enable a critical listener to test the strength of the ideas he or she hears.
5. One aspect of critical listening is being able to understand nonverbal clues. In what two important ways can nonverbal clues affect the meaning of a message?
6. Two active-listening techniques are to think ahead and to give the speaker feedback. What is one way you can use each of these techniques?
7. Name and explain five types of faulty reasoning.
8. Define the propaganda technique called card-stacking.
9. What are three other propaganda techniques?
10. List the four guidelines for giving an oral critique.

## Discussion Questions

1. Discuss the difference between average listening and active, critical listening.
2. Imagine that you are in a class that is reviewing information for a test. Discuss some specific obstacles that might interfere with good listening. Then discuss specific behaviors that can help you to overcome these obstacles.
3. Some feel that one of the major problems people face is the inability to listen to each other—to give each other a fair hearing. The Greek philosopher Zeno of Citium wrote, "The reason why we have two ears and only one mouth is that we may listen the more and talk the less." Discuss the meaning of Zeno's words and explain whether or not you agree with him.
4. James Russell Lowell—an American diplomat, essay-writer, poet, and editor—once wrote, "A wise scepticism is the first attribute of a good critic." Discuss the difference between critical listening and uncritical listening. How does this difference relate to Lowell's statement? Do you think he is advocating a refusal to accept reasonable arguments or proofs? Why or why not?
5. The novelist Joseph Conrad—whose works often deal with how a person's beliefs affect his or her goals and choices in life—wrote, "He who wants to persuade should put his trust not in the right argument, but in the right word. The power of sound has always been greater than the power of sense." Discuss the meaning of Conrad's statement. Then discuss how this quotation relates to the difference between persuasion and propaganda.

# ACTIVITIES

**1. Observing and Analyzing Listening Behavior.**
As you talk with people, you are probably conscious of those who really listen and those who do not. The next time you are talking to a group, notice listening behavior. What indicates that a person is listening carefully or is not? What effect does your listeners' attention or inattention have on you as a speaker? Share your findings with your class.

**2. Understanding Propaganda Techniques.**
Look closely at the cartoon below. What propaganda technique is Charlie Brown's little sister trying to use on him? What technique does Charlie Brown use in return? Explain which propaganda techniques you think are used and how they are intended to affect the listener. Compare your answers to these questions with your classmates' answers.

PEANUTS reprinted by permission of UFS, Inc.

**3. Practicing Listening Skills to Gather Information.**
**A.** Talk with two people who have lived in your neighborhood or nearby for at least twenty years. Ask them to tell you what the area was like when they first lived there. Make no notes while they talk, but listen attentively. After each session, write down the important facts you remember. Share your findings with your classmates.

**B.** Working with a partner, listen to a five-minute segment of a radio news broadcast. Then, write down everything you remember hearing. Compare your notes with your partner's.

**4. Interpreting Nonverbal Clues.**
**A.** As you read the items below, try to picture each scene in your mind. Decide whether the nonverbal signals used in each situation serve to emphasize or to contradict the verbal message. Compare your answers with those of your classmates.

1. Laila has been named valedictorian. On hearing the news, Rhonda, a friend of Laila's, looks away and, in a monotone, mutters, "Congratulations. I'm so happy for you."
2. Brandon's sister Felicia is competing in her first marathon. As Felicia nears the finish line, Brandon claps, cheers wildly, and yells, "Way to go, Fish-face! You can do it!"
3. Your new classmate Travis is eating lunch by himself in the cafeteria. You go over to where he is sitting and ask if you may join him. Travis shrugs and says, "Suit yourself," and returns to the book he is reading.
4. You are worried about your neighbor Mr. Winthrop. Lately, you haven't seen him working in his garden as much as you used to. When you ask him if anything is wrong, he looks thoughtful, slowly shakes his head, and says, "No, nothing. Everything's OK."
5. Todd is applying for a job at a fast-food restaurant. He has just asked

the manager about opportunities for advancement in the business. After clearing her throat a few times, the manager says, "Well, um, . . . you know . . . with hard work and, um, determination, you just might, ah, work your way up to a job like mine someday."

**B.** Working with a partner, review the items you found to be contradictory in Part A. Then, try to make the verbal and nonverbal messages agree. Have one partner revise the nonverbal signals to be consistent with the verbal message. Have the other partner revise the verbal messages to be consistent with the nonverbal signals.

## 5. Identifying Memory Devices and Analyzing Their Usefulness.
Make a list of associations and mnemonic devices you use to remember things. For example, some people remember the spelling of *surgeon* because it has two words in it, *surge* and *on*. Make a class list of memory devices. Discuss what makes some of these devices more useful than others and which new ones you will try.

## 6. Identifying and Evaluating Propaganda Techniques.
Spend one week listening and looking for propaganda techniques. Advertisements, commercials, and political speeches are rich sources, but also read newspaper editorials and listen to other speeches, discussions in school or clubs, and television news and talk shows. Record any examples you find of the propaganda techniques on pages 93–95; list, or be ready to explain, their distortions.

## 7. Identifying Your Negative Listening Habits.

**A.** The following statements identify negative listening habits. Do any of them represent your behavior? For each one that does, indicate possible ways to change your behavior.

1. I may fall asleep in afternoon lectures.
2. There are some people I just can't listen to, no matter what they say.
3. When I'm interested in a topic or when I really think a speaker is wrong, I keep butting in.
4. When someone's voice irritates me, I stop listening.
5. I get so tense when we talk about tests that my mind races and I miss what's being said.

**B.** Read the following statements; then indicate whether each statement applies to you often, seldom, or never. Give yourself three points for each *often,* two for each *seldom,* and one for each *never.* If you score ten points or more, you need to work on improving your listening behavior.

1. I do not let a person complete more than a few sentences before I interrupt.
2. I like to finish people's sentences for them.
3. I fiddle with a pen or a pencil or gaze out the window rather than look at the person who is speaking.
4. I do not question a point, ask for examples, or challenge a speaker.
5. I do not try to summarize the key points that a person has made.

# COMMUNICATION IN THE WORKPLACE

### Background

Effective teachers usually listen carefully to their students to evaluate what their students' needs are.

### Preparing to Do the Job

You are a piano teacher or football coach working with a student. Create a hypothetical practice session in which the student is not performing as well as he or she usually does. Is the student depressed or anxious? Is he or she having problems in school? Write the dialogue of a question-and-answer session between you and the student. As you write the dialogue, consider what clues you should listen and watch for to understand your student's problem.

### Testing Your Skill

Rehearse with a partner, and then present the scene to your class. Ask classmates to evaluate how well you, as the teacher, listened to your student.

# EVERYDAY COMMUNICATION

### Situation

You are a parent having a discussion with your teenage son or daughter about improving his or her performance in school.

### Problem

Teenagers often complain that their parents do not listen to them, and parents commonly have the same complaint about teenagers. Can improved listening skills help parents and teenagers communicate better? Write a short dialogue of the discussion between you and your teenager. As you work on the dialogue, consider what kinds of questions you could ask, and how you could respond to questions and statements from your son or daughter. When should you talk and when should you listen?

### Assessing Your Skill

Present your dialogue in class, and discuss how listening skills can improve parent-teen communication.

105

# Interpersonal Relationships

# CHAPTER 5

▼

# Analyzing Yourself as a Communicator

SCRAPBOOK

## What Is Intrapersonal Communication?

Although you may think of communication primarily as interpersonal, or taking place between you and others, you probably spend a great deal of time talking with yourself. This "self-talk" is called **intrapersonal communication.**

Intrapersonal communication helps you determine what you think and how you behave. Much of your thought and behavior depends on how you perceive the world around you.

Your perceptions affect the way you feel about yourself, your attitudes toward communicating, and your ability to make predictions about others.

# Understanding Perception

Did you enjoy the party? Are you a good student? Do you get along well with your classmates? What kind of car would you like?

The answers to these questions depend on your perceptions. **Perception** is an active process of giving meaning to information you receive from your senses. When your perceptions of the world, yourself, and others are accurate, your communication with yourself and others is likely to be accurate as well.

## Aspects of Perception

Perception is the process by which you select, organize, and interpret information from the sense organs.

**Selection.**   Your body receives sensory stimulation constantly, yet you, like most people, probably focus your attention on relatively few sensory details.

> **EXAMPLE:** As you read this book, sights, sounds, and smells are all around you. If your concentration lapses, the buzz of a lamp or the scent of a flower may capture your attention and break your concentration. However, if you are able to refocus your attention on your reading, the distractions that surround you blend into the background once again.

**Organization.**   Once the brain selects sensory details, it begins to organize them. The brain follows certain principles in making sense out of the selected details. For instance, the brain is likely to perceive even complex sensory information as falling into simple forms and recognizable patterns.

**EXAMPLE:** When Roberto and his friend Scott first entered the new super mall, its arrangement appeared to be a jumble. As they walked along, Roberto began to perceive the mall as being organized in the shape of a plus sign: There were large anchor stores at each of the four ends, restaurants and small shops dotting the main walkways, and an atrium with a fountain and seating areas in the center.

**Interpretation of Sensory Information.**  As the brain selects and organizes the information it receives from all of the senses, it completes the process of perception by interpreting the information. **Interpretation** is the process of explaining the information that has been selected and organized.

Because two people may not select the same sensory details or organize them in the same way, they also may not arrive at the same interpretation of objects, events, or other people. This difference of interpretation is important because it directly affects communication.

**EXAMPLE:** Two classmates, Roberto and Scott, wandered separately from store to store in the super mall. Scott, who could make no sense out of the arrangement of stores, said to himself, "This place is a zoo. I'm never coming back here again. I can't find anything." Roberto, on the other hand, was able to make sense out of the arrangement, and thought to himself, "I love this design; it really works to give me access to all the different stores." When Roberto met up with Scott at the food court, he commented, "This place is really something." Scott replied, "It certainly is." Roberto and Scott misunderstood each other's comments. Roberto assumed that Scott was admiring the mall, while Scott assumed that Roberto agreed with him in disliking the place.

The more unclear or complicated the information, the more difficult it is to interpret, and the greater the likelihood of error. For instance, have you ever been startled by something that you saw from the corner of your eye, only to discover that what you thought you saw was far different from what was actually there? Or have you ever thought a stranger was someone you knew because you saw a hairstyle or gesture that looked familiar?

What do you see in this picture? Do you see an image of an old woman with a large nose or of a young woman in profile?

## Individual Differences in Perception

Perception is affected by individual differences. Each person perceives objects, places, events, and people somewhat differently as a result of individual traits, including physical characteristics, background and experience, selected focus, and current mood and circumstances.

**Physical Characteristics.**   Your perceptions are affected by physical characteristics such as your age, size, health, and gender.

> **EXAMPLE:** Mike tried to take his five-year-old son Jerry on the Junior Racer, a children's ride in an amusement park. As they approached, Jerry began to cry: "I don't want to go on this ride. It's too big." Mike was about to say, "No, this is a little ride," but when he looked at it through Jerry's eyes, he understood why his son was afraid.

**Background and Experience.**   Your unique background and past experiences also affect your perceptions. Your past experiences differ from the experiences of others, and other people do not necessarily share perceptions that you take for granted.

> **EXAMPLE:** Two new friends, Laura and Tanya, were trying to decide where to have lunch. Laura had eaten sushi all her life and suggested that Tanya come with her to her favorite Japanese restaurant. "Oh, gross!" replied Tanya. "How could you stand to eat raw fish?" Laura realized that she should not have assumed her new friend would share her opinion and experience of certain kinds of food.

**Selected Focus.**   At any given time, your mind has a focus that affects how you perceive the environment. This selected focus leads you to notice some things and to ignore others

**EXAMPLE:** In art class Krista is studying fabric design and color. When she stops by a friend's house, she is struck by the unusual geometric patterns in the living room drapes. "Wow," Krista says. "I've been in this house several times and never noticed the design of these drapes."

**Current Mood and Circumstances.**   Immediate circumstances and mood also affect perceptions.

**EXAMPLE:** When you are walking downtown, your perceptions will differ dramatically depending on how you are feeling and what you are thinking about. If you are hungry, you will see everything in terms of food. You may walk right by a sale of your favorite running shoes as you look for a restaurant. If you have read about an increase in crime downtown, you may watch the people around you carefully, and tightly clutch the packages you are carrying.

# ACTIVITY 1

## Analyzing Your Perceptions

Take a minute to perceive everything that is around you. Now close your eyes and describe what you saw to a partner. Open your eyes and look again. What did you miss? Can you explain why you selected the items you were able to describe? What caused you to notice these and not other aspects of the environment?

# Thinking About Your Self-Concept

How you communicate and how you behave depend a great deal on what you think of yourself. This section discusses the formation of the self-concept, the accuracy of your self-concept, and the relation of self-concept to communication.

GARFIELD reprinted by permission of UFS, Inc.

## Forming a Self-Concept

Your **self-concept** represents a collection of perceptions about every aspect of your being, including your physical and mental capabilities, your vocational potential, and your communication abilities. The self-concept is formed through what you see and experience, and through what others tell you about yourself.

**Observation and Experience.** Many of your self-impressions are formed by how you observe yourself. You look at yourself in the mirror and make judgments about your weight, attractiveness, dress, makeup, and hairstyle.

> **EXAMPLE:** Gloria is trying on clothes. What she sees will affect what she thinks about herself. If she likes what she sees, she may say, "This looks great! I can really handle these new styles." If she doesn't like what she sees, she may say, "I've got to cut down on junk food—and it wouldn't hurt to get a little more exercise."

Your impression of yourself is also based on experience. You make judgments about what you are good at and what you like.

> **EXAMPLE:** Since Darnell gets his best grades in French class and sees himself as being able to handle the homework in nearly record time each night, he is likely to say to himself, "I'm really good at foreign language."

In general, the greater the number of positive experiences you have, the more positive your self-concept becomes. Likewise, the greater the number of negative experiences you have, the more negative your self-concept may become.

**What Others Tell You.**    In addition to your own observations and personal experiences, your self-concept is usually affected by what others tell you about yourself.

> **EXAMPLE:** You have just given your interpretation of a character in a play you are studying in English class. One of your classmates says, "I didn't really understand the meaning of the main character's actions in that scene until you explained it—you're really good at analyzing plays."

Positive comments are likely to strengthen your self-concept, especially if you admire and respect the person making the comment about you. You use such comments to confirm, strengthen, or alter your self-concept. The more positive comments you receive about yourself, the more positive your total self-concept usually becomes. You feel better about yourself.

## Developing an Accurate Self-Concept

The accuracy of your self-concept depends on the accuracy of your perceptions. Everyone experiences success and failure, and everyone hears praise and blame. If you remember your most successful experiences and positive responses, your self-concept will probably be positive as well. If, however, you perceive and focus on negative experiences and criticism, your perception will be correspondingly negative and your self-concept will be weak. In neither case does the self-concept necessarily conform to reality. Yet in terms of behavior, your *perception* of yourself—what you *think* you are like—will probably have a far greater effect on your behavior than reality is likely to have.

*I*n your communication journal, write down notes expressing your current observations and feelings about your self-concept. You can organize your comments into three categories: "How I see myself," "How others see me," and "How I wish I were." Compare your comments, and note similarities and differences among your three lists. Then write a short statement that summarizes what you have learned about yourself. Because this information is for your own benefit, you do not have to share it with anyone else unless you feel comfortable revealing your personal thoughts and feelings to your classmates.

## Self-Concept and Communication

Your self-concept affects many aspects of your life, especially your intrapersonal communication: problem solving and decision making, behavior, and processing of feedback.

**Problem Solving and Decision Making.** Your self-concept affects the intrapersonal communication you use in problem solving and decision making. When you are thinking, in a sense you are talking to yourself. Faced with a problem or with the need to make a decision, you may be especially conscious of different, and often competing, mental voices.

**EXAMPLE:** After a party, Miguel had this intrapersonal conversation: "I think I made a good impression on Suki. I think I'm going to give her a call. Wait, but she also talked with a lot of other people. Yes, but she spent a lot more time with me than with anyone else. But then, that doesn't mean she cares about me personally. She probably won't even remember who I am."

Several of Miguel's thoughts are competing. His self-concept is likely to determine which voice he listens to. If Miguel feels good about himself, he will probably conclude that Suki was sincere, and he will call her.

**Behavior.** Self-concept also directly affects your behavior. People with strong self-concepts are likely to focus on positive experiences they have had; people with weaker self-concepts are more likely to focus on negative experiences. This intrapersonal communication will actually influence performance.

**EXAMPLE:** Anton perceives himself as a good public speaker. Concerning a speech assignment, he thinks, "I've got a lot going for me. I'll do well on this assignment." Because he is confident, he stays relaxed, prepares calmly, and practices the speech. Just as he predicted, he gives a good speech and receives a high grade. Bryan, on the other hand, perceives himself as a poor speaker. He thinks, "I know I'll mess up this speech!" Expecting failure, he cannot concentrate on preparing, he does not take time to practice the speech, and he tells himself constantly that he is going to do poorly. Just as he predicted, he gives a poor speech and receives a low grade.

**Processing of Feedback.** Self-concept can also affect how you process the feedback you receive. You are likely to choose to listen to messages that reinforce, or strengthen, your self-perception. In effect, you hear only what you want to hear. However, positive feedback can improve your self-concept.

EXAMPLE: Anton thinks he is a good speaker. If he hears one comment praising his information and one criticizing his eye contact, he will listen to the praise and say, "I guess my eye contact wasn't as good as it could have been, but I'll improve that before the next speech."

If Bryan gets the same comments, he will probably process them differently. He will listen to negative comments about his speech and play down or screen out positive comments. Thus, Bryan will say to himself, "I don't know why I got praise for my material. It wasn't that good; anyone could have found out that information. But my poor eye contact really must have ruined the speech. I'll never get any better."

# ACTI·V·ITY
## 2   Conducting a Self-Concept Check

For each of the following topics, write down the number that most closely represents your self-evaluation in that area.

| Topic | Negative | | Neutral | Positive | |
|---|---|---|---|---|---|
| **1.** My appearance | 1 | 2 | 3 | 4 | 5 |
| **2.** My work habits | 1 | 2 | 3 | 4 | 5 |
| **3.** My accomplishments | 1 | 2 | 3 | 4 | 5 |
| **4.** My scholastic abilities | 1 | 2 | 3 | 4 | 5 |
| **5.** My athletic abilities | 1 | 2 | 3 | 4 | 5 |
| **6.** My social skills | 1 | 2 | 3 | 4 | 5 |

For each topic area for which you recorded a *1* or a *2*, write one example to illustrate this evaluation. Then, for each of these statements, write three examples that give a more positive view. Now reconsider your ratings: Is it possible that you were too hard on yourself?

# Assessing Needs: Sources of Behavior

Why did Maria decide to run for student council president? Why did Tyrone elect a course in psychology rather than computer science? Why did Jasmine stay up so late studying? These questions consider **motives,** the sources of behavior. People display very diverse motives as they respond to biological and social needs.

## Types of Needs

People have the same biological needs: the needs for food, water, and sleep. But social needs vary on the basis of background and experience.

**Interpersonal Needs Theory.** Many social scientists have demonstrated that interpersonal needs influence behavior. For instance, William Schutz, a psychologist, lists three basic interpersonal needs that affect behavior:

- the need to give or receive affection from others
- the need to include others or be included in relationships
- the need to control others or relinquish control to them

People also have needs for pleasure, relaxation, and escape. Thus, people communicate with others to have fun, to unwind, and to fill time while avoiding other activities.

| Common Social Needs | | |
|---|---|---|
| achievement | escape | nurturing |
| affection | inclusion | pleasure |
| control | independence | relaxation |

People's needs differ and change over time. When other people's needs differ significantly from yours and you do not understand that, communication may break down. Moreover, unfulfilled needs can lead to anxiety or unhappiness and may weaken a person's self-concept.

**Maslow's Hierarchy of Needs.** According to Abraham Maslow, a noted psychologist, behavior is motivated by a **hierarchy of needs,** a ranking of five general categories of needs: physiological, safety, love, esteem, and self-actualization. These needs form a pyramid, with the most basic needs at the bottom of the pyramid. Once the basic, lower-level needs are met, people move to higher levels of need.

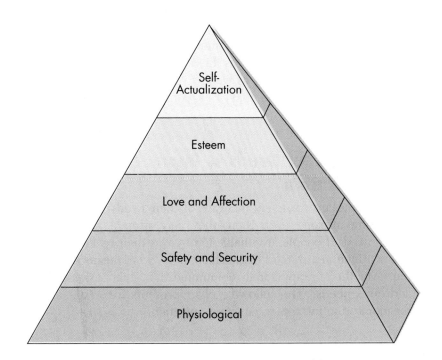

- **Physiological Needs:** The most basic needs are the physiological, or bodily, needs for food, water, and stable body temperature. They form the base of the "needs pyramid." These basic needs must be satisfied before a person can become concerned about needs at higher levels.
- **Safety and Security Needs:** These needs include self-preservation and concern about long-term survival. They motivate people to take care of themselves—for example, to take a course in self-defense. These needs also motivate people to seek stable jobs, to buy insurance, and to save money for the future.
- **Love and Affection Needs:** These needs are met by group and family membership and by the development of friend-ships. People want to feel as though they have someone to count on, especially when they go through hard times.
- **Esteem Needs:** People need status, recognition, and attention. They can meet these needs by gaining expertise in a particular job or area of study, by sharpening athletic skills, or by purchasing products that will make them feel good and look good in the eyes of their peers.
- **Need for Self-actualization:** The drive a person has to be everything that he or she can be, to take full advantage of his or her talents and abilities, is called **self-actualization.**

Seeing needs as a hierarchy helps to explain behavior. For example, when you are hungry or tired, you may not want to talk with a friend or work on your homework. First you need to meet a basic physiological need. This hierarchy helps you understand other people's motivations as well as your own. For example, if a friend needs esteem, he may seek compliments or praise after doing a job well.

## Assessing Your Needs to Improve Communication

Most people are relatively unaware of their needs until they feel something missing; even then, they may attempt to satisfy the wrong need. If people are unable to discover their real needs, they will continue in a state of dissatisfaction. By what means do people improve the intrapersonal communication that assesses and addresses needs? The following chart presents three suggestions for monitoring intrapersonal communication.

## HOW TO > *Monitor Intrapersonal Communication*

1. **Take time to be alone and to think about yourself.** During your time alone, you can evaluate how well you are meeting your personal goals. If you are not meeting those goals, you have a choice: Work out different methods for achieving your goals, or set more realistic personal goals. Try to determine what you really want to do, both in the short term (for instance, three months from now) and in the long term (perhaps next year). For example, maybe you want to be a lifeguard next summer but are not currently qualified for the job. A short-term goal might be to find out how you can become qualified. A long-term goal might be to learn the necessary skills so that you can apply for a job as a lifeguard.

2. **Conduct a self-concept check.** Discover how you are feeling about yourself. If you find aspects of your self-concept that you wish were different, plan ways of making changes. For instance, if being out of shape is causing a negative self-concept, set a goal of walking for thirty minutes three days a week.

3. **Check your ideas with a close friend, relative, or trusted adult.** Make lists of your strengths and weaknesses, your goals, and your methods of achieving those goals. Then, discuss these lists with someone who can help you check the accuracy of your self-concept. For instance, you may believe that people stay aloof from you because they do not like you. However, as you discuss this idea with the person you trust, your confidant may suggest a reason for people's behavior that you have not considered. For instance, your friend may point out that people seem aloof because they see you as having more self-discipline than they have, which in turn makes them feel uncomfortable.

**For Better or For Worse**®                                      **by Lynn Johnston**

## Making Changes in Self-Concept

Even though people are constantly changing physically, they are likely to resist changes in their self-concept. At times, people seem bent on maintaining low impressions of their abilities or performances.

> **EXAMPLE:** In middle school, Josie did not get good grades in math. Later, when Josie took algebra and geometry in high school, she found herself getting above-average grades. However, when a friend asked whether she would take precalculus, Josie said, "No, I've just been lucky—I'm not really very good at math." Josie's self-concept does not reflect her actual ability. Stubbornly maintaining that she cannot do well in math cements artificial limits that may prevent her overall growth.

To make any conscious change in self-concept, you first have to recognize that some kinds of behavior are more likely to get positive responses. Then you need to engage in those kinds of behavior.

As you make positive changes in your self-concept, you are likely to begin getting positive responses from others. If your self-concept tends to be weak, these positive responses may encourage you, proving that it was not *you* that people acted negatively toward, but your former behavior. Keep the following ideas in mind as you consider making changes in your self-concept.

- Ask yourself if you really need to change, or if you are being overly critical of yourself.
- Remember that you cannot change everything and that change takes time.
- Commit yourself to change through self-discipline.
- Seek advice about making changes from parents, friends, teachers, and counselors.

# Interacting with Others

How well you interact with others depends on your attitudes and goals and on your understanding of interpersonal roles.

## Examining Attitudes and Goals

When you approach people, what is your attitude toward communication? Are you positive or negative? What are your communication goals?

**Attitudes.**   **Attitudes** are relatively long-lasting organizations of beliefs that cause you to respond in particular ways. Attitudes include positive or negative evaluations or feelings toward objects, people, and events. Your attitude toward communication depends on your personal orientation, your level of shyness, and your sense of control.

- **Personal Orientation:** Your own attitude toward communication is closely related to your self-concept. Some people see themselves as **extroverted,** social individuals who are relationship-oriented and responsive to the needs of others. Extroverted people are likely to look forward to communicating and interacting with people. Other people may see themselves as **introverted,** or withdrawn, individuals who keep more to themselves and who are less responsive to others' needs. Introverted individuals are less likely to look forward to communication. They tend to look for activities that they can do alone.
- **Level of Shyness:** Your attitude toward communication may depend on your level of shyness. Regardless of how extroverted you might be, you are likely to experience

shyness in some situations. Most people are shy only in particular situations. For instance, some people feel nervous only when they walk into a room of strangers, while others may feel shy only when they are in the company of supervisors, teachers, or other authority figures.

- **Sense of Control:** Your attitude toward communication may be based in part on your sense of control—whether you view life and events as being within your control. People who believe that what happens to them is controlled by forces outside of themselves are less likely to have favorable attitudes toward communication. On the other hand, people who believe that nearly every aspect of life is within their control are more likely to have favorable attitudes toward communication. They see themselves as capable of having an effect on their own lives, others' lives, and their environment.

**Goals.** **Goals** are aims that you hope to achieve or accomplish through communication. Make your goals realistic. Expect to find a summer job as a sales clerk rather than as a sales manager. The better you are at setting and accomplishing realistic goals, the higher your self-esteem will rise. If you have clearly defined goals and if you believe that you have some control over your destiny, then you are more likely to look favorably on communication as a means of achieving your goals.

# Calvin and Hobbes

**by Bill Watterson**

**Your Commitment to Effective Communication.** To begin to improve your communication, you must be committed to communicating well. You must be willing to talk with others in an effort to improve your communication. Most people do not become better communicators without this kind of conscious effort.

## Analyzing Interpersonal Situations

As you have grown up, you have learned to adapt your behavior to particular interpersonal situations. You have probably developed a public as well as a private self. Your public self is shown through a variety of roles that you choose to play. How successful you are in interpersonal situations depends on how accurately you assess the times and places for playing these different roles.

**Your Public and Private Selves.**   Your **public self** is that part of yourself which you choose to share with everyone. You may show a different public self in different circumstances. For example, you might show yourself to be outgoing, confident, and fun loving; you might show yourself to be thoughtful, caring, and cautious; or you might show yourself to be powerful, in charge, and boisterous. Your public self is thus displayed in the various roles you choose to play.

Your **private self** is that part of yourself which is most true to your self-concept. You may choose to show yourself to be outgoing, confident, and fun loving, when in reality you may be just the opposite. Ordinarily you reveal your private self only to those who are close to you.

**Playing Different Roles in Different Circumstances.**   In your interactions with others, you display your public self by playing various roles. A **role** is a pattern of behavior that characterizes a person in a given context, or situation. Based on your self-concept, needs, and attitudes, you learn many roles that you can play. With some of these roles you have great success, and these become roles that you enjoy playing. With others, you do not do as well, and so you may stop trying to play them.

**EXAMPLE:** Whenever Rubén senses tension in his Spanish class, he responds by behaving humorously. The other students laugh, and even the teacher smiles. Since Rubén enjoys this attention, he begins to exhibit similar behavior in similar circumstances. Again, Rubén enjoys the attention it gets him, and the role of class comedian becomes a major part of his public self.

Jason sees the attention Rubén is getting, so he too tries to act up in similar circumstances. However, if the class does not respond as they do for Rubén, Jason is likely to question whether he should continue trying to play the role of comedian. If the class consistently responds in a negative way, Jason will probably stop playing this role.

**Assessing the Time and Place to Play a Role.** The appropriateness of a role depends on the time and the place. You need to assess when a role you are playing is appropriate.

**EXAMPLE:** Rubén has learned that he can behave humorously and get positive reinforcement from his friends and classmates. But Rubén must also learn that this role is not always appropriate. When the situation calls for giving information or solving problems and Rubén tries clowning, his behavior is likely to be disruptive and inappropriate. If Rubén's little brother Juan asks for advice and Rubén tells him a joke, Rubén is likely to get a negative response. He must learn that although there may be room for a little humor in certain contexts, this behavior becomes obnoxious when circumstances call for a serious approach.

Good communicators are adept at a variety of roles. Over time, you learn when the various roles you can play are most appropriate for the situation and for the people with whom you are communicating. When you determine what role to play, you will need to consider the compatibility of needs and the best way to arrive at shared goals.

- **Need Compatibilities:** Often, it is important that the roles you play meet others' needs. When you are talking, what you say will be evaluated by others in terms of their needs. When the role you wish to play is not compatible with others' needs, they will probably assess the role you are playing as inappropriate.

**EXAMPLE:** Gail and George are sharing humorous stories of their work experiences. Marcia gets into the conversation and begins playing the role of advice giver. The other two ignore Marcia's advice and return to their conversation. Because Gail and George are sharing the stories for entertainment, not to get advice, Marcia receives a negative response. The role she is playing is not appropriate to the needs of Gail and George.

- **Shared Goals:** Communication works best when the roles of those involved meet shared goals. Although you may have your own motivation for behaving a certain way at a certain time, the various roles that you play will be considered inappropriate if they do not fit in with the shared goals of your group.

**EXAMPLE:** A committee is trying to complete the final draft of a proposal that it must finish right away. Andrew decides to take his time and to analyze every statement thoroughly. Although careful examination is often necessary, the current shared goal is for the group to complete the task as quickly as possible. Therefore, Andrew's role of careful analyzer is likely to be seen as inappropriate by other committee members at this time.

## ACTIVITY 3

### Assessing Roles

For three days, record the various communication situations you experience. Describe the roles you chose to project in each. Then write an analysis of these roles and observations. To what extent does your communication behavior differ, and to what extent does it remain the same in different situations? What factors in a situation seem to trigger certain behaviors in you? How satisfied are you with the roles that you displayed in each situation? In which situation were you most pleased? least pleased?

# Making Predictions About Others

How well you communicate with others depends at least in part on your ability to make accurate predictions about them. Predictions about others are based on your own self-concept and on your first impressions.

## Basing Predictions on the Self-Concept

Your self-concept not only influences your communication behavior but also affects how you perceive others. The specific influence of your self-concept on your understanding of others can be seen in three areas: accuracy, acceptance, and personality.

**Accuracy.** The more accurate your self-concept, the more accurately you can perceive others. However, if you have difficulty determining your own strengths and weaknesses, you will probably be unable to determine accurately the strengths and weaknesses of others. For example, if Angela fails to see that she tends to be dependent on others, she is not very likely when she meets Mark to see that he is self-centered.

**Acceptance.** The more you accept yourself, the more likely you are to see others favorably. If you have difficulty liking who you are, you will be less likely to care for others. For example, if Sarah likes herself, she is more likely to see positive qualities in other people.

**Personality.** Your personal characteristics influence the type of characteristics you are likely to perceive in others. For example, Taneesha is a very caring person. Given her own level of caring, she perceives that the people she meets are caring as well.

## Basing Predictions on First Impressions

Besides being affected by self-concept, predictions about others are also a result of factors that influence first impressions: physical characteristics, social traits, stereotyping, and emotional states.

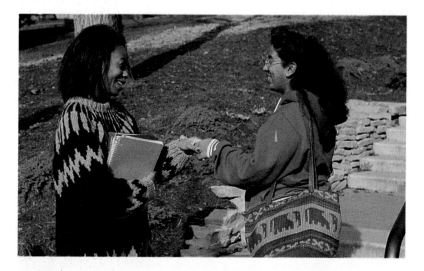

**Physical Characteristics.**   When two people meet, they form first impressions of each other based on physical characteristics. For example, at a party Ken sees an attractive young woman across the room. He taps his friend Dave on the shoulder, points to her, and says, "I've got to meet her." In some cases, merely looking at a photograph may create a strong impression.

**Social Traits.**   First impressions are also made on the basis of perceived social traits. As a result of seeing a single instance of behavior, you may attribute certain traits to people. For example, after a party, Carlos asks Mimi what she thought of Randy. Mimi, who had heard Randy bragging about himself to a group of people, answers, "Randy? He's really self-centered."

Notice that this judgment follows a single episode. Observing a person's behavior in a single situation and basing a judgment on that one situation can lead you to judge a person's other characteristics without further investigation—a tendency known as the **halo effect.**

EXAMPLE: Sonja perceives Francesca as a warm, caring person. Since these characteristics are important to Sonja and are part of her own personality, Francesca has a "halo effect" as far as Sonja is concerned. If a friend accuses Francesca of being aloof, Sonja may rush to Francesca's defense. The halo effect may lead Sonja to assume that Francesca is always friendly.

**Stereotyping.**   **Stereotyping** is assigning characteristics to a person solely on the basis of the person's membership in a certain group. Remember that everyone is a member of some identifiable group. Once you identify a person as a member of a specific group, you must be careful not to judge the individual on the basis of impressions that you associate with the particular group. Remember that each person you meet is a unique individual.

> **EXAMPLE:** When Della is introduced to Carl, a football player, her first impression may be affected by her stereotype of athletes. Because the few athletes she has known didn't do very well in school, Della has always assumed that *all* athletes are poor students. If Della judges Carl on the basis of this stereotype, she may be surprised when she learns that Carl is an honor student.

The problem with stereotypes is that they are often wrong. They can also be terribly hurtful. Stereotypes are oversimplified opinions or uncritical judgments of others formed when people perceive a characteristic in a few members of a group and assume that the characteristic is typical of the entire group. Stereotyping ignores individual differences. In even its mildest form, this particular shortcut will lead to inaccurate predictions about others and thus to ineffective communication.

**Emotional States.**   Your feelings at any given moment also affect your first impressions of others. If you are cheery, your impressions of people are likely to be positive; if you are depressed or angry, your first impressions are likely to be negative.

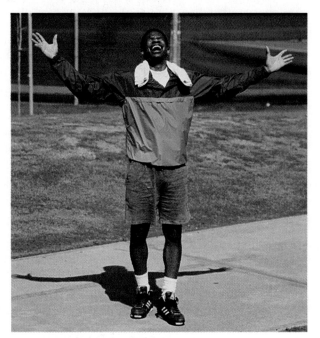

> **EXAMPLE:** Bonnie is having a great day. Dana introduces her to Marsha, a girl who has just transferred from another school. Since Bonnie feels happy, she is willing to see Marsha in a positive light. Bonnie offers to be a friend, saying, "Transferring to a new school has to be tough; if I can help you with anything, I'll be glad to." Linda, on the other hand, is having a bad day. As Dana introduces her to Marsha, she thinks, "Oh, great. A helpless new kid. I hope Dana doesn't expect me to play nanny and show her around."

Your emotional state may also affect the motives you assign to others' behavior. Besides making judgments about people, you also try to construct reasons about why people behave as they do.

**EXAMPLE:** Darlene has agreed to meet Justine right after school. After waiting for half an hour, Darlene begins thinking of reasons why Justine is late. If she is in a good mood, Darlene may decide that Justine's lateness is for a good reason. If she is in a bad mood, Darlene may believe Justine is simply being inconsiderate.

## Confirming Perceptions

Because inaccuracies in perception are common and influence how you communicate, improving perceptual accuracy is an important first step in becoming an effective communicator. The following suggestions can help you to construct a more realistic impression of others as well as to assess the soundness of your perceptions.

## HOW TO *Check Your Perceptions*

1. **Seek more information to verify perceptions.** If your impression of someone is based on only a few pieces of information, you need to learn more before you act on your conclusions. Remember that your perception is subject to change. You can then collect more information to determine whether your original perception is accurate.

2. **Recognize that even if your original perceptions were accurate, people change over time.** You need to make an effort to observe a person's behavior without bias and be prepared to change your perception when it is appropriate. For example, someone you did not like in elementary school may now be a different kind of person.

3. **Talk with the people about whom you are forming perceptions.** The more information you have to work with, the more likely your perceptions are to be accurate. And the best way to get information about people is to talk with them. If you have perceived someone as self-centered or untrustworthy on the basis of one experience, postpone your judgment until you have a chance to get to know the person.

4. **Check perceptions verbally.** Because your judgments affect your ability to communicate effectively, you should try to confirm your perceptions. A **perception check** is a verbal statement that reflects your understanding of another person's nonverbal cues. [See page 28 of Chapter 2.] You should (1) watch the behavior of the other person, (2) ask yourself, "What does that behavior mean to me?" and (3) put your interpretation of the behavior *into words* to verify whether your perception is accurate.

# ACTIVITY 4

## Analyzing Predictions About Others

**T**hink of a recent situation in which you made a prediction about someone. In a paragraph, analyze your perception of that person and how you developed this impression. What was your perception of the person? How was it affected by your self-concept? How was your perception affected by your first impression? How did you confirm your perception of this person? Do you think your perception—your prediction about this person—was accurate?

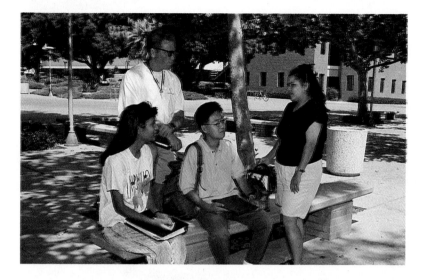

## GUIDELINES

### for Analyzing Yourself as a Communicator

- Do I use intrapersonal communication to assess my perceptions and needs?

- Are my perceptions of myself and others accurate and realistic?

- Am I trying to achieve a positive self-concept?

- Do I have a positive attitude toward interacting with others?

- Have I made a commitment to communicating effectively?

- Am I aware that the roles I adopt must be appropriate to the time and place and to others' needs?

- Do I make accurate predictions about others?

- Do I check my perceptions of others for accuracy?

# IMPROVING EXPRESSION SKILLS

### Best Foot Forward

Many people find that they must sharpen their communication skills in order to advance in their careers. One resource for instruction and practice is a leadership or management-skills trainer.

### Characteristics of a Good Leadership Trainer

A good leadership trainer

❶ helps trainees recognize how self-concept affects their effectiveness in leading others

❷ understands how a trainee's attitudes, goals, and interpersonal roles affect the clarity of his or her communication

❸ assesses trainees' needs to evaluate reasons for actions and attitudes that affect communication

## ACTIVITY

### Situation

You have a classmate who is new to your school, and you would like to get to know him or her better.

### Preparation

Choose a partner to play the role of the new classmate. Ask your partner to tell you about an activity he or she enjoys. What part does your classmate take when he or she is engaged in this activity? Why does the partner enjoy participating in this activity? How did your partner get interested in the activity?

### Analysis and Assessment

After the conversation, write a few sentences, summarizing what you have understood about your partner's goals and attitude about the activity. Then share your findings with your partner. Does he or she agree with what you have written? Discuss how your partner might express ideas differently in order to convey a clearer or more accurate impression of his or her goals and attitudes.

**M**eet the Leadership Trainer

Leadership trainer Martha Lask says, "Many people who have trouble communicating are self-conscious, and they fear being harshly judged by others. If I do my job right, the trainees leave the training session with more self-confidence and a better understanding of how their own perceptions, needs, and goals affect their ability to communicate."

*Martha Lask*

# S★U★M★M★A★R★Y

**ANALYZING YOURSELF AS A COMMUNICATOR** involves intrapersonal communication. This "self-talk" helps you to determine what you think and how you behave. Much of your thought and behavior depends on how you perceive others and the world around you.

- **Understand perception** as a process of selecting, organizing, and interpreting sensory information. Individual differences in perception occur because of physical characteristics, background and experience, selected focus, and current mood and circumstances.

- **Think about your self-concept,** a collection of perceptions based on your own observations and experience as well as what others tell you about yourself. An accurate self-concept helps you with problem solving and decision making; it also affects your behavior and how you process feedback.

- **Assess needs,** your own as well as others', to evaluate reasons for actions and attitudes in order to improve your ability to communicate.

- **Interact with others** by examining your own attitudes and personal goals and analyzing interpersonal situations in which you wish to communicate.

- **Make predictions** about appropriate communication based on your own self-concept and on your impressions about others. Then check your perceptions for accuracy.

## Vocabulary

Look back through this chapter to find the meaning of each of the following terms. Write each term and its meaning in your communication journal.

attitudes, p. 122
extroverted, p. 122
goals, p. 123
halo effect, p. 128
hierarchy of needs, p. 118
interpretation, p. 111
intrapersonal communication, p. 109
introverted, p. 122
motives, p. 118
perception, p. 110
perception check, p. 130
private self, p. 124
public self, p. 124
role, p. 124
self-actualization, p. 119
self-concept, p. 114
stereotyping, p. 129

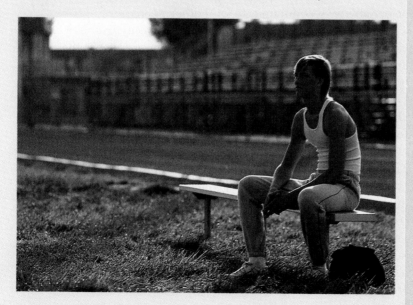

# Review Questions

1. Define *intrapersonal communication* and explain how it is useful.
2. *Perception* is the process of giving meaning to information you receive from your senses. What are three aspects of perception?
3. Individuals often differ in the way they perceive people, places, and things. What are four different factors that may affect perceptions?
4. Define the term *self-concept* and explain how a self-concept is formed.
5. What are the three ways that the self-concept affects someone's intrapersonal communication?
6. From lowest to highest, what are the five levels of needs in the hierarchy of needs as defined by Maslow?
7. Identify three ways that you can monitor your intrapersonal communication.
8. What are three factors that may have an effect on your attitude toward communicating?
9. In many cases, predictions we make about others are affected by our own self-concepts, but these perceptions may also be affected by *stereotyping*. What is stereotyping?
10. A good method for determining the accuracy of your evaluations or judgments is to confirm your understanding with a *perception check*. What is a perception check?

# Discussion Questions

1. Discuss the importance of developing a positive self-concept. Then discuss the ways that a person's positive self-concept can affect his or her ability to communicate with other people.
2. The English writer William Hazlitt once wrote, "He who undervalues himself is justly undervalued by others." Discuss the meaning of this quotation. Do you agree or disagree? Discuss how this quotation relates to intrapersonal communication.
3. Do you consider yourself a good judge of a person's character? Discuss what you think makes someone a good judge of character. Identify several specific characteristics that you think a good judge of character should have.
4. The journalist John Morley wrote, "Labels are devices for saving talkative persons the trouble of thinking." Discuss the meaning of this statement, and explain how this statement relates to the concept of stereotyping.
5. Discuss at least one recent situation that you were involved in (either as a participant or a witness) in which a perception check helped the people involved in the situation to communicate more effectively.

# ACTIVITIES

**1. Developing a Self-Logo.** Develop a logo that represents you. A logo is a distinctive trademark. For example, thumb through magazines to examine the logos for car and clothing companies. Your logo should contain a name and some kind of visual element or illustration. Be prepared to give a short explanation of how the logo you have designed features your key characteristics.

**2. Writing a Tribute or Eulogy.** Every newspaper keeps prewritten statements about people in the news so that it will have an article ready if the paper is ever required to print a tribute or a eulogy in the next edition. If a newspaper kept a file about you, what do you think the article would say? Write a two-paragraph statement that you believe captures your personal qualities.

**3. Analyzing Your Strengths and Weaknesses.** For your own information, copy and then complete the following chart. Because this is primarily for you, you do not need to share your analysis with anyone else.

Contrast your responses in the top and bottom portions of the chart. What have you learned from successful situations that you might use in situations in which you do not handle yourself as well as you would like?

**4. Writing Perception Checks.** For each of the following situations, write a well-phrased perception check—a statement that indicates how you would interpret the emotional state of the person. Then say each statement aloud as if you were speaking to the person described. Does each of your statements sound honest and natural? If not, revise each statement until it does.

a. Natalie comes rushing into her room, throws her books on the floor, and sits at her desk, holding her head between her hands.

b. Franco comes home from football practice with a pale face and slumped shoulders.

c. As you return the sweater you borrowed from Tammy, she stiffens, grabs the sweater, and starts to walk away down the hall.

| Situations I do not handle as well as I would like | How I feel in the situation | How I handle the situation | How I might handle the situation with a greater sense of self-worth |
|---|---|---|---|
| Situations I handle well | How I feel in the situation | How I handle the situation | What gives me a sense of self-worth about the way I handle the situation |

d. Miss Hicks told you earlier today that you could come in after school this afternoon to talk with her about your college search. When you arrive at her office, she looks up at you, squints her eyes, and frowns.

5. **Identifying Occupational Stereotypes.** Make a chart like the one below. To complete the chart, picture a person working in each of the occupations listed. As you picture the person, identify descriptive characteristics for each one. Then answer the following questions.

a. What did you use as a basis for filling in the chart?
b. How well do you think your chart would provide you with information about someone introduced to you as having that occupation?
c. How much do you think the information from your chart would influence your attitude toward the person?
d. What have you learned about stereotyping as a result of completing this activity?

| Occupation | Physical characteristics | Gender | Salary | Education | Leisure activity | Automobile |
|---|---|---|---|---|---|---|
| Television newscaster | | | | | | |
| Department store salesperson | | | | | | |
| High school teacher | | | | | | |
| Doctor | | | | | | |
| Automobile mechanic | | | | | | |
| Clerical worker | | | | | | |
| Construction worker | | | | | | |

# COMMUNICATION IN THE WORKPLACE

### Background
Your attitude about your job is one of the most important factors affecting your performance. Remember that a job can help you fulfill many of your needs, such as providing money for physiological needs like food and shelter.

### Preparing to Do the Job
Study Abraham Maslow's hierarchy of needs on page 119, and consider how a job in your field of interest can help fulfill those needs. What needs are not met by the job you chose? Write a two- or three-page report on how the job you chose can help fulfill your needs. Since you can't count on your job to fulfill all of your needs, include an alternate source of fulfillment for each need.

### Testing Your Skill
Read your report aloud in class, and ask your classmates for feedback. How well did you relate how your chosen job can help fulfill your needs?

# EVERYDAY COMMUNICATION

### Situation
Your self-concept—that is, what you think of yourself—can be influenced by what you admire in other people.

### Problem
In a brief paper, identify a personal hero—perhaps someone you know, a fictional character, a historical figure, or someone in public life—and discuss what you might learn from this person.

### Assessing Your Skill
In your paper, you should consider what admirable traits your subject has. Do you see any of those traits in yourself? Would you like to? How do you think you could develop these traits in yourself? Think of at least three ways you can incorporate these traits into your everyday behavior. Now, imagine that you have incorporated some of these admirable traits. How would your self-concept be affected?

Friendship

# C H A P T E R 6

# Communicating Person to Person

## OBJECTIVES

**After studying this chapter, you should be able to**

**1.** Identify three stages of relationships.

**2.** Build and maintain a personal relationship.

**3.** Respond to others with respect and understanding.

**4.** Communicate thoughts and feelings that are appropriate for your public self and for your private self.

**5.** Disclose your feelings in a useful manner and assert yourself when you need to do so.

**6.** Give and receive constructive criticism.

## What Is Interpersonal Communication?

**Interpersonal communication** is the communication that occurs between two or more people, usually people who have a personal relationship. The spectrum of relationships may range from casual acquaintances to close personal friends or family members. The skills of interpersonal communication include

- developing relationships
- responding to others
- communicating thoughts and feelings
- giving and accepting criticism

Some examples of interpersonal communication include a discussion about work responsibilities with a co-worker, a conversation with a classmate about a math test, and a conversation with a close friend about the friend's fear of driving a car.

In this chapter, you will learn what interpersonal communication skills are and how to use them.

# Developing Relationships

Most of us look forward to starting, building, and maintaining good relationships with others. A good relationship involves interactions with another person that are satisfactory to both of you.

## Recognizing Stages of Relationships

**Acquaintances.**   People you know and talk with when you happen to meet them are **acquaintances.** Your interactions are casual and limited. You might become acquainted with the people who live down the street or with the people who share some of your activities, but you do not make arrangements to spend time with them.

**Friendships.**   You become friends with some people because you enjoy their company. **Friendships** usually begin casually but grow when you find that you like each other and that the relationship is mutually satisfying. While playing tennis with an acquaintance, you might discover that, in addition to your enjoyment of the game, you share other interests. Once your friendship has taken root, you would deliberately plan to spend time together.

**Close Relationships.**   A **close relationship** is one in which people share their deepest feelings with each other. Such a relationship is built on trust and commitment. Close friends go out of their way to help each other; they are concerned about each other. Although a close relationship can involve a romantic attachment, it need not. Close relationships grow when you share the most critical moments of your life with another person, when you share both your sorrows and your joys.

# ACTIVITY 1

## Analyzing Your Personal Relationships

**T**hink about the people you know. Estimate what percentage you would classify as acquaintances, as casual friends, and as close friends. Then make three lists to show what you are likely to talk about with each kind of friend. If you feel comfortable doing so, share your lists with your classmates.

## Building Relationships

A good relationship does not just happen; it must be built through the efforts of both people in the relationship.

**Approaching Others with Empathy.** To create a good relationship, two people must approach each other with **empathy.** Empathizing is "walking in another person's shoes" to understand how that person feels. Since the world you see cannot be exactly the world that someone else sees, being empathetic is not always easy. But when you empathize, others feel that you are trying to understand what happens to them, and they are more likely to trust you.

> **EXAMPLE:** When Latoya tells Trish of her uneasiness in expressing ideas in class, Trish listens carefully to what Latoya says. Since Trish enjoys talking in class, she tries to put herself in Latoya's shoes—she imagines how she would feel if she were a quieter person who was as anxious about speaking up in front of her classmates as Latoya is.

**Sharing Feelings.** It takes two people to have a relationship, and each needs to share in making it work. In a good relationship, each person needs to feel that the other person makes an effort to share feelings so that both people feel that the relationship is equally and fairly balanced.

**CATHY**                                                    **by Cathy Guisewite**

**Establishing Trust.** For relationships to grow, the people involved must begin to trust each other. When you **trust** someone, you feel that you can rely on that person. You have complete confidence in the other person. To establish trust, friends must approach each other with honesty—about themselves and about their feelings toward the other person. At the same time, they must feel secure that what they reveal about themselves will not be used to hurt them in some way.

> **EXAMPLE:** If Trish trusts Latoya enough, she might explain that she dreads band auditions because she fears being beaten out for first chair by her younger sister. But to trust her friend, she must believe that Latoya will not reveal the information or use it to take advantage of her.

**Achieving Personal Growth.** As relationships develop, they also promote personal growth. When you take responsibility in a relationship, for example, you become a more responsible person in other areas of your life. When you improve your communication skills in a relationship, you can also transfer those skills to other areas of your life.

## Maintaining and Improving Relationships

The key to maintaining and improving relationships is good communication. Many people think that once they have begun a friendship it will last forever without additional effort. Nothing could be further from the truth. Even after a relationship appears to be

steady and settled, you need to continue the kinds of communication that helped it to grow in the first place. When you are in a good relationship, remember to

- empathize and be sensitive to the other person's feelings
- demonstrate your support of the other person in times of need
- listen to the other person
- share your feelings
- speak with honesty, while respecting the other person's feelings
- enjoy your relationship

*T*hink of a casual friendship that developed into a closer friendship. What factors allowed the relationship to succeed? How did communication skills play a role in developing the relationship? In your communication journal, write about what you expect of the interactions in a good relationship.

# Responding to Others

Much of your time in interpersonal relationships is spent in responding to what others have to say. Those responses should reflect a sensitivity to the feelings and thoughts of others.

## Respecting Others

**Respect** is a feeling of high regard, honor, or esteem that you have for other people. Here are some of the fundamental ways for showing respect.

- **Treat close friends with courtesy.** Don't make the mistake of thinking you can be rude to a friend and get away with it.
- **Respect the other person's opinions.** You may not always agree, but you should recognize that your friend has a right to his or her own opinions.
- **Be tactful.** Even though you may disagree with the other person, you should take care to do so without being offensive. Try to be sensitive to the other person's feelings.
- **Respect the other person's right to be heard.** Be aware of how long you speak, and do not dominate the discussion.

ACTIVITY 2

### Responding to Others with Respect

**W**ith a friend, identify a topic that the two of you disagree on. Use a tape recorder to record a ten-minute conversation about the topic. Attempt to respect each other's opinions. After you have finished your conversation, play back your audiotape and critique your responses. If you are unable to tape your conversation, ask another person to listen to it and to critique it when you are finished.

## Checking Understanding

Effective responses are thoughtful as well as respectful, and these types of responses are dependent upon a clear understanding of what the other person is saying. A **misunderstanding** is a lack of clear communication that may come about if you

- assume, or take for granted, that you know what the other person means
- do not pay close and careful attention to what the other person is saying
- do not take time to make sure that you understand what has been said

Questioning and paraphrasing are two techniques for making sure that you understand.

**Questioning to Be Sure.**  You have been asking questions since you learned to talk. Generally, you ask questions to obtain information or to engage someone in conversation. To communicate effectively person to person, you also ask questions to make sure that you do not misunderstand what the other person is saying. Here are some examples of questions that attempt to clarify.

- "Are you saying that ____?"
- "Do you think that ____?"
- "What did you mean when you said ____?"
- "Would you mind repeating what you just said? I'm not sure I understand."

**Paraphrasing to Understand Meaning.** **Paraphrasing** means using your own words to restate what another person has said. By paraphrasing someone's words, you let that person know what you think he or she said. In that way, you give the person a chance to correct you if you are mistaken. You can introduce your paraphrase with comments like these:

- "So, what you're saying is _____."
- "I take it that you believe _____."
- "What I heard you say is _____."

WIZARD OF ID By permission of Johnny Hart and Creators Syndicate, Inc.

# A·C·T·I·V·I·T·Y
## 3
### Practicing Questioning and Paraphrasing

**W**orking with a partner, use the following situations as opportunities to practice questioning and paraphrasing. As you each take a part and act out your conversations, try to include other interpersonal communication skills as well—showing empathy, sharing feelings, respecting opinions, taking turns, and using tact.

- It is Friday and Michael is upset because he did not make the basketball team; Jennifer has been looking forward to their date for the Thanksgiving dance all week.
- Margaret is afraid that she will not pass her math course, and she is embarrassed to ask for help; Juana is willing to tutor, but she doesn't know how to approach her friend.
- Melissa wants to try out for the school softball team, but she is afraid that she does not play well enough; Tom would rather have Melissa spend time with him than practice ball.
- John has a part-time job to help save money for college, and he is a little envious of his friend Ian's free time. Ian plans to go to college, but he is really more interested in all of his high school activities than he is in planning for college.

# Communicating Your Thoughts and Feelings

Communication is a two-way street. In addition to responding to what the other person says, you must share things about yourself—your thoughts, your feelings, and your ideas.

## Judging What Is Appropriate to Share

Your **private self** is that part of yourself which is most true to your self-concept, while your **public self** is that part of yourself which you choose to share with others. The following suggestions should help you to judge what to share with others.

1. **Increase the level of sharing gradually.** When you first get to know someone, share information about topics that are of general interest—hobbies, sports, and current events. Wait until you have developed an ongoing relationship to talk about your feelings, attitudes, and private thoughts.

2. **Share private information only with someone you trust.** There is some risk involved in telling about yourself, so share your fears, deep feelings, and secrets with those whom you know you can rely on to keep your confidences.

3. **Continue to share only if the other person confides in you.** You may misread someone and tell more about yourself than the other person shares about himself or herself. If that happens, you might want to avoid sharing too much until your friendship has developed into a closer relationship.

# Disclosing Your Feelings

Even in a close relationship, it is sometimes difficult to handle the sharing of feelings. However, unless you can learn to share feelings with others in a positive way, you will not be able to maintain a relationship of mutual trust.

**Avoid Always Withholding Your Feelings.** Sometimes it is so uncomfortable to disclose your feelings that you withhold, or keep your feelings inside. Psychologists believe that if people constantly withhold feelings they can develop physical problems such as ulcers, high blood pressure, or even cancer, as well as emotional problems such as sadness, depression, or tension.

Although withholding feelings may be wise in some situations, always doing so can have negative effects on relationships. If you care about someone, make it a point to communicate how you feel about what they say and do.

**Avoid Displays of Negative Feelings.** People share their feelings not only with words, but also with actions. Cheering at a pep rally, patting a friend on the back, and sharing a hug are all positive displays of emotion. But displays of negative feelings can actually interfere with communication. Slamming a door behind you, sulking, and shouting certainly show feelings, but they don't tell the other person exactly what you are feeling or why. It is much better to describe your feelings than to display them with negative, or aggressive, behavior.

**Describe Your Feelings.** Instead of withdrawing or displaying your feelings in a negative way, learn how to describe them. When you describe your feelings, try to put your feelings into words in a calm, nonjudgmental way. Describing your feelings in this way will give other people knowledge that will be helpful in future interactions with you.

When you describe your feelings, try to describe, honestly and accurately, what you are experiencing. You may find it easier to be honest if you first accept that it is all right to feel what you are experiencing. To begin with, you may find it easier to describe positive feelings: "I'm so glad you called. I needed to talk to someone." However, as a relationship develops, it becomes important to describe your negative feelings as well. You might begin with something that affects you but not the relationship: "When I stay by myself at night, I really get nervous. Every little noise spooks me."

Then, as you experience success and develop trust in the relationship, learn to describe what bothers you about what the other person has said or done. Describing is especially helpful with negative feelings because it gives the other person helpful information. Remember to describe the situation as it affects you and your feelings.

- "When you criticize how I play when I'm trying my hardest, I feel defeated."
- "When you told him about our conversation, I was angry. I didn't want anyone else to know."
- "I waited for your call before I made plans. I feel left out when you don't let me in on your arrangements."

*T*hink back over the events of the day. Were there any times when you felt particularly happy, angry, disappointed, excited, sad? Jot down a few emotions that you recall. How did you communicate your feelings to others? Write down how you shared the feelings you listed. If you discover that you tended to withhold your feelings or to display them inappropriately, write down what you might have done to describe your emotions positively to someone else.

## Speaking Up for Yourself

Even within caring relationships, people sometimes seem to take advantage of you and to ignore your feelings. It may even seem as if they do not listen to you at all. Sharing your thoughts and feelings under these conditions can be very difficult, but it is sometimes necessary to let another person know exactly what you want.

Psychologists define **assertiveness** as the practice of exercising your personal rights. When you are assertive, you give the reasons why you feel or believe or think as you do and suggest a responsible action from someone in response.

**EXAMPLE:** "I explained to you that I have homework on weeknights. It frustrates me when you expect long phone conversations. I'd like to limit our weeknight calls to thirty minutes."

It is often difficult for quiet people who normally keep things to themselves to speak up. Asserting yourself does not mean being aggressive, but it does mean letting someone know what you want.

# HOW TO Assert Yourself

1. **Avoid language that can lead to arguments.** Do not threaten or criticize. In fact, do not focus on the other person at all; talk about yourself.

2. **Be specific about what you want.** Sometimes you know someone so well that you think the person can read your mind. However, the only way to make sure that the person knows what you want is to say exactly what it is.

3. **Keep a firm but pleasant tone of voice.** Although it is difficult when you are upset, it is very important to control the tone, pitch, and volume of your voice. If you get off to a bad start, stop for a moment and gain control of yourself.

# ACTIVITY 4

## Observing Communication Behavior

For two days, observe people communicating. Note situations in which people withhold their feelings or withdraw (passive behavior), display negative feelings (aggressive behavior), or describe their feelings and speak up for themselves (assertive behavior). Which types of behavior seem to be more productive? With a partner, discuss your observations and write a summary of your findings.

# Giving and Accepting Criticism

In any friendship or close relationship there may be a need for **constructive criticism,** criticism that is beneficial and helpful rather than disapproving. Since people, at one time or another, all find criticism difficult to accept, it is important to express and receive criticism with discretion and care. The information in the following chart will help you to learn how to give and receive constructive criticism.

## HOW TO ▷  *Give and Accept Criticism*

### Giving Criticism

1. **Choose an appropriate time and place.** Try not to criticize someone in front of others. When you discuss a problem, try to choose a time when the other person is relaxed and willing to listen. After you are sure that you have the other person's complete attention, be brief and to the point.

2. **Choose only one or two specific points for criticism.** Do not attempt to recite an entire list of problems. Instead, identify only one, or possibly two, specific actions or statements that you feel need to be changed.

3. **Describe the person's behavior carefully and accurately.** Talk about specific actions, not personality, character, or values. For example, you might say, "I wish you would not interrupt me," rather than "You are the rudest person I know."

4. **Respond to the present, not to the past.** Sometimes it is tempting to bring up unresolved, bad feelings from the past and to rehash old arguments in an attempt to resolve them. However, this is usually not very effective in changing behavior.

5. **Try to include ideas for solutions.** It is usually possible to come up with positive suggestions, and such suggestions show the other person that your intentions are positive.

### Accepting Criticism

1. **Think of criticism as an opportunity for improvement.** When you receive a negative review from someone, try to see it as a chance to learn something about your behavior that you did not know before. Constructive criticism is in your best interest.

2. **Make sure that you understand what you hear.** Don't jump to conclusions about what you think someone means. If you are confused, ask for clarification.

3. **Recognize those who use constructive criticism.** Since giving constructive criticism is not easy, thank the people who take the time to do so.

# ACTIVITY 5

## Analyzing Constructive Criticism

Think about a time when a close friend criticized you for a specific behavior. Analyze the effectiveness of the criticism that you were given by asking yourself the following questions.

1. What specific action, or actions, were criticized? What specific changes were you requested to make in your behavior?
2. Did you accept the criticism constructively? If so, how did you change your behavior? If not, why not?
3. What, if anything, could the person criticizing you have done differently to make the criticism, or the suggestion for change, more constructive?
4. What, if anything, could you have done to make the situation more constructive?

# GUIDELINES

## for Communicating Person to Person

- Do I approach others with empathy (understanding their point of view)?
- Are my close relationships built upon shared feelings and trust?
- Do my relationships allow me to grow as a person?
- Do I put the same energy into maintaining relationships that I put into building them?
- Do I treat friends with courtesy, and do I respect their opinions?
- Am I tactful when I disagree with someone?
- In conversations, do I allow the other person equal opportunity to talk?
- Do I use questioning and paraphrasing to make sure that I know what someone means?
- Do I make good judgments about when to share personal information with friends?
- Do I describe my negative feelings rather than acting them out?
- Am I learning to assert myself and speak up for what I want?
- Do I give criticism so that it is received constructively?
- Do I learn from the helpful comments of my friends, even when an opinion is negative?

# RESOLVING DISPUTES

## Everyone Needs to Be Heard

Mediators help people resolve many kinds of disagreements, including disagreements among people who want to preserve an ongoing personal relationship, whether as casual acquaintances, close friends, or family members.

## Characteristics of an Effective Mediator

An effective mediator

**1** makes sure that each person's side of the issue is clearly stated

**2** makes sure that each person listens respectfully to others

**3** makes sure that each person focuses on the specific actions or words that led to the disagreement, and on his or her own thoughts and feelings about those words or actions

## ACTIVITY

### Situation

You are baby-sitting two young cousins who are arguing about taking turns playing a computer game. The child waiting for a turn becomes angry and calls the other child a "cheater" and a "liar." The child playing the game insists that it isn't the other one's turn yet and becomes upset about being called names.

### Preparation

Your main goal is to resolve the disagreement. How will you get the children to communicate about their responsibility in the argument? You will need to use questioning tactics that will help the children feel comfortable discussing the situation. Make sure each child listens to and understands the other child's thoughts and feelings and that they have agreed on a plan for taking turns.

### Analysis and Assessment

Write a dialogue showing how you would handle the situation. Ask a couple of classmates to read the children's parts, and then present the scene to the class. Have your classmates evaluate the probable effectiveness of your mediation.

## Meet the Mediator

As a professional mediator, Susan Patterson says her goal is "to ensure that each person involved in a dispute is able to express his or her views." She says her job is rewarding: "Often, when each side of a dispute finally hears the opposing side state its case clearly, hurt and anger disappear, and both sides agree on a resolution that everyone involved can accept as fair."

*Susan Patterson*

# S☆U☆M☆M☆A☆R☆Y

**COMMUNICATING PERSON TO PERSON** is sometimes called interpersonal communication. It refers to the communication that occurs between two people who have a personal relationship. Personal relationships range from casual acquaintances to very close friendships or family connections. Good communication skills are important in building and maintaining personal relationships.

- **Develop good relationships** by recognizing the various types of relationships and working to build and maintain them. Approach others with empathy, share your feelings, and establish trust with your friends. Take advantage of good relationships to achieve personal growth.

- **Respond to others with respect.** Treat others with courtesy, respect their opinions, be tactful when disagreeing, and give them a chance to talk during a conversation. To be sure that you know what the other person means, check your perceptions by questioning or paraphrasing what has been said.

- **Communicate your thoughts and feelings** to people with whom you have close relationships, but share only what you feel comfortable sharing. When you disclose your feelings, be careful not to withhold feelings that you need to express. When you have negative feelings toward the other person, describe them rather than acting them out. Be willing to speak up for yourself when you have something to say. Learn to give and receive constructive criticism.

Look back through this chapter to find the meaning of each of the following terms. Write each term and its meaning in your communication journal.

acquaintances, p. 140
assertiveness, p. 148
close relationship, p. 140
constructive criticism, p. 150
empathy, p. 141
friendships, p. 140
interpersonal communication, p. 139
misunderstanding, p. 144
paraphrasing, p. 145
private self, p. 146
public self, p. 146
respect, p. 143
trust, p. 142

# Review Questions

1. What is interpersonal communication?
2. What are the three stages of relationships?
3. When you begin friendships, what are two methods that will help you to build good relationships?
4. What is the importance of trust in a relationship?
5. Why is it important to continue good communication skills as a relationship grows?
6. What are four good ways to show respect to another person in a relationship?
7. What are two methods that can help you to determine whether you understand what another person is saying?
8. What are three techniques for determining what is appropriate to share with someone?
9. What are two positive ways to reveal your feelings to someone else? Why are these methods more effective than withholding feelings or acting them out?
10. List three or four good hints for giving and receiving constructive criticism.

# Discussion Questions

1. Your relationships grow in intensity as you discover what you have in common with other people. Discuss some indicators that tell you a relationship probably will not grow.
2. With your classmates, discuss why empathizing is not as easy as it may sound. What differences between people make it difficult to understand what it is like to be "in the other person's shoes"? What can someone do to better understand the circumstances of someone else?
3. Unfortunately, many people use ineffective methods to reveal their feelings to others. However, their actions represent learned behavior and, like all behavior, it can change. Discuss why it is important to practice describing your feelings and speaking up for yourself assertively.
4. La Rochefoucauld, a seventeenth-century French writer, once wrote, "To listen closely and reply well is the highest perfection we are able to attain in the art of conversation." Discuss the meaning of this quotation. How does it relate to the ability of a good communicator to respond to another person?
5. Konstantin Dankevich, in *The New York Times* (November 19, 1959), wrote, "Only paper flowers are afraid of the rain. We are not afraid of the noble rain of criticism because with it will flourish the magnificent garden of music." Discuss the meaning of this quotation in reference to constructive criticism.

# ACTIVITIES

**1. Making Up Proverbs.** Proverbs are short statements that record the wisdom of a certain time. "Two wrongs do not make a right" is a proverb that might apply to interpersonal communication. Make up one- or two-sentence proverbs for our time about person-to-person communication. Start by trying to think of clever or ironic insights about interpersonal relationships. Perhaps you have learned something about how people relate to one another that strikes you as amusing. Share your proverbs with your classmates.

**2. Writing Paraphrases.** For each of the following statements, write a paraphrase that shows your understanding of the meaning of the statement.

a. "I've been playing piano for eight years, and this is the first time anyone has asked me to perform. Even though I've had recitals, they have been small. I don't know whether I'm ready for a large performance yet."

b. "I asked him if he had had a good time, but all he did was shrug his shoulders. I just can't seem to get him to say anything more. I am really tired of trying to communicate."

c. "I did want to go to that party, but since I didn't get an invitation until just a day before, I decided to stay home. I think she must have found out I was bothered, so she sent me the invitation."

d. "The car is not running right. It doesn't have any pep, and it keeps stalling at lights. People behind me honk and act irritated at me. I am afraid it wasn't a very good buy. It really bugs me."

e. "Ever since we moved to our new house, my dog and cat fight all the time. Mom says one of them may have to go. I don't understand their behavior, and I don't know what to do."

**3. Describing Feelings.**

**A.** Practice describing feelings by acting out with your classmates one of the situations shown below or a specific situation of your own choosing. Positive reactions are easier to act out, but you can handle the negative ones by describing how you feel about the situation.

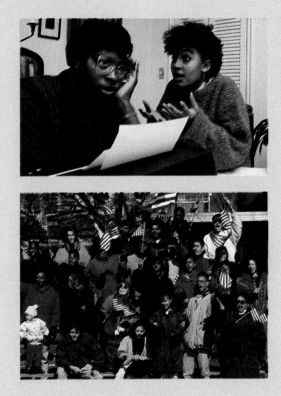

**B.** Imagine that you find yourself in each of the situations described in the following scenes. Describe what your feelings might be, whether positive or negative, about the situation.

1. Someone you don't know very well takes the time to help you with some math problems that stump you. With this help you later get a better test grade than you have ever gotten.

2. Your dad travels for business and doesn't get to come to many of your games. However, he makes the last game of the season, and the team loses.

3. Your friend asks you to go to the haunted house and midnight horror movie on Halloween night. You are baby-sitting later that weekend and know that you might spend the night in fear if you spend Halloween night having scary experiences.

4. Several friends ask you to go on a raft trip down a nearby river after a heavy rainfall. You are not a very strong swimmer, and you know that the current will be strong.

5. You've been looking forward to going to the Winter Carnival at school. You even bought a new outfit and got someone you work with to trade nights. Your date calls you the day before and says, "I'm sorry, I'm not going to be able to make it. I hope you're not mad. Maybe we can go to the dance next weekend."

6. You discover that several people know a secret that you had told a friend in confidence. It affects not only you, since it involves a comment you made about someone else.

**4. Asserting Yourself.** Now that you have practiced describing how you feel, add another dimension. In these situations, show how you want to be treated. Do not yell—describe what you want. First, tell what bothers you. Then describe how you feel about it. Finally, tell how you want the other person to act.

a. You plan to have a few friends over for a cookout. You do not have a lot of money for food, so you limit the invitations to a few close friends. However, one of your friends brings along an extra crowd of people who turn out to be hungry, rowdy, and rude. What do you tell your friend?

b. You come home late from school after practice. You are tired, hungry, dirty, and impatient to get to the movies. The dinner that your mother saved for you was given to the dog; someone is in the bath; and you discover that your sibling has borrowed the sweater you wanted to wear. (Hint: Keep your response specific to the action that you can do something about.)

c. You and a friend have made plans to go skating on Sunday afternoon. At the last minute, your mother decides to go visit a friend of hers that you know and wants you to go with her.

**5. Criticizing Constructively.** The following situations call for constructive criticism. For each situation, write out a dialogue expressing constructive criticism. Share your wording with a small group of classmates in a discussion.

a. You ride to school in a car pool. On the days your friend drives, you are usually late getting to school.

b. A good friend says "like" in every sentence and uses other expressions that you think are immature. It bothers you, and you are aware that other people make fun of it.

c. A friend of yours borrows some tapes and CDs from several friends and forgets to return them. The friends complain to you.

# EVERYDAY COMMUNICATION

### Situation

You are sharing a room with a close friend. The two of you get along, but living together as roommates has highlighted some of the differences between you.

### Problem

You cannot stand dirt or messiness, and you are upset when your roommate leaves books and papers on the floor, damp towels on the chair, and clothing scattered about the room.

### Assessing Your Skill

Can you work out the problem with your roommate and still remain friends? Write a script for a five-minute conversation in which you attempt to resolve the problem. Ask a classmate to read one role while you read the other for your class. Ask classmates to evaluate your effectiveness in expressing your issues and negotiating to resolve them.

# COMMUNICATION IN THE WORKPLACE

### Background

Businesses sometimes hire professionals to train their employees to communicate more effectively with customers.

### Preparing to Do the Job

You and your partner are communications experts. You have been hired to make a presentation that teaches the techniques of positive response and constructive criticism.

### Testing Your Skill

You and your partner should begin with a two-minute speech, explaining positive response and constructive criticism and how they help communication. Then illustrate these techniques in a three-minute, acted-out conversation. Finally, ask your "trainees" if your presentation explained the two concepts and how to use them effectively.

EFFECTIVE COMMUNICATION
TRAINING CLASS
• POSITIVE RESPONSE
• CONSTRUCTIVE CRITICISM

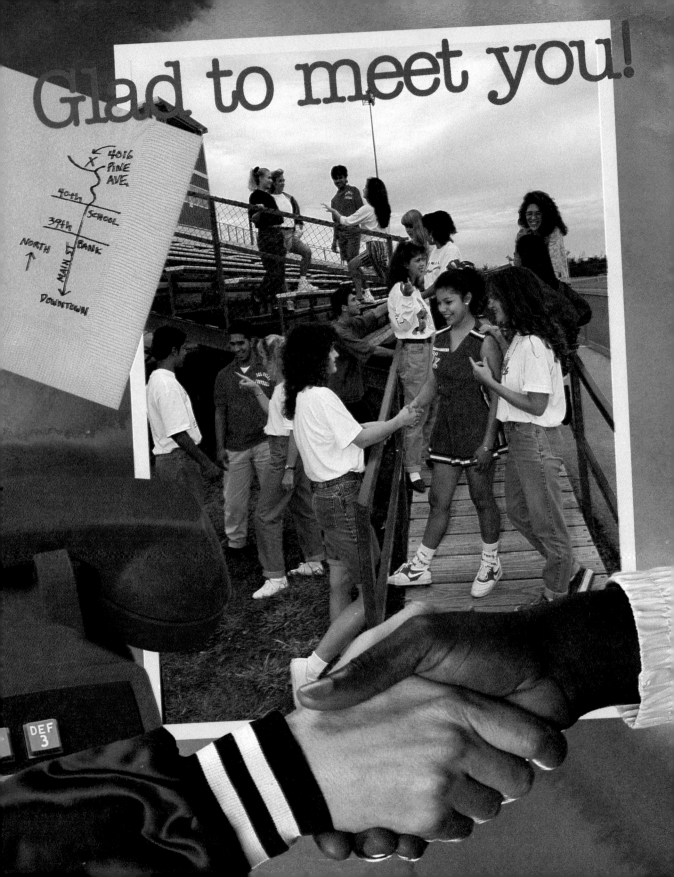
Glad to meet you!

# CHAPTER 7

▼

# Speaking Informally

**OBJECTIVES**

**After studying this chapter, you should be able to**

1. Give clear directions and understand directions that you receive from others.
2. Use the telephone effectively for social and business purposes.
3. Make effective announcements.
4. Introduce people to each other.
5. Identify qualities of a good conversationalist.
6. Start and carry on interesting conversations.
7. Use constructive feedback to solve problems and to settle disagreements.

## What Is Informal Communication?

**Informal communication** involves giving and receiving messages in casual, person-to-person interactions, rather than in structured situations such as formal speeches and debates. Two broad types of informal communication are

- **practical communication,** which is useful, direct, and goal oriented
- **social communication,** which is friendly, cordial, and enjoyable

Examples of practical communication are a phone call to a video store to find out whether a movie you want to rent is available and an announcement over the school's public-address system of a change in schedule for a school club's meeting. An example of social communication is a conversation in the school cafeteria about what took place at the class picnic the previous Saturday.

In this chapter, you will learn skills that will improve your ability to communicate practically and socially.

# Speaking for Practical Purposes

## Giving and Receiving Directions

**Directions** are instructions for finding a particular place. [See Chapter 14 for information about instructions for carrying out a process.]

**Giving Directions.**   When someone needs directions for finding a particular place, your ability to provide clear and accurate information is crucial. To ensure clarity and accuracy, follow these suggestions.

1. *Give directions fluently.* Before you give directions, think through what you want to say. You will be more likely to get through the steps without hesitating or confusing your listener if you are clear in your mind about the best route to take.
2. *Select the simplest route.* Give directions for the easiest way to get to a place for someone who is not familiar with the area. You may know shortcuts, but shortcuts often involve unmarked streets or roads that are difficult to find.
3. *Give directions in a series of logical steps.* The person asking for directions needs to know what to do first, what to do second, and so on.
4. *Use visual terms when possible.* Directions such as *go right* and *turn left* are easier for most people to follow than *turn north* or *go south.* Any landmark that you mention should stand out from its surroundings.
5. *Consider drawing a map.* Unless the directions are extremely simple, you may want to draw a map. A good map includes only those details that the person needs in order to find the way.
6. *Repeat directions, if necessary.* If your instructions are at all complicated, repeat them, using language as close to your original wording as possible. In addition, have the person confirm his or her understanding by repeating the directions to you.

**Receiving Directions.**   When you are asking for directions, you can use the following guidelines to ensure that you receive the information you need.

1. *Ask for directions clearly.* Frame your request so that your listener will understand what you want to know. Be specific. For example, instead of saying, "I'm looking for Computer House," you might say, "I'm looking for a store called Computer House on Adams Avenue. Can you tell me how to get there?"
2. *Listen carefully.* Make sure that you have understood all the steps. If you have a pencil and paper, take notes. Be patient; the person giving you directions is trying to be helpful.

3. *Repeat the directions.* To ensure that you have understood, repeat the directions out loud so that the person who gave them can double-check their accuracy.
4. *Thank the person.* Always thank people who try to help you, even if they give confusing directions. If some of the directions were not clear enough to follow, go part of the way and then ask someone else for further directions.

# ACTIVITY
## 1
### Giving and Receiving Directions

**W**ork with a partner to act out one of the following situations. Choose the situation that you like best and, after practicing, act it out for your classmates. Then listen to your classmates' feedback about the effectiveness of your directions.

1. This is your first day at school. You need to find your way to the lunchroom. Ask for directions from your partner.
2. In your math class, you strike up a conversation with the person sitting behind you, and you invite this person to come to your house after school. Give directions for how to get to your home from the school.
3. Your class is planning a picnic. You have been put in charge of arranging the location. Select a specific location, such as a lakefront picnic area or a hillside park, and give directions to your classmates to guide them to this location.
4. The school chorus is putting on a concert at a local elementary school on an upcoming Saturday afternoon. Another member of the chorus has asked you for directions to get from your school to the elementary school where the concert is to be held. Give the requested directions to your classmate.

Maps like the one shown here are designed to be used by people who have visual impairments.

## Speaking on the Telephone

Although you have probably been using the telephone since early childhood, you can always practice and improve your telephone skills.

**Making a Social Call.** A **social call** is a telephone call made for personal reasons—to talk with family members, friends, or social acquaintances.

1. *Call at appropriate times.* Unless your call is urgent, make it at a time that is convenient for the other person. In most cases, avoid making calls early in the morning, late at night, or at mealtimes. Be aware of time zones across the country. If you place a 9:00 A.M. call from Massachusetts, it may wake up your cousin in California. It is also always polite to ask, "Are you in the middle of something?" or "Can you talk now?"

2. *Dial correctly.* Check the number you are calling and be sure to touch or dial carefully. If you do not recognize the voice that answers the phone, give the number you are calling and ask if you have reached it. If you have made a mistake, apologize for the inconvenience.

3. *Allow time for someone to answer the phone.* You should probably let the phone ring at least six to ten times. Six rings gives the person only about eighteen seconds to reach the phone.

4. *Identify yourself and state your purpose.* When someone answers the telephone, say who you are and ask for the person you wish to speak to. You cannot assume that the person will recognize your voice, and many people become anxious when a caller does not give his or her name.

5. *Use your best vocalization and articulation skills.* Speak clearly, enunciate carefully, and use changes in pitch, loudness, and rate to reinforce the meaning of your words. It is more difficult to distinguish between some sounds on the phone than it is in person.

6. *Keep calls to a reasonable length.* Monopolizing the phone is not considerate to other members of your household. Lengthy phone calls may also be inconvenient for the person you are talking to.

**Receiving a Social Call.** Just as there are procedures to follow when you are making a social call, so are there procedures to follow when receiving a social call.

1. *Answer appropriately.* The best way to answer the telephone is simply to say, "Hello," and wait for the caller to speak. If you hear nothing, hang up. If the caller is not someone you recognize, you will need to be cautious about disclosing personal information. You might ask, "Who is speaking, please?" or "What number are you calling?"

2. *Respond to the situation.* If the caller has dialed a wrong number, respond courteously as you inform the caller of the mistake. If the call is for another person in your household, you might ask, "May I say who's calling?" and then ask the caller to wait while you tell the other person that he or she has a phone call. If the person whom the caller wishes to speak to is not available, offer to take a message. When there is a message, record it clearly and post it where it can be seen.

3. *Do not provide strangers with your name or number.* If a caller is not someone you know, seems confused, or demands your name or number, ask, "What number are you dialing?" If the caller has misdialed, say, "I'm sorry. You've reached the wrong number." If the person in fact dialed your number correctly, suggest a call to directory assistance for the correct number he or she actually wants.

4. *Be honest but courteous.* If you are short of time or are expecting another call, tell your caller. To avoid being rude, you might provide a brief explanation for the reason you need to get off the phone. You might say, "Elena, I just sat down to eat dinner. Can I call you back in about an hour?" or "Sam, I've enjoyed talking to you, but I need to go now. My brother wants to use the phone to get some information about a homework assignment."

**A**ct out the following situations with a partner, showing how you would handle each call. Then ask for and respond to feedback from your classmates.

1. You are baby-sitting for your neighbors, the Garcias, who have gone out for the evening. The phone rings, and the caller asks to speak to Mr. Garcia.
2. There is a new student at school whom you would like to get to know better. You telephone this person and extend an invitation to go bowling with you.
3. Someone whom you would like to get to know just telephoned you for the first time, but you have to get off the phone right away because your mother is expecting an important call.
4. You are visiting a friend's house, and everyone is in the back yard. As you walk back into the house, the phone rings.

**Making a Business Call.**  A **business call** is a call made to a company or organization to request information or help, to make a complaint, or to take care of some other business matter.

In most cases, the same procedures apply to making business calls as apply to making social calls, except that business calls often require you to be more formal. When calling a business, be prepared to identify yourself and to state your purpose promptly.

> EXAMPLE: Hello, my name is Ted Begosian. I'm president of the Student Council at North High School. May I speak with Mr. Moniz? He asked to be informed when we had a calendar of school events available.

In addition, businesses often transfer or route calls. If your call is

- answered by an operator or a secretary, identify the person or department you need to reach
- answered by voice mail (a computerized answering system), leave your name, phone number, and purpose for calling
- put on hold, wait patiently (for a reasonable time)
- transferred to another person, state your name and your purpose again
- cut off accidentally, call back
- answered by a computerized routing system, listen carefully to the options and select the one that will direct your call to the correct person or department

Respond appropriately when the phone is answered. Choose what to say based on whom you have reached and whether the person ought to hear your purpose in full detail.

1. *Be sure you are talking to the right person.* It does you no good to explain your business to the person who answers the phone if he or she is not the proper person. To make sure that you are connected with someone who can help you, you might say something like, "Hello, this is Ellen Cheng. I'm having a problem with a hair dryer I bought from your company recently. Whom should I speak with about this matter?"

2. *Be specific about what you want.* State your request clearly and directly. For example, if you were calling a business-supply store to ask about a specific product, you might say, "Hello, my name is Ellen Cheng. I'm calling to see whether you carry $9\frac{1}{2}$- by 6-inch spiral notebooks with college-ruled paper."

3. *Make sure that the person understands your request.* If the person repeats your request incorrectly or in some other way shows a lack of understanding, stop the person and repeat your request. If you have a complaint, explain what you expect to happen to resolve the difficulty.

4. *Be patient.* No matter how many times you have been transferred, cut off, or put on hold, always be polite as you explain your business clearly and firmly.

**Receiving a Business Call.** You may receive business calls on the job or at home. If you have a job that includes answering the telephone, your employer will give you specific instructions for taking calls. Usually, you will answer the phone by giving the company's name rather than your own.

When you are at home, most of the business calls you receive are **telemarketing** calls, telephone calls from individuals or businesses that want to sell you services or products. Many of these calls are made by professional telemarketing agencies. Such agencies hire people to make calls for the purpose of selling products or getting contributions. If you know you are not interested in buying the product or pledging a contribution, say politely but firmly, "I'm not interested," and hang up. Some calls are generated by computers. For these you need only to hang up if you are not interested.

**Using Answering Machines.** When you call many businesses, as well as some individuals, you may find yourself communicating not with a human but with an answering device. There are several different devices that answer telephone calls.

One common device is an **answering machine,** an independent mechanism hooked up to a telephone line that responds to calls with a tape-recorded or digitally reproduced message.

**Voice mail** is an electronic system that provides the caller with a number of options from which to select, usually by using numbers on a touch-tone telephone pad. A voice-mail system often allows callers the option of recording a message. Voice mail also allows callers to route calls to a specific extension in a business office or request particular information, such as the weather forecast or the caller's bank balance.

Most answering devices follow these procedures.

1. The machine answers the phone.
2. The caller listens to prerecorded instructions. (For voice mail, you may be asked to use your touch-tone keys to route your call.)
3. A tone, a beep, or a series of beeps signals the caller to begin a message.
4. A second tone or beep indicates that the recording time has been used up and that the machine has stopped recording.

When you record a message, listen very carefully to the taped instructions. In most cases, you will be asked to state who you are, as well as the date and time you called. Since you will have a limited amount of time to state your message, make sure it is brief and to the point. If you want someone to return your call, be sure to leave your phone number.

When communicating by answering machine or voice mail, there is always a possibility that a message will be lost. If you leave a message and the person does not return your call within two days or so, you may want to try again.

# A·C·T·I·V·I·T·Y 3

## Practicing Business Calls

Working with a partner, act out one of the following situations. After demonstrating an appropriate response to the situation, ask for and respond to feedback from your classmates on how effectively you have communicated your message.

1. Your parents are buying a new kitchen appliance, and they want you to help them. You call a department store to find out whether it has a specific model of the appliance in stock, what its price is, what its features are, and what colors are available.

2. You headed a drive at your school to collect food and clothing for the homeless. You are calling a local agency to find out where and when you should drop off the donated items.

3. You recently bought a shirt. It shrank and faded the first time you washed it. You call the department store to complain and are directed to leave a recorded message.

4. You get a call from a telemarketer offering you a good deal on a five-year subscription to a magazine that your family does not usually buy.

**Relaying Messages.** When you answer a phone call intended for someone else, it is important to relay an accurate message to the other person. In some cases, passing on the message may be a simple courtesy; in other cases, the message may be of critical importance.

When taking a message, try to make a written note rather than trust your memory, and keep the following points in mind.

1. Take the caller's name and phone number. Even when a return phone call is not requested, the person receiving the message may need to return the call.

2. Offer to take a message. Once the caller has given you the message, it is a good idea to repeat it and make sure that you have recorded it accurately.

3. Make sure that you give the message to the person or post it in a place where it can be clearly seen.

If you take messages from an answering machine, check the directions on the machine before playing back the messages. Some answering machines tape new messages over ones that have been replayed, so it is important to have a pencil and paper ready to note the messages and phone numbers as you hear them.

*** NOTE *** 4pm

Kathy —
JoAnn called —
she'll be here at 2pm
tomorrow (not 1pm) to
pick you up.
Call her back if time
is OK — 555-0099
Bob

## Making Announcements

You may need to make announcements in class, at a school assembly, or over the public-address system. When you are asked to make an announcement, follow these guidelines.

1. *Include all important information.* To make sure you have all the information you need, you might use the reporter's 5W-How? questions: *Who? What? When? Where? Why? How?*

2. *Write out your announcement.* By writing and revising your wording, you can be sure not to forget any major points, and you can make your message interesting. Get your audience's attention by beginning in an interesting or unexpected way.

3. *Rehearse.* Practice emphasizing the key words in your announcement. Speak slowly and clearly. Have someone listen to you as you practice and give you feedback to help you improve your delivery. If you will be using a microphone or public-address system, determine how close to the microphone your mouth should be to get the best sound level.

4. *Deliver your announcement effectively.* Wait until the audience is quiet to begin. Speak loudly enough that everyone can hear you clearly.

# ACTIVITY 4

## Giving Messages and Announcements

Imagine yourself in each of the situations that follow. For each situation, prepare an appropriate response.

1. When you come home one afternoon, you hear the following message on your family's answering machine: "Hello. This is the principal, Mr. Ames, calling from Kaiser Elementary School. It's 2:30 P.M. Shirlene said she wasn't feeling well, so we took her temperature. It was 102 degrees. We have her lying down now in the school nurse's office, but she's definitely a sick little girl. Could somebody come and get her as soon as possible? The phone number here is 555–5100." You realize that the caller made an error, because you do not know anyone named Shirlene.

2. You want to start a new club at school. Your school principal has given you permission to go to each classroom to announce the introductory meeting for the club. In your announcement, give information that students might need in order to motivate them to attend the first meeting. Your announcement should create interest in the club since the school will not sponsor the club unless it has at least ten members. Be sure to state the time and location.

## GUIDELINES
### for Practical Communication

- When I give directions, do I select the simplest route and explain chronological steps in visual terms?

- Do I ask for directions courteously, listen carefully when they are given, and repeat them to make sure that I have understood them?

- When I make a social telephone call, am I considerate of the person receiving the call, and do I identify myself?

- When I make a business telephone call, do I identify myself and state my purpose clearly?

- When I make or receive a business telephone call, am I efficient and courteous?

- When I leave a message on an answering device, is my message clear, specific, and concise?

- Do I relay messages accurately and completely?

- Do I make announcements that are interesting and that are loud enough to be heard by everyone in my audience?

# Speaking for Social Purposes

## Making Introductions

When you meet people you do not know, or when you are with people who do not know each other, you will need to make introductions. The ability to make an **introduction**—to present one person to another or to a group—identifies you as a person who is self-confident and competent.

**Introducing Yourself to Others.**   You will sometimes be faced with situations in which you have to introduce yourself. For example, you might be attending a new school and have to introduce yourself to some other students at a table in the cafeteria, or you might be at a party and not see anyone you know. In such situations, you can introduce yourself by

- greeting the other person
- giving your name
- saying something about yourself and asking a question

EXAMPLE: Hi, I'm José Morales. Mrs. Bellini, our club sponsor, asked me to meet you here and go with you to our school. How was your flight?

When introducing yourself in a business situation, you should greet the other person, give your name, and then state your purpose.

EXAMPLE: Hello. My name is Amy Yamoto. I'm a student at West Township High School, and I would like to ask you how I may apply for a summer job here.

**Introducing Others.** Even though the opportunity or the occasion to introduce people to each other comes up frequently, you might feel rather uncomfortable about how you should go about it. The purpose of introductions is to exchange information, primarily people's names. In years past, people followed elaborate rules regarding introductions, but today, people are usually not as demanding about observing every dictate of formal etiquette in social situations.

In general, any introduction that is conducted in a smooth, comfortable manner and that allows the people involved to exchange names and greet one another politely is considered a successful introduction. Knowing a few simple guidelines about the order of names and the wording of an introduction will help you to manage introductions without awkwardness or embarrassment.

The first issue in making an introduction concerns the **order of names**—the order in which people are presented to each other. The person named first is the person to whom the other person is being introduced.

EXAMPLE: In the following introduction, Tarik is being introduced to Amy: "Amy, I'd like you to meet Tarik Armani. Tarik, this is my neighbor, Amy Beaulieu."

According to tradition, you should first state the name of the person

- who is of higher achievement or earned status ("Dr. Mora, this is my little sister, Ruth.") [Dr. Mora is the school principal and therefore has higher status.]
- who is older ("Mrs. Rosenberg, I'd like to introduce you to Tom Karas, my classmate.") [Mrs. Rosenberg is a retired art teacher.]

If the rules for status and age conflict or do not apply, simply start your introduction by naming the person who is more familiar to you. For example, "Mom, I'd like you to meet my friend, Margaret Browne." As another example, you might say, "Leroy, I want to introduce my next-door neighbor LaKeesha."

The second issue in making an introduction is what wording to use. Although there are many acceptable variations, formal situations usually call for formal language, as well as the use of last names and titles.

**FORMAL WORDING:**

Dr. Klein, I would like to present my friend, Tuan Chin.
Felicia Hernandez, I'd like to introduce Chip Johansen.

**INFORMAL WORDING:**

Paula, have you met Mike?
Bill, this is Sam.
Janelle, Shula.

**Responding to an Introduction.** The best way to respond to an introduction is to politely acknowledge your pleasure at meeting the other person. The simplest response is "Glad to meet you." However, if the person introducing the two of you has added some details about the other person to the introduction, you can express interest by asking a question that allows you to get a conversation started.

**EXAMPLE:** Brian introduces his brother Matt to Angelina: "Angelina, I'd like you to meet my brother Matt. He plays in the school band." Angelina might then say, "Glad to meet you, Matt. What instrument do you play?"

Appropriate behavior during introductions is largely a matter of good manners and good sense. For example, if someone you are introduced to offers to shake your hand, you should do so. However, if shaking hands is inconvenient, it makes sense to ignore the custom and to respond politely in some other way. For example, you might simply smile and nod rather than shake hands in some circumstances. The main idea is to be polite.

**EXAMPLE:** You are at a party. You have food in one hand and a beverage in the other. Because both your hands are encumbered, it makes sense to nod and smile in greeting when you are introduced rather than to try to shake hands. However, if the person you are being introduced to really seems to want to shake hands, then you should put everything down in a gracious manner that does not in any way suggest that you find this maneuver inconvenient. Then you should shake hands politely and cheerfully.

Good sense also dictates when you should stand up for an introduction. In general, you should stand up to indicate respect when you are introduced. However, if standing is awkward, as it might be in a bus or in a theater, it makes better sense to ignore this convention.

# ACTIVITY 5

Explain what you would say and do in each of the following situations.

1. You are at a party at which you know no one except the host, who is busy at the moment. You walk over to a person who also seems a bit lost. How do you introduce yourself?

2. You have an appointment to see Ms. Koriyama at Signature Publishing Company. What would you say when speaking to the receptionist?

3. You wish to introduce your mother to your math teacher, Mr. Canseco. What do you say?

4. You invite a new girl at school to dinner at your house. How would you introduce her to your parents?

5. You are painting the front porch and have paint all over your hands. One of your friends drops by and introduces you to his cousin. What do you do when the cousin tries to shake your hand?

## Developing the Skills of Conversation

**Conversation** is the informal exchange of thoughts and feelings by two or more people. Good conversations enable people to participate in enjoyable exchanges of ideas, get to know new acquaintances, cement old relationships, and influence the thinking and behavior of others. Pleasurable, satisfying conversation depends on the conversational skills of the people participating; these are skills that you can learn.

| Qualities of a Good Conversationalist | |
|---|---|
| **Knowledgeable** | able to speak intelligently about a variety of topics and to share interesting information and insights on several topics |
| **Caring** | able to understand and respond with sensitivity to the feelings, needs, problems, and concerns of others |
| **Encouraging** | able to use questions to draw people out and to get them to talk about themselves and their experiences by asking open questions that prompt people to share |
| **Natural** | able to discuss things that interest themselves and other people without pretending and without attempting to impress anyone |
| **Flexible** | able to listen to the views of others and to keep an open mind when weighing and evaluating others' opinions |
| **Good Listeners** | able to be encouraging and enthusiastic when listening, without interrupting or dominating the conversation |

**Strategies for Conversing.** Great enjoyment can come from a conversation. Good conversationalists are made, not born. The following strategies will enable you to improve your verbal skills and to become a more effective conversationalist.

1. *Ask good questions.* You have been asking questions since you began to talk, but some questioning strategies are more effective than others.

   • **Open questions** are those that must be answered with an explanation. For instance, the question "How do you feel about being elected to the student council?" is an open question. To answer it, the person asked would probably talk about his or her feelings or reactions. Avoid **closed questions**—those that can be answered with *yes* or *no*, or with only a word or two. For instance, if you ask, "Were you glad when you were elected to the student council?" the person could simply answer yes or no, and the conversation would reach a dead end.

- **Follow-up questions** relate to the subject matter of an earlier question. Since carrying on a conversation is a constant exchange, you can use follow-up questions to keep a conversation going.

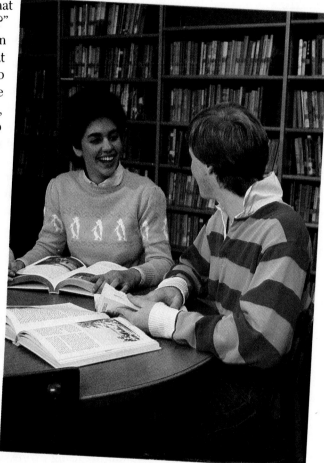

  **EXAMPLE:** You ask Sara, "What have you been doing lately?" Sara answers, "I've been exercising, trying to run at least three miles a day." To encourage her to continue and to begin a conversation, you could ask a follow-up question, such as "Where do you run?" or "How do you find time to run?" or "How long does it usually take you to run three miles?" or "What kind of running shoes do you prefer?" or "Do you ever plan to enter a running race?"

- Questions that relate to a person's interests encourage the person to talk. Since many people often resort to discussing the weather when trying to think of something to say, relate a question about the weather to the person's interests. You might say, "This is the warmest March we've had in years. Do you think you'll start baseball practice early?"

2. *Paraphrase.* **Paraphrasing** is stating in your own words what someone else has said. In a conversation, paraphrasing can help you to

- show that you know how someone feels
- show that you are paying attention
- avoid misunderstandings [See page 144.]

  **EXAMPLE:** You might say, "Let me make sure I understand your point. Are you saying—?" and then paraphrase the key points. The other person can then correct you if your understanding is inaccurate.

**3.** *Use clear, vivid words.* The more specific and concrete your words are, the more likely you are to convey your message accurately. If someone says, "We're planning neat things for the picnic," the listener may be too bored even to wonder what the "neat things" are. However, if someone says, "We're planning a horseshoe tournament and volleyball challenge games for the picnic," the more specific terms help to develop a more interesting conversation.

**4.** *Use appropriate nonverbal cues.* You can use body language—gestures, facial expressions, and movements—to add meaning and emphasis to your words. For example, in telling about a superb play in a volleyball game, you could use your hands to show how you spiked the ball backhanded.

**5.** *Put expression in your voice.* By varying the pitch, volume, and intonation of your voice, you can add power to your conversation and make it more interesting to others. For example, in a description of an incident, such as how you found a five-dollar bill on the sidewalk, the way you vary the pitch and loudness of your voice stresses certain words and creates a sense of excitement.

**6.** *Be aware of your listeners' comfort level.* A good conversationalist is sensitive to other people's feelings. Use good manners.

- Use language and subject matter appropriate to your purpose and your audience.
- Do not criticize people in front of others.
- Try to focus on cheerful subjects.
- Do not ask overly personal questions.
- Do not gossip about people you know.
- When you're talking with someone, stand at a distance that's comfortable for both of you.
- Be polite by using expressions such as *please, thank you,* and *excuse me.*

Drawing by Stevenson; © 1964, 1992 The New Yorker Magazine, Inc.

List qualities that you think make someone a good conversationalist. Your list may be different from the one on page 174. Then, rank these qualities, beginning with the quality you feel is the most important. Discuss your rankings with your classmates to see how their lists compare with yours. On the basis of these characteristics, how do you rate yourself as a conversationalist? In which areas do you feel you might need improvement? Which characteristics do you think might be your particular strengths?

COMMUNICATION JOURNAL

Think about some of the more interesting conversations you have had in the last few weeks. Which of these conversations was the most interesting? What particular features made this conversation so enjoyable? Jot down your observations about this conversation, and draw conclusions about what made the conversation especially memorable.

# Using Constructive Feedback to Resolve Disagreements

A **disagreement** is a difference of opinion among two or more people. Since disagreements are a normal and sometimes necessary part of living, it is important to learn to handle them in a constructive, or positive, way.

The best method of dealing with disagreement is discussion. **Discussion** means talking through a problem, such as a disagreement, by following the problem-solving method. The **problem-solving method** involves identifying the problem, determining its nature and causes, talking about possible ways to solve the problem, and selecting the best way.

Even if discussion does not completely solve a problem that involves disagreement, it gives both parties in the dispute a better understanding of the issues involved. However, since discussion itself may not always be constructive, it is sometimes necessary to control its direction by using the technique of **constructive feedback,** or evaluating a problem to negotiate a solution.

## Resolve Disagreements by Using Constructive Feedback

1. **Agree to a "time out" to settle the dispute.** Try to call a halt or set a specific time to discuss the issues. If one or both parties seem embarrassed, angry, or distressed, set a later time when a discussion of the disagreement may be more productive.

2. **Identify the difficulty to be resolved.** Define the problem in terms of needs, without communicating blame. For instance, you might say, "I feel as though I'm having to do more than my share of the work."

3. **Respond to the action, not the person.** If you say, "What you said made me angry," rather than "You made me angry," you are responding to the action, not to the person. "You made me angry" may sound like a personal attack.

4. **Use "I" messages, not "you" messages.** A **"you" message** is one that expresses a judgment of another person's actions. For example, you might say, "*You* are always trashing our locker." "You" messages often sound as though the speaker were accusing or blaming the other person. As a result, people rarely respond well to them. An **"I" message,** on the other hand, is a statement that begins with "I" and that expresses honestly how you feel as a result of the other person's behavior. For example, you might rephrase the above "you" message as follows: "*I feel angry when you leave your wet socks in our locker.*"

5. **Discuss only the specific, current disagreement to be resolved.** Do not try to discuss several different problems at the same time. Stick to one problem, the one that is bothering you now. Giving a detailed history of the present problem or mentioning problems that you have had with this person in the past will only lead to more arguments.

6. **Be willing to negotiate a solution.** Give your suggestions for how the conflict might be resolved. Also, let the other person give his or her suggestions. Evaluate the solutions together to decide which solutions are fair to both parties. Negotiate until both parties agree on a solution.

FOR BETTER OR FOR WORSE copyright 1992 Lynn Johnston Prod. Reprinted with permission of Universal Press Syndicate. All rights reserved.

# ACTIVITY 7

## Using Constructive Feedback to Settle Disagreements

Working with a partner, act out one of the following situations. Your goal is to settle the disagreement with a discussion that uses constructive feedback to identify the problem and to negotiate a fair solution. Ask a third person to observe your discussions and to evaluate how successfully you and your partner handle the problems.

1. You and a younger relative share a room. You try to keep your side of the room neat, while your roommate not only keeps the other side a mess but also lets his or her mess encroach on your side.

2. For the past three months, you have been working after school at a store. Two other students work with you. After observing and evaluating your tasks, you believe that the manager gives you many more tasks than he or she gives the other two students.

3. You are in a group of five students writing a report for your history class. The report is due in one week. You believe that the group leader has assigned you a topic for which it is difficult to find adequate resource materials. You feel that your topic is more difficult to research than the topics assigned to the other students in the group.

4. You and your sister are saving to buy your parents an anniversary present. You have just found out that your sister has used all of the savings to buy herself a new sweater.

## GUIDELINES

### for Speaking Socially

- When I introduce myself, do I greet the person, give my name, and say something about myself?

- Do I use appropriate language in my introductions?

- Do I draw others into conversation, keep an open mind, and listen with interest?

- In conversation, do I ask effective questions, use nonverbal techniques to add meaning and emphasis, paraphrase to check my understanding, and use clear, vivid words?

- Do I solve problems by giving constructive feedback?

- Do I use constructive feedback to discuss and solve problems?

# PUTTING UNDERSTANDING TO WORK

### Finding a Home

A real estate agent is licensed to represent people who are trying to buy or sell properties. Successful agents are usually able to communicate effectively to understand and meet their clients' needs.

### Characteristics of a Good Real Estate Agent

A good real estate agent

1. builds a file on each client's preferences and needs

2. obtains information about school zones, local real estate laws, and neighborhood characteristics

3. uses constructive feedback to meet the client's needs

4. introduces buyers and sellers

5. uses the telephone efficiently

6. gives accurate, easily understood directions

### Meet the Real Estate Agent

As a real estate agent for seven years, Joe Stewart has found dream homes for many clients. "I communicate with many people every day, either by phone, in person, or by e-mail," he says. "This communication enables me to develop a clear understanding of the client's needs."

*Joe R. Stewart*

## ACTIVITY

### Situation

You are a real estate agent building a profile of a client who wants to buy a house. The client is being transferred to your city by her company.

### Preparation

Make a list of ten questions that can help determine what kind of house your client would like to buy. Is your client married? Does she have children? Would she like a home office? a recreation room? a swimming pool? a large kitchen? What location is preferred?

### Analysis and Assessment

Write a short question-and-answer script in which you ask questions of a client to determine what kind of house and neighborhood the client desires. Recruit a classmate to play the role of your client, and perform the script in class. Ask for feedback from your classmates. Can they think of other questions you could have asked?

# S•U•M•M•A•R•Y

**INFORMAL SPEECH** is the communication that takes place between people in unstructured, unofficial situations. One category of informal speech has a practical purpose—to obtain information or to accomplish a task. Another category has a social purpose—to enjoy an exchange of thoughts and feelings with other people.

- **Give and receive directions** accurately by focusing on simple, direct explanations, using visual words and maps, and repeating directions to clarify and ensure accuracy.
- **Use the telephone efficiently and courteously** for both business and social transactions. When calling, identify yourself, articulate clearly, and be specific about the reason for your call. When answering the phone, answer appropriately, respond courteously and responsibly to the situation, and take messages accurately.
- **Introduce yourself** to others with a greeting and your name. Introduce people to each other smoothly and politely by using an appropriate order of names.
- **Be a good conversationalist** by asking good questions to draw people out, by being sensitive to the feelings and needs of others, and by choosing language and using vocal control to create interest.
- **Use constructive feedback** in discussion to deal with disagreements in a positive way.

## Review Questions

1. One guideline for giving clear directions is to select the simplest route. What are three other guidelines for giving clear directions?
2. When you are making a social call, why is it a good idea to identify yourself to the person who answers the phone?
3. What procedure should you follow to relay messages accurately and effectively?
4. Why is it important to take notes about messages that you hear on an answering machine?
5. According to tradition, when you introduce one person to another, you should name the person of higher status first. What are two other guidelines for introducing one person to another?
6. A good conversationalist can speak on a number of subjects. What are some other qualities of a good conversationalist?
7. Two types of questions are open questions and closed questions. How does an open question differ from a closed question?
8. Why is paraphrasing a good technique to use in a conversation?
9. What are the guidelines for giving constructive feedback?
10. How does an "I" message differ from a "you" message? What effect(s) does each of these kinds of messages have on a listener?

## Discussion Questions

1. In general, which do you think is easier, talking to others face to face or talking on the telephone? Discuss the reasons why people favor one method of communication or the other. What are some situations in which you would prefer one method over the other?
2. Like many modern inventions, the telephone has affected people's lives in both positive and negative ways. First, discuss the benefits of the telephone. For example, it helps you to keep in touch with people who live far away. Then, discuss its drawbacks. For example, a ringing telephone can interrupt a good conversation. What do you imagine would be the benefits and drawbacks of telephones that allow you not just to hear but also to see the person you're talking to?
3. Discuss the different feelings that people have about answering machines. Why do you think some people refuse to leave messages on answering machines? What are some strategies for helping people to become more comfortable with answering machines?
4. William Hazlitt, the English essayist, once wrote, "The art of conversation is the art of hearing as well as of being heard." Discuss the meaning of this quotation. How does it relate to the ability of a good conversationalist to listen?
5. Confucius, the Chinese philosopher, once said, "Learning without thought is labor lost; thought without learning is perilous." How does this quotation relate to what you have learned about problem solving?

# ACTIVITIES

1. **Giving Directions.** You and your family are vacationing in New York City. Your family has planned to spend today exploring Central Park, and they've named you the "official" map reader. Working with a partner, use the map below to give directions for one of the following situations.

   a. You are at Columbus Circle and want to go to the Metropolitan Museum of Art.

   b. You are at Summit Rock, and your little sister says she's hungry. Your brother volunteers to get her a snack.

   c. Your tour of Belvedere Castle just finished, and you have fifteen minutes to get to the Naumberg Bandshell for a free concert.

2. **Making Telephone Calls.** Make a list of three common situations in which you would have to make business calls. Be sure that one of these situations involves making a complaint. Working with a partner, act out each of these situations.

3. **Relaying Messages.** Ask a partner to leave three messages on an answering machine or a tape recorder, each one for a different family member in the particular household. Play back the messages and jot down the important facts in them; paraphrase the messages if necessary. Tell how you would make sure that each family member gets his or her message.

4. **Making Introductions.** Working with some other members of your class, act out introductions for the following situations.

   a. You are at a party where you know very few people. You see a boy or a girl you want to meet.

   b. You and a friend are browsing through a department store. She introduces you to her cousin, who works in the shoe department. You respond to the introduction.

   c. You and a friend are standing in line at the store. You meet your family doctor.

   d. You are with an adult family member at the hardware store. You meet your science teacher.

   e. You are applying for a part-time job at a fast-food restaurant. The manager has just asked you to come into his office for an interview.

5. **Identifying Suitable Topics for Conversation.** You have been invited to a party at a new friend's house. You will not know anyone there except your new friend. List at least five topics that you could use for making conversation with the other people at the party.

**6. Making Announcements.** Prepare a short announcement to be delivered in one of the situations shown below or in a specific situation of your own choosing. Be sure to include in your announcement all important information that your audience would need to know. Then, with a group of your classmates, practice delivering your announcement.

**7. Solving Problems.** Working with a partner, plan a situation in which two friends disagree about what they should do after seeing a third friend cheat on a test. Include enough specific details of the conflict to establish why the two friends disagree. Write key lines of dialogue between the two friends in which they use constructive feedback to settle the dispute. Act out the disagreement and its settlement as an improvisation, with your classmates as the audience.

**8. Paraphrasing During a Conversation.** You are in a conversation in front of the school with friends. Paraphrase the following statements to show your understanding of each person's intended meaning.
  a. Latoya says, "I'd like to try out for the part, but since Dorie's trying out too, I just don't know."
  b. Juan says, "Powell said my last paper was too detailed. This time I left out a lot of details, and he said my analysis was superficial!"
  c. Malcolm says, "The first playoff game is on Tuesday, but that's the same day as choral practice, and I've got a solo to work on."
  d. Heather says, "Dad's got a chance for a promotion, but we'd have to move out of state right in the middle of my junior year!"
  e. Ming says, "The constant rain day after day is starting to get to me. Do you think we're ever going to see the sun again?"

# EVERYDAY COMMUNICATION

## Situation
To sell your car, you have placed a newspaper advertisement with your telephone number. How would you communicate with potential buyers?

### Problem
What description will you give to callers who ask about the car? Where will you meet to show the car, and what directions will you give to guide the caller there? How will you discuss your asking price? Write a question-and-answer script that addresses these questions.

### Assessing Your Skill
Does your script include techniques to answer the caller's questions and resolve disagreements over the price? Are your directions to the meeting place clear and easy to follow? Be prepared to present your script as if you were speaking to the buyer.

# COMMUNICATION IN THE WORKPLACE

## Background
You are a college student with a part-time job at a clothing store. You and another clerk have had a disagreement concerning the sharing of responsibilities in your department.

## Preparing to Do the Job
What would you do to reach an agreement about sharing specific responsibilities, such as stocking shelves, organizing merchandise, answering the phone, waiting on customers, and filling out paperwork?

## Testing Your Skill
Identify the main issues on which you and your co-worker disagree. Then think of strategies you could use to resolve the issues. Prepare a short dialogue in which you use constructive feedback to resolve the disagreements. Be prepared to present your dialogue for your classmates and to ask for their feedback on the effectiveness of your strategies.

# Interviewing

## What Is an Interview?

An **interview** is a formal meeting, usually face to face, in which people obtain information by asking questions. The **interviewer** is the person who conducts the interview by asking questions. The **interviewee** is the person who responds to the interviewer's questions. However, an interview is not a one-way form of communication. The interviewee can also ask questions. Three common types of interviews are

- the **job interview,** in which a personnel director or other person responsible for hiring employees reviews an applicant's qualifications for a job
- the **school interview,** in which an admissions officer interviews an applicant for schooling after high school graduation, such as business, technical, and trade schools; community colleges; or colleges and universities
- the **informative interview,** in which the interviewer gathers information about a topic from a knowledgeable, experienced person

In this chapter, you will learn how to be interviewed for a job or for school admission and how to conduct an informative interview.

# Preparing to Be Interviewed

Since you can expect to face a number of important interviews, you will want to be well prepared for them. The following suggestions can help you get ready for an interview for a job or for school admission.

## Reading the Advertisement Carefully

Often you'll learn about jobs or educational opportunities through advertisements. When reading these advertisements, make sure you understand two things: (1) the type of job or courses being advertised and (2) the qualifications that an applicant must have for the job or courses. Here are two sample advertisements:

The two qualifications for this job as a receptionist are a good telephone voice and good typing skills. If you met these qualifications, you could fill out an application and write a business letter requesting an interview.

RECEPTIONIST
Summer Replacement

Generic Products is looking for a person with a good phone voice to handle our six incoming phone lines. Person must be a good typist. We will train on CRT. Application forms will be provided on Wed. and Fri. at 2693 Spring Ave. Write for interview.

SUMMER BUSINESS PROGRAM

Southern Ohio College is offering the following courses:
**Summer Session I:** Intro to Business 101, Accounting 101, Finance 111
**Summer Session II:** Intro to Business 102, Accounting 102, Finance 112
For more information on admissions and registration, call 555-1234.

By reading this ad, you could tell whether Southern Ohio College was offering a course you wanted. By calling the number provided, you could also learn how to apply for admission as well as how to register.

## Preparing a Résumé

A **résumé** is a brief account of an applicant's educational background and employment experience. Some employers want to receive a cover letter and a résumé before they will ask you to interview. Even if you have sent a résumé ahead, bring a copy to the interview. The résumé will provide a quick overview of data about you and will remind the interviewer of your qualifications after the interview is over.

A résumé is seldom more than one page long. It should include the following information:

- your name, address, and telephone number
- your education, including honors, awards, or special courses
- your previous work experience

| | |
|---|---|
| **ANGELA THOMPSON** | 1632 Morgan Drive<br>Cincinnati, OH 45211<br>(513) 555-5971 |

| | |
|---|---|
| **Work Experience** | DANSON'S DEPARTMENT STORE , Cincinnati, OH<br>    1997 to present<br>Currently working as a Sales Associate in the Misses<br>    Clothing department.<br><br>CINCINNATI HERALD, Cincinnati, OH, 1995–1997<br>Worked as a newspaper carrier. |
| **Education** | CENTRAL HIGH SCHOOL, Cincinnati, OH<br>    1996 to present<br>Currently enrolled as a Junior. |
| **Awards Received** | HONOR ROLL, 1996 to present<br>ALL-STATE BASKETBALL TEAM, 1997 and 1998<br>ALL-REGION CHOIR, 1996–1998<br>ALL-STATE CHOIR, 1997 and 1998<br>STATE QUALIFIER FOR DRAMATIC INTERPRETATION<br>MEDAL, 1997 and 1998 |
| **Interests and Activities** | Theater, Drill Team, Student Council, Varsity Basketball,<br>Choir, Creative Writing, Peer Tutor Program |
| **References** | Mrs. Judith Miller<br>Director, Drama Department, Central High School<br>Fifth & Beech<br>Cincinnati, OH 45219          Tel: 555-3741<br><br>Mr. Paul Shuman<br>Manager, Danson's Department Store<br>4962 Glenway<br>Cincinnati, OH 45238          Tel: 555-6061<br><br>Ms. Donna Groves<br>Basketball Coach, Central High School<br>Fifth & Beech<br>Cincinnati, OH 45219          Tel: 555-3733 |

*I*n your communication journal, make notes about your qualifications, interests, and goals for a job, a career, or further education. As new ideas occur to you, add them to your notes. What do your notes show you about the kind of job or schooling you would enjoy?

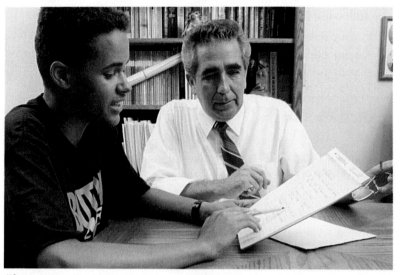

When preparing a résumé, you may want to get advice from a school counselor, job counselor, or other adult.

## Scheduling an Appointment

Usually the business's personnel director or the school's admissions officer will schedule your interview for a specific time. However, if you are asking for an interview, you should set up a time with the interviewer or with his or her assistant. Volunteering to just "show up any time" suggests a lack of understanding of business etiquette. To appear professional, always make an appointment.

### Reporting an Interview Experience

**H**ave you ever been interviewed for a job or for admission to a school? If so, tell your class about your experience and specify the purpose of the interview. Identify the interviewer, and describe the outcome of the interview. If you have not been interviewed, talk with someone who has and report that person's experience.

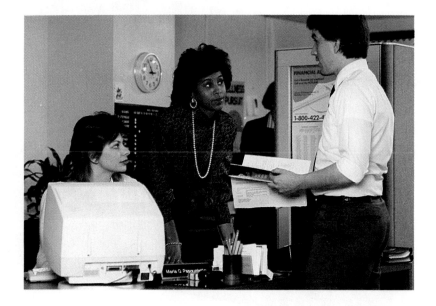

## Determining the Purpose of the Interview

Whether you are being interviewed for a job or for school admission, the interviewer may have several purposes.

Primary, or main, purposes:
- to make sure that you are qualified for the job or school
- to decide if you are the kind of person the company hires or the school admits

Secondary, or additional, purposes:
- to do a preliminary screening interview to determine whether you may proceed in the interview process
- to gather additional information about you

Try to learn the purpose of the interview beforehand so that you can prepare for it.

## Finding Out Information for the Interview

The more you know about the company, the school, or the interviewer, the better you can anticipate and answer questions as well as pose your own. Interviewers will see your knowledge as a sign of interest, initiative, and responsibility; consequently, they will be more likely to feel that talking with you is worth their time. Good sources of useful information include brochures, catalogs, and newspaper and magazine articles. Information may also be available in your school library or career counseling office.

## Knowing What You Want to Say

What do you want the interviewer to remember about you? Make sure that you are prepared to provide sufficient information about your qualifications, goals, and interests. General information is information you would use for any interview. Specific information is information that applies only to the particular job or school. You will need both kinds.

- **Qualifications:**
  What makes you a good candidate for this job or school? Generally, you might state that you have good communi cation skills. But specifically you could note that you type sixty words per minute.

- **Goals:**
  What do you hope to achieve with this job or at this school? Your general goal might be to find a challenging, rewarding career. Your specific goal might be to become a programmer for a computer software company, to design interactive computer games, or to earn a degree in computer science.

- **Interests:**
  How do you spend your spare time? You might say that you generally enjoy several hobbies, but you could specifically mention belonging to your school computer club. Be sure to put special emphasis on those interests that relate to the job or school.

# Knowing What You Want to Ask

A job or school interview is not a one-way form of communication. Although its main focus is on finding out about you, you may also want to ask questions. In order to make good decisions about the job or school, you should feel knowledgeable about the situation. More information may help you decide whether to take the job if it is offered or to attend the school if you are accepted.

Strictly Classified reprinted by permission: Tribune Media Services.

One technique you can use to be sure you obtain the information you need is to prepare a list of questions ahead of time. If your questions are not answered during the interview, request a few moments to ask questions. The following questions are some of the ones you may want to ask.

## Job

What will be my specific duties?
Who will be my supervisor?
If I have questions, whom should I ask?
What kinds of clothes are required? If uniforms are required, who pays for them?
Is there a union?
Will I be expected [ or will I have the opportunity ] to work overtime?
Is there any on-the-job training?

## School

How long is the course of study?
How many credits am I expected to handle [ or am I allowed to take ] each term?
What is the balance between required courses and electives?
Are there any work-study programs?
Besides books, tuition, and fees, what other expenses can I expect?
How can I apply for financial aid and for scholarships?
Are there any job placement services?

# ACTIVITY 2

## Writing a Résumé and Preparing for an Interview

In the classified section of your newspaper, find an advertisement for a job that appeals to you and for which you feel you are qualified. Using the format shown in the example on page 189, write a résumé that you could use if you were applying for this job. Then list both your qualifications and any questions you would ask.

## Rehearsing the Interview

Even though you cannot anticipate every question you may be asked in an interview, rehearsing answers to possible questions and devising follow-up questions will still be helpful. You may want to plan two or three practice sessions before you go. Rehearsing the interview will help you appear to have **poise,** the quality of looking confident and prepared to handle any problem.

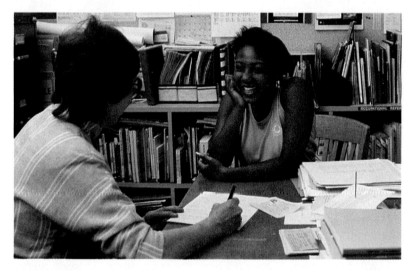

# ACTIVITY 3

## Rehearsing the Interview

Ask a classmate, a parent, or a trusted adult to play the role of interviewer and to ask you questions about the résumé you have developed in Activity 2, above. Try to answer the questions in the same manner that you would answer them in an actual interview. Then review your answers with your partner. Were your answers clear and concise? Which answers do you feel you handled best? Does your interviewer agree that these were your best responses?

# Being Interviewed

After you prepare for being interviewed, you are ready to consider the qualities interviewers look for in applicants and the kinds of questions they may ask.

## What Do Interviewers Look For?

The interviewer wants to know about your knowledge, your interests, and your attitudes. In addition, he or she will be looking for qualities that indicate you are a candidate to consider seriously.

| What Interviewers Look For | |
|---|---|
| **Promptness** | • Arrive on time.<br>• Give yourself more time than you need to get there.<br>• If you know you'll be late, call ahead to tell the interviewer.<br>• If you know you will not be there at all, call ahead to reschedule the interview. |
| **Appearance** | • Dress appropriately.<br>• Groom yourself well.<br>• Do not chew gum. |
| **Poise** | • Maintain an assured, confident manner throughout the interview.<br>• Be prepared. The more prepared you are, the more poised you are likely to be.<br>• To deal with nervousness, focus on the questions one at a time, and on your answers to them. |
| **Flexibility** | • Give answers that reflect your ability to adapt to new situations.<br>• Give at least one specific example to support your answers. |
| **Honesty** | • Be honest.<br>• Avoid the temptation to exaggerate.<br>• If you don't know the answer to a question, say so. |
| **Initiative** | • Give answers that show you are willing to take on new tasks and enterprises. |
| **Communication Skills** | • Develop good written and oral communication skills.<br>• Give answers that reflect your ability to take directions from supervisors; to communicate with fellow employees, teachers, and other students; and to express your thoughts effectively in writing. |

# ACTIVITY 4

Imagine that you are hiring someone for a job. First, write the advertisement detailing the job responsibilities and requirements. (You can get ideas by reviewing the ads in your local newspaper.) Then, discuss with your class the qualities mentioned on page 195 that you would consider the most important in a person applying for this job. Also explain your reasons for choosing these qualities. Finally, discuss with your classmates the similarities and differences in your ideas.

## What Do Interviewers Ask?

Interviewers obtain information by asking questions. No two interviewers will ask exactly the same questions, but you can anticipate four types of questions that they usually will ask:

- questions that request information
- questions that probe deeper
- questions that check understanding
- questions that require you to take a stand

**Questions That Request Information.** Questions that request information consider your current status, background, interests, and goals for the future.

1. **Current status:** Questions about your current status seek to discover where you stand at the moment in school or at work.

   EXAMPLES: What grade are you in now?
   What kind of program are you taking in school?
   What are your duties on your current job?

2. **Background:** Questions about your background seek to learn about your work and school experience, places you have lived, and things you have done.

   EXAMPLES: What experiences have you had that prepare you for this job?
   What courses have you taken that prepare you for this program?
   What are you particularly good at?

3. **Interests:** Questions about your interests seek to gain insight into the kind of person you are.

   EXAMPLES: What do you do in your spare time?
   What are your hobbies?
   If you could travel anywhere in the world, what places would you like to visit?

4. **Goals:** Questions about your goals seek to discover your hopes and plans for the future.

> **EXAMPLES:** If you are hired, how long would you expect to work here?
>
> In five years, what position would you like to hold?
>
> After you graduate from high school, what do you see yourself doing?

**Questions That Probe Deeper.**   Interviewers ask questions that probe deeper to find out more about your answers to other questions. These questions are meant to challenge statements you have made and to find reasons for your actions.

> **EXAMPLES:** You say you quit your newspaper delivery job after three weeks. Why?
>
> You say math is your favorite subject. What in particular do you like about math?
>
> Why do you think that you would be able to handle dictation if you have not had a course in shorthand?

**Questions That Check Understanding.**   Interviewers ask questions to check their understanding of what you have said.

> **EXAMPLES:** Though you took typing, you are not sure that you understand letter-format rules?
>
> Did you say that your grades in English accurately reflect your communication skills?
>
> What I hear you saying is that you would not be able to work on weekends. Is that correct?

**Questions That Require You to Take a Stand.** Interviewers ask questions that require you to take a stand to see how you respond under pressure.

> EXAMPLES: Why do you want to work for this company?
> Why do you want to attend this school?
> What kind of pay do you expect?

[Note: The Equal Employment Opportunity Commission, the EEOC, has written guidelines for the kinds of questions that may or may not be asked. In general, questions about marital status, family, race, physical characteristics, age, and other personal information are not allowed unless they directly bear on an applicant's ability to do the job.]

# HOW TO > *Answer an Interviewer's Questions*

1. **Answer the question the interviewer actually asked.** Listen carefully to be sure you understand the question. Then answer the question the interviewer actually asked, not the one you wish the interviewer had asked. Feel free to use questions that check understanding to clear up any misperceptions.

2. **Answer questions as fully and as honestly as you can.** Don't be afraid to take a few moments to frame, or shape, your responses. Avoid answering simply "yes" or "no" or giving only one- or two-word responses, but keep to the point. Don't go into long-winded explanations. Also, keep in mind the EEOC guidelines mentioned above. You don't have to answer personal questions unless they concern your qualifications for the job.

3. **Frame your answers to present yourself in the best possible light.** Emphasize the reasons that make you a good candidate for the job or the school.

# ACTIVITY 5

## Planning and Conducting a Job Interview

Look again at the job advertisement you wrote in Activity 4 on page 196. Write at least five questions you would ask an applicant for that job. Then, working with a partner, use your questions to conduct an interview, with one of you as the interviewer and the other as the interviewee. Present the interview to the class. Finally, ask your classmates to assess the strengths and weaknesses of the interview and to suggest how the questions and the responses could be improved.

Drawing by Stan Hunt; © 1983 The New Yorker Magazine Inc.

*"I'd just like to say, sir, that I always make a bad first impression."*

# GUIDELINES
## for Being Interviewed

- Do I have a résumé to give the interviewer?
- Have I identified my qualifications, goals, and interests?
- Have I allowed enough time to get to the interview?
- Have I dressed appropriately for the interview?
- Am I prepared to ask and answer questions clearly, honestly, and carefully?
- Do I have questions to ask the interviewer?
- Am I relaxed, enthusiastic, and confident?
- Do I speak clearly?

# Interviewing Others

You can conduct an informative interview with a knowledgeable person to gather information about a topic for an informative speech (see Chapter 14) or a persuasive speech (see Chapter 15). For example, for a speech about placing a local bird on the endangered species list, you could interview a biologist. Identifying the person you want to interview and planning what questions you want to ask will help you prepare for an interview.

*B*rainstorm a list of possible topics for a speech and jot them down in your communication journal. Then, for each topic, try to think of a person whom you could interview to gather information. Write the names or job titles beside the topic.

## Identifying Likely Sources

For any topic, you can probably find several people who can provide good information. Start by listing three or four likely sources. You want someone who can be a **reliable source**—someone who can be depended upon to give accurate information about the subject. A **primary source** is someone who provides information from direct experience. A **secondary source** is someone who provides information that originated with other people.

## HOW TO ⟩ Select Sources to Interview

1. **Is the person knowledgeable about the information you want?** For example, a buyer for a local department store would be a knowledgeable source for a report about the latest fashions.

2. **Is the person a primary source or a secondary source?** Can this source give you information from direct experiences, or does the source obtain information from other people? For example, if a chef tells you how he prepares his famous soufflé, he is a primary source; however, if he tells you how another chef says she prepares the soufflé, he is a secondary source.

3. **Is the person a reliable source?** Can you trust your source to give you dependable, accurate information? For example, a dietician would give accurate information about safe ways to lose weight. You should carefully consider three aspects of reliability:

   - Age: An older person is likely to have had more experience than someone younger and is therefore often perceived as being a more reliable source. However, a younger person may have more recent information that may be more reliable than an older person's experience.
   - Memory: As a rule, the longer ago an event took place, the less reliable a person's remembrance of details about the event will be.
   - Bias: Even the most reliable source will usually have a point of view that may affect the accuracy of information.

## Making an Appointment

Call or write the person you want to interview. Explain why you would like an interview with him or her and what you hope to gain from the interview. Try to arrange an in-person interview. If the person lives far away or if the person's schedule does not permit a face-to-face visit, you may have to conduct the interview by telephone. In either case, set up a specific time and place for the interview. Tell the person how to contact you in case he or she needs to reschedule.

## Preparing a List of Questions

Gather background information about your topic and about the person you are interviewing. Then use this knowledge to prepare intelligent questions. The types of questions you will ask will depend on the information you want.

| Types of Interview Questions | | |
|---|---|---|
| **Type of Question** | **Description** | **Example** |
| **Open Questions** | encourage a person to talk at length, to share feelings and impressions | "How did you first become interested in medicine?" |
| **Closed Questions** | can be answered with "yes" or "no" or a few words; used to obtain specific information quickly | "Where did you do your internship?" |
| **Neutral Questions** | promote objectivity by giving the interviewee no hint of what particular answer you want | "How do you respond when a patient refuses to follow orders?" |
| **Leading Questions** | suggest the answer you expect or desire | "Doesn't it upset you when a patient refuses to follow orders?" |
| **Follow-up Questions** | probe for additional information about a previous question | "What was it about being in medicine that interested you?" |

## Organizing Your List of Questions

You can arrange your questions so that your interview will have a beginning, a middle, and an end.

- Beginning: Try to relieve any tension the interviewee may have by asking easy-to-answer questions.
- Middle: Include questions that aim for specific information and that may take more time for the interviewee to answer.
- End: Conclude by thanking the interviewee for taking time to answer your questions. Give him or her a chance to make additional comments. A good final question is "Is there anything else you think I should know about this topic?"

A·C·T·I·V·I·T·Y 6

### Gathering Information from Others

You are going to give a speech on the popularity of a sport, a television show, or a place to eat. Choose and limit your topic, and then list three people who would be good sources of information about it. Which person would you choose to interview? Why? Next, write six questions to ask this person, and organize them into the most effective order.

# Conducting an Interview

**1. Come prepared to record the interview.**   To prevent distortion of facts, keep a careful record of the interview. If you plan to take notes, leave enough space between the questions you prepared so that you can write down brief answers. If you plan to tape-record the interview, first ask the interviewee's permission. Also be sure that your tape recorder is working well.

**2. Be courteous.**   Show patience, encouragement, and respect as the interviewee answers your questions.

**3. Listen carefully.**   At various points in the interview, paraphrase out loud any answers that seem unclear to you. **Paraphrasing** means stating in your own words the idea or feeling you get from another person's words.

**4. Monitor your nonverbal communication.**   Make sure that your nonverbal reactions—your facial expressions and your gestures— reflect the tone you want to convey. Keep good eye contact, nod to show understanding, and smile occasionally to maintain the friend-liness of the interview.

# ACTIVITY 7

## Conducting an Informative Interview

Working with a partner, conduct the informative interview you developed in Activity 6 on page 202. Present your interview in front of the class. After you finish, discuss with your classmates how effective your questions were and how you might have conducted the interview better.

# Following Up an Interview

After an interview, you should write a short letter to the person who interviewed you or whom you interviewed. This is a courtesy letter to thank the interviewer or the interviewee for taking the time to talk with you.

In a letter to an interviewer, indicate that you look forward to hearing from the company or school as soon as possible. If you interviewed someone, offer to send the interviewee a copy of your article or report as well.

---

1632 Morgan Dr.
Cincinnati, OH 45211
June 4, 1995

Mr. Richard Parker
Director, Marketing Division
Generic Products
2847 Spring Ave.
Cincinnati, OH 45227

Dear Mr. Parker:

Thank you for taking the time to talk with me about the opening for a clerical position in the Marketing Divison of Generic Products. I look forward to hearing from you about my application.

Sincerely yours,

*Angela Thompson*

Angela Thompson

# ACTIVITY 8

## Writing a Follow-up Letter

For Activity 2 on page 194, you selected a job advertisement in the newspaper. Suppose that you have already gone on an interview for the advertised job. Write a follow-up letter to the interviewer. What impression of yourself would you want the interviewer to get from your letter? How would you write your letter in order to give this impression?

## GUIDELINES
### for Interviewing Others

- Do I have a knowledgeable and reliable person to interview for information about my topic?

- Do I have an appointment scheduled at a time that is convenient for the interviewee?

- Do I have an organized list of questions?

- Do I have permission to tape-record the interviewee's responses?

- Do I appear courteous and attentive and listen carefully to the interviewee's answers?

- Do I send appropriate nonverbal messages to the person I am interviewing?

## APPLYING YOURSELF

### Improving Interview Effectiveness

A university admissions officer often interviews a prospective student to determine whether the student and the university are an appropriate match. The admissions officer asks questions aimed at discovering whether an applicant has the necessary qualities to succeed at the university.

### Characteristics of an Effective Admissions Officer

An effective admissions officer

**1** recognizes the qualifications, goals, and interests of an applicant

**2** identifies appropriate questions to ask an applicant

**3** conducts an interview effectively

**4** follows up an interview directly

## ACTIVITY

### Situation

Your best friend has asked you to help him or her rehearse for an upcoming interview for a summer job. This will be your friend's first job, and he or she wants to make a good impression.

### Preparation

Think about how you can help your friend prepare for the interview. What kinds of questions should your friend expect the interviewer to ask, and how should your friend respond? What qualities can your friend accentuate in the interview? What would be appropriate attire? How can your friend effectively follow up the interview?

### Analysis and Assessment

Write a two- or three-page dialogue of your friend's interview. Ask a classmate to play your friend; then rehearse the dialogue and present it in class. Ask for feedback from your classmates on the effectiveness of your interview questions and your friend's responses.

**Meet the Admissions Officer**

"Test scores and transcripts can tell us a lot about a student's preparation and potential," says John W. Lind, Vice President for Enrollment Management at Southwestern University. "We also learn important things from an interview. Was the applicant prompt, poised, and honest? Does the applicant have the initiative necessary to succeed at Southwestern?"

*John W. Lind*

# S•U•M•M•A•R•Y

**INTERVIEWING** is a form of communication in which people obtain information by asking questions or by answering questions. A person who is conducting an interview is the interviewer; the person being interviewed is the interviewee.

- **Prepare to be interviewed** for a job or for school admission by determining the requirements for the job or the school, preparing a résumé, and scheduling an appointment with the interviewer. You should also determine the purpose of the interview and find information about the company, the school, or the interviewer. Think about what you want to say and what you want to ask the interviewer. Then rehearse the questions and answers so that you will be less nervous during the actual interview.

- **Understand qualities** interviewers look for: promptness, appearance, poise, flexibility, honesty, initiative, and communication skills. Also anticipate the kinds of questions the interviewer will probably ask.

- **Prepare to conduct an interview** by determining a knowledgeable and reliable source to interview, making an appointment, and preparing and organizing a list of varied types of questions. Record the interviewee's responses in written notes or in a tape-recording. Be courteous and listen carefully. Also be sure to use nonverbal language that maintains an appropriate tone for the interview.

- **Follow up an interview** with a thank-you letter.

Look back through this chapter and find the meaning of each of the following terms. Write each term and its meaning in your communication journal.

## Review Questions

1. How is an interview different from a question-and-answer session in which an audience asks questions of a speaker?
2. What are at least three things you should do to prepare for an interview?
3. A résumé is a brief account of your experience. In general, what information should you include in your résumé?
4. What is the difference between the general information and the specific information you provide about your qualifications, goals, and interests?
5. Why is it important to rehearse for an interview?
6. What are at least five qualities interviewers look for in an applicant?
7. What are the four types of questions you may be asked during an interview?
8. What three questions should an interviewer ask before choosing a person for an informative interview?
9. What is the difference between an *open* question and a *closed* question? What is the difference between a *neutral* question and a *leading* question?
10. How should you follow up an interview?

## Discussion Questions

1. You are interviewing for a job selling clothing at a department store. Discuss the importance of good appearance in interviewing for that job.
2. The Equal Employment Opportunity Commission (EEOC) does not allow employers to ask prospective employees questions about marriage, religious preference, ethnic background, and other personal matters. Discuss why you think such questions are disallowed.
3. The famous U.S. educator and politician Horace Mann once wrote, "Unfaithfulness in the keeping of an appointment is an act of clear dishonesty. You may as well borrow a person's money as his time." Do you agree or disagree with Mann? Why? What advice do you think Mann would give to a person preparing for an interview?
4. The French philosopher Voltaire suggested, "Judge a man by his questions rather than by his answers." What do you think this quotation means? Discuss what the interviewee can learn from the questions the interviewer asks. Then discuss what the interviewer can learn from the questions the interviewee asks.
5. Interviewers look for honesty in applicants. Discuss with your classmates why this trait is so important and what an applicant can do to establish his or her honesty.

# ACTIVITIES

**1. Analyzing Interviewing Skills.** Watch an interview on a television talk show or news program, and tell your class about it. What kinds of questions did the interviewer ask? How effective were these questions in getting the interviewee to talk? How could the questions have been more effective?

**2. Understanding and Answering a Job Advertisement.** Read the following job advertisement. What type of job is being advertised? What qualifications does an applicant need? List the steps that you would follow in applying for this job. Then, compare your list with a partner's to see if you have included all the necessary steps.

> ### SUMMER HELPER
> Fast-paced and growing florist and gift delivery business looking for a sharp, self-motivated, cheerful customer service clerk. Must have: professional appearance, pleasant phone voice, ability to handle light typing and filing. Must be dependable and reliable. Good pay, some benefits. Send résumé to:
> ### Blooms and More
> 9258 NW Parkway
> Cincinnati, OH 45233

**3. Preparing for and Practicing for a School Interview.**

**A.** Choose a school in which you are interested—a business, technical, or trade school; a community college; or a college or university. Write questions that an interviewer from that school might ask you. Then write your answers to these questions. Compare your questions and answers with those of your classmates.

**B.** Write a letter to the school of your choice asking for an interview.

**C.** Working with a partner, conduct a school interview. Have one person act as the interviewer and the other as the interviewee. Then, invite and respond to feedback from your classmates.

**4. Preparing for a Celebrity Interview.**

**A.** Imagine that you are a journalist. Your next assignment is to interview one of the celebrities shown below or another celebrity of your own choosing. What would your readers be most interested in knowing about the person you interview? Think of at least four general topics that you might have your interviewee address.

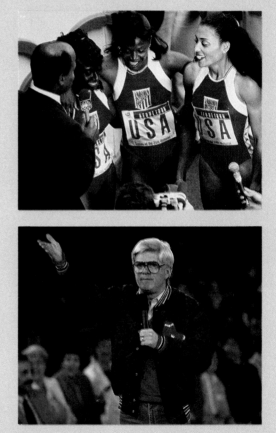

**B.** Using the list of general topics that you made for Part A, think of ten specific questions to ask your interviewee. Try to make most of your questions open ones to encourage the person to talk at length. [For examples of the different types of interview questions, see the chart on page 202.]

**C.** Imagine that your interview has taken place. Follow it up with a thank-you letter. Write a letter to your interviewee, thanking him or her for talking with you. [Use the letter on page 204 as a model of a business letter.] Notice that you will need to make up the interviewee's address.

**5. Preparing for and Practicing for a Job Interview.**

**A.** Imagine you are going to interview for a summer job. List the questions you would expect an interviewer to ask you. Then list your answers to these questions. Compare your questions and answers to those of your classmates.

**B.** Working with a partner, conduct an interview for a summer job. Have one person act as the interviewer and the other as the interviewee. After the interview, listen to and respond to feedback from your classmates.

**6. Identifying Techniques for Reducing Nervousness.** Discuss with your classmates techniques you can use to help reduce your nervousness before an interview. Compile a class list of these techniques, and copy the list in your communication journal. Try to refer to it before you participate in an interview.

**7. Preparing for an Informative Interview.** Think of a sport, a profession, a craft, or a hobby that would make an interesting topic for a speech. [You may wish to refer to pages 216–220 in Chapter 9 for more about generating topic ideas.] Next, identify three people in your community who would be knowledgeable subjects for an informative interview on this topic. Finally, develop at least five questions you might ask each person to gather information about your topic.

**8. Analyzing Nonverbal Communication in an Interview.** In a job interview, an experienced personnel director or other business person who does a great deal of hiring will often form opinions about a job applicant even before the applicant says a word. Such opinions are based on the interviewer's first impression of the applicant. Obviously, creating a good first impression is important to getting an interview off to a positive start.

Think of two different jobs that you would like to apply for. Imagine that you have an interview for each job. How would you try to create a good first impression at each interview? What would you wear to each one? How would you act? Notice the ways in which you adapt your appearance or behavior to each setting. For example, you would probably not wear the same clothes to apply for a pizza delivery driver job that you would wear to an interview for a position as a sales clerk in a department store.

# COMMUNICATION IN THE WORKPLACE

### Background
You are an interviewer asking questions of an applicant for a summer job. You think the applicant is a good candidate, but so far he or she has given only very short answers.

### Preparing to Do the Job
Make a list of at least three skills an interviewer can use to make an applicant more at ease and talkative. Then write a short, three- or four-minute dialogue showing an interviewer using these skills with an applicant.

### Testing Your Skill
Ask a classmate to play the part of the applicant. Then assume the role of the interviewer, and act out your dialogue in class. Afterward, discuss with your classmates the skills necessary for an interviewer to have. Ask your classmates if they thought your interviewing skills would have made them more at ease and talkative.

# EVERYDAY COMMUNICATION

### Situation
You see an ad in the newspaper for a job that interests you. The job requires that you submit a résumé.

### Problem
Assume that you meet the qualifications, and write a résumé to submit with your application. Then prepare for a possible interview. Decide what you would wear and how you would act.

### Assessing Your Skill
Did you choose clothing that would make a positive impression on the interviewer? Are you prepared to identify your strongest qualifications and your career goals? Do you know why you want the job and why you should be hired? Read your answers aloud or act out an interview for your classmates. Ask your classmates to evaluate your performance during the interview. Would they hire you for the job?

# Unit 3

# Public Speaking

Purpose

Explain
Show
Give
Prove
Convince
Motivate

C H A P T E R **9**

# Getting Ready

OBJECTIVES

**After studying this chapter, you should be able to**

1. Select a suitable topic for a speech.
2. Identify qualities that make a good topic for a speech.
3. Tell the difference between a general purpose and a specific purpose.
4. Write a thesis statement.
5. Draw conclusions about the knowledge, interests, and attitudes of your audience.
6. Determine how your occasion will affect your speech.
7. Identify the kinds of information you can use to support your thesis statement.

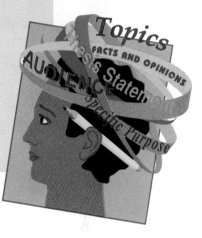

## How to Prepare for a Speech

Your teacher has just given you an assignment: You are to make a five-minute speech to your class a week from today. You probably have many questions. Where should you begin to plan your speech? What topic should you speak about? What do you need to know about your audience, and what will interest them? What kinds of information can you use in your speech?

The key to making a successful speech is to prepare, prepare, prepare. Speakers sometimes think they are so familiar with their topics that they can simply get up and speak about them. But planning a successful speech means thinking about several separate but interrelated parts: choosing your topic; writing your thesis statement; knowing your purpose, audience, and occasion; and supporting your thesis statement. In this chapter, you will learn several useful techniques that will help you with each of these steps.

# Choosing Your Topic

## Generating Topic Ideas

You can begin to find a topic for your speech by thinking about **subject areas,** or general categories, that are interesting and familiar to you. Some common subject areas are jobs and careers, hobbies and activities, past events, current issues, places, processes, and people. However, a general subject area, such as *movies,* is too broad to be covered effectively in one speech. A **topic** suitable for a speech is a specific category within a subject area. A number of techniques can help you get ideas for your topic:

- flipping through magazines and newspapers
- scanning entries of your diary or writing journal
- skimming through an encyclopedia
- interviewing others
- **brainstorming,** or quickly listing possibilities without stopping to evaluate each one

**EXAMPLE:** For his first speech, Joel Foster selected the subject area *hobbies and activities* and brainstormed the following ideas about the subject *football* to find a topic for his speech.

### Football

| | | | |
|---|---|---|---|
| players | offense | defense | passing |
| tackling | plays | calling plays | stadiums |
| rules | injuries | equipment | stretching |
| zones | positions | cheerleaders | coaching |
| practice | strategy | numbers | the ball |
| placekicking | punting | pass patterns | blocking |

*A*s you participate in your daily activities—going to classes, talking to friends, watching television, reading—note subject areas or specific topics that interest you. This list of topics can furnish useful ideas for speech topics.

## Limiting Your Topic

Limit your topic enough so that you can cover it effectively in one speech. Focus on specific aspects, examples, parts, uses, or other features of the topic.

**EXAMPLE:** After brainstorming, Joel selected three topics: *calling plays, pass patterns,* and *placekicking.* Since Joel liked *place-kicking* best, he chose this topic for his speech. But this topic is too broad to be covered effectively in one speech because there are so many different features of placekicking—its use in football strategy, famous plays involving placekicking, and the two different styles of placekicking. For his speech, Joel further limited his topic to *soccer-style placekicking.*

The chart on the following pages shows how you can use questions to narrow a general subject to a suitably limited topic.

## Exploring Subject Areas to Find Speech Topics

| General Subject Areas | Questions to Ask Yourself About This Subject Area | Sample Subjects | Sample Limited Topics |
|---|---|---|---|
| **Jobs and Careers** | 1. Have you ever had a part-time job during the summer or on weekends? If so, what knowledge or experience have you gained that might interest others? | pet-sitting | Five Pointers Every Pet-Sitter Should Know |
| | 2. Are you interested in a specific career? What do you know about it that might interest others? | chemistry<br><br>lawn care | Why I Want to Become a Research Chemist<br>What I Learned About Lawn and Garden Care in My Summer Job |
| **Hobbies and Activities** | 1. What hobby or activity do you enjoy? (Possibilities include coin collecting, raising cats, playing an instrument, or painting.) | baseball cards | How to Collect and Display Baseball Cards |
| | 2. Have you ever participated in an activity or hobby that others might like to know more about? | community theater<br>scuba diving | Participating in Community Theater<br>How I Learned to Scuba Dive |
| **Past Events** | 1. Is there a specific historical event that interests you and that you think would interest others? | the Battle of Gettysburg | How the Battle of Gettysburg Affected the Civil War |
| | 2. What event in your life or someone else's life is significant to you and could be meaningful to others? | my new baby sister | New Baby in the House |

*(continued on next page)*

| General Subject Areas | Questions to Ask Yourself About This Subject Area | Sample Subjects | Sample Limited Topics |
|---|---|---|---|
| **Current Issues** | 1. Is there a recent event in world or national news that you think is important? | peace in the Middle East | Why Resolving the Arab-Israeli Conflict Is Important |
| | 2. What significant events are taking place in your city, county, or state? | our county's programs | Our County's New Youth Activities Program |
| **Places** | 1. What specific place appeals to you for a particular reason? | a fishing location | The Best Place on Lake Texoma to Fish for Bass |
| | 2. What place have you heard about or studied that has importance or significance for others? | the Panama Canal | The Panama Canal's Importance in World Trade |
| **Processes** | 1. What do you know how to do or to make that you could describe to someone else? | models | How to Build a Model Airplane |
| | 2. Are you familiar enough with the way something works that you could explain it to others? | TV sets | How a Television Set's Color Gun Works |
| **People** | 1. Is there a person whose courage, skill, honesty, thoughtfulness, or other quality impresses you? | my grandfather | Why I Admire My Grandfather |
| | 2. What famous person do you find notable or admirable? Why? | Hatshepsut | Hatshepsut, the Woman Who Became Pharaoh |

## Choosing a Subject and Limiting It to a Speech Topic

**S**elect two subject areas and brainstorm ideas about each subject area. When you run out of ideas, put your lists aside. Later, return to your lists to see if you can add more items. After completing your two lists, choose the three items from each list that interest you most. Next, from each group of three items, find the one that you would most like to develop into a speech topic for this subject area. Finally, limit each topic so that it can be covered effectively in one speech.

# Knowing Your Purpose

Your **purpose** is what you intend to achieve in your speech. You will have both a general purpose and a specific purpose.

## General Purpose

Your **general purpose** is the overall intent of your speech. Speeches may be given for several different general purposes, but primarily speeches are intended to inform, to persuade, to entertain or suit a special occasion.

| General Purposes for Speeches | | |
|---|---|---|
| **Purpose** | **Description** | **Examples** |
| **Speech to Inform** | presents new information to an audience or gives new insights into information that an audience already has | • teachers giving class lectures<br>• announcers broadcasting news<br>• supervisors explaining work<br>• procedures<br>[See pages 355–381 for more information about speeches to inform.] |
| **Speech to Persuade** | tries to change an attitude or a belief, or to move an audience to action | • politicians urging voters to support them<br>• lawyers addressing a jury<br>• salespeople convincing consumers to buy products<br>[See pages 383–415 for more information about speeches to persuade.] |
| **Speech to Suit a Special Occasion** | entertains or amuses an audience or recognizes a specific reason for the audience being present and promotes group bonding or social cohesion | • club officers giving a "roast" to a member at a banquet<br>• valedictorians addressing their graduating classmates and parents<br>• officials commemorating the unveiling of a memorial statue<br>[See pages 417–445 for more information about speeches to entertain or to suit a special occasion.] |

## Specific Purpose

The **specific purpose** of a speech is its goal, stated in a complete sentence. If the general purpose of your speech is to inform, then your specific purpose will be a statement of the particular information you will present to the audience.

> **EXAMPLE:** Joel's general purpose in his speech about placekicking is to inform. His specific purpose could be stated in a complete sentence: "I want to explain the steps in soccer-style placekicking."

1. **Express the specific purpose as a declarative sentence.** Soccer-style placekicking is Joel's topic, but it is not a complete thought. A question, such as "How do you placekick?" or a title, such as "Today's Placekicking," does not give any idea of what you will say in the speech. Use a complete declarative sentence, such as "I want to explain the steps in soccer-style placekicking," to state your specific purpose. Remember that your goal is to announce what your topic is and which of its aspects you'll discuss.

2. **State the specific purpose precisely.** The specific purpose, "I want to explain the steps in soccer-style placekicking," is not precise enough. How many steps are in the process? Identify an exact number of steps, points, parts, stages, or reasons to make your specific purpose more precise. An improvement is to state, "I want to explain the four steps in soccer-style placekicking."

3. **Make sure the specific purpose contains only one idea.** Suppose you state your specific purpose as "I want to explain the four steps in soccer-style placekicking and the three steps in punting." This statement of specific purpose contains two separate ideas. Each idea might be good for a specific purpose, but both purposes should not be used in the same speech.

4. **Include words in the specific purpose that show your intent.** In stating your specific purpose, use words that express the general purpose of the speech. For example, if you want to inform, use words like *explain, show,* or *give.* If you want to persuade, use words like *prove, convince,* or *motivate.*

Just as you use increasing powers of magnification to observe more and more closely through a microscope, you use tighter and tighter focus to state your specific purpose.

# ACTIVITY 2

For each of the two topics you chose for Activity 1 on page 220, write a specific speech purpose. Be prepared to discuss with your classmates what particular information you would present about each topic.

# Writing a Thesis Statement

A **thesis statement** is a complete sentence that expresses the speaker's most important idea, or key point, about a topic. A thesis statement guides the development of a speech.

EXAMPLES:

1. **Specific purpose:** "I want to explain the characteristics of the six major classifications of show dogs."
   **Thesis statement:** "Show dogs are classified according to their characteristics as hounds, terriers, working dogs, toys, sporting dogs, and nonsporting dogs."
2. **Specific purpose:** "I want to convince the class that they should read *To Kill a Mockingbird.*"
   **Thesis statement:** "*To Kill a Mockingbird* is an excellent book to read because it features interesting characters, thought-provoking issues, and an exciting plot."

# ACTIVITY 3

Identify each of the following sentences as either a specific purpose sentence or a thesis statement. Be prepared to discuss your answers.

1. The four main components of a computer are the central processing unit, the disk drive(s), the keyboard, and the monitor.
2. I want to explain the three major causes of juvenile delinquency.
3. I want to convince the class of the value of vocational education.
4. You should give to United Appeal because one gift helps many charities.
5. The powers of the presidency are held in check by the legislative and judicial branches of government.

If you already know a great deal about your topic, you can write your thesis statement at this stage of your planning. For most speeches, however, you will need to do some research first.

**EXAMPLE:** Knowing the steps involved in soccer-style place-kicking, Joel Foster can complete his thesis statement at this stage of preparation.

**Subject Area:** football

**Topic:** placekicking

**Limited Topic:** soccer-style placekicking

**General Purpose:** to inform

**Specific Purpose:** I want to explain the four steps in soccer-style placekicking.

**Thesis Statement:** The four steps in soccer-style placekicking are to spot the ball, to mark off the steps, to approach the ball, and to kick the ball.

# ACTIVITY 4

## Writing Thesis Statements

Write a thesis statement for each of the specific purposes you stated in Activity 2 on page 223.

**CATHY**          **by Cathy Guisewite**

Even when you are allowed little preparation time, identifying your purpose, writing a clear thesis statement, and thinking about your audience and the occasion will help you speak more effectively than not planning at all.

# Knowing Your Audience

The people who will hear your speech are your **audience.** Knowing about your audience will help you determine the information you need to include in your speech. You will need to know some defining characteristics of your audience, or **demographic data,** which may include average age, educational background, and cultural heritage. You will also need to determine your audience's knowledge, feelings, and beliefs about the topic.

## Questions About Your Audience

1. Who will be in the audience? Teenage students, elderly retirees, or a mixed group?
2. Are most members of the audience from an urban, a suburban, or a rural environment?
3. How much will the audience know about the topic— a great deal, a moderate amount, or very little?
4. Will the listeners be familiar with specific terms, concepts, or references you will use?
5. Will the audience need any background or technical information in order to understand your speech?
6. Will the audience be very interested, somewhat interested, or uninterested in this topic?
7. Will the audience's attitude toward this topic be positive, neutral, or negative?

For instance, if Joel Foster knows that his audience has no knowledge of soccer-style placekicking, he will need to provide important background information. If Joel plans to speak to the Northside Parents Club, he should select details and information that appeal to the parents' interests. For example, he might explain how soccer-style placekickers learn to focus on the task despite tremendous distractions and pressure. If Joel plans to speak on the same topic to freshman football players, he might actually explain learning how to placekick.

In most speaking situations, you will have to suit your speech to your audience—not find an audience that suits your speech.

# A·C·T·I·V·I·T·Y
## 5  Analyzing an Audience

Considering your classmates as your audience, apply the questions in the chart on page 225 to one of the topics that you chose in Activity 1 on page 220. Explain what effect the answers to these questions will have on the material you will use to present your topic. Also be prepared to discuss your answers with your classmates to see how accurate your analysis is.

# Knowing Your Occasion

Every speech that you prepare will be given for some occasion. The **occasion** of a speech includes the time, place, and all of the other conditions that define the setting in which you will deliver the speech. Knowing the occasion will help you make choices as you develop your speech.

1. **When will your speech be given?** Consider both the date and the time of day. The date of your speech may be the reason for the speech. For example, you might give a speech about Martin Luther King, Jr., on his birthdate or one about the role of women in the work force on a date close to Labor Day. The time of day also affects your speech. At an early morning speech, some members of your audience might be sleepy. Therefore, you might include some audience participation and avoid dimming the lights for a long slide presentation.

2. **Where will your speech be given?** The size of the room, the seating arrangement, and the presence of a speaker's stand can affect your presentation. For example, in a large room, any visual materials should be much larger than those you would use in a small room.

3. **What are the restrictions for your speech?** Any limitations placed on your speech will affect your preparation. For example, a time limit will determine the amount of material you can present. Whether or not you may use notes affects the way you will deliver your speech.

## ACTIVITY 6

### Determining the Effect of Occasion on a Speech

**A**pply to your own speech each of the questions in the chart above concerning occasion. Then discuss how this information will affect the kind of material you will use in your speech.

# Supporting Your Thesis Statement

You need to find information to support your main idea as expressed in your thesis statement. The types of details commonly used to support a thesis include facts, opinions, examples, illustrations, anecdotes, statistics, comparisons, definitions, descriptions, and quotations.

## Facts and Opinions

Statements of **fact** contain information that can be proved, or verified, by testing, by observing, or by consulting reference materials.

*"Just the facts, ma'am."*

**EXAMPLES:**

1. **Fact:** Tin weighs more than aluminum.
   **To verify:** Look up their weights on a periodic chart of elements, or weigh equal amounts of these substances.
2. **Fact:** Some rodents can fly and glide.
   **To verify:** Observe bats and flying squirrels, or read about them in a reference source.
3. **Fact:** Dodecahedrons are twelve-sided.
   **To verify:** Consult a dictionary for a definition, or get a dodecahedron and count the sides.

Statements of **opinion** express personal beliefs or attitudes. Such statements contain personal judgments, which include information that cannot be proved.

**EXAMPLE:**

1. **Opinion:** Roses are more beautiful than tulips.
   **Why?** Beauty is a matter of personal preference.
2. **Opinion:** Spaghetti tastes better than ravioli.
   **Why?** Taste is a matter of personal preference.
3. **Opinion:** The Braves will win tomorrow's game.
   **Why?** Predictions are always opinions.

In some situations, you may seek an expert opinion. An **expert opinion** is a statement of belief about a subject from a person who is recognized as an authority on that subject. For example, a rocket scientist could offer an expert opinion on space travel. Experts can also supply facts. For instance, a high school coach can report on how many college recruiters have visited players on the team. To get an expert's opinion, you could read books or articles written by the expert, request information in a letter, or interview the expert in person or by telephone.

**EXAMPLES:**

1. **Expert opinion:** Book publisher—how the nonfiction market will grow
2. **Expert opinion:** Coach—how college recruiters will judge the team
3. **Expert opinion:** Dietitian—how low-fat cooking improves health

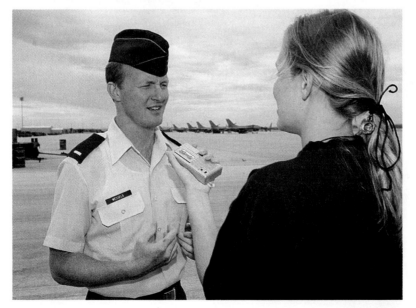

## Examples and Illustrations

An **example** is a single instance that supports or develops a statement. An **illustration** is a detailed example.

**EXAMPLE:** Joel Foster might want to support the idea that soccer-style placekickers are often smaller than other players on a football team. Through reading, Joel might discover this example: Placekicker Jim Breech, at 5′7″ and 165 pounds, was the smallest player on the Cincinnati Bengals in 1992. Joel could expand the Jim Breech example into the following illustration.

Many people who are relatively small are aware that they have little chance of becoming college or professional football players—unless they can placekick. Today, placekickers are the smallest players on the team. For example, consider Jim Breech of the Cincinnati Bengals. Standing only 5′7″ tall and weighing only 165 pounds, he was by far the smallest player on the team's 1992 roster.

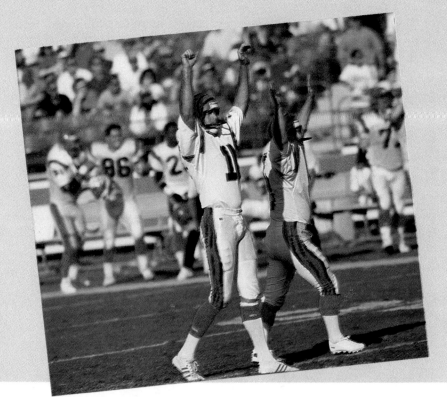

## Anecdotes

**Anecdotes** are brief, often amusing, stories. The purpose of an anecdote is to give information in a form that an audience will remember. Because anecdotes are often entertaining, they can help make your speech more interesting and enjoyable as well as informative.

**EXAMPLE:** Joel might recall a humorous incident that had happened to him the first time he kicked off in a game. He might use that story as part of his speech introduction.

Bill Cosby has entertained millions of people with his anecdotes, which usually contain a kernel of wisdom.

Most people assume that placekicking is simple. I did, in my first game. When the kickoff whistle blew, I ran up to the ball. Just as I launched into a kick hard enough to boot the ball all the way to the end zone, the ball fell off the kicking tee. I kicked at nothing and fell flat on my back. Luckily, the referee had already blown his whistle, so I got a chance to try again. But I never thought of a place kick as simple again.

## Statistics

**Statistics** are numerical facts: "Only six out of every ten registered voters voted in the last school election" or "unemployment recently dropped 2 percent." Citing a few statistics may make your speech more informative, but giving too many statistics can be boring or distracting. Use statistics carefully to add interest or to emphasize a point.

**EXAMPLE:** In his speech on placekicking, Joel could use statistics to show that a large percentage of college placekickers prefer the soccer style: "In the last year, more than 85 percent—that's more than eight out of every ten placekickers on major college teams—kicked soccer style."

## Comparisons

A **comparison** is a statement that shows the similarities between people, places, things, events, or ideas. Comparisons help listeners relate new ideas to familiar concepts.

A **figurative comparison** imaginatively shows similarities between things that are essentially not alike. For example, you may say someone is "as slow as molasses in January" to point out that the person moves slowly.

A **literal comparison** shows the real similarities between things that are essentially alike. For example, if you say, "Tom runs slower than Jorge," you are making a literal comparison.

Occasionally, a comparison is phrased as a **contrast,** highlighting the differences between two things. For instance, you might say, "Unlike last year's ecology club, which consisted primarily of seniors, this year's club has mostly sophomores and juniors as members."

## Definitions

A **definition** explains what a word or a concept means. You should define carefully any words or concepts your audience may not understand.

> **EXAMPLE:** Joel Foster might define *soccer style* this way: "*Soccer style* means approaching the ball at an angle and kicking the ball with the instep as the leg crosses the body."

## Descriptions

A **description** is a word picture of a person, place, thing, or event. Accurate descriptions help people in your audience form mental pictures that correspond to the actual thing described.

> **EXAMPLE:** Joel might describe the proper posture for placekicking: "Before kicking, kickers stand with their arms swinging freely at their sides, weight on the left foot, which is placed slightly ahead of the right, shoulders square to the ground, and eyes fixed on the point where the ball is placed."

## Quotations

A **quotation** expresses someone's exact words. Usually, you express your ideas in your own words. However, in some cases you will use a quotation to express the opinion of an authority or to include a particularly well stated idea. When you use quotations, you must give credit to the source from which the words were taken. (See pages 256–257.) To avoid boring your audience, limit the number and the length of quotations you use.

**EXAMPLE:** To sum up the importance of sportsmanship in football, Joel might use the following quotation by Grantland Rice in *Alumnus Football:* "When the One Great Scorer comes to write against your name—/He marks—not that you won or lost—but how you played the game."

## ACTIVITY 7

### Recognizing Different Kinds of Supporting Information

Read the editorial page of your newspaper. Find examples, illustrations, anecdotes, statistics, comparisons, definitions, descriptions, and quotations that writers use to support main points or to clarify ideas. Share your findings with classmates.

## GUIDELINES

### for Getting Started

- Have I chosen a topic that interests me?

- Have I thought about my own knowledge of this topic?

- Do I know my general purpose?

- Have I clearly identified my specific purpose?

- Do I have a well-worded thesis statement?

- Have I considered my audience—their backgrounds and interests and their knowledge of and attitudes toward my topic?

- Have I considered the occasion of the speech?

- Do I know what types of information I will need to support my main point?

# PREPARING TO SPEAK EFFECTIVELY

## Appreciating Valuable Qualities

An auctioneer is an agent who sells goods at an auction. Some auctioneers specialize in certain goods such as antiques, fine art, automobiles, or collectibles. Others must cultivate a wide range of knowledge because they never know what they will be auctioning next.

## Characteristics of a Good Auctioneer

A good auctioneer

1. identifies and promotes qualities of an item that will bring higher bids

2. speaks knowledgeably and persuasively about a wide variety of items

3. draws conclusions about the audience's knowledge, interests, and attitudes

## ACTIVITY

### Situation

You are an auctioneer preparing to present an item at auction. This item is one of many different items that will be sold at auction in a few days.

### Preparation

Identify an item that you know something about and prepare to answer questions from prospective bidders. What types of questions might they ask? What features make the item unique or enhance its value? Write a brief opening statement in which you discuss the value of the item you chose to auction. Then list five questions you think a potential bidder might ask, and write a brief answer for each question.

### Analysis and Assessment

Deliver your opening statement in class. Then have a partner ask the questions while you answer them. Ask your classmates for feedback about your effectiveness as an auctioneer. Did your responses seem more or less likely to convince the bidders?

## Meet the Auctioneer

Bobby Keilman's specialty is American antiques and collectibles. He receives shipments frequently and spends several hours getting acquainted with each item. "The more I know about a piece, the better I can communicate the value of that piece to the audience," he says. "The better I communicate the value, the more likely it is that we will get a good price."

*Bobby Keilman*

# S•U•M•M•A•R•Y

**GETTING READY** for a speech involves a systematic approach to selecting a suitably limited topic, developing a thesis statement, and finding information to support your thesis. Whether you are giving a speech to inform, to persuade, or to entertain, you can prepare by doing the following activities.

- **Identify subject areas** that are interesting and familiar to you.
- **Determine your topic** and limit it to a manageable size.
- **Identify your general purpose** (to inform, to persuade, or to entertain) and your specific purpose (your particular goal stated in a declarative sentence).
- **Write a thesis statement** that expresses the most important idea you wish to present to your audience.
- **Consider the makeup of your audience:** their demographic features and their knowledge, feelings, and attitudes about your topic.
- **Determine the significance of the occasion** for your speech, and make sure that you know any restrictions that may apply.
- **Support your thesis statement** with appropriate information: facts and opinions, examples and illustrations, anecdotes, statistics, comparisons, definitions, descriptions, or quotations.

## Vocabulary

**Look back through this chapter to find the meaning of each of the following terms. Write each term and its meaning in your communication journal.**

anecdote, p. 231
audience, p. 225
brainstorming,
  p. 216
comparison, p. 232
contrast, p. 232
definition, p. 232
demographic data,
  p. 225
description, p. 232
example, p. 230
expert opinion,
  p. 229
fact, p. 228
figurative comparison,
  p. 232
general purpose,
  p. 220
illustration, p. 230
literal comparison,
  p. 232
occasion, p. 226
opinion, p. 229
purpose, p. 220
quotation, p. 233
specific purpose,
  p. 221
statistics, p. 231
subject area, p. 216
thesis statement,
  p. 223
topic, p. 216

## CHAPTER 9

**Review Questions**

1. After you choose a topic, why should you limit it?
2. List five sources of ideas for speech topics.
3. What are three general purposes for giving a speech?
4. What is the difference between the general purpose and the specific purpose of a speech?
5. How does a specific purpose differ from a thesis statement?
6. Identify the kinds of information that you need to know about your audience.
7. What are three questions you should ask yourself about the occasion of a speech?
8. How does a statement of opinion differ from a statement of fact?
9. How does an illustration differ from an example?
10. How does a literal comparison differ from a figurative comparison?

**Discussion Questions**

1. Discuss why brainstorming is likely to produce better topics for your speeches than just sitting down and trying to come up with a topic. What were the results of your past brainstorming sessions? In what specific ways could you have made these sessions more productive?
2. Discuss with your classmates why it is important to find a topic that interests you and that you know something about. Then discuss the seven subject areas listed in the chart on pages 219–220. What subject areas would you add to this list? Why?
3. You are giving a speech on soccer-style placekicking. Discuss how the following audiences would affect either your specific purpose or your approach.
   a. Boys ages 9–14—very interested in soccer-style placekicking but with very little knowledge of the subject
   b. Senior citizens—not very interested in soccer-style placekicking but with some knowledge of football
   c. Exchange students from China—very interested in learning about football but with little direct knowledge of the game
   d. Male and female high school students—somewhat interested in learning about soccer-style placekicking and with some knowledge of football
4. Ralph Waldo Emerson advised, "Stay at home in your mind. Don't recite other people's opinions. I hate quotations. Tell me what you know." Do you agree with Emerson's statement? Discuss when and where quotations can be used effectively in a speech.

# ACTIVITIES

1. **Identifying Facts and Opinions.** Identify the following statements as fact or opinion. If an opinion is an expert opinion, explain why it qualifies as one.

a. Ronald Reagan first took office as president on January 20, 1981.

b. The mechanic informed my father that our truck needs a new fuel pump.

c. Cheerleading is an enjoyable high school activity.

d. Over 60 percent of the students who take a speech course in our school go on to college.

e. In this school, athletes must maintain a B average to play on teams.

f. As soon as photoelectric cells become more efficient, auto manufacturers will build more electric-powered cars.

g. The decision to close the park was a bad one.

h. According to the almanac, we had a record rainfall last year.

i. That comic strip is very funny.

j. My uncle, who repairs electronic office equipment, thinks voice-operated typewriters will be on the market before the middle of the next decade.

2. **Identifying Comparisons.** Identify each of the following comparisons as either figurative or literal. Explain your reason(s) for classifying each comparison as you did.

a. The cheerleading squad worked as smoothly as a well-oiled machine.

b. Ed Kitt, Central High's center, was about the same size as Miller High's center.

c. A basketball is slightly larger than a soccer ball.

d. Derrick Williams was a tiger on defense during the entire game.

e. The crowd at game time was larger than any other crowd that had attended a Central High game in more than a year.

3. **Limiting a Topic and Developing It into a Thesis Statement.**

A. Choose a subject of your own, select a subject suggested by the photographs below, or select one of the following subjects: basketball, cars, mountains, dogs, or college.

**B.** Working with classmates who have chosen the same subject, brainstorm to come up with a list of twenty-five to thirty topics. Then choose one topic from the list and limit it. Compare your limited topic with your classmates' limited topics.

**C.** For the limited topic you selected in Part A of this activity, write a purpose statement. Then turn your purpose statement into a thesis statement. Finally, compile a list of at least five different kinds of information to support your thesis statement. Share your list with your classmates.

**4. Planning a Speech on a Personal Topic.**

**A.** Take a personal inventory and choose a speech topic from the information you gather on your inventory. Completing the following statements may help you discover a suitable topic.

1. On a Saturday afternoon, I most like to . . .
2. You can always count on me to tell you my opinion about . . .
3. My friends think I'm talented when it comes to . . .
4. If I could be anything I want, I would be . . .
5. I will read almost any book about . . .
6. One day, I hope to be able to . . .
7. I spend most of my spare time . . .
8. My favorite (or least favorite) school subject is . . .
9. When I go to the movies, I most like to see . . .
10. If I could tell you only one thing about me, it would be that I . . .

**B.** Imagine that your general purpose for your speech is to inform your listeners about the topic you have chosen. Brainstorm and identify a specific purpose for your speech.

**C.** Using the specific purpose you stated in Part B of this Activity, write your thesis statement and list five kinds of information you would use in your speech to support this thesis statement.

**5. Analyzing the Use of Statistics in an Article.** Read an article about a local sports team's most recent game. Underline all the statistics used in the article. Could any of the points in the article have been made without statistics? If so, identify which ones.

# EVERYDAY COMMUNICATION

**Situation**
You are at a party. To make a point, you decide to tell your classmates and other friends an amusing story.

**Problem**
Compose a short, three- to four-minute story that illustrates a point and that is suitable for telling in class. Keep in mind your audience, occasion, and purpose for telling the story.

**Assessing Your Skill**
Practice telling your story, and be prepared to present it in class. Also, be ready to take part in a discussion of how you and your classmates planned your stories to suit your purpose (to make a point in an entertaining manner), your audience (classmates and other friends), and the occasion (a group activity).

# COMMUNICATION IN THE WORKPLACE

**Background**
You have been asked to teach a one-hour class on a subject that interests you and about which you have some knowledge.

**Preparing to Do the Job**
Write a short outline of the lecture; then, prepare a three- to five-minute talk that you will give at the beginning of class. Consider ways you can tailor your talk to your students.

**Testing Your Skill**
Your talk should indicate the specific subject matter you will teach (your topic), why you will teach it (your purpose), and how you have tailored your lecture to your students (adaptation to your audience). Practice your talk, and then present it to the class. After giving your talk, ask your classmates for feedback on your teaching plan.

▼

# Gathering Information

## OBJECTIVES

**After studying this chapter, you should be able to**

1. Find information for speeches by using your own experience and observations.
2. Obtain information from others by interviewing, by surveying, or by writing a request letter.
3. Use the library or media center to locate information.
4. Select and use appropriate reference books.
5. Locate newspaper and magazine articles in the library.
6. Use the technologies available in your library (on-line catalog, InfoTrac and other electronic databases, or the interlibrary loan service) to obtain information.
7. Prepare note cards for speeches and identify your sources appropriately.

## Where to Look for Information

We live in the "age of information." Facts, statistics, details, theories, practical advice, studies, and reports are readily available in a variety of media. With a little effort, anyone researching a speech can find enough information to give an interesting and informative presentation. How do you begin to look for the specific information that you need for your speech? Where do you go to find this information? You have three major sources:

- yourself
- other people
- reference materials

In this chapter you will learn how to use these sources and how to record the information you find so that you can incorporate it into your speech.

# Using Your Own Knowledge and Experience

Start your search for information with yourself. Your own experiences and observations will often provide you with valuable details to include in your speech.

## Personal Experience

Before you look anywhere else, think about what information your own experience can provide about your topic. Keep in mind that you chose your topic because you were interested in it and because you already knew something about it.

Take the time to think about experiences you have had that are related to the topic you have chosen. For speech assignments that ask you to talk about something special that happened to you or to demonstrate a product or a procedure, your personal experience alone may provide all the information you need to prepare your speech. Even for topics that require you to find additional information, your experience provides an excellent starting point.

**EXAMPLE:** You might give a speech to your school board members in which you urge that money for the cheerleading squad be increased. In your speech you would be able to share firsthand knowledge about the positive influence cheerleading has in developing responsibility and cooperativeness.

## Observation

Using yourself as a source does not stop with thinking about your own previous experience. You can also gain a great amount of information from observing carefully. For example, if you are planning a speech about bowling techniques, the best way to gather information may be to observe an experienced bowler. Observation can be especially helpful in gathering information for a topic that requires a "how-to" approach.

You can improve your powers of observation by using the following guidelines and by practicing.

# HOW TO > Be an Effective Observer

1. **Make a conscious effort to see and not just to look.** *Looking* means focusing your eyes on some part of the world around you. *Seeing,* on the other hand, requires concentrating, being consciously aware of specific aspects of what you observe. By paying attention, you can see and remember much more about people, things, and events in your life.

2. **Put what you observe into words.** Take the time to *name* and to *describe* aloud everything in your surroundings. Because you will be using your sense of hearing as well as your sense of sight, you will sharpen your focus, and as a result, you will remember more accurately. In addition, by putting what you see into spoken words, you prompt yourself to notice objects and aspects of those objects that you might otherwise miss.

3. **Recognize whether anything is different or unusual about a person, a setting, or an object.** Do you remember those children's puzzles that ask "What's wrong with this picture?" A person in the picture might be wearing two different shoes, or a police officer's uniform might be missing a button. Applying this game to your observations can help you sharpen your attention to detail and remember unusual features.

4. **Take notes on your observations.** When newspaper reporters go to the scene of a news event to gather information, they always have their tape recorders or their pads and pens handy. They never trust their observations to memory alone. Instead, they take quick notes to remind themselves of the exact details of what they have observed. They also ask reporter-style questions, such as *Who? What? Where? When? Why?* and *How?* You can adapt this method of note taking to suit your circumstances by asking questions that organize your observations into categories. As you take notes, be as objective as possible and record the facts as they occur.

*U*se your journal as a place to collect notes on your interests, abilities, activities you enjoy, and experiences you have had. Jot down a few memorable personal experiences and brief notes about what these experiences taught you. Would any of this knowledge make good information for a speech?

# A·C·T·I·V·I·T·Y

## Drawing Information from Observation

**F**ind a topic that you can talk about by using your own experience. Then see how much more you can learn about your topic from planned observation. Observe carefully over a two- to three-day period. Take notes on your observations. Report to your class what additional information you gained from your observations. Ask for and respond to comments from classmates on how you might have improved your observations.

# Collecting Information from Others

Other people can be valuable resources when you are trying to gather information for your speech. Three ways you can collect information from others are the interview, the survey, and the request letter.

## The Interview

For almost any topic, you can obtain valuable information by interviewing. An **interview** is a form of communication in which people gain information by asking questions. Good interviews do not just happen. They are the result of careful planning. [Refer to Chapter 8 for more information about interviewing techniques.]

## The Survey

When you take a **survey**, you question people to obtain information. You select these people at random or from a predetermined list. After you finish your survey, you tally the results. Then, you can support points in your speech with data from your survey.

The survey is a widely used tool for measuring attitudes and opinions. You are probably already familiar with such professional surveys as the Gallup Poll. These professional polls gather people's views about political candidates and controversial issues. The value of a survey is that it allows you to get an impression of people's attitudes very quickly. The problem with a survey is that if it is not carefully conducted, the results can be inaccurate or misleading.

WIZARD OF ID by permission of Johnny Hart and Creators Syndicate, Inc.

# HOW TO > *Conduct a Survey*

1. **Phrase questions clearly and concisely.** Consider the wording of your questions very carefully. Avoid using vague terms that might confuse your survey participants or cause them to give you imprecise or misleading data. For example, if you are surveying for information about which brand of jeans people prefer, the question "What kind of jeans do you like?" is vague. A more focused question is "What brand-name jeans do you prefer?"

2. **Ask enough people.** Since you can rarely ask all the members of a large group, you will usually survey only a representative portion of the group. In a formal survey such as the Gallup Poll, mathematical tables provide data about the number of people that should be polled. For an informal survey in a school, it would be reasonable to poll 5 to 10 percent of the student body. For instance, if your school has a population of five hundred students, you would poll twenty-five to fifty students.

3. **Survey your group at random.** Ideally, a survey canvasses a sample that has all the major characteristics of the entire group that you are gathering information about. In theory, a **random sample** is one in which every member of a group has an equal chance of being selected. One way to set up a random sample is to assign a number to every person in a group, put all the numbers into a container, draw the appropriate percentage of numbers, and then ask those people questions. Another method, called the **fixed-interval method,** is to station yourself at an entrance (for instance, the door to the school cafeteria) and to ask your questions of every fifth person who enters (or every eighth or every tenth, depending on how many people you hope to survey).

# A·CTI·V·ITY 2

## Gathering Information with a Survey

Conduct a survey in your school on the popularity of a certain sport, a particular television show, or a well-known place to eat. First, choose one of these topics. Next, write six survey questions that you will ask about your topic. Organize these questions in the most effective order. Use these questions to survey the student body in your school. Tell your class how many people you surveyed and how you conducted the poll. Report your findings. Ask for and respond to your classmates' evaluations of your survey.

## The Request Letter

If your speech topic is unusual or specialized in some way, you may not have access to people who have information about this topic. An interview or a survey might not be an appropriate method of collecting information from others. However, if you can locate the names of organizations that have knowledge about your topic, you might write a **request letter,** one that asks for information about your topic. Examples of request letters include

- a letter to a political cartoonist, inquiring how he or she began his or her drawing career
- a postcard to a government agency, requesting a free information pamphlet
- a letter to a tourism bureau, seeking information on a state
- a note to a computer company, asking questions about its new computer models

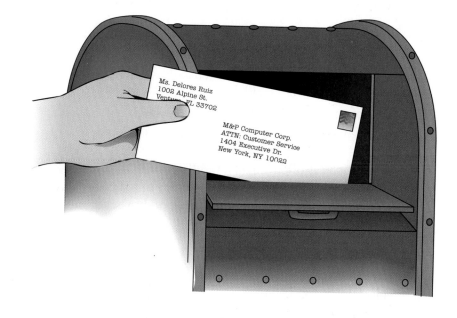

Ms. Delores Ruiz
1002 Alpine St.
Ventura, FL 33702

M&P Computer Corp.
ATTN: Customer Service
1404 Executive Dr.
New York, NY 10022

# HOW TO ▷ *Write a Request Letter*

1. **Allow enough time for the recipient to answer.** You should allow time for the person or organization from whom you are requesting information to receive your letter, to read and respond to your request, and to send you the information you want.

2. **Be clear about what information you need.** Make sure that your request is reasonable and that the recipient will understand exactly what information you need.

3. **Help to make the response easier to send.** You might include a self-addressed, stamped envelope so that it will be easier for the person or organization to mail your reply.

# ACTIVITY 3

## Gathering Information by Letter

With your classmates, brainstorm a list of organizations and individuals that you think might provide helpful information for speech topics. Then select a specific topic, such as the topic you selected for Activity 1 (page 244) or another topic of your own choosing. Identify a particular source from the brainstormed list and compose a request letter, asking for information about this topic.

# Using the Library or Media Center

In many instances, particularly in planning informative and persuasive speeches, you will need to research and read about your topic. By researching, you will be able to

- verify facts that you have already discovered
- find new information that gives your speech depth
- provide background for your topic

Today's library is often called a **media center** because it holds such a wide variety of information resources. Printed material is no longer the only medium for reference sources. In your library you may find reference material in the form of

- books
- magazines, newspapers, and pamphlets
- electronic databases accessed by computer
- videotapes or audiotapes
- photographs, filmstrips, and slides

## The Librarian

Often, the most valuable resource in the library is the librarian. Think of the librarian as an information specialist—someone who can direct you to the most useful tools for your particular research. Make a list of questions that you need to answer about your topic, and show these questions to your librarian. The librarian will be able to suggest the best sources for the information you need.

# The Card Catalog or On-Line Catalog

The **card catalog** lists all the books contained in a particular library. In the card catalog, cards providing information about books are filed alphabetically in three different ways:

- by subject
- by author
- by title

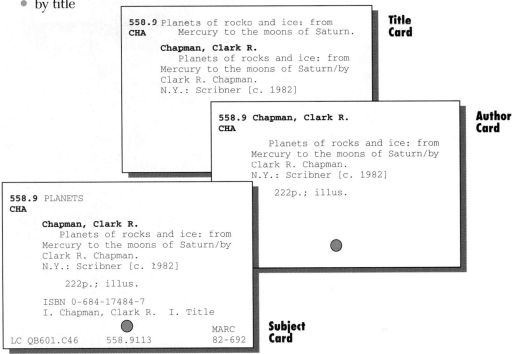

**Title Card**

558.9 Planets of rocks and ice: from
CHA       Mercury to the moons of Saturn.

       **Chapman, Clark R.**
          Planets of rocks and ice: from
       Mercury to the moons of Saturn/by
       Clark R. Chapman.
       N.Y.: Scribner [c. 1982]

**Author Card**

558.9 Chapman, Clark R.
CHA

          Planets of rocks and ice: from
       Mercury to the moons of Saturn/by
       Clark R. Chapman.
       N.Y.: Scribner [c. 1982]

          222p.; illus.

**Subject Card**

558.9 PLANETS
CHA

       **Chapman, Clark R.**
          Planets of rocks and ice: from
       Mercury to the moons of Saturn/by
       Clark R. Chapman.
       N.Y.: Scribner [c. 1982]

          222p.; illus.

       ISBN 0-684-17484-7
       I. Chapman, Clark R.   I. Title

LC QB601.C46      558.9113        MARC
                                  82-692

Some libraries have a **microform catalog** (a microfilm or a microfiche machine) that contains the library's entire listing of books. By turning the dial on a viewer, you can locate the same book information that you would find on card-catalog cards.

Some libraries have an **on-line catalog,** or a computerized card catalog. To use the on-line catalog, you type in the author, title, or subject to find information about the library's resources. The on-line catalog often tells you if the book is checked out or if it is available in another library branch. You can ask your librarian to show you how the cataloging system works.

The key to finding a book is the **call number,** a number-and-letter code assigned to a book according to the classification system used to organize books in the library. All nonfiction books are organized by number, following either the Dewey decimal system or the Library of Congress classification system. Books of fiction are arranged according to the last names of the authors.

## Reference Works

**Reference works** are publications containing useful facts and information. Used for ready reference in the library, many reference books cannot be checked out. The chart on page 251 shows a few reference works that are useful sources for general information.

FOR BETTER OR FOR WORSE copyright 1991 Lynn Johnston Prod.
Reprinted with permission of UNIVERSAL PRESS SYNDICATE. All rights reserved.

## Reference Works

| Type | Description | Examples |
|---|---|---|
| **Encyclopedias (electronic or print)** | • bound volumes or CD-ROM<br>• articles arranged alphabetically by subject<br>• good sources for general information | *Encyclopaedia Britannica*<br>*Encyclopedia Americana*<br>*The World Book Encyclopedia*<br>*Encarta*™ *Multimedia Encyclopedia* |
| **Specialized Encyclopedias** | • helpful in researching specialized fields<br>• contain in-depth information and little-known facts about specific topics | *Reader's Encyclopedia of American Facts and Dates*<br>*The Encyclopedia of World Costume*<br>*The Sports Encyclopedia* |
| **Biographical Sources** | • information about the lives and accomplishments of outstanding people | *Current Biography*<br>*The International Who's Who*<br>*Webster's New Biographical Dictionary* |
| **Atlases** | • maps and geographical information | *Atlas of World Cultures*<br>*National Geographic Atlas of the World* |
| **Almanacs** | • facts, statistics, dates, and general information | *The Information Please Almanac, Atlas and Yearbook*<br>*The World Almanac & Book of Facts* |
| **Dictionaries** | • contain information about how words are spelled, pronounced, or used | *Random House College Dictionary*<br>*Webster's New World Dictionary* |
| **Books of Quotations** | • famous sayings of well-known people<br>• often categorize sayings by subject matter or theme | Bartlett's *Familiar Quotations*<br>*The Oxford Dictionary of Quotations* |
| **Books of Synonyms** | • list more interesting or more exact words to express ideas<br>• may group entries into categories by subject | *Roget's International Thesaurus*<br>*Webster's New Dictionary of Synonyms* |

## Newspaper and Magazine Articles

For current topics, the best sources of information are likely to be newspapers and magazines.

**1. Newspapers.** Your local library probably has an index of articles appearing in the nearest major daily newspaper and an index of articles appearing in the *New York Times.* Even if your library does not carry back issues of the *New York Times,* you will find that when the *Times* index refers to an article on a particular subject, your local paper may have an article on that subject appearing that same day.

**2. Magazines.** Your library probably carries both current and back issues of popular magazines. The *Readers' Guide to Periodical Literature* gives complete reference information for articles in over one hundred popular magazines and journals. The *Readers' Guide* is published yearly with indexes for articles from magazines and journals published the previous year. For each year in progress, the *Readers' Guide* prepares monthly and quarterly indexes.

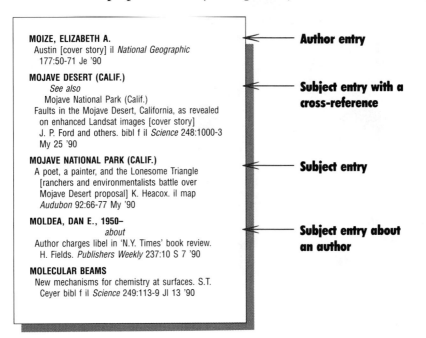

**MOIZE, ELIZABETH A.**
Austin [cover story] il *National Geographic* 177:50-71 Je '90  ← **Author entry**

**MOJAVE DESERT (CALIF.)**
*See also*
Mojave National Park (Calif.)
Faults in the Mojave Desert, California, as revealed on enhanced Landsat images [cover story]
J. P. Ford and others. bibl f il *Science* 248:1000-3 My 25 '90  ← **Subject entry with a cross-reference**

**MOJAVE NATIONAL PARK (CALIF.)**
A poet, a painter, and the Lonesome Triangle [ranchers and environmentalists battle over Mojave Desert proposal] K. Heacox. il map *Audubon* 92:66-77 My '90  ← **Subject entry**

**MOLDEA, DAN E., 1950–**
*about*
Author charges libel in 'N.Y. Times' book review.
H. Fields. *Publishers Weekly* 237:10 S 7 '90  ← **Subject entry about an author**

**MOLECULAR BEAMS**
New mechanisms for chemistry at surfaces. S.T. Ceyer bibl f il *Science* 249:113-9 Jl 13 '90

Each *Readers' Guide* entry gives the article title, author (if the magazine lists one), illustration information, magazine title, volume, page, month, and year. Just as some card catalogs have now been moved to microform and computer, periodical indexes have also been modernized. *The Magazine Index* on microfilm lists articles for hundreds of magazines. Each month, the editors of *The Magazine Index* feature a number of "hot topics" that are arranged in a loose-leaf binder and that are usually kept near the microfilm machine.

A popular magazine and newspaper article index on compact disk is InfoTrac. It is updated monthly and provides an index of general interest magazines from 1985 to the present. To access InfoTrac, use the computer to locate your subject, find the references available, and determine which are the best sources. Often, headings and an **abstract** (a brief statement of the key ideas) are available on the computer. The machine can then print out a listing of just the periodicals that you think will be useful for your speech.

**3. Interlibrary Loan Services.** Libraries, both large and small, may provide **interlibrary loan services.** By means of computers, libraries across the country can access each other's on-line catalogs.

Your librarian can check the listings and can then tell you if a branch library or a library in another city has a book you want. Then, through the interlibrary loan service, your library can request the book for you. Libraries that use this service can increase the number of books available to their borrowers by obtaining materials from more than six thousand other libraries. Sometimes you must pay a fee to use this service.

## Specialty Sources

**1. Microforms.** To save storage space, many libraries miniaturize numerous newspapers and magazines on film. **Microforms** are various types of photographic film bearing the reduced-scale record of printed or graphic material. The two most common types of microforms are **microfilm** (a roll or reel of film) and **microfiche** (a sheet of film).

Microfilm usually comes on a spool holding what looks like a filmstrip. Microfiche is usually on reduced-size pages. Both kinds of microform are used on special microform readers, which magnify the pages to about half the size of an actual newspaper or magazine page. In many cases, you can make copies of the pages you need. If you do not know how to use one of the readers, ask your librarian for help.

**2. Databases.** Some libraries also have access to **electronic databases,** which are extensive collections of information on computer. On-line search services can give you access to more than five hundred databases. There is sometimes a fee charged for the search service, so ask your librarian before using it.

**3. Audiovisual Materials.** Your library may offer recordings, books on audiotape, videocassettes, films, or other audiovisual materials that contain information on your subject. Because each library is different, you will need to check with a librarian to see what is available.

**4. Vertical File.** The **vertical file** is a collection of pamphlets, photographs, and clippings. These materials are not cataloged and are kept in vertical filing cabinets. Many libraries have abandoned the vertical files, but smaller and specialized libraries still maintain the collections. For example, a history library might have a vertical file containing old photographs, newspaper clippings, and other odd-sized material about historical places in the community. Ask your librarian whether your library has a vertical file and how to use it.

**5. Internet or World Wide Web Sources.** Your library/media center may provide a computer with access to the Internet or the World Wide Web for student research. Make certain you have permission and understand required procedures before attempting to access the Internet. Once you're on the Internet, you'll probably use a search engine, such as Infoseek or Yahoo!, to locate information about your topic. Your school librarian or media specialist might have suggestions on how to narrow your topic for the best results. The major issue with research on the Internet is to be certain that your source is reputable, up to date, and authoritative about the topic you are researching. For example, a Web site for a group called Let's Greet Our Alien Visitors would not be a reliable or an authoritative source for information about whether a recent aerial event was a meteor or an intergalactic spacecraft. Be sure to document each source you use, its on-line address, and the identity or professional qualifications of the author or authors of the source material.

# ACTIVITY 4

## Finding Information in a Library

Identify a speech topic. Use the card catalog or on-line catalog to find several books on your topic. For each book, write the call number, title, author, and date of publication. Next, use the *Readers' Guide, The Magazine Index,* or a computerized magazine index to find articles about your topic. List several articles that you think will contain information you can use. Finally, consult several encyclopedias. If any of these have articles on your topic, list the articles under the name of that encyclopedia.

# Recording Your Information

As you find information that you can use in your speech, you will need to record it. One way to do this is to make **note cards** on which you copy the information (or a summary of it) and its source. Use 4- x 6-inch cards, and record each idea separately.

On each card, note the name of the source, the author (if one is given), and the page number. If you have several cards from one source, you might code the cards by number so that you do not have to write the same source information on every card.

Note cards give you flexibility in sorting and arranging information. Remember, though, that you will probably not use all the information you have recorded on your note cards. Before you write your speech, you will select from your note cards only the specific information that is most useful.

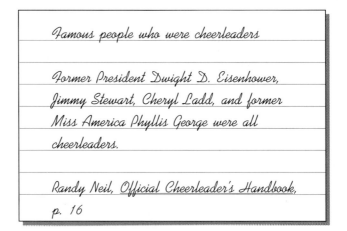

*Famous people who were cheerleaders*

*Former President Dwight D. Eisenhower, Jimmy Stewart, Cheryl Ladd, and former Miss America Phyllis George were all cheerleaders.*

*Randy Neil, Official Cheerleader's Handbook, p. 16*

# Identifying Your Sources

How many sources should you use for a speech? If you are relying on research to give your speech authority, you should probably not have fewer than three. Using only one or two sources may not give you a broad enough range of viewpoints.

The information you use from various sources needs to be credited. Be careful to avoid **plagiarism,** the presentation of another person's words or ideas as if they were your own. You do not need to credit general information—facts that are widely known or that can be found in any number of sources. However, you do need to credit exact quotations, opinions, and information gained from the research or insight of others.

A statement giving credit to the source of quoted material is called a **citation.** In your speech you can give appropriate credit to a source by using a short citation.

- According to an article about interest rates in last week's *Newsweek,* . . .
- In a speech before the Habitat for Humanity organization, former President Carter said . . .
- Martina Browne, in her interesting book on parrots, presents the idea that . . .
- Jim Hawkins, in his book entitled *Cheerleading Is for Me,* suggests that . . .

# ACTIVITY 5

## Preparing Note Cards and Source Citations

Consult the sources you listed for Activity 4 (page 255). Gather information from these sources as if you were going to use it in a speech. Prepare separate note cards for three items of information from these sources. Then, on each note card, write an appropriate citation for each source.

# GUIDELINES

## for Gathering Information

- Have I called upon my prior knowledge or personal experiences for information?

- Have I gained information from my observations?

- Have I interviewed others to gain information?

- Have I conducted surveys as a way of gathering information?

- Have I written to any sources that have information about my subject?

- Have I used the library or other available resources effectively?

- Have I recorded information on note cards?

- Do I know how to cite information from reference sources or from individuals appropriately in my speech?

# COLLECTING RELEVANT INFORMATION

### Helping Careful Consumers

Many newspapers, radio stations, and television news departments have a consumer affairs reporter. These reporters often compare the quality and cost of different brands of consumer items, such as household electronic equipment. They also address product safety issues and answer questions from the public.

### Characteristics of a Good Consumer Affairs Reporter

A good consumer affairs reporter

**1** generates ideas for stories by using prior knowledge and present observations

**2** obtains information by interviewing, surveying, or writing request letters

**3** uses the library or media center to locate relevant information

**4** strives for balance and objectivity when presenting information

## ACTIVITY

### Situation

You are a consumer affairs reporter for a local television station, and your current assignment is to prepare a news report on a consumer item of your choice.

### Meet the Consumer Affairs Reporter

Quita Culpepper, a consumer affairs reporter at a radio station, says, "It's important for me to maintain lines of communication with my listeners so that I know what's important in their lives. Our ratings are directly linked to our ability to deliver what our audience wants and needs."

*Quita Culpepper*

### Preparation

First, pick a specific consumer item to review. Then gather information on several brands of the item by interviewing, surveying, writing request letters, or doing research at the school library or media center. Prepare note cards for a short report on several different brands of the consumer item you chose.

### Analysis and Assessment

Present your report in class as though you were doing a live report for a news program. Then ask for your classmates' feedback on the thoroughness of your research and the quality of your report.

# S✷U✷M✷M✷A✷R✷Y

**GATHERING INFORMATION** for a speech means consulting a number of sources to obtain reliable data.

- **Use your own knowledge and experience** to find material that can be used for your speech. Using yourself as a source means thinking about your own personal experiences to decide what information you already know about your topic. Another way that you can use your own knowledge and experience is by observing closely.
- **Collect information from others** by asking questions and requesting specific information. You can interview other people, conduct a survey, or write a request letter to ask for information from a person or from an organization.
- **Use the library or media center** to find information. You can ask a librarian for help in identifying available resources in the library. A library's card catalog or its on-line catalog can be

used to locate books. Reference works, such as encyclopedias, atlases, or almanacs, are good sources of general information. Most libraries have newspaper and magazine articles that may provide information. Many libraries also provide access to databases and may be able to use interlibrary loan services to provide a wider variety of books. Specialty sources—such as microforms, audiovisual materials, or the Internet—may also be available.

- **Record your information** on 4- x 6-inch index cards. Give citations that identify your sources.

## Review Questions

1. What is the difference between seeing and looking?
2. What are two methods for obtaining a random sample in a survey?
3. How are books listed in the card catalog?
4. What type of information does an encyclopedia have?
5. What type of information can you find in an almanac?
6. What index tells you where you can find information that has recently been in the news?
7. What is the title of an index for magazine articles?
8. In addition to books, magazines, and newspapers, what are two other sources of information found in many libraries?
9. When do you need to give credit for a source?
10. If you plan to write to an organization or individual that may have information about your subject, what are three guidelines you should remember?

## Discussion Questions

1. Suppose that you are giving a speech on one of the following subjects: mechanics, computer games, bicycling, cooking, homework, or dancing. First choose one of these subjects and limit it to a specific topic. Then discuss why you yourself would or would not be an excellent source of information about the topic.
2. Imagine that you want to learn as much as you can from observing firefighters extinguishing a fire, telephone workers installing a telephone, and painters painting a house. Discuss what you should do to become a better and more accurate observer.
3. Suggest several topics on which you could conduct a survey to gather useful information for a speech. Discuss how you would go about conducting a survey on one of these topics. Be sure to mention whom you would survey, the types of questions you would ask, and the number of people you would question.
4. Maya Angelou, poet, playwright, editor, songwriter, singer, teacher, and dancer, spends much time preparing her creative work. In *Singin' and swingin' and gettin' merry like Christmas*, she writes, "Preparation is rarely easy and never beautiful." Discuss whether you feel this description applies to the process of gathering information for a speech. Is the gathering and planning process for a speech similar to other creative preparations?
5. Samuel Johnson, also known as Dr. Johnson, was a noted English lexicographer, critic, and conversationalist. He once wrote, "Knowledge is of two kinds. We know a subject ourselves, or we know where we can find information upon it." First discuss the meaning of this quotation. What is Johnson suggesting? Then discuss how you can make a speech uniquely your own, rather than simply a summary of other people's thoughts.

# ACTIVITIES

**1. Practicing Observation.** Take a minute to look around the classroom. Then cover your eyes and describe a particular part of the room—for instance, the teacher's desk, the back wall, or the area by the doorway. Report your observations carefully. Then open your eyes and compare what you reported with what you can now see.

**2. Using Observation to Play a Game.** Choose a partner and record as many details of his or her appearance as you can in a few minutes. Then leave the room while your partner changes appearance in three subtle, or slightly noticeable, ways. Other class members may suggest changes such as removing one earring, untying one shoelace, or wearing a watch on the opposite wrist. When your partner is ready, return to the classroom and see if, in two minutes, you can identify all three changes.

**3. Identifying Sources for Requesting Information.** Find out the name and position of a person from whom you could request information about each of the following topics:
a. Public television programming
b. History of your town or city
c. Locations and special features of your city's public parks
d. Scheduling of local functions such as concerts and speeches
e. Athletic activities for high school students
f. Consumer information about local businesses
g. Obedience training and health care for pets
h. Employment counseling
i. Fishing regulations
j. Soil and climate conditions for growing a garden

**4. Using Your Powers of Observation.** Have you ever heard the expression "an accident waiting to happen"? Using your powers of observation, find the accidents waiting to happen in the pictures below.

5. **Gathering Information for a Speech.** To prepare an informative speech for your history class, think about national events from 1980 to the present. Then complete the following steps.

   • First select a topic and narrow it.
   • Then list the information you could supply about this topic from your own experience.
   • List five to ten questions you would include in a survey to gather information for your speech.
   • Think about the topic in a new way by listing two to five people from whom you could request information for your speech.
   • Consult the card catalog or on-line catalog in your library. List the titles, authors, and call numbers of five to ten books you would consult for information.
   • Consult the *Readers' Guide to Periodical Literature* or another periodical index. List five to ten articles you would read for information for your speech.
   • Using the books and periodicals you have chosen, create note cards for three items of information from the different books and three items of information from the articles you found in periodicals. On each card, write a general category at the top, a note or quotation in the center, and a source citation at the bottom. Include the author's name, the title of the book or article (also the title of the periodical when citing an article), and the page number.
   • After your teacher has checked your note cards, make photocopies of them (three to a page). Keep the copies in your communication journal to use as models when you make up note cards for your speeches.

6. **Conducting a Survey to Gather Information.** Conduct a survey to find out which singer, musician, or musical group is the most popular with students in your school. To make your survey as accurate as possible, be sure to ask a large random sample of both male and female students from different grade levels. [See pages 244–246 for more information on conducting a survey.] Share your findings with your classmates. What similarities are there among your and your classmates' survey findings? What differences are there? How do you account for these differences?

7. **Using Library Sources to Find Information.** Working alone or with a partner (whichever your teacher directs), consult reference sources in the library to find the answers to the following questions. All of the answers can be found in sources discussed in this chapter. Be prepared to present the answer to each question and to identify the source in which you found that answer.
   a. What is the average rainfall in San Francisco, California; Miami, Florida; and Chicago, Illinois?
   b. What is the origin of the word *tantalize*?
   c. What are the titles of three books by Ernest Hemingway?
   d. When did Arizona become a state?
   e. Who was the twelfth president of the United States?
   f. Who said, "I would rather be right than be President"?
   g. What are the first names of Teddy Roosevelt's mother and father?
   h. What is the motto for the state of Texas?
   i. What movie won the Academy Award for best director in 1983?
   j. Where is the only place in the United States where four states touch at one point?

# COMMUNICATION IN THE WORKPLACE

### Background

You are serving a summer internship at a firm that takes public opinion polls, and your supervisor has asked you to conduct a poll.

### Preparing to do the Job

Begin by identifying a specific topic and a specific group of people whose opinions you want. Then decide what questions you will ask. Write four questions on the topic you have chosen and survey ten people from your target group. Compile the results of your survey.

### Testing Your Skill

Present a report to your class. Tell what you wanted to know (objective), what you asked (questions), who you asked (choices), and what you concluded. Ask for feedback from your classmates about the effectiveness of your survey.

# EVERYDAY COMMUNICATION

### Situation

You have just witnessed a traffic accident, and a police officer has asked you to give an oral description of what you saw.

### Problem

How will you begin your description? What details will you include? In what order will you present your details? What personal opinions and comments will you include? Write a one- or two-page account of your observations.

### Assessing Your Skill

Read your report to your classmates and invite feedback about how well they understand your account. Ask some classmates questions about specific items in your report to assess the effectiveness of your communication. Ask your classmates if your report was clear, and ask how you might improve the account.

▼

# CHAPTER 12

# Using Effective Language

## OBJECTIVES

**After studying this chapter, you should be able to**

1. Explain the differences between good speaking and good writing.
2. Choose the words that most clearly express your thoughts.
3. Explain the difference between specific and general words.
4. Explain how the use of sensory words and figurative language makes language more vivid.
5. Define and give examples of exaggeration, understatement, and irony.
6. List and use different ways to emphasize ideas.
7. Adjust language and tone to suit an audience.

## What Is Effective Language?

Effective language is language that is appropriate for your audience and purpose. The different kinds of language that you use for various audiences and purposes are called **levels of usage.** In English, the levels of usage range from very formal to very informal. For most speakers and occasions, language usage falls somewhere in between the two extremes.

The most widely used variety of English is called **standard American English.** Standard American English allows people from many different regions and cultures to communicate clearly with one another. It is the variety of English that you read and hear most often in books and magazines and on radio and television. It is also the kind of English that people are expected to use in most school and business situations.

As you rehearse a speech, you will need to focus on the language you plan to use when you deliver your presentation.

# Comparing Good Speaking to Good Writing

Although effective spoken language and effective written language have many characteristics in common, they also differ in some significant ways. These differences exist because spoken language does not have the permanence (unless it is taped or recorded in some way) of written language.

## Spoken Language

Spoken language must be immediately understandable, since listeners cannot go back to look at a sentence, a paragraph, or a page the way readers can. However, speakers do have one major advantage over writers. They have, in addition to words, facial expressions, gestures, and tone of voice to help them clarify meaning.

The following list identifies some of the characteristics of spoken language that make it easy for listeners to understand and remember what is said. Spoken language

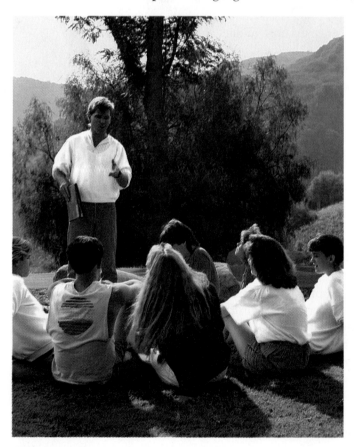

- usually relies on fewer words than written language
- uses shorter, more familiar words and slightly shorter sentences than written language
- uses verbal cues and qualifiers—such as *I think, that is to say,* and *the point I want to make*—to provide hints to listeners
- uses more personal pronouns (*I, you, we, us*) than written language
- uses more informal constructions (contractions, for example) and slang than written language
- uses repetition of words and phrases to aid memory and to reinforce important points

## Written Language

Written language is meant to be read. Even though readers have only the words on the page, they can reread a word, sentence, paragraph, or page to clarify meaning. Also, written language may contain a larger or more complex vocabulary and longer, more complicated sentences than spoken language. Such characteristics of written language often hide the personality of the communicator and often require a more formal level of usage (fewer contractions, personal pronouns, and slang expressions). However, readers can use visual cues (such as punctuation marks, paragraph indents, and bullets) to understand the relationships among ideas, the transitions between ideas, and the overall meaning.

*T*ape-record a public speech such as a sermon or a campaign speech. Listen carefully to the tape to analyze the speaker's use of distinctive spoken-language characteristics in the following areas: choice of vocabulary; variety of sentence length; and use of qualifiers, repetition, personal pronouns, contractions, and slang. Write your observations in your communication journal.

COMMUNICATION JOURNAL

# Choosing the Right Words

To communicate your meaning effectively to your audience, you need to choose the right words—the words that most clearly and exactly express your thoughts. Too often, in both informal conversation and public speaking, people make statements that are not clear.

**UNCLEAR:** I'm going to that place where they have those things I need for class.

**BETTER:** I'm going to that business supply store that carries notebook paper and erasers.

Choosing the right words will help you to express your meaning with **clarity,** or clearness. To develop skill in choosing the right words, try to use

- simple words
- precise words
- specific words
- concrete words

## Simple Words

Your ideas will be easier to understand if you use simple words rather than complex, or difficult, ones. **Simple words** are familiar words, usually of one or two syllables. Difficult words are unfamiliar to many people and often have three syllables or more.

English gives us a wide variety of words that can be used to express various shades of meaning. Too often, however, speakers use difficult or fancy words for no particular reason. For instance, you may wish to express the idea that your brother's hardheaded behavior only exacerbated a problem he was having with his boss. *Exacerbate* is a perfectly good word for expressing the meaning "to increase something's severity." But it would be much simpler to say that your brother's hardheaded behavior only made the problem he was having with his boss worse.

Unless you have some good reason for using difficult or fancy words, select the simplest, most commonly used words that will accurately express your meaning. Using simple words will help your audience to understand what you are saying and will also make your speech sound less stilted.

Reprinted with permission of the authors from *Stockworth: An American CEO*, by Sterling and Selesnick.

Like any good speaker, Stockworth has no use for a speech, or a speechwriter, that uses difficult words rather than simple ones.

Of course, sometimes a less well known word is so accurate or so expressive that no simpler word can be substituted for it without losing an important shade of meaning. However, the less well known word often sounds pretentious, stuffy, not as clear, or simply unnecessary. When you have a choice between words that have nearly the same meaning, choose the simpler word whenever possible.

The chart on page 293 shows some simple words that are often better to use in speaking than their more difficult equivalents.

| Simple Words | Difficult Words |
|---|---|
| cloudy | nebulous |
| spying | espionage |
| wedding | nuptials |
| oily | unctuous |
| avoid | eschew |
| publish | promulgate |
| food | victuals |
| home | residence |

## Precise Words

**Precise words** express your thoughts and feelings accurately, or exactly. You can confuse your listeners if you use vague words that do not clearly express your intended meaning. To choose precise words that clearly and accurately communicate your point, you need to increase your speaking vocabulary to give you choices, and you must be sensitive to differences in meaning.

**VAGUE**    We had a *bad* club meeting yesterday.

**MORE PRECISE**    We had a { *frustrating* / *boring* / *disorganized* / *noisy* / *nonproductive* } club meeting yesterday.

**VAGUE**    The boy *looked* through the window.

**MORE PRECISE**    The boy { *peered* / *gazed* / *squinted* / *glanced* / *spied* } through the window.

As you rehearse your speech, think about your choices in wording and decide whether you have used precise words. If you are not sure, consult a dictionary or a thesaurus (a book of synonyms) to help stimulate your thinking. The thesaurus will give you a range of word choices, while the dictionary will help you to sort out shades of meaning among words that have similar meanings.

**EXAMPLE:** In a speech about football, you are trying to explain that one lineman was able to break up the opposing team's plays because of his speed. As you rehearse, you discover that you have a choice of describing the lineman as *fast* or as *quick.* Even though the two words are similar, they mean something quite different. *Fast* means that a runner can cover a distance in a short period of time; *quick* means that a runner can move or react immediately. This lineman runs no faster than his teammates. However, since he can move forward as soon as the ball is snapped and before opposing players can react, he is quick. Thus, you decide that the word *quick* describes the lineman more precisely than the word *fast* does.

## Specific Words

**Specific words** identify items within a category, while **general words** refer to an entire category. Almost any concept can be made more general or more specific by the words you use to express it.

**EXAMPLE:** *Building* is a general word that encompasses a whole category. Specific words refer to individual items in this category, such as *house, apartment, hotel, City Hall, barn,* and *condominium.*

Specific words help your audience to form a picture in their minds of the specific images that you want them to see.

| General Words | Specific Words |
|---|---|
| She brought them several *things.* | She brought them *pencils, paper,* and *crayons.* |
| A *bird* was at the feeder. | A *blue jay* was at the feeder. |
| He sat reading a *book.* | He sat reading a *paperback novel.* |
| Carmen drove by in her *automobile.* | Carmen drove by in her *convertible sports car.* |

## A·C·T·I·V·I·T·Y 1

### Finding Specific Words

Using a dictionary, a book of synonyms, or your own creativity, find a more specific word or expression for each of the following general terms: *car, office furniture, footwear, cutlery, kitchen utensil, crime, animal, flower, food,* and *music.*

## Concrete Words

**Concrete words** name things that can be perceived by one or more of the five senses. For example, *peanut butter* is a concrete word that names a substance you can touch, taste, smell, and see.

**Abstract words** name things—such as ideas and beliefs—that cannot be perceived by the senses. For example, *fairness* is abstract because it names something you can't touch, smell, hear, taste, or see.

Although concrete words make your speech easier to understand, you need at least some abstract words to identify broader categories. Concrete words can be used to explain the abstract word, as in the following explanation of the word *democracy*.

**EXAMPLE:** We are fighting for democracy. We are fighting for men and women at the voting booth, for workers demanding the right to negotiate, and for students speaking against a proposed law.

## ACTIVITY 2

### Analyzing Word Choice in a Speech

Listen closely to the language used in a passage from a specific speech. Are the key words precise? What other words could have been used? Does the speech contain more specific words than general words? Does it contain more concrete words than abstract words? Report your findings to your class.

# Using Language Expressively

Sometimes ideas are clear, but they lack force—they are not lively or memorable. **Vividness** is the quality of being full of life—of being vigorous or exciting. Good speakers know how to use vivid language that

- captures the imagination
- appeals to the senses
- creates mental pictures

## Sensory Words

One way to make your speech more vivid is to use sensory words. **Sensory words** appeal to one or more of the five senses. To find sensory words, look in a dictionary or a book of synonyms for words that have roughly the same meaning as the word you intend to use but that create a more vivid picture.

| Original Description | More Vivid Description |
|---|---|
| Lena *walked* out of the room. | Lena *stomped* out of the room. |
| The snake *moved* through the grass. | The snake *slithered* through the grass. |
| The *noise* was *loud*. | The *explosion* was *deafening*. |
| Hungrily, Chris *ate* his slice of *fruit*. | Hungrily, Chris *crunched* his slice of *apple*. |

## ACTIVITY 3

### Analyzing Sensory Words

Find a paragraph in a book, magazine, or newspaper that you think is particularly vivid because of its use of sensory words. Identify the senses that these words appeal to. Share your findings with your class.

## Figurative Language

Another way to express an idea vividly is to use figurative language. **Figurative language** consists of figures of speech—words and phrases that are not literally true, but that create a fresh, lively understanding of an idea.

Some of the types of figurative language that you can use to create vivid images in your speeches include

- similes
- metaphors
- exaggerations
- understatements
- irony

**Simile.**   A **simile** is a comparison of two essentially unlike things. In a simile, the comparison is introduced by *like, as,* or a similar word (*seem* or *appear,* for example).

**EXAMPLES:**

- Vicky's criticism was *as sharp as a knife edge.*
- His smile was *as warm as a down comforter.*
- She's got a mind *like a computer.*
- The snow appeared *as flour sifted over the mountains.*

*Eagle's Flight by Bev Doolittle © 1982 The Greenwich Workshop, Inc., 1 Greenwich Place, Shelton, CT 06484*

This painting is a visual representation of a simile from Shakespeare's poem "Venus and Adonis"— "through his mane and tail the high wind sings, / Fanning the hairs, who wave like feathered wings."

**Metaphor.**   A **metaphor** is also a comparison between essentially unlike things. Unlike a simile, a metaphor does not contain the word *like* or *as.* For example, "The lion's eyes glowed like candles in the dark" is a simile; "The lion's eyes were candles in the dark" is a metaphor. Here are some other examples of metaphors.

**EXAMPLES:**

- *The snow was a blanket* over the field.
- *Manuel is a tiger* when he competes.
- *Our offensive line is a wall* of determined players.
- *The sky is a bowl* of pea soup.

## Changing Similes to Metaphors

Each of the following sentences contains a simile. Revise each sentence by changing the simile into a metaphor. The first one has been done for you.

*Simile:* Howie moved like a cat to get to the ground ball.
*Metaphor:* Howie was a cat as he pounced on the ground ball.

1. He sleeps as soundly as a bear in the dead of winter.
2. The icy hill in front of school was like glass. People kept slipping and sliding.
3. The bright green spotlight made Donna look like a frog standing on a lily pad.
4. The baby's cry was like a siren in the night.
5. Her thoughts ran as deep as mountain canyons.

**Exaggeration.** **Exaggeration,** or **hyperbole,** emphasizes or enlarges a description of actions, emotions, or other qualities, such as size or speed. Hyperbole is appropriate only if your listeners know that you are stretching the truth for effect. In its simplest form, hyperbole involves selecting words that magnify to create an effect, usually ironic or humorous.

EXAMPLES:

1. Rather than saying that you are "hungry," you could say that you are "on the verge of starvation."
2. Instead of saying that someone was "embarrassed," you might say that he was "certain that he'd sink into the earth and disappear."
3. Rather than saying that you are "mad" at someone, you could say that you "will never speak to her again in a million years."

Exaggeration plays a major part in many folk tales, such as the tall tales about the giant Paul Bunyan and his blue ox, Babe.

**Understatement.** **Understatement** is the opposite of exaggeration. By describing an idea, an event, or a thing in terms that intentionally diminish or lessen its importance, you can create an ironic or humorous effect.

| Actual Situation | Understatement |
|---|---|
| The batter has struck out five times in one baseball game. | The batter has not done too well today. |
| Yori is running for class president, trying out for the debate team, and auditioning for the school play. | Yori tries to stay busy. |
| Lily ate five sandwiches and drank a quart of milk. | Lily had a hearty snack. |

**Irony.** **Irony** is the use of words to imply something different from, perhaps even the opposite of, what is actually meant.

EXAMPLE: A person may be speaking ironically when he or she says, "I noticed yesterday that Michael just accidently happened to be in the hall by the lockers when Mary Harper walked by on her way to class."

When irony becomes cutting or bitter it is called **sarcasm.**

EXAMPLE: After a boring play, someone leaving the theater may sarcastically say, "That was really an exciting performance. In the middle of the second act, the lady behind me accidentally hit me with her program and woke me up."

# ACTIVITY 5
## Identifying Kinds of Figurative Language

Identify each of the following uses of figurative language as *simile, metaphor, exaggeration, understatement,* or *irony.*

1. The peace was like the eye of a hurricane.
2. Tilly is so strong that she could knock Jupiter out of its orbit.
3. We had a little breeze yesterday—I think it was called a tornado.
4. When he's boxing, his arms are pistons.
5. Don took one of his little naps after dinner last night. I woke him up to go to work this morning.

## Emphasis

**Emphasis** is the force or special attention given to a particular word or point. You can use emphasis to signal to your audience exactly what you want them to remember.

Since emphasis is such a powerful device, you should use it sparingly. If you overuse it, your audience can no longer tell what you intend to stress. Too much emphasis then becomes no emphasis at all.

In Chapter 2, you learned how you can use your gestures and the sound of your voice to create emphasis. You can also create emphasis through repetition and announcement.

**Repetition.**   **Repetition** is saying something more than once. It is the easiest and most common means of showing emphasis.

By using repetition, you tell an audience, "Pay attention—this is really important."

" 'What I Did This Summer.' This summer, I went to camp. I hated it. I hated every minute of it. I hated my counsellor. I hated the food. I hated the woods. I hated the nature walks and the nature talks. I hated the outings. I hated the campfires. I hated the overnights. I hated . . ."

Drawing by H. Martin; © 1985 The New Yorker Magazine, Inc.

**EXAMPLE:** If you were giving a speech on deforestation in the Amazon, you might say the following: "Scientists estimate that as many as fifty million acres of tropical rain forest are destroyed annually. Imagine that—fifty million acres!"

You can use repetition without repeating a statement word for word. Two other forms of repetition are *restatement* and *parallelism.*

**Restatement** is the repetition of an idea using different words.

**EXAMPLE:** You might say, "During the last 200 years, more than 125 species of birds and mammals have become extinct. That's not 125 individuals, but 125 different kinds of animals gone forever." With this restatement, the idea is repeated, but the language is different.

**Parallelism** is the repetition of words, phrases, or sentences to emphasize an idea or a series of ideas.

**EXAMPLE:** Dr. Martin Luther King, Jr., used parallelism in many of his speeches to add power to his statements. Note the use of parallelism in the following excerpt from "I Have a Dream" (reprinted in full in the Appendix of Speeches).

> *There are those who are asking the devotees of civil rights, "When will you be satisfied?" We can never be satisfied as long as the Negro is the victim of the unspeakable horrors of police brutality. We can never be satisfied as long as our bodies, heavy with the fatigue of travel, cannot gain lodging in the motels of the highways and the hotels of the cities. We cannot be satisfied as long as the Negro's basic mobility is from a smaller ghetto to a larger one. We can never be satisfied as long as a Negro in Mississippi cannot vote and a Negro in New York believes he has nothing for which to vote.*

**Announcement.**  Another way of emphasizing a point is to precede what you intend to say with an **announcement** that clearly states your evaluation of that point. For instance, you might use any of the following statements as an announcement.

- Now I come to what I consider my most important point.
- This second idea is the key to understanding the material.
- Pay close attention to the steps of this process. They are a little tricky to follow.
- The formula that I am about to give you is the one that you will use the most in this entire unit.

# ACTIVITY 6

## Identifying Methods for Achieving Emphasis

Read each of the following items. For each item, tell whether it achieves emphasis through *repetition, restatement,* or *announcement.*

1. Three new cases of this deadly disease are reported each week—that's 156 new cases a year!
2. Everyone was amazed by Koslov's margin of two million votes—that's two million votes.
3. Lucas hit .287 last year, just about .300!
4. The United States Coast Guard traces its history back to 1790—that means it is almost as old as this country.
5. Pay attention to this next step. It is crucial to the success of your project.

## Tone

By using **tone,** speakers express their attitudes toward their subjects and their audiences. You can communicate to your audience how you feel about your topic by the tone of your speech. Your tone should also let your audience know how you want them to feel about your topic. You can express tone in two ways:

1. through the sound of your voice
2. through your choice of language

**Vocal Tone.**   Choosing the appropriate tone of voice is essential in delivering the message you intend.

> **EXAMPLE:** If your speech topic is about the dangers of air pollution, you will have a greater appeal to your audience if your tone is concerned and sincere rather than nagging.

**Choice of Language.**   The language you use in your speech will help you to express how you feel about your topic and about your audience. Your language can be *formal, informal,* or somewhere in between. By using informal language, you will express an informal tone. Whichever language you choose needs to be appropriate for the occasion and for your audience.

> **EXAMPLE:** You are speaking before a group of parents and teachers on a formal occasion, such as a ceremony honoring the parent who has volunteered the most time in behalf of the school. For this audience and on this occasion, it would probably not be appropriate to use slang or colloquial expressions, even in an attempt at humor. Instead, choose your words and expressions carefully and use formal language.

## Uses of Formal and Informal Language

| Occasion | Audience | Tone | Language Use |
|---|---|---|---|
| **Awards Ceremony** | school officials and fellow classmates | dignified, polished | *Formal:* Use your best vocabulary, grammar, and syntax. Avoid slang and colloquial expressions. |
| **Meeting to Schedule Events** | student committee | serious, but not stuffy | *Formal to informal:* Use good vocabulary, grammar, and syntax. You may use some slang, colloquial expressions, and personal references (*I, you, we, they*). |
| **Dinner at Home** | family members | chatty, personal | *Informal:* You may use slang, colloquial expressions, and personal references. |

KUDZU by Doug Marlette. By permission of Doug Marlette and Creators Syndicate.

## ACTIVITY 7

### Adjusting Tone for Different Audiences

Prepare a short statement describing how you feel about a school dress code. Prepare this statement as part of the remarks you might make for the following occasions and audiences:

- a class report for your teacher
- a student committee meeting with your peers
- lunch with your friends

Then tell your class how the tone of each statement differs.

# Adjusting Your Vocabulary to Suit Your Audience

Like all groups of people, audiences differ from one to another. You need to be able to adapt your vocabulary to suit your audience. [See Chapter 9 for more information on how to gather important data about your audience.]

Use words that are appropriate for your audience. Obviously, the words you use in a speech to kindergarten students will differ from the words you use in a speech to city council members. Choosing a word that is accurate, specific, and vivid will not matter if your audience does not understand that word.

## Involving Your Audience

Audiences remember more about your speech and respond more favorably to your message when you actively involve them.

You can accomplish this by

- selecting material that relates to your audience's experience
- using personal pronouns to address your audience
- asking rhetorical questions to involve your listeners

**Relate to Your Audience's Experience.** Whenever you have a choice, use material that is closely related to your audience's experience.

> **EXAMPLE:** If you can use only one of two examples—driving a car or flying an airplane—in a speech to your classmates, you will probably want to discuss driving a car, an example that will be more likely to relate to your audience's experience.

**Use Personal Pronouns.**   You give each speech to a specific audience—not to some general or unknown group, but to people who are sitting in front of you. You always want your audience to feel that you are talking with them. One way to do this is to use the personal pronouns *you* and *we* freely.

The pronoun *you* makes an audience feel that you are talking directly to them. The pronoun *we* makes an audience feel that they are joining with you for some shared purpose.

> **EXAMPLE:** Instead of saying, "*One* would think that . . .," say, "*You* would think that. . . ." Instead of saying, "*People* often find that . . .," say, "*We* often find that. . . ."

**Ask Rhetorical Questions.**   A **rhetorical question** is one that is not meant to be answered but that is asked only for effect. Phrasing some key points in the form of rhetorical questions helps to involve your audience by getting them to think actively.

Suppose you are practicing a speech on the history of the bicycle. Instead of beginning, "The bicycle originated in the year . . .," you might try the following phrasing: "Do you know when the first bicycle was built? Can you come up with a specific date? If you think it was during the 1800s, you're absolutely right!"

| Original Phrasing | More Audience-Centered Phrasing |
|---|---|
| Across the country, parents are telling their children to turn off the TV set. However, television can actually help children learn. | Across the country, parents are telling their children to turn off the TV set. But did you know that television can actually help children learn? |
| Although some people think that cars are unreliable, 40 to 45 percent of cars are still on the road after ten years of operation. | Do you think that cars are unreliable? Did you know that 40 to 45 percent of cars are still on the road after ten years of operation? |
| Some people might say, "Don't worry. We've had hurricanes before." But hurricanes are costly. In 1992 Hurricane Andrew cost Floridians more than $10 billion. | Some people might say, "Don't worry. We've had hurricanes before." But hurricanes are costly. Did you know that in 1992 Hurricane Andrew cost Floridians more than $10 billion? |

These rhetorical questions get the point across in a way that involves the audience. As a result, the audience will likely remember the information better and find the information more interesting than if the speaker just stated it directly.

Listen to a speech, paying close attention to the speaker's language. Did it help to involve the audience? If so, write down five specific examples of words or phrases that were particularly suitable. If not, write down some changes that would adapt that language to involve the audience. Be prepared to report your findings and changes to your class.

# ACTIVITY 8

## Adjusting Language to Suit an Audience

Rewrite the following sentences so that they would relate better to an audience of your classmates.

1. One should always brush one's teeth at least twice a day.
2. Athletic programs can build school morale.
3. Driving a car to school can be frustrating.
4. Students should take courses that will benefit them.
5. Some say that the only truly American art form is jazz.

# Avoiding Common Language Problems

Several common problems with language can make your speech less interesting. As a rule, you will want to avoid using

- jargon
- clichés
- euphemisms
- slang
- words that have unintended meanings

## Jargon

**Jargon** is language that is used by people within a particular group or field (such as people who share the same profession, occupation, or hobby), but is not necessarily understood by people outside that group or field. [See Chapter 2, pages 33–34.]

You will need to avoid using jargon in your speeches because it may alienate those members of your audience who are not as familiar with your topic as you are.

**EXAMPLE:** Suppose that you were giving a speech on sailing to an audience that was not familiar with sailing. If you mentioned that sailors often *trim the sails* (adjust the sails to gain full advantage of the wind), you would likely confuse your listeners by your use of jargon.

## Clichés

A **cliché** is a figurative expression that has been used so often that it has lost its power. Overuse of clichés may cause your audience to lose interest in what you have to say. If you want to use figurative language to make your speech more vivid, try to create fresh and original phrases to capture your audience's attention.

| Some Common Clichés | |
|---|---|
| slow as molasses | tried and true |
| eats like a horse | calm, cool, and collected |
| cold as ice | selling like hotcakes |
| fresh as a daisy | cool as a cucumber |
| quiet as a mouse | runs like the wind |
| talks a mile a minute | known far and wide |

# Euphemisms

**Euphemisms** are words or phrases that are used in place of words that are thought to be unpleasant or distasteful. When giving a speech, you can use euphemisms to avoid offending people or hurting their feelings. However, using too many euphemisms can make your speech seem dull.

| Euphemism | More Direct Term |
|-----------|------------------|
| sanitary engineer | garbage collector |
| passed away | died |
| powder room | bathroom |

# Slang

**Slang** is highly informal language that is formed by creating new words or by giving common words new meanings.

| Common Word | Slang Meaning |
|-------------|---------------|
| bad, radical | good, excellent |
| bread, moolah, dough | money |
| sweat, hassle | worry, bother |

Most slang is used for a short time by a particular group of people. For example, in the 1980s, the word *tubular* was surfer's slang for "pleasing, fine." Like *tubular,* most slang expressions die out. A few pass into the mainstream of language.

Slang is generally out of place in public speaking, except when you are giving a very informal speech or when you want to create a particular effect. In formal speaking situations, your audience may react to your use of slang by thinking your words are odd, outdated, or inappropriate.

# Unintended Meanings

**Connotations** are the emotions and associations that are suggested by certain words. [See Chapter 2 for more on connotation.] Because a word can have several connotations, you run a risk of using words in your speech that will have unintended meanings.

However, by listening carefully during your practice sessions, you can avoid many unintended meanings. For instance, as you rehearse your speech, listen carefully to avoid words that stereotype or label people. Listen for the meanings that your words may have for your listeners, not just for the meanings you intend your words to have.

## ACTIVITY 9
### Identifying Common Language Problems in Speeches

Ask one of your classmates to listen to a live or recorded rehearsal of your speech. Have this listener tell you whether you used any jargon, clichés, euphemisms, slang, or words with unintended meanings that should be removed from your speech.

After your partner has evaluated your speech, reverse roles. Listen to your partner's speech and share your evaluation of it.

## GUIDELINES
### for Using Effective Language

- Do I use the most precise words to express my thoughts?

- Do I use specific, rather than general, words?

- Do I use concrete words to make the meanings of abstract words clear to my audience?

- Do I use simple words rather than difficult or pretentious ones?

- Do I use sensory language?

- Do I create fresh figures of speech?

- Do I use different methods to emphasize my ideas?

- Do I use a tone that is appropriate for the audience and the occasion?

- Do I adapt my language to my audience?

- Do I avoid overusing clichés, euphemisms, and slang?

- Do I avoid using language that carries unintended meanings?

# SUITING WORDS TO AUDIENCE

### Selecting Words that Work

The goal when translating or interpreting is to convert a message in the source language into a similar message in the target language. To choose the right words, you have to be fluent in both languages and sensitive to both cultures. A good translator has to consider many other factors, too, including connotation, degree of formality, and shade of meaning.

### Characteristics of a Good Translator

A good translator

1. expresses ideas to appeal to a variety of audiences

2. chooses words that express thoughts clearly and distinguishes specific words from general words

3. uses sensory words and figurative language to make language more vivid

## ACTIVITY

### Situation

As a reporter for a children's television program, your assignment is to take a news story written for an adult special-interest audience and to translate it so that a more general, younger audience can understand it.

### Meet the Translator

"As methods of communication become more and more sophisticated, being understood clearly is increasingly important," says translator Luisa West. "When I can help people who speak different languages and who come from different cultures understand one another and communicate clearly, I find great satisfaction in my work."

*Luisa G. West*

### Preparation

From a newspaper or magazine, choose a news item about a scientific topic, an economic topic, or a topic from another special field. Analyze the article, identifying terms to explain and outlining the most important points. Then, choosing appropriate words, write a version that translates the article for your audience.

### Analysis and Assessment

After you read your translation aloud in class, show your classmates the original news item so they can compare it with your version. How effective was your translation? How might it be improved?

# S•U•M•M•A•R•Y

**USING APPROPRIATE LANGUAGE** in your speeches means using language that is effective and appropriate for your audience and purpose. Selecting the words you want to use to express your message requires careful attention to your language in speech rehearsals.

- **Choose the right words** by selecting simple words, precise words, specific words, and concrete words to help your audience clearly understand your message.
- **Use language expressively** by selecting vivid, sensory words and figurative language to help your audience understand and remember your ideas. Emphasize your ideas by using repetition, restatement, and announcement. Choose words that set a tone which is appropriate to the audience and to the occasion of the speech.
- **Adjust your language to suit your audience** by taking into consideration the vocabulary level appropriate to the audience. To make your speech more audience-centered, you might use personal pronouns or rhetorical questions.
- **Avoid common language problems** such as jargon, clichés, euphemisms, and slang. Be careful that the words you choose do not carry unintended meanings.

Look back through this chapter to find the meaning of each of the following terms. Write each term and its meaning in your communication journal.

abstract words, p. 295
announcement, p. 301
clarity, p. 291
cliché, p. 307
concrete words, p. 295
connotation, p. 308
emphasis, p. 300
euphemism, p. 308
exaggeration, p. 298
figurative language,
 p. 296
general words, p. 294
hyperbole, p. 298
irony, p. 299
jargon, p. 307
levels of usage, p. 289
metaphor, p. 297
parallelism, p. 301
precise words, p. 293
repetition, p. 300
restatement, p. 300
rhetorical question,
 p. 305
sarcasm, p. 299
sensory words, p. 296
simile, p. 297
simple words, p. 292
slang, p. 308
specific words, p. 294
standard American
 English, p. 289
tone, p. 302
understatement, p. 299
vividness, p. 296

## Review Questions

1. Describe four ways in which spoken language differs from written language.
2. When is a word considered precise?
3. List ten specific words that can be used to replace the general term *sport*.
4. Identify an abstract word and give two examples of concrete words that would illustrate or explain it.
5. What are sensory words?
6. How does a simile differ from a metaphor?
7. How does exaggeration differ from understatement?
8. How does irony differ from sarcasm?
9. How does repetition differ from restatement?
10. Identify two methods that can be used to involve your audience in your speech.

## Discussion Questions

1. Figurative language helps make your writing vivid. However, a speech filled with too much figurative language seems "flowery." Discuss with your classmates the use of figurative language. Try to set up guidelines for determining how much figurative language is too much.
2. Many good speakers are witty: They are able to use language in a clever or amusing way. However, wit that contains too much sarcasm can be offensive to other people. La Rochefoucauld, a seventeenth-century French writer, once stated, "The greatest fault of a penetrating wit is to go beyond the mark." First, discuss the meaning of this quotation. Then, discuss the difference between wit and sarcasm.
3. Galen, a Greek physician in the second century A.D., once wrote, "The chief merit of language is clearness, and we know that nothing detracts so much from this as do unfamiliar terms." First, discuss the meaning of Galen's statement. Then, discuss how this statement relates to the idea of keeping the language of your speech simple.
4. A Yiddish proverb says, "Words should be weighed and not counted." First, discuss the meaning of this quotation. Then, discuss how it relates to using appropriate language in your speech.
5. The power of effective speaking has often been recognized throughout the ages. The following advice is found in the *Maxims of Ptahhotep* of ancient Egypt: "Be a craftsman in speech that thou mayest be strong, for the strength of one is the tongue, and speech is mightier than all fighting." First, discuss the meaning of this maxim. Then, discuss how it relates to using appropriate language in your speech.

# ACTIVITIES

### 1. Identifying and Analyzing Elements That Make a Speech Effective.

**A.** Some speakers are famous for their eloquence, or exquisite use of language. One such speaker was the man shown below—Sir Winston Churchill. In the library, find a speech by Churchill. Pay special attention to the words and figures of speech that Churchill used. What specific, concrete words in the speech help to increase the audience's interest and understanding? Identify any metaphors and similes and examples of exaggeration, understatement, and irony.

**B.** Analyze how these figures of speech contribute to the effect that Churchill was trying to have on his listeners. Also identify and analyze the methods Churchill used to emphasize particular ideas. How do these methods affect the tone of the speech? Do they make it dramatic? forceful? dignified? solemn? pompous? Carefully choose several words that state precisely your impression of the tone of his speech. Record your responses to these questions in your communication journal.

### 2. Revising Sentences to Make Word Choice More Precise.

The following sentences contain vague words. Rewrite each sentence by replacing vague words with precise ones to make the meaning of each sentence clearer.

a. A little girl was happily playing with a toy.

b. An irritated police officer was trying to give directions to people.

c. The music of the South is interesting.

d. I got lots of stuff for Christmas.

e. Just go down the road a way and then turn.

### 3. Defining Differences Between Synonyms and Identifying Vivid, Exact Synonyms.

**A.** Immediately following these instructions are lists of several synonyms for the words *best*, *angry*, and *walk*. First, write a definition of each of the synonyms. Make sure that the definition you give for each word describes the special meaning that makes that word different from the other synonyms. Then, study the sentences following the synonyms, and replace the italicized word in each sentence with the synonym of that word that you think creates the most appropriate image.

*best—supreme, maximum, inimitable, peerless, superior*

*angry—irate, irascible, fuming, fierce, hostile, betrayed*

*walk—march, pace, trudge, stalk, strut*

1. What do you think is the *best* price we can get for this product?

2. When she found that she had been overcharged for her prom dress, Erin was *angry*.

3. When he saw that Sal was making fun of him, Ruben *walked* out of the room.

4. Ruben felt *angry* because he had thought that Sal was his friend.

5. When we saw Clara *walk* to the podium, we could tell that she thought that her speech would be the *best* one.

**B.** Using either a dictionary or a book of synonyms, list five words that you think would be good, vivid choices to replace the following words:

happy
said
ran
hit
friend

**4. Analyzing the Language in a Political Speech.** Many politicians are effective speakers. They have to be effective to win elections. Listen to a political speech. Analyze the speaker's use of language. How does the speaker use language effectively? Can you find any weaknesses in the speaker's use of language? If so, identify those weaknesses. Share your findings with your classmates.

**5. Analyzing a Newscaster's Use of Language.** News stories on television can be considered short informative speeches. Listen to your favorite newscaster deliver the top story on the nightly news. In what ways does the newscaster use language effectively? In what ways does he or she use language ineffectively? What advice would you give this person for improving his or her use of language? Share your advice with your classmates.

**6. Completing Similes.** Complete each of the following similes by creating an original comparison. Avoid writing clichés, such as "as sound as a dollar" for the first item.

a. The economy of a nation needs to be as sound as . . .

b. She was a great woman, as courageous as a . . .

c. A tall man, he looked like a . . .

d. Reading a book is like . . .

e. After the war, the peace between the two nations was as fragile as . . .

f. After helping clean up the house all day, I was as tired as . . .

g. That old car he bought looks like . . .

h. When the sun comes out after several days of rain, I feel as . . . as . . .

i. The waves washing up on the loose sand sounded like . . .

j. The light, cool breeze felt like . . .

**7. Analyzing Methods for Achieving Emphasis.** Analyze the methods used to achieve emphasis in two of the student speeches included in the Appendix of Speeches on pages 658–683. Begin by copying the specific words that the speakers use. Then identify whether these words achieve emphasis through repetition or through announcement. Next, briefly state the idea or ideas that are being emphasized in each case. Finally, evaluate the effectiveness of each speaker's use of emphasis, and compare how emphasis was used in each of the two speeches.

Record all of this information in your communication journal and be prepared to share your findings in class discussion.

# COMMUNICATION IN THE WORKPLACE

### Background
Many occupations, such as food preparation, mechanics, teaching, sports, computer programming, or retail sales, use words or phrases all their own. For example, housepainters call a spot that has been left unpainted a *holiday*. This specialized vocabulary is called jargon.

### Preparing to do the Job
Identify five jargon terms from one or several occupations. Find the definitions for these terms and determine what relationship, if any, the jargon meaning has to a more common meaning of each term.

### Testing Your Skill
Report to your class on the terms you chose and on how these terms help people within the occupation communicate more effectively. Can you or classmates think of any ways that the jargon could make communication less effective?

# EVERYDAY COMMUNICATION

### Situation
You have just arrived for the twentieth reunion of your high school graduating class. Despite outward changes, you recognize some familiar voices and speech patterns of friends you haven't seen for years.

### Problem
Which friends would you recognize by their speech? Would you recognize someone's tone of voice? word choice? other distinctive patterns? Working in groups of three, write a two-page dialogue depicting the three of you meeting at your twentieth class reunion and recognizing one another by the way you speak.

### Assessing Your Skill
Present your dialogue in class and respond to your classmates' feedback on how well your team has captured your speech patterns.

# Presenting Your Speech

**OBJECTIVES**

**After studying this chapter, you should be able to**

1. Describe the four methods of delivering a speech and explain the advantages and disadvantages of each.
2. Use effective methods to control stage fright.
3. Explain the effect of your appearance, eye contact, facial expressions, and other nonverbal behavior on your audience.
4. List and explain ways you can improve your vocal skills.
5. Improve your verbal message by concentrating on diction and grammar.
6. Use equipment and materials efficiently.
7. Practice delivering a speech to experience aspects of delivery that include timing, audience feedback, distractions, and unexpected occurrences.
8. Evaluate your delivery of a speech, analyzing both the strengths and the weaknesses.

## How to Present Your Speech

It is your turn to make your first speech in class. You rise from your seat and walk to the front of the room. Setting your notes on the speaker's stand, you pause to look at the audience before you begin. How do you feel? Are you ready?

To present a successful speech, you will need to be well rehearsed and to sound interested in and enthusiastic about your subject. If you are enthusiastic about your subject, you will be less likely to be unnerved by the prospect of giving a speech. In addition, thorough rehearsal will help you to develop the best nonverbal behavior and vocal skills for your particular speech and audience. Careful preparation will even help you to handle unexpected mishaps and distractions that may occur during your speech.

# Comparing Methods of Delivery

A speech can be delivered in one of four ways: impromptu, manuscript, memorized, or extemporaneous.

Although most experienced speakers prefer extemporaneous speaking, each of the four methods of delivery is appropriate for certain circumstances.

## Impromptu

An **impromptu speech** is given on the spur of the moment with no preparation.

**EXAMPLE:** Sometimes, when a celebrity is stopped by reporters and asked to comment on a particular subject, the celebrity's remarks are delivered impromptu. In these instances, the celebrity cannot take the time to prepare a response but simply speaks the words as they come to his or her mind.

## Manuscript

A **manuscript speech** is written out completely and read to the audience.

**EXAMPLE:** Most political speeches are manuscript speeches. By using manuscripts, the speakers avoid the risk of making errors. Reading from their manuscripts provides them assurance that they will not leave out any important points.

## Memorized

A **memorized speech** is written out completely and recited word for word. A memorized speech is actually a manuscript speech committed to memory.

**EXAMPLE:** Contestants in certain competitive speech events often prefer to memorize their speeches because their choice of words plays a large part in how their performances will be evaluated. When writing and revising their written speeches, they take care to choose their words very carefully. By memorizing their speeches, contestants can ensure that their ideas are expressed in the manner they want.

## Extemporaneous

An **extemporaneous speech** is fully outlined and practiced but not memorized. Because the exact wording is left until the speech is given to an audience, the speaker's words sound spontaneous and natural.

**EXAMPLE:** Most professional speakers prefer to speak extemporaneously. They use only a few note cards or perhaps a brief outline. These speakers are thoroughly familiar with their subjects, and they have rehearsed their material. Therefore, they are free to listen and to pay close attention to their audiences' reactions.

## Methods of Delivering Speeches

| Type of Delivery | Description | Advantages | Drawbacks |
|---|---|---|---|
| **Impromptu** | given on the spur of the moment, with no preparation | • allows speaker to respond quickly<br>• sounds natural, spontaneous | • can seem disorganized<br>• may not include all of the important points on the topic<br>• limits a speaker's time to think before responding<br>• may lead to blunders |
| **Manuscript** | written out completely and read to the audience from a prepared script | • can be revised until wording is exact<br>• can be researched so that every key point is supported by details and examples<br>• can be rehearsed and timed exactly | • often sounds stiff, unnatural<br>• may be boring for audience<br>• requires time to plan, write, and revise |
| **Memorized** | written out completely (like a manuscript speech) and then thoroughly memorized | • can be revised until wording is exact<br>• can be researched so that every point is supported by details and examples<br>• can be rehearsed and timed exactly | • must be memorized well enough to sound smooth and natural<br>• requires time to memorize<br>• may increase nervousness and cause speaker to forget |
| **Extemporaneous** | fully prepared (outlined and researched) but not memorized; speaker may use brief outline or note cards | • sounds spontaneous and natural<br>• can be organized in a logical manner<br>• can be researched so that main points are supported<br>• allows for greater flexibility of response to audience feedback | • requires time to prepare outline or notes<br>• requires time to rehearse |

### Analyzing Methods of Delivery

**K**eep a record of the next five speeches you hear. Identify the method that you think was used to deliver each speech: impromptu, manuscript, memorized, or extemporaneous. Which of the speeches are the most effective? What relationships do you notice between effectiveness and method of delivery? Discuss your findings with your classmates.

# Controlling Stage Fright

Are you nervous when you give a speech? If you ask people how they feel about speaking in public, most will admit having feelings of anxiousness. **Stage fright** is the nervousness that speakers feel before and during the presentation of their speeches.

## What You Should Know About Stage Fright

1. **Stage fright is normal.** Beginners as well as experienced speakers feel stage fright before and during a speech. Experienced speakers know that some nervousness is actually beneficial, since people who are a little nervous are more likely to be alert and ready to do their best.

2. **Your audience is not likely to notice your nervousness.** Often, beginning speakers report that they confided in friends that they had felt nervous while speaking, only to hear their friends say, "You didn't seem nervous at all."

3. **Experience and practice will help.** Take advantage of every opportunity you have to speak. With each speech, you will make fewer and fewer mistakes, and your confidence will grow.

**For Better or For Worse®**      **by Lynn Johnston**

## Before Your Speech

1. **Prepare for your speech carefully and completely.** Be sure to set aside enough time to allow yourself to become completely familiar with your material. Leave yourself one or two days just for rehearsal. During that time, even the breaks between rehearsals will help you. Your mind will be working on your speech even when you are not consciously rehearsing.

2. **Look your best.** Dress in the way that gives you the greatest confidence. As a rule, the better you look, the better you will feel. Being appropriately dressed and well groomed when you give your speech will help boost your assurance and lessen your nervousness.

3. **Relax tense muscles.** You are likely to feel most tense shortly before you speak. Therefore, the time immediately before your speech should be spent applying relaxation techniques. Use the techniques shown below.

### Six Steps for Relaxing Tense Muscles

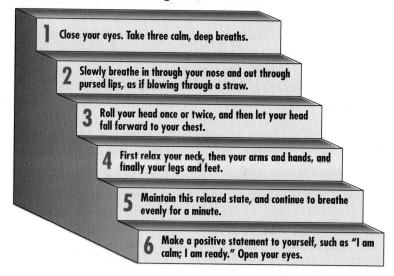

1 Close your eyes. Take three calm, deep breaths.

2 Slowly breathe in through your nose and out through pursed lips, as if blowing through a straw.

3 Roll your head once or twice, and then let your head fall forward to your chest.

4 First relax your neck, then your arms and hands, and finally your legs and feet.

5 Maintain this relaxed state, and continue to breathe evenly for a minute.

6 Make a positive statement to yourself, such as "I am calm; I am ready." Open your eyes.

4. **Give yourself a pep talk.** Immediately before your speech, remind yourself that you are well prepared and that the audience is going to profit from what you have to say.

5. **Be self-assured.** Walk to the speaker's stand with confidence. Let your movements and posture tell your audience that you are prepared to present your speech. Pause a few seconds before you start speaking. Take a deep, steady breath. Then begin your speech.

## During Your Speech

Regardless of how well prepared you are, when you begin to speak, you may still be nervous. Consider the following list of some of the most common sensations. Remember that each of these is a perfectly normal response that is shared by many people. In most cases, you can learn to control your response to these sensations so that they do not affect your delivery.

1. **Queasy feeling, butterflies, sweaty palms, general weakness.** These symptoms may feel strong when you begin speaking, but they lessen quickly once you get into your speech. Remember that these sensations have no direct effect on your delivery. Ignore them and concentrate on expressing your message to your audience.

2. **Dry mouth.** Licking your lips and swallowing often will not diminish the dryness, but they will detract from your appearance. Instead, start your speech slowly and concentrate on what you are saying. As you continue, the dryness in your mouth will subside.

3. **Stumbling over words at the start.** Word fumbles often result from trying to recall the exact words you wrote to express an idea. Practice saying your opening lines several different ways so that you will feel comfortable with a variety of openings as you deliver your speech.

4. **Perspiration, squeaky voice, slight trembling.** Ignore these reactions and focus on your message; your body will return to normal.

5. **Strong desire to quit.** Finish your speech no matter how painful the experience seems at the moment. You will build your confidence by proving to yourself that you can reach your goal and finish your speech.

*K*eep a record of the kinds of nervousness you experience before and during your speeches. Apply the suggestions given in this chapter for handling stage fright. Note which of these suggestions helps you most in managing your nervousness. List other advice or techniques that you have been taught or that you have discovered yourself. Make note of the suggestions that you feel to be most helpful.

**A**t home, practice the relaxation techniques that are recommended for use before your speech. In class, discuss these techniques with your classmates. Tell why you find these techniques helpful. Also ask your classmates for suggestions about managing any specific problems that you may have found when applying these techniques.

# Improving Nonverbal Behavior

Certain nonverbal behaviors can affect your impact on your audience and your ability to achieve your purpose in your speech. Experienced speakers know that their nonverbal behavior has as much—sometimes even more—effect on achieving their goals as the words they speak. For example, if you give your speech with a "deadpan" face or with a scowl, if you shuffle about nervously, or if you look at the floor or at the ceiling, your audience is not going to trust you. Make sure that your nonverbal presentation sends the appropriate message.

## Appearance

Your **appearance** is how you look to your audience. Two key features of your appearance are your clothing and your grooming.

Good appearance is not going to guarantee a good speech, but poor appearance can lessen your chances of achieving your goal. Proper appearance depends on the situation of the speech, but you should always be clean and well groomed, and your clothes should look neat and tidy.

| Common Attire for Specific Speaking Situations | | |
|---|---|---|
| **Situation** | **Men** | **Women** |
| **Informal** | depending on the occasion, jeans or slacks and perhaps a tie or jacket | possibly a skirt or pants and blouse; or a dress |
| **Formal** | perhaps slacks and a jacket; or suit, dress shirt, and tie | perhaps a suit (coordinated skirt or dress pants and jacket) and blouse; or a dress and jacket |

## Eye Contact

**Eye contact** is direct visual contact with the eyes of members of your audience. Your goal in making eye contact with your audience is to give every person listening to you the impression that you are speaking to him or her personally.

Good speakers look randomly at individuals and at groups of individuals distributed widely in the audience. For instance, for a few seconds you might talk to people on the left side of the front row. For the next few seconds you might talk to people at the right rear of the room. By moving randomly from group to group, you can develop a bond with the entire audience. The key is to look at someone or some group at all times.

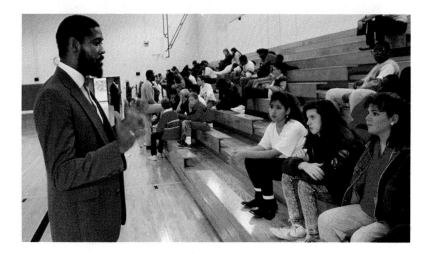

## Facial Expressions

Your facial expression gives your audience clues about the content of your speech. The key to using appropriate facial expressions is to concentrate on what you are saying, not on the fact that you are giving a speech. If you do this, you will be able to avoid two common expression problems: the deadpan and the conflicting expression.

**Deadpan.**  A **deadpan** is an expressionless facial appearance that never changes, regardless of what is being said.

**Conflicting Expression.**  A **conflicting expression** is a facial appearance that does not match a speaker's words or actual feelings. For example, some people develop the habit of smiling when they feel angry or scared. Therefore, if they are a little nervous at the start of a speech, they may start smiling regardless of what they are saying. The conflict between a speaker's verbal expression and facial expression can confuse or annoy an audience.

## Effective Gestures

Beginning speakers often worry about what to do with their hands. When you are standing in front of an audience, you should use the same natural gestures that you use in ordinary conversation.

Since nervousness can affect your gestures, begin your speech with your hands in a neutral position at your sides or resting comfortably on the speaker's stand. Then, as you start to talk, your hands will be free to move normally.

## Good Posture

Good posture creates an impression of confidence and authority. At the start of your speech, stand up straight with both feet firmly on the ground. As you speak, you will naturally shift position, but you should never slump, slouch, or look sloppy.

### ACTIVITY 3

### Evaluating Nonverbal Behavior

Select a partner with whom to exchange feedback about your effective use of nonverbal behavior. Taking turns, let each partner practice approaching the podium, pausing, and then reading the first two paragraphs on the previous page as if they were a brief speech. Have your partner, acting as an audience member, evaluate your nonverbal behavior. Ask for suggestions for improvement.

# Improving Vocal Skills

The sound of your voice plays a major role in your success as a speaker. If you deliver your speech with enthusiasm, your audience will probably share your positive feelings. However, if you are hesitant and seem uncertain, your audience will share your doubt and discomfort.

## Enthusiasm

Show enthusiasm through your voice. **Enthusiasm** is the strong positive feeling speakers show for their topics. Almost all studies show that enthusiasm is the most important factor in determining how much confidence an audience has in a speaker. Listeners who believe that a speaker is truly enthusiastic will become enthusiastic themselves about the speech and about the speaker.

The key to enthusiasm is a positive attitude. You will be enthusiastic about giving your speech if you believe

- your topic is a good one
- you have found excellent supporting material
- your audience will be interested in the material

## Vocalized Pauses

Your effectiveness as a speaker can be weakened by vocalized pauses. **Vocalized pauses** are the meaningless speech sounds that speakers use to fill time. The most common vocalized pauses are *uh, well uh, um,* and *you know.*

Everyone uses these fillers at one time or another in conversation. Most of us do not even hear our vocalized pauses. Because these sounds are not directly related to the meaning of what we are saying, our minds do not usually pay any attention to them. You are likely to insert one or more vocalized pauses when you are

- unprepared for your speech
- searching for the right word
- flustered or embarrassed
- in too much of a hurry

## HOW TO  *Decrease Your Use of Vocalized Pauses*

1. **Find out whether you overuse vocalized pauses.** Focus on overuse, not on the informal slips that nearly everyone makes now and then. You are overusing vocalized pauses if your audience becomes aware of them. You might ask people (including your teacher), "When I talk, are you aware of my use of *uh's, well uh's, um's,* or *you know's?*"

2. **Train your ear to hear your vocalized pauses.** Set up a practice session with a partner who will raise one hand whenever he or she hears you use a vocalized pause. By having someone call your attention to your use of vocalized pauses, you will begin to tune your ear to them.

3. **Train yourself to speak with fewer vocalized pauses.** Once you can hear yourself using vocalized pauses, you can limit their use through practice sessions. As you become more successful at limiting them during rehearsals, you will be able to limit them in your regular speaking.

**For Better or For Worse®**                     **by Lynn Johnston**

FOR BETTER OR FOR WORSE copyright 1986 Lynn Johnston Prod., Inc. Reprinted with permission of UNIVERSAL PRESS SYNDICATE. All rights reserved.

## Articulation, Pronunciation, and Enunciation

In public speaking, you must be careful of your articulation and pronunciation. As you learned in Chapter 3, **articulation** is the shaping of distinct speech sounds into recognizable words. **Pronunciation** is the grouping and accenting of the sounds. [If you have problems with articulation and pronunciation, review the exercises in Chapter 3.]

When you deliver your speech, do your best to enunciate clearly. **Enunciation** refers to the distinctness of the sounds you make.

Good enunciation is clear and precise. Many people suffer from sloppy enunciation. For example, they say

- *probly* for *probably*
- *liberry* for *library*
- *gimme* for *give me*
- *gunna* for *going to*
- *commere* for *come here*

Although sloppy enunciation causes few problems in casual conversation, it is not acceptable when delivering a formal speech.

# HOW TO > *Improve Articulation, Pronunciation, and Enunciation*

- If you have any doubt about the pronunciation of a word, look it up in a dictionary.

- If you have the common faults of slurring sounds and leaving off word endings, practice will help to improve your enunciation. Take ten to fifteen minutes a day to read passages aloud, trying to overaccentuate each of the sounds that give you difficulty.

- If you have a persistent problem of distorting, omitting, substituting, or adding sounds, you may want to work closely with a speech therapist.

## Correcting Vocalization Problems

| Vocal Category | Description | Common Problems | Problem Correction |
|---|---|---|---|
| **Pitch** | highness or lowness of vocal sounds | • monotone—a melody pattern that consists of only one tone | Speak at your optimum pitch, the pitch at which you feel the least strain and have the best resonance. |
| **Volume** | loudness or intensity of speech tones; determined by the force exerted to produce it | • speaking too softly<br>• speaking too loudly | 1. Practice controlling your speaking volume.<br>2. Observe your audience closely. (Are people in the back row straining to hear you? Do people in the front row cringe as if you were shouting at them?)<br>3. Adapt your volume to suit the audience and the speaking environment. |
| **Rate** | the speed at which a speaker speaks | • speaking too quickly<br>• speaking so slowly that the audience is bored | 1. Practice speaking at a steady rate.<br>2. Observe your audience closely. (Does your audience seem to be struggling to keep up with you? Do your listeners seem to be impatient for you to speed up?) |

# ACTIVITY 4

## Evaluating Vocal Skills

Working in small groups of four or five members, have each person stand and talk to the group for two minutes about his or her favorite class. Every time the person says *uh, well uh, you know*, or some other vocalized pause, the other members of the group should each raise a hand. Can anyone get through the entire two minutes without using one vocalized pause? Have the members of the group evaluate and give specific feedback about each speaker's enthusiasm, articulation, pronunciation, enunciation, pitch, volume, and rate.

# Improving Verbal Messages

A verbal message consists not only of the meaning of its words but also of the arrangement of the words in sentences. [You will find more information about verbal messages in Chapter 2.]

## Diction

**Diction** refers to both the words a speaker selects and the specific ways in which the speaker uses these words. No matter what audience you are speaking to, your choice of words can make the difference between a vague, uninteresting message and a clear, effective message.

If you take care when selecting your words, you are more likely to express the precise meaning you intend. Your words should

- be precise, specific, concrete, and simple enough for your listeners to understand your message
- be vivid so that your listeners are able to use your words to create clear mental images of what you are saying
- place emphasis on the most important points of your message
- be fresh, avoiding clichés and overuse of euphemisms or slang

## BLOOM COUNTY                    by Berke Breathed

BLOOM COUNTY by Berke Breathed. © 1984, Washington Post Writers Group. Reprinted with permission.

## Grammar

**Grammar** refers to the rules and conventions for speaking and writing English. When you deliver a formal speech, use standard American English. [See Chapter 12 for additional information about using standard American English.]

| Using Standard American English | |
|---|---|
| **Guideline** | **Example** |
| Use the nominative case for pronouns used as subjects. | *He* and *I* saw an accident. |
| Use the objective case for a pronoun used as the object of a preposition. | The problem is between Jim and *me*. |
| Make sure that a verb agrees with its subject in number. | *One* of the books *is* missing. |
| Use adjectives to modify nouns and pronouns; use adverbs to modify verbs, adjectives, and adverbs. | Her speech was *very good.*<br>He was doing *really well.* |

# ACTIVITY 5

## Evaluating a Speaker's Diction and Grammar

Watch an effective public speaker give a speech. Concentrate on the speaker's diction and grammar. Does the speaker use standard American English? How did the speaker's diction and grammar affect the message of the speech? Share your findings with your classmates.

# Using Speaker's Equipment and Materials

## Speaker's Stand

A **speaker's stand,** or **lectern,** is a piece of furniture designed to hold a speaker's notes or manuscript. The lectern may be an elaborate structure made out of wood or a portable boxlike object that sits on a table, or it may resemble a metal music stand. The top is often slightly tilted so that the speaker can easily see his or her notes, which are kept out of sight of the audience.

## HOW TO ▸ Use a Lectern Properly

1. Practice with a lectern until it becomes an aid, not a crutch. Avoid leaning on or clutching the lectern.

2. If you are allowed notes, you may want to rest them on the stand. You may, instead, prefer to hold your note cards in one hand. This method will give you the freedom to move away from the lectern as you give your speech.

3. Look at your notes when you need to, but do not read from them continuously.

4. As you speak, feel free to stand behind the lectern, beside it, or in front of it.

## Microphone

When speaking to a large audience or in a large auditorium, you will probably want to use a **microphone,** which is simply an electronic device for broadcasting sound. In class you may be asked to use a microphone for one of your speeches just for practice.

Microphones are of three basic types.

1. **The Standing Microphone.** A **standing microphone** is a microphone attached to a stand or lectern. Because this type of microphone picks up sounds only from a narrow range, you will need to speak directly into the microphone for it to work. Do not lean over or put your face too close to the microphone, though. Ordinarily, you will want to maintain a distance of eight to twelve inches from the microphone. To be sure that you are speaking from the correct distance and angle, you should practice with a microphone before giving your speech.

While you are speaking, a standing microphone can sometimes become a distraction, since it may tend to limit your movement. In order to learn how to speak comfortably, you will probably need a few practice sessions to become comfortable with using a standing microphone.

2. **The Hand-held Microphone.** A **hand-held microphone** gives you greater freedom of movement. However, it can be difficult to juggle both the microphone and your speech notes. Some hand-held microphones have long cords that may get caught around objects in the room or may cause you to trip.

3. **The Lavaliere or Clip-on Microphone.** A **lavaliere microphone** is much easier to use than a standing or hand-held microphone because it hangs around your neck. A **clip-on microphone** is attached to your clothing in such a way that it remains at the same distance from your mouth and at the same angle. Once you have either type of microphone properly adjusted, you will have considerable freedom of movement.

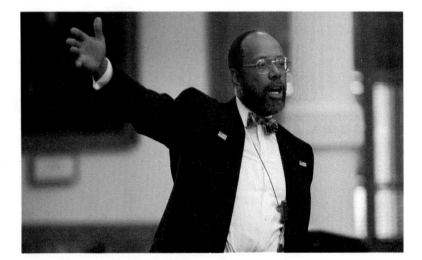

| Practicing with a Microphone | |
|---|---|
| **Situation** | **What to Watch** |
| Pronouncing plosives (*p, b, d, t, k,* and *g*) | The *p* and *b* sounds, especially, can pop and be distorted by a microphone. |
| Pronouncing sibilants (*c, ch, s, th,* and *z*) | The *c* and *s* sounds, especially, can hiss into the microphone. |
| Raising pitch or volume | The microphone may distort sounds or "boom" if your pitch or volume is excessive. |

# ACTIVITY

## 6   Using a Lectern and Microphones

Practice all or a portion of your speech in a classroom that has a lectern. Determine how you will stand at the beginning of your speech. Practice moving away from the lectern and then moving back to it.

If your school has a standing microphone, a hand-held microphone, a clip-on microphone, or all three, practice a part of your speech using one or all of these. For a standing microphone, determine how close to it you should be to achieve the best vocal sound. Find out how much you can move without losing the necessary projection. For a hand-held microphone, determine how close to your mouth it must be to give you the best projection. Walk around with it. Does movement affect your ability to project? For a clip-on microphone, find out how your movements affect the microphone's ability to pick up your voice.

## Audiovisual Materials

**Audiovisual materials** are resources that a speaker uses to clarify or add to the verbal presentation of a speech. Examples include

- audio recordings (cassettes or CDs)
- prerecorded videotapes or videodiscs
- films (usually 8mm or 16mm)
- 35mm slides or 35mm filmstrips
- transparencies
- posters or charts
- multimedia materials (usually stored and presented on a computer)

Audio resources are materials that an audience can hear, such as CDs, records, cassette tapes, or digital sound files stored on a computer. **Visual resources** (sometimes called visual aids) are materials that an audience can see, such as slides, pictures, transparencies, videotapes, and films or animations, graphics, and video images displayed on a computer. In some instances, a person could be considered an audiovisual resource, such as when he or she gives a demonstration or when he or she dresses up in costume to play a particular role.

Even if your time or available materials are limited, you can create your own visual resources by drawing, pasting, or tracing, or by using other common artistic techniques. If you keep the following guidelines in mind, you do not have to be a skilled or talented artist to create an effective visual aid.

# HOW TO > *Make a Visual Aid*

- Identify and select an image or a few words that capture and illustrate an important point of your speech. (See examples on pages 339–340.)

- Make the lettering or images on the visual aid large enough for your audience to see the information clearly, even at a distance.

- Use color to emphasize meaningful details, to show contrast, or to indicate relationships among ideas.

Audio, visual, and multimedia resources can also be created or presented using a computer. Usually, a speaker will present this information using some type of presentation software to put together what is sometimes called a "computer slide show."

The computer can display visual or multimedia materials on its monitor screen or—using a liquid crystal display (LCD) panel or some other type of image-projection system—can project images from the computer onto a large display surface, such as a projection screen. Many types of audiovisual materials can be digitized or downloaded and then stored on the computer to be displayed (with or without audio) at the exact time the speaker wants the audience to view it or hear it.

Do not use audiovisual or multimedia aids during your speech unless you actually want your audience to be looking at or listening to this material. If you display your resource materials before you are ready to make reference to them in your speech, or if you have materials that you pass around before your speech, your audience is more likely to pay attention to these supplementary materials than to listen attentively to you. Therefore, carefully consider the timing and the manner in which you reveal audiovisual materials to your audience.

In addition, you should think about the amount of audiovisual resources you will use. You should use just enough material to illustrate or to emphasize the most important points of information in your speech clearly and vividly. If you have more material than you really need, your audience is likely to become confused or lose their focus on your most significant points.

## Questions About Using Audiovisual Materials

**Will you save time by using an audiovisual aid?** If using an audiovisual aid will save you time in presenting your information, you should probably use it.

**Will an audiovisual aid help you to clarify a point?** Some ideas are easily explained verbally, but others need audiovisual resources to clarify them.

**Will an audiovisual aid help the audience to remember a point?** Not every point in your speech is equally important. Decide which points in your speech will be most clearly and economically emphasized by audiovisual materials.

## ACTIVITY 7

### Analyzing a Speaker's Use of Audiovisual Materials

Watch a television broadcast or a speech in which the speaker uses audiovisual materials. Determine whether these materials are appropriate for the speech. Are they well prepared? Are they used effectively? Would the speech have been as effective without these materials? How does the speaker use these materials—to create interest, to explain, to give examples, or to achieve some other purpose(s)? Share your findings with your classmates.

**FLOWCHART**

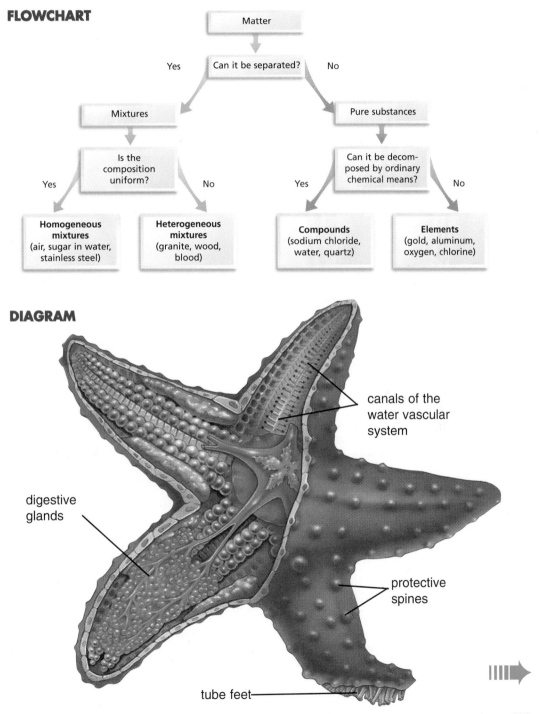

Matter

Can it be separated?

Yes → Mixtures

No → Pure substances

Is the composition uniform?

Yes → **Homogeneous mixtures** (air, sugar in water, stainless steel)

No → **Heterogeneous mixtures** (granite, wood, blood)

Can it be decomposed by ordinary chemical means?

Yes → **Compounds** (sodium chloride, water, quartz)

No → **Elements** (gold, aluminum, oxygen, chlorine)

**DIAGRAM**

canals of the water vascular system

digestive glands

protective spines

tube feet

## LINE GRAPH

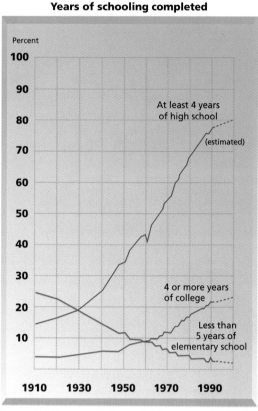

**Years of schooling completed**

Percent

At least 4 years of high school

(estimated)

4 or more years of college

Less than 5 years of elementary school

1910 1930 1950 1970 1990

Sources: U.S. Bureau of the Census; U.S. Department of Education

## PIE GRAPH

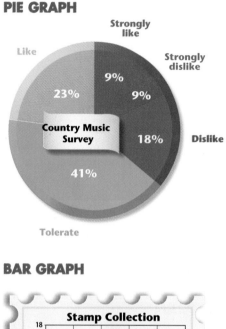

Strongly like

Like

Strongly dislike

9%

23%

9%

Country Music Survey

18% Dislike

41%

Tolerate

## BAR GRAPH

**Stamp Collection**

Number of stamps

18
16
14
12
10
8
6
4
2
0

Below 60 | 60—69 | 70—79 | 80—89 | 90—100

Age of stamps (in years)

## INFORMATION CHART

| Wind Speed in Miles per Hour | 10 | 20 | 30 |
|---|---|---|---|
| Air Temperature 20°F | 3 | –10 | –18 |
| Air Temperature 10°F | –9 | –24 | –33 |
| Air Temperature 0°F | –22 | –39 | –49 |
| Air Temperature –10°F | –34 | –53 | –64 |

# Controlling Other Factors That Affect Delivery

Stage fright and nonverbal, vocal, and verbal messages are not the only factors that may affect the delivery of your speech. You will also need to consider several other factors, such as your timing, your response to audience feedback, your need to handle distractions, and your response to any unexpected events that may affect the delivery of your speech.

## Timing

**Timing** is the controlled pacing of a speech. You time your delivery in two ways: by pacing your delivery so that it fits within a specific time limit and by pacing your delivery of particular words or phrases to give them special attention.

During your rehearsals, you will get an approximate sense of the length of your speech. Experience will help you to judge whether the actual delivery of your speech is likely to take more or less time than your rehearsals take.

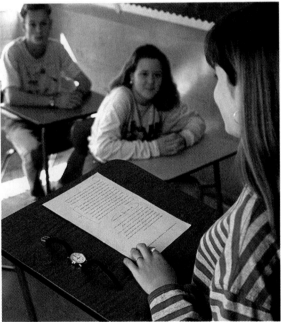

During your speech, your teacher or a classmate may use "countdown" cards so that you can keep track of the time remaining. For example, if the time limit for your speech is five minutes, your timekeeper may hold up a card numbered 4 after the first minute, 3 after two minutes, and so on—to tell you how much time you have left. If you have no timekeeper, you can set a watch on the lectern so that you can glance at it occasionally.

Timing also means pacing your delivery of specific material in your speech to achieve maximum effect. Consider Henny Youngman's old one-line joke, "Take my wife—please." As many times as he tells this joke, it still gets a laugh because of his timing, the way he pauses before he says "please." As you gain experience as a speaker, you will learn how to time the delivery of key sentences in your speech so that you will get the maximum effect out of them.

## Audience Feedback

One test of effective speech delivery is how well the speaker reacts to audience feedback. Effective speakers know when to

- repeat an idea
- talk louder or softer
- speed up or slow down
- shorten discussion of a point that the audience apparently understands
- add to a point the audience has some difficulty grasping

These decisions should be based on how an audience is reacting to a speech as it is being delivered. You cannot make these decisions during rehearsal because you are not practicing in front of the audience that will hear the speech.

At first, you will probably concentrate primarily on delivering the material in the way in which you have rehearsed it. However, with more experience, you will develop the skill of using the audience as a monitor of how you are doing.

## Distractions

In the middle of a speech, noises or interruptions can draw attention away from your speech. Here are some suggestions.

- **Annoying, continuing background noises.** You will have to deal with this type of noise. For instance, you should ignore an air conditioner if it is not excessively loud. If a lawn mower is being operated right outside a window, you will have to close the window or talk louder.

- **Momentary noisy distractions.** Pause until the noise subsides, and then go on as if nothing had happened.
- **Longer noisy distractions.** If you anticipate that the noise will last more than a few seconds, announce that you are going to pause until it subsides. Usually, you will be able to pick up right where you left off. You may find it useful to summarize the point you were making before the distraction and then go on.
- **Hecklers.** Occasionally in a public speech, you will encounter a **heckler,** a person who tries purposely to disturb you while you are speaking. Do not get excited, and do not get into an argument with the heckler. In many situations an audience will quiet a heckler without your having to do anything.

## Unexpected Events

Murphy's Law states that anything that can go wrong will go wrong. Nowhere is this "law" more true than in public speaking. Therefore, a well-prepared speaker leaves nothing to chance and never assumes that everything will go as expected.

If you can face unexpected events with a sense of humor, you can overcome them. If your audience is interested in your speech, they will be willing to tolerate a small amount of distraction.

On October 14, 1912, intrepid speaker Theodore Roosevelt persevered in the face of a serious unexpected event—he was shot. Despite his pain, he insisted on giving his speech. His manuscript, with bullet-holes, is shown below.

Although you cannot anticipate all the frustrating things that might happen, you should consider what you would do in the case of the following unexpected events.

**Dropping Material.**  Whether you drop two or three note cards or a stack of papers, try to go on with your speech as if nothing had happened. If you must retrieve the material, do so as gracefully as possible and continue as if nothing had happened.

**Speaking Without Key Material.**  After starting your speech, you may realize that you do not have with you an important bit of material you need for your speech.

- If the material is readily available—such as at your desk— and is a necessary part of your speech, then excuse yourself to the audience, get the material, return to the lectern, and go on as if nothing has happened.
- If the material is unavailable, either skip any reference to it or think of a way to present the same information in some other manner. If the missing material is a visual aid, for instance, you might give a detailed description of what it would have shown.

**Forgetting a Key Point.**  Anyone is likely to unintentionally leave out some part of a speech. Unless what you have omitted is vital to your audience's understanding, go on without it. However, if the omitted material is vital to the meaning of the speech, then you need to make a comment such as "I forgot to mention a very important point. Let me go over it with you, tell you where it fits, and then go on."

## ACTIVITY 8

### Practicing Delivery

With two or three partners, take turns coping with factors that can affect your delivery of a speech. To practice timing, select a quotation from Bartlett's *Familiar Quotations* and present it to your partners as if you were delivering a short speech. Be sure to pause and add emphasis to convey the meaning of the words as expressively as possible.

Have your partners give you feedback on your performance. For example, they may ask you to repeat a word or to speak more slowly. Respond appropriately to your listeners' feedback.

Take turns practicing how to deal with distractions, such as a pretended interruption for an announcement over the loudspeaker. Discuss with classmates the strategies that you feel were most effective.

# Evaluating Your Delivery

After you finish giving your speech, you should evaluate your delivery. What do you think were your greatest strengths? What do you think were your weaknesses? Use the Guidelines for Delivering a Speech, below, as a basis for making your evaluation. You may want to have one or two of your classmates help you in making your analysis. Your teacher may give you oral or written comments that you can use, too.

## ACTIVITY 9

### Evaluating Delivery of an Extemporaneous Speech

Using the extemporaneous method, deliver a formal speech to your class. Use the Guidelines for Delivering a Speech listed below to evaluate your delivery. Then have the members of your audience identify two aspects of your delivery that you might improve and two aspects of your delivery that they feel are your greatest strengths.

## GUIDELINES
### for Delivering a Speech

- Do I approach the front of the room with confidence?
- Is my appearance appropriate?
- Do I show enthusiasm?
- Is my speaking free of excessive vocalized pauses?
- Do I look at the audience as I talk?
- Are my facial expressions appropriate, and my gestures and movements smooth and natural?
- Are my articulation and pronunciation correct?
- Do I stay within the time limit?
- Do I use the speaker's stand well?
- Do I handle unexpected distractions with ease?
- Do I use audiovisual materials effectively?

# PROVIDERS OF INFORMATION

### Guiding Lights

When visiting a tourist attraction, many people count on tour guides to present accurate, concise, and entertaining information. Tour guides must be prepared to answer many questions and adjust their presentations to accommodate a wide variety of audiences.

### Characteristics of a Good Tour Guide

A good tour guide

1. delivers information clearly and appropriately

2. looks and sounds professional, knowledgeable, and enthusiastic

3. uses eye contact, facial expressions, and other nonverbal communication skills effectively

4. adjusts delivery rate, timing, and volume as needed

5. overcomes distractions and unexpected occurrences

### Meet the Tour Guide

Tour guide Lisa Anderson always shows up at Inner Space Caverns ready for work. "I find I can focus on my audience's needs when I am thoroughly prepared," she says. "During the tour, I try to maintain eye contact with the tourists to be sure I'm holding their interest, and I make adjustments in my presentation as necessary."

*Lisa M. Anderson*

## ACTIVITY

### Situation

You have been chosen to give a new student a thorough five-minute tour of your school. You will have to give this tour during the lunch period when hundreds of students are in the halls and in the cafeteria.

### Preparation

Begin by listing the various things a student at your school must know, such as certain rules, schedules, and important locations, as well as other practical information. Then add some helpful hints and interesting facts to the essentials. Describe the route the tour will take, and list helpful items you will offer the student (a campus map, for example).

### Analysis and Assessment

Make an outline of your tour, keeping your time limit in mind. Refer to the outline as you present the tour in class. Ask your classmates if they think your tour would be effective.

# S★U★M★M★A★R★Y

**PRESENTING YOUR SPEECH** requires effective delivery. There are four methods of delivering a speech: impromptu, manuscript, memorized, and extemporaneous.

- **Control stage fright** by reminding yourself that nearly all speakers are nervous, that audiences are seldom aware of a speaker's nervousness, and that with greater speaking experience, you will learn to control nervousness. Plan and practice your speech carefully. While speaking, you may feel normal symptoms of nervousness. You should ignore them and concentrate on your message.

- **Improve nonverbal behavior** by making sure you present a good appearance, by keeping eye contact with the audience, by maintaining appropriate facial expressions, by using appropriate gestures, and by maintaining good posture.

- **Improve vocal skills** by showing enthusiasm for your topic; by working to eliminate vocalized pauses; and by improving your articulation, pronunciation, and enunciation. Use an appropriate volume, rate, and pitch.

- **Improve verbal messages** by paying attention to your diction and grammar.

- **Use speaker's materials** efficiently. Practice with a speaker's stand, or lectern, and with the various types of microphones. Prepare audiovisual materials, if appropriate.

- **Control other factors that affect delivery** of your speech through practice. Develop a sense of timing, adjust your delivery to respond to audience feedback, and learn to anticipate distractions and unexpected events.

- **Evaluate your delivery** after giving a speech, concentrating on specific areas in which you might make improvements.

## Review Questions

1. One way of delivering a speech is the impromptu method. What are three other ways of delivering a speech?
2. Which of the ways of delivering a speech allows for the most adaptation to the audience?
3. What are five techniques that you can use to reduce nervousness before giving a speech?
4. What are five kinds of nervous sensations that speakers may experience when giving their first few public speeches?
5. Your appearance has a crucial effect on the success of your speech. Why is appearance such an important aspect of nonverbal behavior?
6. Facial expression is another important nonverbal behavior. What is meant by "conflicting expression"?
7. What are vocalized pauses? What is the effect of too many vocalized pauses in a speech?
8. Beginning speakers often have trouble knowing what to do with their notes when they are speaking. What two ways can you handle your notes during your speech?
9. Microphones help you to be heard clearly; however, they can also cause problems. How can a standing microphone cause a distraction?
10. What are three examples of audiovisual materials?

## Discussion Questions

1. Do you believe that most people are nervous about speaking in public? Why do people feel the way they do about public speaking? Working in a small group, share your opinions. On what evidence do you base those opinions?
2. Identify and discuss the kinds of behavior that you find most annoying in public speakers. Why are these kinds of behavior especially annoying?
3. Identify and discuss the kinds of behavior that impress you most in a speaker. Why do they impress you? How might you adopt the behaviors you find particularly impressive?
4. Discuss what you should do if the following situations were to occur while you were giving a speech: (a) you drop material; (b) a loud noise occurs outside; (c) you discover that you have left material at home; (d) you forget to make a certain point.
5. Ralph Waldo Emerson wrote, "There are men whose language is strong and defying enough, yet their eyes and their actions ask leave of other men to live." Working in a small group, discuss the meaning of the quotation. Then discuss how it relates to your own delivery of a speech.

# ACTIVITIES

1. **Identifying Ways of Coping with Nervousness.** Talk with people who give speeches as part of their jobs. Are they nervous before they speak? If so, under what circumstances? How do they cope with that nervousness? Compile a class list of ways to cope with nervousness. Copy this list in your communication journal.

2. **Analyzing Others' Delivery.** While others are giving speeches in class, make notes on their delivery. After everyone has given a speech, review your notes. Identify specific behavior that helped each speaker be more effective and specific behavior that caused the speaker to be less effective. Share your findings with your classmates.

3. **Analyzing Your Own Delivery.**
   A. After you have given your first class speech, use the Guidelines for Delivering a Speech (page 345) to analyze your delivery. Identify your strengths and weaknesses. Once you have arrived at some conclusions about your delivery, ask at least three of your classmates to comment on your conclusions.

   B. If your school has videotape equipment, videotape all or a part of one of your final practice sessions or your actual delivery to the class. Use the Guidelines for Delivering a Speech (page 345) to analyze your delivery. Discuss your conclusions with classmates who saw your delivery.

4. **Analyzing a Professional Speaker's Delivery.**
   A. Watch a professional speaker deliver a speech. Make a list of any vocal or verbal behavior that interferes with or adds to the speaker's effectiveness. Share your findings with your classmates.

B. Look at each of these photographs. Make a list of the nonverbal behaviors that you think might add to or detract from the impact each of these speakers would have on his or her audience. Share your findings with your classmates.

**5. Using Audiovisuals.** Working in a small group, develop a list of informative speech topics or use a list that you've already made. Select ten topics, and list at least five audiovisuals to use with each topic. Try to come up with a variety of materials that a speaker could prepare, such as photographs, illustrations, and charts or graphs of statistical information. In addition, list manufactured materials that a speaker might use, such as tape recordings, compact discs, videocassettes, slides, and filmstrips. You may wish to talk to the media specialist at your school about the availability of such materials.

**6. Preparing for the Unexpected.** An unexpected event, whether it is a fire drill or a simple memory lapse, can fluster a beginning speaker. To recover gracefully from such an event, you need to be prepared. But how can you prepare yourself for the unexpected? One way is to act out "What-if?" situations.

With a small group of classmates as your audience, deliver a speech that you've prepared or given before. It is the job of your group to try to fluster you. They might rearrange or remove your notes, make noises, appear to be asleep, or even heckle you. As each person in the group delivers his or her speech, try coming up with new and different ways to distract the speaker. Remember, the more situations you can imagine and act out, the better prepared you'll be when the unexpected happens.

**7. Inventing Effective Gestures.** Long ago, students of elocution (public speaking) were required to learn and to use a number of standard gestures when they gave speeches or recited pieces of literature in public. These gestures were often quite formal and theatrical: They had to be. Before the invention of the microphone and loudspeaker, an orator could not be certain that everyone in a large auditorium was always able to hear the speech. By watching the speaker's gestures and facial expressions, people in the audience could fill in any parts of the speech they hadn't heard.

Here are two illustrations from an elocution textbook published in 1874. What do you think these gestures mean?

The gesture shown on the left expresses anger and determination. The gesture shown on the right shows the first of a series of seven items that the speaker will mention, with gesture to match, in order of each item's importance.

Working on your own, invent five gestures for speakers today to use. Remember, gestures can reveal a speaker's attitude to a subject, his or her physical position in relation to the subject, and even the relationships among various examples or ideas. Demonstrate each of your gestures to a partner to find out if the meaning is as clear to another person as it is to you.

# EVERYDAY COMMUNICATION

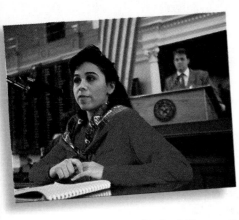

### Situation
You have been asked to speak before a group you belong to—perhaps a scout troop, a sports team, a hobby club, or your family—about methods you find effective in controlling stage fright.

### Problem
Write a ten-minute speech and deliver it to your classmates.

### Assessing Your Skill
Discuss with your classmates the methods you have recommended. In what ways are your methods different from or similar to those discussed on pages 321–323?

# COMMUNICATION IN THE WORKPLACE

### Background
You are working in a hotel and an impatient guest stops you in the hall to ask for help. You are in a hurry yourself because you must be in a staff meeting in the manager's office in five minutes.

### Preparing to Do the Job
Describe the situation. What is the guest's question? How will you respond to the guest so that your reply is courteous and helpful, yet brief? Is the guest a child or an adult? Is the person alone?

### Testing Your Skill
Write a one- or two-page dialogue of your exchange with the guest. Use good grammar and diction, and don't forget to include descriptions of appropriate nonverbal behavior. With a classmate, practice your delivery and timing. Present the dialogue to the class, and ask your classmates for feedback on how well you handled the situation.

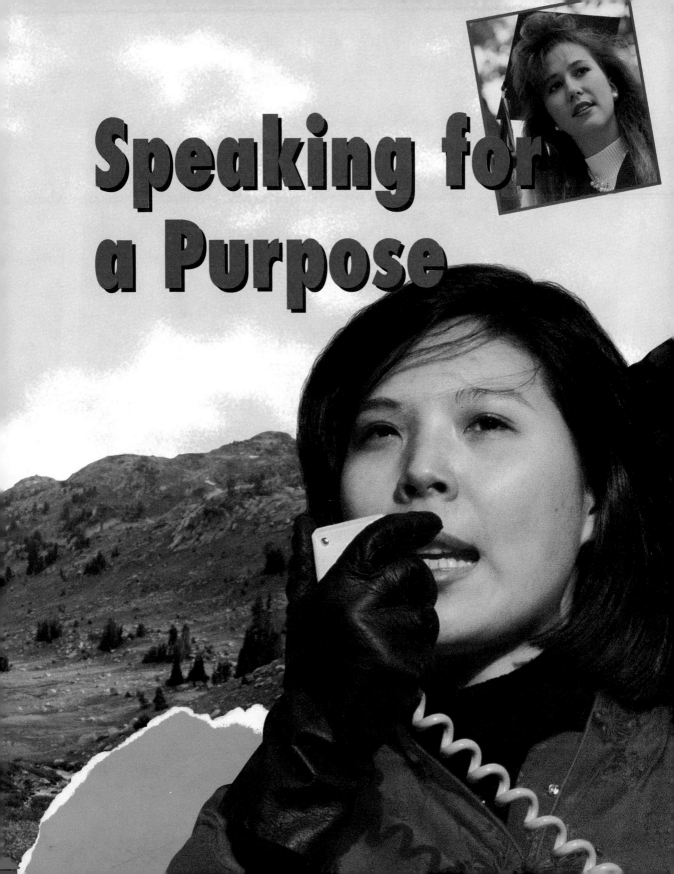

# Speaking for
# a Purpose

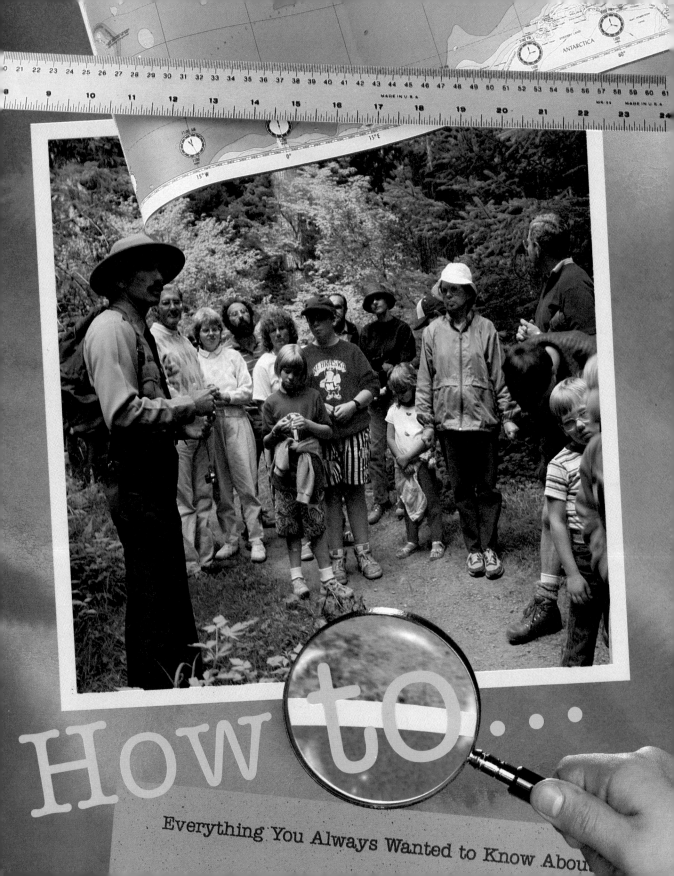

How to...

Everything You Always Wanted to Know About

▼

# Speaking to Inform

**14**

✔ 1.
✔ 2.
✔ 3.
✔ 4.
✔ 5.

## What Is an Informative Speech?

An **informative speech** provides information to an audience. The aims of an informative speech are to help your audience to understand and to remember the information you are presenting.

The two most common types of informative speeches are

- the **expository speech,** which gives information about a specific subject
- the **process speech,** or how-to speech, which explains how to do something, how to make something, or how something works

Some common informative speaking situations include a college recruiter telling graduating seniors about scholarships, a paramedic explaining how to perform CPR, a firefighter telling about household safety tips, and a student reporting on advertising in presidential elections.

In this chapter, you will learn how to develop both types of informative speeches. In addition, you will find suggestions about ways to present information that will increase your audience's understanding.

# Planning an Informative Speech

## Choosing a Topic

For any type of informative speech, you should select a topic that you are interested in and that you already know something about. The following charts list appropriate topics for the two types of informative speeches.

| Possible Topics for Expository Speeches |
| --- |
| • Education of women in colonial America |
| • The influence of African masks on modern sculpture |
| • Changes in the ozone layer above Antarctica |
| • Cliff dwellings of the Anasazi |
| • Three types of extrasensory perception |
| • Cartoon images in American pop art |

| Possible Topics for Process Speeches | |
| --- | --- |
| How to Do Something | • How to use a compass<br>• How to select in-line skates<br>• How to repair a bicycle hand brake |
| How to Make Something | • How to prepare healthy snacks<br>• How to build a bookcase<br>• How to make origami flowers |
| How Something Works | • How an automatic teller machine works<br>• How a microwave works<br>• How a helicopter flies |

In some cases, you will not be able to choose a topic of your own. You may be assigned a broad subject area from which you will be expected to select a specific topic, or you may be assigned a topic that needs to be limited further.

Always look carefully at a topic you have been assigned to see if it has been limited to a manageable size. If the topic is too broad, consider particular features or a specific perspective from which the topic can be examined. [For more information about limiting a topic, see pages 217–219.]

## Knowing Your Purpose

Your general purpose in an expository or a process speech is to inform your audience. Your specific purpose relates to your topic and to the specific information you want to convey. [For more information on stating a specific purpose and writing a thesis statement, see pages 221–224 of Chapter 9.]

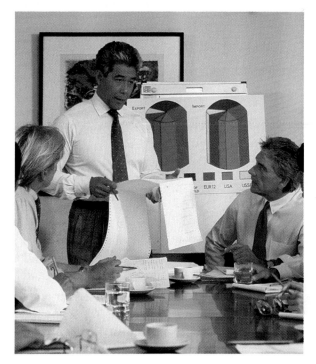

EXAMPLES:

1. For an expository speech, you might state your specific purpose as "I want to explain the three major steps in the evolution of the computer."
2. For a process speech, you could state your specific purpose as "I want to explain how to perform a soccer-style place kick."

## Gathering Information

The more convincingly you can show your listeners that you know about your topic, the more likely they are to pay attention and to remember what you say.

You might begin gathering information by thinking of what you already know about your topic. To locate more information, use library resources, interview a knowledgeable person, survey a group of people, or write a request letter to obtain information. [For more help on sources of information, see pages 242–255 of Chapter 10.]

# ACTIVITY
## 1
### Developing a Topic for an Informative Speech

Make a list of five subjects that interest you. Then select one and limit it to a suitable topic (see pages 217–219). Is the topic more appropriate for an expository speech or a process speech? State a specific purpose for your speech, and list at least two sources of information you would use to gather material for your speech.

# Preparing to Speak

## Preparing Your Introduction

Introductions for informative speeches can vary in length depending on the topic, the audience's interest level, and the audience's knowledge about the subject. Keep in mind that an introduction for an informative speech should

- attract the audience's attention
- focus attention on the subject
- gain the audience's goodwill

You can use any of the common methods for beginning a speech—a startling statement, a question, a quotation, a story, or a personal reference—in an informative speech. [See pages 271–273 of Chapter 11 for a discussion of these methods.] You might try different introductions and then choose the one that you think would most appeal to your audience.

**EXAMPLE:** Latice chose a topic for a process speech—how to fold napkins. She thought of two approaches to interest others: the first based on people's curiosity and the second based on people's desire to please others.

➤ Have you ever seen and admired the special ways napkins are folded for elegant dinners shown on television programs? Have you wanted to know how to make beautifully folded napkins? Actually, napkin folding is not as difficult as it may seem. In the next few minutes, I will show you two of the most attractive ways of folding napkins.

➤ Think of a time when your family prepared a meal for a special occasion. Did you ever wonder what you could have done to give that meal a memorable touch? One way is to use a technique seen at elegant dinners on television programs: Fold the napkins in a unique, formal manner.

Reprinted with permission of the authors from *Stockworth: An American CEO*, by Sterling and Selesnick.

*J*ot down a brief description of a speaking situation in which you were interested in listening to information about a topic. Why did you want to learn more about this specific topic? In what ways did the introductions contribute to your interest?

## Organizing the Body of an Informative Speech

You can select from a variety of ways to organize the body of your informative speech. [For a general discussion of these methods, see Chapter 11.] The following list gives specific suggestions about applying these methods to organize an informative speech.

**1. Chronological Order.** **Chronological order** arranges details or events according to the order in which they occurred in time. Chronological order is often useful for expository speeches that present a history of something, as in the following outline.

**Specific Purpose:** I want to explain the three major steps in the evolution of the computer.

    **I.** The first electronic computers used vacuum tubes and were so large that each took up an entire room.
    **II.** The second electronic computers used transistors and were considerably smaller than the earlier computers.
   **III.** The third generation of computers uses microchips and has been further reduced in size.

Chronological order is also used in process speeches that explain procedures or events step by step.

To make remembering easier for your audience, group the steps in chronological order under broad headings. Your audience members can remember four main points, each with four subdivisions, much better than they can remember sixteen main points.

**EXAMPLE:** The first outline in the chart on page 361 shows a series of twelve steps. The second outline shows how these steps can be grouped under major headings.

**Specific Purpose:** I want to explain how a dishwasher works.

   **I.** In the first step, the drain is closed and soapy water fills the lower portion of the washer.
  **II.** In the second step, an electric coil heats the soapy water.
 **III.** In the third step, the heated, soapy water is siphoned through rotating blades and sprayed onto the dishes.
  **IV.** In the fourth step, the soapy water is drained, and clean water is heated and then used to rinse the dishes.

**Specific Purpose:** I want to explain how to perform a soccer-style place kick.

<table>
<tr><td>

**WEAK: 12 steps**

I. Spot the ball on the tee.
II. Face the goal posts.
III. Take three steps back.
IV. Take two steps left.
V. Stand facing right goal post.
VI. Take three steps toward the ball.
VII. Contact ground on left heel.
VIII. Swing right leg through.
IX. Keep toe pointed.
X. Lock knee.
XI. Strike ball at a spot one third up from ground.
XII. Kick with instep.

</td><td>

**BETTER: 4 steps with subdivisions**

I. Spot the ball on the tee.
II. Mark off steps.
   A. Face the goal posts.
   B. Take three steps back and two to the left.
   C. Stand facing right goal post.
III. Step toward the ball.
   A. Take three steps, beginning with left foot.
   B. On third step, contact ground with left heel.
IV. Kick the ball.
   A. Swing right leg through.
   B. Keep toe pointed.
   C. Lock knee.
   D. Strike ball at a spot one third up from ground.
   E. Kick with instep.

</td></tr>
</table>

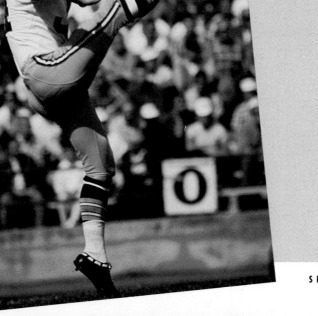

**2. Topical Order.**   In **topical order,** a topic is broken down into its parts and then arranged in an order determined by the speaker and stated in the specific purpose. This is the most common method for organizing expository speeches.

> **Specific Purpose:** I want to explain the three major types of extrasensory perception.
>   **I.** One type is telepathy.
>  **II.** A second type is clairvoyance.
> **III.** A third type is precognition.

Topical order is also used for a process speech that addresses more than one main point. In this method of organization, the main points are arranged in topical order, and then their subdivisions are arranged chronologically.

> **Specific Purpose:** I want to explain two simple but attractive ways of folding napkins.
>   **I.** One way is the fan fold.
>       **A.** The first step is . . .
>       **B.** The second step is . . .
>       **C.** The third step is . . .
>  **II.** A second way is the turtle fold.
>       **A.** The first step is . . .
>       **B.** The second step is . . .
>       **C.** The third step is . . .

**3. Spatial Order.**   In **spatial order,** details are arranged according to their position in space. This arrangement is often used for descriptions.

> **Specific Purpose:** I want to explain what a typical word-processing unit looks like.
>   **I.** Immediately in front of the operator is a standard computer keyboard.
>  **II.** Directly above the computer keyboard is a monitor screen.
> **III.** Below or to the right of the computer keyboard is a disk drive.

Animal Crackers by Roger Bollen. Reprinted by permission: Tribune Media Services.

**4. Climactic Order.** **Climactic order** arranges items according to their order of importance, usually starting with the least important item of information and ending with the item of information that is the most important.

**Specific Purpose:** I want to explain three requirements for being a good football coach.
  **I.** A good coach must have an ability to recognize raw talent in new players.
  **II.** More important, a good coach must understand the mechanics of the sport.
  **III.** Most important, a good coach must be able to motivate players to do their best.

**5. Cause-and-Effect Order.** In **cause-and-effect order,** information is arranged to show causes or conditions and the effects or results of those causes or conditions.

**Specific Purpose:** I want to explain the relationship between high interest rates for consumers and the onset of a recession in the general economy.
  **I.** High interest rates for consumers make consumers more reluctant to borrow and drive down consumer demand for financing to make purchases.
  **II.** A reduction in consumer purchases calls for a decrease in production of manufactured goods, which then causes more unemployment.
  **III.** The result is a recession, or a downward trend in the overall economy.

**6. Comparison-and-Contrast Order.** In **comparison-and-contrast order,** items of information are arranged to show the similarities and differences between the items.

**Specific Purpose:** As pets, dogs and cats are different in two ways but have one trait in common.
   **I.** Dogs tend to show more devotion to owners than most cats do.
   **II.** Cats generally show more independence and self-sufficiency than most dogs do.
   **III.** Both dogs and cats can be affectionate pets.

## Preparing Your Conclusion

The conclusion of an informative speech usually includes a summary of the main points. [See Chapter 11 for more on conclusions.]

**EXAMPLE:** The expository speech on extrasensory perception, outlined on page 362, might end with this statement: "So we can see that extrasensory perception includes telepathy, clairvoyance, and precognition."

Since a process speech aims to have the audience master the key steps of the process, an effective conclusion often includes a summary of those steps.

**EXAMPLE:** The speech about how high interest rates contribute to starting a recession might conclude with the statement, "When high interest rates reduce consumer spending, the decrease in sales causes cutbacks in production, resulting in layoffs and the beginning of a recession."

Many speakers end with a quotation, an anecdote, or a final thought that makes the conclusion more memorable.

# ACTIVITY
## 2
### Preparing Your Informative Speech

Using the topic and the specific purpose you developed in Activity 1 (page 357), prepare an introduction for your speech. Next, decide which type of organization will best fit your topic and purpose. Be prepared to explain your decision. For a process speech, list the main points of the information or the main steps in the process. If your list has more than five steps, group the steps into categories. Finally, prepare a conclusion for your speech.

# Adapting Your Speech to Suit Your Audience

To help your listeners understand and recall the information you present, you will often need to adapt your speech to suit their experience, needs, and interests.

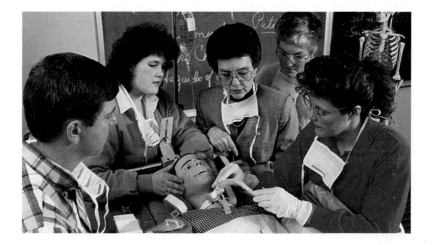

## Experience

Since your listeners may lose interest if they cannot figure out what your information has to do with them, you will need to relate your speech to your audience's experience. Some topics are easy to relate to an audience's needs and interests—for instance, telling high school seniors how to improve their SAT scores.

When your audience is not knowledgeable about your topic, you should relate it to a topic that they may know more about. For example, an expository speech about building the Egyptian pyramids might be more interesting to an audience if you compare ancient and modern building methods.

## Familiarity

Your audience is unlikely to be familiar with all of the information you plan to include in your speech. You might poll some of the members of your audience before giving your speech to find out the extent of their knowledge.

**EXAMPLE:** Rico, who raises show dogs, had planned to give a speech on the different types of dogs. He had assumed everyone in class knew that dogs were classified into six groups:

working dogs, terriers, sporting dogs, nonsporting dogs, hounds, and toys. However, when he asked several of his classmates, most of them could not name the categories. Rico therefore made sure that he included more background information in his speech.

## Technical Knowledge

Avoid using details and terms that are meaningful only to an expert. Unless you are actually talking to an audience of specialists about your topic, adapt the level of technical language in your speech to the audience's level of understanding.

**EXAMPLE:** If you are speaking to a group of electronic hobbyists, you can use technical terms to explain how a picture is formed on a television screen. However, for other audiences, you might simply say that the picture tube shoots beams of light onto the television screen in patterns that create pictures.

## Details

Especially with process speeches, you will need to include enough details to explain the procedure clearly and comprehensively. Your audience may not know how to perform the process you are explaining, so do not assume that they will be able to notice or to supply missing details.

**EXAMPLE:** A group of complete beginners might have problems understanding this explanation of how to check the oil level in a car:

> To check the oil level, remove the dipstick, wipe it clean, reinsert it, and remove it again. Read the level on the dipstick to see if you need to add oil.

Your inexperienced listeners may not know (1) what a dipstick is and (2) how to find it. Here is an example of a more complete explanation:

> To check the oil level, first find and remove the dipstick, a long, thin piece of metal with a handle (usually a loop) that goes into the engine itself. On many engines, the dipstick is in plain view, but on some models, you must look for it. Remove the dipstick and wipe it clean on an oil rag or a paper towel. Then reinsert it and remove it again. The oil will leave a line on the dipstick. If the line is near the "Full" mark, you have no problem. If it is near the "Add" mark, though, you need to add oil.

## Essential Steps

In a process speech, take care not to overwhelm your audience by telling every possible detail of the process. Include just enough details so that the information is clear.

**EXAMPLE:** A speech on how to bowl might include the following steps:

> Hold the ball in front of you in your right hand. As you take a short, sliding step with your right foot, push the ball out in front of you. On your second step, begin a pendulum swing with the ball. By your third step, the ball should have swung behind you. On your fourth and final step, swing the ball forward and slide on your left foot. Release the ball as it passes your leg. Let your right arm continue to swing forward in your follow-through.

This explanation focuses only on essentials. If you tried to include every movement of every part of a bowler's body, you would risk confusing your listeners.

## ACTIVITY 3

### Considering Your Audience

For an audience survey, prepare three or four questions about the information you plan to present in your speech. Include technical terms and major concepts you want to discuss. Ask various people in your school to answer the questions. Then write a paragraph explaining what you have learned and what adjustments you should make to adapt your speech to your audience's level of understanding.

# Helping Listeners Retain Information

You can use a number of methods and devices to help your audience understand and remember the information you are presenting.

**1. Mnemonic Devices.** A **mnemonic device** helps the memory by providing easy-to-remember associations.

| Mnemonic Devices | |
|---|---|
| **Type** | **Examples** |
| **Rhyme**—a short poem or rhymed phrase | In fourteen hundred and ninety-two, Columbus sailed the ocean blue. *(to remember date of Columbus's voyage)* |
| **Acronym**—a word made out of the first letters of the words in a phrase or the items in a list | H.O.M.E.S. *(to remember the names of the five Great Lakes:* **H***uron,* **O***ntario,* **M***ichigan,* **E***rie, and* **S***uperior)* |

**2. Audiovisual Materials.** **Audiovisual materials** are resources that a speaker uses to

- save time in explanation
- clarify a point
- help an audience remember important material

Sometimes you can find audiovisual materials—such as charts, diagrams, photographs, cassette tapes, graphs, or maps—already prepared. For example, you may obtain audiovisual materials through your local, state, or national government agencies. You can also make suitable visuals yourself. [See Chapter 13, page 336, for more about making visual materials.]

**3. Demonstrations.** In a **demonstration,** a speaker performs the steps of a process to help listeners understand it and learn how to perform it themselves. A speaker might also ask a well-qualified person to demonstrate. For a speech on giving artificial respiration, for example, you could ask a paramedic to demonstrate while you explain the process.

Using a demonstration is appropriate when

- the process to be demonstrated is relatively simple and has a manageable number of steps
- the demonstrator is able to complete the demonstration smoothly
- the audience can see everything that is being done

PEANUTS reprinted by permission of UFS, Inc.

In a **partial demonstration,** either some of the parts of the demonstration are already completed or the size of items is exaggerated so the audience can see them clearly.

EXAMPLES:

1. To show how to patch a hole in plasterboard, you could avoid delay by bringing two containers with premeasured amounts of water and dry plaster and demonstrating how to mix them. While giving more details about the mixture, you could show a third container with the proper mixture ready to use. Then you could go on to your next step.

2. To show how to sew a button on a coat, you might use items of an exaggerated size: a cardboard button about the diameter of a dinner plate, and a sharpened pencil with string tied to the end to represent the needle and thread. Then everyone in your audience could see the process.

## ACTIVITY 4

### Preparing a Memory Device

Using the topic you began to prepare in Activity 2 on page 364, create a device to help your audience understand and remember information about your topic. Be prepared to explain how this memory device would help you present information more effectively than you could with words alone.

# Delivering Your Speech

Any speech will be more effective if it is delivered well. [In preparing to deliver your informative speech, keep in mind the guidelines discussed in Chapter 13.]

**1. Credibility.**   A speaker's **credibility** is the amount of trust and belief the speaker inspires in an audience. You want to establish yourself as a speaker whom the audience can trust to give accurate information. One way to do this is to tell the audience a little about your background or experience to let your audience know what makes you qualified to talk about your topic. Be thoroughly prepared, but if you do not know something or if experts are still debating a point, freely admit this.

**2. Enthusiasm.**   Be enthusiastic about your topic. Your audience will probably find it difficult to become excited about the topic you are speaking about if you do not seem to find it important or interesting. The more enthusiasm you show, the more likely you are to get and to hold the audience's attention.

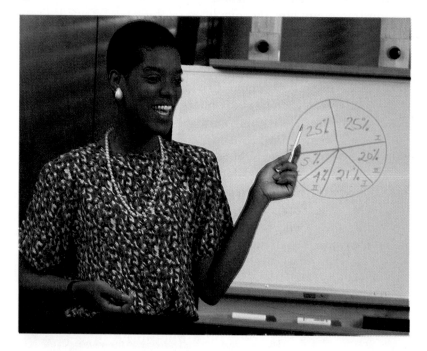

**3. Eye Contact.**   Establish eye contact with your listeners. If you look at the members of your audience, they will look at you. If you fail to establish eye contact, the members of the audience will let their eyes—and their attention—wander. [See Chapter 13 for more information about eye contact.]

**4. Vocal Variety and Emphasis.**   Vary your tone, rate, volume, and pitch to emphasize key points and to make your speech more interesting. [See Chapter 3 for more about using your voice effectively.]

**5. Clear Articulation and Enunciation.**   Be careful not to slur your words. When you speak clearly, your audience will find listening to your message easy and enjoyable.

**6. Good Pronunciation.**   Your pronunciation can either help or hurt your credibility. If you mispronounce key words in your speech, your listeners will begin to question whether you have a thorough knowledge of your subject.

## A·C·T·I·V·I·T·Y
### 5
### Evaluating Your Delivery

Record a rehearsal of your informative speech (or have someone listen carefully to your rehearsal). Rate yourself (or have your partner rate you) on your enthusiasm, your vocal emphasis and variety, your articulation and enunciation, and your pronunciation. Identify two specific improvements that you plan to make in delivering your speech.

# Conducting a Question-and-Answer Session

Question-and-answer sessions often follow informative speeches. These sessions allow the audience to clarify ideas and to get more information. Plan to set aside one third to one half of your time for questions and answers—for example, for a thirty-minute speech, reserve ten to fifteen minutes for questions.

People are sometimes reluctant to ask questions, so you will need to let the audience know in advance that you are truly interested in answering their questions. For example, you might say, "As I'm going along, make note of any places where I haven't been clear or where you would like more detail—and I'll answer your questions at the end."

Another way to encourage your audience to answer questions is to conclude by saying something like this: "What I've said may have started you thinking about ideas that I didn't cover or that you'd like to have explained further. I'll be happy to answer your questions."

1. **See to it that people ask questions rather than give speeches.** If someone starts talking but no question comes forth within the first few sentences, interrupt politely to make sure that the person has a question.

2. **Call on people from all parts of the audience.** Avoid calling only on those in the middle of the audience or those seated in the first few rows. Give everyone a chance to ask a first question before calling on those with second questions.

3. **Try to answer all questions briefly.** Remember that you have a time limit. Reply succinctly to give as many people as possible a chance to ask their questions.

4. **If you cannot answer a question, feel free to say so.** It is much better to say, "I'm sorry, I really don't have an answer for that" than to stall or try to answer questions you are not prepared to answer. You can always offer to locate the information and provide it later.

## ACTIVITY 6

### Rehearsing Answers to Potential Questions from Your Audience

After you rehearse your speech, rehearse answers to potential questions. Either ask yourself questions or have a friend listen to your speech and then ask you questions. Locate any additional information the questions raise that your speech did not answer.

## Responding to Feedback

In an informative speech, you are trying to reach as many people as possible with your information, so you should watch for signs of inattention or lack of understanding: yawning, papers rustling, feet shuffling, and coughing. If you see your listeners adopting these behaviors, begin at once to think of ways to recapture their attention, such as varying your voice, increasing your movements, and making gestures.

As you gain speaking experience, you will become more aware of audience behavior. The mark of a truly effective speaker is the ability to adapt to these signs and regain the audience's interest quickly and smoothly.

When you speak, how aware are you of what your audience is doing? When your next speech is over, write down some of the behavior that you observed during your speech. What behavior, if any, affected your delivery? What did you do to keep or regain the audience's attention?

## Evaluating Informative Speeches

After your classmates have presented their speeches, you will probably be called upon to give an oral or a written critique of each speaker's effectiveness. [For a more detailed discussion of oral and written critiques, see Chapter 4.]

Remember that the purpose of an informative speech is to help an audience understand and remember the information presented. Therefore, a critique of an informative speech should focus on the effectiveness of what the speaker said and did to help the audience understand and remember information.

## ACTIVITY 7

### Giving a Critique of an Informative Speech

Working with a partner, find an informative speech in an issue of *Vital Speeches of the Day*. Have your partner deliver this speech to you as if he or she were presenting it to an entire audience. Then, using the Evaluation Checklist on page 375, give an oral critique. Finally, provide a written critique.

PEANUTS reprinted by permission of UFS, Inc.

## FOR INFORMATIVE SPEECHES

### for an Expository Speech

- Have I selected and limited an appropriate topic?

- Have I clearly stated a specific purpose?

- Have I gathered information from a variety of sources?

- Does the topic relate to my audience's experience?

- Does the introduction spark my audience's interest in learning more about my topic?

- Is the material well organized?

- Is the information new, or does it offer new insights?

- Can I use audiovisual materials to help my audience understand and remember information?

### for a Process Speech

- Have I selected a process that interests me and that I know how to perform?

- Have I clearly stated a specific purpose?

- Have I organized the steps in the process clearly?

- Will my presentation help the audience visualize the process?

- Have I adapted the speech to my audience?

- Can I deliver the speech confidently?

- Can I respond appropriately to audience feedback?

# EVALUATION ✓ CHECKLIST

## for Informative Speeches

**Organization:**

Was the purpose of the speech clear?

Did the introduction gain attention? Did it clarify the purpose?

Was each of the main ideas or major steps easily identifiable?

Did the main ideas follow a consistent pattern?

Did the speaker use good transitions?

Did the conclusion summarize the key ideas? Did it close the speech on a high note?

**Content:**

Did the speaker seem to understand the topic?

Did the speaker consider the audience's interest, knowledge, and attitude?

Was enough information given to make the key ideas or points of the speech understandable?

Were audiovisual materials used effectively?

Were materials provided to help the audience remember the key ideas?

**Language:**

Was the language precise?

Were the words specific and concrete?

Did the speaker use words that the audience could understand?

Did the speaker emphasize key ideas?

Was the tone appropriate for the audience and the occasion?

**Delivery:**

Did the speaker seem confident?

Was the speaker's appearance appropriate?

Did the speaker show enthusiasm?

Did the speaker look at the audience during the speech?

Were facial expressions, gestures, and movements natural?

Were the speaker's articulation, enunciation, and pronunciation correct?

**Additional Comments:**


**Evaluation:**

# SHARING KNOWLEDGE

## Spreading Useful Information

Many jobs require good public-speaking skills in order to spread information about goods and services being offered and to attract potential customers.

## Characteristics of a Good Informative Speaker

A good informative speaker

1. identifies the aims, types, and defining features of an informative speech

2. develops an effective informative speech, using an appropriate topic

3. adapts information to help an audience understand and remember it

4. conducts a question-and-answer session after the speech

## Meet the Informative Speaker

Architect Ben Obregon specializes in providing information about designing and building straw-bale houses. "Straw-bale construction is growing in popularity, but most people still don't realize how sturdy and well-insulated a straw-bale house can be," Obregon says. "I consider it part of my job to speak to as many groups as possible and to explain it so that any audience will understand and appreciate it."

*Ben Obregon*

## ACTIVITY

### Situation

The president of a local service organization has asked you to deliver an informative speech on a particular topic at the group's next meeting. You are considered an expert on the topic.

### Preparation

First, choose a topic you know well or can easily research. Then identify your audience. How can you use their interests and level of experience to draw their attention to your topic? Determine the best way to present your ideas clearly and completely. Consider a visual aid or two, and allow time for a question-and-answer session.

### Analysis and Assessment

Write a two- or three-page informative speech. Practice the speech, and then deliver it in class. Ask for feedback from your classmates on the effectiveness of your presentation.

# S•U•M•M•A•R•Y

**AN INFORMATIVE SPEECH** helps an audience understand and remember the material presented. The two types of informative speeches are expository speeches and process speeches. An expository speech gives information on a specific topic. A process, or how-to, speech tells how to do something, how to make something, or how something works. Use the following pointers to develop an informative speech:

- **Choose a topic** that you are interested in and that you already know something about. Limit your topic to a manageable size.
- **Gather information** from a variety of sources: your own experience and observations, interviews or surveys, and written sources.
- **Organize your speech** into three parts: an introduction, a body, and a conclusion. Organize the body of your speech in one of the following orders: chronological, spatial, topical, climactic, cause-and-effect, or comparison-and-contrast.
- **Adapt your speech** to your audience's experience, interests, and knowledge.
- **Deliver your speech** expressively. Use audiovisual materials if they save time, clarify an idea, or emphasize a point. Throughout the speech, evaluate and respond to audience feedback. After the speech, leave time for a question-and-answer session. Answer questions carefully and fully.
- **Evaluate an informative speech** with an oral or written critique by focusing on what the speaker did to help the audience understand and remember the information presented.

Look back through this chapter to find the meaning of each of the following terms. Write each term and its meaning in your communication journal.

**audiovisual materials,** p. 368
**cause-and-effect order,** p. 363
**chronological order,** p. 359
**climactic order,** p. 363
**comparison-and-contrast order,** p. 364
**credibility,** p. 370
**demonstration,** p. 368
**expository speech,** p. 355
**informative speech,** p. 355
**mnemonic device,** p. 368
**partial demonstration,** p. 369
**process speech,** p. 355
**spatial order,** p. 362
**topical order,** p. 362

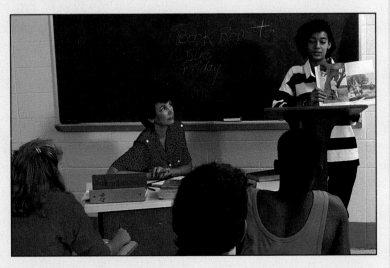

## Review Questions

1. What are the major goals that an effective informative speech should accomplish?
2. Identify the three kinds of processes that can be explained in process speeches.
3. What should an effective introduction to an informative speech accomplish?
4. In what cases would chronological order be an especially good organizational pattern to use in developing the body of an informative speech?
5. What should you do when you find you have as many as fifteen steps in a process speech?
6. What does an effective conclusion of an informative speech accomplish?
7. What are three ways that you can adapt your speech to your audience?
8. When should audiovisual materials be used in an informative speech?
9. What is the difference between a demonstration and a partial demonstration?
10. "Call on people from all parts of the audience" is one guideline for handling the question-and-answer session following an informative speech. What are three other guidelines?

## Discussion Questions

1. You are giving a speech on a subject that interests you a great deal, but you think that this subject might not have a very strong appeal to your audience. Discuss with your classmates how you might prepare an introduction that would arouse your audience's interest in this subject.
2. Think of the courses that you take in school. In which of these courses would you like to see more demonstrations? How would additional demonstrations make it easier for you to learn? Discuss your answers with your classmates.
3. Discuss the reasons for including a summary as part of the conclusion of an informative speech.
4. Samuel Johnson once wrote, "Man is not weak, knowledge is more than equivalent to force. The master of mechanics laughs at strength." First, discuss the meaning of this quotation. Then, discuss how various types of knowledge can be used in developing an informative speech.
5. Long ago, the Greek philosopher Heraclitus claimed, "Eyes are more accurate witnesses than ears." Discuss how this quotation relates to the need to include a demonstration in your process speech.

# ACTIVITIES

1. **Testing Your Memory.** Read the following paragraph in order to remember it.

   *Go straight until you come to a fork in the road. Then turn left and keep going until you see the third four-way stop. Now turn right and go until you come to an overpass. Turn right again at the street immediately before the overpass. Continue for three stop signs and you will see a church with a steeple. You want the white building directly across from the church.*

   Now cover the paragraph and write the directions as you remember them. After you finish, check your version of the directions against the paragraph.

2. **Using Spatial Order to Organize Details for a Speech.**

   **A.** Select an object, a location, or a landscape (such as one shown in the pictures on this page) as the topic for an informative speech. You may also select a topic of your own. Identify the component parts of the topic you have selected, and arrange the details of your description in a specific spatial order.

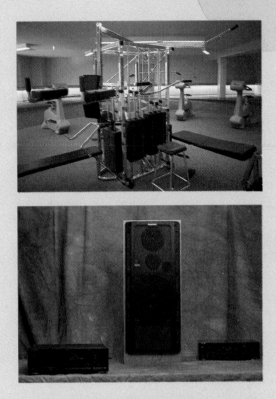

   **B.** Present your informative speech to your classmates. After you complete your speech, ask your listeners to draw a sketch and label the parts of the object or location you are describing. Was your description clear enough to help your audience to visualize the object or location clearly?

3. **Giving an Informative Speech.** Choose a common object in your classroom, such as an eraser, a wastebasket, or a window; or choose an idea or emotion such as courage, equality, or anger. Write a short definition of the object or idea you chose. Present your definition as a short informative speech. Ask your listeners to use the Evaluation Checklist for Informative Speeches (page 375) to evaluate your delivery. Conduct a question-and-answer session following your speech, and respond to your listeners' feedback.

4. **Giving an Informative Speech.** Choose a topic you are studying in another class, such as the discovery of radioactive elements by the Curies or a landmark Supreme Court ruling. Research this topic by consulting three different sources. Using your notes from your research, prepare a brief extemporaneous report on your topic. Include citations for at least two of your sources. Present your report in class. Ask your listeners to critique your speech by using the Evaluation Checklist for Informative Speeches (page 375).

5. **Giving a Process Speech on How to Do Something.** Write a list of five processes that you know how to do well. Which process can you explain completely in less than five minutes? Jot down the steps of the process, and using only this brief list, deliver a short extemporaneous speech explaining the process. If necessary, use audiovisual materials in your speech. Ask your classmates to use the Evaluation Checklist for Informative Speeches (page 375) to evaluate your presentation.

6. **Giving a Process Speech on How to Make Something.** Think back to a project you have completed in which you made something, such as a special meal, a computer program, a video, or a piece of art. Review the steps in the process and write them down in order. Also list all the materials you needed. Organize your lists into an outline that you can use to present a speech giving complete directions for following the process. Deliver your speech to your classmates. Try to use notes as little as possible, but be careful not to leave out any steps or materials. Ask your listeners to use the Evaluation Checklist for Informative Speeches (page 375) to give you a critique of your presentation.

7. **Giving a Process Speech on How Something Works.** Think of the many simple tools and devices you commonly use (for example, a pencil sharpener, a can opener, an eraser, or a bicycle pump). Read two or three short explanations of how one of these common tools or devices works. Using the best information from your sources, write a two- or three-page explanation of your own. Present your explanation in a speech to your class. Use audiovisual materials to demonstrate the item that you are explaining. Conduct a question-and-answer session following your speech, and respond to your audience's feedback. Ask your listeners to use the Evaluation Checklist for Informative Speeches (page 375) to critique your presentation.

8. **Identifying the Uses of Demonstrations.** Prepare a list of twenty jobs that would require a demonstration of something. For example, a vacuum-cleaner salesperson would likely be required to demonstrate how a vacuum cleaner works or a person selling a time-saving food processor might be required to demonstrate how easily or simply the processor works. Share your list of jobs with your classmates. After eliminating duplications, select a combined list of twenty jobs that the class feels are most likely to require demonstrations.

9. **Giving an Oral Critique of an Informative Speech.** Using the Evaluation Checklist for Informative Speeches (page 375), prepare a careful critique of an informative speech delivered by one of your classmates. Present your critique orally in class. Ask your classmates to evaluate your critique, and respond to the feedback they give you.

# EVERYDAY COMMUNICATION

### Situation

Your friend has asked for your honest opinion about a report, short story, poem, or drawing that he or she has written or created. Your reaction is generally favorable, but you see some flaws.

### Problem

What will you say to your friend? First, identify the situation. Which of your friends has asked your opinion? What have you been asked to critique? What is good about it? What is flawed?

### Assessing Your Skill

Write a one- or two-page critique that expresses your overall favorable impression as well as your reservations. Be prepared to present your critique in class. Ask your classmates for feedback on the helpfulness and tactfulness of your comments.

# COMMUNICATION IN THE WORKPLACE

### Background

You have been asked to teach a group of co-workers how to operate a particular piece of machinery or office equipment. How will you go about doing so?

### Preparing to Do the Job

First, identify the people you will teach and a piece of machinery or office equipment that you believe you could teach someone to use. Make a list of the steps that have to be followed to operate the equipment, along with any other details that you think would be helpful to learners.

### Testing Your Skill

Adapt your instructions to suit the experience, familiarity, and technical knowledge of your listeners. Be prepared to present your lesson in class, and to respond to feedback on how well you have explained the process of operating the equipment.

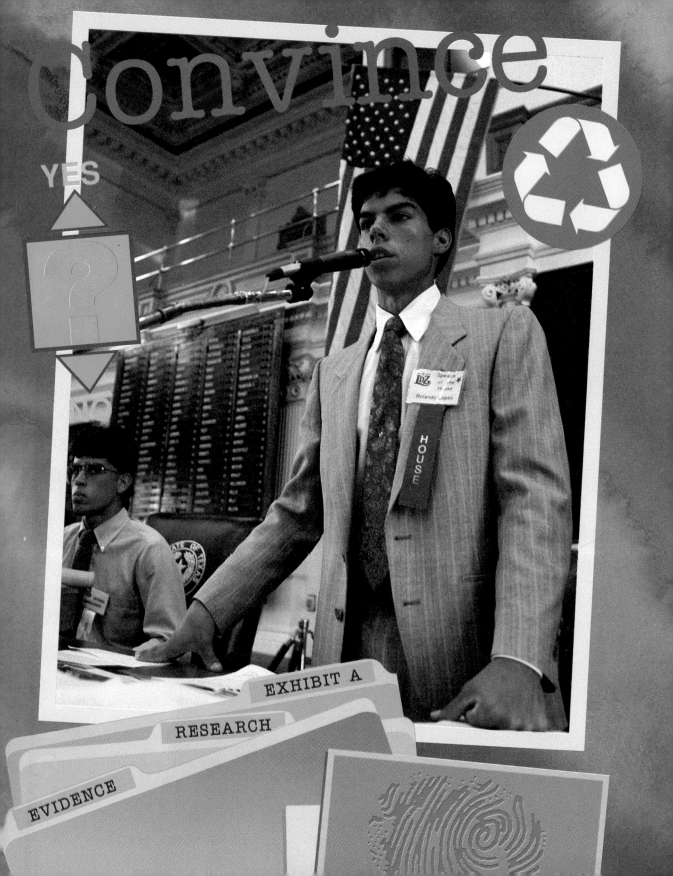

## CHAPTER 15

# Speaking to Persuade

C H A P T E R 15

**OBJECTIVES**

**After studying this chapter, you should be able to**

1. Define *persuasive speaking.*
2. Select a persuasive speech topic and develop it into a persuasive speech.
3. Use logical reasoning, consisting of reasons and evidence, to support and develop points in your speech.
4. Develop appropriate emotional appeals to support and develop points in your speech.
5. Establish your credibility while meeting ethical standards for public speaking.
6. Evaluate a persuasive speech.

## What Is a Persuasive Speech?

Any time you try to convince someone to think, believe, or act as you want them to, you are speaking to persuade. A **persuasive speech** is one that

- establishes a fact
- changes a belief
- moves an audience to act on a policy

How successful you are in presenting a persuasive speech depends on what you say and how you say it—your content and delivery.

In this chapter you will learn how to select and limit a suitable topic and to develop it into a persuasive speech. You will also learn how to apply logical reasoning by developing reasons and supporting them with evidence, how to develop emotional appeals to support your ideas, and how to establish your credibility with your listeners. You will learn how to adapt your speech to your audience and how to deliver it convincingly.

# Preparing a Persuasive Speech

In planning a persuasive speech, you consider the same elements you do for any type of speech: topic, purpose, and audience. You already know what the general purpose of your speech is: to persuade. Knowing your choices within that general purpose will help you make decisions about the other elements of your speech, such as the organizational pattern you use.

## Understanding the Types of Persuasion

Persuasion stems from the idea that people can hold different views on a topic and that it is open to question as to which viewpoint is the better one. Your goal as a speaker is to support your viewpoint so that the audience will adopt it. In this way, persuasive speeches deal with three types of questions that can be answered in more than one way:

- questions of fact
- questions of belief
- questions of policy

A **question of fact** concerns statements that can be seen as either true or false. You offer proof to support a statement of fact, but the audience determines whether you have convincingly proved that the statement of fact is true.

**EXAMPLES:**
1. Recycling can (cannot) save local communities money.
2. Coffee drinkers have (do not have) a higher risk of heart disease.
3. The space program does (does not) contribute to our national security.

A **question of belief** focuses on what is right or wrong, good or bad, best or worst, moral or immoral. While you cannot prove that a belief is true or false, you can supply convincing information to justify a belief.

**EXAMPLES:**
1. Small schools are (are not) better for most students than large schools are.
2. Elvis Presley was (was not) the greatest rock-and-roll performer ever.
3. It is (is not) wrong to avoid jury duty.

A **question of policy** focuses on a particular action. You try to convince the audience to act on some policy or to agree that some policy should be changed.

**EXAMPLES:**

1. The senior class should (should not) vote for Ann Welch.
2. High school athletes should (should not) be required to maintain a B average to compete interscholastically.
3. Funding for space exploration should (should not) be increased.

# ACTIVITY 1

## Identifying Persuasive Statements

Identify each of the following statements as a question of fact, a question of belief, or a question of policy.

1. Seattle does not deserve its reputation for having an extremely rainy climate.
2. The United States should abolish the electoral college.
3. South High has a better basketball team than North High.
4. You should watch the documentary about jobs for teenagers.
5. Illiteracy continues to be an important national problem.

## Choosing and Limiting a Topic

With the techniques you learned in Chapter 9 (pages 215–239), you can find many topics for persuasive speeches. A good persuasive topic is one that

- you feel strongly about
- other people may have different views on

**EXAMPLE:** For her persuasive speech, Gloria Marcus chose the subject area *current events* and brainstormed about upcoming events at her school. From her list of ideas, she chose *the election of class officers* and limited it to the topic *Ann Welch's candidacy for senior class president.* Gloria felt strongly that Ann should be elected, and she knew that other students supported other candidates.

# ACTIVITY 2

## Developing a Topic for a Persuasive Speech

In Chapter 9 (pages 216–219) you learned several techniques for generating a topic. Using those techniques, select and limit a topic that is suitable for a persuasive speech. Be sure your topic meets the two criteria, or standards, for a good persuasive topic: that it is one that you feel strongly about and that it is one that other people may have different views on. You and your classmates might want to discuss and compare the topics you have developed.

## Writing Your Thesis Statement

Once you have chosen a topic, your next step is to state your specific purpose. [For more information on how to state your specific purpose, see pages 221–222 of Chapter 9.] This statement will be the basis for your thesis statement, a complete sentence that can state any one of the following three items:

- the fact you want to establish
- the belief you want to establish or change
- the policy you want your audience to support or act on

Almost any thesis statement can be worded so that it makes your specific goal clear.

**EXAMPLE:** Gloria could have written any of these thesis statements for her speech on Ann Welch's candidacy (she actually wrote the third one):

- Fact: Ann Welch is qualified for the job of senior class president.
- Belief: Ann Welch is the best candidate for senior class president.
- Policy: You should vote for Ann Welch for senior class president.

# ACTIVITY 3

## Writing Your Thesis Statement

Using the topic you developed in Activity 2 on page 386, write a thesis statement for your persuasive speech. Decide whether your thesis will deal with a question of fact, of belief, or of policy. Check that the wording of the thesis makes clear the viewpoint your speech will support.

# Using Persuasive Techniques

To get people to think, to believe, or to act the way you want them to, you can use three persuasive techniques:

- applying logical reasoning—to convince the audience by using rational argument
- appealing to the emotions—to affect how the people in the audience feel so that they will agree with you
- establishing your credibility—to make the audience believe in you

Effective persuasive speakers often use all three of these techniques within a single speech.

## Applying Logical Reasoning

Applying **logical reasoning** means building an argument that is based on reasons supported by evidence. [For more information on identifying faulty reasoning, see pages 90–92 of Chapter 4.]

A **reason** is a statement that explains or justifies your thesis. It answers the question "Why?"

**EXAMPLE:** You want to persuade your classmates to see the drama club's production of *Grease*. You might use statements such as these as your reasons:

- *Grease* is one of the most popular musicals of all time.
- The music is excellent.
- The acting and dancing are outstanding.

**Evidence** is material that establishes the soundness of each reason. For instance, to establish that *Grease* is one of the most popular musicals of all time, you could cite the fact that the *World Almanac* lists *Grease* as one of the longest-running Broadway shows ever.

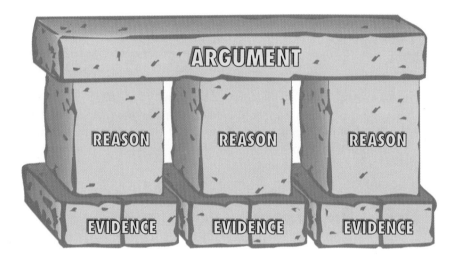

**Finding and Evaluating Reasons.**   To find reasons to support your thesis, you can use three sources:

- yourself
- other people
- reference materials

[For help with finding and using different sources of information for a speech, see pages 242–255 of Chapter 10.] For some topics, you can begin drawing on your own knowledge and experience. For other topics, you will also need to talk to other people and to conduct research using a variety of reference materials.

**EXAMPLE:** From Gloria's own experience, she knew that Ann Welch had held a variety of elective and appointive positions. As one of her reasons, she listed Ann's leadership experience.

Next, Gloria talked to other people—students, teachers, and school officials—about Ann's candidacy. Many of these people mentioned Ann's efforts on behalf of her fellow students. (Such comments are called **testimonials,** statements attesting to the worth of someone or something.) These comments led Gloria to her second reason: Ann's willingness to work hard.

Finally, Gloria found several articles and editorials by and about Ann in current and back issues of the school paper. From them she learned about Ann's hopes for the senior class. As her third reason Gloria listed Ann's interesting ideas for the coming school year.

# HOW TO > *Evaluate Reasons*

1. **Is each reason relevant to your thesis?** Each of your reasons should directly support your thesis. Set aside any that don't answer the question "Why?" in relation to your thesis. For example, Gloria might have listed as one of her reasons Ann's ambition to become the first woman to be elected president of the United States. That ambition does not directly support Gloria's thesis that Ann should be elected president of the senior class.

2. **Is each reason distinct?** Each reason should be separate from each of your other reasons and from your thesis. For example, the statement "Ann Welch has held several elective and appointive positions" merely restates Gloria's first reason, Ann's leadership experience, and should be set aside.

3. **Does each reason provide strong support for the thesis?** For example, if Gloria discovered that Ann's leadership experience was actually very limited, she would need to look for reasons that provided stronger support for her thesis.

4. **Will the audience consider the reason important?** For example, Gloria had to decide whether her fellow seniors would consider leadership experience, hard work, and fresh ideas important factors in selecting a class president.

5. **Do you have just enough reasons?** An effective persuasive speech usually presents two or three reasons. If you present fewer, your audience may feel that you have not answered the question "Why?" to their satisfaction. If you present more than five or six, they may be overwhelmed and lose the thread of your argument.

**Supporting Reasons with Evidence.**   In your speech you will support each of your reasons with evidence. For a persuasive speech, two of the types of details you learned about in Chapter 9 (pages 228–229) are particularly effective evidence: facts and expert opinions. You should offer at least two pieces of evidence for each of your reasons. If you offer any fewer than two pieces of evidence, the audience may not take your reasons seriously.

BORN LOSER reprinted by permission of NEA, Inc.

A **fact** is an item of information or a statement that can be verified, or checked, by testing, by observing, or by consulting reference materials.

**EXAMPLE:** As evidence of Ann's leadership experience, Gloria cited two facts: that Ann was vice-president of her sophomore class and that Ann is editor of the school paper. Both of these statements can be verified.

An **expert opinion** is a statement of belief about a subject by a knowledgeable person recognized as an authority on that subject. Such statements cannot be proved, because they express value judgments. Expert opinion is not always perceived by an audience to be as strong as factual evidence. In some cases, however, expert opinions are as effective as facts.

**EXAMPLE:** One of Gloria's reasons is that Ann is a hard worker. Gloria could support that reason with factual evidence: what posts Ann has held and what she has accomplished. Still, the term *hard worker* involves a value judgment about what constitutes hard work. That is, different people can hold different views about what characterizes hard work.

To further support her point, Gloria could interview the school paper's faculty adviser. That teacher's testimonial that Ann is a hard worker would be considered an expert opinion because of the teacher's years of experience working with other student editors.

1. **Is the evidence relevant to the reason it supports?** The facts or expert testimony you present should relate to the particular reason you are trying to support. For example, saying that Ann Welch is an honor roll student would not help Gloria support her first reason, Ann's leadership experience. However, Gloria could state that Ann helped establish a volunteer tutoring service.

2. **Is the evidence verifiable and reliable?** You should be able to check the accuracy of any facts you cite to support a reason. An expert opinion should come from someone knowledgeable about the topic—someone recognized as an authority on the subject. For example, Ann's piano teacher would not be a reliable source for information about Ann's willingness to work hard on school projects.

3. **Is there enough evidence?** Your purpose is to persuade your audience. You want your listeners to adopt your point of view or to take a specific action. To get them to do so, you must provide sufficient proof—usually two pieces of evidence for each reason.

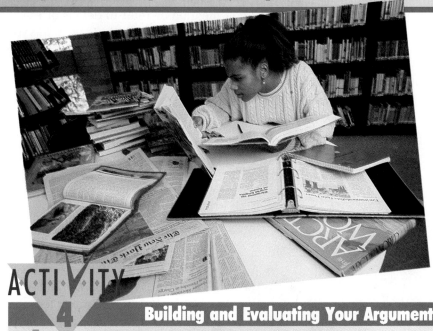

## ACTIVITY 4

### Building and Evaluating Your Argument

List at least two reasons to support the thesis statement you wrote for Activity 3 on page 387. Using the questions on page 389, evaluate your reasons to determine whether they build the argument you want to make. Then gather at least two pieces of evidence to support each reason, and evaluate your evidence with the questions above. Remember to use the sources of information you learned about on pages 242–255 of Chapter 10.

# Developing Emotional Appeals

An **emotional appeal** is a statement that arouses strong feelings—pleasure or anger, joy or sadness, pride or shame—in an audience. This type of statement may be effective for a persuasive speech that focuses on urging action. In such a speech, you don't simply want your listeners to agree with you; you want them to translate that agreement into action. And many people will not do so until their emotions become involved. For example, some of Gloria's classmates might believe that Ann would make a good senior class president, but they will not take the time to vote. Gloria needs to spur them to action.

You can develop emotional appeals for any persuasive speech in three ways:

- by citing specifics
- by using vivid language
- by including personal references

**Citing Specifics.** When you cite specifics, you mention or refer to details or examples that clearly illustrate a point you want to make. By citing specifics, you may remove any uncertainty your audience may have about your meaning.

**GENERAL STATEMENT:** Ann Welch is a hard worker.

**SPECIFIC EXAMPLE:** When Ann thought that students weren't being rewarded for their efforts to clean up the schoolyard, she arranged to take the principal on a tour of the school grounds and pointed out exactly what the students had done.

The words *hard worker* alone are not likely to arouse strong feelings. Most people are accustomed to hearing these words without giving them much thought. But by specifying *how* Ann works hard on behalf of her fellow students, Gloria appeals to her classmates' pride, thus getting them emotionally involved.

**Using Vivid Language.**  When you use descriptive language effectively, you enable your listeners to picture situations that you are referring to. [For more information on using vivid language, see pages 296–303 of Chapter 12.]

BLAND STATEMENT: Ann Welch knows how to stay cool in an emergency.

VIVID DEVELOPMENT: Last April 25 during lunch, Ann was outside enjoying the fresh air along with hundreds of other students. Suddenly, the wind picked up, coal-black clouds began building, and lightning crackled the sky. Recognizing the threat of a tornado and the danger of panic, Ann quickly got a few friends together and worked out a plan to lead the students calmly to the school basement. As a result of her swift action, not a single person was injured in the move to safety.

**Including Personal References.**  When you refer to the audience directly or when you relate the topic you are discussing to the audience's direct experience, you are using personal references. By using personal references, you make your listeners feel that they have a personal stake in the topic and you increase their interest.

TOO IMPERSONAL: Ann Welch plans to make graduation ceremonies better.

PERSONAL REFERENCE TO AUDIENCE: You've worked hard for your diploma, and you deserve to have your achievement recognized in front of the school community and your family and friends. Ann Welch will propose a graduation policy that calls for every one of you to receive your diploma in person. School officials will individually name graduates and award their diplomas. This policy will guarantee you the individual recognition you deserve.

# Establishing Your Credibility

**Credibility** is the quality of being believable. Think about the people you trust. You probably consider them trustworthy because you see them as competent, sincere, and dynamic. Your success as a speaker hinges on convincing your audience that you possess those three characteristics.

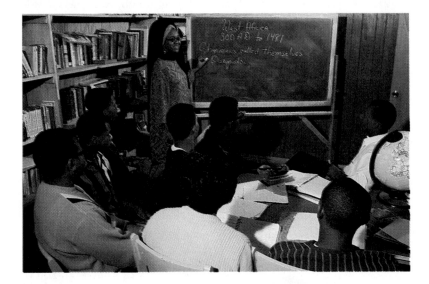

**Competence.**  **Competence** is the state of being well qualified. It comes from knowledge and preparation. To establish your competence, you have to *know* your topic thoroughly and *show* that you are knowledgeable. The more you know about a topic and the better prepared you are, the more likely it is that your audience will believe you.

EXAMPLES:

1. You want to convince your classmates to buy a certain brand of running shoes. To establish your competence, you could show how much you know about the construction of these shoes and the anatomy of the human foot. Showing how this particular type of shoe protects the runner's foot would more likely persuade the audience than just saying that the shoe looks good or is popular.
2. Gloria established her competence by showing that she knew Ann's experience, achievements, and ideas in detail.

**Sincerity.**  **Sincerity** is the quality of being genuine. It is primarily conveyed by your tone of voice, and it usually can't be faked. To establish your sincerity, you have to genuinely care about both your topic and your audience.

**EXAMPLE:** If Gloria truly cares about the senior class and really thinks that Ann is the best candidate, her speech will probably sound sincere. If not, her delivery will lack the sincerity necessary to establish her credibility.

**Dynamism.** **Dynamism** is the quality of being energetic and enthusiastic. It is expressed by your tone of voice as well as by your nonverbal behavior—your appearance, eye contact, facial expressions, gestures, and posture. Enthusiasm is contagious. The more dynamic you are, the more receptive to your ideas your audience is likely to be.

*A*s you watch television and listen to the radio, make notes in your journal about the emotional appeals advertisers use to convince you to buy their products. Also try to note when advertisers use logical reasoning and how they try to establish their credibility with you as a consumer.

## Meeting Ethical Standards

**Ethical standards** are society's guidelines for right, just, and moral behavior. Violating ethical standards can destroy a speaker's credibility. It is unethical for public speakers

- to lie or deceive
- to distort
- to engage in name-calling
- to attack a person or an idea without giving evidence
- to deny the opposition the right to reply

Your goal is to persuade the people in your audience, not to manipulate them. Persuasion uses logical reasoning and emotional appeals to convince your listeners to agree with you of their own free will. You want them to adopt your viewpoint or to take specific action, but you are not coercing, or forcing, them to do so. By contrast, **manipulation** is the shrewd or devious management of facts for your own purpose. It is based on the unethical distortion of information: withholding key information, presenting half-truths, or purposely misrepresenting ideas and details.

Calvin and Hobbes, copyright 1989 Watterson. Distributed by Universal Press Syndicate. Reprinted with permission. All rights reserved.

If you try to manipulate your audience or follow any other unethical practices, you will probably fail to achieve your goal. Once your listeners discover that you have deceived them, you lose your credibility and become totally ineffective. As you develop any persuasive speech, be aware of the close relationship between manipulation and the use of propaganda techniques. Take care to base your argument on sound logical reasoning and valid emotional appeals. [For information on spotting propaganda techniques, see pages 92–95 of Chapter 4.]

ACTI·V·ITY

5

## Developing Emotional Appeals and Credibility for a Persuasive Speech

Identify at least one emotional appeal that you can use to develop your thesis statement. Why do you think this method will be effective? What do your classmates think about its effectiveness?

Next indicate the best method you can use to establish your credibility on your topic. What information can you give to show your competence? What can you do to establish your sincerity?

# Adapting Your Persuasive Speech to Your Audience

Before you decide how to organize your material, you ought to consider two things: one, the possible makeup of your audience, and two, how best to adapt your speech to that particular audience. With the persuasive speech more than with any other, adapting your speech so that it both reaches and moves your audience is crucial to your success.

Although the individual members of any audience may have many different attitudes about a topic, an audience as a whole can be classified as

- mostly favorable
- mostly neutral
- mostly apathetic
- mostly hostile

To determine your audience's attitude toward your topic, you can use the questions in Chapter 9 (page 225). You may also want to conduct a poll.

**EXAMPLE:** A few days before delivering her speech, Gloria gave each person in class the questionnaire on the next page. Gloria's goal was to determine how her audience felt about the candidates for senior class president. Knowing her audience's attitudes, Gloria could make adjustments in her reasons and evidence to build a more convincing argument.

## QUESTIONNAIRE FOR STUDENT ELECTIONS

**1.** If elections for senior class president were held today, who would you vote for?

_____

**2.** For each candidate, indicate the letter of the phrase that best summarizes your feelings about that person:

Bill Garver _____
Jack Phillips _____
Laura Simpson _____
Ann Welch _____

**A.** I am strongly in favor of his/her candidacy.
**B.** I am somewhat in favor of his/her candidacy.
**C.** I have no strong feelings one way or the other about his/her candidacy.
**D.** I don't know much about him/her, or I am not interested in the election.
**E.** I am somewhat opposed to his/her candidacy.
**F.** I am strongly opposed to his/her candidacy.

When you cannot circulate such a questionnaire, base your prediction of your audience's attitude on what you do know about their interests and values.

## Adapting to a Favorable Audience

A **favorable audience** is one in which the majority of the listeners agree, from slightly to completely, with your thesis. Listeners with this type of favorable attitude need to have their existing feelings strengthened to such a degree that they will act on their feelings.

> **EXAMPLE:** Gloria found that most of the class already seemed to favor Ann Welch. Yet, no one can ever be sure what voters will do. Thus, Gloria's goal was to sustain and build on her listeners' favorable attitude so they would, indeed, vote for Ann.

## Adapting to a Neutral Audience

A **neutral audience** is one in which the majority of the listeners have not reached a decision about your thesis. Neutral audiences will generally give all sides an equal hearing. They need information to persuade them to take a stand.

> **EXAMPLE:** If Gloria faced a neutral audience, she could supply her listeners with such a wealth of information that they would decide that their best course was to vote for Ann.

## Adapting to an Apathetic Audience

An **apathetic audience** is one in which a majority of the listeners have no interest in your thesis. Other than a hostile audience, an apathetic audience is the most difficult to persuade. Such listeners need to be shown how your thesis affects them personally.

> **EXAMPLE:** If Gloria faced an apathetic audience, she could show her listeners how voting—and, specifically, voting for Ann—would give them a say in how the senior class is run.

## Adapting to a Hostile Audience

A **hostile audience** is one in which the majority of the listeners oppose your thesis. With some topics, especially highly controversial ones, you may notice that many people in a hostile audience may specifically object to your proposal, while others may favor a different one. Such listeners need to be shown that they are being fair in listening to you, that what you have to say matters to them, and that you are worth listening to. One speech probably will not sway them completely, but it may open their minds to your thesis.

**EXAMPLE:** If Gloria faced a hostile audience, she could compliment her listeners on their fairness in listening to her and acknowledge the validity of their point of view. Establishing her credibility would be particularly important, as would using logical reasoning.

This approach also works well when you address a radio or television audience. It is unlikely that you will drive away any listeners who already favor your proposal, and your approach may convince some neutral listeners and stir some apathetic ones.

## ACTIVITY 6

### Using a Questionnaire to Identify Audience Attitudes

Make up a questionnaire on your topic. Your questionnaire can be similar to the one on page 398. Hand out your questionnaire to every person in your audience. Then collect the questionnaires, and tabulate the responses with a checklist like the one following. Use the results to determine the final wording of your thesis statement and to review the appropriateness of your reasons and evidence.

_____ Strongly in favor     _____ Apathetic or uninformed
_____ Slightly in favor     _____ Slightly against
_____ Neutral     _____ Strongly against

After you tabulate your results and consider how they might affect your argument, discuss your findings with your classmates. What did they learn by using a questionnaire?

# Organizing Your Speech

For the most part, the way you organize your speech will be guided by your impression of your audience's attitude and by the nature of your material. Persuasive speeches are organized according to two approaches: deductive and inductive.

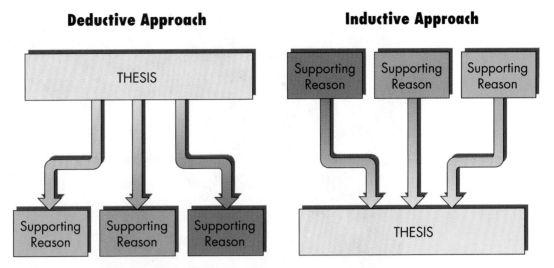

**Deductive Approach**

THESIS

Supporting Reason · Supporting Reason · Supporting Reason

**Inductive Approach**

Supporting Reason · Supporting Reason · Supporting Reason

THESIS

With the deductive approach, the thesis is stated first and then reasons are presented that support the thesis. With the inductive approach, a number of reasons are stated which then build to the statement of the thesis.

## Using a Deductive Approach

In a **deductive approach,** you begin with your thesis and then present reasons to support it. When you organize your material deductively, you try to move your audience from the general to the specific. Three types of deductive approaches are

- the statement-of-reasons method
- the problem-solution method
- the comparative advantage method

While all of these methods are deductive, each of them has its own special format for presenting information, making it particularly useful in certain circumstances.

**Statement-of-Reasons Method.** The **statement-of-reasons method** is the classic deductive approach in which the thesis is stated directly and followed by supporting reasons. This method works well with a favorable audience, since your listeners are not likely to be turned off by a direct approach.

**Thesis:** You should vote for Ann Welch for senior class president.
    **I.** Ann Welch has proven leadership experience.
    **II.** Ann Welch is a hard worker who will work for you.
    **III.** Ann Welch has fresh ideas that will benefit you.

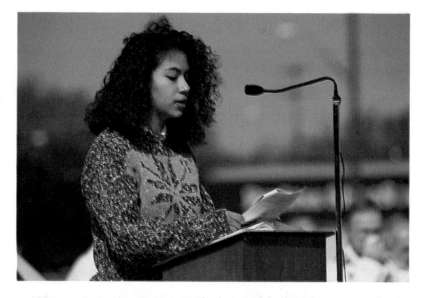

**Problem-Solution Method.** With the **problem-solution method,** you first present a problem and then offer at least one possible solution for that problem. You continue with this pattern for each problem you have identified.

This method works well with both favorable and neutral audiences. It can also succeed with apathetic audiences if you personalize both the problem and the solution convincingly.

**Thesis:** You should vote for Ann Welch for senior class president.
  I. Our senior class members face several problems. [Problem]
    A. Students don't feel they have any input.
    B. Teachers don't respect student opinion.
  II. Ann Welch can solve each of these problems. [Solution]
    A. Ann Welch can generate student interest.
    B. Ann Welch is respected by the faculty.

**Comparative Advantage Method.** The **comparative advantage method** presents each reason as a benefit to the audience. Sometimes the advantage of each reason is stated directly, using words like *more* or *better;* other times it is simply implied, or suggested. This method works well with neutral audiences. By directly presenting the benefits, you might sway a neutral audience to adopt your viewpoint.

**Thesis:** You should vote for Ann Welch for senior class president.

   **I.** Ann Welch has more experience than any other candidate.

  **II.** Ann Welch has shown the ability to work harder than any other candidate.

 **III.** Ann Welch's fresh ideas will benefit you more than any other candidate's ideas will.

## Using an Inductive Approach

In an **inductive approach,** you begin with your reasons and lead up to your thesis. When you organize your material inductively, you try to move your audience from the specific to the general. The inductive approach is the opposite of the deductive approach you have just read about. Three types of inductive approaches are

- the criteria-satisfaction method
- the negative method
- the Monroe motivated sequence

**Criteria-Satisfaction Method.** The **criteria-satisfaction method** has the purpose of getting the audience to agree to the soundness of certain criteria, or standards. Then you show how your proposal satisfies those criteria. This method is especially useful with hostile audience members who need to be shown that what you have to say matters to them and that you are worth listening to.

   **I.** Most of us are likely to agree on the criteria for class president.
-    **A.** A class president should have proven leadership experience.
-    **B.** A class president should have a record as a hard worker.
-    **C.** A class president should have fresh ideas.

  **II.** Ann Welch meets all three of these criteria.
-    **A.** Ann Welch has considerable leadership experience.
-    **B.** Ann Welch has proven to be a hard worker.
-    **C.** Ann Welch has fresh ideas that will benefit you.

 **III.** **Thesis:** You should vote for Ann Welch for senior class president.

You have to satisfy criteria in all areas of life. This photograph shows an example of a vehicle that did not meet the clearance criteria for this bridge.

**Negative Method.**   With the **negative method,** you show that no option other than the one you propose is acceptable. This method can work well with a hostile audience if you give your listeners enough solid evidence to convince them to agree with every one of your reasons.

> **I.** Bill Garver has no real leadership experience.
> **II.** Laura Simpson has no real leadership experience.
> **III.** Jack Phillips has a little experience but has not shown an inclination to be willing to pitch in with the work.
> **IV.** Ann Welch has leadership experience, has proven herself to be a hard worker, and has fresh ideas.
> **V. Thesis:** You should vote for Ann Welch for senior class president.

**Monroe Motivated Sequence.**   The **Monroe motivated sequence,** developed by Professor Alan H. Monroe, is based on the premise that in order to convince an audience to act, a speaker must

1. draw *attention* to the problem
2. show a *need* for some action
3. outline a plan that will *satisfy* that need
4. help the audience *visualize* the benefits of that plan of action
5. suggest a specific *action* that puts the plan into practice

I. We all saw how last year's senior class floundered for lack of leadership. [Attention]
II. Yet, the senior class is the class with the greatest expectations in high school. [Need]
III. A strong leader can restore class spirit and help our class accomplish its goals. [Satisfaction]
IV. Led by a president with a clear vision of this class's potential, proven leadership experiences, and a commitment to hard work, this class can go down in history. [Visualization]
V. **Thesis:** You should vote for Ann Welch, a hard-working, proven leader with a vision. [Action]

## ACTIVITY 7

### Organizing Your Persuasive Speech

Select one of the six methods of organization, either deductive or inductive, and outline the main points of your speech. Be prepared to explain why you chose this method.

# Delivering Your Speech Convincingly

Delivery is important in any speech, but it is especially critical in a persuasive speech. Anything less than your most dynamic delivery will diminish your chances of persuading your audience.

## Using Visual Materials

Since an audience can grasp information better by seeing and hearing it than by hearing it alone, look for opportunities to use visual materials in your persuasive speech.

Charts, graphs, films, slides, and photographs can help listeners visualize a need, motivating them to action. For example, to persuade an audience to support relief efforts for hurricane victims, a speaker could dramatize the need by showing photographs of people left homeless by the storm.

However, if you include visuals, beware of their overuse. No doubt you have had the experience of sitting in a darkened room as a speaker showed slides. The first few slides may have aroused your interest, and the next few may have held it. Beyond that, however, you were probably more ready to go to sleep than to pay attention to the speaker.

## Responding to Feedback

While you speak, your audience will be giving you subtle (and at times, not-so-subtle) feedback that will help you determine how you are doing. Be sure to respond to that feedback. For example, if your audience shows signs of boredom, boost the energy level of your delivery. Also be alert for shifts in attitude. For example, if a neutral audience begins to show signs of doubt, spend more time detailing your evidence.

Don't treat your speech as though it were engraved in stone. Feel free to add to a point, shorten a point, speed up, slow down, or even insert some humor if the feedback from your audience suggests the need for it.

## ACTIVITY 8

### Rehearsing Your Persuasive Speech

Using the outline you developed for Activity 7 on page 405, rehearse your persuasive speech thoroughly. Mark the ideas that you feel should be given special vocal emphasis, and work to achieve that emphasis. Then decide what kinds of visual materials, if any, you will use, and gather or prepare those materials. Be prepared to give your persuasive speech in class.

# Evaluating a Persuasive Speech

Both oral and written critiques are as essential for persuasive speeches as they are for informative speeches. However, while an informative speech critique focuses on the speaker's efforts to help the audience understand and remember the information, a critique of a persuasive speech focuses on the speaker's efforts to motivate the audience to believe a thesis or to act upon it. Such a critique, whether oral or written, evaluates the speaker's organization, content, language, and delivery.

You can use the Evaluation Checklist on page 409 as the basis for an oral or written critique of a persuasive speech. [For more about oral or written critiques, see pages 96–99 of Chapter 4.]

In your communication journal, make notes about the instances of persuasive speaking that you encounter daily. For example, did you try to convince a parent to let you go to the football game or to the dance on Saturday? What reasons and evidence did you present? What emotional appeals did you use? How did you try to establish your credibility, so you would be allowed to go? Perhaps you have seen a political advertisement on television lately. What was the ad trying to convince you to do or to believe? What reasons and emotional appeals did it use? What did the ad do to make you want to believe it?

# ACTIVITY 9

## Giving an Oral Critique of a Persuasive Speech

In an issue of *Vital Speeches of the Day*, find a persuasive speech that you think is especially effective. Prepare and give an oral critique of this speech. Be sure your critique explains why you think the speech is particularly effective. What reasons and evidence does the speaker give? What emotional appeals does the speaker use? How does the speaker establish his or her credibility and adapt to the audience?

The best way to develop a persuasive argument is to be persuaded yourself, like the people shown in this photograph.

## GUIDELINES
### for Persuasive Speeches

- Is my specific purpose clearly stated in my thesis?
- Have I provided good reasons to support my thesis?
- Have I provided evidence to support each reason?
- Have I provided enough reasons and evidence to build a convincing argument?
- Have I analyzed my audience?
- Have I adapted my material to meet audience attitudes?
- Have I used emotional appeals appropriately?
- Have I organized my speech in a way that is likely to motivate the audience?
- Have I established my credibility on my topic?
- Can I use verbal and nonverbal skills to present my speech convincingly?

# EVALUATION  CHECKLIST

## *for Persuasive Speeches*

**Organization:**

Did the introduction gain the audience's attention?

Did the thesis statement clearly indicate the specific purpose of the speech?

Was each of the reasons clearly identifiable and logically organized?

Did the conclusion summarize the key points? Did it close the speech on a high point?

**Content:**

Did the speaker seem knowledgeable about the topic?

Did the speaker consider the audience's interest, knowledge, and attitudes?

Was enough specific information given to make the key points of the speech understandable?

Did visual materials help the audience remember the key ideas?

Were reasons presented to support the thesis?

Did the evidence strongly support the reasons presented?

Did the speaker use any emotional appeals to motivate the audience?

Did the speaker build or maintain credibility?

Did the speaker present the speech ethically?

**Language:**

Was the language precise?

Were the words specific and concrete?

Did the speaker use words that the audience could understand?

Did the speaker emphasize key ideas?

Was the tone appropriate for the audience and the occasion?

**Delivery:**

Did the speaker seem confident and enthusiastic?

Did the speaker look at the audience during the speech?

Were the speaker's facial expressions, gestures, and movements natural?

Were the speaker's articulation, enunciation, and pronunciation correct?

**Additional comments:**


**Evaluation:**

# RAISING MONEY

### Sharing the Wealth

People who raise money for charitable organizations must use their communication skills to persuade people and groups to donate money. One of the most effective methods of fundraising is to speak persuasively before a wide variety of groups and convince people to contribute.

### Characteristics of a Good Fundraising Speaker

When speaking in public, a good fundraiser

1. delivers a committed, persuasive speech

2. presents and develops ideas logically

3. develops appropriate emotional appeals to emphasize key points

4. establishes credibility by maintaining ethical standards for public speaking

## ACTIVITY

### Situation

As chairperson of a committee formed to raise money for a plaque honoring a local dignitary, you have been asked to speak at the next meeting of a local service organization. Your job is to convince the audience to contribute money.

### Meet the Fundraiser

Gene Attal has been raising funds for Seton Medical Center for more than two decades. "As a speaker, I try to appeal to the audience's emotions with examples of people who need Seton's help," he says. "But I also try to appeal to the audience's logic, because they must be convinced that Seton is capable of helping these people and is worthy of a contribution."

*Gene Attal*

### Preparation

First, choose as the honoree someone you know well or can easily research. Then decide what organization you will be addressing and what sort of speech might be most effective. Are you more likely to succeed by using logical reasoning, an emotional appeal, or some combination of both? How will you establish credibility? Finally, prepare a short persuasive speech in which you ask the audience to contribute money as a group or as individuals.

### Analysis and Assessment

Present your speech to the class, and ask for feedback from your classmates. Was your presentation convincing? Why or why not?

# S☆U☆M☆M☆A☆R☆Y

**A SPEECH TO PERSUADE** establishes a fact, strengthens or changes a person's beliefs, or moves a person to action.

- **Choose a topic** that you feel strongly about and that other people may have different views on.
- **Write a thesis statement** that addresses a question of fact, of belief, or of policy.
- **Use persuasive techniques** to convince your audience. You might (1) use logical reasoning by providing sound reasons and valid evidence, including facts (verifiable statements) and expert opinions (statements by knowledgeable people); or (2) appeal to your listeners' emotions by citing specifics, using vivid language, and including personal references.
- **Establish your credibility** by emphasizing your competence, knowledge of the topic, sincerity and goodwill toward the audience, and enthusiasm about the subject.
- **Meet ethical standards** when you speak. Lying, distorting, and name-calling have no place in persuasive speaking.
- **Adapt your speech** to your audience's attitude toward your topic—favorable, neutral or undecided, apathetic, or hostile.
- **Organize your speech** to present your reasons and evidence in either a deductive or an inductive pattern.
- **Deliver your speech** as convincingly as possible. Use visual materials, and respond to audience feedback.
- **Evaluate a persuasive speech** by focusing on how the speaker motivated the audience to believe the thesis or to act upon it.

## Vocabulary

Look back through this chapter to find the meaning of each of the following terms. Write each term and its meaning in your communication journal.

apathetic audience, p. 399
comparative advantage method, p. 402
competence, p. 394
credibility, p. 394
criteria-satisfaction method, p. 403
deductive approach, p. 401
dynamism, p. 395
emotional appeal, p. 392
ethical standards, p. 395
evidence, p. 388
expert opinion, p. 390
fact, p. 390
favorable audience, p. 399
hostile audience, p. 400
inductive approach, p. 403
logical reasoning, p. 387
manipulation, p. 396
Monroe motivated sequence, p. 404
negative method, p. 404
neutral audience, p. 399
persuasive speech, p. 383
problem-solution method, p. 402
question of belief, p. 384
question of fact, p. 384
question of policy, p. 384
reason, p. 387
sincerity, p. 394
statement-of-reasons method, p. 401
testimonials, p. 389

# Review Questions

1. Both an informative and a persuasive speech provide information. What makes a persuasive speech different from an informative speech?
2. One kind of persuasive speech establishes a fact. What do the two other kinds of persuasive speeches do?
3. You should support your thesis with reasons. What two types of evidence should you use to support your reasons?
4. Using logical reasoning is one technique of persuasion. What are two other techniques of persuasion?
5. One way of appealing to emotions is to use specific words and details. What are two other ways of appealing to emotions?
6. To give your speech effectively, you must establish credibility. What are the three elements of speaker credibility?
7. What is the difference between persuading and manipulating an audience?
8. When you use deductive organization, you state your thesis first and then give your reasons. What are three types of deductive organization?
9. When you use inductive organization, you state your reasons first and lead up to your thesis statement. What are three types of inductive organization?
10. A critique of an informative speech focuses on the speaker's ability to help the audience understand and remember the material. On what does a critique of a persuasive speech focus?

# Discussion Questions

1. Audience analysis is extremely important for effective persuasive speaking. Discuss why a speaker needs to approach each audience differently.
2. You are giving a speech to three different audiences. First identify these audiences. Then discuss what you would do differently to adapt your speech to each of them.
3. All of us have encountered unethical speakers at one time or another. First discuss the question, "Does the end ever justify the means in public speaking?" Then discuss the methods used by unethical speakers to manipulate their audiences.
4. Blaise Pascal, a French mathematician, wrote, "People are generally better persuaded by the reasons which they have themselves discovered than by those which have come into the minds of others." Discuss how this quotation relates to the persuasive speech.
5. In the eighteenth century, an English writer who used the pseudonym of Junius (and whose identity is still uncertain) wrote, "By persuading others, we convince ourselves." Discuss how this quotation relates to you as a persuasive speaker.

# ACTIVITIES

**1. Identifying Types of Persuasion.** Identify each of the following statements as a question of fact, a question of belief, or a question of policy.

a. The Lindale Eagles will win the regional football championship.

b. Students should receive job training while they are in high school.

c. The defendant did commit the crime of which he is accused.

d. We must act globally to combat the "greenhouse effect."

e. Katherine Hepburn single-handedly changed Hollywood's rather narrow image of a leading lady.

**2. Examining Techniques of Persuasion.**

**A.** Find five different advertisements. Label each one according to its primary audience appeal. Is its appeal based on logical reasoning? emotional appeals? the credibility of the source? Explain your answers.

**B.** Select a persuasive speech from an issue of *Vital Speeches of the Day.* Identify portions of the speech that contain logical reasoning, make emotional appeals, and establish credibility. Be prepared to read these portions to the class and to discuss the techniques of persuasion they use.

**3. Identifying Logical and Emotional Appeals.** Identify each of the following statements as representing a logical appeal or an emotional appeal.

a. According to one study, illiteracy costs the U.S. government and taxpayers approximately $120 billion a year.

b. Sixty percent of prison inmates are unable to read.

c. You and I have to spend our hard-earned dollars on taxes to pay for prisons.

d. Literacy programs benefit everyone in the community by lowering crime rates and increasing local workers' abilities to handle higher-skilled employment.

e. You can make a difference in your community by volunteering to become a reading tutor and helping someone who is illiterate learn to read or someone whose reading is deficient improve his or her skills.

**4. Giving a Persuasive Speech That Establishes or Changes a Belief.** First, look at the photograph below (or another picture of your own choosing), and think of an issue that the scene in the photograph raises. Then, think of an improvement that would address the issue, and write it as a thesis that addresses a question of belief. For instance, you might state, "Community involvement is the best way to combat our litter problem." Outline a logical argument for making the improvement, and present it in an extemporaneous speech to your class. Finally, ask your classmates to use the Evaluation Checklist for Persuasive Speeches on page 409 to give an oral critique of your speech.

**5. Identifying Inductive and Deductive Approaches.** Identify each of the following arguments as inductive or deductive in approach. Then label each argument according to its method of organization.

a. **Thesis:** My family should buy a new car.
    I. Our old car is giving us problems.
        A. It gets poor gas mileage.
        B. It breaks down regularly.
    II. A new car would solve these problems.
        A. It would get better gas mileage.
        B. It would be less likely to break down.

b. I. Our family agrees on the criteria for a family car.
        A. A family car should get good gas mileage.
        B. A family car should be reliable.
        C. A family car should have room for the whole family.
    II. This minivan meets all these criteria.
        A. This minivan gets good gas mileage.
        B. It is reliable.
        C. It has room for the whole family.
    III. **Thesis:** My family should buy this new minivan.

c. I. That sports car doesn't have room for the whole family.
    II. That station wagon has room for the whole family, but it doesn't get good gas mileage.
    III. That sedan has room for the whole family, but it has very little cargo space.
    IV. This minivan has room for the whole family, gets good gas mileage, and has plenty of cargo space.
    V. **Thesis:** Our family should buy this minivan.

**6. Analyzing a Persuasive Speech.** Briefly outline the main points of a persuasive speech from *Vital Speeches of the Day*. Which of the six organizational patterns (deductive or inductive) did the speaker use? How effective was the speaker's argument? What were its strengths and weaknesses? Be prepared to discuss the main points you outlined and your analysis of the speech.

**7. Giving a Persuasive Speech That Establishes a Fact.** Think of a statement that concerns you and that can be proven true or false—for example, homework does (or does not) help students learn a subject thoroughly. First, state your thesis to address a question of fact. Organize your information and identify whether you use a deductive or an inductive approach. Deliver your speech to your class. Ask your classmates to use the Evaluation Checklist for Persuasive Speeches (page 409) to give you an oral critique of your speech.

**8. Giving a Persuasive Speech That Changes a Policy.** Think of a policy you would like to see changed at your school. Clearly identify the policy and the change you would like to see made. Then state this change in a thesis that addresses a question of policy. Organize your supporting facts and other information in a brief outline that will fit easily on a 3- x 5-inch or 4- x 6-inch card. Using only the outline on your card, deliver your speech to your class. Then conduct a question-and-answer session about the policy change you presented as well as the strengths and weaknesses of your speech.

# COMMUNICATION IN THE WORKPLACE

### Background

You are a sales representative for a product or service you believe in. To overcome customer resistance, such as preference for a competing brand or objections to price, you must use strong persuasive skills.

### Preparing to Do the Job

Identify your product or service and your customer. Then write a three- or four-minute sales pitch to present to your first customer. List the three strongest objections you think your customer might have, and make sure you address these objections in your sales pitch.

### Testing Your Skill

Present your sales talk in class, using visual materials if possible. Ask your classmates to give you feedback about the persuasiveness of your sales talk. Would they buy the product or service?

# EVERYDAY COMMUNICATION

### Situation

Think of a recent conversation in which persuasive speaking played a part. Identify some ideas or points that you wish you had thought of during the conversation.

### Problem

Outline the original discussion. Who was involved? Who said what? What was the outcome? Then decide exactly when and how you should have presented the ideas that occurred to you later.

### Assessing Your Skill

Write a brief dialogue of the discussion, inserting your new ideas where they would have had the greatest effect. Be prepared to explain the differences between your dialogue and the original discussion. Present your dialogue in class, and ask for feedback on how effectively you presented your opinions in the two situations.

415

Congratulations!

CHAPTER

C H A P T E R

**16**

# Speaking for a
# Special Occasion

**After studying this chapter, you should be able to**

1. Choose and limit a topic, identify purpose, think about an appropriate tone, gather information, and prepare to deliver a special-occasion speech.
2. Adapt a special-occasion speech to an audience.
3. Evaluate a special-occasion speech.
4. Plan and deliver the following types of special-occasion speeches: a graduation speech, a speech of introduction, a speech of presentation, a speech of acceptance, a commemorative speech, and an "after-dinner" speech.
5. Recognize the rules for extemporaneous and impromptu speeches in a competition.

## What Is a Special-Occasion Speech?

In an informative or persuasive speech (see Chapters 14 and 15), you have a definite purpose—to inform or to persuade. Accordingly, your purpose as a speaker is the most important factor in determining what you say and how you say it. However, not every speech is controlled by purpose. In a **special-occasion speech** the occasion itself sets the tone of the speech and determines its content. These occasions are often rituals that mark important events in our lives and promote group bonding or social cohesion.

Special-occasion speeches are given in a wide variety of real-life speaking situations: Speaking at a graduation ceremony, introducing a speaker to your club, and presenting your coach with a gift at a sports banquet are all examples of special-occasion speeches. In this chapter you will learn how to develop various kinds of speeches for special occasions.

# Planning a Speech for a Special Occasion

Most special-occasion speeches are not impromptu. You usually know that you will be asked to speak and have time to plan what you are going to say. You can use the suggestions on pages 418–426 to develop any kind of special-occasion speech. [For specific suggestions regarding several common types of special-occasion speeches, see pages 427–437.]

## Choosing and Limiting a Topic

Choosing a topic is often not a problem for special-occasion speeches because the occasion itself frequently determines the topic. For example, in a graduation speech, you will probably talk about your school experience or about what graduation means to you. Try to focus on something specific. Limit your topic to a small, coherent piece of the larger topic.

| Special-Occasion Topics | | |
| --- | --- | --- |
| **Occasion** | **Large Topic** | **Limited Topic** |
| **Graduation speech** | Your experience at Shaw High School | A few specific experiences and why you'll always remember them |
| **Introducing a speaker** | The speaker's whole life and career | Four reasons why you should listen carefully to this speaker |
| **Presenting an award** | The recipient's whole life and career | The recipient's actions and qualities that led to this honor |

# Identifying Your Purpose

Knowing your purpose will help you to decide on the tone and content of your speech. Two questions can help you to identify whether your purpose is to inform, to persuade, or to entertain your audience.

- **What does the occasion require?** Most occasions have a built-in purpose. For example, suppose that for an upcoming assembly you have been asked to introduce the main speaker, an astronaut who had graduated from your high school. Your purpose is to inform: to give the audience information about the astronaut's accomplishments and career.
- **What does the audience expect?** Rude and sarcastic jokes in a graduation speech would be out of place—even shocking. However, the audience would probably expect some humor as a graduation speaker prepared the way for his or her more serious or reflective remarks. In the same way, some humor about the guest of honor would be expected in some "after-dinner" speeches in which the audience expects to be entertained.

# Thinking About Tone

Because occasions vary, some speeches for special occasions are informal and humorous, while others are both formal and serious. The tone of a speech should fit the occasion. **Tone** is the feeling a speaker reveals or conveys about his or her topic. The tone you adopt is determined by the content of your speech, the language you use, and the amount of humor you include.

| Tone | How Tone Is Achieved |
|---|---|
| **Formal tone** (often used for a graduation speech, a speech of introduction, or similar types of speeches) | • complete sentences<br>• an appropriate amount of humor<br>• no slang or idioms<br>• serious ideas<br>• often impersonal but can include personal reflections<br>• serious attention to structure of speech |
| **Informal tone** (often used for an "after-dinner" speech, a story, or similar types of speeches) | • slang, idioms, contractions<br>• humorous anecdotes<br>• other kinds of humor<br>• a few sentence fragments<br>• personal—tell about yourself<br>• structure less important |

## Gathering Information

For most special-occasion speeches, you carry around all the information you need right in your head—in your memories and thoughts. In Chapter 9 (see pages 216–219) you learned some techniques for getting that information on paper. Here are some additional ways to gather information for your speech.

- **Idea starters:** For the introduction, the body, and the conclusion of your speech, you may be able to use facts, quotations, anecdotes, humorous incidents, definitions, personal experiences, personal opinions (beliefs, hopes, wishes), current events (newspaper stories, magazine articles, TV or radio news), and audiovisuals (posters, photos, charts, music).

- **Talking to people:** Because no two people experience an event in exactly the same way, others may be able to fill in specific details you do not recall about an event. For example, as preparation for your speech at a sports banquet, you might ask several teammates, "What were you thinking when Melissa threw that final pitch in the last inning of the championship game?" For most speeches, teachers and other trusted adults can also advise you on the kinds of information your speech should contain as well as give you other tips on how to make your speech successful.

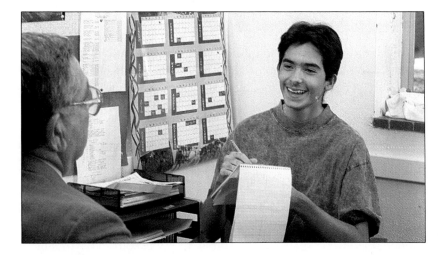

# ACTIVITY

## Analyzing Special-Occasion Speeches

For each speech outlined below, tell what you think the purpose is and what the tone of the speech should be. Then jot down two ideas or details you might include in each speech.

1. You are the president of the drama club. For the upcoming last club meeting of the school year, you have been asked to present an award to the club's faculty adviser.
2. You have been asked to present the main speaker at your state's annual student government association meeting. Teachers and students from the entire state are in the audience. The main speaker is your state's first woman governor.
3. You have been chosen to give a two-minute speech on scholarship at the induction ceremony of the National Honor Society. Other speakers will talk about membership qualifications and service projects for the year. In the audience are current National Honor Society members, students who are about to be inducted, and their parents and friends.
4. You have won the essay contest on free enterprise sponsored by business owners in your community. The award will be presented to you after lunch at the business club's next monthly meeting.
5. You are the captain of your high school's swimming team. You have been asked to speak at the dedication ceremony for your community's recently built natatorium. Because the new facility was funded by state and local sources, prominent state and local politicians, as well as teachers, students, and community members, will be present.

# Preparing Your Speech

Once you have clearly identified your purpose and your audience and have made some notes about what you might include in your speech, you are ready to transform your rough notes and general ideas into a speech.

## HOW TO > Prepare a Special-Occasion Speech

1. **Focus on what is important.** No matter how much your topic interests them, everyone in your audience has a limited attention span. If you ramble, they will start to daydream or fall asleep. As you prepare your speech, avoid wordiness. Get to the point.

2. **Keep it simple.** Everyday conversation is generally easy to listen to and to understand, but speeches often contain complex ideas. Listeners cannot go back to something that has confused them in a speech. Keep your language simple and make your ideas easy to follow. Explain complicated ideas carefully.

3. **Support what you say with specifics.** Back up your statements with examples, anecdotes, facts, or statistics. When you state a fact or opinion, your audience needs to hear reasons or evidence to understand why you believe the statement to be true.

4. **Pay attention to structure.** Experienced speakers advise: "Tell them what you're going to tell them; then tell them; then tell them what you told them." Start with an intriguing introduction, and end with a definite conclusion. [See pages 270–274 of Chapter 11 for information on writing introductions and conclusions.]

   One device that lends structure to a speech is **repetition,** the repeating of a sentence or a phrase that runs like a refrain throughout the speech—for example, the "I have a dream" refrain in the famous speech by Dr. Martin Luther King, Jr. (page 680). Speech writers aim for a slogan or sentence that the audience will remember. A graduation speaker, for example, might repeat "We are the future" at appropriate places in the speech.

## Adapting Your Speech to Your Audience

When you give a special-occasion speech, your audience is likely to consist of your peers—fellow students who share common interests and experiences. They may be members of your club, your graduating class, or your tennis team. Since you know them fairly well, you can draw on your own observations and experience to adapt your speech to fit your classmates' interests, needs, and expectations.

**Attention Span.** A captive audience sitting through a long program, such as a graduation ceremony, will not pay attention for very long to a dull speech. Recapture lost attention by using your voice with power and cadence. You might also consider cutting some material and proceeding to the end.

Attention span is usually not a problem if your audience is there by choice. If you are talking to the computer club about a contest for developing new software, for instance, the members will listen carefully because they are interested in what you are saying. If you are presenting an award to this year's outstanding school soccer player, the members of the soccer team will probably pay close attention to your comments.

**Knowledge, Needs, and Interests.** Every listener should feel as if you are talking directly to him or her. For this reason, you should include specific suggestions and examples, provide needed background information, and define technical terms. For example, for a speech introducing a state representative to a group of high school seniors, you might identify the specific district that the elected official represents. You might also mention committees on which he or she serves.

**Expectations.** Your audience will have certain expectations that you should aim to meet. For instance, an audience would not expect to hear a graduation speech made up primarily of jokes.

Here are three ways to determine what your audience will expect from your speech:

1. Refer to the suggestions on pages 427–437 for developing the type of special-occasion speech you plan to make.
2. Listen to other people's speeches for similar occasions, and pay attention to the audience's reactions.
3. Ask for advice from teachers and advisers, especially those who have listened for many years to the kind of speech you are going to make.

PEANUTS reprinted by permission of UFS, Inc.

# ACTIVITY 2

## Preparing a Special-Occasion Speech

Look back at the five speech occasions listed in Activity 1 on page 421. Choose one situation and fill out a chart like the one at the top of the following page. You may also want to work with a classmate to develop two different attention-getting introductions for the speech you have chosen. [Review pages 270–273 in Chapter 11 for more help with writing introductions.]

*(continued on next page)*

*Planning a Special-Occasion Speech*

Occasion: _____

Purpose: _____

Audience: _____

Topic: _____

Introduction: _____

Body (specific details): _____

Conclusion: _____

# Delivering Your Speech

All the principles of effective delivery that you studied in Chapter 13 (pages 317–345) apply to several different types of speeches, including special-occasion speeches. Rehearsing is one way to increase the chances that you will present your speech with the most effective delivery possible. The more you rehearse, the more comfortable you will be when you deliver your speech. By knowing your speech well, you will be able to maintain eye contact with your audience while only occasionally glancing down at your manuscript or notes. Keep the following suggestions in mind as you rehearse your speech.

- **Rehearse by yourself.** Say your speech aloud in front of a full-length mirror. Figure out where to pause, where your voice should rise for emphasis, and where it should fall. You may even want to mark your manuscript with a colored pencil to show word groupings, pauses, and inflections for emphasis. [See pages 63–64 for more information on inflection.]

    Remember that many special-occasion speeches are for pleasant occasions. In such cases, a deadly serious, wooden tone of voice is inappropriate. Always try to give your speech a dash of liveliness. Keep your volume up as you vary your tone and phrasing.

- **Rehearse before an audience.** Find people who are similar to the members of your expected audience, and ask them for some suggestions on what might improve your speech. You might get together with five or six classmates, listen to each other's speeches, and comment on them. [See the Evaluation Checklist on page 439.] If the drama or speech department in your school has a video camera you can borrow, ask someone to film you as you practice delivering your speech. Then watch the video carefully and critically.

Thinking about your rehearsals for a speech will help you deliver your speech better. In your communication journal, make notes about your rehearsals by yourself in front of a mirror and those before an audience. What do you think you do well when you give your speech? What do you need to improve?

## Evaluating Special-Occasion Speeches

In real life, there are no grades at the end of a special-occasion speech. Your audience may applaud politely or enthusiastically or not at all. In speech class, however, you may often be asked to critique your classmates' speeches. Whether oral or written, your critique should evaluate the speaker's organization, content, language, and delivery. [See pages 96–98 for more information on oral and written critiques.]

You can use the Evaluation Checklist on page 439 to evaluate a special-occasion speech. Because special-occasion speeches vary a good deal, not all of the questions apply to every type of speech.

ACTIVITY 3

### Evaluating a Special-Occasion Speech

Using the Evaluation Checklist on page 439, evaluate a special-occasion speech you have heard on television or on the radio, at school or a community event, or at a family gathering. What did you notice about what the speaker said? about the tone of the speech? about the audience at that occasion? about the speaker's delivery of the speech? Was the speech memorable or outstanding in any way? Why?

# Understanding Types of Special-Occasion Speeches

In this section you will focus on specific types of special-occasion speeches. If someday you accept an Oscar for an Academy Award or nominate a candidate for president of the United States, you can apply the principles you learn in this section to plan your speech.

## Preparing a Graduation Speech

**Occasion.**   A **graduation speech** is a formal address made at a commencement ceremony in honor of the occasion. Actually, a graduation ceremony may include several speeches, such as those given by students, administrators, and a featured or main speaker. After the speeches, the graduates receive their diplomas.

**Audience.**   The audience at a graduation ceremony is usually made up of graduating students, their families, friends, and teachers. The graduates are often excited, and their parents and families are proud and happy. Thus, although typically cheerful and positive in attitude toward the speaker, the listeners may likely be restless. Remember that your listeners are eagerly waiting for the presentation of diplomas. They will be grateful for a short speech: ten to twenty minutes long. Your senior-class adviser will tell you how long your speech should be.

**Content and Tone.**   Certain ideas and approaches are expected in a graduation speech. Use the following suggestions to develop your speech.

- Tell brief anecdotes, not long stories.
- Include some humor, but avoid silliness and disrespect.
- Evaluate the school experience without slapstick or anger.
- Include expected topics: congratulating graduates, acknowledging teachers, looking back, looking ahead.
- Offer optimistic and inspirational advice.
- Use formal and dignified language.

# ACTI·VITY 4

**Y**ou are a featured speaker at your class's graduation from high school. Plan and write a five-minute speech. Find a partner and listen to each other's graduation speeches. Then use the Evaluation Checklist on page 439 to critique each other's speeches, providing three or four specific, positive suggestions for improvement.

## Preparing a Speech of Introduction

**Occasion.**   A **speech of introduction** is a formal speech for the purpose of gaining the audience's attention and setting the stage for the speaker or program that follows. For example, a speech of introduction may precede a dramatic reading or oral interpretation to provide background for the audience that will help them understand the dramatization they are about to hear. In many cases, a speech of introduction is used to introduce the main speaker that an audience has come to hear.

**Purposes.**   Your first purpose is to inform the audience about the speaker and the topic: to tell them just enough to pique their curiosity and to convince them that the speaker is worth listening to. A second purpose is to make the speaker feel welcome.

**Audience.**   Most audiences have a wide range of attention spans. You need to capture your listeners' attention immediately and to keep your introduction brief. Most introductions should run no longer than two minutes; some may be as short as half a minute. Remember that the audience still has to listen to the speaker's speech.

**Content and Tone.** Your audience will expect answers to three basic questions: *Who is the speaker? What will the speaker talk about? Why should I listen?* Use the following suggestions to develop your speech.

- Make your speech brief.
- Pronounce the speaker's name and official title correctly.
- Use the title the speaker wants you to use—for example, Dr. Janice Goodstein.
- Include accurate facts about the speaker's qualifications and experience, but avoid too many details and too much personal information.
- Adopt a formal, respectful tone.
- End your speech of introduction with a formal welcome: "I'd like you to welcome Dr. Janice Goodstein to our psychology club meeting."

## ACTIVITY 5

### Introducing a Speaker

Choose a classmate and write a one- or two-minute speech of introduction that you would give if that classmate were the main speaker at a school assembly. Think of a topic your classmate will speak about, and tell why he or she is an expert on that topic. Use factual information about your classmate. Practice your speech and then deliver it before the class.

## Preparing a Speech of Presentation

**Occasion.** People often receive awards, honors, or gifts for special achievements or for special occasions. For example, your principal might present a plaque to the school's outstanding student volunteer, or an actor might receive an Oscar for a movie role. At these times, a speaker gives a **speech of presentation** to honor the person who is being recognized and to present the actual award or gift.

**Audience.** Whether friends, family members, or colleagues, the audience members for a speech of presentation are usually people who either know or care about the person receiving the award. They are interested in hearing about the person's accomplishments that led to the honor. They are also eager to see the person receive the award or gift, so a brief speech of presentation—no more than five minutes long—is appropriate.

**Content and Tone.** Unless it is important to surprise the award's recipient, the speaker usually names the person early in the speech. Use the following suggestions to develop your speech.

- Explain why the award or gift is given, who gives the award, and how the person's qualities or achievements led to this honor.
- Tell a brief anecdote to illustrate the recipient's actions or personal qualities.
- Read aloud the inscription on a plaque or trophy to satisfy the audience's curiosity.
- Adopt a respectful tone, but also consider using a warm and personal tone, depending on the award itself and on how well you and the audience know the recipient.

## Preparing a Speech of Acceptance

**Occasion.** A **speech of acceptance** is one given by a person who has received an honor, an award, or a gift. In the speech, the recipient usually expresses his or her appreciation.

**Audience.** Like the audience for a speech of presentation, the audience for a speech of acceptance is usually made up of the recipient's friends, family members, and colleagues. The audience members are certainly interested in the speaker's thank-you remarks, but they would most enjoy a brief speech of acceptance—two to three minutes long at most.

**Content and Tone.** A speech of acceptance acknowledges the people who have given the award or gift, as well as the people who helped the speaker to achieve it. You might use one or some of the following suggestions in your acceptance speech.

- Convey a simple, direct thank you.
- Include a brief anecdote to entertain your listeners and perhaps strengthen your connection with them.
- Mention what you think the honor might mean to you in the future.
- Accept with a sense of pride and honor, not false modesty and embarrassment.
- Adopt a warm, personal tone.

# ACTIVITY

## 6 Preparing Speeches of Presentation and Acceptance

Working with a partner, identify a speech occasion for receiving an honor or award. Prepare a speech of presentation, giving the award to your partner. Next, have your partner prepare a speech of presentation to give you the award. Each of you should then become a recipient, and prepare a speech of acceptance for the award. Refer to the Guidelines for Special-Occasion Speeches on page 438 as you prepare your speeches.

# Preparing a Commemorative Speech

**Occasion.**   A **commemorative speech** is given to mark an important event or to honor a person. For example, your mayor may give a commemorative speech to dedicate a monument at a local Civil War battlefield. A commemorative speech that honors a living person is called a **testimonial speech;** one that honors a person who has died recently is called a **eulogy.**

**Audience.**   The audience at a commemorative speech usually has some vital interest in the event or in the person being honored. You may attend the mayor's dedication speech, for example, because one of your ancestors played an important role in the battle that is being remembered. While the audience wants to hear what the speaker has to say, the speaker should still strive to be brief. There may be other speakers who are also presenting their comments about the event or the person.

**Content and Tone.**   Commemorative speeches can be given at occasions that range from being joyful to being very sad. Use the following suggestions to develop a commemorative speech for a particular occasion.

- Discuss the significance of the event or the person being honored.
- Include brief anecdotes to illustrate your points. Even in the case of a eulogy, which is often given at a funeral service, you may include a light anecdote to illustrate the person's best qualities.
- Include details and ideas that honor the person or the event.
- Adopt a respectful tone. Depending on the specific occasion and your connection to the person or event, you may also want to convey a warm, personal tone. Try to avoid slang and informal language, however.

# ACTIVITY 7

## Preparing a Commemorative Speech

**Y**our school has just built a new facility that will improve the quality of education you and your classmates receive (for example, a new media center or a computer lab). Decide what kind of facility you would like to talk about, and prepare a commemorative speech to mark and celebrate its opening.

## Preparing an "After-Dinner" Speech

**Occasion.** An **"after-dinner" speech** is the featured entertainment at a meeting or at a special occasion, such as an awards banquet. Usually, the audience eats first; then there may be a brief business meeting, followed by one or more speakers.

**Audience.** Members of the audience may know each other and share a common experience (owning a business) or interest (drama). If they have just eaten a meal, they have been sitting still for a long time. They may listen patiently for a while but may become restless before very long. Your purpose is to entertain them briefly—no more than five minutes if there are several speakers, and no more than ten minutes if you are the only speaker.

**Content and Tone.** Choose a topic that will appeal to your audience's interests and concerns. For example, for an audience of amateur photographers, you might talk about the topic "Great Pictures That Got Away." For an audience of parents, you might choose a serious topic, such as "How to Talk to Your Teenager," and treat it lightly. Use the following suggestions to develop your "after-dinner" speech.

- Include an introduction that captures your audience's interest and communicates that your speech is intended to be amusing.
- In the body of your speech, use a series of brief stories and examples related to your topic.
- Convey a light and amusing tone by using informal language.

## ACTIVITY 8

### Planning an "After-Dinner" Speech

You have been invited to be the only speaker at the next meeting of a school club. (For this speech you can choose a club that you currently belong to or one you are interested in joining.) Brainstorm possible topics that would appeal to your audience—perhaps a serious topic that you would like to treat humorously. Then choose one topic and think of at least three brief anecdotes and examples to include in your "after-dinner" speech.

## Preparing an Extemporaneous Speech for Competition

**Occasion.** The National Forensic League sponsors high school speech and debate competitions all over the country. [See Chapter 18 for more about debate.] An **extemporaneous speech** for a competition is one that requires speakers to give seven-minute speeches after only thirty minutes of preparation time. Speakers compete in two divisions with topics that have a persuasive purpose and that deal with either international or domestic (United States) issues, such as nuclear war or national health insurance.

An extemporaneous speaking team amasses current evidence about the topics—newspaper and magazine articles, statistics, quotations, and excerpts from books. Each piece of evidence has a **citation** that tells its source and date, and files are updated throughout the year. Team members study each folder carefully to become familiar with the evidence.

The heart of an extemporaneous speaking competition is the preparation room or area, where speakers wait until it is their turn to speak. Thirty minutes before their turn to speak, the speakers reach into an official envelope and draw out three topics. They must immediately choose one of the three. Speakers consult the team's files on the topic, make notes, and quickly rehearse the speech. Speakers are not allowed to look at any written material when they deliver their speeches.

**Audience.** A judge or panel of judges listens to each speech and awards points based on the speaker's content and delivery. After several preliminary rounds (with different topics for each round), the highest-ranking speakers compete in quarterfinal, semifinal, and final rounds.

**Content and Tone.** Use the following suggestions to develop an extemporaneous speech.

- Take a stand and line up supporting evidence. State an opinion clearly, and back it up with statistics, facts, and examples.
- Stick to the topic. **Topicality,** or relating everything directly to the topic you have chosen, is a requirement in extemporaneous speeches. You will lose points if you wander from your topic as stated in the question.
- Pay attention to tone and structure. Create a definite beginning, middle, and end. Make sure that you state the topic in your introduction.
- Sound confident. You want your audience to believe that you are in control and that you know what you are talking about. Send these messages nonverbally by keeping your voice steady, showing enthusiasm, and having a relaxed body posture.
- Express your ideas clearly. Remember that you don't need to choose "difficult" words to show that you know what you are talking about. Use simple, direct language and complete sentences.

# Giving an Impromptu Speech in a Competition

**Occasion.** An **impromptu speech** for a speech contest requires speakers to give a five-minute speech after five minutes or less of preparation. With so little preparation time, impromptu speakers rely almost entirely on their ability to "think on their feet." They must formulate their ideas quickly. Their goal is simple: to be articulate, or to express their ideas clearly. Impromptu speakers must also maintain their poise to convey the impression that they can calmly and coherently speak on any topic.

Impromptu speakers do not prepare evidence folders: They would not have time to look at them, and impromptu topics are not often about current events for which speakers would require evidence. Topics in impromptu speech competitions vary widely and are usually a single word or phrase. Some contests require speakers to respond to a quotation, question, or statement.

From the three topics drawn from an envelope, an impromptu speaker chooses the one he or she knows most about. In most impromptu speech tournaments, speakers have up to five minutes to prepare, but sometimes they must begin speaking right after they choose a topic.

**Audience.** Judges award each speaker points for content and delivery. Just as in extemporaneous speech contests, the highest-ranking speakers move into the final rounds.

**Content and Tone.** Use the following suggestions as you prepare for an impromptu speech in a competition.

- Follow a simple structure: an attention-getting introduction, then the main ideas with supporting details, and finally an effective conclusion.
- Use clear, coherent language.
- Try to project confidence.
- Adopt a tone that is appropriate to the topic, from personal topics (responsibility, friends) to formal ones (world hunger, voter apathy).

"The picture's pretty bleak, gentlemen. ... The world's climates are changing, the mammals are taking over, and we all have a brain about the size of a walnut."

# ACTIVITY 9

## Giving an Impromptu Speech

Work with five or six students. Put at least twenty slips of paper with impromptu speech topics into an envelope. Topics can be single words, phrases, quotations, questions, or statements. Have each person pick three topics and choose one for a two-minute impromptu speech. Allow for five minutes of preparation time. Take turns until each person has given an impromptu speech. Then, discuss how you would evaluate each speech if you were a judge at a competition.

## GUIDELINES

### *for Special-Occasion Speeches*

- Have I chosen a limited topic appropriate for the occasion?

- Have I identified my purpose?

- Have I gathered information to support what I say?

- Have I written an attention-getting opener and a strong conclusion?

- Have I adapted the speech to my audience's needs, knowledge, interests, and expectations?

- Is my speech too long or too short?

- Is my tone appropriate for the occasion?

- Have I practiced the speech enough so that I can deliver it confidently and maintain eye contact with the audience?

- Can I use humor to make my speech more entertaining?

# EVALUATION  CHECKLIST

## *for Special-Occasion Speeches*

**Organization:**
> Did the introduction catch the audience's attention?
> Were the speaker's ideas easy to follow?
> Did the speaker use good transitions between major points?
> Was there an effective conclusion?

**Content:**
> Was the speech an appropriate length for the particular occasion?
> Did the speaker provide any necessary background information the audience might need?
> Was the content appropriate for the occasion?
> Did the speaker consider the audience's interests, needs, and expectations?
> Was the tone appropriate for the occasion?

**Language:**
> Did the speaker choose words that created a tone appropriate for the particular occasion?
> Did the speaker use words that the audience could understand?
> Did the speaker define any technical terms?

**Delivery:**
> Did the speaker seem confident?
> Was the speaker's attitude appropriate for the occasion?
> Did the speaker look at the audience during the speech?
> Was the speaker easy to hear and understand?
> Did the speaker pronounce words and names correctly?

**Additional Comments:**

**Evaluation:**

# SPEAKING FOR A SPECIAL EVENT

### Rising to the Occasion

Toastmasters is an international organization that is dedicated to helping its members improve their public speaking skills. Toastmasters clubs meet regularly to give members an opportunity to practice their speaking skills and get constructive feedback from other members.

### Characteristics of a Good Toastmaster

A good Toastmaster

1. chooses and limits a speech topic
2. prepares and delivers special-occasion speeches
3. adapts a special-occasion speech to suit a particular audience
4. evaluates a special-occasion speech

## A·C·T·I·V·I·T·Y

### Situation

A classmate of yours has been chosen to be a foreign exchange student, and you have been asked to prepare a speech for his or her going-away party.

### Preparation

You want to congratulate your friend, wish him or her well, and express your feelings about the event. Some of your reactions may be difficult to talk about. For example, you will probably wish your friend were not leaving the country. How will you be honest without detracting from the celebration?

### Meet the Toastmaster

Toastmaster Huy-Suong N. Bui recognizes that public speaking skills play an important role in most people's professional lives. "Your success in business is based on how effectively you communicate," she says. "Through participation in the Toastmasters, people from all backgrounds learn to speak effectively, conduct a meeting, manage a department or business, and to lead, delegate, and motivate. You learn all this by doing—by actually speaking to groups."

*Huysuong N Bui*

### Analysis and Assessment

Using wording and tone appropriate to the occasion, prepare a brief (one-page) special-occasion "bon voyage" speech. Present your short speech in class as if you were one of the speakers at the going-away party. Ask your classmates to describe how your friend and the other guests would react to your speech.

# S·U·M·M·A·R·Y

**SPEAKING FOR A SPECIAL OCCASION** involves a situation in which the occasion itself sets the tone of the speech and determines its content.

- **Plan a special-occasion speech** by limiting your topic and identifying your purpose and tone according to the occasion. Some special-occasion speeches require a formal tone, while others require an informal tone. Gather information by using idea starters and by talking to other people.

- **Prepare your special-occasion speech** by focusing on your key ideas, supporting your ideas with specifics, eliminating wordiness, and keeping your language and ideas easy to understand.

- **Adapt your speech** to the audience's expectations, attention span, knowledge, needs, and interests.

- **Rehearse your speech** by yourself and before an audience so that you can deliver it without reading it. Mark your speech for pauses, emphasis, and word groupings. Deliver your speech in a relaxed manner, maintaining eye contact and varying your voice. Be sure to pronounce words correctly and to enunciate clearly.

- **Evaluate a special-occasion speech** using the Evaluation Checklist on page 439.

- **Understand that different types of speeches are appropriate** in various special occasions. Be familiar with the kinds of special-occasion speeches presented in this chapter.

## Vocabulary

Look back through this chapter to find the meaning of each of the following terms. Write each term and its meaning in your communication journal.

"after-dinner" speech, p. 433
citation, p. 434
commemorative speech, p. 432
eulogy, p. 432
extemporaneous speech, p. 434
graduation speech, p. 427
impromptu speech, p. 436
repetition, p. 422
special-occasion speech, p. 417
speech of acceptance, p. 430
speech of introduction, p. 428
speech of presentation, p. 429
testimonial speech, p. 432
tone, p. 419
topicality, p. 435

## Review Questions

1. Identify two specific purposes a special-occasion speech might have. Give an example of each.
2. Name two types of special-occasion speeches for which a formal tone is appropriate. How would you achieve a formal tone?
3. Name a type of special-occasion speech for which an informal tone is suitable. How would you achieve an informal tone?
4. Why would talking to other people sometimes be helpful in gathering information and details for a special-occasion speech?
5. Why is structure important in a special-occasion speech?
6. What are three considerations you should take into account when adapting your special-occasion speech to your audience?
7. What topics are appropriate in a graduation speech? in a speech of introduction?
8. How are a speech of presentation and a speech of acceptance related?
9. What is the main purpose of a commemorative speech? of an "after-dinner" speech?
10. What is the difference between extemporaneous and impromptu speeches for competition?

## Discussion Questions

1. Of all the special-occasion speeches mentioned in this chapter, which one do you think you would be most comfortable giving? Which one would make you feel most uncomfortable? Discuss your responses with your classmates. See if you can find reasons why certain types of speeches make you feel more comfortable.
2. Discuss how the occasion itself determines the type of speech you give in a particular situation. Also discuss how the occasion affects the tone you adopt in your speech.
3. Discuss the role of anecdotes and humor in special-occasion speeches, and tell when both are or are not appropriate.
4. Samuel Johnson, the English essayist and poet, wrote "Praise, like gold and diamonds, owes its value only to its scarcity." First, discuss the meaning of this quotation. Next, discuss how this quotation applies to a speech of presentation. Then, discuss the ways in which this quotation relates to someone who is making a speech of acceptance.
5. Discuss with your classmates the meaning of the ceremony held by your school to commemorate the graduation of the senior class. Who participates in this ceremony? How many speakers usually give speeches, including speeches of introduction? How many speeches could be considered main or featured speeches? What expectations does the audience have of the speeches made on this occasion?

# ACTIVITIES

**1. Preparing a Graduation Speech.** Prepare a three-minute graduation speech to be given before the graduates of an extracurricular program, such as a museum art class, a gymnastics team, or a community music program. Be sure to include topics that will interest the graduates and their friends and families. Deliver your speech to your classmates. Then ask them to use the Evaluation Checklist on page 439 to determine the strengths and weaknesses of your speech.

**2. Preparing a Speech of Presentation.**
   **A.** Using a literature or humanities textbook or current magazines and newspapers, select an author, an artist, or a musician you would like to honor. Decide what type of award you would like to bestow on this person. The award may be real or imaginary, serious or humorous. For example, you might choose to award your favorite columnist a Pulitzer Prize. Or, you might "honor" the rock musician whose guitar riffs are the most repetitive, by presenting him or her with a Golden Snore Award.
   **B.** Prepare a three-minute speech of presentation for the award. In your speech, be sure to explain the significance of the award and to state the reasons why the recipient deserves the honor. Deliver your speech to a group of classmates. Ask them to use the Evaluation Checklist on page 439 to evaluate your speech.

**3. Giving a Commemorative Speech.**
   **A.** Using a social studies or history textbook, select a historic event that interests you and that you would like to commemorate. If you are not very familiar with the event, do some research to learn more about the event's participants, its causes and outcomes, and its lasting significance.
   **B.** Prepare a three-minute commemorative speech in which you dedicate a monument erected to honor and remember this historic event. Be sure to take into account your audience's knowledge (or lack of knowledge) of the event. Also, point out what, specifically, makes this event worthy of commemoration. Deliver your speech to a small group of classmates, and ask them to use the Evaluation Checklist on page 439 to evaluate your speech.

**4. Preparing an "After-Dinner" Speech.** Prepare a five-minute "after-dinner" speech for a banquet. For example, you might prepare a speech for your swim team's awards banquet or for your youth group's annual retreat. Deliver your speech to a small group of classmates. After you speak, ask your classmates to evaluate your speech with the Evaluation Checklist on page 439.

**5. Observing and Critiquing Special-Occasion Speeches.** Watch an awards presentation on television. For example, you might choose a ceremony for one of the awards like the ones shown in these photographs or for another prestigious award of your own choosing. Prepare a short written critique of one presentation speech and one acceptance speech you observe during the program. What could each speaker have done differently? Refer to the Evaluation Checklist on page 439 to develop your critiques.

**6. Developing Standards for Impromptu and Extemporaneous Speech Contests.** In impromptu and extemporaneous speaking competitions, judges evaluate each speaker's performance, considering the short preparation time and the tense situation. For each type of speech, develop at least three standards, or criteria, you would use if you were a judge evaluating speakers. Be prepared to explain why speakers should meet each standard in the competition.

**7. Giving an Impromptu Speech.** Using a five-minute preparation time, prepare a two-minute impromptu speech. In your speech, you should try to explain the meaning of any one of the following quotations. Deliver your speech to a small group of your classmates. After you speak, discuss with your classmates specific suggestions for making improvements in your impromptu speaking style.

**a.** "This above all: to thine own self be true, / And it must follow, as the night the day, / Thou canst not then be false to any man."

—William Shakespeare, from *Hamlet*

**b.** "Iron rusts from disuse; stagnant water loses its purity and in cold weather becomes frozen; even so does inaction sap the vigor of the mind."

—Leonardo da Vinci, from *The Notebooks [1508–1518]*

**c.** "I started with this idea in my head, 'There's two things I've got a right to . . . death or liberty.'"

—Sarah Bradford, from *Scenes in the Life of Harriet Tubman*

**d.** "'Hope' is the thing with feathers— / That perches in the soul— / And sings the tune without the words— / And never stops—at all—"

—Emily Dickinson, from *No. 254*

**e.** "Conversation . . . is the art of never appearing a bore, of knowing how to say everything interestingly, to entertain with no matter what, to be charming with nothing at all."

—Guy de Maupassant, from *Sur l'Eau (On the Water)*

**8. Planning an Extemporaneous Speech for a Competition.** Using a thirty-minute preparation time, plan a seven-minute extemporaneous speech that outlines your opinion and reasons that support it. Use the following question for your topic: "Should this state pass a law limiting the times and number of hours teenagers can work during the school year?" In your plan, also indicate how you would gather information to support your reasons.

# COMMUNICATION IN THE WORKPLACE

### Background

You have been asked to introduce a community representative who will speak to your school at an assembly.

### Preparing to Do the Job

Prepare a two-minute speech of introduction for a community representative. Select a real person, if possible. In your speech, briefly give the speaker's background and identify the topic of the speech. You may need to do some research to find specific information about the person or to clearly identify the topic.

### Testing Your Skill

Be prepared to deliver your speech to your class. Afterward, ask your classmates to evaluate your performance. Did they have a clear understanding of the topic and the speaker's qualifications? Would they be interested in hearing the speaker that you introduced? Why or why not?

# EVERYDAY COMMUNICATION

### Situation

You are the student representative on your community's board of education. The board members have asked you to present the "Teacher of the Year" award to Ms. Sanchez, the band director.

### Problem

Prepare a three-minute speech for the presentation of Ms. Sanchez's award. In your speech, make reference to the award's inscription: "With gratitude for your willing leadership and encouragement of all student musicians."

### Assessing Your Skill

Deliver your presentation to the class. Ask your classmates for feedback on your presentation of the award.

445

Unit 5

# Democratic Processes

consensus

C H A P T E R **17**

# Group Discussion

**OBJECTIVES**

**After studying this chapter, you should be able to**

1. Define *group discussion*.
2. Plan a discussion by determining a purpose and format, choosing a topic, wording a discussion question, and preparing an outline.
3. Carry out the roles of leader, secretary, and participant in group discussions.
4. Resolve conflict in discussions.
5. Reach group decisions by decree, by voting, or by consensus.
6. Evaluate a discussion.

## What Is Group Discussion?

More than likely you have participated in group discussion in many of your cooperative learning projects. **Group discussion** is a goal-oriented form of communication. It is the face-to-face communication of a small number of people who meet for a specific purpose, such as to arrive at a decision, to brainstorm ideas, to share information, or to solve a problem.

In planning a group discussion, it is important to consider the *who, where,* and *when* of the meeting. Five to seven people are enough to stir up a lively discussion but not so many that members will feel uncomfortable. Also, an odd number of members prevents tied votes, or deadlocks. Members should work in a comfortable, well-lighted environment and should sit either in a circle (for a private discussion) or in a semicircle (for a public discussion with an audience). To be effective, members should be well rested and should limit their sessions to short time periods, usually no more than an hour in length.

# Planning a Group Discussion

Planning and participating in an effective group discussion means thinking about and dealing with several interrelated parts of the discussion:

- determining a purpose and a format
- choosing a topic
- wording a discussion question
- identifying the types of discussion questions
- preparing an outline

## Determining a Purpose and a Format

Members of a discussion group do not meet simply for the sake of discussion. The group has a goal or a purpose, and the discussion is intended to accomplish that goal or purpose. The following chart lists several of the many purposes that group discussions can serve.

| Purposes for Discussion | |
|---|---|
| • to arrive at a solution to a problem | • to negotiate agreements |
| • to brainstorm ideas | • to resolve conflicts |
| • to learn cooperatively | • to share information |
| • to make a decision | • to stimulate thought or action |
| • to make plans | • to strengthen bonds among people |

To be successful, your discussion group needs more than a purpose, or reason, for meeting. You must also choose an appropriate **discussion format.** Group discussion formats may be either public or private.

**Public Discussion Formats.**   When group discussions are held in front of an audience, you can use one of the following public discussion formats: panel, symposium, or forum.

- A **panel format** is used when a group of experts discusses a topic to provide information and opinions that another group can use to reach a decision or to find a solution.

    EXAMPLE: A town council invites a panel of experts, such as engineers, waste disposal experts, and environmentalists, to discuss the plans for building a new incinerator plant.

- A **symposium format** is used when several people present short, prepared speeches on the same topic and then discuss among themselves the ideas presented in the speeches.

    EXAMPLE: A university invites a symposium of people, such as a campus police officer, a college student, and a professor, to discuss ways to improve campus security.

- A **forum format** is used when a panel or a symposium is opened up to questions or comments from the audience.

    EXAMPLE: A company invites a symposium of productivity and time-management experts to discuss ways of improving worker efficiency. After the experts have presented their prepared speeches, the moderator invites questions from the audience.

**Private Discussion Formats.** When group discussions are held in closed session, you can use one of the following private discussion formats: free-form, moderated free-form, standing committee, ad hoc committee, round-table, or progressive.

- A **free-form format** is used when group members discuss a topic at will in no particular order.
- A **moderated free-form format** is used when a moderator, or leader, introduces the topic to be discussed and recognizes individuals to speak.
- A **standing committee format** is used when a small group of people is asked to study problems that fall within their scope of duties or functions and then to make recommendations to the organization of which they are a part.

  EXAMPLE: An organization asks its budget committee to discuss a problem related to dues. The members of the committee discuss the problem in a private meeting and then present their proposed solution to the organization's leaders or perhaps to the entire organization.

- An **ad hoc committee format** is used when a group is formed to study a single issue or to accomplish a single task. Unlike a standing committee, which handles various issues or tasks over a long period of time, an ad hoc committee is formed to do a particular job and then is disbanded when its job is completed.

  EXAMPLE: A college board of trustees forms an ad hoc committee to search for a new college president.

- A **round-table format** is used when each member of a group discussion gives a brief report on some aspect of a topic and then the group as a whole discusses the separate reports.

  EXAMPLE: A museum of African American culture holds a round-table discussion on "African Americans in the Arts." After reports by each member on the different arts—for example, music, dance, painting, sculpture, and theater—the group as a whole discusses the breadth and depth of the African American contribution to the arts in the United States.

- A **progressive format** is used when a large group of people is divided into smaller groups, each of which discusses a different aspect of the topic. This format is particularly helpful when everyone in the group is not prepared to discuss the entire question.

"Oddly enough, language has proved no problem."

## Choosing a Topic

Without a topic, there is nothing to discuss. A discussion can be held on almost any topic. Often the topic is chosen for the group.

**EXAMPLES:**

1. A principal asks a group of teachers to find possible solutions to the problem of an overcrowded student parking lot.
2. A nonprofit organization asks a group of architects to devise a workable plan for adding a new wing to the public library.

Sometimes a group is asked to select its own topic. If you are in a group that is given this opportunity, here are a few guidelines that you should keep in mind to help you choose an appropriate topic.

## HOW TO ▷ *Choose a Discussion Topic*

1. **Choose an interesting topic.** The topic should be interesting to all or most members of the discussion group and to the audience if the discussion is to be public.

2. **Choose a topic about which group members are informed.** The members of the discussion group should know enough about the topic to be able to make a valuable contribution to the discussion.

3. **Choose a significant topic.** Members should feel that time spent discussing the topic is time well spent.

4. **Choose a properly limited topic.** The topic should be narrow enough to be dealt with effectively in the time available.

# ACTIVITY 1

## Choosing Topics and Formats

**F**orm a discussion group of five to seven classmates. Brainstorm to come up with a list of ten group discussion topics. For example, you might list censorship of movies as one topic. Then decide within your group which discussion format you would use to discuss each topic.

## Wording a Discussion Question

Once you have chosen the topic for your group discussion, you will need to phrase, or word, the topic as a question. A well-phrased discussion question should meet the following requirements.

**1. The question's wording should be clear and concise.** If the wording is vague, the group will not know what it is trying to achieve or how to proceed.

> **VAGUE:** Should the curriculum be looked into?
> **CONCISE:** Should each course in the high school's curriculum be reevaluated to make sure that it meets the goals set by the state board of education?

**2. The question's wording should promote objective discussion.** If the wording is subjective, it could sway the group to reach the answer or solution implied by the question.

> **SUBJECTIVE:** Should our ridiculously low standards for high school athletic eligibility be raised?
> **OBJECTIVE:** Should our high school's minimum standards for athletic eligibility be revised?

**3. The question's wording should allow for more than a yes or no answer.** If the wording requires only a yes or no answer, the group may not fully discuss all of the issues of the topic.

> **REQUIRES YES OR NO:** Should a student who cheats on a test receive an F?
> **REQUIRES A DISCUSSION:** What should the policy be for dealing with students who cheat on tests?

*I*n your communication journal, keep a list of questions that could be used for a group discussion. Add ideas to this list as they occur to you.

COMMUNICATION JOURNAL

# Identifying Types of Discussion Questions

There are three major types of discussion questions: questions of fact, questions of value, and questions of policy. Understanding the category that a discussion question belongs to helps the group to determine an effective organization, or plan, for dealing with the topic.

- A **question of fact** asks for evidence that can be gathered from observation, experimentation, or authoritative sources to determine what is true.

  EXAMPLES:
  1. How much has the space program cost Americans, and what return have they received for their investment?
  2. What effect did the arrival of the Europeans have on the native peoples of the Americas in the late fifteenth and early sixteenth centuries?

- A **question of value** asks for an evaluation of one or more persons, places, things, or ideas and often contains words such as *effective, good, worthy, better,* or their opposites. To answer a question of value, a group must make a judgment.

  EXAMPLES:
  1. Has the space program brought about better living conditions for ordinary Americans?
  2. What valuable aspects of indigenous culture disappeared as a result of contacts between Europeans and the native peoples of the Americas?

- A **question of policy** asks what action, if any, should be taken and often includes the word *should.* By far the greatest number of questions examined by discussion groups in everyday situations are questions of policy.

  EXAMPLES:
  1. Should funding for the space program be increased, decreased, or maintained at current levels?
  2. What efforts should be made to restore parts of the indigenous cultures that were destroyed by the coming of Europeans to the Americas?

## Preparing an Outline

The next step in planning a discussion is to prepare an outline. A **discussion outline** usually consists of questions about the topic that the group members should address. Group members should decide on the specific wording and order of these questions or issues for the outline they will follow. Very few groups follow an outline point by point throughout a discussion. However, following the main points of the outline will help group members avoid straying from the topic and from their purpose. There are three ways to prepare an outline, depending on whether the discussion question is one of fact, of value, or of policy.

**Outline for Questions of Fact.**   The main points in this type of outline should ask group members

1. to define key words
2. to find information that supports the definitions
3. to determine what circumstances might affect the answer

**Discussion Question:** Does our high school adequately prepare students for their lives after graduation?
  I. What do we mean by *adequately*?
  II. How can we measure students' employment or academic experiences after graduation?
  III. What effect might current economic conditions have on students' lives after graduation?

**Outline for Questions of Value.**  The main points in this type of outline should ask group members

1. to determine the criteria, or standards of value, for making the judgment
2. to determine the information relevant to the discussion question
3. to match the information with the criteria
4. to determine what circumstances might affect the decision

**Discussion Question:** Is our high school the best high school in the area?

I. What are the criteria for determining the "best" high school?
II. What facts need to be considered in comparing our high school to other high schools in the area?
III. Do the facts show that our high school meets more of the criteria than other high schools in the area meet?
IV. Are there any other circumstances that affect the evaluation?

**Outline for Questions of Policy.**  The main points in this type of outline are based on John Dewey's five steps of reflective thinking. These steps are particularly useful if the group purpose is to solve a problem. Group members should

1. define the problem
2. analyze the problem
3. suggest possible solutions
4. select the best solution
5. suggest ways of carrying out the solution

**Discussion Question:** What should be done to lower student absenteeism in our high school?

I. How many students are absent each day?
II. What are the effects of absenteeism?
III. What are some possible solutions to the absenteeism problem?
IV. Which solution will reduce the problem and limit its effects?
V. How will the solution be carried out?

Because no two discussion questions are the same, no two outlines will follow exactly the same format. Each of the outlines that have been provided on the preceding pages applies only to the specific discussion question that it illustrates. However, as you can tell from these examples, every outline should help the discussion group to

- define key terms
- present relevant information
- address all relevant facets of the question
- allow for opposing views
- conclude with a tangible outcome

## ACTIVITY 2

### Planning a Discussion

Form a discussion group with four or six of your classmates. With the other members of your group, decide on a purpose, format, and discussion topic. If your group has difficulty deciding on a topic, you may want to review the information on how to choose a discussion topic on page 453. Then write a discussion question on your topic and tell whether the question is a question of fact, a question of value, or a question of policy. Finally, work as a group to develop a tentative outline for a discussion of your topic.

# Performing Different Roles in a Discussion

Each member of a discussion group has some role, or task, to perform. In most discussion groups, there are three distinct roles: the leader, the secretary or recorder, and the participants.

## Leading a Discussion

**Leadership** is the ability to guide a group toward its goal. When a person is appointed leader, he or she may adopt one of the following styles of leadership.

| Styles of Leadership | | | |
| --- | --- | --- | --- |
| **Style** | **Description** | **Advantages** | **Disadvantages** |
| **Laissez-faire (or nondirective) leadership** | responsibilities are shared by all members of the group | works well if several members assume the leadership role | may not provide sufficient guidance |
| **Authoritarian (or directive) leadership** | responsibilities are given to one leader | works well if time is short and all members want or need total direction | can be oppressive, create resentments, and hinder communication |
| **Democratic (or supportive) leadership** | leader suggests procedures, asks other members for ideas | works well if members are willing to contribute | may take too long; can be ineffective if members do not contribute |

A leader's responsibilities include selecting a time and place to meet, distributing an outline in advance of the meeting, and making sure that the meeting place is set up properly. When conducting a group discussion, a leader is responsible for

- introducing the discussion
- keeping the discussion moving
- moderating the discussion
- keeping the discussion on track
- concluding the discussion

**Introducing the Discussion.** Usually, the leader introduces the discussion question and reviews the tentative outline. After a brief discussion of the outline, the group may decide to change it or to follow it closely. Then the group leader presents any essential background information that the group needs and moderates a brief discussion of key terms related to the discussion question.

**Keeping the Discussion Moving.** An effective leader keeps the discussion moving by having a prepared list of questions that are related to the group's outline and that encourage others to contribute their own ideas, facts, and opinions.

An effective leader also summarizes when the group reaches a decision or agreement. For example, the leader may say, "Then we are all agreed that the class gift will be a world atlas for the library." By summarizing, the leader helps the group keep track of its progress.

Drawing by Maslin; © 1985 The New Yorker Magazine Inc.

*"And now at this point in the meeting I'd like to shift the blame away from me and onto someone else."*

**Moderating the Discussion.** Another important responsibility of the group leader is making sure that everyone has an equal chance to participate. The leader should recognize speakers, solicit reactions from members who have not contributed, and moderate interchanges between members.

Moderating interchanges between members sometimes means calming tensions that arise. In any good discussion, some group members are likely to pursue their points aggressively. An effective leader breaks in before individuals become angry.

EXAMPLES:

1. When one person interrupts another person, the leader might say, "Kim, I don't think you are letting José make his point. Would you go over that again, José?"
2. When two members are building up to an argument, the leader might say, "You two are on opposite sides of this issue, but let's discuss possible points of agreement."

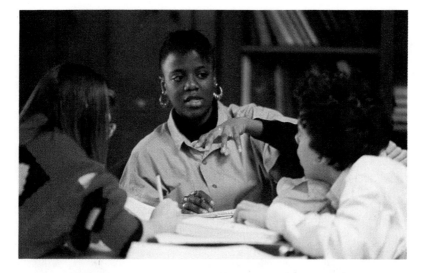

**Keeping the Discussion on Track.** Whenever a group discussion veers off course, the leader should steer the conversation back to the question and issues at hand. In this way the leader helps to ensure that the group will accomplish its purpose.

**Concluding the Discussion.** Accomplishing the purpose of the discussion often requires taking a final vote or summarizing what has been said. It is the group leader's responsibility to conduct the vote and to summarize the major points made during the entire discussion. Sometimes a leader may ask the group's secretary to summarize the discussion. After the vote and summary, the leader gives members a chance to comment on the summary and modify it.

# ACTIVITY 3

Listen to a group discussion in a class, at work, or in a club meeting. What kind of leadership style does the leader use: laissez-faire, authoritarian, or democratic? How can you tell? What are some examples that illustrate that kind of style? How effective is the leader? How do you account for the leader's effectiveness or ineffectiveness? If you had been the leader, what would you have done differently? Share your findings with your classmates.

## Serving as a Secretary, or Recorder

Sometimes members of a discussion group agree on six or eight points during a meeting, but a week later no one remembers precisely what those decisions were. A good written record can eliminate confusion and prevent disagreement.

A **secretary,** or **recorder,** for the group should record

- major points of agreement or decisions made
- definitions of key terms
- issues that the group wishes to return to at a later time
- major points of disagreement
- issues that seem important during the discussion

At the end of the discussion, the secretary will either record the summary given by the group leader or present a summary at the leader's request.

## Participating in a Discussion

Participating in a discussion is more than just being present. Communicating effectively in a group discussion involves

- preparing to participate
- taking an active part
- listening carefully
- listening critically
- respecting all group members
- using an appropriate speaking voice

**Preparing to Participate.**   Before group members take part in a discussion, they should prepare for the discussion by

- studying the outline
- thinking about the discussion question
- doing research on the discussion question, if necessary

Research can include considering one's own experiences, asking others for information and opinions about the discussion question, and studying relevant materials in a library or media center. [See Chapter 10 for more information on research.]

Before the group discussion, evaluate your understanding of the discussion outline, the discussion question, and any background research. Then take some time to strengthen any area in which you are weak. You are reasonably well prepared for a discussion if you have completed the tasks in the following chart.

## HOW TO > Prepare for a Group Discussion

1. **Define the topic to be discussed or the problem to be solved.** Know exactly what it is that the group must make decisions about.

2. **Analyze the problem.** Break the discussion question down into its parts.

3. **Evaluate the facts you have gathered.** Separate fact from opinion. Eliminate facts that are not relevant to the ideas being considered.

4. **Sort your notes.** Select the most important facts and arrange them in a logical order.

5. **Identify incomplete information.** Make plans to complete your research.

6. **Consider several different solutions.** Think of a number of different ways to resolve the problem.

7. **Keep an open mind.** Don't decide the issue until you have heard all the facts.

**Taking an Active Part.**   During the discussion, participate fully. Share information that you have gathered about the discussion topic, ask questions often to clarify what other group members are saying, and respond directly to the statements made by other group members.

**Listening Carefully.**   Participants in discussions often concentrate so hard on what they want to say that they do not listen closely to other group members. Yet, some of the best participants are those who concentrate on understanding what is being said. This allows them to ask penetrating questions, to give appropriate examples, and to recognize areas of agreement or disagreement.

**Listening Critically.**   Listening critically involves weighing and evaluating comments made by other group members. You can do this by asking yourself the following questions.

- What was the source of the information presented, and was it reliable?
- What were the reasons, or bases, for that conclusion or opinion?
- Are any facts or ideas contradictory?
- Does the conclusion or opinion follow logically from the evidence presented?

As you listen to other group members, take notes on what they say. Doing so will help you to avoid misinterpreting other speakers' statements and to refer specifically to what other speakers have said when you are speaking.

**Respecting All Group Members.** When you are in disagreement with someone else in a group, you may have difficulty restraining negative emotions. However, doing so is essential to the effectiveness of the group.

- Don't stifle group creativity by making negative evaluations of others' ideas.
- Let others finish talking before you comment.
- Even if you feel frustrated, avoid becoming abusive or short-tempered.
- Never make personal remarks. Instead, focus your comments on facts and issues.
- Show in your attitude that you respect others' opinions, values, beliefs, and ideas.

**Using an Appropriate Speaking Voice.** In all discussions, public or private, it is important that you

- speak loudly enough to be heard
- enunciate clearly
- adopt a tone that is appropriate for the audience and the occasion of the discussion

# ACTIVITY 4

## Solving Problems Through Group Discussion

In your discussion group, brainstorm a list of problems that exist in your school or community. Then select one of the problems and follow these steps to arrive at a possible solution.

1. Define the problem as a clearly stated question that contains one main idea. For example: *How can we stop automobile thefts from occurring in the school parking lots?*
2. Analyze the problem by examining its details. For example: *Under what specific circumstances have automobile thefts occurred? Have there been witnesses? Have students kept their cars locked?*
3. Determine possible solutions. Brainstorm as many solutions as possible—no matter how bizarre and far-fetched some may seem—to encourage creativity among all participants.
4. Select the best solution or combination of solutions. Consider how much the solution will cost, how easily it can be implemented, and whether it will create other problems.
5. Present a brief summary to your class of the problem your group has discussed and the solution or solutions suggested.

# Managing Group Conflict

**Conflict** is a form of disagreement. In any group discussion, conflict may arise between members of the group. Some conflict is desirable because it leads group members to put forward their best efforts and arguments. However, too much conflict can make constructive discussion impossible. To prevent conflict from becoming disruptive, group members need to

- recognize when conflict is developing
- diagnose the nature of the conflict
- help the group to defuse or resolve the conflict

## Recognizing Conflict

Conflict often begins innocently as a genuine disagreement over some point.

> **EXAMPLE:** In a meeting of the editorial board of a school newspaper, two editors might disagree about which of two stories deserves the leading place on the first page. If their agreement remains a healthy exchange about the pros and cons of the two choices, there is no problem. However, if the disagreement goes beyond an objective weighing of the two positions, someone, usually the group leader, will recognize that a disruptive conflict is developing.

One sure sign of disruptive conflict is the unwillingness of one group member to hear another out. Other signs include the use of derogatory remarks rather than logical argument and the inability or unwillingness of one group member to recognize the worth or reasonableness of another member's statement or idea.

# Diagnosing and Resolving Conflict

Once conflict is recognized, it should be diagnosed so that it can be resolved. Usually this means redirecting the attention of the people who are in conflict toward the issue at hand.

| Managing Group Conflict | | |
|---|---|---|
| **Problem** | **Cause** | **Possible Solution** |
| **Group members arguing about what to discuss next** | Conflict concerning outline for discussion | Refer to outline for discussion. |
| **Group members arguing about a point that has been discussed** | Conflict over differences in recollection | Read record of discussion, and review facts and reasoning. |
| **Group members arguing about whether something is true** | Conflict concerning factual information | Analyze and evaluate information; if necessary, find additional supporting information. |
| **Group members arguing over the meaning or significance of facts or other points of discussion** | Conflict over interpretation | Analyze facts or points of discussion and their relationships to each other and to the topic of discussion. |
| **Group members arguing over what is "more important" or "better"** | Conflict concerning value of information | Identify and establish criteria for determining value of information. |
| **Group members arguing about solution to question** | Conflict over goals, methods of discussion, or results of discussion | Review and evaluate goals, methods used to reach solutions, and solutions. |
| **Group members interrupting** | Group members being disrespectful | Remind group of purpose of discussion and call on all members to show tolerance and respect. |
| **Group members trying to defeat one another rather than focusing on ideas or issues** | Group members competing rather than cooperating | Focus attention on the ideas or issues being disputed; remind group members that they should attack the problem or question, not one another. |

Watch a television discussion program. Make notes in your journal about any conflicts that arose during the discussion. Determine what caused the conflict in each case and then note what could have been done to resolve it. Also note whether the members of the discussion group and the moderator of the group dealt with the conflict effectively.

# A·C·T·I·V·I·TY
## 5    Analyzing Conflict in Group Discussions

Recall a group discussion in which you participated and in which conflicts developed among group members. What were the factors that contributed to the conflicts? How effective were the group leader and the other members of the group in dealing with the conflicts? Were the conflicts resolved? If so, how? If not, what do you think could have been done? Share your experiences and your views with your classmates.

## Reaching a Group Decision

Very often, the major goal of a group is to reach a decision. Groups usually arrive at decisions in one of three ways: by decree, by voting, or by consensus.

### Decision by Decree

A decision by **decree** occurs when the group leader dictates the group's decision. Often when a group is being run in a directive, authoritarian way, the leader will listen to group comments and then state a decision. Decision by decree is quick and easy, but it tends to be counterproductive because it lowers group morale. If the members of a group have no voice in the decision making, then they are unlikely to work hard to carry out the decision.

### Decision by Voting

There are times when a group just cannot seem to agree on key points, and yet the group must arrive at a decision. In such circumstances, the group should take a **vote.** Before the group votes, its leader should state clearly the options being voted on. The option that receives a **majority** (more than half) of the votes wins. Unfortunately, voting inevitably results in winners and losers. Since losers can sometimes become disgruntled, voting is not always the ideal way to come to a decision.

## Decision by Consensus

By far the best way of arriving at a decision is by consensus. A **consensus** is arrived at when the group's decision is worded in such a way that the entire group can agree on it. If the members of the group cannot agree on a point, but the group desires that a consensus be reached, then the group should reword the point or continue discussion until consensus is reached.

Groups must be careful, however, to avoid achieving a **false consensus,** one that does not reflect the actual views of the group members. This can occur when a question or option is made so vague that it causes conflict in interpretation. [See chart on page 467.]

"*Then, gentlemen, it is the consensus of this meeting that we say nothing, do nothing, and hope it all blows over before our next meeting.*"

**T**hink about the last group that you worked in. Were the group's decisions made by decree, by vote, or by consensus? What effect did the method of arriving at decisions have on the group's morale? Discuss your views with your classmates.

# Evaluating Group Discussion

How much you improve your discussion skills will depend on how you take advantage of criticism. Group discussions are evaluated by observers. Each observer takes careful notes of what happens. Since you are likely to work as both an observer and a participant, you should know how group discussions are evaluated.

**Individual Participation.** One way to evaluate a group discussion is to concentrate on what each person in the group is doing. Each speaker can be rated on a scale of 1 to 5 on the characteristics that have been discussed. The evaluation shows the observer's reactions to each group member's performance.

| Sample Evaluation Form for Group Discussion | | | | | |
|---|---|---|---|---|---|
| **Name** | **Contributed Information** | **Asked Questions** | **Followed Plan** | **Paid Attention** | **Showed Courtesy** |
| | | | | | |
| | | | | | |

**The Discussion Process.** A second way to evaluate a group discussion is to focus on the discussion process. To do this, you should have some record of who is talking and to whom he or she is speaking. Then after the discussion, you can make your judgment about the balance of participation.

An effective method for keeping this record is to diagram the discussion process. On a sheet of paper, draw separate boxes to represent each of the individuals involved in the discussion. Then label each box with a participant's initials. Place the leader's initials at the top. Draw an arrow from each box to each one of the other boxes. (The resulting diagram will look something like a multi-pointed star with the boxes at the points.)

Each time one of the participants speaks to another individual, place a mark on the line that connects the boxes containing these individuals' initials. (Place this mark closest to the box of the individual who made the remark. However, if a speaker makes a comment intended for the entire group, place a mark inside the box containing that speaker's initials.) Using this method, you can evaluate whether the discussion involved the entire group.

**Quality of the Discussion.**   A third way to evaluate a discussion is to focus on the quality of the discussion. To do so, you should answer the following questions.

- Was the group goal clearly stated as a question of fact, of value, or of policy?
- Did the group have a discussion outline?
- Were conclusions that were drawn based on information presented in the discussion?
- Was the decision defensible?

## ACTIVITY 7
### Evaluating Group Discussion

Listen to a group discussion, either a live discussion or a radio or television program. Choose a method of evaluation and evaluate the discussion. Share your evaluation with your classmates.

## GUIDELINES
### for Participating in Group Discussion

- Am I prepared?
- Do I share information objectively?
- Do I ask questions?
- Do I try to help the group stay on track?
- Do I evaluate information that is presented?
- Am I respectful of others' views?
- Do I cooperate?
- Do I speak loudly and clearly enough for everyone to understand?
- Do I understand and carry out the responsibilities of leadership?
- Am I able to identify and help manage conflict?

# DISCUSSING AND DECIDING

### Contributing to a Group Discussion

Governmental bodies such as your local school board depend on strong leadership to keep group discussion on track and productive. A school board president must be able to plan and conduct a discussion effectively.

### Characteristics of an Effective School Board President

An effective school board president

1. determines a purpose and format for a group discussion and prepares an outline to follow

2. carries out the role of leader as well as participant in group discussions

3. recognizes and helps resolve conflict in discussions

4. helps the group reach decisions

**Meet the School Board President**

Lupe Costilla has led many discussions in her tenure as a school board president. "The most important thing is to do your homework," she says. "The more you know about an issue, the easier it is to keep the discussion on track, resolve any conflicts that might arise, and facilitate decision making."

*Lupe Costilla*

## ACTIVITY

### Situation

A community service club you belong to has raised $500 through car washes and bake sales. As president of the club, it's your job to lead a discussion among club members to decide how to spend the money.

### Preparation

Decide which discussion format you would like to use, and come up with some of your own suggestions about how to spend the money. You will want to come up with suggestions that would be of service to your community. Prepare a discussion outline by making a list of eight to ten questions that you can use to lead the discussion.

### Analysis and Assessment

Recruit a few classmates to act as club members. In class, lead a brief discussion of your questions among these members. Resolve any conflicts, and then reach a group decision by decree, by voting, or by consensus. The rest of the class should evaluate the discussion using an evaluation form such as the one on page 470 or the guidelines on page 471.

# S•U•M•M•A•R•Y

**GROUP DISCUSSION** is the face-to-face communication of a small number of people who meet for a specific purpose. You can plan and participate in a group discussion by thinking about and dealing with the interrelated parts of the discussion.

- **Plan a group discussion** by determining a purpose and a format, choosing a topic, wording the discussion question appropriately, indentifying the type of discussion question, and preparing an outline for the discussion.

- **Perform the different roles in a discussion** by selecting a specific role to play. The discussion leader should introduce the discussion, keep it moving, moderate the discussion, keep it on track, and conclude the discussion. The secretary should record major points of agreement and decisions made by the group, definitions of key terms, issues to be discussed at a later time, major points of disagreement, and important issues raised during the discussion. Participants in a discussion should prepare by studying the discussion outline, thinking about the discussion question, and doing research on the discussion question, if necessary.

- **Manage group conflict** by recognizing that a conflict is developing, by diagnosing the nature of the conflict, and by helping the group to defuse or resolve the conflict.

- **Reach a group decision** by decree, by voting, or by consensus. Consensus is preferred but cannot always be achieved.

- **Evaluate a discussion** by analyzing the contributions of all of the participants.

## Vocabulary

Look back through this chapter to find the meaning of each of the following terms, and write it in your communication journal.

ad hoc committee format, *p. 452*
authoritarian (or directive) leadership, *p. 459*
conflict, *p. 466*
consensus, *p. 469*
decree, *p. 468*
democratic (or supportive) leadership, *p. 459*
discussion format, *p. 451*
discussion outline, *p. 456*
false consensus, *p. 469*
forum format, *p. 451*
free-form format, *p. 452*
group discussion, *p. 449*
laissez-faire (or nondirective) leadership, *p. 459*
leadership, *p. 459*
majority, *p. 469*
moderated free-form format, *p. 452*
panel format, *p. 451*
progressive format, *p. 452*
question of fact, *p. 455*
question of policy, *p. 455*
question of value, *p. 455*
round-table format, *p. 452*
secretary (or recorder), *p. 462*
standing committee format, *p. 452*
symposium format, *p. 451*
vote, *p. 468*

# Review Questions

1. What is a group discussion?

2. What are some purposes that a discussion can serve? (Name at least four.)

3. A panel is a group of people who discuss a topic of mutual interest to them and to their audience. What is the difference between a panel and a symposium?

4. What is the difference between a free-form discussion format and a moderated free-form format? between a standing committee format and an ad hoc committee format?

5. One type of discussion question is a question of fact. What are two other types?

6. One style of leadership is laissez-faire. Name two other styles of leadership. What are the responsibilities of a group leader using each of these styles?

7. What is the job of the secretary, or recorder?

8. One major responsibility of a participant is to share information. What are three other responsibilities of a participant in a group discussion?

9. Disagreements between group members can turn into disruptive conflicts. What can a group leader do to manage conflict in a discussion?

10. A group decision can be reached by decree, by voting, or by consensus. Why is consensus the most effective method?

# Discussion Questions

1. Discuss with your classmates why discussion groups are a necessary part of a democratic society. In what ways do discussion groups help participants voice their opinions? How do group members keep the power of leaders in check?

2. Some people feel too shy to express their opinions in group discussions. Discuss ways in which a person can overcome shyness. Then discuss ways in which an effective leader can help and encourage a shy group member.

3. Conflict is likely to arise in group discussions. Discuss ways to recognize a conflict before it becomes a serious disagreement. Then discuss ways in which a good leader can manage the conflict.

4. Compare and contrast the effectiveness of groups led by laissez-faire, authoritarian, and democratic leaders. List some specific examples of situations in which each type of leadership would be appropriate.

5. *Vogue* magazine once defined *camel* as "a horse planned by a committee." First, discuss the meaning of this comment. Then discuss how the comment illuminates certain weaknesses of the group decision-making process. Finally, discuss whether the strengths of the group decision-making process outweigh its weaknesses.

# ACTIVITIES

**CHAPTER 17**

**1. Choosing Topics and Questions for Group Discussion.**

   **A.** Think about your school. List five issues facing your school that would be suitable for group discussion. For example, you might list pass/fail grading, the need for new gym equipment, changes in graduation requirements, or the dress code.

   **B.** Turn each of the topics you listed in Part A of this Activity into a discussion question. Then identify each question as a question of fact, of value, or of policy.

**2. Analyzing Your Role in a Group.** On a sheet of notebook paper, copy the pattern of circles shown below. Write your name and a personal description in the center circle. Then, in the outer circles, write the names of the different groups to which you belong, such as your family and your speech class. On your paper, describe your role in each group. What effect do other group members have on the way you see yourself in the group? Do you act sometimes as a leader and sometimes as a participant? What is your main leadership style?

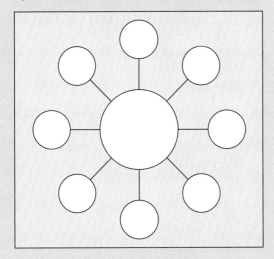

**3. Analyzing a Public Meeting.** Attend a public forum, a city council meeting, a school board meeting, or any other type of public meeting such as the one shown below. Report afterward on such items as the number of people in attendance, the number of participants, the way the meeting was conducted, the topics discussed, and the action taken.

**4. Preparing an Outline for Group Discussion.** First read each of the following questions. Decide whether each is a question of fact, a question of value, or a question of policy. Then prepare an outline for a group discussion on each of the questions. You may want to refer to the example outlines on pages 456–457.

   a. What are the advantages and the disadvantages of a liberal arts education?

   b. What role should the federal government play in supporting the arts in this country?

   c. In what ways are young children influenced by television?

   d. What should the foreign language requirement be for high school students?

   e. What was the funniest movie produced last year?

**5. Understanding the Effect of Seating Arrangements.** A group's seating arrangement can affect both the interaction among group members and the kind of leadership that is appropriate for the group.

**A.** Working with a group of your classmates, answer the following questions. Then compare your answers to those of others in the class.

1. In your experience, how does where a person sits affect the way he or she acts in a group?

2. Which of the seating arrangements shown below is best suited to a private group discussion? to a public group discussion?

3. The seating arrangements shown below are just a few of the many arrangements that are possible. Think of some other arrangements and the situations in which they might be used, such as a panel discussion with two opposing factions or a pep talk before a football game. Draw a simple diagram of each arrangement you think of.

**B.** With your group, answer the following questions. You may want to rearrange your own chairs in order to experiment with some different seating arrangements.

1. In each of the seating arrangements shown in the diagram on this page, where would the discussion leader most likely sit?

2. Which of the seating arrangements shown would best suit an authoritarian leader? a laissez-faire leader? a democratic leader? Give reasons for your answers.

3. How important is it for the leader to be in a position where he or she can see and be seen by all of the group members?

4. One of the discussion leader's responsibilities is to arrange the meeting space. If you were leading a discussion group, which of the seating arrangements shown here would you choose to encourage active participation from all group members? Explain your choice.

**6. Analyzing Public Group Discussion.**

**A.** Study your daily newspaper. Look for reports of meetings of Congress, of the state legislature, of the city council, and of local clubs. Then prepare a list of eight or ten topics that are being resolved through public group discussion.

**B.** Classify the level of interest of each topic as local, state, national, or international. Then identify specific groups that would be concerned with these topics.

# EVERYDAY COMMUNICATION

### Situation
You are married and have children. Your family needs to make a decision, and you have called a conference to discuss it.

### Problem
Identify the members of your family and the issue that your family needs to discuss. Write a two- or three-minute informative speech about how you would lead the discussion. [For more information on informative speeches, see Chapter 14.]

### Assessing Your Skill
Be sure to discuss your leadership style, the method your family would use to arrive at a decision, the part that each family member would play in the discussion, and the decision that would be reached through the discussion. Present your speech in class. Invite feedback from your classmates on the effectiveness of your leadership style.

# COMMUNICATION IN THE WORKPLACE

### Background
You are running a small business. You have had a good year, but lately business has slowed. To help decide how to deal with the decline, you gather your employees for a group meeting.

### Preparing to Do the Job
Begin by identifying the business you are running, who your employees are, and what each of them could contribute to the discussion. Then decide which issues you will discuss with your employees and how you will prepare for and conduct the meeting.

### Testing Your Skill
Write a three- or four-page dialogue of your group discussion that ends with a conclusion about what caused the decline and a decision on how to reverse the decline. Present your dialogue in class, and respond to feedback on the effectiveness of your discussion.

REAL-LIFE COMMUNICATION

Pros & Cons

# Debate

## OBJECTIVES

**After studying this chapter, you should be able to**
1. Identify the specialized features of debate.
2. Identify three kinds of propositions.
3. Identify three debate formats.
4. Prepare to debate by discovering issues and organizing proof.
5. Recognize the responsibilities of the affirmative and negative sides in constructive speeches.
6. Define *refutation* and *rebuttal*.
7. Recognize criteria, or standards, for judging a debate.

## What Is Debate?

**Debate** is formalized public speaking in which participants prepare and present speeches on opposite sides of an issue to determine which side has the stronger arguments. Even if you do not participate in competitive debate, knowing its principles of clear thinking will help you in many speaking situations.

Debate as a means of decision making goes back to the ancient Greeks. Today, debate is an essential element of the democratic process in the United States: In legislative assemblies, courtrooms, and other public forums, debates have led to decisions on personal freedom, civil rights, and war and peace. In the past thirty years, presidential debates have also played a prominent role in elections.

In this chapter you will learn about the features and principles of debate as they are used in three different debate formats:

- formal or traditional debate
- cross-examination debate
- Lincoln-Douglas debate

# Understanding the Features of Debate

As a specialized form of public speaking, debate has several unique features. These features include speakers on two sides of a controversial issue who present speeches that build arguments for and against a proposition.

## Controversy

Debate begins with a controversy expressed in a proposition. A **proposition** is a statement that asserts a fact, makes a value judgment, or recommends a policy. A proposition must deal with a controversial question—one that has valid evidence for two sides of an issue that divides public opinion. [For more information on propositions, see pages 482–484 of this chapter.]

## Speakers on Two Sides

The two sides in a debate are called the *affirmative* and the *negative.* The affirmative side supports the debate proposition. The negative side opposes it. For instance, if the proposition to be debated were "*Resolved,* That the minimum age for obtaining a driver's license should be raised to eighteen," the affirmative side in the debate would support the change, and the negative side would oppose it.

The speakers on opposing sides take turns presenting their arguments. In formal debate and cross-examination debate, each side has two speakers. The two speakers work as a team with

each person having different responsibilities at different times. In Lincoln-Douglas debate, each side has only one speaker. In the cross-examination and Lincoln-Douglas debate formats, speakers also question, or cross-examine, the opposing speaker. In all debate formats, the affirmative side always begins and ends the debate.

## Identifying Affirmative and Negative Positions in Debate

Imagine that you will participate in a debate on the proposition *"Resolved,* That public schools should adopt a year-round schedule." (1) What will be the affirmative side? (2) What will be the negative side? (3) Which side will go first?

## Status Quo

The existing state of affairs is called the **status quo.** Debate assumes that the status quo is satisfactory until proven otherwise.

> **EXAMPLE:** The minimum age for obtaining a driver's license in most states is sixteen. Sixteen is neither the only age that could be considered nor necessarily the best age. However, sixteen is the status quo. It will continue to be the law until enough evidence is presented to change it.

Because the affirmative side seeks a change from the status quo, speakers on that side have the **burden of proof,** the obligation to present arguments for changing the status quo. Until this burden of proof is met, the negative side has nothing to do. Therefore, the affirmative goes first and presents a strong enough argument in favor of the change to force the negative to reply.

## Constructive and Rebuttal Speeches

Any debate format is based on two kinds of speeches: a **constructive speech,** which builds an argument, and a **rebuttal speech,** which rebuilds it.

## Calvin and Hobbes                                                    by Bill Watterson

During the constructive speeches, the affirmative and negative speakers establish reasons for the superiority of their side. During the rebuttal speeches, each speaker does two things: rebuilds arguments that have been questioned or attacked and refutes, or attacks, an argument raised by the other side. Refutation leads to verbal clashes that make debate exciting.

*B*esides being used in high school contests, debate is basic to public discussion. In your communication journal, take notes about how speakers on television and radio use the features of debate. For example, listen to news analysis programs and talk shows. What issues do the speakers discuss? How controversial are the issues? How clear is each speaker's position on the issue? What kinds of propositions do they argue? Do the speakers build arguments to establish the superiority of their positions? Do they refute arguments raised by the other side? How effective are the speakers?

## The Proposition

Debate focuses on a controversial topic stated in a proposition, or resolution. Every year, national debate organizations select the propositions that high school debaters will use in their contests. There are three types of propositions:

- propositions of fact
- propositions of value
- propositions of policy

**Propositions of Fact.** **Propositions of fact** make statements about what has happened, is happening, or will happen. This type of proposition is most common in courts of law, where people search out reasons and evidence to prove or disprove the proposition—to determine what is true or false.

**EXAMPLES:**
- Anita Jones is not legally bound by the terms of the contract.
- Chris Smith is guilty of damaging clothes at the Plaza Department Store.
- Tom Green is the legal owner of the 1987 automobile in question.

**Propositions of Value.** **Propositions of value** express judgments about the relative merit of a person, place, or thing—the value object. Propositions of value always include evaluative words such as *effective, good, worthy, better,* or their opposites. Although debaters can set up criteria for determining what is "best," "effective," or "easier" and can measure the objects against those criteria, they cannot verify the findings. Therefore, the result is a matter of judgment, not a matter of fact.

EXAMPLES:

- *Resolved,* That Parker High has the best football team in the state.
- *Resolved,* That personal freedom is more important than law.
- *Resolved,* That computer language is easier to master than a foreign language.

**Propositions of Policy.** **Propositions of policy** focus on specific plans of action. The word *should* in propositions of policy makes this type of proposition the easiest to recognize and the easiest to phrase.

EXAMPLES:

- *Resolved,* That solar-energy research should be significantly increased.
- *Resolved,* That the United States should adopt a national health insurance program for all citizens.
- *Resolved,* That more vigorous academic standards for language arts and mathematics should be established in United States secondary schools.

1. **Does the proposition give the burden of proof to the affirmative?** The proposition should be worded to change an idea, an institution, or a current policy or to express a value judgment. For example, the proposition of policy "*Resolved,* That the federal income tax should be abolished" is stated correctly because abolishing the tax would be a change from current policy. If the proposition were worded, "*Resolved,* That the federal income tax should be continued," it would be incorrect because this statement would place the burden of proof on the negative side.

2. **Does the proposition contain only one topic?** The proposition "*Resolved,* That the Murray High School football and basketball programs should be abolished" is incorrect because it contains two topics. Either topic (the football program or the basketball program) is debatable, but both cannot be debated at the same time.

3. **Are the words used in the proposition clear?** For instance, the proposition "*Resolved,* That qualifications for welfare recipients should be reevaluated" is not clearly stated. The words *should be reevaluated* do not suggest a specific plan of action. The word *reevaluated* needs to be replaced with a word or phrase that specifies the reevaluation, such as *broadened* or *made more restrictive.*

# A·C·T·I·V·I·T·Y 2

## Identifying the Types of Propositions

Identify each proposition below as a proposition of fact, of value, or of policy.

1. All high school students should be required to take a foreign language.
2. The advantages of wearing seat belts outweigh any risks.
3. Ann Welch is an effective president of the senior class.
4. All young people should be required to participate in a year of public service.
5. Park Hills has a better football team than North Hills has.

# Understanding Debate Formats

High school students usually participate in three different debate formats:

- formal or traditional debate
- cross-examination debate
- Lincoln-Douglas debate

These debate formats differ in three important ways:
1. number of speakers
2. time schedules for the speakers
3. types of propositions used
While the time schedules vary, the affirmative and negative sides in each format speak for the same total amount of time.

## Traditional Debate

**Traditional,** or **formal, debate** involves two affirmative speakers and two negative speakers who argue a proposition of policy. Each speaker speaks twice within set time limits—once in a constructive speech and once in a rebuttal speech. The two affirmative speakers act as one team, and the two negative speakers act as the other. The two teams typically follow this schedule.

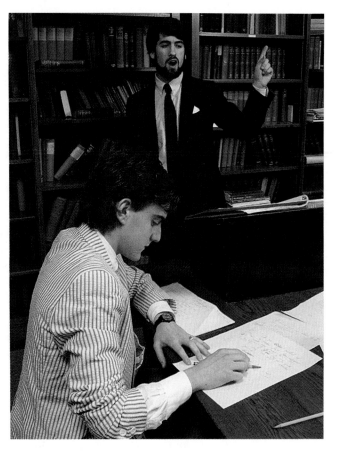

| Traditional Debate | | | |
|---|---|---|---|
| **Constructive Speeches** | | **Rebuttal Speeches** | |
| **1st Affirmative** | 10 minutes | **1st Negative** | 5 minutes |
| **1st Negative** | 10 minutes | **1st Affirmative** | 5 minutes |
| **2nd Affirmative** | 10 minutes | **2nd Negative** | 5 minutes |
| **2nd Negative** | 10 minutes | **2nd Affirmative** | 5 minutes |

## Cross-Examination Debate

**Cross-examination debate** takes place between two affirmative speakers and two negative speakers who argue a proposition of policy. It differs from traditional debate by including brief cross-examination periods in which the participants question their opponents. This give-and-take between speakers provides for a lively exchange of ideas. The cross-examination period specifically allows a speaker to clarify issues and to highlight the opposing side's weaknesses for the judge. Although time limits may vary, the following schedule is frequently used.

| Cross-Examination Debate | |
| --- | --- |
| **1st Affirmative** | 8-minute constructive speech |
| **2nd Negative** | 3-minute questioning of 1st Affirmative |
| **1st Negative** | 8-minute constructive speech |
| **1st Affirmative** | 3-minute questioning of 1st Negative |
| **2nd Affirmative** | 8-minute constructive speech |
| **1st Negative** | 3-minute questioning of 2nd Affirmative |
| **2nd Negative** | 8-minute constructive speech |
| **2nd Affirmative** | 3-minute questioning of 2nd Negative |
| **1st Negative** | 5-minute rebuttal speech and summary |
| **1st Affirmative** | 5-minute rebuttal speech and summary |
| **2nd Negative** | 5-minute rebuttal speech and summary |
| **2nd Affirmative** | 5-minute rebuttal speech and summary |

## Lincoln-Douglas Debate

**Lincoln-Douglas debate** involves one affirmative speaker and one negative speaker who argue a proposition of value. The name of this format comes from a series of debates between Abraham Lincoln and Stephen A. Douglas in the 1858 Illinois senatorial race.

The Lincoln-Douglas format is well suited to classroom practice, because it focuses on the skills of individual debaters and takes less time than formal debate. At the same time, it includes all the same elements of argument, reasoning, refutation, and rebuttal as the other two debate formats. It also includes cross-examination periods. In a typical Lincoln-Douglas debate, each speaker has thirteen minutes for constructive and rebuttal speeches, as well as a three-minute cross-examination period.

| Lincoln-Douglas Debate | |
|---|---|
| **Affirmative** | 6-minute constructive speech |
| **Negative** | 3-minute questioning of the Affirmative |
| **Negative** | 7-minute constructive speech and refutation |
| **Affirmative** | 3-minute questioning of the Negative |
| **Affirmative** | 4-minute rebuttal speech |
| **Negative** | 6-minute rebuttal speech and summary |
| **Affirmative** | 3-minute rebuttal speech and summary |

Lincoln-Douglas debate deals with values, not policy. The word *should* never appears in a proposition of value because the affirmative side is not called upon to prove the need for a policy change. The affirmative side simply argues the truth or merit of its proposition, and the negative side argues the falsity of that proposition. Neither side considers solutions or new policies to enact. While the arguments in formal debate rely on factual evidence, the arguments in Lincoln-Douglas debate emphasize evidence consisting of the logical analysis of philosophical issues. This format promotes exploration and increased understanding of our values and beliefs.

Lincoln-Douglas debate argues four basic types of values: moral, utilitarian, social, and aesthetic. Any combination of these values may be used to either defend or deny a proposition of value.

EXAMPLES:
- In the proposition "*Resolved,* That war is a moral way to settle disputes between nations," the debaters may argue the morality of war, the utility of war, or the social necessity of war.
- In the proposition "*Resolved,* That protection of the environment is more desirable than economic development," the debaters may argue the morality of endangering the environment, the usefulness of the environment as opposed to the usefulness of development, society's need to grow economically, and the aesthetic values of preserving nature.

# Preparing Yourself for Debate

Your preparation for the debate—regardless of the debate format you are using—will include identifying or discovering the key issues that are central to your proposition. You will also have to find reasons and evidence that relate to the debate proposition. [See pages 248–255 of Chapter 10 for more help on gathering information.]

## Recognizing Key Issues

In order to debate effectively, debaters need to identify the key issues that are central to the proposition. **Key issues** are the points of disagreement in the debate—questions that a speaker must answer satisfactorily in order to justify the adoption or rejection of a proposition. The affirmative must answer *yes* to the questions; the negative must answer *no.* Whether yes or no, each answer must be supported with reasons and evidence.

## Using Stock Issues

Since the time of the ancient Greeks, debaters have looked for help in discovering key issues. One method that continues to be helpful, regardless of which of the three types of propositions the speakers are debating, is the use of stock issues. **Stock issues** are a formula of set questions that are adapted to the particular debate topic. Different sets of stock issues apply to propositions of policy and to propositions of value.

**Stock Issues for Propositions of Policy.** In formal debate and cross-examination debate, debaters use four basic stock issues to discover the key questions in a proposition of policy. These stock issues are:

1. **Ill:** Is there a problem with the current situation?
2. **Blame:** Is the current policy responsible for the problem?
3. **Cure:** Will the proposition solve the problem?
4. **Cost:** What are the costs of the proposition?

Both the affirmative and the negative speakers can use these stock issues to analyze the proposition and construct their cases.

EXAMPLE: *Resolved,* That Social Security benefits for the elderly should be lowered significantly.

I. Is the level of Social Security benefits for the elderly causing a problem? [This question meets the stock issue of ill: *Are there significant harms or needs within the present situation to warrant a change in policy as specified in the proposition?*] Subissues suggest potential problems with the status quo:
   A. Is the economy being adversely affected?
   B. Are the benefits received by the elderly unfair?

II. Is the current policy on Social Security benefits responsible for the ills? [This question meets the stock issue of blame: *Is the present system inherently responsible?*]

III. Are there facts to support the statement that lowering benefits will solve the problems? [This question meets the stock issue of cure: *Will the proposal remove the ills?*]
   A. Will lowering benefits help the economy?
   B. Will lowering benefits make for more equitable treatment of the elderly?

IV. What are the consequences of lowering benefits? [This question meets the stock issue of cost: *What are the consequences of changing the system?*]
   A. Will lowering benefits work? [This subissue questions the practicality of the solution.]
      1. Is it feasible to lower benefits?
      2. Will lowering benefits upset the system?
   B. Are there facts to prove that the advantages of lowering benefits outweigh the disadvantages? [This subissue questions the desirability of decreasing benefits.]
      1. Will the proposal alienate the elderly?
      2. Will the economy be stimulated?

**Stock Issues for Propositions of Value.** In Lincoln-Douglas debate, speakers can use the following stock issues to explore a proposition that affirms a value judgment or evaluation.

1. What are the criteria, or standards of judgment, for making the evaluation?
2. Does this particular case meet the criteria?

**EXAMPLE:** *Resolved,* That SAT tests are effective predictors of college success.

I. What are the criteria for determining whether a test is an "effective predictor of college success"? [This question asks *By what criteria is the value object to be judged?*] The subissues offer possible criteria:
   A. Is the correlation of high test scores with high college grades an important criterion?
   B. Is the correlation of low test scores with low college grades an important criterion?

II. Does the available information show that SAT tests meet the key criteria? [This question asks *Do indicators show that the value object conforms to the criteria?*]
   A. Is there information to show that people with high scores do well in college?
   B. Is there information to show that people with low scores do poorly in college?

## The Proof

In a debate, **proof** is the reasons and evidence given to answer the questions in the stock issues. You should gather more reasons and evidence than you will be able to use in the debate's time period.

**For Better or For Worse**®                                    **by Lynn Johnston**

**Reasons.** **Reasons** are statements that justify the proposition. As you conduct your research, be sure to take note of reasons that support both the affirmative and the negative positions, regardless of which side of the debate you are on. Knowing the reasons for the opposition's point of view will make you aware of the evidence that may be used against your argument. This will help you to strengthen your own case. Also, you may be asked to argue either side of a proposition.

EXAMPLE: *Resolved,* That law enforcement agencies should be given greater freedom in investigating and prosecuting crime.

**Stock Issue:** Is there a problem?
A. To what extent are law enforcement agencies hampered by restrictions placed on how they investigate and prosecute crime?
B. What potential harms may result from the current restrictions?
C. What are the limits of an individual's rights?
D. What criteria are used to determine when current restrictions are too strict?
E. Can the problem be solved under the status quo?

**Affirmative Reasons:**
1. Recent Supreme Court decisions have unduly restricted law enforcement agencies in investigating and prosecuting crime.
2. Judicial restrictions have caused much of the increase in crime.
3. Criminal suspects are able to take advantage of various technicalities in the current system of laws to escape jury trial.

**Negative Reasons:**
1. Law enforcement agencies are not unduly restricted in their investigation and prosecution of crime.
2. Judicial restrictions contribute very little to increasing the crime rate.
3. Suspects and defendants who profit from limits imposed on law enforcement agencies are taking advantage of rights guaranteed by the Constitution.

**Stock Issue:** Would greater freedom for law enforcement agencies solve the problem?
A. Would the plan for granting greater freedom to law enforcement agencies be practical?
B. Would greater freedom be the best way of solving the problem?

**Affirmative Reasons:**
1. Greater freedom for law enforcement agencies would allow more evidence to be gathered and put before juries.
2. Greater freedom for law enforcement agencies would lead to more convictions, which in turn would reverse the alarmingly high crime rate.
3. Greater freedom for law enforcement agencies would not create new problems.

**Negative Reasons:**
1. Those who commit crimes can be convicted within the existing framework if law enforcement agencies respect the law in collecting evidence.
2. Greater freedom would have little effect on crime.
3. Greater freedom would give law enforcement agencies too much power, which some officials would be tempted to abuse.

**Evidence.**    To debate, you also need **evidence,** the facts and opinions given to support each reason. You need to gather examples, statistics, and quotations that support your reasons. Write your pieces of evidence on note cards following the guidelines discussed on page 256 in Chapter 10.

EXAMPLE: You might create the following note card about giving greater freedom to law enforcement agencies. Then you could evaluate this particular piece of evidence using the questions in the how-to chart on page 493. [For more information on reasons and evidence, see pages 387–391 of Chapter 15.]

---

*Undue Restrictions*

*According to William Long, Superior Court Judge, King County, Washington, the question of unlawful searches and seizures "has become so highly technical that an officer who goes into a hotel room with a search warrant for one piece of evidence and finds something else can't use that other evidence. It's suppressed, so the criminal can go free."*

*"How Much Crime Can America Take?"*
*U.S. News and World Report,*
*April 20, 1964, p. 66*

---

1. **Is the evidence recent enough to be relevant to today's problems?** Out-of-date evidence is likely to be irrelevant to a current debate. For instance, the quotation in *U.S. News and World Report* is dated 1964. Criminal law has changed a great deal since then.

2. **Is the evidence well documented?** Where did the evidence come from? Who said it? The quotation from *U.S. News and World Report* is well documented.

3. **Is the source reliable?** Can you believe the source? In this example, *U.S. News and World Report* is a widely quoted, credible national news magazine. The source of the quotation, a superior court judge from Washington, is a reliable source on legal matters.

4. **Is the evidence objective?** Is the evidence inclined to be partial to either side of an issue? For the quotation in the example, you would need to determine whether William Long had an objective viewpoint.

# ACTIVITY 3

## Developing Reasons and Evidence

Using the steps given below, develop reasons and evidence for a policy debate on the following proposition: "*Resolved,* That the United States government should increase preservation of wilderness areas."

1. List potential questions (subissues) under the four stock issues (ill, blame, cure, and cost) that are relevant to the proposition.

2. List three affirmative and three negative reasons under your proposition. (These reasons are likely to relate to at least one of the stock issues—see pages 491–492 for examples.)

3. Prepare fifteen evidence cards to be turned in to your teacher. Record your information as suggested in the sample note card on page 492.

# Developing the Constructive Speech

Your next step in preparing for a debate is to develop a constructive speech, which builds an argument for an affirmative or a negative case. A **case** consists of the reasons and evidence on which you base your position.

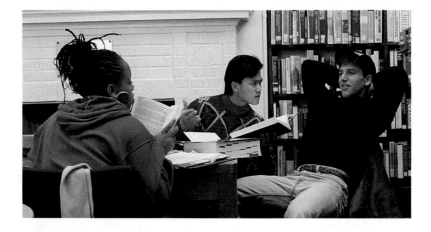

## The Affirmative Case

The **affirmative case** presents reasons and evidence that support a proposition. In formal or cross-examination debate, the affirmative case indicates a problem with the present system and shows why the plan of action in the proposition offers the best solution. In Lincoln-Douglas debate, the affirmative case defends the criteria for making the value judgment stated in the proposition.

Because the affirmative always has the burden of proof, the affirmative argument needs to present a ***prima facie* case,** one that contains enough reasons and evidence to win a debate if the other side presented no argument. (*Prima facie* means "at first sight.") A *prima facie* case convinces a debate judge that the affirmative argument is valid. If the affirmative side cannot build a *prima facie* case, there is no need for negative argument and, consequently, no reason for debate.

After you have gathered reasons and evidence, you should select the most powerful ones for presenting your case in a limited time—probably two to four reasons. In Lincoln-Douglas debate, you will organize the affirmative case in a straightforward way: Define any terms, outline the issues to be debated, and justify why those are the key issues. For traditional or cross-examination debate, you should also consider a pattern of organization: the problem-solution pattern or the comparative advantages pattern.

**Problem-Solution Pattern.**  The **problem-solution pattern** (also called the "need-plan pattern") organizes information to present both a problem and a solution to that problem. This pattern has at least three parts that attempt to prove

- that a significant problem exists
- that adopting the proposal will help to solve the problem
- that adopting the proposal is the best way to solve the problem

**EXAMPLE:** *Resolved,* That law enforcement agencies should be given greater freedom in investigating and prosecuting crime.

 I.   Restrictive Supreme Court rulings on government law enforcement agencies have resulted in an increase in the crime rate.

 II.  Our plan for greater freedom for these agencies would work to solve this problem.

 III. Our plan for greater freedom would be the best way to solve this problem.

**Comparative Advantages Pattern.**  The **comparative advantages pattern** organizes information to demonstrate that the proposal would have significant advantages over the status quo. This pattern differs from the problem-solution pattern in two important ways:

- The plan is always presented and discussed in detail at the beginning of the proposal.
- The plan focuses on the two to four advantages of the proposition over the status quo.

**EXAMPLE:** *Resolved,* That law enforcement agencies should be given greater freedom in investigating and prosecuting crime.

 I.   [A detailed explanation of the specific points of the proposal is given here.]

 II.  The proposal would be comparatively advantageous to the status quo for the following reasons:

   A.  Greater freedom for law enforcement agencies would contribute to protection of all citizens by lowering the crime rate.

   B.  Greater freedom for these agencies would create more effective deterrence to crime, thereby helping to prevent young people from pursuing criminal activities.

In the comparative advantages pattern, you still must consider whether a problem exists. However, instead of identifying a serious problem that cannot be solved by the status quo and then giving a solution, you suggest a new proposal whose benefits would be so significant that the plan should be adopted whether a problem exists or not.

**EXAMPLE:** If you are able to show your friend that another route to school is shorter, has fewer traffic lights, and will get him to school faster than the route he now takes, your friend may try the route because it is comparatively advantageous. The question is not whether something is wrong with the old route, but whether the new route is *significantly* better. Your friend will not adopt the new route to save only fifteen seconds on a thirty-minute drive.

## The Negative Case

The negative side's main goals are to develop the negative constructive case and to attack the affirmative's argument. The **negative case** gives reasons and evidence that

- act as straight refutation of the affirmative case
- defend the status quo
- for policy propositions, present a counterplan

The organization of negative speeches depends on which of these three courses the speech will take.

**Straight Refutation.** **Straight refutation** means that the entire negative case will be a denial of each affirmative argument stated—whatever reasons the affirmative team presents.

**EXAMPLE:**

**Affirmative Case:**
   **I.** Restrictive Supreme Court rulings on law enforcement agencies have resulted in a continued increase in the crime rate.

   **II.** Our plan for greater freedom for these agencies would work to solve this problem.

   **III.** Our plan for greater freedom would be the best way to solve this problem.

**Negative Case Using Straight Refutation:**
   **I.** Supreme Court rulings have not been the cause of the increase in the crime rate.

   **II.** Giving greater freedom to law enforcement agencies would not work to solve this problem.

   **III.** Giving greater freedom to law enforcement agencies would actually create more problems.

**Defense of the Status Quo.** To defend the status quo, the negative team explains the status quo and shows either how it is already meeting the problem or how it could meet the problem.

EXAMPLE:

### Negative Case Defending the Status Quo:

    **I.** Under the present system, police have the tools to cope with the increase in the crime rate.

    **II.** The present system works better than would giving greater freedom to law enforcement agencies.

    **III.** The present system has more benefits and fewer disadvantages than would giving greater freedom to law enforcement agencies.

The defense of the status quo has a major advantage. The negative team stands for something rather than simply being against the affirmative. This forces the affirmative to go on the defensive. Instead of just supporting its own case, the affirmative side must also attack the constructive arguments of the negative side. The major disadvantage of defending the status quo is that it requires the negative side to construct two arguments: one for the status quo and one against the proposition for change.

**Counterplan.** A **counterplan** is a different solution. Ordinarily, only the solution suggested in the policy proposition is debated. However, if the negative side agrees that a problem exists, it can present a solution that differs substantially from the affirmative's proposition. The debate then becomes a clash between the relative merits of the two solutions.

EXAMPLE:

### Negative Case Counterplan:

    **I.** The negative agrees that the crime rate has risen.

    **II.** The best solution to this problem would be to involve more citizens in crime prevention programs.

    **III.** Increased citizen participation in crime prevention would work better to lower the crime rate than would giving law enforcement agencies greater freedom.

    **IV.** More citizen participation in crime prevention would have more benefits and fewer disadvantages than would giving law enforcement agencies more freedom.

The advantage of the counterplan is that it may catch the affirmative side off guard. In effect, when the negative side proposes a counterplan, the first affirmative speech has been wasted. If the negative side believes that the status quo has weaknesses, it is better off presenting a minor repair than defending the status quo.

## Selecting Reasons for Different Patterns of Argument

Imagine that you are on the affirmative side debating the policy proposition "*Resolved,* That the United States should substantially reduce its foreign policy commitments." In your research you have discovered the numbered reasons listed below. First, select the reasons you would choose for a problem-solution pattern. Next, select the reasons you would choose for a comparative advantages pattern. Finally, imagine that you are on the negative side and that you are using the straight refutation pattern. List the reasons you would use *against* the reasons you selected for the comparative advantages pattern.

1. Our foreign policy commitments have led to the loss of valuable friendships and prestige.
2. Our foreign policy commitments have significantly weakened the national defense.
3. Our foreign policy commitments have not significantly aided underdeveloped nations.
4. Our foreign policy commitments have not deterred aggression.
5. Our foreign policy commitments have weakened regional alliances.
6. Reducing commitments would better enable us to meet the goals of our foreign policy as set forth by the administration.
7. Reducing commitments would allow us to strengthen ties with traditional allies.
8. Reducing commitments would result in fewer problems than the present policy is causing.

# Considering Refutation and Rebuttal

**Refutation** means attacking the argument of the opposition. **Rebuttal** means rebuilding your argument after it has been attacked.

## Refutation

No matter which side you have taken in a debate, you may refute your opposition's quantity of evidence, quality of evidence, and reasoning from the evidence.

**Quantity of Evidence.** Any reason presented in a debate must be supported with evidence. Sometimes debaters give little or no supporting evidence. In such cases, the opposing team may simply refute an argument on that basis—lack of evidence.

**EXAMPLE:** A debater gives little or no evidence to support the following reason: "Supreme Court decisions have unduly restricted law enforcement agencies." An opposing debater could refute by saying, "The affirmative has asserted that Supreme Court decisions have unduly restricted law enforcement agencies. We remind the affirmative that they have the burden of proof, and until we hear evidence to support the assertion, we need not reply to it."

**Quality of Evidence.**   A more effective method of refutation is to attack the quality of the evidence presented. If sheer number of evidence cards were most important, judges would need only to count cards and would not have to weigh arguments. One statement by a law enforcement officer about the effects of a court decision on crime could be worth far more than interviews with a dozen random citizens.

**Reasoning from the Evidence.**   The most effective form of refutation is to attack the opposition's reasoning from the evidence. Each argument is composed of at least three elements: (1) evidence or data from which a conclusion is drawn, (2) the conclusion itself, and (3) the reasoning that links the evidence and the conclusion. Most debates involve four common types of reasoning: generalization, causation, analogy, and sign.

PEANUTS reprinted by permission of UFS, Inc.

**1. Generalization.**   A **generalization** is a conclusion based on one or more specific instances.

> **EXAMPLES:**
> - You noticed in your math class that Heather had a pocket calculator, Tim had a pocket calculator, and Tanya had a pocket calculator. If you concluded from these instances that all your classmates had pocket calculators, you would be reasoning by generalization.
> - In the debate about giving law enforcement agencies more freedom, your opponent might argue that for the past twenty-five years most Supreme Court decisions related to

investigation and prosecution of crime have restricted law enforcement agencies. He or she might cite three examples: the Mapp decision, the Mallory decision, and the Miranda decision. Thus, your opponent would be generalizing, using specific instances as the basis for a conclusion: that most Supreme Court decisions have restricted law enforcement agencies.

You can refute such a generalization by asking the following three questions:

- **Are enough instances cited?** Two or three examples are seldom enough to draw a generalization.
- **Are the specific instances typical of all possible instances?** If examples are very unusual, they do not provide a sound basis for a generalization. Other people will discount or dismiss such unusual examples.
- **Are there any negative instances, or instances that prove the opposite?** If negative instances can be found, they may disprove the generalization.

**2. Causation.** A **causation argument** provides a conclusion that is a direct result or a direct effect of one or more particular sources or conditions.

EXAMPLES:

- Your friend Heather told you that she studies math at least one hour a night. If you concluded that Heather will get a good grade in math, you would be reasoning by causation. Your reasoning is probably sound: Studying at least one hour a night often helps to produce good grades.

- Your opponent might argue that the crime rate has risen dramatically as a direct result of Supreme Court decisions restricting law enforcement agencies. Thus, your opponent would be presuming a causal relationship between Supreme Court actions and the crime rate. However, a rise in the crime rate does not necessarily mean that there is a causal relationship between that rise and the Supreme Court decisions.

To refute a causal relationship, ask the following two questions:

- **Are the items of evidence important enough to lead to the conclusion?** If the effect can be explained without the information being cited as evidence, then that information does not describe an important cause.
- **Do other factors really cause the effect?** If other sources or conditions seem more important in bringing about the effect, then you can question the causal relationship in the information presented as evidence.

**3. Analogy.** An argument can be based on an **analogy,** which is a comparison of something with a similar event, state, or set of circumstances.

EXAMPLES:

- A classmate, Jorge, has been elected to the National Honor Society. You recall that he is a junior, has a B average, and is active both in Glee Club and on the school newspaper. If you concluded that another classmate, Arletha, ought to have been elected to the National Honor Society because her background is similar to Jorge's, you would be reasoning by analogy.
- During a debate on crime, your opponent might argue that when law enforcement agencies in another country similar to ours (perhaps England or Canada) were given increased freedom, the crime rate there went down. If your opponent reasoned that the United States should give increased freedom to law enforcement agencies because the crime rate decreased when England or Canada relaxed controls over its law enforcement agencies, your opponent would be reasoning by analogy.

To refute an analogy, ask the following two questions:

- **Are the subjects that are being compared similar in all important ways?** Are criminal activity and the legal system in the United States similar to those in England or Canada? If subjects do not have significant similarities, then they are not really comparable.

- **Are any of the differences between the two subjects important to the conclusion?** Do the crime rate and legal system in the United States differ in important ways from those in England or Canada? If so, then an analogy drawn between the United States and either of the other two countries may not be sound.

**4. Sign.** A **sign argument** draws a conclusion based on certain signs or indicators.

**EXAMPLES:**
- You see that your brother's eyes are watering and that his nose is running. If you concluded that he has a cold, you would be reasoning by sign.
- Your opponent might argue that the steady increase in the percentage of unsolved crimes is a sign of undue restrictions on law enforcement agencies.

To refute a sign argument, ask the following questions:

- **Do the signs given as evidence always indicate the conclusion?** Do watering eyes and a runny nose always indicate a cold? If not, they are not reliable indicators of the conclusion.
- **Are enough signs present?** Are the two signs, watering eyes and a runny nose, enough to indicate a cold? If not, the presence of the signs does not necessarily imply the conclusion.
- **Are there contradictory signs?** Is your brother alert and energetic? If so, he may not have a cold.

# HOW TO › *Refute an Argument*

1. **State clearly and concisely the argument you are going to refute.** For example, you might say, "The affirmative has argued that Supreme Court decisions have unduly restricted law enforcement agencies in the investigation of crime."

2. **State what you will prove.** Tell the audience how you plan to proceed so that they can follow your thinking. For example, you might say, "We on the negative side are going to argue that although law enforcement agencies are indeed restricted, there is no reason to believe that the restrictions are either undue or unnecessary."

3. **Present the proof completely with documented evidence.** For example, you might present facts, statistics, and quotations to back up your assertion that the restrictions are neither undue nor unnecessary.

4. **Draw a conclusion.** You cannot rely on the audience or the judge to draw the proper conclusion for you. Do not go on to another argument until you have drawn your conclusion. For example, you might say, "Therefore, we can see that although the police are restricted, the restrictions can hardly be labeled undue or unnecessary. Until the affirmative team can offer more evidence, we are going to have to conclude that these needed restrictions do not hamper law enforcement agencies."

## ACTIVITY 5

### Identifying Arguments and Questioning Their Reasoning

Identify the following arguments as generalization, causation, analogy, or sign. Then, for each of the six arguments, write two questions that you need to ask about that kind of reasoning.

1. After our neighbor painted his house, the leaves on the tree in front of our house started to turn brown. The paint must have had some poison in it.
2. Most of us got our lowest golf scores on the fifth hole. The fifth hole must be the easiest.
3. We think it's the measles. He has a fever and has broken out in a rash.
4. The plan worked well for North High's junior class. It will probably work for our junior class.
5. We're probably going to have a bad storm. The sky has filled with very dark clouds, the wind has started to blow, and lightning is flashing.
6. Each of the drivers got a flat tire at the intersection of Main Street and West Avenue. There must be something hazardous on the road.

## Rebuttal

Whereas *refutation* means attacking an argument, *rebuttal* means rebuilding an argument. Both sides have a chance to rescue points from their original arguments that have been attacked. Rebuttal is very similar to refutation in form.

**HOW TO** > *Develop a Rebuttal*

1. **Restate the argument you made originally.** You might say, "We first argued that Supreme Court decisions have unduly restricted law enforcement agencies."

2. **State what your opponent said against your original point.** For example, you might say, "The negative argued that although law enforcement agencies are indeed restricted, there is no reason to believe that the restrictions are either undue or unnecessary."

3. **State your position on your opponent's attack.** You might say, "You will see that the negative side's evidence is far outweighed by evidence from all over the country."

4. **Present the proof completely, with documented evidence.** Use facts, statistics, examples, details, and quotations to support statements you make in rebuttal. For example, you might give a recent quotation from a police commissioner stating that court decisions have hampered efforts to indict and prosecute felons.

5. **Draw a conclusion.** You might say, "Therefore, we can see that even though the negative presented some isolated evidence in support of its attack, the bulk of the evidence supports our point that court decisions have unduly restricted law enforcement agencies."

In your communication journal, keep a list of ideas that you might develop into debate topics. Some ideas for topics may spring to mind immediately, but others may occur to you as you attend class, talk with friends or relatives, listen to the news on television or radio, or read newspaper or magazine articles. When you have accumulated several good ideas, state each of them as debate propositions. Practice writing all three types: propositions of fact, propositions of value, and propositions of policy.

Shoe, by Jeff MacNelly, reprinted by permission: Tribune Media Services.

## Creating a Flow Sheet

Listening is a critical debate skill. Your ability to debate effectively depends on your immediate understanding of each speech. To keep track of the flow, or progress, of arguments, take notes on each speech and, in parentheses, remind yourself how you will respond to each of the opposition's points. [For more on critical-listening skills, see pages 84–87 of Chapter 4.]

Make careful outline notes of each speech on a **flow sheet,** a record of the progress of arguments. Use an 8-1/2 × 14-inch legal pad turned sideways. Draw eight columns on the page. Then take notes on each speech as it is given. Accurately write each of the reasons presented, and include an abbreviated sketch of the evidence. Getting each speech down on paper in a separate column will help you to see the flow of the major arguments throughout the debate. This can help you to plan an effective strategy.

# SAMPLE FLOW SHEET

**PROPOSITION:** *Resolved,* That law enforcement agencies should be given greater freedom in investigating and prosecuting crime.

| 1st Aff. Constructive | 1st Neg. Constructive | 2nd Aff. Constructive | 2nd Neg. Constructive |
|---|---|---|---|
| **I.** Restrictive Supr. Court rulings on law enforcement have resulted in continued increase of major crime. | Status quo is okay. | Supr. Court rulings show status quo not effective. | Aff. plan is not effective.<br><br>Disadvantages:<br>1. Reduce individual freedom. |
| **A.** Violent crime up 200% since 1961. | **1.** Rise in crime rate not linked to Supr. Court rulings. | **1.** Supr. Court rulings linked directly to 200% increase in crime rate. | **2.** Threaten civil liberties. |
| **B.** Crime up 25% in past 5 years. | **2.** Rise in crime rate due to increase in population. | **2.** Crime rate has grown 8 times faster than population. | **3.** Increase court backlog. Disadvantages 1, 2, and 3 outweigh the possible decrease in street crime. |
| **II.** Giving greater freedom would solve these problems. | | | |
| **A.** Police can work more effectively with fewer restrictions. | **1.** Police will be tempted to abuse authority. | **1.** Police work better without Supr. Court rulings. | |
| **B.** Crime rate will decrease. | **2.** Crime rate will increase due to more arrests for minor crimes. | **2.** Crime rate will fall: no link with number of arrests. | |
| **III.** Giving greater freedom would be the best solution to the problem. | | | |
| **A.** It would reduce street crime. | Citizens' crime watch would be better solution. | **1.** Crime watch is not enough. | |
| **B.** It would reduce the number of victims. | ∅ | **2.** Argument for reduced number of victims—dropped. | |

| 1st Neg. Rebuttal | 1st Aff. Rebuttal | 2nd Neg. Rebuttal | 2nd Aff. Rebuttal |
|---|---|---|---|
| Status quo is okay. | Status quo is not working. | Status quo is okay. | Increase in crime means status quo is not okay. |
| | Aff. plan will not create disadvantages. 1. Will not reduce individual freedom; instead will protect. | Disadvantages 1 and 2: will reduce freedom and cause loss of civil liberties. | Only affects criminals; does not harm individual civil liberties. |
| | 2. Hurts only criminal; helps victim & society. | | |
| | 3. Backlog already exists. | ∅ | Disadvantage 3 dropped. |
| Population growth does not accurately reflect crime rate. | Crime rate increase of 25% in past 5 yrs. must be considered. | | |
| ∅ | Neg. argument dropped on Point II. | ∅ | Aff. wins Point II. |
| ∅ | Aff. proves that greater freedom is a solution. | | Greater freedom from Supr. Court rulings will solve problems. |
| Alternate solutions to giving police more power: Citizens' groups can work if crime decreases. | Aff. plan is best method. | | |
| Number of victims is not an issue | Citizens' groups can't eliminate crime and can't aid victims. | ∅ | Point III dropped. Increased freedom is best way to solve problem and reduce crime rate. |

# Preparing the Debate Brief

The **debate brief** is a complete outline of the affirmative and negative cases. It is written before the debate and includes each side's reasons with an outline of the evidence to support each reason. Each item in the outline is written as a complete sentence.

*Resolved,* That law enforcement agencies should be given greater freedom in investigating and prosecuting crime.

## Affirmative

I. Restrictive Supreme Court rulings on law enforcement have resulted in continued increase of major crime.
   A. Violent crime has increased; it has shown an increase of 200% since 1961.
   B. The general crime rate has increased by 25% during the last 5 years, an increase that was considerably greater than the increase in population over the same period of time.

II. Removing the restrictions on law enforcement agencies would improve protection for all citizens.
   A. Law enforcement officials would be free to perform their work more effectively.
   B. Because they will be able to work with fewer restrictions, law enforcement officials will be able to collect more evidence and solve more crimes.
   C. The crime rate will decrease as people recognize that they do not have the legal loopholes to escape the law.

III. Giving law enforcement agencies greater freedom is the best solution to the problem of crime in the United States.
   A. Other solutions, like citizens' crime watches, are only partially effective. Law enforcement agencies still have to have the freedom to investigate and prosecute.
   B. It would reduce crime, and because fewer crimes would be committed, it would reduce the number of victims.

## Negative

I. The current restrictions are not necessarily the cause of the increase in the crime rate.
   A. There is no evidence of a direct link between the rulings of the Supreme Court and an increase in crime.
   B. The rise in the crime rate is directly related to an increase in population.

II. Giving greater freedom to law enforcement agencies would not improve the protections for citizens.
   A. Removal of safeguards to citizens will lead to abuse of authority.
   B. Rather than decreasing, the crime rate would increase as more people are arrested for minor infractions.

III. Giving greater freedom to law enforcement agencies is not the best solution to the problem of the growing crime rate because it would create other problems.
   A. It would lead to a loss of civil liberties and threaten every citizen's right to freedom from harassment.
   B. The increase in arrests for minor crimes would increase the backlog in the court system.

# ACTIVITY 6

## Writing a Debate Brief

Choose a format for a debate. Decide on a proposition. Establish the affirmative and negative sides; then write a debate brief that identifies the specific arguments each side would present.

# Judging Debates

A debate is not like a soccer game in which each goal made leads to a point scored. Debate is more like skating or gymnastics, in which each judge estimates how well each performer met a standard. Criteria for judging are fairly uniform, but applying the criteria is difficult, and two or more judges may disagree in their decisions. The following chart presents criteria for judging a policy debate using the traditional or cross-examination format.

| Judging a Policy Debate | | |
| --- | --- | --- |
| **Pattern** | **Affirmative Must Prove** | **Negative Must Prove** |
| **Problem-Solution** | 1. that there is a significant problem<br>2. that its proposition will solve the problem<br>3. that its proposition offers the best solution | 1. that no problem exists<br><br>2. that the affirmative's proposition would not solve the problem<br>3. that the affirmative's proposition either is not the best way to solve the problem or will cause new problems<br>[**Note:** The negative needs to defeat only one of the affirmative's three issues.] |
| **Comparative Advantages** | 1. that its proposition offers significant advantages over the status quo<br>2. that its proposition will not create significant problems when implemented | 1. that the advantages are not significant<br><br>2. that significant disadvantages will result<br><br>[**Note:** The negative needs to defeat only one of the affirmative's two issues.] |

In many close debates, neither side actually wins an issue. Instead, the debate is decided by determining which side demonstrated superior skill in several possible areas: analysis, evidence, reasoning, organization, refutation, and presentation (expression, delivery, and rate). If no issues are decisively won or lost, the side with the most speaker's points is judged the winner.

For each debate, the judge completes a ballot. A ballot usually provides a place to insert speaker's points. It also contains sufficient space for comments about each speaker and a place to indicate who won. No one standard ballot exists for all high school debates, but the examples shown below are representative models.

Lincoln-Douglas debates are judged in much the same way that traditional and cross-examination debates are. The winner in a Lincoln-Douglas debate is the speaker who earns more points in organization, reasoning, delivery, supporting evidence, and persuasive argumentation of values. The ballot for a Lincoln-Douglas debate is shown below.

DEBATE BALLOT
**University Interscholastic League**
Conference: _____ Date: _____ Judge: _____ Room: _____ Round: _____
Affirmative Team #_____ Negative Team #_____
Circle the number on each category below representing your evaluation of each speaker:

1—Below Average          2—Average

| 1st Aff. Speaker | 2nd Aff. Speaker | Voting Criteria |
|---|---|---|
| 1  2  3  4 | 1  2  3  4 | Analysis |
| 1  2  3  4 | 1  2  3  4 | Organization |
| 1  2  3  4 | 1  2  3  4 | Refutation |
| 1  2  3  4 | 1  2  3  4 | Oral Style |
| 1  2  3  4 | 1  2  3  4 | Speed of Delive |

Total Points ____   Total Points ____

**AFFIRMATIVE CRITICISM:**                    NE

Rank each debater in order of excellence (1st for best, 2

1st Aff. (Name)                Rank (____)   1st

2nd Aff. (Name)                Rank (____)   2nd

The significant clash(es)/issue(s) used as the basis for my

In my judgment, the _____
(Affirmative or Negative)

LINCOLN-DOUGLAS DEBATE BALLOT
**University Interscholastic League**
Conference: _____ Date: _____ Judge: _____ Room: _____ Round: _____
Affirmative #: _____ Negative #: _____
Circle the one number representing your evaluation of each speaker:

| | Superior | Excellent | Good | Average |
|---|---|---|---|---|
| Affirmative | 25 24 23 22 21 | 20 19 18 17 16 | 15 14 13 12 11 | 10 9 8 7 6 |
| Negative | 25 24 23 22 21 | 20 19 18 17 16 | 15 14 13 12 11 | 10 9 8 7 6 |

| AFFIRMATIVE | NEGATIVE |
|---|---|
| Analysis: | Analysis: |
| Argumentation: | Argumentation: |
| Presentation: | Presentation: |

Reason for Decision:

In my judgment, _____ debater # _____ won the debate.
(affirmative or negative)

Judge's Signature

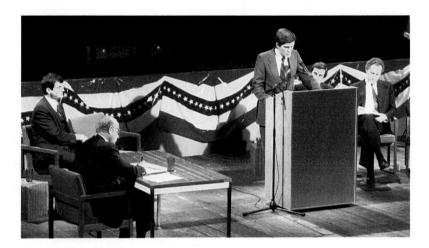

# ACTIVITY 7

## Judging a Debate

Imagine that you are judging a debate. What issues would the affirmative side have to win in order to win the debate? What issues would the negative side have to win? Listen to a classroom debate and decide who won the issues. Also, give your evaluation of how each speaker performed in analysis, evidence, reasoning, organization, refutation, and presentation.

## GUIDELINES

### for Participating in Debate

- Do I understand the debate proposition?
- Have I determined the key issues for the debate?
- Have I researched the topic carefully to develop reasons and evidence?
- Have I developed a case that is consistent with the material?
- Have I prepared a brief of my case?
- Have I anticipated the arguments of my opponent?
- Am I prepared to refute the arguments of my opponent?
- Am I prepared to rebuild the arguments my opponent attacks?
- Have I practiced?

# EVALUATING DEBATE

### Choosing a Winner

The chairperson, or chair, is responsible for making sure that the debate that occurs during group meetings is as organized, courteous, and fair as possible.

### Characteristics of an Effective Chairperson

An effective chairperson

**1** understands the procedures for conducting a debate

**2** makes sure that both sides in the debate are able to follow the appropriate order for speaking and observe the time limits allowed

**3** evaluates a debate properly

## **M**eet the Chairperson

Frances Battise has served as chairperson of the Alabama-Coushatta Tribal Council in Livingston, Texas. She says one of the most important jobs is making sure all sides of an issue get a fair hearing. "Every issue of debate has at least two sides, and some have many sides," Battise says. "The chairperson tries to make sure that everyone gets a chance to participate in the debate."

*Frances Battise, RN*

## ACTIVITY

### Situation

You are a member of a local group that is trying to determine which side of an issue to support. You and your fellow members have been asked to evaluate a public debate on this issue and assess the performance of each debate participant.

### Preparation

Working with one or more classmates, watch a live debate, or locate a videotape or a cassette recording of a debate through your school's library or media center. Take notes, and then use the criteria given in this chapter to evaluate the performance of each participant. Keep in mind that you may not necessarily agree with the winner's opinion; you are simply evaluating his or her methods of debating the issue.

### Analysis and Assessment

Based on your notes on the participants' effectiveness in the debate, decide which side was the winner. Discuss your decision with your classmates, and explain the reasons for your choice. Then ask for feedback from your classmates on the soundness of your reasoning.

# S⭐U⭐M⭐M⭐A⭐R⭐Y

**DEBATE** is a form of decision making in which two or more people present speeches on opposing sides—the affirmative and the negative—of a public issue.

- **A debate centers on a proposition,** which clearly states a position on a specific topic. Propositions give the burden of proof to the affirmative side. They should be clearly worded and should deal with only one controversial topic.
- **Debate can follow any number of formats.** The most common formats are traditional, cross-examination, and Lincoln-Douglas.
- **A case** consists of the reasons and evidence that a side uses as a foundation for its position.
- **Constructive speeches** build arguments on both sides of the proposition. Depending on the type of proposition, both the affirmative and negative sides select patterns for organizing their arguments.
- **Refutation** is the attacking of ideas. Refutation may be based on the amount, the quality, or the reasoning of the evidence. **Rebuttal** is the rebuilding of an argument.
- **A debate brief** is an outline of the affirmative case, the negative case, or both. The debate brief includes all the reasons given for the case and key evidence that supports the reasons.
- **Debates are judged on two criteria:** which side gave the better argument concerning the issues and which side did the better job of debating.

# Review Questions

1. Give an example of each of the three types of debate propositions: propositions of fact, propositions of value, and propositions of policy.
2. List the three standard debate formats and explain how they are alike and how they differ.
3. What are the stock issues for a proposition of policy? What are the stock issues for a proposition of value?
4. One way to organize the affirmative case for a proposition of policy is to use the problem-solution pattern. What is another way to organize the affirmative case?
5. One way to organize a negative case is to use the straight refutation approach. What are two other ways that a negative case can be organized?
6. What is a weakness of defending the status quo in the negative case?
7. Explain the difference between refutation and rebuttal and give at least one example of each.
8. One basis for refutation is the opposition's insufficient quantity of evidence. What are two other grounds for refuting the opposition's arguments?
9. One common type of reasoning is generalization. What are three other types of reasoning from the evidence?
10. What is the purpose of the flow sheet? of the debate brief?

# Discussion Questions

1. Discuss some possible reasons why the tradition developed that the affirmative side always presents its case before the negative side in a debate.
2. Identify the major differences between a traditional or a cross-examination debate and a Lincoln-Douglas debate. Then, discuss cases in which each of these debate formats would be most appropriate.
3. The French mathematician and philosopher Blaise Pascal wrote, "When we wish to correct with advantage, and to show another that he errs, we must notice from what side he views the matter, for on that side it is usually true." First, discuss the meaning of this quotation. Then, discuss how it relates to the issues of refutation and rebuttal in debate.
4. Discuss why effective debating involves more than building solid arguments on the issues.
5. The famous English physician and writer Thomas Fuller wrote, "Argument seldom convinces anyone contrary to his inclinations." First, discuss the meaning of this quotation. Then, discuss how it relates to debate.

# ACTIVITIES

1. **Revising the Wording of Propositions.** Rewrite the following propositions to meet the three guidelines for wording a proposition given on page 484.

   a. All American auto makers should be required to install both driver's and passenger's side air bags on all models of their automobiles.

   b. The system of funding public elementary education through property taxes should be reconsidered.

   c. An equal rights amendment should not be adopted.

   d. The current method for responding to stated complaints by customers interacting with personnel in both retail sales and in customer service should be altered in favor of customer satisfaction.

   e. Motorcycle manufacturers should be permitted to produce for private ownership motorcycles that can exceed the legal speed limit by more than ten miles an hour.

2. **Organizing Support for an Issue.**

   **A.** Select a stock issue on a policy of your own choice. Then, write the affirmative and the negative reasons that make up the proof for this issue. Finally, find three pieces of evidence to support each reason. Be prepared to discuss why the evidence that you have found through your research provides convincing support for the affirmative position and negative position.

   **B.** Use either a problem-solution pattern or a comparative advantages pattern to organize the reasons and evidence you have gathered for Part A. Be sure that you have identified the status quo clearly, and be specific about how your reasons and evidence resolve the issue.

3. **Understanding the Importance of a Historical Debate.** Prepare an informative report on a presidential election-year debate or on other famous debates or series of presidential debates of your own choice. Identify, if possible, the most significant issue about which the participants disagreed. In proposition form, state each side's position on this issue.

   As you investigate your topic, research the effects that this particular debate or series of debates had on people's thinking about the central issue or on the outcome of the election. Present your finished report to your class.

Example: Jimmy Carter-Ronald Reagan debate in 1980

Example: George Bush-Bill Clinton-Ross Perot debate in 1992

**4. Choosing Topics and Propositions for Debate.** List three topics that you believe are worthy of debate. For each topic, write three debate propositions: a proposition of fact, a proposition of value, and a proposition of policy. Then list each set of propositions in your order of preference, giving the one you would most enjoy debating first.

**5. Preparing for a Values Debate.**

**A.** Select one of the following propositions of value or a proposition of your own choice for debate. Then list the key issues for the proposition that you selected.

1. *Resolved,* That the spirit of the law is more important than the letter of the law.

2. *Resolved,* That American presidential campaigns are too long.

3. *Resolved,* That plagiarism is morally wrong.

**B.** Select a partner, choose a side, and prepare to debate the proposition you selected in Part A. Identify the stock issues for the proposition, and develop reasons and evidence to support them. Prepare a file of evidence cards to use as you develop your case. Predict your opponent's arguments, and be prepared to discuss why your arguments are sound.

**6. Preparing for a Policy Debate.**

**A.** Select one of the following propositions of policy or a proposition of your own choice for debate. Then list the key issues for the proposition that you selected.

1. *Resolved,* That the minimum age to obtain a driver's license should be raised to eighteen.

2. *Resolved,* That all fifty states should follow the same yearly schedule for public schooling.

3. *Resolved,* That cat owners should be required to keep their pets on a leash.

**B.** Select a partner, choose a side, and prepare to debate the proposition you chose for Part A. Make sure that your issues can be supported by specific reasons. Prepare a file of evidence cards that you can use in developing your case. Identify the pattern or approach you will use to organize your evidence. Predict your opposition's likely arguments for the constructive speeches and for rebuttal and refutation. Be prepared to discuss why your position is more sound and more convincing than the opposing position.

# EVERYDAY COMMUNICATION

### Situation
Attend a debate concerning a controversial topic that interests you. If you are unable to attend a live debate, watch one on television or view a video recording of a presidential debate.

### Problem
Listen to the debate carefully and chart it on a flow sheet. Use the judging criteria on pages 509–510 to write a brief report on the main features of the debate—the proposition, the affirmative and negative cases, the issues, any refutation or rebuttal, and the outcome. In your report, make sure you give your evaluation of the debate. Who do you think won? Why? What were the strong points and weak points of the opposing arguments?

### Assessing Your Skill
Be prepared to read your report in class and conduct a question-and-answer session with your classmates.

# COMMUNICATION IN THE WORKPLACE

### Background
You are an attorney preparing the argument for your next case.

### Preparing to Do the Job
Begin by defining your position and the specifics of your case. Will you present the affirmative or negative side—that is, are you the defense attorney or the prosecutor? What legal issues will you debate? Who is your client? What arguments will you offer to support your position?

### Testing Your Skill
Write a brief speech presenting your case. Be prepared to deliver your speech in class and to conduct a question-and-answer session in which you defend your position against issues and arguments offered by your classmates. Ask your teacher or classmates to evaluate your presentation according to the guidelines on page 511.

Agenda

STUDENT COUNCIL
BALLOT

Chairperson
☒ Sylvia Garza
☐ Lee Kim
☐ Mark Rob

▼

# Parliamentary Procedure

## What Is Parliamentary Procedure?

Members of the prom committee are meeting to decide on the entertainment, and opinions differ as to what type of band should be hired. Committee members are shouting out their opinions to be heard by the group. One student, who strongly supports a rock-and-roll band, is arguing with another student, who prefers a rap band for the occasion. Several students believe that they have a majority in favor of hiring a jazz band, but they cannot get the group's attention in order to call a vote.

Without a system for an efficient and productive exchange of ideas, people with differing opinions are likely to spend long hours in heated debate that may never lead to a satisfactory resolution. **Parliamentary procedure,** a set of rules for conducting orderly meetings, was developed to prevent such inefficiency. The three major functions of parliamentary procedure are to ensure that meetings run smoothly, to help a group focus on the issues that are most important to the entire membership, and to ensure that meetings are run according to democratic principles.

# Understanding the Principles of Parliamentary Procedure

Many groups—governmental, business, educational, and social—conduct their business at meetings to which all members are invited. Based on the rules and customs of the early British Parliament, the set of rules for conducting meetings is called **parliamentary procedure.**

To maintain order, group meetings are generally conducted according to the following five principles of parliamentary procedure.

| Principles of Parliamentary Procedure* | | |
|---|---|---|
| **Principle** | **Explanation** | **Advantage** |
| **Only One Item at a Time** | Only one matter of business may be considered at a time. | helps to maintain order |
| **Open Discussion** | Everyone has a right to express an opinion, and each opinion is treated as valuable. | enables the group to come to an informed decision |
| **Equality of Voting Rights** | Every member has the right to vote, and each vote is counted as equal. | ensures a fair vote |
| **The Majority Rules** | The minority agrees to accept the decisions of the majority. Most votes require a **simple majority,** which consists of at least one more than half of those voting. Special situations need a two-thirds majority. | assures that the collective judgment of the group prevails; saves time |
| **Protection of Minority Rights** | • When any motion infringes on personal rights, at least two thirds of those present and voting must affirm that motion for it to pass.<br>• Rules give minority opinion an equal right to be heard on all motions. | assures that each motion is carefully considered from all viewpoints |

\* For a complete discussion of parliamentary procedure, consult *Robert's Rules of Order, Newly Revised.*

## Public Record

All proceedings included in a meeting are considered to be a matter of public record. The group's secretary takes **minutes,** a written and official record of the meeting's proceedings. These minutes are read and presented for an approval vote at the next scheduled meeting. They are kept in the official files of the organization.

## A·C·T·I·V·I·T·Y
### 1    Analyzing a Group Meeting

Plan with a classmate to attend a meeting of a formal group, such as a town council. Note when the group used parliamentary procedure. How were the rights of individuals protected? How did the members benefit from observing the principles of parliamentary procedure? Discuss these questions with your classmate.

## Running a Meeting

The rules of parliamentary procedure cover almost all situations that might arise during a meeting: the writing of the constitution and bylaws, the duties of officers, and the specific rules governing debate. An organization can also create its own set of rules, to be included in the organization's constitution and bylaws.

Although all of these rules and procedures are important, the ones that are most vital to you in your role as a potential leader or member of an organization are those that deal directly with running a meeting.

## Calling a Meeting

When a meeting is planned, members must be given notice, usually ten days in advance, that the group will assemble. Notice should be provided to members in writing, and commonly an **agenda,** a short list of items to be discussed, is included. This practice ensures that all members are aware of the group's planned activity and have an opportunity to participate.

Advance notice is important for special meetings or meetings for a group that does not meet on a regular basis. If officers fail to give members advance notice, any business conducted at a meeting can be nullified. In addition, if it can be proved that officers planned to hold a secret meeting, they can be removed from office.

## The Quorum

At the beginning of a meeting, the chairperson must always make sure that a quorum is present. A **quorum** is the minimum number of members that must be present for the group to conduct business. A quorum can be set at any number. For most groups, the quorum is set at 40 to 60 percent of the membership. For very large organizations, 20 percent of the membership often constitutes a quorum. If no number is set by an organization, then the quorum is one person more than 50 percent of the membership.

The quorum should be high enough that the business conducted represents the thinking of the organization as a whole. However, it must be low enough that a reasonably well attended meeting is likely to have enough members to conduct business.

ACTIVITY
2

### Setting a Quorum

Investigate the quorum requirements of two groups that meet on your school campus or in your community. Ask the officers or members of each group why they chose high or low quorum requirements, and report your findings to the class. Suppose that your class were going to function as an organization. What number would you suggest as a quorum? Why?

# Order of Business

The order of business for a meeting involves the sequence of items on the agenda. Most formal organizations use the following standard items, which are suggested in *Robert's Rules of Order*.

1. Call to order
2. Reading and approval of minutes from previous meeting
3. Officers' reports
4. Standing committee reports
5. Special committee reports
6. Old business
7. New business
8. Announcements
9. Adjournment

A group can follow this standard order of business or set its own order of business in its bylaws. Even when an order is set, items can be shifted with the consent of the group.

# ACTIVITY 3

## Writing an Agenda for a Group Meeting

Imagine that your class functions as an organization. At the last meeting the group members elected class officers for the year, and at the upcoming meeting they will begin to consider new business. Write an agenda that could be used for that meeting. Be creative, but make sure that you include the standard items listed under "Order of Business." Then share your agenda with your classmates and respond to feedback from them.

# Understanding the Duties of Officers

Parliamentary organizations have at least three key officers. The chairperson presides, or exercises control, over meetings. When the chairperson is absent, the vice-chairperson presides. The secretary keeps an accurate, official record of each meeting, the minutes.

## The Chairperson

The **chairperson,** or chair, is responsible for running pleasant, efficient meetings and for protecting the rights of everyone at the meetings. To do so, the chairperson should have a mastery of parliamentary procedure. The chairperson should

- govern the group by parliamentary procedure, an established organizational pattern that members can agree on
- educate the members of the organization by explaining procedures whenever necessary, so that everyone under-stands what is taking place and why it is taking place
- maintain order by insisting that all members follow parliamentary procedure during meetings
- be fair in recognizing members to speak

Procedure calls for a member to raise one hand (or to stand at large meetings) to be recognized. In small groups, people may just speak out. Effective chairpersons try to ensure fair speaking order, to avoid having especially outspoken people dominate the meeting.

1. Give the person who made the motion the right to speak first.

2. Call on each person by name.

3. If possible, try to alternate speakers so that the different sides of an issue are presented in a balanced discussion.

4. Be sure that everyone has a chance to speak once before anyone gets the chance to speak for a second time.

5. Maintain good eye contact with the whole group. The chair should not always look at the same section of the group or at the same person whenever a debate begins.

## The Vice-Chairperson

The **vice-chairperson** assumes the duties of the chair when the chair is unable to do so. The vice-chair also assumes the duties of the chair when the chair steps down to debate a motion. Once a chair steps down, he or she cannot resume the role of chair until that particular motion is voted upon.

## The Secretary

The **secretary,** the major recording officer and keeper of records, must be trustworthy and accurate. The primary role of the secretary during a meeting is to take the minutes. Policy demands that proceedings be a matter of public record. Therefore, the minutes are kept on file.

A secretary can keep an official record of a meeting with handwritten notes and electronic devices.

## What to Include in the Minutes

1. The kind of meeting (regular or special)
2. The name of the organization
3. The date, hour, and place of the meeting
4. The name of the presiding officer
5. The number of members present and the names of absentees
6. The action taken on minutes of the previous meeting
7. Committee reports
8. Each main motion, the name of the person introducing it, and the action taken
9. Points of order and appeals
10. Any material that in the future may be helpful in explaining what was done at the meeting
11. The program, if any, such as a special presentation, speech, ceremony, or entertainment
12. The time of adjournment

# A·C·T·I·V·I·T·Y 4

## Evaluating the Performance of Officers

Attend a meeting of a group in your school or community that uses parliamentary procedure. Note how each of the club officers performs his or her duties. Be especially aware of how the chairperson ensures that everyone's rights are protected during debate on any motions that are presented. How well does the chair maintain order? How does the chair maintain fairness in recognizing members to speak? Comment on any failures you note during the proceedings, and suggest ways that they could have been avoided by adhering to parliamentary procedure.

Do you think that you would like to be an officer of an organization? If so, which office most appeals to you? In your journal, list the responsibilities of that office. Then examine your character traits, your strengths and weaknesses, and your likes and dislikes. Evaluate whether or not you would be a good candidate for the office.

COMMUNICATION JOURNAL

# Understanding Motions

In a parliamentary organization, all of the business in a meeting is handled through the making of motions. A **motion** is a proposal for action made by a member. There can be no discussion unless there is a motion before the members. Once a motion is made, the members must act on it in some way.

## Classification of Motions

In most groups you will use five classifications of motions:

- main
- subsidiary
- privileged
- incidental
- renewal

**Main Motions.**    **Main motions** are those that set forth new items of business to be considered. Ordinarily, they must be made first; many of the motions in the other classifications are used in response to main motions. There can be only one main motion on the floor at a time.

EXAMPLES:

- I move that club members actively participate in the drive to eradicate illiteracy.
- I move that we hold a Valentine's dance on February 14.
- I move that club members volunteer to work one hour a week at the local day-care center.

**Subsidiary Motions.** **Subsidiary motions** allow members to change or dispose of a main motion that is being discussed.

1. The motion to **lay on the table** calls for a temporary postponement of action until someone makes a motion to remove the original motion from the table.
2. The motion to move the **previous question** calls for a vote to stop discussion on a motion.
3. The motion to **limit debate** calls for a time limit on individual speeches or on the entire debate; the motion to **extend debate** moves that debate be extended to allow more complete discussion of the issue.
4. The motion to **postpone to a definite time** calls for a postponement of action until a particular time set by the person making the motion.
5. The motion to **refer to a committee** calls for shifting discussion of the matter at hand to a smaller group meeting at some other time.
6. The motion to **amend** calls for an alteration in the wording of a motion.
7. The motion to **postpone indefinitely** calls for a postponement of discussion for that session and thus prevents the main motion from coming to a vote.

**Privileged Motions.** **Privileged motions** concern the running of the meeting itself. Because of their urgent nature, they take precedence over all other classes of motions.

1. The motion to **adjourn** calls for the meeting to close.
2. The motion to **recess** calls for a break during the meeting.
3. The motion **question of privilege** calls for immediate action on such things as heating, lighting, ventilation, and disturbances.

4. The motion **call for the orders of the day** alerts the chairperson that a scheduled event has been overlooked.

**Incidental Motions.** The motions that relate to questions of procedure arising out of the discussion are called **incidental motions**. There are a number of these incidental motions that are commonly used.

1. The motion to **appeal** is used to force the chairperson to submit a disputed ruling made by the chairperson to a vote by the entire group.
2. The motion to **close nominations** calls for an end to the process of nominating persons for offices.
3. The motion **division of assembly** requires the chairperson to call for a second vote. This second vote will preferably be conducted by a method other than the method used to conduct the first vote.
4. The motion **division of question** requires the chairperson to divide a motion with more than one part into its various parts. Dividing a question allows each part to be discussed and voted on separately.
5. The motion to raise a question of **parliamentary inquiry** is made to request information about whether making a motion would be in order. This motion is always made to the chair.
6. The motion **object to consideration** allows the group to dismiss a main motion that is irrelevant, that is considered inappropriate, or that is for some other reason deemed undesirable. Objections to consideration must be made before any debate of the main motion begins and before any subsidiary motions are made.

7. A motion to **reopen nominations** is made to allow more nominations to be made after nominations have been closed.

8. A motion to **suspend the rules** calls for the suspension, during the current meeting, of any standing rule that the organization may have. Such suspensions are generally intended to allow members to do something not normally allowed by the rules.

9. A motion to **establish the method of voting** calls for the chairperson to take the vote in the manner stated in the motion (for instance, by secret ballot or by a show of hands).

10. A move to **withdraw a motion** gives the person who made the motion permission to remove it from consideration.

11. The motion **point of order** calls attention to a violation of parliamentary procedure.

"You *can't* move we adjourn, Wilson. We just started."

**Renewal Motions.**   **Renewal motions** get discussion reopened on decisions that have already been made. There are three renewal motions that you will use.

1. The motion to **reconsider** calls for discussion of a motion that has already been passed.

2. The motion to **rescind** calls for the cancellation of action taken on a previous motion.

3. The motion to **take from the table** calls for reopening discussion of a motion that had earlier been laid on the table by a subsidiary motion.

Business in a formal parliamentary body, whether large or small, is conducted through *motions.*

## Precedence of Motions

Perhaps the main appeal of parliamentary procedure is its orderliness. The motions that are listed on pages 527–530 are presented in the order in which they can be introduced. The order in which the motions must be voted on or acted upon is called the **order of precedence.** Privileged and subsidiary motions are ranked above main motions in the following order.

| | |
|---|---|
| **Privileged Motions** | 1. Adjourn |
| | 2. Recess |
| | 3. Question of privilege |
| | 4. Call for the orders of the day |
| **Subsidiary Motions** | 5. Lay on the table |
| | 6. Previous question |
| | 7. Limit debate or extend debate |
| | 8. Postpone to a definite time |
| | 9. Refer to a committee |
| | 10. Amend |
| | 11. Postpone indefinitely |
| **Main Motions** | 12. Any main motion |

A motion of higher precedence is in order when a motion of lower precedence is on the floor.

**EXAMPLE:** Suppose that the main motion before a student council meeting is "to hold a dance in the school gym on Saturday, March 15, beginning at 8:00 P.M." If while the motion is being debated someone moves "to lay the motion on the table" (number 5 in precedence), this motion takes precedence over the main motion (number 12). If after the motion "to lay on the table" is seconded, or supported by another person, someone else moves "to postpone discussion of the main motion until the next meeting" (number 8), this motion is out of order because "lay on the table" (number 5) is of higher precedence than "postpone to a definite time" (number 8).

Note that incidental motions and renewal motions are not ranked in order of precedence. They are dealt with as they are made rather than in a sequential order of preference.

## Table of Parliamentary Motions

The following table gives a concise overview of the rules governing motions. The first column, labeled "Rank," gives the order of preference. Needing a **second** means that a person other than the person making the motion must indicate that he or she is willing to have the group consider the motion. **Debatable** refers to whether that motion can be discussed by the group before it is voted upon. **Amendable** refers to whether any changes in the motion are allowed.

# TABLE OF PARLIAMENTARY MOTIONS

## Privileged, Subsidiary, and Main Motions

| Rank | Name of Motion | Interrupt a Speaker? | Need a Second? | Debatable? | Amendable? | Vote |
|---|---|---|---|---|---|---|
| 1. | Adjourn | no | yes | no | no | maj. |
| 2. | Recess | no | yes | yes | yes | maj. |
| 3. | Question of privilege | yes | no | no | no | none |
| 4. | Call for the orders of the day | yes | no | no | no | none |
| 5. | Lay on the table | no | yes | no | no | maj. |
| 6. | Previous question | no | yes | no | no | 2/3 |
| 7. | Limit or extend debate | no | yes | yes | yes | 2/3 |
| 8. | Postpone to a definite time | no | yes | yes | yes | maj. |
| 9. | Refer to a committee | no | yes | yes | yes | maj. |
| 10. | Amend | no | yes | yes | yes | maj. |
| 11. | Postpone indefinitely | no | yes | yes | no | maj. |
| 12. | Any main motion | no | yes | yes | yes | maj. |

## Incidental Motions

| Name of Motion | Interrupt a Speaker? | Need a Second? | Debatable? | Amendable? | Vote |
|---|---|---|---|---|---|
| Appeal | yes | yes | yes | no | maj. |
| Close nominations | no | yes | no | yes | 2/3 |
| Division of assembly | yes | no | no | no | none |
| Division of question | yes | no | no | yes | none |
| Parliamentary inquiry | yes | no | no | no | none |
| Point of order | yes | no | no | no | none |
| Object to consideration | yes | no | no | no | 2/3 |
| Reopen nominations | no | yes | no | yes | maj. |
| Suspend the rules | no | yes | no | no | 2/3 |
| Voting, motions relating to | no | yes | no | yes | maj. |
| Withdraw a motion, leave to | yes | no | no | no | maj. |

## Renewal Motions

| Name of Motion | Interrupt a Speaker? | Need a Second? | Debatable? | Amendable? | Vote |
|---|---|---|---|---|---|
| Reconsider | no | yes | yes | no | maj. |
| Rescind | no | yes | yes | yes | 2/3 |
| Take from the table | no | yes | no | no | maj. |

## Understanding Motions

The key to understanding and using motions is to know when a motion is in order, whether it is debatable or amendable, and what vote it requires to pass. Use the table on page 533 to help you complete the following activities.

1. Indicate whether each of the following motions is amendable.
   a. Take a recess
   b. Main motion
   c. Lay on the table
   d. Postpone to a definite time
   e. Adjourn
2. Indicate what vote (no vote, simple majority, or two-thirds majority) each of the following motions requires to pass.
   a. Call for the orders of the day
   b. Close nominations
   c. Take from the table
   d. Previous question
   e. Amend
3. For each of the following situations, indicate whether the second motion is in order.
   a. Diego moves to have a party. Paul moves to amend the motion.
   b. Ella moves to take a recess. Wenona moves to lay on the table the motion about having a party.
   c. Heather moves to postpone the motion until the next meeting. Tyrone moves to adjourn.
   d. Juan moves to redecorate the meeting room. Joan moves to refer the motion to a committee.
   e. Tanya moves to amend the motion to redecorate the meeting room. Sylvia moves the previous question.

# Using Motions

Each parliamentary motion has its own specific characteristics and uses. Each has its own particular function in parliamentary proceedings.

## Getting a Motion on the Floor

According to the rules of parliamentary procedure, no discussion is in order unless a motion is on the floor. The procedure for making a motion involves the following steps.

1. The chairperson grants the floor by stating the member's name, for example, "Tom" or "Mrs. Lopez."

2. The person makes a motion, such as "I move that the annual dance be held at 8:00 P.M., Saturday, June 4, at the Topper Club."

3. Another member then seconds the motion by calling out, "I second the motion" or simply "Second." The member who seconds does not have to be recognized. Since seconding only indicates willingness to have the motion discussed, the seconder need not be in favor of the motion. If no one calls out a second, the chair asks, "Is there a second?"

4. If the chair does not hear a second, he or she says, "The motion fails for lack of a second. Is there further business?" If the chair does hear a second, the chair says, "It has been moved and seconded that the annual dance be held at 8:00 P.M., Saturday, June 4, at the Topper Club. Is there any discussion?"

5. After discussion of a main motion (or immediately in cases when no discussion is allowed), the chair calls for a vote.

WIZARD OF ID by permission of Johnny Hart and Creators Syndicate, Inc.

## Changing the Motion

A main motion can be changed in several ways during the discussion preceding the vote. It can be withdrawn or amended.

**Withdraw the Motion.** If a motion is so poorly phrased that it is difficult to understand, the person who made the motion can ask to withdraw it. Usually, the motion is withdrawn if the person who originally seconded it gives permission. However, the chair must get the consent of the group. If someone objects, a vote is taken. If a majority favors withdrawing, the motion may be withdrawn.

**Amend the Motion.** At any time during discussion of a motion, any member can move to amend or change the wording of a motion. The following rules govern the amending of a motion.

1. An amendment must be specific when it is put before a group. The following chart outlines the five different ways to amend the motion "I move to hold the annual Spring Dance at 8:00 P.M., Saturday, June 4, at the Topper Club."

| Way to Amend | Example of Motion to Amend |
|---|---|
| **Inserting** | "I move to amend the motion by inserting the word *Formal* after *Spring*." |
| **Adding** | "I move to amend the motion by adding the words *Lower Pavilion* after *Club*." |
| **Striking out** | "I move to amend the motion by striking out the word *annual*." |
| **Striking out and inserting** | "I move to amend the motion by striking out 8 and inserting 9." |
| **Substituting** | "I move to amend the motion by substituting for it the following motion: To hold a picnic at 2:00 P.M., June 4, at Parker Field." |

2. Only one primary amendment and one secondary amendment may be considered at a time. A **primary amendment** is an amendment of the main motion. A **secondary amendment** is an amendment of a primary amendment.

3. An amendment must be germane to a motion. To be **germane** means that the amendment must in some way relate to the issue of the original motion.

   **EXAMPLE:** If a member moved to amend the annual dance motion by adding "and that eating shall be allowed at group meetings," the amendment would not be germane.

4. An amendment cannot be made by inserting the word *not* into the main motion.

# ACTIVITY 6

## Making and Amending Motions

Suppose you belong to an organization and want to propose buying a lectern for the meeting room. Write down the steps you will follow to get the motion before the group. Practice saying the steps aloud. Next, amend the motion to propose buying a gavel instead of a lectern. Write how you will make such an amendment. Practice the wording aloud.

## Putting Off Discussion

There are several parliamentary procedures available to group members when they wish to delay discussion of a motion either temporarily or permanently.

1. If a certain motion seems inappropriate for the group's consideration, a member can **object to consideration.** This motion is in order before any debate on the motion occurs.

   **EXAMPLE:** If at the meeting of the junior class one student moved "to ask the principal to purchase supplies for Mrs. Kwan's tenth-grade homeroom," another student could object to consideration of the question on the grounds that it is irrelevant to the ordinary business of the group since that business is supposed to pertain to eleventh-grade issues.

2. If a member believes that group discussion of a subject would be more appropriate either later in the meeting or

at a different meeting, he or she can move to **postpone to a definite time.** This is a motion to defer the group's action temporarily.

**EXAMPLE:** If a motion requiring data about finances is before the group and the class treasurer has not yet arrived, a member can move to delay consideration of the subject until the treasurer gets to the meeting.

**3.** If a member believes that a motion should be delayed but is not sure exactly when would be the best time to return to it, he or she can move "to lay the motion on the table." This motion places the main motion on the secretary's table, where it stays until someone moves to take it from the table.

To **lay on the table** is probably the best known of the delaying motions, but it is also the most abused. The most frequent misuse is in specifying a time.

**EXAMPLE:** The wording "I move to lay the motion on the table until next week" is improper since the motion to lay on the table cannot specify any time limit. If a member wants the motion set aside at this meeting but brought up at the next meeting, then he or she should move to postpone it, not to lay it on the table.

## Expressing Disagreement

Even when parliamentary procedure is used to govern the proceedings of a meeting, situations that are out of order may occasionally arise. If a member believes that the rules of parliamentary procedure have been violated, there are two courses of action.

1. A member can rise to a **point of order** at any time. When someone stands and says, "Point of order," the chair will ask that person to state the point (even if doing so interrupts another speaker). If the speaker is correct, the chair will change the procedure accordingly.

2. A member can **appeal** the decision of the chair. If a member believes that the chair has made a decision that does not seem in keeping with the parliamentary rules used by the group, that member can appeal the decision. With this motion a member calls upon the chair to open discussion on the merits of the judgment and then to put the question to a vote. If a majority of those voting support the person making the appeal, then the chair's decision is reversed.

## Dealing with Complicated or Time-Consuming Subjects

When a member thinks that the subject under discussion is too complicated or too time-consuming for the group to consider, he or she can refer the motion to a committee. The purpose of this motion is to have a smaller group consider the matter in detail to save time for the larger group. Many organizations run almost entirely under a committee structure by requiring that every motion come through a committee before it can be debated on the floor. Most organizations have at least a few standing committees, each considering a certain type of question, so that most business is reviewed by a committee before being sent to the entire organization for consideration.

A member who makes a motion to **refer to committee** may wish to designate the makeup of the committee and its authority.

**EXAMPLE:** Someone might say, "I move to refer the motion to a committee of three members appointed by the chair with instructions to report back to this group at our next regular meeting."

## Controlling Length of Debate

Before debate begins on any issue, or even during the debate itself, a member can move to **limit** or to **extend debate.**

**EXAMPLE:** If, in today's debate, you fear that everyone might want to speak at great length, you might say, "I move to limit speeches to three minutes each" or "I move to limit the total discussion to one hour."

If a member wishes not just to control the length of speeches or the debate but to stop the meeting completely, he or she can move to **recess,** which will stop the meeting for a few minutes, or move to **adjourn,** which will end the meeting for the day.

# Voting on a Motion

After discussion of a main motion (or immediately in cases when no discussion is allowed), the chair calls for a vote. Ordinarily an oral vote is taken, with members saying either "aye," "no," or "abstain" aloud. A vote to **abstain** indicates that the member does not wish to support or to oppose a motion that is being voted upon. If a member of the group wishes to vote by some other method, a motion about how to vote is always in order. Voting may be done by a show of hands, by standing, by secret ballot, or by **roll-call vote,** in which the secretary calls out each member's name and records his or her response. Votes are counted by the chairperson or the secretary or sometimes by both. Except when a two-thirds majority is required, all motions require a simple majority vote.

# When the Vote Is Too Close to Call

When a vote is taken and the outcome is too close to call either way, the group always has the right to assure itself that the votes are counted correctly. The motion **division of assembly** requires the chairperson to call for a second vote. By using this motion (or by just calling out, "Division"), a member can indicate his or her opinion that the vote is close enough to require a recount. It is preferable that the second vote be conducted by another method. For example, if the first vote was taken by voice, the second count will be taken by show of hands or by standing.

Drawing by Joe Mirachi; © 1979 The New Yorker Magazine, Inc.

*"All who thought my little joke very funny say 'Aye.'"*

# Breaking a Tie

One of the chair's most important rights is the right to vote to break a tie. Therefore, if a motion requiring a majority has fifteen aye votes and fifteen no votes, the chair may vote. However, the chair can never be forced to vote. If the chair refuses to vote when there is a tie, the motion fails for lack of a majority. Breaking a tie is not the chair's only opportunity to vote. The chair may vote any time that his or her vote will affect the outcome.

## Changing the Outcome After the Vote

Parliamentary procedure allows for people to change their minds on an issue. Any time after a motion has been passed, a member of the group may move to **rescind** it. To rescind means to cancel the action taken on a previous motion.

A member may also move to **reconsider** a motion any time within the same meeting or at the next meeting. This motion means that a member is asking the group for permission to reopen discussion on the question. If the motion to reconsider passes, then discussion is reopened, and eventually another vote will be taken. If the motion to reconsider fails, then the group moves on to other business.

In order to prevent abuse of the motion to reconsider, parliamentary law requires the member calling for reconsideration to have voted on the winning side. This ensures that a member who voted on the losing side does not use this motion to delay the proceedings or to obstruct the will of the majority.

MOTION TO RECONSIDER

## Bringing a Motion to a Vote

There are two ways to bring a motion to a vote.

1. Informally, a member simply calls out, "Question." Although anyone who wishes to discuss the motion further has the right to do so, the knowledge that at least one person wants to get on to the vote may lead others to show a similar feeling. Also, a chairperson may say, "It sounds as if some of you believe we have exhausted meaningful discussion. Are we ready to get on to the vote?"

2. More formally, a member who is ready to vote raises one hand to be recognized. When called on by the chair, he or she makes the motion "to move the previous question" to see whether the group wants to stop discussion and vote on the motion. A positive vote on the motion to move the previous question means

that no further discussion of the current motion is allowed. The chair subsequently calls for a vote on the main motion before the group.

# ACTIVITY 7

## Observing Voting Procedures

Some television channels carry the proceedings of local legislative bodies. Check your local TV listings to see if any program like this is available to you. If so, follow the proceedings and pay particular attention to the voting procedures. Report your findings to your class.

Reprinted with special permission of King Features Syndicate, Inc.

# GUIDELINES

## for Using Parliamentary Procedure

- Do I know the duties of the chairperson, the vice-chairperson, and the secretary?
- Do I know the meanings and uses of parliamentary motions?
- Do I understand when a motion is in order?
- Do I know how to make commonly used motions?
- Do I know how to change a motion?
- Do I know how to express disagreement?
- Do I know what motions relate to voting?

# PLAYING BY THE RULES

### Observing Parliamentary Procedure at Work

For lawmakers, mastering parliamentary procedure is especially important. The United States Congress and many state legislatures use *Robert's Rules of Order*, but each body also has many special rules.

### Characteristics of an Effective Legislator

An effective legislator

1️⃣ understands and applies the principles of parliamentary procedure to conduct meetings effectively

2️⃣ makes motions

3️⃣ applies the procedures for calling and completing a vote

## ACTIVITY

### Situation

You are helping to organize a new citizens' advocacy group in your community. To conduct group meetings in an organized way, you need to understand and apply parliamentary procedure.

### Preparation

Attend a meeting of a local group that conducts its official business according to the principles of parliamentary procedure. For example, you might attend a meeting of your school board or town council. As you listen, pay close attention to how the rules of parliamentary procedure affect how group members speak and reach decisions. If the group departs from what this chapter outlines, make note of it. After the meeting, try to obtain a copy of the minutes and review them to confirm your observations.

### Analysis and Assessment

Prepare a one-page report on your observations. Present the report in class, and ask your classmates for feedback. Do your classmates agree with your observations? If not, how do their observations differ?

### Meet the Legislator

"Parliamentary procedure can be a powerful instrument for accomplishing legislative goals in an orderly manner," Texas State Senator Gonzalo Barrientos says. The rules seem complicated to many people at first, but they ensure that there is a process in place to proceed in an orderly manner. "The rules of order are used by many groups all over the world, and so—once you learn these rules—you can more easily understand how other groups conduct their normal decision-making processes."

*Gonzalo Barrientos*

# S☆U☆M☆M☆A☆R☆Y

**PARLIAMENTARY PROCEDURE,** a set of rules for conducting meetings, is designed to allow free debate among members while maintaining order and ensuring that all members have an opportunity to be heard.

- **Understand the principles of parliamentary procedure,** which follow certain basic ideas: only one item may be considered at a time; everyone has a right to express an opinion, and each opinion is valued; every member has a right to vote, and each vote is counted as equal; the group always follows the opinion of the majority; minority rights are protected; and the minutes of the meetings are public record.
- **Run meetings** by using rules of parliamentary procedure that cover calling meetings, setting the quorum, and establishing the order of business.
- **Understand the duties of officers** and their responsibilities. The chairperson runs the meeting; the vice-chairperson assumes the duties of the chair when the chair is unable to do so; and the secretary keeps the minutes.
- **Understand motions,** proposals for action made by a member. Once a motion is made, members must act on it in some way. Motions are classified as main, subsidiary, privileged, incidental, and renewal. The motions in each classification have specific characteristics, ranks, and uses, and are governed by specific rules.
- **Use motions** to initiate action.
- **Vote on a motion** with a method that allows members to express their opinions clearly. Voting is usually done by voice or by hand, but it can also be done by ballot or roll call.

## Review Questions

1. One function of parliamentary procedure is to ensure that meetings run smoothly. What are the other functions of parliamentary procedure?
2. Parliamentary procedure is based on five principles. What are they?
3. What are the duties of the chairperson, the vice-chairperson, and the secretary?
4. Privileged motions have to do with the conduct of meetings. With what are subsidiary motions concerned?
5. Incidental motions relate to questions of procedure that arise from debate. What is the purpose of renewal motions?
6. *Precedence* refers to the ordering or ranking of motions. List privileged motions and subsidiary motions in order of precedence.
7. What are the five steps for getting a motion on the floor?
8. One way of changing the wording of a motion is by amendment. In what five ways may an amendment be put before a group?
9. What are the ways of delaying a discussion or a vote on a motion?
10. After a main motion has been discussed, the chair calls for a vote. What methods may be used for voting?

## Discussion Questions

1. Discuss parliamentary procedure as a democratic process. To what extent are the rights of the minority protected? To what extent are the rights of the majority protected? What are the pros and cons of majority rule? In addition to voting, what other aspects of parliamentary procedure promote democratic processes?
2. Discuss whether parliamentary procedure can be used at every kind of meeting. For what types of meetings is it most appropriate? Are there any types of meetings in which parliamentary procedure is not appropriate?
3. Discuss the circumstances under which it is better to postpone a motion to a definite time rather than to lay it on the table.
4. Discuss the reasons why some motions take a two-thirds vote to pass, while others take only a simple majority.
5. Henry David Thoreau wrote, "A wise man will not leave the right to the mercy of chance, nor wish it to prevail through the power of the majority. There is but little virtue in the action of masses of men." First discuss the meaning of the quotation. Can you think of any historical instances in which Thoreau's quotation proved true? How can a minority gain power over a majority? Then discuss what the chair can do in situations when a small minority dominates the meeting.

# ACTIVITIES

## 1. Explaining How and Why Parliamentary Procedure Is Used.

**A.** Prepare a short informative speech explaining the rules governing the precedence of motions. After your speech, ask your classmates for oral critiques of your speech.

**B.** Prepare a persuasive speech telling why meetings should be held according to the rules of parliamentary procedure.

## 2. Dealing with Disagreement in a Meeting.

The picture below illustrates what can happen in even the most formal and orderly meetings when debate becomes heated.

**A.** Working with a group of classmates, imagine yourselves in such a situation. What can be done to restore order when a disagreement arises?

**B.** With your classmates, choose a topic for debate and have two members or two factions take opposing sides on the issue. As the debate gets more heated, have each other member of the class act as chairperson and try to settle the conflict.

**C.** With a small group, think of some ways to prevent an outburst like the one shown below. How might the chairperson take the group's emotional "temperature"? What could he or she do to keep the meeting orderly? In what ways might the protection of minority rights help to ensure that a meeting runs smoothly?

3. **Understanding Motions.** You are the parliamentarian of the student council. Answer each of the following questions according to the rules of parliamentary procedure.

   a. The nomination of new officers to the student council was discussed at last week's meeting. Carla moves to reopen nominations this week. Does she need a second?

   b. Brandon is reading the minutes of last week's meeting. Amy interrupts him and moves to postpone indefinitely the reading of the minutes. Is Amy out of order?

   c. Maxine moves to postpone debate on fund-raising activities until next week's meeting at 3:30 P.M. on Tuesday. Jesse moves to amend Maxine's motion by striking *3:30* and inserting *3:45*. Is Jesse allowed to make this motion for amendment?

   d. Because there are many items on the agenda, Reggie moves to save time by limiting individual speeches on each item to two minutes. Pat, the chairperson, opens this motion to debate. Is Pat out of order?

   e. Karl's motion to adjourn has been seconded and is now put to the vote. Does the motion require a two-thirds majority in favor of it to pass?

4. **Running a Meeting According to Parliamentary Procedure.**

   **A.** Run a meeting according to parliamentary procedure. Plan to have each member of the class submit a motion (such as "I move that *Oklahoma!* be selected as the junior class musical this year"). Before the meeting, have an agenda committee composed of three members of the class word the motions and set up an agenda. Have a second committee of three members set up rules to govern discussion. Make sure that these rules cover maximum length of speeches, number of times a person may speak on one motion, and method of determining the chairperson for each debate.

   Each member of the class should be prepared to present a short speech supporting the motion he or she submits. Discuss each motion until it is passed, defeated, or delayed.

   **B.** Have each member of the class act as chair in a discussion of a motion. Other class members should contribute to the discussion by making privileged, subsidiary, or incidental motions. The chair will rule on each motion and will conduct the discussion until the motion is passed, defeated, or delayed by passage of some other motion. First, have a short practice round in which mistakes are called to the chair's attention so that the chair can correct them. In a second round, have the chair step down when he or she makes a mistake, and have another student take over as chair. The goal is for the chair to get through an entire motion without making a procedural mistake.

   **C.** Practice voting by voice, by show of hands, by rising, by roll call, and by written ballot on such things as appointing a committee, changing the time or place meetings will be held, and other actions that might be proposed as motions in a meeting.

# COMMUNICATION IN THE WORKPLACE

## Background
You are in business and plan to attend a meeting of a governmental body to oppose a regulation that affects your company.

### Preparing to Do the Job
Identify your company and the governmental body. Do you work for a large corporation, for a regional firm, or for yourself? Are you addressing a federal, state, or local agency? Next, identify the regulation. What will it govern? Why is it being enacted? Finally, specify your arguments against the regulation. Why exactly do you oppose it?

### Testing Your Skill
Write a three- or four-page dialogue of an open meeting in which you present your views. Use at least three parliamentary motions. Present your dialogue in class, and conduct a question-and-answer session on your use of parliamentary procedure.

# EVERYDAY COMMUNICATION

## Situation
You have recently moved into your first house or apartment. You read in a newsletter from your homeowners' or renters' association that a regulation you oppose will be discussed at the next meeting.

## Problem
You decide to attend the meeting and express your opinion. Assume the meeting is conducted according to parliamentary procedure.

## Assessing Your Skill
Consider how the regulation will affect you. Then identify how others at the meeting feel about the regulation. How many are for it? How many are opposed? What are their reasons? Would you be more willing to support the regulation if it were amended? Write a two- or three-page informative speech narrating what you would do. Be prepared to present your speech and to respond to feedback from your classmates.

town
meowner's
ssociation

Unit 6

# Performing Arts

HOT

COLD

Forward, the Light Brigade!

# CHAPTER 20

▼

# Oral Interpretation

**After studying this chapter, you should be able to**

1. Select a work of literature for oral interpretation.
2. Analyze the literature to determine its meaning and mood.
3. Prepare and present an oral interpretation of a piece of literature.
4. Participate in a choral speaking performance.
5. Participate in reader's theater.

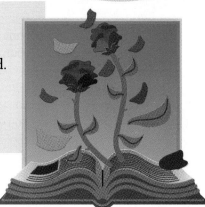

## What Is Oral Interpretation?

Oral interpretation is a performance art. The speaker attempts to communicate his or her sense of the meaning and beauty of a work of literature by reading it aloud to an audience. An oral interpretation is generally thought of as a reading performance by a single interpreter. Two related forms are

- *choral speaking,* in which a group of people combine their voices in a group reading of a poem
- *reader's theater,* in which a group of people read and interpret a play

Both the interpreter and the audience benefit from the oral performance. By experimenting with the use of voice, facial expression, and gesture, the interpreter learns more about the piece of literature as he or she studies and prepares to interpret it. Through the reading performance, the listener sees a work of literature come alive. In fact, some people enjoy a work of literature when it is interpreted aloud much more than when it is read silently.

In this chapter, you will learn how to perform an oral interpretation, how to speak in a choral group, and how to perform in a reader's theater.

# Choosing Literature for Interpretation

An **oral interpretation** involves the presentation of a work of literature to a group of listeners in order to express the meaning contained in the literary work. Therefore, an oral interpretation is only as good as the literature being interpreted. Your choice of a selection for your interpretation should be based not only on your interests but also on your knowledge of literature. You may find suitable choices among a variety of types of literature.

## Recognizing Types of Literature

What is **literature?** It is writing as an art form. Literature expresses ideas of permanent or universal interest, and it is characterized by excellence of form or expression.

**Prose.**  Prose is writing that corresponds to everyday patterns of speech. It is usually divided into nonfiction and fiction.

- **Nonfiction** tells about real people and real events. It is the truth as the author understands it. A *biography*, for example, is an account of a person's life written by someone else. An *autobiography*, in contrast, is an account of the writer's own life. Another popular form of nonfiction is the essay, a short piece of writing that presents an author's thoughts or feelings on some subject. A *personal essay* usually focuses on the writer's feelings and responses to an experience. A *formal essay* attempts to analyze a topic from a more objective point of view.
- **Fiction** is writing drawn from the writer's imagination. Although fiction may be based on actual events or real people, the facts merely serve as a starting point for the author's imagination. Two of the most common forms of fiction are the *novel* and the *short story*.

**Poetry.**   Poetry appeals to emotion and imagination through the creative arrangement of words on the basis of their sounds and meanings. In contrast to the everyday speech patterns of prose, poetry is compressed, musical language.

Poetry is a natural form for oral interpretation because it has its roots in the oral tradition. When written language was unavailable and all stories had to be passed along orally, the rhythms and rhymes of poetry helped people to remember the words. Although many modern poets write in free verse, which does not have a regular rhythm or rhyme scheme, they use other sound effects that enhance an oral reading.

**Drama.**   A drama is a story that is written to be acted out for an audience. Like short stories and novels, drama focuses on character and conflict, developed by the use of dialogue. Although most drama is prose, you will find some plays—Shakespeare's plays, for example—that are written in poetry.

*A*s you read textbooks for other classes, or as you read magazines, newspapers, or books, you may come across items that you would like to share with others in an oral interpretation. Keep a list of these items in your communication journal. When you need material for oral interpretation, this list will be a valuable source. You might also make notes about what parts of the pieces you would like to emphasize.

COMMUNICATION JOURNAL

## Identifying Suitable Selections

Whether you choose prose, poetry, or drama for oral interpretation, your first consideration should be your own interests. If you don't enjoy and appreciate the selection yourself, there is no point in sharing it with others.

In addition to your own interests, here are some other factors to consider as you make your choice.

**Universal Appeal.**   One characteristic of good literature is that it has **universal appeal**—relevance, or a relationship, to the experience of all human beings. This does not mean that everyone will like the selection, but it does mean that it will be of interest to most people. The following poem is an example of a piece of literature with universal appeal.

**Dreams**

*Hold fast to dreams*
*For if dreams die*
*Life is a broken-winged bird*
*That cannot fly.*

*Hold fast to dreams*
*For when dreams go*
*Life is a barren field*
*Frozen with snow.*

—Langston Hughes

Why does this poem have universal appeal? It deals with a subject that most of us experience in one way or another: We discover that our dreams are fading and we don't know what to do about it. For an oral interpretation, a selection with universal appeal has the advantage of being likely to interest the audience.

**Ideas and Insights.**   Most good literature offers readers **insight,** or important ideas or new perceptions of life. Sometimes the writers are merely putting into words the ideas and insights that we have not been able to express for ourselves. For example, when Langston Hughes calls life without dreams "a barren field / Frozen with snow," he gives us an insight into what our own lives might be like if we gave up our dreams. Selecting a piece of literature that offers new ideas or insights is another way of ensuring that your audience will be interested in your interpretation.

**Emotional Appeal.**   Another factor to consider in choosing a selection is its **emotional appeal** to your audience. Most good literature appeals to the emotions and to feelings, as well as to the mind. Sometimes the emotional appeal is a result of the ideas in the literature, and sometimes it is a result of the language itself. In this poem by Leroy V. Quintana, the emotional appeal is a result of both the subject of the poem and the language the poet uses.

### Legacy II

*Grandfather never went to school*
*spoke only a few words of English,*
*a quiet man; when he talked*
*talked about simple things*

*planting corn or about the weather*
*sometimes about herding sheep as a child.*
*One day pointed to the four directions*
*taught me their names*
        *El Norte*
*Poniente*        *Oriente*
      *El Sur*
*He spoke their names as if they were*
*one of only a handful of things*
*a man needed to know*

*Now I look back*
*only two generations removed*
*realize I am nothing but a poor fool*
*who went to college*

*trying to find my way back*
*to the center of the world*
*where Grandfather stood*
*that day*

**—Leroy V. Quintana**

The subject of this poem, the speaker's memory of and sense of gratitude for the wisdom given by a grandfather, arouses our feelings of nostalgia. But the language tugs at our emotions as well. Notice the choice of simple words and phrases and the lack of punctuation, which helps create a conversational rhythm.

**Technical Quality.** Not all literature is equally well written. Choose a work that has **technical quality,** meaning that it is constructed well. Are the ideas expressed clearly? Is the language precise and vivid? As a rule, the better a work is written, the easier it is to read aloud.

**Appropriateness for the Occasion.** In addition to being a great piece of literature, the work you choose must be appropriate for your purpose and occasion. First, the ideas and the tone should be appropriate. For example, to celebrate your grandmother's birthday, you might choose a selection that praises a grandmother; for an engagement party or wedding, you might choose a love poem.

Second, the length must be appropriate. For example, if you have a time limit of five minutes for your performance, you cannot read a twenty-page short story. You may have to use an excerpt or a shorter work.

## A·C·T·I·V·I·TY
### 1
### Identifying a Selection for Oral Interpretation

Refer to your communication journal or do some reading, and prepare a list of three or four of your favorite works of literature. Evaluate the appropriateness of each work for an oral interpretation by considering whether the selection has (1) universal appeal, (2) ideas and insights, (3) emotional appeal, (4) technical quality, and (5) appropriateness for a class reading. Identify, from your list, your choice of a selection that you think would work best for an oral interpretation.

## Understanding Your Selection

Before you can interpret a selection for other people, you must have a good understanding of it yourself. You need to have a good sense of what the writer tried to accomplish, as well as what the writer did accomplish.

You should keep in mind, however, that there may be more than one way to interpret a piece of literature. Just as no two people bring identical interests and needs to a reading, no two people will respond to the literature and interpret it in exactly the same way. Nevertheless, to prepare a good oral interpretation, you should learn as much as you can about your selection.

## Meaning

In your interpretation you will be attempting to convey the main idea of the selection. To do that, you have to think about the meaning of the individual words as well as the meaning of the work as a whole. What does this word mean and why does the author use it here? What does it all add up to? What's the point?

As you read the following poem, think about the meaning of the individual words, as well as the meaning of the entire poem.

### Grass

*Pile the bodies high at Austerlitz*

*   *and Waterloo.*

*Shovel them under and let me work—*

*   *I am the grass; I cover all.*

*And pile them high at Gettysburg*

*And pile them high at Ypres and Verdun.*

*Shovel them under and let me work.*

*Two years, ten years, and passengers*

*   *ask the conductor:*

*   *What place is this?*

*   *Where are we now?*

*   *I am the grass.*

*   *Let me work.*

*   —Carl Sandburg*

Since the vocabulary of this poem is simple, you probably would not have to look up word meanings as such, but you might need to check specific references. If you looked up *Austerlitz, Waterloo, Gettysburg, Ypres,* and *Verdun,* for example, you would learn that they are all sites of famous battles, battles that together took the lives of millions of men. With this knowledge, it becomes easy to understand the other references to "piling bodies high."

*Analyze a Selection*

1. **Look up the meanings of unfamiliar words.** Find the definitions of words you do not know in a good dictionary.

2. **Pay attention to denotations and connotations of words.** In addition to the dictionary definition, or denotation, of the word, pay attention to its connotation, the feelings it arouses.

3. **Look up specific references to places, people, and events.** You might consult encyclopedias, biographies, or textbooks.

4. **Find information about the author and this particular work.** Study the author's background to find out why, when, and where the piece was written.

5. **Think about the writer's choice of words.** Why was one word chosen over another?

6. **Look up the pronunciation of any word you are unsure of.** Correct pronunciation will be very important when you perform your oral reading.

7. **Paraphrase the work.** Try to put the work into your own words to be sure you understand its meaning.

## The Speaker

Before you can orally interpret a piece of literature, you need to know who is speaking. Sometimes, particularly in prose, the author speaks directly to the reader. At other times, the author speaks to the reader indirectly, through the voice of a character or a role the author has assumed. In fiction, a fictional **speaker** or narrator is often a character in the story or novel. To adequately interpret a piece of literature, you will have to stand in the speaker's shoes and assume his or her voice.

CALVIN & HOBBES, copyright 1988 Watterson. Distributed by UNIVERSAL PRESS SYNDICATE. Reprinted with permission. All rights reserved.

The character speaking in Edgar Allan Poe's short story "The Cask of Amontillado" is the voice of Montresor, a madman. In the following excerpt, Montresor is explaining how he planned his revenge on Fortunato. To interpret this story successfully, you would have to tell the story as if you were this madman.

*The thousand injuries of Fortunato I had borne as I best could; but when he ventured upon insult, I vowed revenge. You, who so well know the nature of my soul, will not suppose, however, that I gave utterance to a threat. At length I would be avenged; this was a point definitively settled—but the very definitiveness with which it was resolved, precluded the idea of risk. I must not only punish, but punish with impunity. A wrong is unredressed when retribution overtakes its redresser. It is equally unredressed when the avenger fails to make himself felt as such to him who has done the wrong.*

*It must be understood, that neither by word nor deed had I given Fortunato cause to doubt my good-will. I continued, as was my wont, to smile in his face, and he did not perceive that my smile now was at the thought of his immolation.*

## The Audience

Another key to a good interpretation is knowing the audience that the author or the speaker is addressing. The way that people speak to an audience is directly affected by their relationship to the audience.

For example, most literary selections do not have a narrator. However, in some selections the speaker reveals his or her feelings directly to the audience and may, in some instances, address the audience as if the individual readers were close friends.

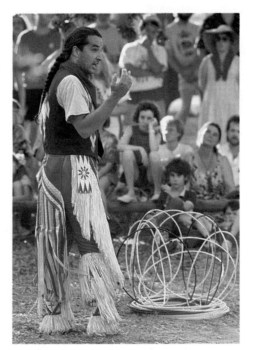

| Audience | Relationships |
|---|---|
| **General readers** | • relatively distant because the author/speaker does not know the individuals in the audience; most literature written for this audience |
| **The writer himself or herself** | • personal, private writing such as that found in diaries and journals |
| **A character within the story or poem** | • personal address that is affected by the fictional relationship between the speaker and the character; may be friendly, hostile, or loving, and so forth; listener may be superior or inferior in status to speaker |

In the following excerpt from Robert Browning's poem "My Last Duchess," the speaker is the Duke of Ferrara, a fictional Renaissance nobleman. What can you tell about the audience he is speaking to?

*That's my last Duchess painted on the wall,*

*Looking as if she were alive. I call*

*That piece a wonder, now: Frà Pandolf's[1] hands*

*Worked busily a day, and there she stands.*

*Will 't please you sit and look at her? . . .*

You can tell the Duke is speaking to a character in the poem because of the last line. He asks the other character, an envoy who is of inferior rank to the Duke, to sit down and look at a picture of his last Duchess. If you were interpreting this poem, you would read it as though you were talking to a single person alone in a room, and you would try to reflect the personal relationship between the Duke and the envoy.

## Mood

The **mood** of a piece of literature is the emotional tone it exhibits. Although emotional tone is not equally strong in all works of literature, recognizing the tone or mood will help you with your

[1] **Frà Pandolf:** an imaginary monk and painter of the Italian Renaissance period. *Frà* means "Brother."

interpretation. If the mood is somber or sad, for example, you wouldn't want to read the piece in a happy, lively voice. Writers convey mood through the words they choose, through rhythm, and through setting. Think about the plaintive repetition of *who* in "Abuelito Who" and the setting of "The Cask of Amontillado" in dark, eerie, empty catacombs.

# ACTIVITY 2

## Understanding a Literary Work

Choose a selection that you believe is appropriate for an oral interpretation. It may be the selection you identified in Activity 1 on page 558. Use these questions to develop your understanding of the work.

1. Do you think this work has universal appeal? If so, what is that appeal?
2. What is the central meaning of this piece of literature?
3. Who is the speaker, and how would an understanding of that speaker's characteristics affect an interpretation of the work?
4. What audience is the speaker addressing, and how would the relationship between the speaker and the audience affect an interpretation of the work?
5. What is the mood of this work? How do you know, and how would it affect your interpretation?

# Preparing Your Presentation

Your oral interpretation will consist of two parts: an introduction to the material and the reading itself. Both must be planned and rehearsed before you perform.

## Preparing an Introduction

The purpose of your introduction is to gain the interest of your audience and to provide information they will need in order to understand and enjoy your presentation. The following suggestions will help you identify information you may wish to include in your introduction.

1. Give your reasons for choosing the particular selection you are presenting.
2. Identify the author and the title of the selection.
3. Provide background information about the author or the selection. For example, explain the author's reasons for writing this piece or tell when and where it was written.
4. If you are using a portion of a play or story, review the action that precedes the passage and introduce any characters involved with it.
5. Describe any special features of the setting.
6. Be brief. The most important part of the presentation is the oral interpretation of the selection itself.

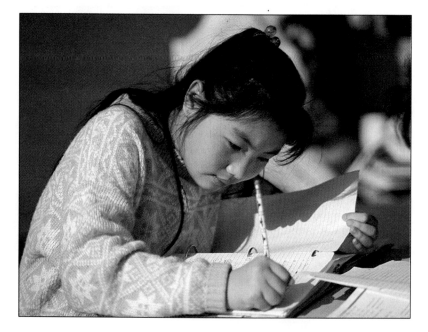

# Considering Punctuation and Word Groupings

In silent reading, punctuation serves as a guide to accurate understanding. However, in oral reading, you need to vary your vocalization, articulation, pauses, and gestures to punctuate words and sentences and to group ideas. The following chart outlines some of the techniques that you can use to indicate punctuation and word groups in an oral reading.

| Punctuation Appearing in the Selection | Oral Technique Used in Interpreting the Selection | Marks Made to Prepare the Reading Manuscript |
|---|---|---|
| **Commas, semicolons, colons, dashes, and periods** | Use pauses of varying lengths. | Use a slash (/) to indicate short pauses, a double slash (//) for longer pauses. |
| **Words in parentheses** | Pause and lower volume. | Mark parentheses or highlight in color. |
| **Italicized or underlined words** | Use louder volume, with stress placed on the words for emphasis. | Highlight italicized or underscored words. |
| **Words inside quotation marks** | Use a variety of changes in voice, such as changes in volume, quality, rate, and use of accents. | Underscore, mark pauses, or use colored highlights to indicate treatment of different characters. |
| **Question marks** | Use a rising inflection. | Mark an arrow with rising curve. |
| **Meaningful word groups such as clauses and phrases** | Emphasize meaning by using a variety of changes in voice quality, volume, or rate. | Mark specific word groups, underscore for emphasis, or use colored highlights. |

# Preparing a Manuscript

Even if you are planning to interpret a selection from memory, it is still a good idea to have the manuscript in view. In most cases, the manuscript should be typed (double-spaced) and marked in ways that will help you with your reading. For example, you might highlight or underline words you want to emphasize, or you might provide phonetic spellings for words you have difficulty pronouncing. On the next page, you will see an example of a manuscript that has been marked for an oral interpretation.

How do I love thee?//Let me <u>count</u> the ways./
<mark>I love thee</mark> to the depth and breadth and <u>height</u>
<u>My soul can reach,</u>/when feeling out of sight
<u>For the ends of Being and ideal Grace</u>.//
<mark>I love thee</mark> to the level of every day's
<u>Most quiet need,</u> by sun and candlelight.
<mark>I love thee</mark> freely, as men strive for Right;/
<mark>I love thee</mark> purely, as they turn from Praise.//
<mark>I love thee</mark> with the passion put to use
In my old griefs,/and with my <u>childhood</u>'s faith.//
<mark>I love thee</mark> with a love I seemed to lose
With my lost saints—<mark>I love thee</mark> with the breath,
Smiles, tears, of <u>all my life!</u>—and,(if God choose,)
I shall but love thee <u>better</u> after death. //

Elizabeth Barrett Browning, "Sonnet 43"

## Practicing Your Delivery

For a good performance, you must practice. Remember that an oral interpretation is more than just sight reading. Here are some general guidelines that you can follow during practice sessions to help you sharpen your presentation.

1. Record your practice sessions on audiotape or videotape, and then carefully evaluate your presentation. Make any necessary changes.
2. Experiment with different ways of expressing ideas or lines or words.
3. Practice reading the work several times, until you are convinced that your interpretation is as effective as you can make it.
4. Practice the gestures and facial expressions you will use. Make sure that they help to express the meaning and the mood of the material.

As you practice your reading, remember that the success of an oral interpretation is in part due to the effective use of emphasis, rate of speaking, and vocal quality and tone.

**Emphasis.**   The **emphasis** you place on a word or phrase influences the meaning you communicate to your audience. You can use both stress and pauses to emphasize.

**Rate.**   Changes in **rate** also affect meaning and mood. For example, a slower rate is usually more appropriate for a selection that is sad or serious. A lighter, faster rate may suggest happiness and joy, or it may suggest excitement and fear. When reading a poem, pay close attention to the rhythm the poet has created, and try to adjust your reading rate to that rhythm. Finally, remember that most selections should be read at a moderate rate, neither too fast nor too slow. Don't rush through your presentation.

**Voice Quality and Tone.**   Your voice quality and your tone can also reflect meaning and mood. Think about the way your voice sounds when you say "No!" in a happy, excited way as opposed to the way you say it when you are angry. With practice, you can control the quality and tone of your voice to reflect the meaning and mood of the selection you are reading.

With a partner, practice reading the following excerpt from Gary Soto's short story "The Jacket," which is about a boy who is humiliated by the ugly jacket his mother has bought for him. Take turns reading the selection and evaluating your delivery on the basis of (1) emphasis, (2) rate, and (3) voice quality.

That was the first afternoon with my new jacket. The next day I wore it to sixth grade and got a D on a math quiz. During the morning recess Frankie T., the playground terrorist, pushed me to the ground and told me to stay there until recess was over. My best friend, Steve Negrete, ate an apple while looking at me, and the girls turned away to whisper on the monkey bars. The teachers were no help: they looked my way and talked about how foolish I looked in my new jacket. I saw their heads bob with laughter, their hands half-covering their mouths.

Even though it was cold, I took off the jacket during lunch and played kickball in a thin shirt, my arms feeling like braille from goose bumps. But when I returned to class I slipped the jacket on and shivered until I was warm. I sat on my hands, heating them up, while my teeth chattered like a cup of crooked dice. Finally warm, I slid out of the jacket but a few minutes later put it back on when the fire bell rang. We paraded out into the yard where we, the sixth graders, walked past all the other grades to stand against the back fence. Everybody saw me. Although they didn't say out loud, "Man, that's ugly," I heard the buzz-buzz of gossip and even laughter that I knew was meant for me.

# Interpreting Literary Selections

## Prose

**Prose** is the normal form of written or spoken language; it is any type of speech or writing that is not poetry. Examples of prose writing include works of fiction, such as short stories and novels, and works of nonfiction, such as essays and biographies. Fiction works generally include certain literary elements, such as characters, setting, plot, and theme, that you will need to consider when you are adapting a selection for an oral interpretation. Other concerns that you will need to address are the point of view expressed, the length of the selection, and the process of condensing the material.

**Point of View.** The **point of view** refers to who is telling the story. You will need to consider the point of view to determine the voice to use when you are reading aloud.

## Point of View

| Type | Interpretation | Example |
|------|----------------|---------|
| **First Person, Main Character:** speaker has a primary role in story; referred to with pronoun *I* | Reader adopts a voice to suit the personality and vocal qualities of this main character, a character who has a personal stake in what happens. | "I left the woods for as good a reason as I went there. Perhaps it seemed to me that I had several more lives to live, and could not spare any more time for that one."<br>—Henry David Thoreau, from *Walden* |
| **First Person, Observer:** speaker is only indirectly involved in the conflict of the story; referred to with pronoun *I* | Reader takes on the vocal qualities of this observer, a character who can be relatively objective because he or she often watches instead of participating in the action of the story. | "One confidential evening, not three months ago, Lionel Wallace told me this story of the Door in the Wall. And at the time I thought that so far as he was concerned it was a true story."<br>—H. G. Wells, from "The Door in the Wall" |
| **Third Person, Limited or Omniscient:** speaker is outside the story; uses third-person pronouns—*he, she, they* | Reader retains his or her own vocal qualities; thus, reader narrates the story objectively, as a commentator rather than a participant in the action of the story. | "Granny wished the old days were back again with the children young and everything to be done over. It had been a hard pull, but not too much for her. When she thought of all the food she had cooked, and all the clothes she had cut and sewed, and all the gardens she had made—well, the children showed it. There they were, made out of her, and they couldn't get away from that."<br>—Katherine Anne Porter, from "The Jilting of Granny Weatherall" |

**Length.** Since most prose pieces—short stories, novels, and essays—are fairly long, you may not have time to read the entire piece aloud. In some works, you might be able to find a part that will stand on its own well enough to be read by itself. For example, a description or a bit of dialogue might work well for oral interpretation.

At other times you may need to **condense,** or cut, the work. Such cuts can be used not only to shorten a work, but also to remove portions that are inappropriate for the audience or that do not lend themselves to oral presentation.

# HOW TO > *Condense Prose*

1. Cut descriptive and narrative passages that are not essential to the story line.

2. Eliminate or condense flashbacks.

3. Cut quotation tags, such as "he said" or "Mary replied," as well as descriptions of the way each character speaks.

4. Eliminate repetitive material that is not essential to the story or essay.

5. Cut references to events or characters not directly involved in the portion of the work you are reading.

# ACTIVITY 4

## Giving an Oral Interpretation of a Prose Selection

Choose a work of prose you would like to share with your classmates. Study it carefully to make sure you understand its meaning, point of view, and mood. If you need to, condense it using the guidelines at the top of this page. Practice your delivery, and then give an oral interpretation for your classmates.

# Poetry

**Poetry** is compressed, highly charged language that appeals to our emotions and imaginations. Usually, a poem is arranged in lines with a regular rhythm and often with a definite rhyme scheme. Poets often use various other literary elements, including figurative language, imagery, and repetition, to heighten feeling and suggest meaning.

**Rhythm.** **Rhythm,** a rise and fall of the voice created by the flow of stressed and unstressed syllables, is far more important in poetry than in prose. Although it occurs in all speech, it is deliberately used by poets to create a musical quality, as well as to bring out the meaning of the poem.

In an oral interpretation of a poem, you can use your awareness of the pattern of stressed and unstressed syllables to bring out the poem's music and meaning. Notice the rocking, lilting rhythm in the following stanza from the poem "Recuerdo." (*Recuerdo* is a Spanish word meaning "remembrance" or "souvenir.")

If you were to read the following stanza aloud, you would want to use the rhythm of the syllables to express the happiness of the speaker's memories. As shown above the first line, the symbol ( ´ ) is used to identify stressed syllables, and the symbol ( ˘ ) is used to identify unstressed syllables.

*from* **Recuerdo**

*We were very tired, we were very merry—*
*We had gone back and forth all night on the ferry.*
*It was bare and bright, and smelled like a stable—*
*But we looked into a fire, we leaned across a table,*
*We lay on a hill-top underneath the moon;*
*And the whistles kept blowing, and the dawn came soon.*

*—Edna St. Vincent Millay*

As another example, read the following excerpt from Alfred, Lord Tennyson's poem "The Charge of the Light Brigade," a poem about a cavalry brigade that was sent into a battle impossible to win. Notice, as you read the stanza on page 572, how the rhythm in the poem captures the onrushing doom of the galloping cavalry.

> "Forward, the Light Brigade!"
> Was there a man dismayed?
> Not though the soldier knew
>   Someone had blundered.
> Theirs not to make reply,
> Theirs not to reason why,
> Theirs but to do and die,
> Into the valley of Death
>   Rode the six hundred.

If the poem you are reading is written in **free verse,** as is most modern poetry, you will not find regular rhythmic patterns. Instead, you will find rhythms more like that of natural speech. Rhythm is still used to create a musical quality, however, as you can see in the following free verse poem.

### Ornamental Sketch with Verbs

Sunset runs in a stream
over the brows of buildings
    dropping west to the river,
turns the street to a gilded stagger,
makes the girl on skates,
    the man with the block of ice,
    the basement landlady calling her cat
    creatures in a dream,

scales with salamander-red
    the window-pitted walls,
hairs the gutters with brindled light,
helmets cars and boys on bikes
and double-dazzles
    the policeman's portly coat
halos the coal truck where
    nuggets race from a golden sled,

*festoons lampposts to fantastic trees.*
*lacquers sooty roofs and pavements,*
*floats in every puddle*
   *pinks of cloud*
*flamingos all the pigeons,*
*grands all dogs to chows,*
*enchants the ash can into urns*
   *and fire-escapes to Orleans balconies.*
                    **—May Swenson**

**Repeated Sounds.**   **Repetition** is another way to add musical quality to poetry. It may affect your interpretation in two ways.

1. Repeated sounds may highlight meaning. For example, a repeated word or a phrase may indicate its importance.
2. You should give repeated sounds neither more nor less emphasis than they deserve. For example, the rhymed words at the ends of lines of poetry are not always the most important.

| Some Types of Repeated Sounds | |
| --- | --- |
| **Form of Repetition** | **Example** |
| Repetition of words or phrases | and night is an ocean<br>and night strikes sparks<br>   —Octavio Paz, "Two Bodies" |
| Repetition of consonant sounds, usually at the beginning of words: alliteration | helmets cars and boys on bikes<br>and double-dazzles<br>   —May Swenson, from "Ornamental<br>   Sketch with Verbs" |
| Repetition of sound in two or more words that appear close together: rhyme | Theirs not to make reply,<br>Theirs not to reason why,<br>Theirs but to do and die:<br>   —Alfred, Lord Tennyson, from "The<br>   Charge of the Light Brigade" |

**Punctuation and Line Length.**   Because poetry is written in lines, it is tempting to pause at the end of each one. As in prose, however, the meaningful unit of a poem is the sentence. When you read a poem, use the punctuation marks—commas, periods, and so forth—to determine when to pause. Otherwise your reading will emphasize words and ideas that the poet did not intend to emphasize so explicitly.

**Figures of Speech and Sensory Images.** Although both prose and poetry may contain figures of speech and sensory images, they are far more important in poetry. **Figures of speech** are words and phrases that compare two things that are basically very dissimilar. They are not meant to be taken literally.

For example, in his poem "Fog," Carl Sandburg describes the fog coming in "on little cat feet." Understanding that figure of speech will help you see how the fog creeps in silently, and it would probably affect your oral reading of the poem.

**Sensory images** are words and phrases that evoke mental pictures by appealing to the senses—sight, hearing, smell, taste, or touch. To interpret or read a poem expressively, you need to be aware of these images. For example, in Matthew Arnold's "Dover Beach," the poet uses images that appeal to the sense of hearing: ". . . the grating roar/Of pebbles which the waves draw back, and fling,/At their return, up the high strand,/Begin, and cease, and then again begin,/With tremulous cadence slow, and bring/The eternal note of sadness in." Compare the images in Arnold's lines to these images by William Wordsworth that appeal to the sense of sight: "A violet by a mossy stone,/Half hidden from the eye!/Fair as a star, when only one/Is shining in the sky." These images appeal to the senses by stirring up remembered impressions or feelings.

**Choral Speaking.** Poetry is often performed for an audience through **choral speaking,** an oral interpretation in which several voices speak together in a group. Choral speaking works well with poetry because of poetry's tight structure and musical sounds.

The goal in choral work is to maintain a coordinated ensemble sound, a sound that may include solo voices as well as group voices. A choral reading group is often put together in an arrangement of voices similar to that of a singing chorus: soprano, alto, tenor, and bass. Combinations of voices are then used to create special effects. For example, the soprano and tenor voices speaking in unison will give an effect different from the effect of the alto and bass voices together.

In planning a group oral interpretation, keep the following suggestions in mind.

1. Each reader should have a copy of the script and should highlight or underline the lines he or she will be reading.
2. Readers should learn the rhythm of the work and practice starting and stopping at the same time.
3. Although there is little movement in choral speaking, some coordinated movements may be planned. Such movements might include turning or bowing heads, raising a hand or an arm, or swaying from side to side.

Today, choral speaking is used in some plays to represent an entire group of people or some nonhuman force. Especially with a complex poem, a choral reading can add power and heighten the emotional impact of the reading.

# ACTIVITY 5

Work with a group of eight students whose voices can be divided into four pairs: two sopranos, two tenors, two altos, and two basses. Prepare a reading of Carl Sandburg's poem "Chicago," which is given below.

First analyze the poem, then decide which passages will be read by each vocal pair. For example, for the five lines that open the poem, the altos might read the first line, the tenors the second, the sopranos the third, and the basses the fourth. The entire group could read the fifth line. Practice your presentation and perform it for your class.

> *Hog Butcher for the World,*
> *Toolmaker, Stacker of Wheat,*
> *Player with Railroads and the Nation's Freight Handler;*
> *Stormy, husky, brawling*
> *City of the Big Shoulders:*

*They tell me you are wicked and I believe them, for I have seen your*
    *painted women under the gas lamps luring the farm boys.*
*And they tell me you are crooked and I answer: Yes, it is true I have*
    *seen the gunman kill and go free to kill again.*
*And they tell me you are brutal and my reply is: On the faces of women*
    *and children I have seen the marks of wanton hunger.*
*And having answered so I turn once more to those who sneer at this my*
    *city, and I give them back the sneer and say to them:*
*Come and show me another city with lifted head singing so proud to be*
    *alive and coarse and strong and cunning.*
*Flinging magnetic curses amid the toil of piling job on job, here is a*
    *tall bold slugger set vivid against the little soft cities;*
*Fierce as a dog with tongue lapping for action, cunning as a savage pitted*
    *against the wilderness,*
> *Bareheaded,*
> *Shoveling,*
> *Wrecking,*
> *Planning,*
> *Building, breaking, rebuilding*
*Under the smoke, dust all over his mouth, laughing with white teeth,*
*Under the terrible burden of destiny laughing as a young man laughs,*
*Laughing even as an ignorant fighter laughs who has never lost a battle,*
*Bragging and laughing that under his wrist is the pulse, and under his*
    *ribs the heart of the people,*
> *Laughing!*
*Laughing the stormy, husky, brawling laughter of Youth, half-naked,*
    *sweating, proud to be Hog Butcher, Toolmaker, Stacker of Wheat,*
    *Player with Railroads and Freight Handler to the Nation.*

## Drama

A **drama** is a story that is written to be acted out on a stage. The playwright usually emphasizes literary elements such as character, conflict, and action, which are developed in a play by the use of dialogue and action. Since dramas are meant to be performed, they often make excellent material for oral interpretation.

**Characters.**   The fact that a play is meant to be performed on a stage with different characters talking to one another presents a difficult problem for the single oral interpreter. How do you show a difference between the characters? The following suggestions may help you to solve this problem.

1. So that you won't have to read for several different characters, select a scene or portion of the play that has only one or two characters.
2. Use different vocal characteristics for each character. For example, you might change your rate, pitch, or accent when you switch from one character to another.
3. Employ different body language and posture for each character.

**Physical Action.**   While performers in a play are free to use their entire bodies and the entire stage to play their parts, you do not act out an oral interpretation. Your actions should be limited to small, subtle movements. For example, you could turn your head in a different direction to indicate where your characters are. If you feel the audience needs to know something about the action, you may describe it briefly in your introduction.

**Length.**  The guidelines for condensing prose (page 570) apply to drama as well, but here are some additional points to keep in mind when you need to condense a section from a dramatic work when preparing it for an oral interpretation.

1. Cut characters that are not essential to the major action of the play.
2. Cut material from the passage that comments on action that has taken place earlier in the play.
3. Cut or condense parts that involve a great deal of stage action but have little or no dialogue.

# A·C·T·I·V·I·TY
## 6
## Preparing an Oral Interpretation of a Dramatic Passage

Prepare an oral reading of the following passage from the play *Antigone* by Jean Anouilh.

In this scene the young woman Antigone confronts her uncle, Creon, the king of Thebes. Antigone's brother Polyneices has rebelled against the state and has been killed in battle. As an example to other would-be rebels, Creon has decreed that Polyneices' body be left in the open to rot. However, to leave a body unburied is profoundly against Greek religion. Antigone, who feels that her duty to her brother must be honored, has defied Creon's order by attempting to bury Polyneices, even though she knows the penalty for her disobedience is death. As the scene opens, Antigone has just been caught and brought before her uncle, Creon, the king.

CREON.  Had you told anybody what you meant to do?

ANTIGONE.  No.

CREON.  Did you meet anyone on your way—coming or going?

ANTIGONE.  No, nobody.

CREON.  Sure of that, are you?

ANTIGONE.  Perfectly sure.

CREON.  Very well. Now listen to me. You will go straight to your room. When you get there, you will go to bed. You will say that you are not well and that you have not been out since yesterday. Your nurse will tell the same story. [*He looks toward arch, through which the* GUARDS *have exited.*] And I'll dispose of those three men.

ANTIGONE.  Uncle Creon, you are going to a lot of trouble for no good reason. You must know that I'll do it all over again tonight.

*(continued on next page)*

[*A pause. They look one another in the eye.*]

**CREON.** Why did you try to bury your brother?

**ANTIGONE.** I owed it to him.

**CREON.** I had forbidden it.

**ANTIGONE.** I owed it to him. Those who are not buried wander eternally and find no rest. Everybody knows that. I owe it to my brother to unlock the house of the dead in which my father and my mother are waiting to welcome him. Polyneices has earned his rest.

**CREON.** Polyneices was a rebel and a traitor, and you know it.

**ANTIGONE.** He was my brother, and he was a human being. Who, except you, wants my brother's body to rot in a field? Does God want that? Do the people want it?

**CREON.** God and the people of Thebes are not concerned in this. You heard my edict. It was proclaimed throughout Thebes. You read my edict. It was posted up on the city walls.

**ANTIGONE.** Of course I did.

**CREON.** You knew the punishment I decreed for any person who attempted to give him burial.

**ANTIGONE.** Yes, I knew the punishment.

**CREON.** Did you by any chance act on the assumption that a daughter of Oedipus, a daughter of Oedipus' stubborn pride, was above the law?

**ANTIGONE.** No, I did not act on that assumption.

**CREON.** Because if you had acted on that assumption, Antigone, you would have been deeply wrong. Nobody has a more sacred obligation to obey the law than those who make the law. You are a daughter of lawmakers, a daughter of kings, Antigone. You must observe the law.

**ANTIGONE.** Had I been a scullery maid washing my dishes when that law was read aloud to me, I should have scrubbed the greasy water from my arms and gone out in my apron to bury my brother.

**CREON.** What nonsense! If you had been a scullery maid, there would have been no doubt in your mind about the seriousness of that edict. You would have known that it meant death; and you would have been satisfied to weep for your brother in your kitchen. But you! You thought that because you come of the royal line, because you were my niece and were going to marry my son, I shouldn't dare have you killed.

**ANTIGONE.** You are mistaken. Quite the contrary. I never doubted for an instant that you would have me put to death.

# Participating in Reader's Theater

A popular form of oral interpretation is known as **reader's theater.** It can take many forms. At its simplest, a group of readers sits in a circle and reads a play aloud. Each person reads one or more parts, and the group is its own audience. While an individual can enjoy reading a play silently, the conflict and excitement of a drama is much more apparent in a group oral reading.

More often, reader's theater is performed for an audience. The readers sit or stand facing the audience and read the roles they have been assigned. In contrast to a play, in which the actors talk directly to each other and appear to ignore the audience, in reader's theater the performers acknowledge the presence of the audience and read toward them. A narrator may be used to describe the setting of the play and the physical appearance of the characters, and, where a cut version of a play is being presented, give needed background information.

## Techniques for Reader's Theater

1. Readers can stand or sit. They may sit when they are not in a scene and rise as their characters enter.
2. A character who is in a scene but is silent or uninvolved may stand with his or her back to the audience.
3. Scripts may be carried by hand, or stands may be used.
4. Everyone may dress in clothes of a similar design and color, or items of clothing may be used as clues to character.
5. Movements and gestures are suggested or symbolic. Two characters who share a scene, for example, may move forward to be in front of the group.

## Selecting Material

Some plays are more suitable than others for reader's theater. Comedies that have knockabout action lose much of their appeal when this is omitted. Plays presented directly to an audience are especially effective as reader's theater. These include Greek tragedies, such as Sophocles' *Antigone*, and twentieth-century plays, such as Thornton Wilder's *Our Town*.

Reader's theater need not be confined to plays. Poems, stories, myths, and sections of novels can be adapted for use in an effective program that an audience will enjoy.

## ACTIVITY 7

### Reading a Scene from a Play

With two or three of your classmates, select a scene from a play to perform in a reader's theater. Be sure that it is a scene that has no more than three or four characters. Decide who will read each part, and then practice together. Concentrate on oral expression, and allow yourselves only a few subtle gestures and movements. Decide how you will dress and whether you will sit or stand as you are reading. Finally, perform the scene for the entire class.

## GUIDELINES

### for Giving an Oral Interpretation

- Does my selection have the characteristics of good literature?
- Do I understand the meaning and the mood of the work?
- Have I prepared an effective introduction to the selection?
- Have I prepared a manuscript to guide my delivery?
- Have I practiced my reading thoroughly?
- Have I taken into consideration the special features of the form—prose, poetry, or drama—that I am interpreting?
- Do I use my voice to punctuate and group ideas?
- Do I use both stress and pauses to emphasize important words and ideas?
- Do I control my rate of speaking to reflect meaning and mood?
- Do I control my voice quality and tone to reflect meaning and mood?

# PRESENTING A STORY EFFECTIVELY

### Telling Tales

Storytelling is a tradition as old as language itself. That tradition is kept alive today by storyteller clubs and by public libraries, many of which hold regular story readings for children.

### Characteristics of an Effective Storyteller

An effective storyteller

1. selects a story for oral interpretation

2. makes sure the story is appropriate for the audience and occasion

3. analyzes the story to determine which parts should be narrated and which should be treated as dialogue spoken by the characters in the story

4. uses voice quality and tone as well as body language to convey meaning

## ACTIVITY

### Situation

You have a summer job at a local library. The person who reads stories for children each week is sick, and your supervisor has asked you to fill in.

### Preparation

Choose a children's story—perhaps one of Aesop's fables—that illustrates an important truth about life. Familiarize yourself with the story, and then practice your delivery using a mirror to check your use of facial expressions, body language, and gestures. When reading the dialogue, use paralanguage cues, such as tone of voice and rate of speech, to bring the story's characters to life.

### Analysis and Assessment

Present your interpretation to the class, and then ask your classmates for feedback. Discuss how a young child might respond to your storytelling performance.

## Meet the Storyteller

Ken Masters performs Native American stories for children at public libraries throughout the United States. "Storytelling is like creating a movie in the mind by using your voice, your eyes, and your gestures," he says. "If I am telling a new story or one hundreds of years old, I practice by hearing myself tell it many times. This helps me grasp the meaning and mood before presenting the story in public."

# S✪U✪M✪M✪A✪R✪Y

**ORAL INTERPRETATION** is a performance art in which the speaker communicates his or her sense of the meaning and beauty of a work of literature by reading it aloud. Two related performing arts are choral speaking and reader's theater. In choral speaking, a group of people combine their voices to read a poem. In reader's theater, a group of people interpret a play by reading it aloud, rather than acting it out. Keep the following points in mind as you practice the art of oral interpretation:

- **Select literature** that interests you and that has universal appeal, ideas and insights about life, emotional appeal, and good technical quality.
- **Develop an understanding** of a piece of literature by identifying the central meaning of the work, the speaker and his or her relationship to the audience, and the mood.
- **Consider the special characteristics** of a work when preparing an interpretation. With prose, consider point of view and length. With poetry, consider rhythm, line length and punctuation, sounds, figures of speech, and sensory images. With drama, consider character development, physical action, and length.
- **Use changes in voice** such as volume, rate, inflection, stress, pauses, and accents to reflect the meaning and mood of the work being interpreted.
- **Coordinate your rhythm, timing, and movements** with other performers in a choral speaking performance.
- **Use reader's theater** to communicate the meaning and mood of a play without physical action, scenery, or complicated sets.

## Vocabulary

Look back through this chapter to find the meaning of each of the following terms. Write each term and its meaning in your communication journal.

choral speaking, p. 575
condense, p. 569
drama, p. 577
emotional appeal, p. 556
emphasis, p. 567
fiction, p. 554
figures of speech, p. 574
free verse, p. 572
insight, p. 556
literature, p. 554
mood, p. 562
nonfiction, p. 554
oral interpretation, p. 554
poetry, p. 571
point of view, p. 568
prose, p. 568
rate, p. 567
reader's theater, p. 580
repetition, p. 573
rhythm, p. 571
sensory images, p. 574
speaker, p. 560
technical quality, p. 558
universal appeal, p. 555

# Review Questions

1. What is oral interpretation?
2. List three kinds of literature that are appropriate for an oral reading.
3. Universal appeal is one factor to consider when you are choosing a literary selection to interpret. What are four other factors that you should consider?
4. Understanding meaning is one aspect of understanding a work of literature. What are three other elements that you should understand before you interpret a selection for other people?
5. What kinds of information about a selection and its author might you include in an introduction?
6. Explain the difference between first-person narration and third-person narration, and list some ways in which each type of narration affects oral interpretation.
7. What distinguishes poetry from prose?
8. How is choral speaking both similar to and different from an individual interpretation?
9. In an oral reading of drama, how could you show where the characters are?
10. If you were participating in a reader's theater presentation, how could you show that your character was not a participant in the scene at the moment?

# Discussion Questions

1. Discuss the ways in which preparation for an oral reading differs from preparation for a speech.
2. Discuss the circumstances under which choral speaking should be considered for oral interpretation, and list at least three works of literature that lend themselves to choral speaking.
3. Three elements contribute to a successful oral interpretation—the quality of the material, the preparation of the interpreter, and the goodwill of the audience. Discuss the role of each of these elements.
4. American playwright Thornton Wilder once wrote, "The less seen, the more heard." First, discuss the meaning of this quotation. Think of some examples that illustrate this idea. Then explain how this quotation relates to oral interpretation.
5. The Greek philosopher Epictetus once wrote, "First learn the meaning of what you say, and then speak." First, discuss the meaning of this quotation. Do you agree or disagree with the philosopher's statement? Think of specific examples that can be used to support your opinion. Then discuss whether this quotation applies to oral interpretation.

# ACTIVITIES

**1. Choosing a Selection That Suits a Particular Audience.** Imagine that you have been asked to present an oral interpretation in each of the situations that are pictured below. Working with a partner, choose a piece of literature that is appropriate for each occasion. Consider selections that might amuse, teach, or otherwise entertain the audience as well as selections that might inspire or uplift your listeners. Compare your selections with those of the rest of the class.

**2. Analyzing Oral Reading.** Stop for a few minutes to think about the number and kinds of situations during the past few days in which someone has read material to you. The situation might involve someone reading to you either in person or on television or on the radio. Would any of these readings be called "oral interpretation"? Why or why not?

**3. Reading and Analyzing Poetry.**

**A.** First, practice reading the following poems aloud. In your reading, try to discover and follow the rhythm intended by the poet. Then, identify examples of figurative language and sensory images in the two poems. With your classmates, discuss how the rhythm, figurative language, and sensory images affect the meaning and mood of the poem.

1. *I've got the children to tend*
   *The clothes to mend*
   *The floor to mop*
   *The food to shop*
   *Then the chicken to fry*
   *The baby to dry*
   *I got company to feed*
   *The garden to weed*
   *I've got the shirts to press*
   *The tots to dress*
   *The cane to be cut*
   *I gotta clean up this hut*
   *Then see about the sick*
   *And the cotton to pick*

   *Shine on me, sunshine*
   *Rain on me, rain*
   *Fall softly, dewdrops*
   *And cool my brow again.*

   *Storm, blow me from here*
   *With your fiercest wind*
   *Let me float across the sky*
   *'Til I can rest again.*

   *Fall gently, snowflakes*
   *Cover me with white*
   *Cold icy kisses and*
   *Let me rest tonight.*

   *Sun, rain, curving sky*
   *Mountain, oceans, leaf and stone*
   *Star shine, moon glow*
   *You're all that I can call my own.*

   —Maya Angelou, "Woman Work"

2. *I wandered lonely as a cloud*
    *That floats on high o'er vales*
        *and hills,*
    *When all at once I saw a crowd,*
    *A host, of golden daffodils;*
    *Beside the lake, beneath the trees,*
    *Fluttering and dancing in the*
        *breeze.*

    —**William Wordsworth, from
    "I Wandered Lonely as a Cloud"**

**B.** Identify the repeated sounds in each of the following poems. Then read the poems aloud and discuss with your classmates how reading aloud helps communicate the meanings of specific words and the meaning of the total poem.

1. *It is blue-butterfly day here in*
        *spring,*
    *And with these sky-flakes down in*
        *flurry on flurry*
    *There is more unmixed color on*
        *the wing*
    *Than flowers will show for days*
        *unless they hurry.*

    *But these are flowers that fly and*
        *all but sing:*
    *And now from having ridden out*
        *desire*
    *They lie closed over in the wind*
        *and cling*
    *Where wheels have freshly sliced*
        *the April mire.*

        —**Robert Frost, "Blue-Butterfly
        Day"**

2. *I never saw a moor—*
    *I never saw the sea—*
    *Yet know I how the heather looks*
    *And what a billow be.*

*I never spoke with God*
*Nor visited in Heaven—*
*Yet certain am I of the spot*
*As if the checks were given.*

        —**Emily Dickinson, "I Never
        Saw a Moor"**

**4. Choosing Selections for Oral Interpretation.**

**A.** Working in a group, list the types of literature and the specific selections that are enjoyed most by each person in the group. Then study the list to determine which selections would be suited to oral interpretation.

**B.** Using an anthology of literature, choose one example of each of the major types of literature (prose, poetry, drama) that you think would be a good selection for an oral reading. Be prepared to discuss why you made each selection.

**5. Using Vocal Techniques to Communicate Meaning and Mood.**

**A.** Select a short work and read it aloud to show how vocal punctuation can be used to change the meanings of words and ideas. Discuss your reading with your classmates after you have finished.

**B.** Select two poems that are totally different in mood. Explain how you would read each poem to show the differences in mood between them.

**6. Reading a Prose Selection Aloud.** Bring a favorite story to class and read it (or a portion) aloud. Be sure that you understand the story. Consider the speaker and the point of view. Prepare an introduction and a manuscript for your reading. Use your vocal skills to express the meaning and mood. When you finish your reading, briefly discuss the story's meaning and conduct a question-and-answer session.

# COMMUNICATION IN THE WORKPLACE

**Background**

You work for a company that produces audiotapes of books. Your assignment is to identify an autobiography or a biography to record.

### Preparing to Do the Job

First, do some research in the library to find a good biography or autobiography. If you cannot find one that interests you, ask your English teacher or librarian to recommend one. Read or skim the book and select a portion that you could read aloud in five or ten minutes.

### Testing Your Skill

Prepare an introduction and practice reading the selection aloud. Then, if you have access to a tape recorder, prepare an audiotape. If not, prepare an oral reading. Play the tape or read the selection for your classmates; then lead a discussion about the advantages and disadvantages of books on tape.

# EVERYDAY COMMUNICATION

**Situation**

You are a camp counselor with a group of young children and have promised to read a story to them.

**Problem**

What story would you read them? How would you present it? What gestures would you use to enliven your reading? First, identify the ages of the children, and then select a story appropriate for that age group. Make sure the story is one that you can read in less than ten minutes; otherwise, the children may become bored.

**Assessing Your Skill**

Practice reading the story in a way that will make it entertaining and interesting for young children. If possible, try your reading out on some children, then read your story to your class. Ask for feedback from your classmates. Ask for suggestions for improving your reading.

Encore!

# 21

# Theater

**After studying this chapter, you should be able to**
1. Trace the historical development of drama.
2. Explain the difference between formal and informal theater.
3. Prepare yourself to act in a play.
4. Contribute to the production of a play in a nonacting role.
5. Participate in an informal theater performance.

## What Is Drama?

**Drama** is an art form in which a story dealing with a human conflict is acted out on a stage. Unlike other art forms, such as music, sculpture, and dance, drama often incorporates all the other art forms. The excitement of theater is created by the interaction of performers playing their parts and an audience reacting to them.

The two basic types of drama are

- **formal theater,** in which the actors follow a script for the dialogue and the actions of the play
- **informal theater,** in which the actors rely on their imaginations to generate the story, dialogue, and movement

Some examples of formal theater include school plays, Broadway plays, and repertory theater. Movies and television dramas have much in common with formal theater, with the major difference being that movies and television dramas are not performed for a live audience. Because acting is performed for a camera, actions, gestures, and voice must be more natural. Some examples of informal theater are the mime who performs at a street festival and the person who tells stories around the campfire at a summer camp.

In this chapter you will learn how to participate in both formal and informal theater.

# Understanding the Development of the Theater

The roots of theater are deep. It is likely that in prehistoric times, people acted out scenes as part of religious ritual. In these scenes myths might have been acted out and heroic deeds re-created. Such scenes probably included choral chants, singing, mime, and dance.

## A Brief History

**Greek Theater.** Formal theater began in ancient Greece as a religious celebration associated with the worship of Dionysus, the god of wine. These festivals lasted five or six days, with the final three days devoted to dramas that competed for annual prizes. Records dating from about 534 B.C. show that the actor and dramatist Thespis won the first contest. The word *thespian,* meaning "actor," comes from his name.

The first formal theater was founded in Athens in the fifth century B.C. The plays were presented with one, two, or three actors playing all the parts and with a **chorus** that gave background information and commented on the action. All participants wore masks, and all parts were played by men.

Greek dramas were presented in an amphitheater setting that had a round playing area with an altar, a building or scene house used for changing, and seats most of the way around the playing area. There was no raised stage with a framing arch as there is in most modern theaters.

Greek drama followed certain principles.

- The drama was designed to bring about a catharsis, a release of emotions, in the audience.
- The main characters in the drama were of noble birth. In tragedies the main character suffered a fall from grace, usually as a result of a tragic flaw in his or her nature.
- The drama was written in poetic language.

**Roman Theater.** About 200 B.C., Rome overtook Athens as the cultural center for drama. Surviving Roman dramas are considered inferior to the Greek dramas they imitated. However, the Romans made major contributions to the theater's physical setting by developing a more modern elevated stage.

**Theater in the Middle Ages.** With the decline and fall of Rome, formal theater disappeared for centuries. Beginning in the tenth century, the Church began giving presentations dealing with biblical events and parables. These continued through the Middle Ages until the sixteenth century. In England groups of players constructed pageant wagons, providing a movable stage for acting out religious stories or events. Each scene of their dramas was presented at a different place in town, with the crowd of spectators following in a sort of miniature pilgrimage. Three types of plays were developed during this period.

- **Miracle plays** dramatized events from the Bible.
- **Mystery plays** presented events from the saints' lives.
- **Morality plays** presented allegorical stories in which characters personified religious or moral abstractions.

**Renaissance Theater.** From about 1300 to 1600, an era called the Renaissance (literally, "rebirth") brought renewed interest in Greek and Roman plays. In addition, original comedies, tragedies, and **pastoral plays** (love stories in idealized woodland settings) were created and performed. A major contribution was Italy's **commedia dell'arte,** popular comedy in which professional actors improvised, or made up, their roles as stock characters in humorous, standardized situations.

A conjectural reconstruction of the Globe Theater (1599–1613)

*Globe Playhouse (c. 1599–1613).* Reconstruction drawing by C. Walter Hodges.

English Renaissance drama flourished between 1590 and 1630. Three events in this period brought about the development of the English theater: the development of secular (nonreligious) themes, the rise of professionalism in both acting and play writing, and the performance of plays in English rather than in Latin.

The Elizabethan theater period was named for Elizabeth I (1533–1603), queen of England from 1558 to 1603. William Shakespeare (1564–1616), regarded as one of the world's greatest playwrights, wrote and performed during this age. His plays include tragedies, comedies, and histories (dramas based on historical events).

The French theater blossomed at the end of the Renaissance with the works of Molière (1622–1673), considered a comic genius. His plays ridicule people, ideas, hypocrisy, medicine, and forced marriages.

**Restoration Theater.** After 1660, a new era of drama began in England. This period, called the Restoration after the restoration of the royal family of Stuart to the throne in 1660, continued until 1700. Restoration comedy, also called **comedy of manners,** satirizes social customs. During this period, women were allowed to appear on stage for the first time in England.

**Nineteenth-Century Theater.** During the nineteenth century, Romanticism flourished throughout Europe. In general, during the Romantic Period, the belief in the reliance on reason was replaced by the belief that human beings should be guided by feelings and emotions. Playwrights during this period experimented with a great variety of new themes and characterizations. Many plays were made into operas, an elaborate form of musical theater still performed today.

Late in the nineteenth century, **modern drama** was born with the works of such dramatists as Henrik Ibsen (1828–1906) in Norway, August Strindberg (1849–1912) in Sweden, Anton Chekhov (1860–1904) in Russia, and John Galsworthy (1867–1933) and Bernard Shaw (1856–1950) in Great Britain. This early modern period was marked by realism, a movement to portray people and situations as they really are in everyday life.

**Contemporary Theater.** During the past few decades playwrights have experimented with many styles of theater. One of the most interesting styles to emerge has been the **theater of the absurd.** In this style, life is viewed as meaningless and people's strivings as absurd, since they cannot do anything to improve the human lot.

Today, many different styles of theater coexist, with no one style dominating. Revivals provide opportunities to see the styles of the past, while experimental theater presentations allow us to watch new theatrical styles emerging.

## Understanding the Characteristics and Types of Drama

The most important characteristics of drama are (1) that it tells a story, and (2) that performers interact with a live audience.

In formal theater the actors follow a complete script, which provides both the dialogue and directions for the action in the play. Formal plays are traditionally classified as either comedy or tragedy. These two forms are often defined by how they end— a **comedy** has a happy ending and a **tragedy** has a sad or disastrous ending. Comedy is also often characterized by exaggerated or eccentric behavior. Its primary goal is to entertain people and to make them laugh, but it can be scornful as well as humorous. A tragedy tells a story of serious and important events in which the main character comes to an unhappy end. In classical tragedy, highborn people fall to ruin, usually as a result of some "tragic flaw." Today we usually call serious plays "dramas" rather than "tragedies."

Informal theater is more spontaneous than formal theater: The actors do not follow a complete script. Another characteristic of informal theater is that it may be performed anywhere. For example, pantomime, a nonverbal form of theater, often takes place in an urban space—a courtyard or street corner where people gather. Storytelling, another form of informal theater, might take place around a campfire or in someone's living room.

# A·C·T·I·V·I·T·Y
## 1
### Listing Favorite Comedies and Tragedies

Work with a group of your classmates. Make a list of movie and television comedies you have seen and enjoyed. Then make a list of tragedies, or serious dramas, you have enjoyed. Share your lists with your entire class.

# Acting in a Formal Play

Suppose you want to try out for a formal play and have been given a script. Your audition is next week. What should you do to prepare yourself?

## Understanding the Script

First, of course, you should read the play thoroughly several times. As you read, pay special attention to

- the theme, or meaning, of the play
- the relationships among characters
- the mood or atmosphere of the play
- the setting of each scene and act
- the sequence of events
- the climax, or highest point of interest

These readings will give you a basic understanding of the play and will prepare you for auditions and rehearsals.

## Auditioning and Rehearsing

**Participating in Auditions.**  The play's director announces when auditions will be held. Sometimes you are expected to be familiar with the part you are auditioning for; in such cases, you will probably be asked to prepare a short piece from that role. After obtaining a copy of the play, practice the portion you will use in your audition. Here are some suggestions for preparing for the audition.

- Practice reading the part aloud, not silently.
- Think about how the character should look and how you can make yourself look more like the character.
- Think about how the character would sound, and practice reading in his or her voice.

Occasionally a director asks people to read a part "cold," without having had a chance to practice. When that happens, you should still try to concentrate on the way the character should look and sound, and move into that role.

**Attending Rehearsals.** When you accept a part in a play, you become a member of the **cast,** the ensemble of actors. Becoming a cast member means that you agree to attend all rehearsals and performances. Even people with the smallest parts are expected to attend all rehearsals unless they are specifically excused by the director. If you know you will be late to a rehearsal, you must notify your director in advance.

## Analyzing a Character

By studying the script carefully, you can begin to understand your character's motivations, why the character acts as he or she does. An author may reveal the motivations and personality of a character through

- stage directions that say what the character looks and sounds like
- what the character says and does
- what other characters say

Another way of getting insight into your character is to observe how real people behave when they are in situations like those being portrayed in the play. An accomplished actor is a keen observer of human nature. You may also use your own experience. If your character, for example, has to make an agonizing choice, you might try to remember how you felt when you yourself had to make a difficult decision.

After you understand why your character behaves as he or she does, you can begin to explore how you will portray that behavior. You will decide how the character walks (quickly or slowly), stands (upright, stooped, slouched), sounds (soft-spoken, abrasive, boisterous), and acts (angry, nervous, happy) in various situations.

Of course, any of the decisions you make may be changed as you practice your part and as other actors develop their characters. There is rarely one "right" way to play a character. Inevitably, different actors will find different facets of a character to emphasize.

It is important to remember that, although some behavior is virtually universal, a good actor goes beyond trite, conventional responses. For example, in the play *The Diary of Anne Frank*, Anne Frank is a thirteen-year-old girl. An actress could play the part simply by thinking of how any girl that age behaves. However, to portray Anne successfully, a performer must be sensitive to the girl's peculiar situation. In other words, an actress would need to get beyond the stereotype to uncover what makes Anne special. Playing her as a typical thirteen-year-old girl would not work well because Anne's circumstances made her life and her actions unique. Even when a character lives a fairly normal life, unlike Anne's, you should always work on portraying those special traits and features that make the character special.

Although stereotypes help us identify common or average human traits, the effective performer must go beyond the stereotypes. Perhaps the most important task an actor faces in playing a role is creating a unique individual on the stage.

## Understanding Relationships Among Characters

Since your character is not alone on the stage, you must study the other characters and their relationships to the character you are playing. Ask yourself the following questions.

- What is your character's place in the total play? Is he or she the **protagonist,** the main character, in the play? Or is he or she the **antagonist,** the main opponent of the protagonist?
- If your character is neither the protagonist nor the antagonist, what is his or her relationship to these characters?
- What is your character's relationship to minor characters in the play?
- If there are family relationships, what are they like? Are they tense and distrustful? supportive?
- What is the background of these characters' relationships? Why do they like or dislike one another?

Once you understand the relationships among the characters, you can adapt your behavior—the way you look at another character, your gestures, your tone of voice—to illustrate those relationships.

## Developing a Character's Voice

The character's voice is as important as his or her dialogue and actions. By concentrating on projection, rate, and pitch, you can create a voice that is interesting as well as one that helps to reveal the character and his or her motivations.

**Projection.** Since theaters and auditoriums may not have public-address systems, voice projection—the volume and force of the voice—is extremely important. You will need to practice projecting your voice so that it can be heard in the back of the auditorium. Since it is difficult to do this while controlling your voice so that it doesn't become harsh or indistinct, you will probably need to practice the technique.

**Rate.** A good actor controls the rate of his or her speech to suggest emotions or feelings. For example, you might speak quickly if your character is excited but slow down your speech if your character is feeling lonely or depressed.

**Pitch.** You can use pitch—the highness or lowness of your voice—to suggest the feelings and tensions of your character. Remember that rising inflections communicate uncertainty and surprise and that falling inflections communicate certainty and the completion of a thought.

# A·C·T·I·V·I·T·Y 2

## Analyzing a Characterization

Watch a film or a play of your choice. As you are viewing the film or play, choose one actor to study. Use these questions to analyze how the actor develops the character he or she is playing.

1. How does the way the actor talks—rate, pitch, inflections, accents—reflect the personality of the character he or she is playing?
2. How do the movements and nonverbal behaviors of the actor reflect the personality of the character?
3. Does the actor present a fully developed character or a stereotype?
4. What are the relationships between this character and the other characters in the play or film? How do the actor's nonverbal behaviors suggest those relationships?

## Memorizing Lines

Some people have more trouble than others do in learning lines. Nevertheless, at some point in the rehearsal schedule, performers are expected to be "off book," that is, to have mastered their lines so that they can concentrate on character development. Remember that in addition to learning your lines, you must also know your cues. There are several traditional methods for learning lines. Use one or all of them.

## HOW TO > *Learn Lines*

1. **Ask another person to cue you.** Get another person to speak your cues to you and then, script in hand, follow along to make sure you are saying your lines correctly.

2. **Using a blank piece of paper, cover your lines so that you can only see your cue.** Say your lines to yourself; then uncover the lines to see if you were correct.

3. **Read your cues into a tape recorder.** Leave pauses so that when you play the tape, you can say your lines in between the cues.

4. **Run lines as frequently as possible.** Use time when you are not on stage to practice lines with other actors.

5. **Associate lines with movement.** As you learn your lines, walk through the acting you will perform, including movements such as walking, sitting, turning, or handling props.

## Learning Movement

One of the major questions that beginning performers have is what to do with their bodies while on stage. Most play scripts provide each actor with general directions, which are often enclosed in parentheses or brackets. For example, the script will specify when to come on stage and when to leave. However, stage directions may be less specific about how and where a performer should move while on stage.

The director plans the movements of all the actors on the stage. The overall plan for actor movement is called **blocking.**

A theatrical stage is divided into nine parts [see the diagram on page 601]. *Upstage* is farthest from the audience; *downstage* is closest to the audience. These terms were inherited from old theaters, where the stage floor slanted downward, or "raked," so that people sitting in the audience could see better. In modern theaters the stage is flat, and the auditorium seating is slanted.

**Areas of a Stage**

Upstage

| Offstage Right | Up Right | Up Center | Up Left | Offstage Left |

| Center Right | Center | Center Left |

| Down Right | Down Center | Down Left |

Downstage

Audience

Stage directions are given from the vantage point of the actor as he or she faces the audience. Thus, "stage right" will refer to your right, not the audience's right. During early rehearsals the director will work through each scene in the play, giving each actor his or her blocking. For example, as you deliver a line of dialogue, you may need to move from a chair at downstage left and walk behind a sofa as another character replies. When the director gives you your blocking, be sure to write it down. Use a pencil (blocking may be changed later), and save time by using the simple abbreviations given on the next page.

Stage movement always has a purpose. Sometimes it is simply to get the actor from one place to another. Mostly, however, movement occurs for dramatic effect; that is, movement is motivated by what the character is saying or thinking. In general, characters move when they say their own lines and are still when others are speaking. Sometimes, to create a particular effect, this general rule is broken.

A good director will maintain visual balance throughout the play by coordinating the actors' movements so that the actors are in complementary areas of the stage. Thus, sometimes actors may be moved into specific positions so that they contribute to the complete stage picture.

## Abbreviations for Stage Directions

| | | | |
|---|---|---|---|
| **UR** | Upper Right | ↑ | Voice up |
| **UC** | Upper Center | ↓ | Voice down |
| **UL** | Upper Left | **¼ L** | Turn ¼ away from center front toward stage left |
| **CR** | Center Right | | |
| **C** | Center | **¼ R** | Turn ¼ away from center front toward stage right |
| **CL** | Center Left | | |
| **LR** | Lower Right | **PSL** | Stand in profile toward stage left |
| **LC** | Lower Center | | |
| **LL** | Lower Left | **PSR** | Stand in profile toward stage right |
| **D** | Downstage | | |
| **U** | Upstage | **¾ USL** | Turn ¾ away from facing center front toward upper stage left |
| **XC** | Cross Center Stage | | |
| **XSL** | Cross Stage Left | **¾ USR** | Turn ¾ away from facing center front toward upper stage right |
| **XSR** | Cross Stage Right | | |
| **XDR** | Cross Down Right | **( )** | Stage directions, usually enclosed in parentheses |
| **XUR** | Cross Up Right | | |
| **XDL** | Cross Down Left | _____ | Underline words which are to be emphasized |
| **XUL** | Cross Up Left | | |
| **⌢X⌢** | Cross on curved line | ✕ | Cut |

## Samples of Script Marked with Stage Directions
### Scene from Act 1 of
#### THE DIARY OF ANNE FRANK

Ⓟ Peter Van Daan
Ⓚ Mrs. Van Daan
Ⓥ Mr. Van Daan

PDSL

**Peter Van Daan** *is standing at the window of the room on the right.*

**Mrs. Van Daan** *(rising, nervous, excited).* Something's happened to them! I <u>know</u> it!
XCL

**Mr. Van Daan.** Now, Kerli!   XUC

**Mrs. Van Daan.** Mr. Frank said they'd be here at seven o'clock. He said . . .   ¼ L

**Mr. Van Daan.** They have two miles to walk. You can't expect . . .   XDC

**Mrs. Van Daan.** They've been picked up. That's what's happened. They've been taken.   XDR

**Mr. Van Daan** *(indicates that he hears someone coming).* You see?   PSL   ↑

**Peter Van Daan** *(takes up his carrier and his schoolbag, etc., and goes into the main room as Mr. Frank comes up the stairwell from below).*   move UC and down stairs, XC

## Maintaining Intensity

**Intensity** is the depth of feeling a performer has for a part. Whether or not you have been able to bring a character to life at every rehearsal, you must do so when the curtain goes up. Act as if the dramatic action is happening for the very first time. You must respond on stage with the energy that a real person would show if he or she were in the character's circumstances in real life. In a way, you must be more real than life.

## HOW TO ⟩ Prepare to Act a Role

1. **Understand the script.** Read the script carefully and be sure that you have a clear idea of the meaning of the play.

2. **Analyze the characters.** You should be aware of what motivates your character and why this person acts and speaks the way he or she does in the course of the play. In addition, you will need to understand the relationships between your character and the other characters in the play.

3. **Develop a fully rounded portrayal of the character you play.** As you rehearse, you learn the words your character speaks. At the same time, practice using your voice, your movements on stage, and your gestures to express the character you are playing.

4. **"Become" your character.** When you are on stage, your words and movements must be consistent with the character you are playing.

## ACTIVITY 3

### Practicing a Speaking Role

Follow these steps to practice a speaking role in the excerpt from *The Diary of Anne Frank* on the next page.

1. Using some or all of the strategies listed on page 600, memorize Mrs. Van Daan's or Mr. Frank's lines.
2. Outline the character's movement on the stage.
3. Analyze the relationships among the characters, and identify verbal and nonverbal behavior you could use to show those relationships.
4. As other students read their parts, perform the role you have studied.

# The Diary of Anne Frank

*by Frances Goodrich and Albert Hackett*

### Act One, Scene 2

*It is early morning, July, 1942.* Mr. Van Daan, *a tall, portly man in his late forties, is in the main room, pacing up and down, nervously smoking a cigarette. His clothes and overcoat are expensive and well cut.* Mrs. Van Daan *sits on the couch, clutching her possessions—a hatbox, bags, etc. She is a pretty woman in her early forties. She wears a fur coat over her other clothes.* Peter Van Daan *is standing at the window of the room on the right, looking down at the street below. He is a shy, awkward boy of sixteen. He wears a cap, a raincoat, and long Dutch trousers, like "plus fours."[1] At his feet is a black case, a carrier for his cat. The yellow Star of David[2] is conspicuous on all of their clothes.*

**MRS. VAN DAAN** (*rising, nervous, excited*). Something's happened to them! I know it!

**MR. VAN DAAN.** Now, Kerli!

**MRS. VAN DAAN.** Mr. Frank said they'd be here at seven o'clock. He said…

**MR. VAN DAAN.** They have two miles to walk. You can't expect…

**MRS. VAN DAAN.** They've been picked up. That's what happened. They've been taken…

[Mr. Van Daan *indicates that he hears someone coming.*]

**MR. VAN DAAN.** You see?

[Peter *takes up his carrier and his schoolbag, etc., and goes into the main room as* Mr. Frank *comes up the stairwell from below. His movements are brisk, his manner confident. He wears an overcoat and carries his hat and a small cardboard box. He crosses to the* Van Daans, *shaking hands with each of them.*]

**MR. FRANK.** Mrs. Van Daan, Mr. Van Daan, Peter. [*Then in explanation of their lateness*] There were too many of the Green Police[3] on the streets… we had to take the long way around.

[*Up the steps come* Margot Frank, Mrs. Frank, Miep (*not pregnant now*), *and* Mr. Kraler. *All of them carry bags, packages, and so forth. The Star of David is conspicuous on all of the* Franks' *clothing.* Margot *is eighteen, beautiful, quiet, shy.* Mrs. Frank *is a young mother, gently bred, reserved. She, like* Mr. Frank, *has a slight German accent.* Mr. Kraler *is a Dutchman, dependable, kindly.*

*As* Mr. Kraler *and* Miep *go upstage to put down their parcels,* Mrs. Frank *turns back to call* Anne.]

**MRS. FRANK.** Anne?

[Anne *comes running up the stairs. She is thirteen, quick in her movements, interested in everything, mercurial[4] in her emotions. She wears a cape, long wool socks, and carries a schoolbag.*]

**MR. FRANK** (*introducing them*). My wife, Edith. Mr. and Mrs. Van Daan [Mrs. Frank *hurries over, shaking hands with them.*]…their son, Peter…my daughters, Margot and Anne. [Anne *gives a polite little curtsy as she shakes* Mr. Van Daan's *hand.*]

---

[1] **"plus fours":** baggy trousers gathered under the knee; also called *knickers.*
[2] **Star of David:** a six-pointed star, a symbol of Judaism that Nazis required Jews to sew on all their clothing for identification as Jews.
[3] **Green Police:** Nazi police who wore green uniforms.
[4] **mercurial:** quickly changeable.

# Producing a Formal Play

A play is more than just actors on stage. What goes on behind the scenes? Who pulls it all together?

Many people with a variety of responsibilities take part in producing a play. You will have a greater understanding and appreciation of drama if you understand more about the complete process of producing a play.

## Selecting a Play

Before the producer or director can do anything else, a play must be selected. Some make the choice without any advisors; others use a play-reading committee. No matter who makes the decision, however, the following questions should be answered satisfactorily.

- How large is the cast? Do we have enough actors for all of the parts?
- What is the composition of the cast? How many males and how many females are there? What special skills are needed?
- What are the technical requirements? Is our stage large enough? Do we have the budget for lighting and costumes? Can we build the sets or are they too complicated?
- Is the play appropriate for our audience? Is it both emotionally and intellectually suitable? Will our audience enjoy this play?
- How much is the royalty, the payment of money for the right to produce the show? Can we afford it?

To find plays, you could start with drama anthologies in your school or city library. You also could consult the publication *Dramatics*, which lists and reviews plays. The following list identifies several frequently performed plays.

**MUSICALS:** *The Music Man, Little Mary Sunshine, Carousel, Oliver!, The Wiz, The King and I, West Side Story*

**COMEDIES:** *Auntie Mame, The Boy Friend, Charley's Aunt, Arsenic and Old Lace, Harvey, Life with Father, Blithe Spirit*

**DRAMAS:** *Our Town, A Streetcar Named Desire, A Raisin in the Sun, Dark of the Moon, I Remember Mama, The Diary of Anne Frank*

**W**orking in a group, select one of the plays listed at the bottom of the previous page. Read the play and then use the questions given above the list to decide whether you could produce this play in your high school.

## Organizing Auditions

**The Structure of the Audition.**   Most high school and college plays are cast through **auditions**—formal tryouts in which people have a chance to show their abilities. Usually these auditions are open to anyone who wishes to try out for a part. A director who has a particular person in mind for a part may give that person an audition before the open auditions. Many professional shows are cast in this way. At times, auditions are closed, which means that only those who meet specific conditions are allowed to try out. For example, tryouts may be open only to people with singing or dancing experience in shows or only to students in the junior class.

Sometimes a separate audition is held for each type of part. For example, auditions for singers may be held one day, auditions for lead speaking parts a second day, and auditions for all other parts a third day.

At the beginning of auditions, the director usually asks everyone to fill out an audition form. An audition form asks for previous productions, personal information such as weight and height, any roles played, and identification of possible conflicts with the proposed rehearsal schedule.

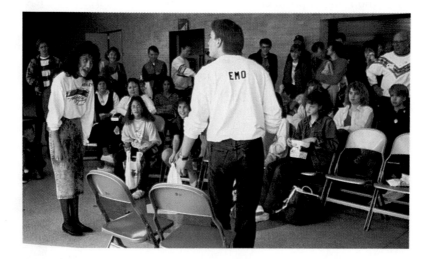

**Casting.** Ordinarily, the director decides who will be in the cast after he or she has heard everyone audition. During auditions the director looks for specific characteristics from the actors trying out for the parts. These characteristics may include an actor's experience, physical build, or vocal qualities. A director may also consider other qualities needed to portray a particular character.

During the audition period, the director will also be selecting people to work on the various backstage crews. Remember that you can show your interest and learn something about the theater by volunteering to become a member of the stage crew.

# ACTIVITY 5

## Organizing an Audition

**W**ith a partner, select a play with which you are both familiar. If you wish, you may use the play you selected and read for Activity 4 on page 606. Then develop a plan for auditioning and selecting cast members for the play. Decide whether you would have open or closed auditions, whether you would have a separate audition for each type of part, and what information you would ask for on an audition form. After you have finished your audition plan, be prepared to explain your decisions to other members of your class.

## Structuring Rehearsals

**Rehearsals,** or practice sessions, may be conducted for a period of from two to ten weeks, depending upon the experience of the cast and the complexity of the play. Musicals, for example, demand more rehearsal time.

Early in the rehearsal schedule, the performers usually practice scene by scene. For example, one entire rehearsal might be devoted to one complicated scene. As performance time nears, more of the play is covered at every rehearsal. Often, during the last ten rehearsals, the entire play may be rehearsed. At any stage of a rehearsal, the director may make suggestions to the actors as they are working. At the end of each rehearsal, the director gives the cast feedback about the portion rehearsed.

During the last week or so of rehearsals, the technical aspects of the show are added. Scenery is finished and lighting is coordinated. In the last two or three rehearsals, called **dress rehearsals,** every aspect of the show is rehearsed just as it will be done at the time of performance. Often, a small audience is invited to attend.

## Gathering Information About Auditions and Rehearsals

**M**eet with someone who is directing an upcoming play, such as a teacher in your school or a director for a community theater in your area. Ask the following questions concerning auditions and the rehearsal schedule, and report your findings to your classmates.

1. How many parts are in the play?
2. What are the parts in the play?
3. Will those who try out need to be familiar with the play?
4. Will those who try out need to have any special skills, such as singing or dancing ability?
5. How long a period is scheduled for rehearsals?
6. How long will each rehearsal be?
7. What time do rehearsals begin and what time do they end?
8. Which days of the week will rehearsals be held?
9. When will all actors need to know all their lines?
10. When are dress rehearsals scheduled?

## Working in Nonacting Roles

There are many nonacting roles that are essential to a successful theater production, and many people enjoy working in these areas. Some people prefer to work in one of the technical or production aspects of a play rather than to act a role on stage. Nonacting roles include responsibilities such as directing or producing the play, building and painting the set, finding or making props, making or preparing costumes, running lights or sound during the play, and selling tickets or seating patrons.

Nonacting roles not only are necessary to the production of a play, but also are fun to accomplish. Following are some of the important roles in production.

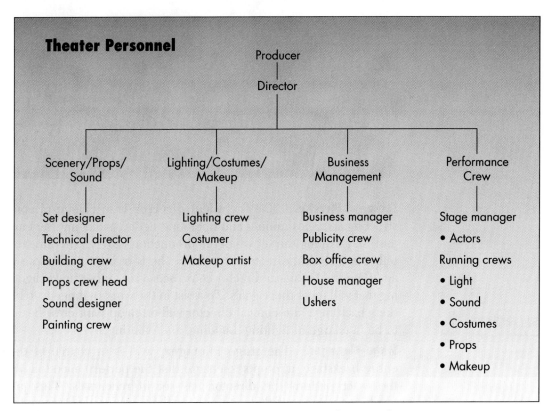

**Theater Personnel**

Producer

Director

| Scenery/Props/Sound | Lighting/Costumes/Makeup | Business Management | Performance Crew |
|---|---|---|---|
| Set designer | Lighting crew | Business manager | Stage manager |
| Technical director | Costumer | Publicity crew | • Actors |
| Building crew | Makeup artist | Box office crew | Running crews |
| Props crew head | | House manager | • Light |
| Sound designer | | Ushers | • Sound |
| Painting crew | | | • Costumes |
| | | | • Props |
| | | | • Makeup |

**Producer.** As the head administrator of a dramatic production, the **producer** is the person who is responsible for bringing together the script, the theater, and the director. In professional theater, the producer also arranges the financing for a show. Although the role of producer is separate from the role of director in professional theater, in high school theater the producer is usually also the director.

**Director.** The **director** is in charge of selecting the play, casting the parts, coaching the actors, and coordinating the work of the set designer and the costumer. Although the teacher in charge of drama will most likely direct the major productions, students often are able to gain experience in directing scenes, one-act plays, and other short productions. If you are interested in directing, you may be able to assist the teacher or the director in carrying out the many tasks a director must do.

**Technical Director.** The **technical director** is in charge of constructing sets, positioning and operating lights, managing the curtain, and striking the set when the production is over. The director tells the technical director what he or she is trying to accomplish, and then the technical director constructs a set and arranges lighting that will meet those goals. To assist in the work that needs to be done backstage, a technical director will often appoint crew heads to be in charge of lighting, building, and painting.

**Stage Manager.** The **stage manager,** who is in charge of the entire backstage, attempts to ensure that the performance follows the exact pattern the director has set in rehearsals. This job involves making sure that actors are in their proper places to go on stage, cuing actors (helping them learn when they go on and when they speak), prompting when necessary, and in general helping rehearsals run smoothly. The stage manager records all of the director's instructions about blocking, cues, and sound effects in a master prompt book so that anyone at any time can see the movement of a scene. Once the production begins, the stage manager takes over many of the director's chores, such as managing the actors and the overall production of the show.

**Set Designer.** The **set designer** is responsible for designing all visual elements, including stage sets and lighting, that will be used for the production. The set designer works closely with the director to design a set and lighting that will create the proper atmosphere for the play. A successful set will create a mood that will help the audience to better understand the meaning and intent of the show. For instance, cheerful colors will usually be used for a comedy or a musical, while the set for a serious drama will commonly employ darker, more somber tones.

After the designer has a basic concept of how the set will look, he or she creates a **floor plan,** which is a diagram that shows the positions of walls, entrances, and furnishings on the stage. The set designer draws separate designs for each of the different settings in a particular play. Although some plays, such as *The Diary of Anne Frank,* have only one set for the entire production, other plays have two, three, or even more different sets. Below is an example of a floor plan.

**Set Design for
The Diary of Anne Frank**

**Costumer.** The **costumer** is in charge of the performers' attire. Costumes must reflect the period in which the play is set, and they may also reveal aspects of a character's age, personality, job, and social standing. For contemporary plays, the costumer may be limited to simply offering ideas about what each of the actors may wear. Some plays, however, make special demands. For example, when a theater group produces a historical play or a play set in an exotic or a fantasy location, the costumer will have to make or rent appropriate costumes.

**Business Manager.** The **business manager** takes care of the financial matters that relate to the production—paying bills, issuing and keeping track of tickets, filing receipts, and keeping good records. The business manager may also be responsible for printing programs. A program includes listings of the cast in order of appearance, of the production staff, and of committees and crews. Programs also carry "acknowledgments" for those who lent assistance. For example, if a florist donated the plants for a wedding scene, the florist's name would be acknowledged on the program.

The business manager is also likely to be in charge of publicity for the show. Publicity may involve making posters, submitting articles about the show to the school or local newspaper, and writing press releases for local radio or television stations.

**House Manager.** The **house manager** is in charge of the ushers, who seat the audience. Being house manager involves selecting the ushers, coordinating their dress, and supplying them with programs. The house manager is also in charge of checking house lighting, air conditioning, heating, and ventilation.

**Makeup Artist.** Since stage makeup is different from regular makeup, productions assign someone to be the **makeup artist** responsible for using special theatrical makeup techniques. After a foundation has been applied, highlights and shadow are used to suggest age and character. Sometimes wigs, hairpieces, beards, and mustaches are made. The makeup artist sometimes uses latex to create three-dimensional skin textures or to give a young actor the look of old age. In large productions a makeup crew will be used. Actors may assist in doing their makeup. For example, they may do the basic makeup, with a makeup artist applying the finishing touches.

**Property Crew Head.** Properties (or "props") consist of furniture and items such as pictures, bookcases, and carpets. They also include hand props, such as swords, crockery, and walking sticks. The **property crew head** is responsible for collecting these items and making them available during rehearsals and performances.

# ACTIVITY 7

## Choosing Production Roles

**R**eview the explanation of nonacting production work (pages 608–612), and think about your special skills or talents and how they would be useful in taking on the various responsibilities that are involved in producing a play. Then choose the nonacting role you would be most interested in. Finally, get together with a group of three or four classmates to discuss your preferences as well as your reasons for those preferences.

COMMUNICATION JOURNAL

*A*fter each rehearsal, if you have a role in a play, or after each work session, if you have a backstage job, record in your journal exactly what happened during the day's session. Later, when you go back and reread your entries, you will probably be surprised to discover that while little progress seems to be made in each daily session, great strides have been made over the course of five or six sessions.

# Participating in Informal Theater

Participating in informal theater can be very rewarding. Informal theater gives a performer the opportunity to gain theatrical experience without requiring the time, expense, or other complications of being involved in a formal production.

## Pantomiming

**Pantomime** is dramatic communication performed entirely without words. Do you remember times when you silently mimicked the way a person put on makeup or answered the telephone? Such mimicry is an example of pantomime.

Professional mimes (pantomimists), like the world-famous French master mime Marcel Marceau, frequently amaze audiences with their ability to communicate using no words at all. Mimes rely entirely on gesture, facial expression, and movement to represent action and express meaning. Every action performed by a mime—even the smallest movement of a finger or the slightest change of expression—is designed to carry meaning.

Pantomiming is an art form itself, but it is also good practice for learning to express physical and mental states. For example, trying to pantomime such actions as picking a flower, meeting a new friend, catching a ball, polishing a car, or digging a ditch can help you develop a heightened awareness of the feelings associated with those actions and can prepare you for other, more formal, acting experiences.

**Identifying a Situation.**   When you are trying to decide on the subject of a pantomime, think of a situation, a little story. For example, you might think of a pitcher trying to strike out a batter, a person pestered by ants at a picnic, a child trying to tie her shoe, or a teenager who has locked himself out of his car. Notice how each of these situations has the potential for some conflict and suspense. Once you have thought of a good situation, you can begin to think of the character and how you will show his or her actions and feelings.

**Observing People.**   One of the keys to a good pantomime is accuracy of detail. The audience has to be able to recognize the process that the movements are suggesting. The best way of identifying those details is by observing other people as they go through similar situations.

For example, if you were going to pantomime someone trying to carry an awkward armload of packages, it would probably be a good idea to watch someone who is trying to handle an actual stack of packages. Here are some examples of the kinds of questions you might ask yourself to guide your observation.

- *Is there a conflict in this situation?* What does the person do when he or she first becomes frustrated or realizes there is a problem? For example, what does the person do when he or she first discovers that the packages are awkward to carry?

- *What kinds of expressions do you see on the person's face?* Do the person's lips pucker or do the corners of the person's mouth turn down?

- *What happens with the rest of the person's body?* Does the person contort his or her body to try to hold the packages and keep them balanced?

- *What is the sequence of actions?* Step by step, what actions does the person take in trying to resolve the problem? How do the person's emotions build?

- *How does the person solve the problem?* Does the person manage to balance the packages, drop them all and stomp on them, or find someone to help carry some of the load?

PEANUTS reprinted by permission of UFS, Inc.

**Practicing.**   Pantomiming is like formal acting in the sense that much practice is necessary for a good performance, and the best way to practice pantomiming is to watch yourself in a mirror. For example, suppose you are going to pantomime the situation in which the small child is trying to tie a shoelace, and you have begun your preparation by observing such a child.

You could try mimicking the child's behavior while you watch yourself in a mirror. Observing yourself, you might decide that your pantomime is not dramatic enough and might try to think of something to improve it. Perhaps just as you have finally succeeded in forming a bow, you tug on the shoelaces to tighten the knot and one of the laces breaks. You could then try out that action in front of the mirror to see if it would make your performance more dramatic.

**Joining a Group.**   Eventually you may want to work with others to create more complicated scenes. Suppose, for example, you wanted to pantomime a crowd reacting to a football play that resulted in the winning touchdown being scored in a tense, hotly contested game. You and one, two, or three others could sit on a bench facing an audience of classmates. Then each of you could act out various kinds of behavior, such as jumping up and down or hugging each other.

**Performing.**   As with any other performance art, a successful pantomime depends on your ability to create a complete experience for your audience. The following list identifies some of the things you can do to create that experience.

**1.** Do not use a verbal introduction. Let the pantomime speak for itself.

**2.** Remain in character from the time you appear before the audience until you leave.

**3.** As you perform, keep in mind what the person would be thinking. It will help you to focus your emotions and your actions. Also, if your actions have no thought behind them, they will seem unnatural.

4. Remember to use your eyes, your mouth, and subtle movements of your hands and arms to suggest your thoughts and feelings.
5. Exaggerate your gestures slightly so that the audience can see them and recognize what they mean.
6. Use sound effects—squeaks, groans, clicks, and so forth—only if they are critical to setting up the situation.

## Improvising

**Improvisation** is a form of drama that is spontaneous rather than planned. It is performed without scripts or rehearsal. One important difference between improvisation and pantomime is that the former includes speech as well as action. Like a formal play, improvisation includes at least the following three basic elements: a dramatic situation, dialogue, and characterization.

**A Dramatic Situation.** Although life itself may be viewed as drama, just showing life as it occurs would not be very effective as theater. Whether you are doing improvisation or creating a play, your situation must be dramatic. A **dramatic situation** is one in which the characters are facing a situation that forces them to act. Whatever they choose to do, or not do, will have consequences.

Without a dramatic situation, an improvisation is unlikely to hold an audience's interest. For example, an audience would soon lose interest in a dialogue between you and your partner in which the two of you chatted aimlessly about the weather. If, on the other

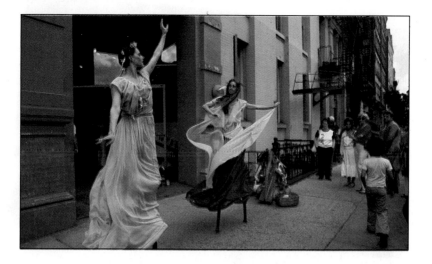

hand, you play a student who has been wrongly accused by a teacher of cheating on an important exam, your solution to this problem could provide dramatic interest.

**Dialogue.** **Dialogue** is the conversation that occurs between two or more characters in a drama. Although dialogue originally applied to conversation between just two people (*di-* is a Greek prefix meaning "two"), it is now used to apply to all conversation in a play. The term **monologue** refers to an extended speech by one person.

There is a major difference between dialogue in a formal play and dialogue in an improvisation, however. Improvisation has no scripts. The actors know the situation and they make up the dialogue as they go along. The only requirement is that they try to be true to the situation and maintain their characters.

**Characterization.** **Characterization** means the portrayal of the physical, intellectual, and emotional traits of each character. During rehearsals for a formal play, you have many opportunities to think about how you will portray a character. [See pages 596–599.] But during an improvisation, you will have to react spontaneously. Still, the nature of the situation will help you determine what you will say. For example, if you were portraying one person as a spoiled brat, you would want to exhibit the kinds of behavior that you would expect from such a person in such circumstances. You would be quick to anger, and perhaps you would whine and cry.

Whatever type of character you decide to develop, be consistent throughout the improvisation, whether it is supposed to last for one minute or for ten minutes. In addition, never stop acting in the middle of an improvisation. Keep in mind that you are creating an illusion. To do so, you must be consistent and stay in character.

# ACTIVITY 8

## Pantomiming and Improvising

First, pantomime one of the following situations. Then, working with a partner, develop one of the situations into an improvisation.

1. You walk by a pet shop, see a dog in the window, go into the shop to ask about the dog, and are so taken with it that you buy it.
2. You order a sandwich and a glass of milk, and you get a bowl of soup and a glass of soda water.
3. You ask a person you do not know very well out on a date for the first time.
4. You walk into a china shop carrying a large package.
5. You are watching a sporting event on television, and your favorite team is losing.

## Storytelling

**The History of Storytelling.**   Human beings have always been story-tellers: Our ancestors told stories in their caves, in their tents, and in their huts. Before there was a written language, people told stories to pass along their heritage and traditions, as well as to entertain. Storytelling did not die when the printing press was invented. It is still alive and well, and it is an art you can learn and use.

**Identifying a Good Story.**   You can find ideas for a story almost anywhere. You may think of a story one of your grandparents told you, or you may remember something that happened to you. You can even pick up ideas from newspapers and television news programs.

Your story can be based on fact, or it can be totally imaginary. The important thing is that your story be entertaining. Here are some guidelines for thinking of a good story.

1. To flesh out the ideas for your story, answer the questions *Who? What? Where? When? Why?* and *How?*
2. Be sure there is some kind of conflict and suspense. You want your audience to be eager to find out what happens next.
3. Your story should build up to a high point of tension or interest, and the ending should resolve the conflict and end the suspense.
4. You should include details drawn from your senses of sight, hearing, touch, taste, and smell. Sensory details will help your readers to picture the scene and actions in their own minds.
5. If you have a point to make in your story, let the outcome or resolution make it for you. Do not say "and the moral is" or "and that's why this story is important."

**Telling the Story.** The act of storytelling is mostly verbal, but a good storyteller does not rely on words alone. Facial expressions, gestures, and other movements help to create the complete performance. For example, if you were telling a story about a ghost, you might jump and throw your hands in the air as if frightened when telling about the ghost's surprising appearance.

In storytelling, however, the voice is the primary instrument of performing. To make a story come to life for your audience, you need to make use of these vocal techniques.

- Remember that inflections—upward or downward glides of pitch—communicate feelings. Change the pitch of your voice to suggest strong feelings or tensions, or to suggest that another character is speaking.
- Control the volume of your voice to heighten the suspense of the story, as well as to make sure that everyone in your audience can hear you.
- Control the rate of your speech. You can speed up a little or slow down slightly to reflect the pace of the action, but be careful not to talk so quickly that you lose your audience.

# ACTIVITY 9

## Telling a Story

Select a story that you can tell to students your own age. It can be one you have heard from someone else or one you create yourself, but it should have conflict and suspense. Practice telling the story in an entertaining way. You might videotape yourself or ask a friend to be your audience and critique your performance. Be sure you are using your voice as well as facial expressions and gestures to make the story more interesting. After you have practiced thoroughly, tell the story to your entire class.

© Mell Lazarus. By permission of Mell Lazarus and Creators Syndicate.

## GUIDELINES

### for Taking Part in a Play

- Have I analyzed the play completely?
- Do I understand the motivations behind my character's actions?
- Do I understand the other characters in the play?
- Have I chosen the gestures, movements, and voice that best portray my character?
- Have I taken advantage of my own powers of observation to bring truth to the character?
- Have I relied on stereotyped reactions, or have I created uniquely appropriate, fully rounded human responses for my character?
- Have I memorized my lines?
- Can I bring intensity to the performance?
- Do I play the role with enough diversity?
- Is my portrayal true to the character?

# UNDERSTANDING THEATER PROCESS

### Putting on a Show

A theater director selects the play, casts the parts, coaches the actors, and supervises the set design and costuming. In some cases, the director also performs the tasks of a producer, such as negotiating for theater space or arranging financing.

### Characteristics of an Effective Theater Director

An effective theater director can

1. analyze a script for cast, set, and crew needs

2. create and communicate a production style to cast and designers

3. evaluate rehearsal progress to give appropriate feedback to cast and crew

4. supervise the production of a play

## ACTIVITY

### Situation

The editor of your school newspaper has assigned you to interview someone who is involved in the local community theater or in your school drama club. The person may specialize in acting, directing, set design, costume design, or any aspect of community theater.

### Meet the Director

Theater director Rick Schiller says communication skills are vital in theater. "For a play to work, I have to be able to communicate with the actors and crew. I also have to be able to listen. Theater is a collaborative art. As the artistic leader of the production, I depend on my ability to encourage each person to bring ideas and creativity to the process."

*Rick Schiller*

### Preparation

Find someone to interview, then generate several questions to ask him or her. For example, you could start by asking why he or she chose to participate in community theater. Take your complete list of questions along to the interview. Listen carefully to the interviewee and take accurate notes, asking follow-up questions as necessary to clarify the responses to your original questions.

### Analysis and Assessment

Write a short summary of what you learned about theater, and share your findings with the class. Ask your classmates for feedback. Do they have any questions you didn't think of?

# S·U·M·M·A·R·Y

**THE THEATER,** an art form in which a story of human conflict is acted out before an audience, includes two major types of theater: formal and informal. Formal theater is planned and rehearsed, and the actors follow a script for their dialogue and actions. Informal theater is more spontaneous and free-flowing.

- **Understand the historical development** of the theater and the basic characteristics of formal and informal drama.
- **Audition for a role** in a formal play by reading the play thoroughly, practicing the part aloud, and thinking about the nature of a character.
- **Analyze a character** to determine his or her motivations and relationships with other characters.
- **Develop a character's voice** by concentrating on projection, rate, and pitch to create an interesting voice that reveals your character's personality and motivations.
- **Use movement** to reveal your character's personality and motivations.
- **Select a play** for production by considering the audience, the casting requirements, and the technical requirements.
- **Use your knowledge** of auditioning, casting, and rehearsal procedures to facilitate a play's production.
- **Work in a production area** not only for enjoyment, but also to learn more about the theater.
- **Participate in informal theater** by performing pantomime, improvisation, or storytelling.

## Review Questions

1. What is the difference between formal and informal theater?
2. Formal drama began in ancient Greece as part of religious ceremonies. Part of the ceremony was devoted to annual theatrical competitions. Who was Thespis?
3. One method for learning lines is to ask another person to cue you. What are four other methods for learning lines?
4. Stage directions that appear in the script or that are given by the director tell the actors where and how to move on the stage. What is meant by "stage right"?
5. How does blocking help the actors determine their movements on the stage?
6. One factor to consider when deciding whether a play is worth producing is the interest of your audience. What are two other factors to consider?
7. Opening night is preceded by many rehearsals. What is the purpose of a dress rehearsal?
8. An actor is responsible for "creating" a believable character that works in the context of a particular play. What are the responsibilities of a director?
9. Many people work behind the scenes to make a theatrical production a success. What are the responsibilities of a stage manager?
10. Both pantomime and improvisation are types of informal theater. How does improvisation differ from pantomime?

## Discussion Questions

1. Research and prepare a three- to five-minute oral report on one of the following periods of drama: Greek, Roman, Medieval, Renaissance, Elizabethan, Restoration, Romantic, Realistic. Consider what influence the style of this period had on the dramatic periods that followed it. List the period's leading playwrights and the titles of their most famous works. Then, discuss each of these periods with your classmates.
2. Discuss the role of the director in bringing a play to the stage. How does the director's role in an amateur company differ from that in a professional company?
3. Discuss the responsibilities of the actor during auditions and rehearsals versus the responsibilities of the director.
4. Discuss and give several examples of the actor's use of voice and physical movement in both formal theater and informal theater.
5. The poet and literary critic T. S. Eliot was quoted in the *New York Post* (Sept. 22, 1963) as saying, "A play should give you something to think about. When I see a play and understand it the first time, then I know it can't be much good." First, discuss the meaning of this quotation. Then, discuss whether or not you agree with it.

# ACTI⋁ITIES

**1. Reporting on Nonacting Areas of a Production.** Watch a community theater or professional theater production. Then prepare and give an extemporaneous oral report discussing the costumes, scenery, and lighting for the play. How appropriate were they to the action and meaning of the play? Can you think of any changes that would have made them better?

**2. Presenting a Dramatic Scene.** Working with three or four of your classmates, select a scene from a play that you could perform. Choose one group member to direct the scene, and divide the acting roles among the other members of your group. Memorize lines, block movements, and rehearse your scene before presenting it to the class. After you have completed the performance, discuss with the class what you have learned about characterization and movement.

**3. Participating in Pantomime.**
**A.** Working in a group, identify the kinds of gestures, facial expressions, and movements that would be needed to pantomime the following situations:
  1. Dealing with a vending machine that has taken your money without giving you the merchandise you wanted
  2. Trying to keep a kite in the air
  3. Walking barefoot across hot sand or a hot street
  4. Carrying a large box down a flight of stairs
  5. Planting a garden

**B.** Pantomime actions that would be characteristic of the following things:
  1. A photocopy machine making a copy
  2. A dog begging for a treat
  3. A tree in a spring breeze
  4. A bird preening itself
  5. A balloon slowly deflating

**4. Presenting an Improvisation.** Working with a partner, improvise one of the situations shown in the following pictures or another situation of your own choosing. Act out your improvisation. Then ask your classmates to identify the situation you portrayed.

5. **Reporting on an Audition.** Attend an audition for a play—a school play, a neighborhood play, or a community theater play. Be prepared to tell the class how the audition was held. Where did the audition take place? Who was there? What did those who were auditioning have to do? Did the director indicate how he or she would decide whom to cast for specific roles?

6. **Interpreting a Role in a Play.** Working with a partner, decide how you will present the lines of dialogue given below. How will you interpret each role? Are the speakers acquaintances or co-workers? Do they feel friendly, neutral, or hostile toward each other? Is one speaker a man and the other a woman? Are they both men?

   After you have determined who the speakers are and what the relationship between them is, think of ways to portray each character. Present your dialogue to the class. Then, compare your interpretation with those of your classmates.

*Speaker #1:* Hey, over here.
*Speaker #2:* There you are!
*Speaker #1:* Great weather we're having today!
*Speaker #2:* Uh, huh. Have you been waiting long?
*Speaker #1:* Not very long. Please sit down.
*Speaker #2:* Thanks.
*Speaker #1:* So, what have you been up to?
*Speaker #2:* Nothing much. How about you?

7. **Observing and Recording Mannerisms.** Many of the very best actors are also keen observers of human nature. Such actors have a huge supply of observed gestures, accents, and mannerisms from which they can draw to create a new character.

   Observe the mannerisms or actions of five people whom you know well or whom you see on a regular basis, such as your lab partner in science or the school bus driver. Record these observations in your communication journal. Then, list at least five specific mannerisms or actions that you would adopt to characterize each person you observed.

8. **Giving Stage Directions.**

   A. Familiarize yourself with the scene from *Antigone* on pages 578–579. As you read, imagine that you are a director blocking this scene. How might you use stage movement to heighten the dramatic effect of the scene? What movements would be appropriate for Creon? for Antigone? How would you make sure the stage appeared balanced?

   B. Working with several of your classmates, block the scene from *Antigone*. As you decide which movements work best, mark a copy of the script with specific stage directions. [Use the chart and the example on page 602 as a model.] Compare your group's blocking of the scene with that of another group in the class.

# EVERYDAY COMMUNICATION

### Situation
You have been asked to train the new employees who will work at the counter of a health food restaurant. Since they must meet the public and represent the company, they are required to play a specific role.

### Problem
You will need to address the issue of costumes or uniforms and how they should be worn. You will also need to provide scripts (precise words and lines) for greeting customers, taking orders, and handling complaints. Finally, you will have to instruct the employees in using specific, nonverbal behaviors and physical actions that are appropriate for the job.

### Assessing Your Skill
Prepare a five- to ten-minute portion of a training session in which you teach someone how to do this job. Present the lesson to your class, and ask for feedback from your classmates.

# COMMUNICATION IN THE WORKPLACE

### Background
Your boss, the editor of the local newspaper, has asked you to write a review that identifies the strengths and weaknesses of your local community theater's new play.

### Preparing to Do the Job
You will need to see a production to review. If possible, attend a theatrical production by a school or community theater group. If not, view a video recording of a stage production that interests you.

### Testing Your Skill
Jot down your impressions as you watch the performance or as soon afterward as possible. Also, you may want to find out what other critics have said about the play or performers. Write a one- or two-page review giving your opinion of the strengths and weaknesses of the performance. Share your review with your classmates and ask for feedback.

627

mass media

"STUDENTS: The MOVIE"

| PROD. | SCENE | 3 | TAKE |
|---|---|---|---|
| ROLL 5 | CLASSROOM (Int.) | | 2 |

DIRECTOR BOYD-ALVAREZ

CAMERA CHEN

Day  Nite  Int.  Ext  Nos
AMBER  Sync

▼

C H A P T E R **22**

# Radio and Television

**After studying this chapter, you should be able to**

1. Summarize the history of radio and television and describe current trends in both fields.
2. Explain and give examples of how the mass media, including radio and television, affect culture.
3. Plan and produce a mock radio talk show.
4. Plan and produce a radio drama.
5. Plan and produce a mock television news story.
6. Prepare a public service announcement.

## What Are Radio and Television?

Radio and television are two forms of electronic mass media. Because they deal in oral and visual messages, they involve speaking and listening skills.

Four common forms of radio and television presentations are

- the **radio talk show,** in which a moderator and one or more guests discuss a topic
- the **radio drama,** in which actors present an oral performance of a play or radio script
- the **television news story,** in which a reporter or newscaster uses videotape to illustrate a current news event
- the **public service announcement (PSA),** in which a brief persuasive message is presented

These presentations cover all types of subjects and issues. For example, on a radio talk show the moderator and guests might discuss a current controversy over the lack of new textbooks in local schools. A television station might carry a public service announcement urging people to register to vote.

# Tracing the Development of Radio and Television

The printing press, invented by Johannes Gutenberg in the 1430s, was the first example of **mass media**—practical methods for communicating with a mass, or large group, of people. Before Gutenberg, books were extremely difficult to make and therefore too costly to be widely distributed. After Gutenberg, books began to be mass-produced, and an explosion of literacy occurred.

Since the time of Gutenberg, many other mass media have appeared, including newspapers, magazines, films, and billboards. The most influential mass media in our time are radio and television.

## The Origins of Radio and Television

**The Emergence of Radio.** In the late 1800s, people had two means of long-distance communication—the telegraph and the telephone. In 1895, Guglielmo Marconi, an Italian inventor, created the first radio communication. By 1901, Marconi's equipment was sending signals across the Atlantic Ocean. The following chart shows some of the major events in radio's early history.

| Date | Event |
|------|-------|
| 1910 | Lee De Forest produces a program starring tenor Enrico Caruso singing from New York's Metropolitan Opera House. |
| 1916 | First experimental programs are broadcast. |
| 1920 | KDKA, first professional station, broadcasts election of President Warren G. Harding. |
| 1925–26 | Radio's Golden Age begins: Soap operas, afternoon children's serials, and nighttime comedies and dramas become popular. |
| 1926 | NBC, first permanent national network, is created. |
| 1941–45 | President Franklin Roosevelt uses "fireside chats" to rally people to support World War II. |
| 1950 | Radio's Golden Age ends as television challenges radio's popularity. |

**The Emergence of Television.** The groundwork for television was laid in the 1870s when it was discovered that there was a way to transform light variations into electrical signals. Both a mechanical scanning disc and the first photoelectric cells were designed just a few years later. However, it was not until 1923—when V. K. Zworykin applied for a patent on the iconoscope, an all-electric television tube—that the development of television broadcasting became possible.

By the late 1920s, the technology for sending and receiving television signals had been invented, and in the 1930s the first television broadcasts began. However, the cost of television and the coming of World War II delayed until the late 1940s the emergence of television as an important communication medium. By the 1950s, television had become popular enough to challenge radio. Some people even predicted that radio would disappear altogether. In 1950, only 9 percent of U.S. households had television sets, but just fifteen years later, in 1965, 95 percent of households had at least one set. In a short period of about forty years, television had become a fixture in almost every household in the United States.

**Radio's Response to Television.** Radio stayed alive despite the success of television by adopting new formats. A **format** is a particular combination of content and style. Increasingly, radio stations began concentrating on music, news, and talk formats and left comedic and dramatic programming to the visual medium of television.

## Radio and Television Today

**Radio Today.**   Far from disappearing, radio is more popular than ever before. There are now more than ten thousand radio stations in the United States, and in 1990 alone, more than twenty-one million radio sets were sold.

The popularity of modern radio is partly due to the development of portable receiving devices. Millions of people listen to radios in their cars, at work, and at play—places where television sets are not commonly found. Another reason for the continued popularity of radio is its ability to be audience specific. Being small, most radio stations can target their programming and advertising to specific audiences. As a result, whoever you are, you can probably find a radio station with a format tailored to your interests.

Although music stations are by far the most common type of radio station today, news and talk radio stations are becoming increasingly popular. A talk radio station typically mixes news reports with moderated, live "call-in" programs in which listeners express their opinions on various topics.

Independent college radio stations are often nontraditional types of radio stations. College radio stations are often very small and are frequently staffed by nonprofessionals—students who are learning about broadcasting. Because they often do not have to earn profits and are usually staffed by students, college radio stations are often creative in their programming. They may play avant-garde music or hold discussions of controversial subjects. They have returned to radio some of the excitement (and some of the pitfalls) of the days of live radio programming.

**Television Today.**   No one would dispute the importance and popularity of television today. Nearly every home in America has at least one television set, and by the time the average American reaches the age of thirty, he or she has logged over thirty-five thousand hours in front of the television.

Although most early television programs were **live** (transmitted as they occurred), most of today's programs are **prerecorded** (recorded earlier for later broadcast). The exceptions are generally newscasts, most of which are live, and some talk and interview shows.

In the United States, there are two kinds of television stations: commercial stations and noncommercial, or educational, stations. The commercial stations are funded by advertisers. The noncommercial stations are funded by a combination of government money, private donations, and subscriptions. Noncommercial stations typically air children's shows, news programs, nature studies, classic films, biographies, political or social documentaries, and science and arts programming. Commercial stations also show some of the same types of programs, but they are largely dominated by situation comedies, dramas, and talk shows.

In recent years cable television and home satellite dishes have had a tremendous effect on the quality of reception and variety of programs available to Americans. **Cable television** brings programs over cables into people's homes, while home satellite dishes pick up signals from the commercial satellites used by the networks and television stations. **Pay television** is a type of cable television in which people pay a fee to watch a particular program, usually a movie, a sports event, or a concert. **Pay-cable television** is a regular subscription service that brings a variety of programs into the home on one channel in exchange for a monthly fee.

In the United States, the three major television networks saw their markets erode during the 1980s and early 1990s as a result of the viewing options made possible by means of cable and satellite. During the 1980s the number of cable television subscribers jumped from a little over fifteen million to more than fifty million. Several pay-cable channels emerged during this period, including Home Box Office, The Disney Channel, The Movie Channel, The Learning Channel, and Bravo! Many of these pay-cable channels develop their own programs.

# ACTIVITY 1

## Comparing Radio and Television Programming

With a partner, survey the radio and television programming available in your community. Gather your information by listening and viewing as well as by studying program guides and listings. How does the radio programming differ from the television programming? How are the radio and television progamming alike? How does the programming vary according to time of day or evening? What do these differences indicate about the reasons people listen to the radio or watch television? Share your findings in a class discussion.

## Trends for the Future

Predicting the future of any technology is a risky business. There was a time, for example, when popular storytellers predicted travel to the moon in hot-air balloons! However, there are some emerging technologies and trends in the television and radio industries that bear watching.

| Emerging Audio and Video Technologies | |
|---|---|
| **High-Definition Television (HDTV)** | creates a sharper image due to its higher **resolution,** (a more detailed definition of an image achieved by using a greater number of picture cells, or pixels, to create the image) |
| **Digital Recording** | a technique that converts sounds or images into groups of electronic bits and stores them on a specific medium; during playback, the recorded bits are read electronically, often by means of a laser beam |
| **Information Network** | single machine (combination telephone, computer, compact disc player, television, radio, and electronic newspaper) in the home connected by fiber-optic cables to a nationwide or worldwide information network |
| **Interactive Television** | system that allows the viewer to interact with and respond to what is seen on the television screen, using one or more special communication devices |

# The Effects of Radio and Television

The mass media are powerful communication tools because they reach so many people. With the mass production of newspapers, magazines, and books in the nineteenth century, people came to be influenced by what they read as well as by those around them. When radio, and then television, came along, these media were even more influential because they reached more people more quickly.

**The Power of Electronic Media.** In 1938, Orson Welles dramatically demonstrated the power of radio by presenting a story about an invasion from Mars as though it were a series of news bulletins. Thousands of people panicked, believing that the United States was being attacked by Martians.

In the 1950s and 1960s, the commercial side of television helped to produce the world's first mass consumer economy. A large and powerful advertising industry grew up around television, and enormous sums of money were spent convincing viewers to buy everything from automobiles to cereal. In 1960, the power of television was demonstrated when a little-known senator named John Kennedy challenged a well-known, popular vice-president, Richard Nixon, in a series of televised debates. Kennedy won both the debate and the presidential election.

Today, a presidential election can be influenced by a single statement broadcast on the evening news. In addition, images from across the globe of wars, floods, and famines come directly into our living rooms and arouse our sympathy or our wrath. People all over the world watch American television programs. Advertisers influence how viewers spend their money and how they think of themselves. In short, life in the twentieth century has been powerfully influenced by the broadcast media.

**The Values Presented in the Electronic Media.** Unfortunately, the values that the media teach may not always be the values that are in the best interests of society. Radio and television advertising, for example, has been criticized for presenting a view of the world in which happiness seems to be a result of what people have and what they can buy.

# Calvin and Hobbes                            by Bill Watterson

Commercial television has drawn fire in recent years for its violence, its promotion through advertising of materialistic values and waste, and its tendency to stereotype women, minorities, teenagers, elderly people, and just about everyone else. In addition, commercial news programs have been criticized for oversimplifying issues. For example, the broadcast news has been criticized for providing one- or two-second statements, called **sound bites,** instead of in-depth analyses.

Finally, commercial television is often attacked for sensationalizing the news and for concentrating on negative aspects of social and political life. It has been shown, for example, that the more television people watch, the more violent and dangerous they believe the world to be.

On the positive side, both commercial and noncommercial television serve necessary functions: They draw together people from diverse backgrounds and give them a shared culture, and they expose people to information and issues about which they might otherwise have been unaware.

**The Critical Audience.** The power and influence of the media and its potential to affect the audience make it essential that we all become critical viewers and listeners. When you listen to the radio or television, be aware of the purposes of the programming. Is the program attempting to entertain, to inform, or to persuade you to buy something? Analyzing the program's basic purpose will enable you to make the first step toward controlling the effects that the media may have on you.

> ## HOW TO > *View and Listen Critically*

1. **Identify the purpose of the program.** Try to analyze the aim or goal of what you are listening to or viewing. Is the program attempting to entertain you, to inform you, or to persuade you?

2. **Analyze the values or assumptions that the program represents.** What ideas does the program take for granted? For example, if the purpose of the program is to entertain, determine whether the humorous portions of the program could be considered derogatory or insulting to any group of people. If the purpose of the program is to inform or to persuade, be sure to think about the information presented to distinguish between actual, provable facts and someone's preferences or opinions. [See pages 228–229 for more on facts and opinions.] You will need to think carefully about the information presented to identify the sources of information, their reliability, and any biases they might have. You should be able to verify the accuracy of facts and statistics.

3. **Make your own judgment.** Remember that information that is presented to you through the mass media often represents someone else's opinion or point of view. Even seemingly objective images and pictures may distort reality. If you listen and observe carefully and evaluate media presentations critically, you will become an informed, intelligent listener or viewer.

*F*or a period of one week, keep a record in your communication journal of everything you listen to on the radio or watch on television. Note all commercials, songs, and news stories that you are exposed to and every instance of stereotyping or violence that you encounter. At the end of the week, look over your notes and ask yourself these questions: What messages am I exposed to in the media? What are advertisers telling me that I need? What stereotypes have been reinforced by my media usage this week? How much violence did I hear about or watch each day? What, if anything, did I learn from the media during the week? After you have completed your inventory, compare your findings with those of your classmates.

# Preparing a Radio Talk Show

## The Format of a Talk Show

Talk radio is one of the most rapidly growing forms of radio programming today. Formats for talk radio programs differ considerably, but a common format runs like this:

- A host, or moderator, appears in a regular time slot—fifteen minutes to an hour each day.
- At the beginning of the show, the host introduces some issue that will be of interest to many listeners. Often this is an issue raised by some recent news event that is summarized by the host.
- Then the host introduces a guest or a panel of guests to discuss the issue.

Generally, the guest or guests on radio talk shows are celebrities, politicians, authors, or journalists. In addition there are sometimes knowledgeable commentators, or pundits, who appear regularly with the host and his or her guests. After an open discussion in which the host, the guests, and the pundits address the issue, the host then takes telephone calls from listeners, who are invited to ask questions or to comment on the issue.

## Skills Needed for a Talk Show

There are only two roles in a radio talk show—host or guest. Although the speaking and listening skills needed on a radio talk show are similar to those needed in other speech situations, remembering the following guidelines will help you prepare for any talk show appearance.

Participate in a Radio Talk Show

1. **Use your voice effectively.** Remember to control the volume, rate, and pitch of your voice to create interest and to communicate clearly. [See pages 53–73 for more about using your voice.] Be sure you are familiar with the type of microphone being used, and take care with plosives (*p, b, d, t, k, g*), sounds that can be distorted by microphones. [See pages 333–335.]

2. **If you are the host, you should lead the discussion and keep it moving.** Before the show, prepare by identifying an issue or topic that will be of interest to your listening audience. Look for current issues in the news or current topics of discussion in the community. As the program begins, introduce your guests and refer to them by name when asking them questions or commenting on their responses. As the program proceeds, use three types of questions to stimulate discussion: questions that request information, questions that probe deeper, and questions that check your understanding. [See pages 173–176 for more information about conversational skills and pages 196–198 for more about being an effective interviewer.] Remember to demonstrate respect for the opinions of others. [See pages 141–143.]

3. **If you are the guest, you should speak up to express your ideas and opinions.** A talk show, by definition, requires its participants to communicate their ideas. [See page 638.] Participants should use questioning and paraphrasing to clarify ideas and shared perceptions. [See pages 144–145.] Talk show guests should respect the opinions of other guests and of the host, and take turns in the discussion. A talk show guest should speak up about his or her ideas, but he or she should also remember that he or she may politely refuse to discuss topics that he or she feels are too private or not appropriate for the discussion. [See pages 146–149.]

# ACTIVITY 2

## Planning and Producing a Radio Talk Show

**W**ork with a small group of classmates to plan your own fifteen-minute radio talk show. Choose one person to act as the host while the others in the group act as guests. Identify an issue that members of the group care about deeply—one that is likely to get a response from them. Plan an opening, or introductory, statement by the host as well as the questions that the host will ask the guests. Present your radio talk show to your class, allowing a five-minute period in which you will take questions or comments from your "listeners"—the other members of your class who are not in your group. If you have facilities available to do so, perform your talk show using microphones and a tape recorder.

# Preparing a Radio Drama

Radio's Golden Age was a time when hundreds of thousands of listeners regularly gathered around their radio sets to hear comedy sketches and radio dramas. Some of the dramas produced on radio, like Lucille Fletcher's *The Hitchhiker,* Orson Welles's version of *The War of the Worlds,* and W. W. Jacobs's *The Monkey's Paw,* have become classics. Many people who remember radio dramas from their childhoods consider this medium to be the most moving of all theatrical forms—more so than live theater or television or film.

The power of radio drama lies in its appeal to the imagination. Viewers of live theater, television, or film are limited by what the visual medium actually shows them. Listeners to a radio drama, on the other hand, are limited only by their imaginations. When a radio program's narrator describes a ghostly figure standing by a roadside, the listener is invited to reach inside himself or herself and to conjure up a figure more ghastly than any actual picture might be.

Orson Welles is shown here during the radio broadcast of *The War of the Worlds.* At the time, he was unaware of the panic that his radio play was causing among thousands of his listeners.

## The Format of a Radio Drama

The script of a radio drama contains sound effects, music, dialogue, acting instructions, and narration.

**Sound Effects.**   In a radio script, the abbreviation SFX stands for "sound effects." To a great extent, sound effects play the same role in radio drama that pictures play in television drama. Sound effects help to set the scene and to establish the mood, or atmosphere. They also help to reveal the actions taking place. For example, the sound of a doorbell lets the audience know that someone is at the door.

**Music.**   Music is an important part of most radio, television, and film drama. In television and film, music often plays continuously under the action and mirrors in its emotional quality the emotions that the director wants the audience to feel. For example, a chase scene might be accompanied by fast-paced music, and a tender scene between a child and his father might be accompanied by a soft children's melody.

In radio dramas, music rarely plays continuously in the background. Instead, musical cues are used to open and to close scenes. These cues act as transitions to move the audience from one scene to another. The chart below shows some instructions that are commonly used for music.

| Audio Script Terminology | |
| --- | --- |
| **GOES UNDER** | The music is heard quietly in the background and fades as someone begins to speak. |
| **UP AND OUT** | The music returns to its full volume at the end of a scene. |
| **UP AND OVER** | The music rises in volume until it drowns out the voices. |
| **UP TO ESTABLISH** | Music is played at full volume at the beginning of a scene. |

**Dialogue.**   The words actually spoken by the characters in a radio play are referred to as **dialogue.** Obviously, most of the work in a radio drama is done by the dialogue. The audience cannot see the setting or the costumes or the expressions on actors' faces, so dialogue, music, and sound effects must convey all of those things.

**Acting Instructions.** Some scripts for radio dramas include acting instructions that are embedded in the lines of dialogue. These acting instructions often appear in parentheses and in italics; they tell how the characters are feeling or describe how the characters' lines are to be delivered. In well-written radio dramas, acting instructions are usually unnecessary because the characters' emotions or tones of voice are clear from the situation and from what is being said.

**Narration.** Many radio dramas include a **narrator** or announcer whose job it is to introduce the scenes, to provide transitions, and to conclude the program. The words spoken by the narrator or announcer are called **narration.**

---

## Excerpt from a Radio Drama

*SFX: WIND AND SEA. FOGHORN IN DISTANCE.*
*MUSIC: TIN WHISTLE PLAYS "THE GREAT SILKIE," GOES UNDER.*

**NARRATOR:** Ten miles off the Welsh coast, a fishing boat, the *Swansea,* casts its nets into dark, churning waters. It's an ancient act, casting nets upon the sea, an act that, for all its familiarity, remains mysterious. One never knows what the abyss will yield up to the world of sunlight and air.

**MATE:** Captain, you'd better have a look at this. There's something strange caught in our nets, abeam, port side.

**CAPTAIN O'DONNELL:** *(Annoyed)* What do you mean, something strange?

**MATE:** I don't know . . . something.

**CAPTAIN:** Well, clear the net and get on with your fishing. What's the matter with you?

**MATE:** I think you'd better go above and have a look for yourself.

*SFX: FOOTSTEPS OF CAPTAIN AND MATE UP LADDER AND ACROSS THE DECK. GULLS CRYING.*

**CAPTAIN:** You called me on deck for this? Come on, lad, are you daft? You'd think you'd never seen a dead seal before.

**MATE:** Captain, that's not a dead seal. It's, it's . . . I don't know what it is.

**CAPTAIN:** Well, haul it up an' let's have a look.

*SFX: WATER SLOSHING. HEAVY WEIGHT BEING LIFTED. EXCLAMATIONS OF SURPRISE FROM THE SAILORS.*

*(continued on next page)*

> **MATE:** What do you make of it?
>
> **SAILOR:** Some sort of monster if you ask me.
>
> **MATE:** Ever seen the like?
>
> **CAPTAIN:** Not while awake I haven't.
>
> **MATE:** Me neither. Looks almost human, doesn't it?
>
> **CAPTAIN:** Never seen the like of it.
>
> **SAILOR:** Some sort of monster.
>
> **MATE:** Almost like . . . a girl.
>
> *SFX: WIND AND SEA. MUSIC: "THE GREAT SILKIE" UP AND OUT.*

## The Literary Elements of a Radio Drama

A radio drama contains elements that are common to all works of literature, such as setting, mood, characters, conflict, and plot. [See pages 558–563 and pages 596–599 for information about how these elements are handled in adaptations of literary works.] For radio dramas, these literary elements are handled in specific ways. For example, the mood may be established by music or the setting may be explained by the narrator.

## Skills Needed to Perform in a Radio Drama

Since actors in a radio drama cannot be seen by the audience, scripts can be read rather than memorized. Actors also do not have to worry about physical actions. However, the absence of visual cues makes an actor's voice crucial to the success of a radio drama.

# HOW TO > *Participate in a Radio Drama*

1. **Use your voice effectively.** Vary the pitch, rate, and volume of your voice to convey the emotions of the character. [See pages 596–599.]

2. **Prepare a reading script.** Mark a copy of your script so that you can see where you need to use changes in pitch, rate, volume, and stress. [See pages 565–566.]

3. **Use the microphone correctly.** Before the performance, practice using the microphone. [See pages 333–335.] During the performance, hold your script carefully to avoid making noise with the paper.

## ACTIVITY 3

**W**ork together with a group of classmates to write and produce your own radio drama. You can create an original script or adapt a published story. Work out a plan for sound effects and music to establish the settings and to create the moods. Write a script for your radio play. Follow the format of the sample on pages 642–643. After you have completed the script, assign parts and present the radio play in front of the class (or record it for playback in class). If possible, include appropriate sound effects in your presentation.

# Preparing a Television News Story

Television news programs have a large impact on public opinion. The creation and presentation of a television news story involve three areas of responsibility: script preparation, technical production, and on-air performance.

## Script Preparation

A television script has two parts—a **video,** or picture, section and an **audio,** or sound, section. The video section describes the video footage and sound effects in the script. The audio section presents the words to be spoken. The following chart identifies some of the terms used in the typical script on the next page.

| Video Script Terminology | |
|---|---|
| **COVER** | videotape of scene used in conjunction with the anchor's or the reporter's voice |
| **CU** | close-up, a picture of something or someone taken at close range |
| **OUT** | last words of videotaped segment |
| **SOT** | sound on tape, a videotape clip containing sound |
| **SUPER** | superimposed letters or graphics, often used to identify persons appearing in newscasts |
| **TIME** | length of time, in seconds, of videotaped segment |
| **TRACK UP** | begin playing videotape |
| **V/O** | **voice-over,** a voice played without an accompanying picture of the speaker, usually over a film of some scene |

| | Script for Television News Story | |
|---|---|
| **Video** | **Audio** |
| Anchor lead-in | In a visit today to Diego Rivera High School, Governor Gonzales announced his new Computers for Kids program. Financed entirely by private contributions from individuals and businesses, Computers for Kids aims to provide computers for every elementary and secondary school classroom in the state by the year 2005. |
| SOT (CU of Gov. Gonzales) SUPER: Governor Gonzales | TRACK UP OUT: ". . . for the twenty-first century." TIME: 23 |
| V/O transition COVER of students gathered around computer<br><br>V/O Set-up shot of Myra Rodriguez | Reaction from teachers and students has been largely enthusiastic. Students at Rivera High now typically wait in long lines to get access to computers, but that will soon be a thing of the past.<br><br>Of course, the introduction of computers into daily classroom instruction will require teachers to master this new technology. |
| SOT (CU of Ms. Rodriguez) SUPER: Myra Rodriguez, English Teacher | TRACK UP OUT: ". . . if only I had the time." TIME: 18 |
| V/O Shot of school<br><br>SUPER: 1–800–555–2343 | Word processing, spreadsheets, databases, programming— providing classrooms with computers will open up a new world of learning to students at this high school and soon at every high school across the state. Within a few years, every elementary classroom will be provided with computers. Businesses and individuals interested in donating to Computers for Kids can call the governor's office at 1–800–555–2343. |

## On-Air Performance

Speaking skills, although important in all areas of television production, are of primary importance for the people who present the news. Because television is a visual medium, the presenters, like actors on stage or in films, must communicate nonverbally as well as verbally.

**Types of News Talent.** Not all performers on a television news show have the same responsibility. A newscaster or news **anchor** may be responsible for writing and editing news stories as well as for reading them accurately on the air. A reporter may be responsible for preparing stories for newscasters as well as for presenting live on-scene reports. A **commentator** may have responsibility for analysis of the news. Unlike the typical newswriter, who attempts to present an unbiased, factual report, a commentator often expresses his or her personal opinions about the news.

**Skills Needed for On-Air Performance.** Television **talent**—the performers who appear on camera—must be able to communicate well both verbally and nonverbally. In addition, television performers must understand the technical aspects of television production that affect their performance. For example, most television stations have a **teleprompter** that scrolls the script for performers to read. When using a teleprompter, performers have to avoid staring at it. They also have to be prepared to handle a script themselves if something goes wrong with the teleprompter.

In low-budget video productions, performers may need to read **cue cards**—large sheets of cardboard with handwritten script or notes. The danger of cue cards is that they may get mixed up; again, the performer has to be prepared to continue with the report if the cue cards are lost or out of order.

The guidelines on the following page identify other points that you will need to remember when you are preparing to perform in a television news show.

*Perform for a Television Newscast*

1. **Practice using a teleprompter or cue cards.** Rehearse several times in advance of a performance with the actual equipment you will use.

2. **Know the meaning of production cues.** Learn to respond to any hand signals used to relay the director's instructions for time cues, directional cues, and audio cues.

3. **Look into the camera.** When speaking directly to the video audience, look into whichever camera is on. The "on camera" is indicated by a red light. The only exception is that when you are talking to another person, you should maintain eye contact with that person, not with the camera.

4. **Look your best.** Recognize that your appearance—attire, hairstyle, and so forth—is important. It will create an image of you as a person and as a personality.

## ACTIVITY 4

### Writing and Presenting a Television News Story

**W**ork with two classmates to write and produce a television news story about an event at your school, such as a speech tournament, a drama club rehearsal, a football game, or a class activity. One person can perform as anchor or newscaster, one as field reporter, and one can prepare the scripts. You will need an introduction to the story, and you may need to interview a participant in the event. Present your story to your class. If you have access to a video camera, you can actually film footage to show as part of your news story.

# Preparing a Public Service Announcement for Television

A **public service announcement,** often called a **PSA,** communicates an informative or persuasive message that is in the community interest. For example, a museum might give information about a new exhibit, or a local charity might seek donations.

In terms of technical and artistic requirements, there is little difference between a PSA and an ad. Both are produced with careful attention to budgets, and both must fit into time slots of less than sixty seconds. The creator of a PSA, like the creator of an ad, will probably plan every aspect of the spot.

# The Storyboard

The tool most often used in planning all aspects of a video production, such as a PSA or a commercial production, is a **storyboard,** a layout that shows all of the pictures (usually shown in sketches), video, and audio cues that accompany the written script. The chart below defines some of the technical terms used to identify camera shots in television scripts.

The drawing at the left is a frame from an actual storyboard. The photograph at the right is a still shot showing this scene as it appeared in the film.

| Video Terminology | |
|---|---|
| **INT** | interior, inside |
| **EXT** | exterior, outside |
| **CU** | close-up |
| **ECU** | extreme close-up |
| **Pull back** | move camera away from subject |
| **Zoom in** | move camera toward subject |
| **Angle on** | shot that will include the subject |
| **Cut to** | abrupt change to a new picture |
| **Pan** | move camera from right to left or left to right |
| **Point-of-view shot** | view as seen by one of characters |
| **Tight shot** | view of subject and little, if anything, else |

Using a storyboard, a director can work out exactly what he or she wants to say in dialogue, to show in pictures, and to express by using nonverbal cues such as music and sound effects. The more carefully a project is planned, the more likely that the production time and costs will be kept within acceptable limits.

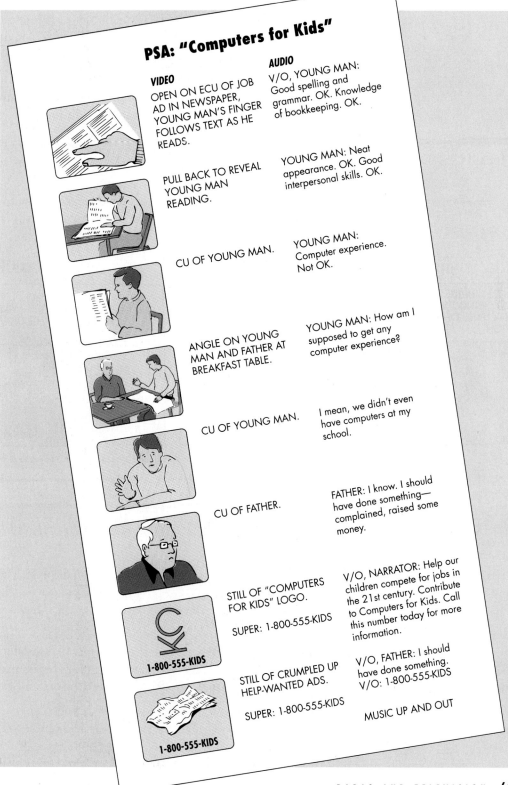

# PSA: "Computers for Kids"

**VIDEO**

**AUDIO**

OPEN ON ECU OF JOB AD IN NEWSPAPER, YOUNG MAN'S FINGER FOLLOWS TEXT AS HE READS.

V/O, YOUNG MAN: Good spelling and grammar. OK. Knowledge of bookkeeping. OK.

PULL BACK TO REVEAL YOUNG MAN READING.

YOUNG MAN: Neat appearance. OK. Good interpersonal skills. OK.

CU OF YOUNG MAN.

YOUNG MAN: Computer experience. Not OK.

ANGLE ON YOUNG MAN AND FATHER AT BREAKFAST TABLE.

YOUNG MAN: How am I supposed to get any computer experience?

CU OF YOUNG MAN.

I mean, we didn't even have computers at my school.

CU OF FATHER.

FATHER: I know. I should have done something— complained, raised some money.

STILL OF "COMPUTERS FOR KIDS" LOGO.

SUPER: 1-800-555-KIDS

V/O, NARRATOR: Help our children compete for jobs in the 21st century. Contribute to Computers for Kids. Call this number today for more information.

**1-800-555-KIDS**

STILL OF CRUMPLED UP HELP-WANTED ADS.

SUPER: 1-800-555-KIDS

V/O, FATHER: I should have done something. V/O: 1-800-555-KIDS

MUSIC UP AND OUT

**1-800-555-KIDS**

## Performance Skills

Acting in a public service announcement requires the same kinds of communication skills that are needed by performers in a television news show (pages 645–647).

- Speaking: Performers need to control the volume, rate, and pitch of their speaking voices. [See pages 53–73 for more about using your voice effectively.]
- Nonverbal communication: Performers need to control their gestures, posture, and movement. [See pages 36–37 and 600–603.]
- Technical understanding: Performers need to know how to respond to camera, use microphones, use scripts, and so forth.

**FUNKY WINKERBEAN**            **BY TOM BATIUK**

Reprinted with special permission of North America Syndicate

## HOW TO ▷ *Prepare a Public Service Announcement*

1. **Identify the main idea.** Focus on the essential meaning of the informative or persuasive message you want to communicate. Decide what the audio portion will do and what the video portion of the message will do.

2. **Plan the audio and video portions of the presentation.** Create a storyboard that identifies the visuals or pictures, the video and audio cues, and the audio script. Use standard audio and video terminology on the storyboard. Use the storyboard as a guide for the production of the PSA. It will tell the director, the camera person, the audio person, and the actors what to do.

3. **Rehearse, then present, the PSA.** Practice and rehearse the announcement several times before recording or performing it.

**W**orking with two or three classmates, choose an issue for a public service announcement. Select an issue from the following list or choose one of your own: air pollution, eating healthful foods, littering, recycling, staying in school, voting.

Plan a thirty-second PSA, and make a storyboard showing the video and audio portions. If possible, film your announcement with a video camera. If video equipment is unavailable, present your PSA to your class as a live performance.

# Evaluating Radio and Television Presentations

Because a media presentation has many elements, you will need to focus on specific aspects that you wish to analyze. Decide whether to analyze the program from the point of view of a viewer or from the vantage point of a performer or director. Use the following guidelines as a basis for your critique. [For information about giving oral or written critiques, see pages 96–98.]

## GUIDELINES

### for Radio and Television Presentations

- For a radio talk show, did the host identify an issue of interest to the listening audience and question the guests effectively? Did the guests express their ideas effectively while respecting the ideas of others? Did all participants use their voices and their microphones effectively?

- For a radio drama, was the presentation effective in telling a complete story? Did the sound effects and music set the mood and convey information about the action and the setting? Did the actors' voices convey emotions appropriately?

- For a television news story, to what extent did the reporter convey facts instead of opinion? Did the reporter or anchor use equipment, such as cameras and microphones, effectively? Did the video and audio portions work together well to tell the news story?

- For a public service announcement on television, did the announcement convey clear information or an effective persuasive message? Did the video and audio portions work together to convey the message?

# PREPARING FOR MEDIA PRESENTATION

### Delivering the News

Reporters who present the news on television must have excellent verbal and nonverbal communication skills. In addition, they must understand the technical aspects of television production that affect their on-air performance.

### Characteristics of an Effective News Reporter

An effective news reporter

**1** knows how to plan and produce a variety of news stories

**2** presents balanced, unbiased reports

**3** uses good verbal skills, speaking clearly and with appropriate voice effects, pauses, and emphasis

**4** uses good nonverbal cues such as gestures, posture, and movement

## A·C·T·I·V·I·T·Y

### Situation

You are applying for a summer internship at a local television news station. You have been asked to prepare and present a short news bulletin to demonstrate your knowledge of news reporting.

### Meet the News Reporter

"A news reporter not only has to know how to convey meaning clearly," says veteran news reporter Catenya McHenry. "You also have to understand how to present the material effectively, watching your pace and speaking with the right emphasis, because it all affects your ability to communicate with your audience."

*Catenya McHenry*

### Preparation

Write a news bulletin about a recent event that happened to you or someone you know. The event can be serious or funny, and it does not need to be of major importance. Plan an attention-getting lead-in and an effective conclusion. Practice delivering the bulletin with cue cards until you feel that you sound like a newscaster.

### Analysis and Assessment

Present your bulletin to the class, and ask for feedback from your classmates. Did they find your presentation authentic and effective? Ask your classmates to suggest areas for improvement.

# S✪U✪M✪M✪A✪R✪Y

**UNDERSTANDING RADIO AND TELEVISION** is essential for anyone living in today's society. These media influence people's behavior and beliefs. You need to be a critical listener and viewer and to know how to use these common media to convey messages.

- **Understand developments** in technology that affect the ways radio and television have influenced society in the past and are likely to influence society in the future.
- **Listen and view critically,** with an understanding of both the negative and the positive effects of radio and television on individuals, on society, and on culture.
- **Prepare a radio talk show** by fitting the format, identifying and introducing an issue, and expressing opinions about the issue in a discussion.
- **Prepare a radio drama** by preparing a script that contains narration, acting, sound effects, and music. Then rehearse and present a convincing performance.
- **Prepare a television news story** by preparing a script that contains both audio and video cues.
- **Prepare a public service announcement (PSA)** by using a storyboard as a planning tool to anticipate all aspects of the video and audio portions of the presentation.
- **Evaluate radio and televison presentations** by identifying the purpose of the presentation and then analyzing how well the program achieved the purpose.

## Vocabulary

Look back through this chapter to find the meaning of each of the following terms. Write each term and its meaning in your communication journal.

anchor, p. 646
audio, p. 644
cable television, p. 633
commentator, p. 646
cue cards, p. 646
dialogue, p. 641
digital recording, p. 634
format, p. 631
high-definition television (HDTV), p. 634
information network, p. 634
interactive television, p. 634
live, p. 633
mass media, p. 630
narration, p. 642
narrator, p. 642
pay-cable television, p. 633
pay television, p. 633
prerecorded, p. 633
public service announcement (PSA), p. 647
radio drama, p. 629
radio talk show, p. 629
resolution, p. 634
sound bites, p. 636
storyboard, p. 648
talent, p. 646
teleprompter, p. 646
television news story, p. 629
video, p. 644
voice-over, p. 644

## Review Questions

1. What are radio and television?
2. What are the *mass media?*
3. How did radio manage to survive despite the emergence of television?
4. What are the differences between commercial and noncommercial television stations?
5. What are four emerging technologies in the mass media today?
6. What kinds of subjects are generally discussed on radio talk shows?
7. What are three major means by which ideas and events are conveyed in a radio drama?
8. What are two of the skills needed by participants in a radio talk show?
9. What are two of the skills needed by the talent in television news shows?
10. What is the purpose of a storyboard, and what does it contain?

## Discussion Questions

1. The mass media caused the emergence of a mass culture. Millions of people heard the same messages, adopted the same beliefs, and bought the same products because they were influenced by the same media. The technology of cable and the resulting emergence of numerous specialized channels may be changing all that. Instead of millions of people all tuning in to the same television network, individuals can now choose the programs that best suit them. What effect do you think this change might have on the culture of the United States?
2. Orson Welles's airing of *The War of the Worlds,* Roosevelt's "fireside chats," and the Nixon-Kennedy television debates all demonstrated the power of radio and television to sway people. Can you think of other examples in the present time period of the power of radio and television to sway public opinion or to bring about change in people's actions or beliefs? Explain your answer.
3. During the 1992 presidential election campaign, all the major candidates for president and vice-president were guests at least once on radio talk shows. What does this tell us about such shows? What role do you think such shows play in a democracy?
4. The United States is a diverse, or pluralistic, society. How is that diversity reflected in contemporary radio and television?
5. Advertisers on radio and television are often criticized for using unfair or misleading persuasive techniques. Review the discussion of these techniques on pages 92–95 of Chapter 4. Then discuss with your classmates the use of these techniques in popular radio and television advertisements. Are children especially vulnerable to misleading ads? Explain.

# ACTIVITIES

1. **Giving a Report on Radio or Television Production.** Visit a local radio or television station and watch a show being produced. Notice the use of microphones, cameras, cue cards, teleprompters or scripts, and hand signals. Prepare a three- to five-minute report with at least one visual aid. Rehearse your report and present it to your class. Leave time for a short question-and-answer session after your talk.

2. **Analyzing Current Technological Trends.** Research an emerging television or film technology such as fiber-optic cabling, interactive television, high-definition television, pay-cable television, digital editing, or virtual reality. Hold a class discussion in which each participant presents one new technology. Then, discuss the impact these new technologies might have on society.

3. **Understanding Television Genres.**
   A. Working with your classmates, identify as many different genres, or types, of television programs as you can. Some common genres include situation comedies, talk shows, game shows, soap operas, news programs, and mysteries. List the genres on a chalkboard or on an overhead transparency.

   B. Working with a small group of your classmates, choose one of the genres the class identified in Part A and analyze some of the genre's characteristics. One way to do this would be to select several representative shows within the genre and to determine what characteristics they have in common. Present your findings to the class. Be prepared to discuss television shows that seem to fit in more than one genre.

4. **Analyzing and Predicting Trends in Popular Television Programming.**
   A. Look at the following chart that lists the most popular television shows of the past four decades. What does this chart tell you about the television-viewing habits of people in the United States? What types of shows have been consistently popular? What do changes in the types of popular programming reflect about society's changing interests or needs? If you are not familiar with some of the shows mentioned, you can see reruns of many of them on cable TV. Or you can ask an older friend or family member who remembers the show to tell you what it was about. Working with a group of your classmates, prepare a short presentation about the television trends that you have identified.

## MOST POPULAR TV SHOWS, BY DECADE

These charts are based on a show's average rating throughout each decade, and are thus an indication of both popularity and longevity.

| Decade and program | Decade and program |
|---|---|
| **1950–59** | **1960–69** |
| 1. A. Godfrey's Talent Scouts | 1. Bonanza |
| 2. I Love Lucy | 2. The Red Skelton Show |
| 3. You Bet Your Life | 3. The Andy Griffith Show |
| 4. Dragnet | 4. The Beverly Hillbillies |
| 5. The Jack Benny Show | 5. The Ed Sullivan Show |
| 6. A. Godfrey and Friends | 6. The Lucy Show/Here's Lucy |
| 7. Gunsmoke | 7. The Jackie Gleason Show |
| 8. The Red Skelton Show | 8. Bewitched |
| 9. December Bride | 9. Gomer Pyle |
| 10. I've Got a Secret | 10. Candid Camera |
| **1970–79** | **1980–89** |
| 1. All in the Family | 1. 60 Minutes |
| 2. M*A*S*H | 2. Dallas |
| 3. Hawaii Five-O | 3. The Cosby Show |
| 4. Happy Days | 4. Dynasty |
| 5. The Waltons | 5. Knots Landing |
| 6. The Mary Tyler Moore Show | 6. Cheers |
| 7. Sanford & Son | 7. Magnum, P.I. |
| 8. One Day at a Time | 8. Murder, She Wrote |
| 9. Three's Company | 9. Who's the Boss? |
| 10. 60 Minutes | 10. Family Ties |

**B.** Working with a partner, make some predictions about television-viewing trends of the 1990s. You may want to base your predictions on information in almanacs or on trends you have observed among your own family members, friends, and classmates. Compare your predictions with those of your classmates.

5. **Evaluating the Quality of Television.** Although many critics have panned television as being mindless or devoid of programs that enrich viewers' intelligence, others have praised television because it brings the whole world into viewers' living rooms. Prepare a list of programs that you feel are particularly mindless and a separate list of programs that you feel are particularly noteworthy. Present your lists to the class. Then debate the question "What is the value of television?"

6. **Analyzing Television News Programs.** Watch several television news programs with different formats, including local evening news programs, national evening news programs, and moderated news discussion programs. Compare and contrast the different formats. Which do the best job of presenting the issues in all their complexity? Which are the most in-depth? Which provide the most coverage of events? Which are the most interesting? Answer these questions in a comparison-and-contrast essay.

7. **Analyzing Television and Radio Usage.** Survey the students in your school to find out their habits of radio and television usage. Make up a questionnaire that deals with hours spent listening or viewing, preferred programming, parental guidance or lack thereof, differences between weekday and weekend listening and viewing, and other important information. Identify what you see as the most interesting or important results of your survey. Share your findings with your classmates in a class discussion. You may find it helpful to arrange your data in an expanded version of a chart like this one.

| Categories of viewing | Freshmen | Sophomores | Juniors | Seniors |
|---|---|---|---|---|
| Average hours of viewing per week | | | | |
| Hours watching news per week | | | | |
| Hours watching comedies per week | | | | |
| Hours watching dramas per week | | | | |
| Hours watching talk shows or information programs | | | | |
| Number of hours viewing with parent present | | | | |

# COMMUNICATION IN THE WORKPLACE

### Background

You are the host of a television show for teenagers. Each week, you invite one or two people to talk with you about a community issue.

### Preparing to Do the Job

Select an issue appropriate for a fifteen-minute program, and invite two other people to join you in a discussion of the issue. You can invite two classmates, or two adults from your community who are particularly interested in the issue. [For more information about organizing and participating in a group discussion, see Chapter 17.]

### Testing Your Skill

Prepare the questions that you will ask, and schedule the session. Make an audiotape and play it for the class, or conduct the session live in front of the class. Be prepared for a class discussion of how well you moderated the talk show.

# EVERYDAY COMMUNICATION

### Situation

You are a volunteer for a guide-dog training program, and your supervisor has asked you to write a script and produce a public service announcement to promote the program.

### Problem

What is your target audience? Would an informative or a persuasive message work better with this audience? [For more information about persuasive techniques, see pages 387–396.] What will your narrative (audio) be? What visuals or images will you show?

### Assessing Your Skill

Use your answers to these questions to create a storyboard. If possible, find some other students to help you videotape and produce your public service announcement for your class. If not, present your idea to the class as you would to your supervisor. Ask for feedback.

REAL-LIFE COMMUNICATION

# APPENDIX OF SPEECHES

*Note to the student: Keep in mind that speeches are created to be spoken. As you read the following speeches, try to say them aloud. Often, an oral reading will reveal facets of a speech, such as rhyme, alliteration, rhythm, and emphasis, that may go unnoticed in a silent reading.*

## INFORMATIVE SPEECH: EXPOSITORY SPEECH

### "The Future We Predict Isn't Inevitable: Reframing Our Success in the Modern World"

Melodie Lancaster

> *Melodie Lancaster, President of Lancaster Resources, presented this speech to the Symposium for the Houston Council of the American Business Women's Association in 1992. In her speech, Ms. Lancaster explains why working people need to come to a new understanding of "success in the modern world." She holds that, while change is inevitable, the future we plan for is not. Therefore, we must make plans that allow for change. A good informative speech presents new information to an audience in an interesting way. How well does this speech meet these criteria? What specific facts and details does Ms. Lancaster give to support her assertion that workers will need to be willing to change in order for them to succeed in the job market of the future?*

Thank you for the warm welcome. It's a privilege to take part in this program, to share the fellowship of this superb organization. I'd like to begin with a quote from Charles Handy's book, *The Age of Unreason*, which strikes at the heart of what I'd like you to remember today.

"The future we predict today isn't inevitable," he writes. "We can influence it if we know what we want it to be . . . We can take charge of our own destinies in a time of change." Is what Professor Handy is saying a contradiction? After all, change for most of us implies confusion, doubt, uneasiness. Control implies a firm grip.

To be in control is like the airline pilot who flies a flight plan to a certain city. She knows the route, but can't assume all will go smoothly. There could be storms, mechanical failure, and many other unforeseen problems. So, the pilot needs to be ready for all contingencies. This takes training and planning. If something unexpected happens, she has options: a change of course, a diversion for repairs, or an alternate destination.

You and I are much like that pilot. We are on a career journey. We also are facing an unpredictable working environment—unlike our parents and their parents experienced. How we see ourselves on this journey is really the key to success. We could fear what's ahead—a natural reaction. But the wisest course is to take control, and use change to our advantage. We can do this provided we have the right information and act upon it. We can do this provided we open our minds to new ideas and new opportunities. How we get there from here is what I'd like to talk about today.

Do you like change? Do any of us really relish a dramatic change in our routine? Most would answer "no" even though we Americans are a very mobile people. It's human to feel a tightness in our bodies when we're facing some new adventure. There are some exceptions, of course. Slow change becomes part of our routine.

If you are 45 years old or older, all this has happened since you were born: television, penicillin, polio vaccine, xerox, plastic anything, frisbees and the Pill. How about FM radio, VCR's, computers, CD's, computer dating, electric typewriters, artificial hearts, word processors, and guys with earrings.

And ballpoint pens, air conditioning, drip-dry clothes, space walks, moon landings and Mars probes. Pancake make-up, microwave ovens, househusbands, weirdos, nerds, and McDonalds. Michael Jackson, Madonna and New Kids on the Block. Swing, rock, rap, and country.

Speaking of change, I remember the day when Neil Armstrong took that first step on the moon, and the thrill of accomplishment all of us felt. I don't believe anyone was really surprised we went to the moon. Science fiction writers and movies created moon travel long before the first rocket was on the pad. What no one predicted, and the most astonishing part of the trip, was we watched that step in our living rooms through the magic of television.

It took us ten years to get to the moon, and decades more preparing for it. That's why what has happened over the past five years is even more incredible. The social and political changes sweeping Eastern Europe still are unimaginable. Nothing in our memory compares to the end of the Cold War, and even more, the rise of enterprise from the ashes of communism.

What's even more unsettling is the vast social and political changes we've seen are compounded by equally jarring change in the business world. Suddenly, our companies are fighting for survival against foreign ones in our own backyard. Today's business fortunes also hinge on keeping products and services in tune with the vibrations of the consumer's ever changing tastes.

In this new world, we've even coined a brash new language. Restructuring, and downsizing, and outsourcing, and mergers, and sell offs. And to go with the new language we are seeing a different face to American business. A face that also keeps changing with the times. Corporations are shrinking, and I believe this trend will continue.

We also find the relationship between employers and employees decidedly different than just a few years ago. Twenty years ago, the average employee began and ended a career with the same company. He or she looked to the company for security, and expected the company to take charge of career development.

You won't find that kind of paternalism as much any more, just as you won't find the intense loyalty that employees used to give their corporations. What you will find is a much greater emphasis on decentral authority.

Decision making is now the province of "profit centers." Teamwork is stressed to improve efficiency and cut waste, and the key to success is individual achievement and accountability. The people who do the best will be the people who are the best prepared.

Going to work without knowing when the next shoe will fall isn't a pleasant experience for anybody, but the uncertainty isn't likely to end. Our best hope is to accept change as the norm. We need to begin reframing the challenge of career. The business climate isn't something to overcome.

Instead, it's a time to use change as an opportunity. So, I'd like to go over some trends and suggest how you might prepare yourselves to take advantage of them.

*First, success in today's business world takes more knowledge.* Most of us grew up during an age when a strong back counted the most. Even nations achieved power because they had natural resources and material wealth. Today, virtually every industry or business you can name is "knowledge intensive."

The image of the petroleum industry, for example, is more appropriately a computer than a roustabout on a drilling platform. Finding, producing and marketing petroleum can take dozens of disciplines—from political science, to environmental engineering, to law. It's not just the oil business. It's every business. Indeed, the main objective of business today is marshalling intellectual capital and making the most of it.

The shift to a knowledge base means you need more education and training to get a good job. Even entry level people must have computer skills. As recently as the mid-1980s, 22 percent of the nation's jobs required a college degree. By the year 2000, half of all jobs will require education beyond high school. Most of them will be filled with college graduates.

We also know that 75 percent of the jobs created in Texas during the next decade will be in the service industries, which require technical skills.

*Second, as corporations shrink, the opportunities for entrepreneurship grow.* Restructuring often is seen as wholesale loss of jobs. However, just because a corporation is smaller, doesn't mean its responsibilities are fewer. Those tasks are now being contracted to consultants.

This is cost effective, because the company doesn't have to pay retirement, health and other large costs. There are other sound reasons: Consultants are focused on the job at hand. They are there when the company needs them, and are not caught up in company politics and turf battles. The temporary employee also is becoming a permanent fixture.

The Department of Labor estimates that by the year 2000, eighty percent of America's jobs will be in the service sector, which uses 75 percent of the nation's temporary employees. Temporaries are in demand because more and more people are interested in part-time work.

What's more, information technology innovation, such as computers and fax machines, have created an ideal marriage of suburbanites and their downtown counterparts. The company benefits from greater productivity.

The employee benefits because there are no traffic jams to fight and more time for family and other interests. In fact, the experts believe by the 21st century only half of all workers will be what we now call "full time." They will then join the ranks of a "new minority" in our country.

*Third, our population is growing older, and the demand for older workers is also growing.* In just eight years, the average employee will be 39 years old. As baby boomers reach middle age, I believe they will find their age a plus. This marks a move away from previous trends of hiring less experienced people, while providing on-the-job training. Even though corporations spent between $30 billion and $50 billion on training and remediation last year, companies were looking for experienced, seasoned people.

*Fourth, the ability to communicate is essential—for people with jobs, those looking for jobs, and corporations seeking to reach the public.* Ideas are driving the economy of the future. Communicating ideas is the fuel that makes the engine run. No company is insulated from public scrutiny, even those that do not sell directly to the public. Today, perception is reality for the bulk of the population—whether it's business practices or environmental sensitivity.

The need to communicate extends to everyone. With the need for greater personal accountability and responsibility comes the need to market ideas.

Which brings me to the "Dear Abby" part of my speech this afternoon—some advice based on my own experience talking with and working with thousands of people. I have three suggestions:

*Ladies and gentlemen, learn to be properly selfish.* In these times you and you alone must take charge of your career. Know the market, and understand the marketable skills that are needed, and develop them. Set firm goals, and have the conviction to go after them. By all means, don't waste your time blaming your problems on someone else.

*Second, frame your career goals to reflect the modern business world.* Some of you here will have "A" career in life. But the chances are good the average person will have three or more. Even more to the point, the career path you follow tomorrow may not even exist today.

*Finally, never, ever believe this world is static. If people think it can be done, then the chances are it will be done.*

Listen to these pearls of wisdom:

—In 1895 Lord Kelvin, a noted British physicist said: "Heavier than air flying machines are impossible."

—Here's one by the late Joseph Kennedy who declared: "I have no political ambitions for myself or my children."

—*Business Week* wrote this in 1979: "With over 50 foreign cars on sale here, the Japanese auto industry isn't likely to carve out a big slice of the U.S. market." And, as Admiral Frank Knox put it on December 5, 1941: "No matter what happens, the U.S. Navy is not going to be caught napping."

I say to you, "Don't dare get caught napping." Have courage. Have convictions, and do the very best you can. We recall the story of the three stonemasons who were asked what they were doing. The first said, "I am laying brick." The second replied, "I am making a foundation." And the third said: " I am building a cathedral." Let's you and I set our sights that high. Let's build cathedrals of success today, tomorrow and the day after tomorrow.

# INFORMATIVE SPEECH: EXPOSITORY SPEECH

## "The Green Mountain Boys"

### W. Benson Chiles, student speaker

*In this contest-winning speech, which placed first in the 1986 Texas State Competition, W. Benson Chiles sings the praises of the patriotic Americans known as the Green Mountain Boys. The goal of his speech is to paint a vivid picture of the role that the Green Mountain Boys played during the Revolutionary era. By outlining their valor and accomplishments, Mr. Chiles presents them as examples of all the heroes who have answered the call to defend their country. What does Chiles do to show that the acts of the Green Mountain Boys are the epitome of the spirit which brought freedom to our land? What elements does he use to inspire patriotism in the audience?*

Ethan Allen, Seth Warner, Stephen Fay, Zadock Remington, Colonel James Easton, Major Brown, Captain Edward Mott, Captain Samuel Herrick. Gentlemen, our basic freedoms are in peril. The time has come to fight.

Almost ten years prior to the Revolutionary War, these men answered a roll call when they banded together in an effort to protect local property rights from royal decrees. Named after area mountains, the Green Mountain Boys played a substantial role in the American Revolution. Men like the Green Mountain Boys were the backbone for America during the Revolutionary era. Untrained and ununiformed, these men had a divine sense of righteousness and freedom when they volunteered for demanding military campaigns. This individualism and independence, which became so prevalent in the American militia of the time, provided the desire and commitment necessary to defeat such a world power as Britain. Nonconformity had grown in individuals from the necessity to survive and the opportunity to prosper in the new land, America. The acts of the Green Mountain Boys are the epitome of the boldness of spirit which brought freedom to our land.

At the outset of the War when battles were fought at Lexington and Concord, Ethan Allen, the original leader of the Green Mountain Boys began collaborating with other area leaders to find ways to assist America in the War with their mother country. With some discussion, they agreed on an attack of Fort Ticonderoga, a vital British stronghold which contained many needed weapons. This fort was the main barrier between American and British Canadian colonies because of its strategic location on Lake Champlain. On the night of May 9, 1775, after marching sixty miles and recruiting over two hundred Green Mountain Boys from cities along the way, Allen and his men stood at Hands Cove ready to cross the lake and attack the fort. With some difficulty they procured enough boats to make the crossing and just before dawn they stormed the fort and forced the British to surrender their valuable asset.

Americans gained three beneficial results from this victory. First, the Americans now controlled the route to Canada, allowing General Richard Montgomery's army to capture Montreal in the winter of 1775–1776. Second, it gave Americans confidence and courage to continue in the War. Third, the weapons confiscated from the fort were very instrumental in driving the British from the city of Boston later in the War.

But things did not continue to turn out so well for the Green Mountain Boys. Ethan Allen, being his usual brash self, made a premature attack on Montreal and was captured in the process, eliminating himself from the remainder of the War. Fortunately though, Seth Warner provided very capable leadership for the Green Mountain Boys who became a well-trained, disciplined fighting force.

When the British began sending reinforcements to Canada for full scale attack on America, the Green Mountain Boys again rose to the call and helped defend Fort Ticonderoga and added a decisive victory at Longueuil. But the most exciting and important victory for the Green Mountain Boys came at the Battle of Bennington, where they marched to the rescue of retreating American troops and defeated the army of Johnny Burgoyne.

The Green Mountain Boys, with their flaming spirit, gave America the winning edge over their red-coated foes of Britain by clearing a path to Canada. These men risked their lives for the freedoms which they held true, stated by Thomas Jefferson in the Declaration of Independence. The Green Mountain Boys, in their quest for freedom, began the spark and the fire which has historically remained as an ember capable of being rekindled during our country's time of need. As we know, this ember was rekindled in World War I when our young men left their farms to answer an overseas call to stop a wave of oppression that had developed in Europe. And again our patriots rekindled the fire in the early 1940's by openly enlisting in World War II to halt the onslaught of Hitler and his army. Even today, the flame of patriotism is there to be rekindled when called upon because of that small band of men, whose rough disposition and independent spirit helped lead us to victory and freedom.

So, when we think of the Green Mountain Boys' roll call, we will remember the heroes who answered roll in World War I and World War II and know that the future holds many more heroes who will also risk their lives to answer the roll call of freedom.


# INFORMATIVE SPEECH: PROCESS SPEECH

## "The Half-Time Show"

Monica Seebohm, student speaker

> *In this speech, student Monica Seebohm presents the steps involved in putting on a half-time show at a football game. The effectiveness of a process speech depends upon how clearly and thoroughly the steps of the process are presented and explained. After hearing a process speech, members of the audience should be able to list the steps of the process and either perform them to carry out the process or understand each of them clearly and thereby gain an understanding of the full process. How clearly has Ms. Seebohm stated the five steps of putting on a half-time show? Is her speech aimed at enabling her audience to perform or to understand the process she is presenting? Note how the introduction and the conclusion of the speech are tied together. How does linking the beginning and the ending of the speech in this way contribute to the effectiveness of the speech?*

Football is an American tradition. But when the half-time whistle blows, the spectators who rush out to get a snack are missing a second American tradition. This tradition is the half-time show. Millions of American high-school and college students are involved in marching band programs. But many of the fans don't appreciate or understand the time, the work, and the effort that goes into putting a half-time show on the field. For the next four minutes, I want to familiarize you with the steps involved in putting on a half-time show.

The first step in putting on a half-time show is for the leader to plan the routines that the band will execute. Half-time shows are planned in the summertime, weeks before the first practice. The band director thinks of the various routines and sets them up on paper on grids like this one. This grid resembles a football field with each instrumental section of the band denoted by a different symbol [visual aid 1]. Suppose that as a part of the show the director wanted the band to move in unison onto the field and then break into four blocks. He would draw the following grid [visual aid 2]. A complete half-time show might require twenty or thirty such grids, each indicating the number of steps and the direction.

The second step in putting on a half-time show is for the band leader to familiarize the section leaders with the formations he has planned. Section leaders meet with the band director once a week to discuss the drill. Each section leader is in charge of four or eight band members on the field, so if the band consists of eighty band members, the director would meet with ten to twenty section leaders. It is in these discussions that problems members may encounter are worked out. It's a lot easier to remedy a collision on paper than it is to remedy a collision on the football field. When the section leaders understand the movements of their units, they are ready to show members of their sections the various movements involved in each of the formations.

The third step in putting on a half-time show is for section leaders to work with their band members so that they can follow their various assignments.

There are six contemporary concepts of marching maneuvers: unison band, follow-the-leader, movable block, squad-four, step-two, and circular. Members of the band might learn some or all of these in order to carry out various maneuvers. This one example of a formation that might be used at the very beginning of the show illustrates a "movable block," a concept in which the band divides into symmetrical or asymmetrical units with each unit moving through the routine as a unit [visual aid 2 again].

The movements of a band are orchestrated to musical beats. And each move is organized to a count of eight. For example, it takes eight steps, or beats, to move five yards. This is what is referred to as marching "eight to five." When you watch a band on the football field and they march in straight lines, it is because all band members are taking the same size steps and are marching eight steps for each five-yard line [visual aid 3]. During a routine, squad members move to the command of military-like instructions from each squad leader. Key commands include "About face," which means you have to turn directly around; "Left face," which means you have to do a sharp turn to the left; and "Drag turn right," which means making a slow marching turn to the right [speaker demonstrates each command as she speaks].

As you march, you follow field markings to give you directions [visual aid 2 again]. Yard lines are your most important signposts; they let you know where you are as you march across the field. Hash marks are also very important, because they let you know how far off the sideline you are and how far from the middle of the field you are. And the press box can also be very important for you if you get mixed up and you are not quite sure of which side is the home side.

The next step in putting on a half-time show is to practice the drill. The entire band meets to work on drill together. The routine should flow as it did on the grid. The various squads should fit together to form the entire marching band. For instance, suppose at the start of the show, all the band is lined up on the sideline between the forty-yard lines, facing the playing field. To get started, the squad leader yells, "Forward march." Everyone in the band then marches out toward the sideline on the other side of the field. The first line members move "eight to five" until they reach their stopping point. Each of the next lines takes slightly shorter steps, being sure to stay in a straight line, until the band is properly spaced on the field [visual aid 4]. As soon as that point is reached, the squad leader says, "Left face." While members in Section C left face and march left as they learned in practice, section D marches right, and sections A and B continue forward. At that point the leader says, "Continue for eight, about face and return for eight." At this time sections A and B move right face and left space respectively for sixteen steps [visual aid 5]. If every member of the band has moved properly, the entire band will have completed the first stage of a formation.

The final step in putting on a half-time show is completion of the show itself. Early the day of the game all the members assemble in uniform to polish each step. Five minutes before half time, the band assembles on the sideline. The half-time whistle blows and it's showtime. For the next ten minutes it is the band's responsibility to entertain that crowd.

At the end of the show, as band members march off the football field with pride in a job well done, they may forget the steps of planning, teaching leaders, teaching members, coordinating, and practice; but they will certainly remember the fun of the show itself. Next time you're at a football game and the half-time whistle blows, skip the snack and enjoy the performance.

# PERSUASIVE SPEECH

## "Woman's Right to the Suffrage"

Susan B. Anthony

> *Susan B. Anthony, a leader in the women's rights movement during the late 1800's, was arrested and fined in Rochester, New York, for trying to vote in the 1872 presidential election (nearly fifty years before the passage of the women's suffrage amendment). This persuasive speech is her defense of her action. Notice how tightly she packages her argument in this short speech—every word is precisely chosen to fit into the line of defense she presents. What does she use as the basis for her justification of her action? What question does she see as the only relevant one in this case? What point or points do you find most convincing in her argument?*

Friends and Fellow Citizens: I stand before you tonight under indictment for the alleged crime of having voted at the last Presidential election, without having a lawful right to vote. It shall be my work this evening to prove to you that, in thus voting, I not only committed no crime, but instead, simply exercised my citizen's rights, guaranteed to me and all United States citizens by the national Constitution, beyond the power of any state to deny.

"We, the people of the United States, in order to form a more perfect union, establish justice, insure domestic tranquility, provide for the common defense, promote the general welfare, and secure the blessings of liberty to ourselves and our posterity, do ordain and establish this Constitution for the United States of America."°

It was we, the people; not we, the white male citizens; nor yet we, the male citizens; but we, the whole people who formed the Union. And we formed it, not to give the blessings of liberty, but to secure them; not to the half of ourselves and the half of our posterity, but to the whole people, women as well as men. And it is a downright mockery to talk to women of their enjoyment of the blessings of liberty while they are denied the use of the only means of securing them provided by this democratic-republican government—the ballot.

For any state to make sex qualification that must ever result in the disfranchisement of one entire half of the people is to pass a bill of attainder, or an *ex post facto* law, and is therefore a violation of the supreme law of the land. By it the blessings of liberty are forever withheld from women and their female posterity. To them this government has no just powers derived from the consent of the governed. To them this government is not a democracy. It is not a republic. It is an odious aristocracy; a hateful oligarchy of sex; the most hateful aristocracy ever established on the face of the globe. An oligarchy of wealth, where the rich govern the poor, or an oligarchy of learning, where the educated govern the ignorant, might be endured; but this oligarchy of sex, which makes father, brothers, husband, sons, the oligarchs over the mother and sisters, the wife and daughters of every household—which ordains all men sovereigns, all women subjects, carries dissension, discord, and rebellion into every home of the nation.

Webster, Worcester, and Bouvier all define a citizen to be a person in the United States, entitled to vote and hold office.

The only question left to be settled now is: Are women persons? And I hardly believe any of our opponents will have the hardihood to say they are not. Being persons, then, women are citizens; and no State has a right to make any law, or to enforce any old law, that shall abridge their privileges or immunities. Hence, every discrimination against women in the constitutions and laws of the several States is today null and void.

°The preamble to the Constitution.


## PERSUASIVE SPEECH

### *from* "An Indian's View of Indian Affairs"

### Chief Joseph of the Nez Perce

> *Chief Joseph of the Nez Perce was an eloquent spokesman for the rights of his people. A brilliant tactician, Chief Joseph led his warriors in a prolonged conflict with the U.S. Army, but in 1877, he was forced to surrender. Two years later, Chief Joseph's views of Native American life were published in the* North American Review. *His story moved many readers, and the public became increasingly aware of the plight of the Nez Perce. What are some of the logical and emotional appeals that Chief Joseph uses to persuade his audience to view Native Americans differently? What specific support does he give for his idea that his people should be free to go wherever they choose? Does Chief Joseph convince you that the government has treated the Nez Perce unfairly?*

. . . I have heard talk and talk, but nothing is done. Good words do not last long unless they amount to something. Words do not pay for my dead people. They do not pay for my country, now overrun by white men. They do not protect my father's grave. They do not pay for all my horses and cattle. Good words will not give me back my children. Good words will not make good the promise of your War chief General Miles. Good words will not give my people good health and stop them from dying. Good words will not get my people a home where they can live in peace and take care of themselves.

I am tired of talk that comes to nothing. It makes my heart sick when I remember all the good words and all the broken promises. There has been too much talking by men who had no right to talk. Too many misrepresentations have been made, too many misunderstandings have come up between the white men about the Indians.

If the white man wants to live in peace with the Indian he can live in peace. There need be no trouble. Treat all men alike. Give them the same law. Give them an even chance to live and grow. All men were made by the same Great Spirit Chief. They are all brothers. The earth is the mother of all people, and all people should have equal rights upon it.

You might as well expect the rivers to run backward as that any man who was born a free man should be contented when penned up and denied liberty to go where he pleases. If you tie a horse to a stake, do you expect he will grow fat? If you pen an Indian up on a small spot of earth, and compel him to stay there, he will not be contented, nor will he grow and prosper. I have asked some of the great white chiefs where they get their authority to say to the Indian that he shall stay in one place, while he sees white men going where they please. They cannot tell me.

I only ask of the government to be treated as all other men are treated. If I cannot go to my own home, let me have a home in some country where my people will not die so fast. . . .

When I think of our condition my heart is heavy. I see men of my race treated as outlaws and driven from country to country or shot down like animals.

I know that my race must change. We cannot hold our own with white men as we are. We ask only an even chance to live as other men live. We ask to be recognized as men. We ask that the same law shall work alike on all men. If the Indian breaks the law, punish him by the law. If the white man breaks the law, punish him also.

Let me be a free man—free to travel, free to stop, free to work, free to trade where I choose, free to choose my own teachers, free to follow the religion of my fathers, free to think and talk and act for myself—and I will obey every law, or submit to the penalty.

Whenever the white man treats an Indian as they treat each other, then we will have no more wars. We shall all be alike—brothers of one father and one mother, with one mother, with one sky above us and one country around us, and one government for all. Then the Great Spirit Chief who rules above will smile upon this land, and send rain to wash out the bloody spots made by brothers' hands from the face of the earth.

For this time the Indian race are waiting and praying. I hope that no more groans of wounded men and women will ever go to the ear of the Great Spirit Chief above, and that all people may be one people.

## PERSUASIVE SPEECH

### "Fat Chance"

Jennifer Cober, student speaker

> *In this contest-winning speech, Jennifer Cober makes an engaging appeal for people to evaluate others based on an appreciation of who they are inside, not based on what they look like on the outside. She advances her argument effectively, using touches of humor to remind her listeners of the sympathy toward others that all people should share. In her conclusion, she cites a personal incident to support her main point. What methods does she use in her introduction that make her audience trust and like her as a speaker? Which points do you find most convincing or memorable?*

All right. I know what you're thinking. You're looking at me and you're saying to yourself, "Who is this play-bunny pinup,—this fine and feminine machine, this love goddess from above?" And then, of course, your next question is, "When did she realize she didn't quite have that perfect body she'd always dreamed of?" Well, maybe it was when my speech coach entered me into a reading . . . by myself. Or maybe it has to do with the fact that when a salesman tells me a pair of shoes look good on my feet, I have to take his word for it. Or maybe it has to do with the fact that I needed a nap after climbing a flight of stairs.

You see my problem is, I think about food all day long. Once, I tried to forget about food and just read a book, but all I could find was *The Grapes of Wrath* and *Goodbye, Mr. Chips*. So I turned on the television set. It was the *Fortune Cookie,* starring Jack Lemmon. I was frustrated and upset, so I went to see my doctor. I told him I felt fine, but every time I looked in the a mirror, I wanted to throw up. He said he didn't know what was wrong with me, but he was sure I had no visual problems. He suggested that I start an exercise program and that's exactly what I did. But, I was unenthusiastic about the task that lay before me—of exercise. But all that changed when I met Biff—two *f*s.

He was my aerobics instructor and he had a body that just didn't stop. I pictured myself walking into my aerobics class like Jamie Lee Curtis in the movie *Perfect,* surrounded by hard-bodied, sweaty men in spandex. Instead, I felt more like Hoss on *Bonanza.* I was surrounded by three old men and a herd of cattle. I mean, I knew exercise would be bad, but I hadn't expected this. I had been misled.

Anyone that tells you that losing weight is a simple problem with a simple solution is either (A) lying, (B) badly misinformed, or (C) a cheerleader. The same goes for anyone that tells you that all you need to be thin for life is a little gumption and a strict diet. The truth is that an estimated 80 million Americans are overweight; 15 percent are under the age of thirty. According to Weight Watchers, a national weight-loss and health organization, overweight people have a disease, like alcoholism. They're literally addicted to food. With some 57 percent of our population over their ideal weight, we are right to be concerned and even alarmed at this problem.

But why do so many overweight people see the word *diet* and run? Well, maybe it's because the first three letters of the word spell *die.* It's not that fat people aren't trying to lose weight—we are. Fat people enrich the promoters of the weight-loss industry to the tune of some 10 billion dollars a year. This money goes toward diet books, diet pills, doctors' fees, health clubs and spas, and a variety of other gimmicks that couldn't possibly reduce anything except maybe your bank account. The extent to which this nonsense is believed shows today's extreme passion for slimness.

You know, many of us were brought up on the idea that there's something wrong with hungers of the flesh, that the body should be treated like a temple. Well now we're subscribing to new ideas—a new religion if you will—the religion of weight loss. *Slenderness* and *fitness* are watchwords of this new religion. Physical perfection is now a form of eternal salvation and diet messiahs abound, each propounding the virtues of his or her system with the passions of a tent preacher seeking converts. Each has his or her own faithful disciples spreading the gospel to every heathen, tellin' them to forsake of their fatness, and repent their high-calorie ways.

Now being thin isn't only fashionable, it's righteous. As a result, Americans are in a frenzy to be thin and they seem willing to try almost anything to get that way. One report in a bulletin sent to the American Heart Association states that there is now a tablet on the market that when taken releases a hormone in the body similar to that of the hormone released during exercise. It actually makes your body think it's working out. It's called passive exercise and it gives a whole new meaning to the phrase, "I'm on the pill." While this example may be funny, there are plenty that aren't.

This growing and spreading social malady has claimed such victims as a college co-ed who, convinced that he was just too fat, starved himself to death. A young woman suffering from a host of illnesses, who finally confesses to her doctor that she's been taking forty laxatives a day, every day, to control her weight. These are not isolated cases. They represent the hundreds of thousands of Americans that have fallen prey to the idea that in order to be successful, in order to fit in, in order to win, we have to be thin.

There are no easy answers to losing weight. If you are looking for one, then you're listening to the wrong person. What I will give you is the truth. It is possible to get thin and to stay that way. According to Dr. Alvin Feinstein of Yale University, the key to losing weight is to lose it gradually. His studies show that an overwhelming majority of those who have successfully lost weight quickly will regain their lost weight plus an additional fifteen to twenty pounds within six months.

Let's face it. Who am I to tell you to lose weight? I mean I am eighteen years old and my mother still gets morning sickness. Last week, a peeping Tom actually booed me. Why should you listen to me? Well, I'll tell you. Last summer I lost fifty pounds. I was happier, healthier, and most of all, I was thinner. I ate a lot of lettuce and lean chicken breasts, drank a lot of tea and coffee, and I was losing weight. I thought I was doing myself a favor; that is, until the night of October twelfth when I found myself lying on my back and facing a bright light. I was having emergency surgery to remove my gallbladder. My yo-yo dieting had caused me a serious health problem that I could no longer ignore. All of a sudden, being fat wasn't funny any more. The jokes were old and the laughter had stopped.

Like so many other groups in American society, fat people are longing to find that magic bullet—the simpler the better—to cure their never ending problem. Every decade has had its own magical bullets. The '60s brought diet drinks; the '70s fad was low carbohydrates; the '80s brought us diet pills and walk-in diet clinics. And now in the '90s we have fat substitutes, which allow us to take in a greater amount of food with less fat and calorie content. But once these magic bullets have made their way through the American digestive system, fat people will be just as fat, if not fatter, and having failed again, they'll retreat back to their dandy excuses: "I'm not fat. I'm big boned." "I have a gland problem." "I'm just fat because it runs in my family." "I'm not overweight; I'm under tall."

A growing alternative to those of us that have tried to lose weight and failed seems to be the ever-popular Oprah Winfrey attitude, "I can't lose weight, so I'm just going to accept myself as I am." And, maybe a small percentage of them *can* do this. A very small percentage. A tiny percentage. All right, four people who've never left their dairy farm in Wisconsin. The point is, no one who's invested time and energy into losing weight will ever be truly happy with themselves fat. According to Dr. Gabe Mirkin's book *Getting Thin,* he tells us there are three key things that overweight people must realize. First of all, dieting may not be only a matter of what you eat, but in what amount. A balanced diet can include some of your favorite foods—eaten in moderation. Dieting doesn't have to be all raw fruits and vegetables, but you have to eat in portions that are adequate to your particular weight-loss needs.

Secondly, Dr. Mirkin tells us that not all fat is bad. He says that while having too much body fat is hazardous to your health, the storage of fat is vital to our very existence. Without body fat, camels couldn't cross the desert; seals couldn't reproduce; birds couldn't migrate; bears couldn't survive long winters, and Roseanne Barr just wouldn't be funny. You see society must stop viewing fat as the enemy and realize its assets to the human body. It can be a great source of energy and warmth.

Finally, Dr. Mirkin suggests an exercise program. He suggests aerobic exercise for overweight people because it raises the heart level without straining the heart beyond its capacity. According to Dr. Kenneth H. Cooper, aerobics is the most widely accepted form of exercise, endured by more people in more different forms than any other type. It's so efficient. It is the official form of exercise of the United States Air Force. And don't those guys look good?

My aerobic class is going really great. I'm under a physician's care now; I'm eating right; and most of all I'm exercising. You see, if we can all just forget the magic bullets and the excuses, we can realize that our fate, as a healthier and more aware nation, is much more than just a fat chance.

## PERSUASIVE SPEECH

### "With Rest, You Get Noise"

Brian Eanes, student speaker

> *In this contest-winning speech, Brian Eanes tries to persuade his listeners to accept the relationship between hard work and top-quality results. He cites the positive value of working hard in order to achieve excellence, contending that too many people in our society are*

*willing to accept and to give less than the best. However, he does not suggest that we exhaust ourselves, only that we commit ourselves fully to achieving all that we are capable of achieving and that we always strive to do the best we can in all our endeavors.*

At the age of eight, Arnold Schwarzenegger looked—just like I look. Well, can you see it? I'll grant it I am a bit older than eight, and Arnold does have a slight head start on me at the moment, but it could happen. Me and a two-handed broadsword and Conan the well muscled, and all it would take is . . . a miracle!

Well, fortunately for me and for the Schwarzeneggers of the past, Robert Penn Warren contends that *work* is a four-letter word for *miracle*. Arnold Schwarzenegger seemed to sense the truth of this observation. He knew the price he'd have to pay to achieve the body of a modern Adonis, and he decided that he was willing to make the payment. He struggled through years of pain and hard work to improve his physique and to reach his ultimate goal—to be . . . an actor. Well, anyway his effort allowed him to accomplish things that no one would have believed of him at the age of eight.

Pablo Casals, world's renowned cellist, also achieved his status through struggle and hard work. Once when Casals was touring, his traveling companion noticed that the maestro continually practiced, until his hands literally hurt. Now, since Casals was in his 70s, and well in control of his talent, the young friend suggested that the cellist rest. But Casals exploded. He pounded his fist against the arms of his chair and said, "Rest, never! With rest, you get noise. It takes pain to make music."

Life is a struggle. And yes, to make beautiful music it will probably hurt, somewhere along the line, but to understand the kind of hurt, we first need to understand what Casals might have meant by "pain." Now pain is not always physical. Hurt—"I want to make music." And, even if it is physical, it may not be the result of some external blow. Rather the pain of the struggle could emerge from the inner turmoil of having to make a difficult decision, or from long practicing to improve a talent, or perhaps from the simple business of daily survival. So the pain is the struggle itself. And according to Perry Pascarella in his book, *The New Achievers,* we are no longer willing to struggle unless the reward-to-effort ratio is greatly in favor of the payback. Honest effort it seems has become passé and therein lies the problem. We are afraid of the pain involved in the struggle to achieve. Now as a result of this negative view, life can become stale, and people will stagnate.

Frederick Douglass, a man who escaped slavery and then struggled to secure freedom for others, states in his autobiography, *Narrative of the Life,* "If there is no pain, there is no progress. Those who demand one without the other are men who want crops without plowing up the ground. They want rain without thunder. They want the ocean without the roar of its mighty waters." We can never further the world while we're unwilling to sacrifice and take part in individual struggles. Now this is not to say that all personal struggles have a great effect on the condition of the world, but they do have a great deal to do with our personal lives.

Nevertheless, the *Harvard Business Review* states that society today is suffering from a productivity panic caused by low commitment to work and effort. We want knowledge without study, success without sacrifice, responsibility without consequence. But commitment to an idea is as important, if not more so than the initial decision to commit. Robert Ard, the president of the Black Leadership Council, helps explain the difference between involvement and commitment when he says, "When you look at a plate of ham and eggs, you know that the chicken was involved, but the pig was committed."

Commitment is not something that can be sloughed off at the first sign of trouble. It is an absolute decision to follow through, come hell or high water. And most of the time you can count on both. Pain will occur, but the struggle to prevail will bring us into self-fulfillment unknown to the undecided and the lazy. As Shakespeare's King Lear agonizes, "Nothing can come of nothing."

A pearl is a beautiful example of growth through pain. The process begins when a single grain of sand slips into the shell of an oyster. The sand lies on the oyster irritating it, causing it to secrete a healing liquid that surrounds the grain of sand. Now, this process continues until the sand is completely covered with a thick, solid layer of the healing enzymes, so that the oyster is no longer in pain. So you see, through the pain of the oyster, a pearl is created. Just as through our pain, our struggle, we produce valuable gems—those personal accomplishments we call our own.

Okay, so we know there's value in effort. Struggle matters. The problem is we have no guarantee of the outcome. It's a scary thought to work, to struggle, to suffer the pain, and then have nothing come of it. It's also frustrating, not to mention annoying, especially when we see others getting what we know we deserve. Somehow everything we've endured seems futile.

An old Burmese proverb defines *futility* as "playing a harp before a buffalo." And now, since there's no old Burmese here to explain, I'd like to take a stab. The point is that we won't get a positive reaction from plucking harp strings in front of a large, hairy beast. On top of that, buffalo are tone deaf. So all we're doing is wasting our time and annoying the buffalo.

But the value of struggle is not always the outcome. In his book *Man's Search for Meaning*, Viktor Frankl tells of his personal struggle to survive a Nazi concentration camp. Day after day, he saw men die. But day after day, he saw men give to one another. The meaning of their lives was in their struggle. That many died brutally was not as important as the fact that while they lived, they struggled grandly. As Frankl states, "Struggle has value. Victory is an aftertaste."

Now, in defense of victory, I'd like to say that the winning can certainly be fun. In our society it's hard to convince people otherwise. "Put forth effort and you'll be happy as a clam" just doesn't seem to cut it. But to be able to reflect on the struggle and say, "I tried" is a valuable thing. No struggle is futile. There is a victory whether we reach the goal or not.

So, how do we sell the idea of struggle? How do we convince people that suffering is good for them? Well, it's easy to explain, but difficult to carry out. It's simply a change in attitude. First, we need to understand that to succeed and progress, we need struggle, and there will be pain. Pain of work, pain of disappointment, pain of endurance. Yes, to get the fruit, we've to climb the tree. We must be the pig and commit to our ideas and beliefs, for without commitment, it's too easy to jump back and say, "Well, uh, maybe not." And it's not good to leave an easy out. Too many times we choose to take it, rather than to stay the course.

Next, we need to remember that through the pain of the struggle, life can and will improve. There may be pain, but there will be progress, and life without either pain or progress is a life of boredom and stagnation.

Philosopher Arthur Schopenhauer puts it this way: "Life swings like a pendulum backward and forward, between pain and boredom." Struggle changes the color of an ordinarily gray world.

And last, don't fear futility. Since nowhere these struggles are futile, these fears are groundless. Not long before she died of cancer, Gilda Radner's autobiography appeared for the first time on the best-seller list. Entitled, *It's Always Something,* the book traces a variety of her struggles to achieve as a wife, an actress, a friend, a comedienne, a humanitarian. She had a great gift to make people laugh, a gift to bring joy. But, as she points out, laughter is born of pain. Her greatest struggle was for life and in the end, she lost a valiant battle. But the strength that she gave to others, the fun and the love she shared endured beyond the pain. An end will come to every struggle, and even if the outcome isn't positive, the struggle remains a learning, growing experience. Our resolve must be to endure despite the pain. If we begin to enjoy the struggle, we can begin to enjoy life. An old English proverb claims, "Nothing is got without pain, but dirt and long nails."

Let's struggle to extend our repertoire of accomplishments beyond these two, and remember, with rest you get noise. It takes pain to make a life.

# SPECIAL-OCCASION SPEECH: GRADUATION SPEECH

## University of Colorado School of Medicine Graduation

Antonia C. Novello, M.D., M.P.H.

*In 1990, Antonia C. Novello was named Surgeon General of the United States—the first Hispanic and the first woman to be appointed to this position. Dr. Novello's own childhood health problems and her experiences as a public health physician make her uniquely qualified to address medical school graduates. As the main commencement speaker, Dr. Novello sets three goals for her speech: to congratulate, to counsel, and to challenge the graduates. How does she meet these goals? How does she offer optimistic and inspirational advice to the graduates?*

Good morning, Dean Krugman, honored guests, members of the 1992 graduating class University of Colorado, esteemed faculty, parents, friends, ladies and gentlemen. I am honored that you have invited me here today to share this most significant day. You will come to think of this day as one of the proudest and most unforgettable days of your lives.

I am especially honored to be here because the University of Colorado School of Medicine is one of the jewels in the crown of American medicine. This excellent institution has it all—outstanding research, outstanding clinical training, and an outstanding faculty. It also has an outstanding history. As we stand here today, it is hard to imagine that the University of Colorado School of Medicine opened its doors in 1883 with two students and two senior faculty members. Today, the School of Medicine is the largest medical school in the Rocky Mountain Region.

But that growth tells only part of the story. This institution can be proud of the medical developments that have taken place here including the first totally man-made enzyme, the development of the first Child Health Associate Program in the country, and the identification of the "battered child" syndrome.

Also, your recruitment of women into medicine—44 percent of your graduating class today—is and has been exemplary. You members of the class of 1992 should feel proud to have attended a school with such credentials and such commitment to women and their careers.

I am also impressed by the scholarly dedication the 125 of you who are graduating today have shown to the profession of medicine in your years as students here at the University of Colorado. I have been told that one of you will graduate with both an M.D. and a Ph.D.; another of you will graduate with an M.D. and an M.P.H.; three of you have participated in the Public Health Service's COSTEP program; and some of you will stay behind to do work with the underserved.

I also understand you have shown an unusual amount of romantic commitment—six pairs of couples coming together in one class! This must be some sort of record for your school, or should I say, the weather!

But perhaps most impressive is the number of you who will enter the fields of Family Medicine, Internal Medicine, and Pediatrics, with one of you entering a combined Internal Medicine/Pediatrics program. When 50 percent of you are entering these fields, compared with the national average of 38 percent, this University should be proud of this accomplishment.

But truly, I am here because your class is small enough to be personal and large enough to be powerful! So what better than to have the first female Hispanic Surgeon General this country has ever had to address you this morning? My office, like your class, is small but powerful in messages and commitment.

This is why it is such a joy for me to join you today in celebrating this outstanding institution and to share your pride in these fine young men and women who will now carry your legacy into the future: your graduating class of 1992.

I stand before you today to do three things: to congratulate you, to counsel you, and to challenge you.

Congratulations. Just think of it—in one month you can finally start paying off your student loans. I do want to congratulate you on your entry into the profession of medicine. Yes, you are now back at the entry level.

As I'm sure you've heard from your previous high school and college commencement speakers, "Today marks not an end, but a beginning."

A cliché? Sure it is—but, like most clichés, it contains a kernel of wisdom, especially for physicians.

Think about it. Most of the science and technology you have learned will soon be obsolete. Even worse, in ten years you probably won't remember more than 10 percent of all the facts you have had crammed into your heads. While I doubt that this frightens you, I hope it will trouble you—trouble you enough that you will continue to learn.

It troubles me that so much of medical education must be spent in the drudgery of memorizing facts: the Krebs cycle, origins and insertions of obscure muscles, the pathophysiology of Tsutsuga-mushi fever, and so little time spent in the conceptual teachings of public health, prevention, and common sense.

Now of course, facts are necessary. They are the building blocks of our knowledge. Without them, scientific judgment is impossible, honesty is irrelevant, and compassion is fraudulent. However, facts change. That is why, for me, the true purpose of a medical education is not merely the accumulation of facts but the creating of a habit of mind, a way of being. By this I mean: The complete health professional must be humble in what facts he or she does not know.

Socrates said that if he was wiser than all the rest in Ancient Greece, it was only because he was aware of what he didn't know. That is why I prefer to evaluate health professionals not so much on the answers they give but on the questions they ask.

So while I congratulate you most warmly today, I urge you to embark upon a lifelong quest of learning, of healing, of caring . . . but, above all, of questioning. No matter what specific specialty path you choose, you will be at the center of ever more complex questions. Dealing with them will require that you maintain your curiosity and continue to study science and technology, balanced by a lifelong interest in the humanities and compassion for your fellow human beings.

You stand upon the shoulders of your faculty, just as they stood upon the shoulders of their predecessors. And, like them, you too will one day pass the torch to a new generation of professionals. It is important that you continue to question, to challenge ideas, and to test new ones, for this is truly how we learn and how life and science advance.

So my dear graduates, cherish and advance your profession. In the words of Hippocrates, "Whenever the art of medicine is loved, there also is love of humanity."

And now, my Counsel.

Sir William Osler, in his farewell address to American medical students, said, "To each one of you, the practice of medicine will be very much as you make it—to one a worry, a care, a perpetual annoyance; to another a daily joy and a life of as much happiness and usefulness as can well fall to the lot of man." And so I counsel you now to set your goals. After all, if you don't know where you're going, you're already there!

What kind of physician will you be? I want you to be known not only for your triumphs but also for your dreams. So plan thoughtfully and realistically, but dare to reach for the stars.

When I was a little girl growing up in Puerto Rico, I harbored a dream—a secret dream to become a doctor. Not just any kind of doctor—but a pediatrician. I dreamed only of caring for the children in my hometown of Fajardo.

After I completed my pediatric residency, I was drawn into a subspecialty, nephrology, largely because one of my aunts, really a second mother to me, had died of end-stage renal disease. Still later, I became interested in broader community-health issues, so I joined the Public Health Service and earned an M.P.H. degree. I have loved every step along the way. For me, my professional career has been a journey, not a destination.

That is why when Secretary Sullivan and President Bush asked me to become Surgeon General, I was stunned—stunned and honored. The first woman, and the first Hispanic, Surgeon General of the United States. And all of this the result of the secret, simple dream of a little girl whose only wish was to become a small-town pediatrician on a Caribbean island.

I share something of my own story with you not because I enjoy talking about myself. I don't. But the mere notion that I am the Surgeon General of this country today means that dreams do come true—sometimes in ways we never imagine. So I counsel all of you to dream and to think big. Don't listen to those who say that the American dream is dead. I stand before you as living proof that in this country anything is possible. Believe that you can and will make a difference, and be prepared for opportunities that will surely come your way.

It also helps, of course, to be lucky, but I'll tell you another secret: For me, luck is when preparation meets opportunity. Therefore, the harder I've worked, the luckier I seem to get.

We must also remember that our work as professionals defines us as human beings. As it has been said, "Much of the good and the bad you will ever do in this world will come through your work."

How will you view your work? The author Robert Bella describes three types of work: First, there's the job where the goal is simply making money and supporting your family. Then there's the career where you trace your progress through various appointments and achievements. Finally, there's the calling—the ideal blending of activity and character that makes work inseparable from life.

My friends, I hope you are not just looking for a job. I hope you are not just planning a career. I hope each and every one of you has a calling—a physicianly calling.

I know that you will do well. Your faculty has seen to that. But I pray you will do good.

One word of caution, though, from one who sat where you are today twenty-two years ago—the world owes you nothing! To expect the world to treat you fairly because you're a good person and a graduate of this university is like expecting a raging bull not to charge you because you're a vegetarian!

The road to success has no short cuts or fast lanes. There can be no avoiding your responsibility to give something back to the community and to those responsible for you being here today.

So work hard, and avoid Kuschner's pillars of despair: complacency, mediocrity, and indifference. And beware those enemies of tranquility: avarice, ambition, envy, anger, and pride.

Will you be happy in your work? I hope so. But how will you do it? Riches, fame, and power will not make you happy. In fact, the happiest physicians and health-care professionals I know are those who go about their everyday lives doing good things for other people without asking, "What's in it for me?"

We must remember that service is the rent you pay for living—not only when you have reached your life's goal but also while working toward achieving it. After all, what you will be, you are now becoming.

The importance of this service attitude is painfully obvious in today's world. My friends, there is a spiritual vacuum in America's society today. There is too much of what-can-I-get, rather than what-can-I-give. It has been said that we are in need of a little more heart, a little more brotherhood, less personal greed, more personal good, more service to others. This is why, while I fervently wish you much happiness in your work, I caution you not to seek happiness for happiness sake. If you do good, happiness, believe me, will seek you. It will creep silently into your lives from many sources: the heartfelt "thank you" from a grateful patient, the quiet discovery in a laboratory, the well-crafted lecture, the scientific paper, the book, or the public policy that may affect the lives of millions. Medicine, you see, offers many paths to happiness. So I counsel you not to be good doctors or good health-care professionals only. First and foremost, be good men and good women.

Do not forget to put balance in your lives: family, friends, leisure time, hobbies, social causes, volunteerism, and religion. Only by maintaining your own health—physical, mental, and spiritual—will you be able to look after the health of others.

Now, I would like to offer you some challenges.

All of us will be living in a much different world in the very near future. While the challenges you will face may be too numerous to mention, I will briefly outline ten that I believe deserve special consideration.

Challenge number one is the challenge of new scientific discoveries and exploding technologies. Class of 1992, the future is now. Consider just one example: At the National Institutes of Health, we are supporting the human genome project to decipher the information encoded on the human chromosome. Gene mapping will help scientists understand inherited disorders and may lead to new ways to diagnose, treat, and even prevent such disorders. This new research, and the possibilities it presents, will be as revolutionary as the discoveries of Harvey, Pasteur, and Lister.

The physician of the future will soon be asked to practice medicine at a new genetic and molecular level, utilizing the most sophisticated biotechnological instrumentation.

The second challenge to you, however, is to not neglect public and preventive health while you serve the gods of High-Tech. I am concerned that American medicine is perfecting the biotechnology side of medicine and resisting and/or neglecting the prevention side. After all, the top ten causes of premature death in our nation are preventable.

It is estimated, for example, that we could eliminate 45 percent of deaths from cardiovascular disease, 23 percent of deaths from cancer, and more than 50 percent of the disabling complications of diabetes by adopting prevention in our daily lives. Preventive medicine, however, has not been viewed as the responsibility of those engaged in curative care. And, indeed, this is not what most of us have been trained to do.

If we are to offer the best care possible and be ready for the medical practice of the future, we must become skilled in areas that up to now have not been emphasized in our medical curricula. The physicians of tomorrow, therefore, will have to rediscover the true practice of medicine—which is greater than the treatment of illness alone—or they will be practicing medicine in a vacuum.

Challenge number three is the challenge of shifting demographics in our society. In a country of 250 million people, with more than half of them women, with more than 15 percent of our population African American, more than 10 percent Hispanic, almost one in five of our citizens being under twelve years of age, and more than one in ten over sixty-five, we need to recognize that the role of the health-care professional will have to change in order to accommodate the shifts in demographics and the special needs of emerging communities.

My dear colleagues, you will work in places you never thought of finding yourselves in, and you will care for people you may never have dreamed existed. My friends, welcome to medicine—the ultimate equal-opportunity employer! If we are to strive toward accomplishing the goals set forth in "Healthy People 2000," we must somehow find a way of serving the patients' needs while accommodating the realities of the community in which we serve.

Challenge number four threatens to shake American medicine to its core: the challenge of access for all our citizens to adequate health care. Access is not now available for some deceptively simple reasons. Either no one is there to provide it, or no one can afford it, or no one knows how to go about getting the one that is there—even if it is available.

In addressing the issue of access to care, we must continue to recruit, train, and retain more women and minority health-care providers. Both are seriously underrepresented in health occupations, especially as physicians.

Additionally, we must be forever cognizant that the containment of health-care costs is not the responsibility of a few but rather the responsibility of all.

In addition, for a program to work, it must be sensitive to the language and the culture of the people it serves. As professionals, we should not design programs for communities unless we have walked in their shoes and on their streets. You must know Harlem to design a program for Harlem, and you must know the barrios of Texas to be able to work there.

In expanding access, we must view our patients as our partners in health care. Too often, patients are viewed as supplicants of care who are seen at the convenience of the provider.

The overall atmosphere at some medical-care facilities is not conducive to a patient's self-worth, to the care of the poor, to the needs of working mothers, and/or to the tolerance of the language illiterate. Clinic hours are most often scheduled for the convenience of the provider rather than the convenience of the patient; waiting periods are commonly prolonged; and the facilities are frequently inconveniently located.

Perhaps the biggest challenge regarding access is to create a true under-one-roof, comprehensive, family-based, community-centered, high-quality health-care delivery system. A health-care system, as the President has said, that is user-friendly, efficient and secure, and meets the four A's—accessibility, affordability, accountability, and to be sure, affability, as well.

Challenge number five is related to the challenge of access to health care and I address it especially to those of you who will be attracted to careers in academic medicine.

Academic medicine is a noble calling, but it too must respond to broader societal needs if medicine is to be relevant to our nation's future. The time of the "ivory tower" is over. Each community member should benefit from the talents available in our schools of medicine and our schools of public health. In the future, we will need less emphasis on publishing and more on practicing, less emphasis on tenure and more on teaching, less grantsmanship and more grit. I'd like to see more professors, sleeves rolled-up high, out there on the clinical firing line.

And in turn, I would like to see our universities rewarding these professors for excellence in teaching, in clinical care, and in community involvement. The academicians of the future must, in a word, be encouraged to and rewarded for "taking their gowns to town."

My sixth challenge is one that is dear to my heart as a pediatrician. I'm talking, of course, about our nation's children. Now, it is true that the overall health profile of American children has improved dramatically during this century. Childhood diseases that once struck terror in the hearts of parents—such as polio, diphtheria, and scarlet fever—have been virtually eliminated through improved public-health measures. But like a picture-perfect apple with a worm inside, frightening disparities lurk beneath the surface of this rosy picture of progress.

It is known that every eight seconds a child drops out of school. Every twenty-six seconds a child runs away from home. Every thirteen seconds a child is abused. Every sixty-four seconds a teenager has a baby. Every seven minutes a minor is arrested for a drug offense. Every fifty-three minutes a child dies of the effects of poverty. My friends, these are not statistics from some third world country: These things are happening right here in the United States of America as I speak to you. These modern-day medical tragedies are every bit as devastating as the epidemics of yesterday.

As we search for answers, let's not forget to ask the right questions. And let's not pass the buck. These contemporary American epidemics will not be cured by simply throwing money at them or by packaging new federal programs. Society's problems are medicine's problems. Children generally do as we do, not as we say. Values are more easily caught than taught. So let us start teaching by example. There is a critical role for each and every one of us to play.

My seventh challenge is the challenge of AIDS. No other public-health problem in modern history has had the impact that AIDS is having upon our society. We now find ourselves facing the grim reality reported by the World Health Organization's latest figures: ten to twelve million people have become infected with the HIV virus since the beginning of the epidemic. Over one million of those infections have occurred since April, 1991, and well over 90 percent of infected adults acquired their infection from heterosexual intercourse.

For the year 2000, the WHO projects that there will be nearly forty million total HIV infections in men, women, and children around the world. And by the end of the decade, it is expected that more than ten million children will be orphaned as their mothers or both parents die of AIDS—ten million orphaned children that will sadly have to bear the stigma of the disease, even when all of them won't harbor the virus.

With increasingly heterosexual transmission of the AIDS virus, the HIV epidemic will undoubtedly be the greatest challenge of your medical generation.

The urgency of reaching large numbers of persons in our communities who are not yet infected, but may be at high risk, will increasingly be a major challenge for all of us as health professionals. The knowledge and skill which will be required in the provision of the entire spectrum of health care for HIV will challenge all our creativity and imagination; and for this, we must be prepared. But please, I urge you to remember that behind each one of the AIDS statistics I have just mentioned, there is a human being in need of our compassion and care.

Challenge number eight is another that I have addressed as your Surgeon General: the challenge of violence in our society. Physicians are used to thinking that the issue of violence is the responsibility of other groups—the police, the courts, politicians, the media, the church. I would suggest, however, that this thinking needs revision. Violence is a legitimate public-health concern. It is your challenge—and mine.

Violence permeates every corner of our land—it destroys our cities, it destroys our communities, and it destroys our families. Homicidal violence is now a leading cause of death among our youth. The recent catastrophe in Los Angeles must stand as a grim reminder that America is divided against itself. We, as a society, must search for new solutions to preserve the unique vision of our great nation. If we are to remain a beacon to the world of freedom, justice, and equal opportunity, we must first deliver on those promises to our own citizens.

Physicians, as the guardians of lives, must speak up. We must get informed, get involved, and get in charge. Violence will stop when we stop accepting it as a way of life. We must insist—no more violence!

Challenge number nine is the challenge of working as a team with others. Physicians will not be able to solve the challenge of ravages like AIDS and violence on their own. You must learn to work effectively with other members of the health-care team as you will no longer be the sole proprietors of the state of America's health in the medical world you inherit. By this, I mean that you must work with other professionals who have expertise in their areas of competence, at least equal to your own: nurses, physician assistants, therapists of various types, dentists, engineers, researchers, pharmacists, administrators, police, judges, legislators—and yes, even lawyers.

My tenth and final challenge is the challenge of communication. As medical science becomes more complex, you will have to communicate effectively and become an educator of your community. This is crucial now, especially when the layperson is sometimes as knowledgeable as the provider. You will be a guide, a voice, an advisor, as well as a person of considerable power, in helping patients make correct decisions. If any of my previous nine challenges are to be overcome, they must be cogently and clearly addressed by sensible and sensitive communicators. In this effort, we physicians must be aware that our detached stance, so widely used to protect us from our own feelings, might prevent us from getting close to the people entrusted in our care.

So before you are tempted to astound your patients with your new knowledge, take a moment to listen. Believe me, if you want to develop better doctor-patient relationships, you will do it sooner by listening rather than talking. I urge you to bring empathy to your work—to see with your patient's eyes, to hear with your patient's ears, to feel with your patient's heart.

So there you have it: a top-ten list of challenges from your Surgeon General. A "hit list" if you will, but of the healthiest variety. The going will be tough, but as I look out at the class of 1992, I am encouraged. Sitting before me I see our new generation of clinicians, teachers, researchers, communicators, administrators, and public-policy makers. I believe you are ready to meet these and all the other challenges that lurk in wait for you. Together, we can do what none of us can do alone.

In closing, I would like to pay special tribute to your families who have sacrificed to get you here and your faculty that has prepared you so well. The degrees you are receiving today testify to the support you have received from them along the way. As a matter of fact, this day is theirs every bit as much as yours. They are the bows from which you, as arrows, are sent forth. And as Gibran has written so eloquently, "Just as the Archer loves the arrow that flies, so too does he love the bow that gives them flight."

Today, it has been my distinct honor to congratulate, counsel, and challenge. The rest is up to you. May you seize this day and all others that are to follow to bring honor to your alma mater, joy to your family and friends, comfort to your patients, and true happiness to yourselves.

I pray that you do not lose your sense of who you really are, where your roots are, and who helped you in getting to this point. Most importantly, do not forget the impact of this great institution in molding your life and professional future. University of Colorado graduates of the Class of 1992, may you think clearly, act decisively, and care tenderly.

Thank you very much and God bless you.


# SPECIAL-OCCASION SPEECH: SPEECH OF INTRODUCTION

## Introduction of Gertrude Lawrence to the New York Advertising Club

### G. Lynn Sumner, President of the New York Advertising Club

*Often, the most difficult task in a speech of introduction is to praise the speaker without embarrassing him or her or setting expectations so high that they cannot possibly be met. In this introduction, G. Lynn Sumner does an excellent job of praising Gertrude Lawrence and getting the audience ready to listen to her speech. What means does Ms. Sumner use to build her credibility? What does she do to set the tone for her speech? In what ways does Ms. Sumner praise Gertrude Lawrence and build the audience's enthusiasm? If you had been in the audience, what would your reaction have been to this speech?*

It is a traditional example of the busman's holiday that when a sailor gets a day's shore leave, he goes rowing in Central Park. And if you would know what advertising men are doing these autumn nights—well, they are flocking to the Morosco Theatre, where some aspects of the advertising business have been cleverly put into a play called *Skylark*. The scintillating star of that play—Miss Gertrude Lawrence—is our special guest of honor today. That is the reason why we had no trouble whatever getting a complete set of our vice presidents at the head table.

In *Skylark*, Miss Lawrence plays a familiar part—the neglected wife of an advertising agency executive who is so busy with his clients and his speculative plans for prospective clients that he too often forgets to come home. Of course this is just a play—just a comedy—all in fun—for I am very sure that if Miss Lawrence were *really* the wife of an advertising executive, his chief problem would be to keep his mind on his work.

From observation of her theatre audiences, supplemented by observations of this audience, Miss Lawrence has some observations of her own to make about advertising and advertising men. I hope she doesn't pull her punches. It is a great pleasure to present one of the most charming and talented actresses of the English and American stage—Miss Gertrude Lawrence.

## SPECIAL-OCCASION SPEECH: SPEECH OF PRESENTATION

### Presentation of Honorary Citizenship to Sir Winston Churchill

### President John F. Kennedy

> *A speech of presentation is often given at a ceremony in which an honor, an award, a prize, or a gift is bestowed upon someone. Although a speech of presentation sometimes includes a long tribute to the recipient, for the most part it is a fairly short, formal statement of why the person is being recognized. At the very least, the speech of presentation should discuss the nature or importance of the award or gift and the accomplishments of the individual. In the following short speech, note how President Kennedy highlights why Winston Churchill had earned the honor he is being given. Why is this occasion a unique one in United States history? How does Kennedy justify bestowing this honor on Churchill?*

Ladies and gentlemen, Members of Congress, Members of the Cabinet, His Excellency the British Ambassador, Ambassadors of the Commonwealth, old friends of Sir Winston led by Mr. Baruch, ladies and gentlemen: We gather today at a moment unique in the history of the United States.

This is the first time that the United States Congress has solemnly resolved that the President of the United States shall proclaim an honorary citizenship for the citizen of another country, and in joining me to perform this happy duty the Congress gives Sir Winston Churchill a distinction shared only with the Marquis de Lafayette.

In naming him an honorary citizen, I only propose a formal recognition of the place he has long since won in the history of freedom and in the affections of my, and now his, fellow countrymen.

Whenever and wherever tyranny threatened, he has always championed liberty. Facing firmly toward the future, he has never forgotten the past. Serving six monarchs of his native Great Britain, he has served all men's freedom and dignity.

In the dark days and darker nights when Britain stood alone—and most men save Englishmen despaired of England's life—he mobilized the English language and sent it into battle. The incandescent quality of his words illuminated the courage of his countrymen.

Indifferent himself to danger, he wept over the sorrows of others. A child of the House of Commons, he became in time its father. Accustomed to the hardships of battle, he has no distaste for pleasure.

Now his stately ship of life, having weathered the severest storms of a troubled century, is anchored in tranquil waters, proof that courage and faith and the zest for freedom are truly indestructible. The record of his triumphant passage will inspire free hearts all over the globe.

By adding his name to our rolls, we mean to honor him, but his acceptance honors us far more. For no statement or proclamation can enrich his name now; the name Sir Winston Churchill is already legend.

## SPECIAL-OCCASION SPEECH: SPEECH OF ACCEPTANCE

### Nobel Peace Prize Speech of Acceptance

### Elie Wiesel

> *The purpose of a speech of acceptance is to express appreciation for receiving an award. Most speeches of acceptance include a brief thanks to those responsible for giving the award and, if appropriate, thanks to any who share in the honor. In the following speech,*

*the writer Elie Wiesel, a survivor of the Nazi concentration camps, accepts the 1986 Nobel Prize for Peace. Seeking to avert new holocausts, Wiesel has worked to draw attention to the plight of Cambodians, Soviet Jews, South African blacks, and other victims of persecution throughout the world. In his speech, Wiesel accepts the prize not only for himself but also for the other survivors of the Holocaust and, by extension, all persecuted people. What light does the speech throw on Wiesel's past experiences and their effects on his present values and behavior? In what ways is this speech also a call to action?*

It is with a profound sense of humility that I accept the honor you have chosen to bestow upon me. I know: your choice transcends me. This both frightens and pleases me.

It frightens me because I wonder: do I have the right to represent the multitudes who have perished? Do I have the right to accept this great honor on their behalf? I do not. That would be presumptuous. No one may speak for the dead, no one may interpret their mutilated dreams and visions.

It pleases me because I may say that this honor belongs to all the survivors and their children, and through us, to the Jewish people with whose destiny I have always been identified.

I remember: it happened yesterday or eternities ago. A young Jewish boy discovering the kingdom of night. I remember his bewilderment, I remember his anguish. It all happened so fast. The ghetto. The deportation. The sealed cattle car. The fiery altar upon which the history of our people and the future of mankind were meant to be sacrificed.

I remember: he asked his father: "Can this be true? This is the 20th century, not the Middle Ages. Who would allow such crimes to be committed? How could the world remain silent?"

And now the boy is turning to me: "Tell me," he asks. "What have you done with your life?"

And I tell him that I have tried. That I have tried to keep memory alive, that I have tried to fight those who would forget. Because if we forget, we are guilty, we are accomplices.

And then I explained to him how naive we were, that the world did know and remain silent. And that is why I swore never to be silent whenever and wherever human beings endure suffering and humiliation. We must always take sides. Neutrality helps the oppressor, never the victim. Silence encourages the tormentor, never the tormented.

Sometimes we must interfere. When human lives are endangered, when human dignity is in jeopardy, national borders and sensitivities become irrelevant. Wherever men or women are persecuted because of their race, religion or political views, that place must—at that moment—become the center of our universe.

Of course, since I am a Jew profoundly rooted in my people's memory and tradition, my first response is to Jewish fears, Jewish needs, Jewish crises. For I belong to a traumatized generation, one that experienced the abandonment and solitude of our people. It would be unnatural for me not to make Jewish priorities my own: Israel, Soviet Jewry, Jews in Arab lands.

But there are others as important to me. Apartheid is, in my view, as abhorrent as anti-Semitism. To me, Andrei Sakharov's isolation is as much a disgrace as Iosif Begun's imprisonment. As is the denial of Solidarity and its leader Lech Walesa's right to dissent. And Nelson Mandela's interminable imprisonment.

There is so much injustice and suffering crying out for our attention: victims of hunger, or racism and political persecution, writers and poets, prisoners in so many lands governed by the left and by the right. Human rights are being violated on every continent. More people are oppressed than free.

And then, too, there are the Palestinians to whose plight I am sensitive but whose methods I deplore. Violence and terrorism are not the answer. Something must be done about their suffering, and soon. I trust Israel, for I have faith in the Jewish people. Let Israel be given a chance, let hatred and danger be removed from her horizons, and there will be peace in and around the Holy Land.

Yes, I have faith. Faith in God and even in His creation. Without it no action would be possible. And action is the only remedy to indifference: the most insidious danger of all. Isn't this the meaning of Alfred Nobel's legacy? Wasn't his fear of war a shield against war?

There is much to be done, there is much that can be done. One person—a Raoul Wallenberg, an Albert Schweitzer, one person of integrity, can make a difference, a difference of life and death. As long as one dissident is in prison, our freedom will not be true. As long as one child is hungry, our lives will be filled with anguish and shame.

What all these victims need above all is to know that they are not alone: that we are not forgetting them, that when their voices are stifled we shall lend them ours, that while their freedom depends on ours, the quality of our freedom depends on theirs.

That is what I say to the young Jewish boy wondering what I have done with his years. It is in his name that I speak to you and that I express to you my deepest gratitude. No one is as capable of gratitude as one who has emerged from the kingdom of night.

We know that every moment is a moment of grace, every hour an offering; not to share them would mean to betray them. Our lives no longer belong to us alone; they belong to all those who need us desperately.

Thank you Chairman Aarvik. Thank you members of the Nobel Committee. Thank you people of Norway, for declaring on this singular occasion that our survival has meaning for mankind.


## SPECIAL-OCCASION SPEECH: COMMEMORATIVE SPEECH

### "I Have a Dream"

### Dr. Martin Luther King, Jr.

*In August 1963, more than 200,000 people attended a rally in Washington, D.C., to focus attention on demands for equality in jobs and civil rights. For many people the high point of the day was the delivery of the famous "I Have a Dream" speech by Dr. Martin Luther King, Jr. A commemorative speech marks an important event. In his speech, Dr. King stresses that the time has come to pursue the group's goal of making racial justice a reality. In stirring language, he identifies the trials and tribulations of many in his audience; however, rather than allowing his audience to "wallow in the valley of despair," he outlines the challenge of the future—his dream for the people. The power, motivation, and inspiration of Dr. King's speech are developed through his skillful use of repetition, parallelism, and metaphor. Beginning in the fourth paragraph with his reference to "cashing a check," how does Dr. King use metaphor to heighten the impact of his message on his audience? What is the effect of repetition and parallelism in the "I have a dream" section in the latter part of the speech? In your opinion, what is the most inspirational passage in Dr. King's speech? How does Dr. King's use of language make this passage powerful?*

I am happy to join with you today in what will go down in history as the greatest demonstration for freedom in the history of our nation.

Five score years ago, a great American, in whose symbolic shadow we stand today, signed the Emancipation Proclamation. This momentous decree came as a great beacon light of hope to millions of Negro slaves, who had been seared in the flames of withering injustice. It came as a joyous daybreak to end the long night of their captivity.

But one hundred years later, the Negro is still not free. One hundred years later, the life of the Negro is still sadly crippled by the manacles of segregation and the chains of discrimination. One hundred years later, the Negro lives on a lonely island of poverty in the midst of a vast ocean of material prosperity. One hundred years later, the Negro is still languished in the corners of American society and finds himself an exile in his own land. So we have come here today to dramatize a shameful condition.

In a sense we've come to our nation's Capitol to cash a check. When the architects of our republic wrote the magnificent words of the Constitution and the Declaration of Independence, they were signing a promissory note to which every American was to fall heir. This note was a promise that all men—yes, black men as well as white men—would be guaranteed the unalienable rights of life, liberty, and the pursuit of happiness.

It is obvious today that America has defaulted on this promissory note insofar as her citizens of color are concerned. Instead of honoring this sacred obligation, America has given the Negro people a bad check; a check which has come back marked "insufficient funds." But we refuse to believe that the bank of justice is bankrupt. We refuse to believe that there are insufficient funds in the great vaults of opportunity of this nation. So we've come to cash this check—a check that will give us upon demand the riches of freedom and the security of justice. We have also come to this hallowed spot to remind America of the fierce urgency of *now*. This is no time to engage in the luxury of cooling off or to take the tranquilizing drug of gradualism. *Now is the time* to make real the promises of Democracy. *Now is the time* to rise from the dark and desolate valley of segregation to the sunlight of racial justice. *Now is the time* to lift our nation from the quicksands of racial injustice to the solid rock of brotherhood. *Now is the time* to make justice a reality for all of God's children.

It would be fatal for the nation to overlook the urgency of the moment. This sweltering summer of the Negro's legitimate discontent will not pass until there is an invigorating autumn of freedom and equality. Nineteen sixty-three is not an end, but a beginning. Those who hope that the Negro needed to blow off steam and will now be content will have a rude awakening if the nation returns to business as usual. There will be neither rest nor tranquility in America until the Negro is granted his citizenship rights. The whirlwinds of revolt will continue to shake the foundations of our nation until the bright day of justice emerges.

But there is something that I must say to my people who stand on the warm threshold which leads into the palace of justice. In the process of gaining our rightful place we must not be guilty of wrongful deeds. Let us not seek to satisfy our thirst for freedom by drinking from the cup of bitterness and hatred.

We must forever conduct our struggle on the high plane of dignity and discipline. We must not allow our creative protest to degenerate into physical violence. Again and again we must rise to the majestic heights of meeting physical force with soul force. The marvelous new militancy which has engulfed the Negro community must not lead us to a distrust of all white people, for many of our white brothers, as evidenced by their presence here today, have come to realize that their destiny is tied up with our destiny. And they have come to realize that their freedom is inextricably bound to our freedom. We cannot walk alone.

And as we walk we must make the pledge that we shall always march ahead. We cannot turn back. There are those who ask the devotees of civil rights, "When will you be satisfied?" We can never be satisfied as long as the Negro is the victim of the unspeakable horrors of police brutality. We can never be satisfied as long as our bodies, heavy with the fatigue of travel, cannot gain lodging in the motels of the highways and the hotels of the cities. We cannot be satisfied as long as the Negro's basic mobility is from a smaller ghetto to a larger one. We can never be satisfied as long as our children are stripped of their selfhood and robbed of their dignity by signs stating "For Whites Only." We cannot be satisfied as long as a Negro in Mississippi cannot vote and a Negro in New York believes he has nothing for which to vote. No, no, we are not satisfied, and we will not be satisfied until justice rolls down like waters and righteousness like a mighty stream.

I am not unmindful that some of you have come here out of great trials and tribulations. Some of you have come fresh from narrow jail cells. Some of you have come from areas where your quest for freedom left you battered by the storms of persecution and staggered by the winds of police brutality. You have been the veterans of creative suffering. Continue to work with the faith that unearned suffering is redemptive.

Go back to Mississippi, go back to Alabama, go back to South Carolina, go back to Georgia, go back to Louisiana, go back to the slums and ghettos of our Northern cities knowing that somehow this situation can and will be changed. Let us not wallow in the valley of despair.

I say to you today, my friends, so even though we face the difficulties of today and tomorrow, I still have a dream. It is a dream deeply rooted in the American dream.

I have a dream that one day this nation will rise up and live out the true meaning of its creed: "We hold these truths to be self-evident; that all men are created equal."

I have a dream that one day on the red hills of Georgia the sons of former slaves and the sons of former slaveowners will be able to sit down together at the table of brotherhood; I have a dream—

That one day even the state of Mississippi, a state sweltering with the heat of injustice, sweltering with the heat of oppression, will be transformed into an oasis of freedom and justice; I have a dream—

That my four little children will one day live in a nation where they will not be judged by the color of their skin but by the content of their character; I have a dream today.

I have a dream that one day down in Alabama, with its vicious racists, with its governor having his lips dripping with the words of interposition and nullification, one day right there in Alabama little black boys and black girls will be able to join hands with little white boys and white girls as sisters and brothers; I have a dream today.

I have a dream that one day every valley shall be exalted, every hill and mountain shall be made low, and rough places will be made plane and crooked places will be made straight, and the glory of the Lord shall be revealed, and all flesh shall see it together.

This is our hope. This is the faith that I go back to the South with. With this faith we will be able to hew out of the mountain of despair a stone of hope. With this faith we will be able to transform the jangling discords of our nation into a beautiful symphony of brotherhood. With this faith we will be able to work together, to pray together, to struggle together, to go to jail together, to stand up for freedom together, knowing that we will be free one day.

This will be the day . . . This will be the day when all of God's children will be able to sing with new meaning. "My country 'tis of thee, sweet land of liberty, of thee I sing. Land where my fathers died, land of the pilgrim's pride, from every mountainside, let freedom ring," and if America is to be a great nation—this must become true.

So let freedom ring—from the prodigious hilltops of New Hampshire, let freedom ring; from the mighty mountains of New York, let freedom ring—from the heightening Alleghenies of Pennsylvania!

Let freedom ring from the snowcapped Rockies of Colorado!

Let freedom ring from the curvaceous slopes of California!

But not only that; let freedom ring from Stone Mountain of Georgia!

Let freedom ring from Lookout Mountain of Tennessee!

Let freedom ring from every hill and molehill of Mississippi. From every mountainside, let freedom ring, and when this happens . . .

When we allow freedom to ring, when we let it ring from every village and every hamlet, from every state and every city, we will be able to speed up that day when all of God's children, black men and white men, Jews and Gentiles, Protestants and Catholics, will be able to join hands and sing in the words of the old Negro spiritual, "Free at last! free at last! thank God almighty, we are free at last!"

# SPECIAL-OCCASION SPEECH: COMMEMORATIVE SPEECH

## "The Gettysburg Address"

### President Abraham Lincoln

*A commemorative speech is given to dedicate a memorial, park, building, or some other place or thing for a particular purpose. On November 19, 1863, Abraham Lincoln presented a speech to dedicate the National Soldiers' Cemetery at Gettysburg, Pennsylvania. Before President Lincoln's speech, Edward Everett, president of Harvard, senator, and orator of the day, had delivered a two-hour analysis of the battles at Gettysburg. Following this lengthy tribute, President Lincoln presented his three-minute dedication. His speech has been hailed as the finest example of its kind—and is certainly the most widely quoted of American speeches. What does Lincoln do in the speech to build force behind the word* dedicated? *In your opinion, what qualities in the speech have caused it to endure as one of the world's great statements?*

Fourscore and seven years ago our fathers brought forth on this continent a new nation, conceived in liberty, and dedicated to the proposition that all men are created equal.

Now we are engaged in a great civil war, testing whether that nation, or any nation so conceived and so dedicated, can long endure. We are met on a great battlefield of that war. We have come to dedicate a portion of that field as a final resting-place for those who here gave their lives that that nation might live. It is altogether fitting and proper that we should do this.

But, in a larger sense, we cannot dedicate—we cannot consecrate—we cannot hallow—this ground. The brave men, living and dead, who struggled here, have consecrated it far above our poor power to add or detract. The world will little note nor long remember what we say here, but it can never forget what they did here. It is for us, the living, rather, to be dedicated here to the unfinished work which they who fought here have thus far so nobly advanced. It is rather for us to be here dedicated to the great task remaining before us—that from these honored dead we take increased devotion to that cause for which they gave the last full measure of devotion; that we here highly resolve that these dead shall not have died in vain; that this nation, under God, shall have a new birth of freedom; and that government of the people, by the people, for the people, shall not perish from the earth.

# GLOSSARY

**A**

**abstain** a type of vote in a parliamentary meeting that indicates that a person does not wish to support or to oppose a motion that is being voted upon (p. 540)

**abstract** a brief statement of the key ideas of an article in a periodical (p. 253)

**abstract words** words that name things, such as ideas and beliefs, that cannot be perceived by the senses (p. 295)

**acquaintances** people that a person knows and talks with when he or she happens to meet them (p. 140)

**ad hoc committee format** a type of private group discussion in which a group is formed to study a single issue or to accomplish a single task (p. 452)

**adjourn** a privileged motion calling for the close of a meeting (p. 528)

**affirmative case** in debate, the reasons and evidence presented that support a proposition (p. 494)

**"after-dinner" speech** the featured entertainment at a meeting or at a special occasion (p. 433)

**agenda** a short list of items to be discussed at a group meeting (p. 522)

**amend** a subsidiary motion calling for an alteration in the wording of a motion (p. 528)

**amendable** refers to whether any changes in a motion are allowed (p. 532)

**analogy** a form of reasoning by comparison (p. 91; *also*, p. 501)

**anchor** a performer on a television news show who may be responsible for writing and editing news stories as well as for reading them accurately on the air (p. 646)

**anecdote** a brief, often amusing, story (p. 231)

**announcement** a statement of a speaker's evaluation of a point, given to emphasize that point (p. 301)

**answering machine** an independent mechanism hooked up to a telephone line that responds to calls with a tape-recorded or digitally reproduced message (p. 166)

**antagonist** the main opponent of the protagonist in a play (p. 598)

**apathetic audience** an audience in which a majority of listeners have no interest in the speaker's thesis (p. 399)

**appeal** an incidental motion used to force the chairperson to submit a disputed ruling made by the chairperson to a vote by the entire group (p. 529)

**appearance** how a speaker looks to his or her audience (p. 324)

**articulation** the shaping of distinct speech sounds into recognizable words (p. 59; *also*, p. 328)

**assertiveness** the practice of exercising one's personal rights (p. 148)

**association** the process of tying a behavior to some vivid mental image (p. 88)

**attention** sustained interest (p. 271)

**attitudes** organizations of beliefs that cause a person to respond in particular ways (p. 122)

**audience** the listeners or spectators attending a presentation or performance; the people who hear a speech (p. 11; *also*, p. 225)

**audio** the section of a television script that shows the words to be spoken (p. 644)

**audiovisual materials** resources that a speaker uses to clarify or to add to the verbal presentation of a speech (p. 335; *also*, p. 368)

**audition** a formal tryout in which people have a chance to show their abilities (p. 606)

**authoritarian leadership** a style of leadership in which responsibilities are given to one leader; also called *directive* (p. 459)

**B**

**bandwagon** a propaganda technique that encourages people to act because everyone else is doing it (p. 94)

**begging the question** assuming the truth of a statement before it is proven (p. 90)

**blocking** the overall plan for actor movement in a play (p. 600)

**body** the portion of a speech in which the main points are developed (p. 266)

**body language** the use of facial expression, eye contact, gestures, posture, and movement to communicate (p. 36)

**brainstorming** quickly listing possibilities about a topic without stopping to evaluate each one (p. 216)

**breathiness** a quality of voice that results from too much unvoiced air escaping through the vocal folds as a person is speaking (p. 68)

**burden of proof** the obligation of the affirmative team in a debate to present arguments for changing the status quo (p. 481)

**business call** a telephone call made to a company or organization to request information or help, to make a complaint, or to take care of some other business matter (p. 164)

**business manager** the person in charge of financial matters that relate to a dramatic production (p. 612)

**cable television** a television-distribution system that brings programs over cables into people's homes (p. 633)

**call for the orders of the day** a privileged motion that alerts the chairperson that a scheduled event has been overlooked (p. 529)

**call number** a number-and-letter code assigned to a book according to the classification system used to organize books in a library (p. 250)

**card catalog** a collection of cards arranged by subject, author, and title, listing all the books in a particular library (p. 249)

**card-stacking** a propaganda technique in which only partial information is presented so as to leave an inaccurate impression (p. 94)

**case** the reasons and evidence on which a debate team bases its position (p. 494)

**cast** an ensemble of actors (p. 596)

**causation argument** an argument in which the conclusion is a direct result or effect of one or more particular sources or conditions (p. 500)

**cause-and-effect order** an order in which information is arranged to show causes or conditions and the effects or results of those causes or conditions (p. 363)

**cavity** a partially enclosed area (p. 57)

**chairperson** in a parliamentary organization, the officer who is responsible for running pleasant, efficient meetings and for protecting the rights of everyone at the meetings; also called *chair* (p. 524)

**channels** the means for sending communication (p. 4)

**characterization** the portrayal of the traits of each character in a play (p. 617)

**choral speaking** an oral interpretation in which several voices speak together in a group (p. 575)

**chorus** in Greek theater, a group of people who gave background information and commented on the action (p. 590)

**chronological order** a pattern for arranging details or events according to the order in which they happen in time (p. 267; *also*, p. 359)

**circumflex** an up-and-down inflection (p. 64)

**citation** a statement giving credit to the source of quoted material (p. 257; *also*, p. 434)

**clarity** the clearness of expression (p. 291)

**cliché** a figurative expression that has been used so often that it has lost its power (p. 307)

**climactic order** a pattern of organization in which items are arranged according to their order of importance (p. 363)

**closed questions** questions that can be answered with *yes* or *no* or with only one or two words (p. 174; *also*, p. 202)

**close nominations** an incidental motion that calls for an end to the process of nominating persons for office (p. 529)

**close relationship** one in which people share their deepest feelings with each other (p. 140)

**comedy** drama that usually has a happy ending and that is often characterized by exaggerated or eccentric behavior (p. 593)

**comedy of manners** a form of drama, popular in England during the Restoration (1660–1700), that satirizes social customs (p. 592)

**commedia dell'arte** popular Italian Renaissance comedy in which professional actors improvised their roles as stock characters in humorous, standardized situations (p. 592)

**commemorative speech** a speech given to mark an important event or to honor a person (p. 432)

**commentator** a performer on a television news show who may have responsibility for analysis of the news, often expressing his or her personal opinions about the news (p. 646)

**communication** the process of sharing information by using symbols to send and receive messages (p. 3)

**comparative advantage method** a common deductive approach for presenting information in which each reason is presented as a benefit to the audience (p. 402)

**comparative advantages pattern** in debate, a pattern for organizing information to demonstrate that the proposal stated in the proposition would have significant advantages over the status quo (p. 495)

**comparison** a statement that shows the similarities between people, places, things, events, or ideas (p. 232)

**comparison-and-contrast order** a pattern of organization in which items of information are arranged to show the similarities and differences between them (p. 364)

**competence** the state of being well qualified (p. 394)

**conclusion** the final portion of a speech (p. 273)

**concrete words** words that name things that can be perceived by one or more of the five senses (p. 295)

**condense** to cut, or shorten, a work (p. 569)

**conflict** in group discussion, a form of disagreement (p. 466)

**conflicting expression** a facial appearance that does not match a speaker's words or actual feelings (p. 325)

**connotation** the hidden meaning of a word; the feelings and associations that a word evokes (p. 32; *also*, p. 95, p. 308, p. 560)

**consensus** a group decision that is worded in such a way that the entire group can agree on it (p. 469)

**constructive criticism** criticism that is beneficial and helpful rather than disapproving (p. 150)

**constructive feedback** the technique of evaluating a problem to negotiate a solution (p. 177)

**constructive speech** in debate, the speech that builds an argument (p. 481)

**context** the surrounding words and sentences (p. 85)

**contrast** a statement that highlights the differences between two things (p. 232)

**conventional** accepted by a large number of people (p. 29)

**conversation** the informal exchange of thoughts and feelings by two or more people (p. 173)

**costumer** the person in charge of the performers' attire in a theatrical production (p. 611)

**counterplan** in debate, the negative side's presentation of a solution that differs substantially from the affirmative side's proposition (p. 497)

**credibility** the amount of trust and belief the speaker inspires in an audience (p. 370); the quality of being believable (p. 394)

**criteria-satisfaction method** an inductive method for organizing information in which a speaker first gets the audience to agree with the soundness of certain criteria and then shows how the speaker's proposal will satisfy those criteria (p. 403)

**critical listening** comprehending what is being said while also testing the strength of the ideas (p. 84)

**critique** an analysis and evaluation (p. 96)

**cross-examination debate** a debate format that involves two affirmative and two negative speakers who argue a proposition of policy, but that includes brief cross-examination periods in which the participants question their opponents (p. 485)

**cue cards** large sheets of cardboard with handwritten script or notes that television performers read on the air (p. 646)

**cues** the signals of nonverbal communication, such as body language, appearance, and the sound of the voice (p. 28)

**cultural characteristics** a person's age, religion, and national and ethnic background (p. 14)

**deadpan** an expressionless facial appearance that never changes, regardless of what is being said (p. 325)

**debatable** refers to whether a motion can be discussed by the group before it is voted upon (p. 532)

**debate** formalized public speaking in which participants prepare and present speeches on opposite sides of an issue to determine which side has the stronger arguments (p. 479; *also,* p. 11)

**debate brief** a complete outline of the affirmative and the negative cases in a debate (p. 508)

**decoding** finding the meaning of verbal and nonverbal signals (p. 16)

**decree** a decision dictated by a group leader (p. 468)

**deductive approach** a method for organizing information in which the thesis is stated first and then reasons are presented to support it (p. 401)

**definition** an explanation of what a word or a concept means (p. 232)

**democratic leadership** a style of leadership in which the leader suggests procedures but also asks the other group members for ideas; also called *supportive* (p. 459)

**demographic data** the defining characteristics of an audience, such as average age, educational background, and cultural heritage (p. 225)

**demonstration** a procedure in which a speaker performs the steps of a process in order to help listeners understand it and learn how to perform it themselves (p. 368)

**denotation** the dictionary meaning of a word (p. 31; *also,* p. 95; p. 560)

**description** a word picture of a person, place, thing, or event (p. 232)

**dialect** a regional or cultural variety of language differing from standard American English in pronunciation, grammar, or word choice (p. 33)

**dialogue** the conversation that occurs between two or more characters in a drama (p. 617); the words actually spoken by the characters in a radio play (p. 641)

**diaphragm** a dome-shaped muscle at the base of the lungs (p. 54)

**diction** the words a speaker selects and the specific ways in which the speaker uses these words (p. 331)

**digital recording** a technique that converts sounds or images into groups of electronic bits and stores them on a specific medium; during playback, the recorded bits are read electronically, often by means of a laser beam (p. 634)

**directions** the instructions for finding a particular place (p. 160)

**director** the person in charge of selecting a play, casting the parts, coaching the actors, and coordinating the work of the set designer and the costumer (p. 609)

**disagreement** a difference of opinion among two or more people (p. 177)

**discussion** the process of talking through a problem, such as a disagreement, by following the problem-solving method (p. 177)

**discussion format** a public or private plan and procedure for conducting a group discussion (p. 451)

**discussion outline** an outline that usually consists of questions about the topic that the group members should address (p. 456)

**division of assembly** an incidental motion that requires the chairperson to call for a second vote, which will preferably be conducted by a method other than the method used to conduct the first vote (p. 529)

**division of question** an incidental motion that requires the chairperson to divide a motion with more than one part into its various parts (p. 529)

**drama** an artistic form of communication in which a story dealing with human conflict is acted out on a stage (p. 589; *also,* p. 11, p. 577)

**dramatic situation** in a play, an occasion in which the characters face a situation that forces them to act (p. 616)

**dress rehearsals** the last two or three practice sessions of a play in which every aspect of the show is rehearsed just as it will be done at the time of the performance (p. 607)

**dynamism** the quality of being energetic and enthusiastic (p. 395)

**electronic communication** forms of mass communication, including radio, television, and video (p. 12)

**electronic databases** extensive collections of information on computer (p. 254)

**emotional appeals** statements used to arouse emotional reactions (p. 95; *also,* p. 392, p. 556)

**empathy** an attempt to understand how another person feels (p. 141)

**emphasis** the force or special attention given to a particular word or point (p. 300; *also,* p. 567)

**encoding** the process of turning ideas and feelings into verbal and nonverbal symbols (p. 15)

**enthusiasm** the strong positive feeling speakers show for their topics (p. 327)

**enunciation** the distinctness of the sounds a speaker makes (p. 328)

**environment** all features of the immediate surroundings, including color, lighting, sound, and space (p. 41)

**establish the method of voting** an incidental motion that calls for the chairperson to take a vote in the manner stated in the motion (p. 530)

**ethical standards** society's guidelines for right, just, and moral behavior (p. 395)

**eulogy** a commemorative speech that honors a person who has recently died (p. 432)

**euphemism** a word or phrase that is used in place of words that are thought to be unpleasant or distasteful (p. 308)

**evidence** material that establishes the soundness of a reason (p. 388; *also,* p. 492)

**exaggeration** a form of figurative language that emphasizes or enlarges a description of actions, emotions, or other qualities (p. 298)

**example** a single instance that supports or develops a statement (p. 230)

**expert opinion** a statement of belief about a subject by a knowledgeable person recognized as an authority on that subject (p. 229; *also,* p. 390)

**expository speech** a speech which gives information about a specific subject (p. 355)

**extemporaneous speech** a speech that is fully outlined and practiced but not memorized (p. 319; *also,* p. 434)

**extend debate** (See *limit or extend debate.*)

**extroverted** describes social individuals who are relationship-oriented and responsive to the needs of others (p. 122)

**eye contact** a speaker's direct visual contact with the eyes of members of an audience (p. 325)

**fact** an item of information or a statement that can be proved, or verified, by testing, by observing, or by consulting reference materials (p. 228; *also,* p. 390)

**false analogy** an analogy that draws invalid conclusions from weak or often far-fetched comparisons (p. 91)

**false consensus** a group decision that does not reflect the actual views of group members (p. 469)

**false premise** a premise that is untrue or distorted (p. 91)

**faulty reasoning** a mistake in logic (p. 90)

**favorable audience** an audience in which the majority of listeners agree, from slightly to completely, with the speaker's thesis (p. 399)

**feedback** a return message (p. 4)

**fiction** writing drawn from the writer's imagination (p. 554)

**figurative comparison** a statement that imaginatively shows similarities between things that are essentially not alike (p. 232)

**figurative language** words and phrases that are not literally true, but that create a fresh, lively understanding of an idea (p. 296)

**figures of speech** words and phrases that compare two things that are basically very dissimilar (p. 574)

**fixed-interval method** a method of surveying in which the information-seeker asks questions of a specific proportion of people who pass by (p. 245)

**floor plan**   a diagram that shows the positions of walls, entrances, and furnishings on a stage (p. 611)

**flow sheet**   a record of the progress of arguments in a debate (p. 505)

**follow-up questions**   questions that relate to the subject matter of an earlier question (p. 175; *also,* p. 202)

**formal outline**   a short skeleton of a speech written in complete sentences (p. 275)

**formal settings**   communication situations that people can prepare for ahead of time, such as interviews, group discussions, and debates (p. 9)

**formal theater**   a type of drama in which the actors follow a script for the dialogue and the actions of a play (p. 589)

**format**   a particular combination of content and style at a radio station (p. 631)

**forum format**   a type of public group discussion in which a panel or a symposium is opened up to questions or comments from the audience (p. 451)

**free-form format**   a type of private group discussion in which group members discuss a topic at will in no particular order (p. 452)

**free verse**   a form of poetry that uses the rhythms of natural speech (p. 572)

**fricatives**   the consonant sounds that make a friction-like noise (p. 61)

**friendships**   mutually satisfying relationships (p. 140)

**generalizations**   general conclusions or opinions drawn from particular observations (p. 90; *also,* p. 499)

**generalize**   in language learning, to apply a rule of language to all cases (p. 30)

**general purpose**   the overall intent of a speech (p. 220)

**general words**   words that refer to an entire category of items (p. 294)

**germane**   a requirement in parliamentary procedure that an amendment must in some way relate to the issue of the original motion (p. 537)

**glides**   the sounds that result from the gliding movements of the articulators (p. 61)

**goal**   the speaker's purpose for giving a speech (p. 84)

**goals**   aims that a person hopes to achieve or accomplish through communication (p. 123)

**goodwill**   an audience's respect or positive feeling for a speaker as a person (p. 271)

**graduation speech**   a formal address made at a commencement ceremony in honor of the occasion (p. 427)

**grammar**   the rules and conventions for speaking and writing a language, such as English (p. 331)

**group discussion**   a face-to-face communication of a small number of people who meet for a specific purpose, such as to arrive at a decision, to brainstorm ideas, to share information, or to solve a problem (p. 449; *also,* p. 10)

**halo effect**   based on observing a person's behavior in a single situation; judgment of a person's other characteristics without further investigation (p. 128)

**hand-held microphone**   a microphone that is meant to be held in the hand (p. 334)

**harshness**   a quality of voice characterized by an unpleasant, grating sound that may also be hard or metallic (p. 68)

**hasty generalizations**   conclusions or opinions that are drawn from very few observations or that ignore exceptions (p. 90)

**hearing**   the ability to detect sounds (p. 81)

**heckler**   a person who tries purposely to disturb a speaker (p. 343)

**hierarchy of needs**   developed by Abraham Maslow, a ranking of five general categories of needs: physiological, safety, love, esteem, and self-actualization (p. 118)

**high-definition television (HDTV)**   a video technology that creates a sharper image due to its higher resolution (p. 634)

**hoarseness**   a quality of voice characterized by a thickness of sound or by a muffled or rasping sound (p. 69)

**hostile audience**   an audience in which the majority of the listeners oppose the speaker's thesis (p. 400)

**house manager**   the person in charge of the theater ushers, house lighting, air conditioning, heating, and ventilation (p. 612)

**hyperbole**   (See *exaggeration.*)

**illustration**   a detailed example (p. 230)

**"I" message**   a statement that begins with "I" and that expresses honestly how a person feels as a result of another person's behavior (p. 178)

**impromptu speech**   a speech given on the spur of the moment with no preparation (p. 318; *also,* p. 436)

**improvisation**   a form of drama that is spontaneous rather than planned (p. 616)

**incidental motions**   in a parliamentary meeting, proposals that relate to questions of procedure arising out of the discussion (p. 529)

**individual characteristics** a person's personality, interests, and aspirations (p. 14)

**inductive approach** a method for organizing information that begins with the speaker's reasons and leads up to the thesis (p. 403)

**inflection** the upward or downward glide of pitch as a person speaks (p. 63)

**informal communication** giving and receiving messages in casual, person-to-person interactions (p. 159)

**informal settings** the casual, unstructured situations in which most communication occurs (p. 9)

**informal theater** a type of drama in which the actors rely on their imaginations to generate the story, dialogue, and movement (p. 589)

**information network** a single machine in the home connected by fiber-optic cables to a nationwide or worldwide information network (p. 634)

**informative interview** an interview in which the interviewer gathers information about a topic from a knowledgeable, experienced person (p. 187)

**informative speech** a speech that provides information to an audience (p. 355)

**insight** important ideas or new perceptions of life (p. 556)

**intensity** the depth of feeling a performer has for a part (p. 603)

**interactive television** a device allowing a viewer to interact with and respond to what is seen on the television screen (p. 634)

**interest** the involvement or concern an audience shows about a topic (p. 271)

**interference** anything that gets in the way of clear communication (p. 17)

**interlibrary loan services** the use of computers to access other libraries' on-line catalogs in order to locate and request specific reference materials (p. 254)

**interpersonal communication** the communication that occurs between two or more people (p. 3; *also,* p. 139)

**interpretation** the process of explaining the information that has been selected and organized (p. 111)

**interview** a formal meeting, usually face to face, in which people obtain information by asking questions (p. 187; *also,* p. 10, p. 244)

**interviewee** the person who responds to the interviewer's questions (p. 187)

**interviewer** the person who conducts an interview by asking questions (p. 187)

**intimate space** the distance, usually about eighteen inches, at which people feel comfortable communicating with family members and close friends (p. 42)

**intrapersonal communication** self-talk (p. 109)

**introduction** the beginning of a speech (p. 270); the presentation of one person to another or to a group (p. 170)

**introverted** describes withdrawn individuals who may prefer to keep to themselves rather than to seek involvement with others through social interaction (p. 122)

**irony** the use of words to imply something different from, perhaps even the opposite of, what is actually meant (p. 299)

**irrelevant evidence** information that has nothing to do with the argument being made (p. 92)

**jargon** language that is used by people within a particular group or field, but is not necessarily understood by those outside the group (p. 307; *also,* p. 33)

**job interview** an interview in which a person responsible for hiring employees reviews an applicant's qualifications for a job (p. 187)

**key** the average pitch at which a person speaks (p. 62)

**key issues** the points of disagreement in a debate (p. 488)

**laissez-faire leadership** a style of leadership in which responsibilities are shared by all members of the group; also called *nondirective* (p. 459)

**larynx** the voice box (p. 54)

**lavaliere or clip-on microphone** a small portable microphone that hangs on a cord around the neck or that is clipped to an article of clothing (p. 334)

**lay on the table** a subsidiary motion that calls for a temporary postponement of action until someone makes a motion to remove the original motion from the table (p. 528)

**leadership** the ability to guide a group toward its goal (p. 459)

**leading question** a question that suggests the answer that is expected or desired (p. 202)

**lectern** (See *speaker's stand.*)

**levels of usage** the different kinds of language used for various audiences and purposes (p. 289)

**limit or extend debate** a subsidiary motion that calls for setting a time limit on individual speeches or for extending the debate to allow more complete discussion of the issue (p. 528)

**Lincoln-Douglas debate** a form of debate in which only one affirmative and one negative speaker argue a proposition of value (p. 486)

**listening** getting meaning from sounds that are heard (p. 81)

**literal comparison** a statement that shows the real similarities between things that are essentially alike (p. 232)

**literature** writing as an art form that expresses ideas of permanent or universal interest and that is characterized by excellence of form and expression (p. 554)

**live** television programming that is transmitted as it occurs (p. 633)

**loaded words** words that evoke very strong positive or negative attitudes toward a person, group, or idea (p. 95)

**logical reasoning** the use of reasons supported by evidence to build an argument (p. 387)

**loudness** (See *volume.*)

**main ideas** the speaker's most important points (p. 84)

**main motions** in a parliamentary meeting, proposals that set forth new items of business to be considered (p. 527)

**main points** the major ideas of a speech under which the supporting information is organized (p. 266)

**majority** in voting, the side that wins because over half of the voters support that position (p. 469)

**makeup artist** the person in a dramatic production responsible for using the special techniques needed for theatrical makeup (p. 612)

**manipulation** the shrewd or devious management of facts for one's own purposes (p. 396)

**manuscript speech** a speech that is written out completely and read to an audience (p. 318)

**masking** adopting facial expressions normally associated with one feeling to disguise other, true feelings (p. 36)

**mass media** practical methods for communicating with a mass, or large group, of people, including newspapers, magazines, films, billboards, radio, and television (p. 630)

**media center** a term for today's library, so called because it holds such a wide variety of information sources (p. 248)

**melody** the variations in pitch that help to give expression to a person's voice (p. 63)

**memorized speech** a speech that is written out completely and recited word for word from memory (p. 319)

**message** ideas and feelings that make up the content of communication (p. 4; *also*, p. 27)

**metaphor** a comparison between essentially unlike things without using the words *like* or *as* (p. 297)

**microfiche** a sheet of film that bears the reduced-scale record of printed or graphic material (p. 254)

**microfilm** a roll or reel of film that bears the reduced-scale record of printed or graphic material (p. 254)

**microform catalog** a microfilm or microfiche machine that contains the library's entire listing of books (p. 249)

**microforms** various types of photographic film bearing the reduced-scale record of printed or graphic material (p. 254)

**microphone** an electronic device for broadcasting sound (p. 333)

**minutes** the written and official record of a meeting's proceedings (p. 521)

**miracle plays** medieval plays that dramatized events from the Bible (p. 591)

**misunderstanding** a lack of clear communication (p. 144)

**mnemonic devices** rhymes, acronyms, or other wordplay that are used to help people remember information (p. 88; *also*, p. 368)

**moderated free-form format** a type of private group discussion in which a moderator, or leader, introduces the discussion topic and recognizes individuals to speak (p. 452)

**modern drama** the period of drama, beginning late in the nineteenth century, noted for its use of realism (p. 593)

**monologue** an extended speech by one character (p. 617)

**monotone** a melody pattern that consists of only one tone (p. 63)

**Monroe motivated sequence** an inductive method for presenting information that includes five steps: drawing attention to a problem, showing a need for action, outlining a plan to satisfy that need, visualizing benefits, and suggesting a specific action (p. 404)

**mood** the emotional tone that a piece of literature exhibits (p. 562)

**morality plays** medieval plays that presented allegorical stories in which characters personified religious or moral abstractions (p. 591)

**motion** a proposal for action made by a member of a parliamentary organization (p. 527)

**motives** the sources of behavior (p. 118)

**mystery plays** medieval plays that presented events from saints' lives (p. 591)

**name-calling** labeling intended to arouse powerful negative feelings (p. 94)

**narration** an account of the details of a story or an event; the words spoken by a narrator or announcer (p. 642)

**narrator** in a radio drama, an announcer who introduces the scenes, provides transitions, and concludes the program (p. 642)

**nasal cavity** the nose (p. 58)

**nasality** a quality of voice characterized by too much nasal resonance of all vocal sounds (p. 67)

**nasals** sounds resonated in the nasal cavity (p. 61)

**negative case** in debate, the reasons and evidence that refute the affirmative case, defend the status quo, or present a counterplan (p. 496)

**negative method** an inductive method for organizing information in which the speaker shows that no option other than the one the speaker proposes is acceptable (p. 404)

**neutral audience** an audience in which the majority of the listeners have not reached a decision about a speaker's thesis (p. 399)

**neutral question** a question that promotes objectivity by giving no hint of what particular answer a person wants (p. 202)

**nonfiction** prose that tells about real people and real events (p. 554)

**nonverbal clues** indicators of the social meaning of communication, such as eye contact, posture, and facial expression (p. 86)

**nonverbal language** communication without words (p. 28)

**nonverbal symbols** any means used to communicate without words, including gestures, sounds, facial expressions, and body movements (p. 4)

**note cards** cards used to record information (or a summary of it) and its source (p. 256)

**object to consideration** an incidental motion that allows the group to dismiss a main motion that is irrelevant, inappropriate, or otherwise undesirable (p. 529)

**occasion** the time, the place, and all of the other conditions that define the setting in which a person delivers a speech (p. 226)

**on-line catalog** a computerized card catalog (p. 249)

**open questions** questions that must be answered with explanations (p. 174; *also,* p. 202)

**opinion** a personal belief or attitude (p. 229)

**optimum pitch** the pitch at which a person speaks with the least strain and with the best resonance (p. 62)

**oral cavity** the mouth (p. 58)

**oral interpretation** the presentation of a work of literature to a group of listeners in order to express the meaning contained in the literary work (p. 554)

**oral reading** a performing art in which literature is read aloud and interpreted for an audience (p. 11)

**order of names** the order in which people are presented to each other (p. 171)

**order of precedence** in parliamentary meeting, the order in which motions must be voted or acted upon (p. 531)

**panel format** a type of public group discussion in which a group of experts discusses a topic to provide information and opinions that another group can use to reach a decision or to find a solution (p. 451)

**pantomime** dramatic communication performed entirely without words (p. 613)

**paralanguage** a type of nonverbal communication that uses voice variation and non-word sounds to accompany a verbal message (p. 40)

**parallelism** the repetition of words, phrases, or sentences to emphasize an idea or a series of ideas (p. 301)

**paraphrasing** using one's own words to restate what another person has said (p. 145; *also,* p. 175, p. 203)

**parliamentary inquiry** an incidental motion made to request information about whether making a motion would be in order (p. 529)

**parliamentary procedure** a set of rules for conducting orderly meetings (p. 519; *also,* p. 11)

**partial demonstration** a demonstration in which either some of the parts are already completed or the size of items is exaggerated so the audience can see them clearly (p. 369)

**pastoral plays** Renaissance plays that presented love stories in idealized woodland settings (p. 592)

**pay-cable television** a regular subscription service that brings a variety of programs into the home on one channel in exchange for a monthly fee (p. 633)

**pay television** a type of cable television in which people pay a fee to watch a particular program (p. 633)

**perception** an active process of giving meaning to information a person receives from the senses (p. 110)

**perception check** a verbal response stating one person's understanding of someone else's nonverbal behavior (p. 36; *also,* p. 130)

**personal reference** a speech introduction in which the speaker relates the speech topic directly to the audience's experience (p. 272)

**personal space** the distance, from eighteen inches to four feet, at which conversations occur between acquaintances (p. 43)

**persuasion** the attempt to convince others to do something or to change a belief of their own free will (p. 92)

**persuasive speech** a speech that establishes a fact, changes a belief, or moves an audience to act on a policy (p. 383)

**pharyngeal cavity** the throat (p. 58)

**physical noise** any sound that prevents a person from being heard (p. 17)

**pitch** the highness or lowness of a sound (p. 62)

**plagiarism** the presentation of another person's words or ideas as if they were the speaker's own (p. 256)

**plosives** the consonant sounds that form a small explosion when spoken (p. 61)

**poetry** compressed, highly charged language that appeals to emotions and the imagination, usually arranged in lines with a regular rhythm and often with a definite rhyme scheme (p. 571)

**point of order** an incidental motion that calls attention to a violation of parliamentary procedure (p. 530)

**point of view** refers to who is telling the story (p. 568)

**poise** the quality of looking confident and prepared to handle any problem (p. 194)

**postpone indefinitely** a subsidiary motion that calls for postponement of discussion for that session and thus prevents the main motion from coming to a vote (p. 528)

**postpone to a definite time** a subsidiary motion that calls for a postponement of action until a particular time set by the person making the motion (p. 528)

**practical communication** a type of informal communication which is useful, direct, and goal oriented (p. 159)

**precise words** words that express a person's thoughts or feelings accurately or exactly (p. 293)

**prejudice** a prejudgment or bias; a belief that may not be grounded in facts (p. 83)

**premise** in an argument, a stated or implied starting point that is assumed to be true (p. 91)

**prerecorded** describes television programming that is recorded earlier for later broadcast (p. 633)

**previous question** a subsidiary motion that calls for a vote to stop discussion on a motion (p. 528)

*prima facie* **case** a case that contains enough reasons and evidence to win a debate if the other side presented no argument (p. 494)

**primary amendment** an amendment of a main motion (p. 537)

**primary source** someone who provides information from direct experience (p. 200)

**private self** the aspects of a person that are most true to his or her self-concept (p. 124; *also*, p. 146)

**privileged motions** in a parliamentary meeting, proposals that concern the running of the meeting itself (p. 528)

**problem-solution method** a deductive approach for presenting information in which the speaker first presents the problem and then offers at least one possible solution for that problem (p. 402)

**problem-solution pattern** in debate, a pattern for organizing information to prove that a significant problem exists, that adopting the proposal will help solve the problem, and that adopting the proposal is the best way to solve the problem; also called *need-plan pattern* (p. 495)

**problem-solving method** a four-part method that involves identifying the problem, determining its nature and causes, talking about possible ways to solve the problem, and selecting the best way (p. 177)

**process speech** an informative speech that explains how to do something, how to make something, or how something works; also called a *how-to speech* (p. 355)

**producer** the head administrator of a dramatic production, responsible for bringing together the script, the theater, the director, and, in the case of professional theater, the financing for a show (p. 609)

**progressive format** a type of private group discussion in which a large group of people is divided into smaller groups, each of which discusses a different aspect of the topic (p. 452)

**pronunciation** the combining of precisely articulated speech sounds into distinct words (p. 59; *also*, p. 328)

**proof** in debate, the reasons and evidence given to answer the questions in the stock issues (p. 490)

**propaganda** a form of persuasion that deliberately discourages people from thinking for themselves (p. 92)

**property crew head** the person responsible for collecting properties (or "props") and making them available during both rehearsals and performances (p. 612)

**proposition** in debate, a statement that asserts a fact, makes a value judgment, or recommends a policy (p. 480)

**propositions of fact** in debate, statements about what has happened, is happening, or will happen (p. 482)

**propositions of policy** in debate, statements that focus on specific plans of action (p. 483)

**propositions of value** in debate, statements that express judgments about the relative merit of a person, place, or thing (p. 483)

**prose** the normal form of written or spoken language; any type of speech or writing that is not poetry (p. 568)

**protagonist** the main character in a play (p. 598)

**psychological noise** the thoughts and feelings that distract people from listening to what is said (p. 17)

**public self** the aspects of a person that the person chooses to share with everyone (p. 124; *also*, p. 146)

**public service announcement (PSA)** a brief persuasive or informative message presented on radio and television (p. 647)

**public space** the distance, beyond twelve feet between speaker and audience, at which such types of communication as public speeches or oral readings take place (p. 44)

**public speaking** a formal speaking situation in which one person addresses an audience of many individuals to entertain, inform, or persuade them (p. 11)

**purpose** what a speaker intends to achieve in a speech (p. 220)

**quality** the tone of a person's voice (p. 67)

**question of belief** in persuasion, a statement that focuses on what is right or wrong, good or bad, best or worst, moral or immoral (p. 384)

**question of fact** in persuasion, a statement that focuses on what is either true or false (p. 384); a discussion question that asks for evidence that can be gathered from observation, experimentation, or authoritative sources to determine what is true (p. 455)

**question of policy** in persuasion, a statement that focuses on a particular action (p. 384); a discussion question that asks what action, if any, should be taken (p. 455)

**question of privilege** a privileged motion that calls for immediate action on such things as ventilation, heating, lighting, and disturbances (p. 528)

**question of value** a discussion question that asks for an evaluation of one or more persons, places, things, or ideas (p. 455)

**quorum** the minimum number of members that must be present for a group to conduct business (p. 522)

**quotation** a statement of someone's exact words (p. 233)

**R**

**radio drama** a radio presentation in which actors present an oral performance of a play or radio script (p. 629)

**radio talk show** a radio presentation in which a moderator and one or more guests discuss a topic (p. 629)

**random sample** a sample in which, in theory, every member of a group has an equal chance of being selected (p. 245)

**range** the spread between the lowest and the highest notes that a person can speak comfortably (p. 63)

**rate** the speed at which a person talks (p. 66) or reads a selection aloud (p. 567)

**reader's theater** a form of oral interpretation in which a group of people read and interpret a play (p. 580)

**reason** a statement that explains or justifies a speaker's thesis or proposition (p. 387; *also* p. 491)

**rebuttal** in debate, rebuilding an argument after it has been attacked (p. 498)

**rebuttal speech** in debate, the speech that rebuilds an argument (p. 481)

**receiver** the person who receives a message (p. 4)

**recess** a privileged motion that calls for a short break during a meeting (p. 528)

**recommendation** a short statement that tells an audience the specific behavior the speaker wants them to follow (p. 274)

**reconsider** a renewal motion that calls for discussion of a motion that has already been passed (p. 530)

**recorder** (See *secretary*.)

**reference works** publications containing useful facts and information (p. 250)

**refer to a committee** a subsidiary motion that calls for shifting discussion of the matter at hand to a smaller group meeting at some other time (p. 528)

**refutation** in debate, an attack on the argument of the opposition (p. 498)

**rehearsals** practice sessions (p. 607; *also*, p. 279)

**reliable source** a person who can be depended on to give accurate information (p. 200)

**renewal motions** in a parliamentary meeting, proposals that get discussion reopened on decisions that have already been made (p. 530)

**reopen nominations** an incidental motion made to allow more nominations to be made after nominations have been closed (p. 530)

**repetition** the use of the same word, phrase, or sentence each time a new point is raised (p. 84); for emphasis, saying something more than once (p. 300); the repeating of a sentence or a phrase that runs like a refrain throughout a speech (p. 422); repeated sounds (p. 573)

**request letter** a letter that asks for information about a topic (p. 246)

**rescind** a renewal motion that calls for the cancellation of action taken on a previous motion (p. 530)

**resolution** the sharpness of a video image, due to the number of picture cells, or pixels (p. 634)

**resonance** the reinforcement of sound produced by vibration (p. 56)

**resonators** the bones of the chest, neck, and head and the cavities of the throat, nose, and mouth, which reinforce sound (p. 56)

**respect** a feeling of high regard, honor, or esteem that a person has for others (p. 143)

**restatement** the repetition of an idea using different words (p. 300)

**résumé** a brief account of an applicant's educational background and employment experience (p. 189)

**rhetorical question** a question that is not meant to be answered but that is asked only for effect (p. 305)

**rhythm** a rise and fall of the voice created by the flow of stressed and unstressed syllables (p. 571)

**role** a pattern of behavior that characterizes a person in a given context or situation (p. 124)

**roll-call vote** a vote in which the secretary calls out each member's name and records his or her response (p. 540)

**round-table format** a type of private group discussion in which each member of a group discussion gives a brief report on some aspect of a topic and then the group as a whole discusses the separate reports (p. 452)

**sarcasm** cutting or bitter irony (p. 299)

**school interview** an interview in which an admissions officer interviews an applicant for schooling after high school graduation (p. 187)

**second** an indication that a person other than the person making a motion is willing to have the group consider the motion (p. 532)

**secondary amendment** an amendment of a primary amendment (p. 537)

**secondary source** someone or something that provides information that originated with other people (p. 200)

**secretary** also called a *recorder,* a member of a discussion group who records what happened in the discussion (p. 462); the major recording officer and keeper of records in a parliamentary organization (p. 525)

**self-actualization** the drive a person has to take full advantage of his or her talents and abilities (p. 119)

**self-concept** a collection of perceptions about every aspect of a person's being (p. 114)

**semantic noise** interference caused by words that trigger strong negative feelings against the speaker or the content of the speech (p. 18)

**sender** the person who sends a message (p. 4)

**sensory images** words and phrases that evoke mental pictures by appealing to the senses—sight, hearing, smell, taste, or touch (p. 574)

**sensory words** words that appeal to one or more of the five senses (p. 296)

**set designer** the person responsible for designing all visual elements, including stage sets and lighting, that will be used in a production (p. 610)

**signal words** words that indicate that a list, contrast, or connection is about to be made (p. 85)

**sign argument** an argument that draws a conclusion based on certain signs or indicators (p. 502)

**simile** a comparison of two essentially unlike things using the words *like* or *as* (p. 297)

**simple majority** a majority that consists of at least one more than half the number of people voting (p. 520)

**simple words** familiar words, usually of one or two syllables (p. 292)

**sincerity** the quality of being genuine (p. 394)

**slang** highly informal language that is formed by creating new words or giving common words new meanings (p. 308; *also,* p. 33)

**social call** a telephone call made for personal reasons (p. 162)

**social communication** a type of informal communication which is friendly, cordial, and enjoyable (p. 159)

**social space** the distance, from four to twelve feet, at which interviews and formal conversations occur (p. 43)

**sociological characteristics** a person's affiliations, educational background, and occupation (p. 14)

**sound bites** one- or two-second statements in broadcast news (p. 636)

**spatial order** a pattern of organization in which items are arranged according to their position in space (p. 268; *also,* p. 362)

**speaker** in fiction, the voice of a character or a role the author has assumed (p. 560)

**speaker's stand** a piece of furniture designed to hold a speaker's notes or manuscript (p. 332)

**special-occasion speech** a speech in which the occasion itself sets the tone and determines the content of the speech (p. 417)

**specific purpose** the specific goal of a speech, stated in a complete sentence (p. 221)

**specific words** words that identify items within a category (p. 294)

**speech of acceptance**   a speech in which the recipient of an honor, award, or gift expresses appreciation for the honor (p. 430)

**speech of introduction**   a formal speech for the purpose of gaining the audience's attention and setting the stage for the speaker or program that follows (p. 428)

**speech of presentation**   a speech given to present an honor, award, or gift and to honor the person being recognized (p. 429)

**stage fright**   the nervousness that speakers feel before and during the presentation of their speeches (p. 321)

**stage manager**   the person who is in charge of the entire backstage and attempts to ensure that the performance follows the exact pattern the director has set in rehearsals (p. 610)

**standard American English**   language that follows the rules and guidelines found in grammar and composition books (p. 33; *also*, p. 289)

**standing committee format**   a type of private group discussion in which a small group of people is asked to study problems that fall within their scope of duties or functions and then to make recommendations to the organization of which they are a part (p. 452)

**standing microphone**   a microphone attached to a stand or lectern (p. 333)

**startling statement**   in a speech introduction, a brief statement that surprises the audience and thus catches their attention (p. 272)

**statement-of-reasons method**   the classic deductive method for presenting information in which the thesis is stated directly, followed by reasons supporting it (p. 401)

**statistics**   numerical facts (p. 231)

**status quo**   the existing state of affairs (p. 481)

**step**   an abrupt change in pitch (p. 64)

**stereotype**   a biased belief about a whole group of people based on insufficient or irrelevant evidence (p. 94)

**stereotyping**   assigning characteristics to a person solely on the basis of the person's membership in a certain group (p. 129)

**stirring ending**   a speech conclusion that helps intensify the emotion, or feeling, that the speaker wants the audience to experience (p. 274)

**stock issues**   in debate, a formula of set questions that are adapted to a particular debate topic (p. 488)

**storyboard**   a layout that identifies the pictures, video, and audio cues that accompany the written script for a video production (p. 648)

**straight refutation**   in debate, a type of organization in which the entire negative case is a denial of each affirmative argument stated (p. 496)

**subject area**   a general category (p. 216)

**sublanguage**   a subsystem of an established language (p. 33)

**subsidiary motions**   in a parliamentary meeting, proposals that allow members to change or dispose of a main motion being discussed (p. 528)

**summary**   a short restatement of key information (p. 274)

**supporting details**   the examples, facts, statistics, reasons, anecdotes, or expert testimony that a speaker uses to back up main ideas (p. 85)

**survey**   a method of gathering information by questioning people selected at random or from a predetermined list (p. 244)

**suspend the rules**   an incidental motion that calls for suspension, during the current meeting, of any standing rule that the organization may have (p. 530)

**symbol**   something that stands for something else (p. 29)

**symposium format**   a type of public discussion in which several people present short, prepared speeches on the same topic and then discuss among themselves the ideas presented in the speeches (p. 451)

**system**   a group of elements that work together (p. 29)

**take from the table**   a renewal motion that calls for reopening discussion of a motion that had earlier been laid on the table by a subsidiary motion (p. 530)

**talent**   the television performers who appear on camera (p. 646)

**technical director**   the person in charge of constructing sets, positioning and operating lights, managing the curtain, and striking the set when the production is over (p. 610)

**technical quality**   in literature, refers to being well constructed (p. 558)

**telemarketing**   a sales method that uses telephone calls to sell services or products (p. 165)

**teleprompter**   a mechanical device that scrolls the script for a television performer to read (p. 646)

**television news story**   a television presentation in which a reporter or newscaster uses videotape to illustrate a current news event (p. 629)

**testimonials**   statements attesting to the worth of someone or something (p. 389)

**testimonial speech**   a commemorative speech that honors a living person (p. 432)

**theater of the absurd**   a contemporary style of drama in which life is viewed as meaningless and people's strivings as absurd (p. 593)

**thesis statement**   a complete sentence that expresses the speaker's most important idea, or key point, about a topic (p. 223)

**thespian**   an actor (p. 590)

**timing**   the controlled pacing of a speech (p. 341)

**tone**   the speaker's attitude or feeling toward a subject and an audience (p. 302; *also,* p. 419)

**topic**   a specific category within a subject area (p. 216)

**topicality**   in an extemporaneous speech competition, relating everything directly to the topic the speaker has chosen (p. 435)

**topical order**   a pattern of organization in which a topic is broken down into parts that are then arranged in an order determined by the speaker (p. 268; *also,* p. 362)

**trachea**   the windpipe (p. 54)

**traditional debate**   a debate format that involves two affirmative speakers and two negative speakers who argue a proposition of policy; also called *formal debate* (p. 485)

**tragedy**   drama that usually has a sad or disastrous ending and that tells a story of serious and important events in which the main character comes to an unhappy end (p. 593)

**transfer**   a propaganda method that builds a connection between things that are not logically connected (p. 93)

**transitional devices**   bridges between ideas (p. 275)

**trust**   a feeling that a person can rely on someone else (p. 142)

**understatement**   the opposite of exaggeration; the statement of an idea, an event, or a thing in terms that intentionally diminish or lessen its importance (p. 299)

**unity**   the organization of a speech so that all its parts fit together to make a whole and all of the information relates to the specific purpose (p. 270)

**universal appeal**   relevance, or relationship, to the experience of all human beings (p. 555)

**verbal language**   a system of spoken and written words (p. 28)

**verbal symbols**   words (p. 4)

**vertical file**   a collection of pamphlets, photographs, and clippings kept in vertical filing cabinets in some libraries (p. 255)

**vice-chairperson**   an officer of a parliamentary organization who assumes the duties of the chair when the chair is unable to do so (p. 525)

**video**   the section of a television script that describes the video footage and sound effects (p. 644)

**visual resources**   materials that an audience can see, such as slides, pictures, transparencies, videotapes, or films (p. 336)

**vividness**   the quality of being vigorous, exciting, or full of life (p. 296)

**vocal folds**   the muscles of the larynx; also called *vocal cords* (p. 54)

**vocalized pauses**   the meaningless speech sounds that speakers use to fill time (p. 327)

**voiced**   describes sounds made by vibrations of the vocal folds (p. 61)

**voiceless**   describes sounds made when the vocal folds are open so that air breathed out does not vibrate them (p. 61)

**voice mail**   an electronic system that provides the caller with a number of options from which to select, usually by using numbers on a touch-tone telephone pad (p. 166)

**voice-over**   a voice played without an accompanying picture of the speaker, usually over a film of some scene (p. 644)

**volume**   the intensity of sound (p. 65)

**vote**   a method for reaching a group decision in which the opinion held by the majority of the members of a group is adopted as the decision of the entire group (p. 468)

**withdraw a motion**   an incidental motion that gives the person who made the motion permission to remove it from consideration (p. 530)

**"you" message**   a statement that expresses a judgment of another person's actions (p. 178)

# INDEX

phrasing, 454
types of, 455
Dispute resolution, 152
Distractions, 342–43
hecklers, 343
Division of assembly, 529, 541
"Door in the Wall, The," 569
Douglas, Stephen A., 486
Downstage, 600–601
Drama, 11–12, 555, 589 (*See also* Theater.)
Drama, interpreting, 577–78 (*See also* Acting; Oral interpretation; Theater.)
characterization, 596–99, 617
condensing, 578
distinguishing characters, 577
physical action, 577
placement of characters, 601
"Dreams," 556
Dress rehearsal, 607
Dynamism of speaker, 395

Electronic communication, 12
Electronic media, 635
importance of critical viewing and listening, 636–37
values presented in, 636
Eliot, T. S., 624
Elizabethan drama, 592
Emerson, Ralph Waldo, 236, 284, 348
Emotion, 556–57
Emotional appeals, 392–93, 556–57
as propaganda technique, 95
Empathy, 141
Emphasis, 87, 300–301, 371, 567
announcement, 301
parallelism, 301
repetition, 300
restatement, 300
Encoding of information, 15–16
Encyclopedias, 251
Enthusiasm, of speaker, 327, 370
Enunciation, 328–29, 371
Environment, listening, 83
Environment, speaking, 41–44
color and, 41–42
lighting and, 41–42
sound and, 41–42
space and, 41–44
Epictetus, 584
Equipment, 332–35
lecterns, using, 332–33
microphones, using, 333–35

Ethical standards, 395–96
persuasion vs. manipulation, 396
Etiquette, 171
Eulogy, 432
Euphemisms, 308
Evaluating, listening and, 96–99
Evaluating group discussion, 470–71
focus on discussion, 470–71
focus on participation, 470
focus on quality, 471
Evidence (*See also* Reasoning.)
evaluating, 493
irrelevant, 493
note cards in gathering, 492
supporting, in debate, 492–93
Exaggeration, 298
in pantomime, 616
Examples as support, 230
Exhalation, 55
Experience, personal, as information source, 242–43
Expert opinions, 229, 390
Expository speech, 355
Expression, conflicting, 325 (*See also* Body language; Facial expression.)
Extemporaneous speech, 319, 434–35
Extraneous sounds, use of, 40
Eye contact, 36–37, 325 (*See also* Audience; Feedback.)
during speech, 325, 370
guidelines for, 325
impression created by, 325
in television, 646–47

Facial expression, 36–37, 325 (*See also* Nonverbal communication.)
conflicting expression, 325
deadpan, 325
Facts, 228, 390
as support, 228
opinions vs., 228–29
propositions of, in debate, 482
False analogies, 91
False consensus, 469
False premises, 91
*Familiar Quotations* (Bartlett's), 49
Faulty reasoning, 90–96
Favorable audience, 399
Feedback from audience, 342, 372–73, 406
audience inattention, 372
responding to, 372, 406
Feedback from others 4–6, 17, 342 (*See also* Nonverbal

communication; Paraphrasing.)
Feelings, in literature, 556–58
Fiction, 554 (*See also* Oral interpretation.)
Figurative comparison, 232
Figurative language, 296–99, 574
exaggeration, 298
imagery, 574
irony, 299
metaphor, 297–98
simile, 297–98
understatement, 299
vivid images, 296–97
Fixed-interval method, 245
Fletcher, Lucille, 640
Floor plan of stage, 611
Flow sheet for debate, 505–507
"Fog," 574
Following up an interview, 204–205
Follow-up questions, 175, 202
Forensics (*See* Debate.)
Formal communicating settings, 9–12
Formal outline for speech, 275–78
Formal tone, 420
Forum discussion format, 451
Free-form discussion format, 452
Fricatives, sound classification, 61
Friendships, 140
Fright, stage, 321–24
Frost, Robert, 586
Fuller, Thomas, 514

Galen, 312
Galsworthy, John, 593
Generalization, 90
hasty, 90
General purpose of speech, 220–21, 357, 384, 419
General words, 294
Generators of vocal sound, 54–56
diaphragm, 54
larynx, 54
trachea, 54
vocal folds (cords), 54–55
Germane amendments, 537
Gestures during speech, 36–37, 326, 575 (*See also* Body language; Nonverbal communication.)
naturalness of, 326
Getting started on your speech, 235
Glides, sound classification, 61
Goodwill, building audience's, 271
Graduation speech, preparation of, 427

Negative method, 404
Negative side, in debate, 480–81
    case of, 496–97
    choices of approach, 496–97
    counterplan, 497
    defense of status quo, 497
    goals of, 496
    straight refutation, 496
Nervousness, 321–24
Networks, radio and television, 630, 633
Neutral audience, 399
Newspaper articles, 252
*New York Times,* The, 48, 252
Nixon, Richard, 635
Noise, as interference, 17–18
    physical, 17
    psychological, 17–18
    semantic, 18
Noise, distracting, during speech, 342–43
Nonactors, in theater, 608–613
    business manager, 612
    costumer, 611
    director, 609–610
    house manager, 612
    makeup artist, 612
    producer, 609
    property crew head, 612
    set designer, 610–11
    stage manager, 610
    technical director, 610
Nondirective leadership, 459
Nonfiction, 554
Nonverbal behavior, improving, 324–26
    appearance, 324
    eye contact, 325
    facial expression, 325
    gestures, 326
    posture, 326
Nonverbal communication, 28, 36–45 (*See also* Appearance; Body language; Facial expression; Paralanguage; Personal space.)
    analyzing, 36–37
    and verbal communication, 40–41
    clues, 86
    contradiction, 87
    cues, 28, 36
    defined, 28
    effective use of, 44
    emphasis, 87
    functions of, 37
    importance of, 36
    pantomime as, 49
    skills, 19

    steps in, 45
    use of, 36–39, 45
Nonverbal symbols, 4–6
Nose, 58
Note cards, 256–57, 280, 492
Notes, use in speech rehearsal, 280–81
Note taking
    in debate, 505–507
    when observing, 243
Novello, Antonia, 671–677

## O

Objective discussion, 454
Observation, as information source, 243–44
    guidelines for, 243
    naming and describing, 243
    putting into words, 243
    recognizing differences, 243
    "seeing" vs. "looking," 243
    taking notes on, 243–44
Observation, using, in pantomime, 614
Occasion, knowing your, 226–27
    date and time, 227
    location, 227
    restrictions, 227
Occasion for oral reading, 558
*OED (Oxford English Dictionary),* 31
Officers of organizations, 524–26
    chairperson, 524–25
    secretary, 525
    vice-chairperson, 525
Olmos, Edward James, 50
Open vs. closed questions, 174, 202, 454
Opinions
    as support, 229
    expert, 229, 390
    facts vs., 229
Optimum pitch, 62
Oral cavity, 58
Oral critique, 97, 407–408
Oral interpretation, 553–87
    appropriateness for occasion, 558
    choosing material, 554–58
    guidelines for delivery, 566–68, 581
    interpreting drama, 577–79
    interpreting poetry, 571–76
    interpreting prose, 568–70
    introduction for, 564
    purpose of, 553
    speaker of, 560–61
    technical quality, 558

    understanding the selection, 558–63
Oral reading, 11–12
Order, 267–68, 359–64
    cause-and-effect, 363
    chronological, 267, 359–60
    climactic, 363
    comparison-and-contrast, 364
    spatial, 268, 362
    topical, 268, 362
Order of business, 523
Order of precedence, 531–32
Organization of a speech, 265–79, 400–405 (*See also* Informative speech; Persuasive speech; Process speech; Special-occasion speech.)
Organization of interview, 202
    beginning, 202
    end, 202
    middle, 202
Organization patterns, 267–69
Organizing information, 400–405
    deductive approach, 401–403
    inductive approach, 403–405
Others as information source, 200–201, 244–47
    interview, 201–203, 244
    request letter, 246–47
    survey, 244–46
*Our Town,* 581
Outline, 275–78
    of debate, 505–508
    of discussion, 456–58
Outline of a speech, formal, 275–78
    guidelines for, 276
    parallel language in, 276
    purposes of, 276
    rehearsal and, 276, 279–81
    sample of, 277–78
*Oxford English Dictionary (OED),* 31

## P

Pacing of material, 341
Panel discussion format, 451
Pantomime, 49, 613–16 (*See also* Body language, Informal theater.)
    detail and, 614
    exaggeration and, 616
    observation and, 614
    practice, 615
    sound effects in, 616
Paralanguage, 40–41 (*See also* Vocalized pauses; Vocal variation.)

# ACKNOWLEDGMENTS

For permission to reprint copyrighted material, grateful acknowledgment is made to the following sources:

**Cambridge University Press:** From "The Little Dog" from *Mountains and Molehills* by Frances Cornford. Published by Cambridge University Press, 1934.

**Ronald L. Dodson, Theater/Forensic Director, Westlake High School, Austin, Texas:** "The Green Mountain Boys," speech by W. Benson Chiles.

**Monica L. Haakonsen:** "The Half-Time Show" by Monica Seebohm.

**Harcourt Brace & Company:** From "The Jilting of Granny Weatherall" from *Flowering Judas and Other Stories* by Katherine Anne Porter. Copyright 1930 and renewed © 1958 by Katherine Anne Porter.

**The Heirs to the Estate of Martin Luther King, Jr., c/o Writers House, Inc., as agent for the proprietor:** "I Have a Dream" by Martin Luther King, Jr. Copyright © 1963 by Martin Luther King, Jr., copyright renewed © 1991 by Coretta Scott King.

**Alfred A. Knopf, Inc.:** "Dreams" from *The Dream Keeper and Other Poems* by Langston Hughes. Copyright 1932 by Alfred A. Knopf, Inc.; copyright renewed © 1960 by Langston Hughes.

**Melodie Lancaster:** "The Future We Predict Isn't Inevitable: Reframing Our Success in the Modern World" by Melodie Lancaster, delivered to the Symposium for the Houston Council, American Business Women's Association, Houston, Texas, February 29, 1992.

**National Forensics League:** "Fat Chance" by Jennifer Cober, Barbe High School, Lake Charles, Louisiana. "With Rest, You Get Noise" by Brian Eanes, Churchill High School, San Antonio, Texas.

**New Directions Publishing Corp.:** "Two Bodies" from *Selected Poems of Octavio Paz,* edited by Eliot Weinberger. Copyright © 1963, 1973 by Octavio Paz and Muriel Rukeyser.

**The Nobel Foundation:** "Nobel Peace Prize Speech of Acceptance" by Elie Wiesel. Copyright © 1986 by The Nobel Foundation.

**Leroy V. Quintana:** "Legacy II" by Leroy V. Quintana from *The Face of Poetry,* edited by L. H. Clark and Mary MacArthur. Copyright © 1979 by Leroy V. Quintana.

**Random House, Inc.:** From "Woman Work" from *And Still I Rise* by Maya Angelou. Copyright © 1978 by Maya Angelou. From *Antigone* by Jean Anouilh. Copyright © 1946 by Random House, Inc.; copyright renewed © 1974 by Lewis Galantiere. From "Scene II" from *The Diary of Anne Frank* by Albert Hackett and Frances Goodrich Hackett. Copyright © 1954, 1956 as an unpublished work; copyright © 1956 by Albert Hackett, Frances Goodrich Hackett and Otto Frank.

**Gary Soto and Bookstop Literary Agency:** From "The Jacket" from *Small Faces* by Gary Soto. Copyright © 1986 by Gary Soto. All rights reserved.

**The Literary Estate of May Swenson:** From "Ornamental Sketch with Verbs" from *To Mix with Time* by May Swenson. Copyright © 1955 and renewed © 1983 by May Swenson.

**U.S. News & World Report, Inc.:** From "The First Defect Is Among the Judges Themselves," interview with William G. Long, Superior Court Judge, King County (Seattle), Washington, from "How Much Crime Can America Take?," interviews with law-enforcement officials from *U.S. News & World Report,* April 20, 1964. Copyright © 1964 by U.S. News & World Report, Inc.

**The H. W. Wilson Company:** "Introduction of Gertrude Lawrence to the New York Advertising Club" by G. Lynn Sumner from *I Am Happy to Present: A Book of Introductions,* compiled by Guy R. Lyle and Kevin Guingah. Copyright © 1968 by The H. W. Wilson Company. Entries from "Moize, Elizabeth A." through "Molecular Beams" from *Readers' Guide to Periodical Literature,* 1990, p. 1238. Copyright © 1990 by The H. W. Wilson Company.

# PHOTO CREDITS

Abbreviations used: (t) top, (c) center, (b) bottom, (l) left, (r) right, (bckgrd) background

**COVER:** (tl), Ed Bock/The Stock Market; (tr-bckgd), Rene Sheret/Tony Stone Images; (tr)(bl)(br), Michelle Bridwell/HRW Photo; (bc), Peter Van Steen/HRW Photo

**TABLE OF CONTENTS:** iv(br), Robert Daemmrich/The Image Works; v(tr), Steve Satushek/The Image Bank; vi(tr), David E. Kennedy/TexaStock; vi(br), Michelle Bridwell/HRW Photo; vii(tr), James Sugar/Black Star; viii(tr), David Young-Wolff/PhotoEdit; viii(br), Michelle Bridwell/HRW Photo; ix(br), Jeffrey Sylvester/FPG International, Inc.; x(br), David R. Frazier Photolibrary; xi(br), David Young-Wolff/PhotoEdit; xii(cl), mga/Photri, Inc.; xii(br), Ells Herwig/The Picture Cube; xiii(br), Robert Daemmrich/Stock Boston; xiv(tr), Eric Beggs/HRW Photo; xiv(br), Michelle Bridwell/HRW Photo; xv(br), Robert Daemmrich/Stock Boston; xvi(cr), Mike Wilson/FPG International, Inc.; xvii(cr), Comstock/Comstock, Inc.; xviii(br), David E. Kennedy/TexaStock; xix(cr), mga/Photri, Inc.; xxi(bl), Garry Gay/The Image Bank; xxii(tr), Michelle Bridwell/HRW; xxii(bc), Paul Light/Lightwave

**UNIT 1 OPENER:** xxiv(tr), Michael Sullivan/TexaStock; xxiv(c), T. Rosenthal/SuperStock; xxiv(bl), Craig Tuttle/The Stock Market; xxiv-1(bc), Anthony Edgeworth/The Stock Market; 1(tc), Elizabeth Crews/Stock Boston; 1(c), Oscar Palmquist/Lightwave

**CHAPTER 1:** 2(c), Michelle Bridwell/HRW Photo; 3(cr), David Young-Wolff/PhotoEdit; 5(c), Daniel Schaefer/HRW Photo; 7(bl), Tony Freeman/PhotoEdit; 10(cr), Nita Winter/The Image Works; 10(b), Tony Freeman/PhotoEdit; 1(tc), Robert Daemmrich/The Image Works; 12(tc), Will and Deni McIntyre/Tony Stone Images/Allstock; 12(bl), Martin Miller/Positive Images; 15(tc), Lisa Law/The Image Works; 16(bl), David Young-Wolff/PhotoEdit; 16(br), Robert Kristofik/The Image Bank; 20(br), Michelle Bridwell/HRW Photo; 21(b), Robert E. Daemmrich/Tony Stone Images; 23(tr), David Young-Wolff/PhotoEdit; 23(cr), Michael Sullivan/TexaStock; 23(br), Miro Vintoniv/Stock Boston; 25(cl), Richard Hutchings/PhotoEdit; 25(br), Michelle Bridwell/HRW Photo

**CHAPTER 2:** 26(tl), Steve Satushek/The Image Bank; 26(tr), Michelle Bridwell/HRW Photo; 26(bl), Mary Kate Denny/PhotoEdit; 26(bl), Stock Editions/HRW Photo; 29(c), North Wind Picture Archives; 31(tr), Kevin Vandivier/HRW; 35(cr), Richard Hutchings/PhotoEdit; 38(br), Jane Sobel/The Image Bank; 39(bc), W.B. Spunbarg/PhotoEdit; 40(tc), Bob Daemmrich/The Image Works; 41(br), Arthur Grace/Stock Boston; 42(bc), MUG SHOTS/The Stock Market; 43(tc), /David R. Frazier Photolibrary; 43(bc), /David R. Frazier Photolibrary; 45(tl), Lawrence Migdale/Stock Boston; 45(cr), Richard Hutchings/Photo Researchers, Inc.; 46(br), Michelle Bridwell/HRW Photo; 47(bl), Spencer Grant/Stock Boston; 49(tr), Ralph Barrera/TexaStock; 49(cr), Laimute Druskis/Stock Boston; 49(br), Jim Pickerell/Stock Boston; 50(tr), Mitzi Trumbo/Shooting Star International; 50(cr), Kobal Collection/SuperStock; 50(bl), Warner Bros./Shooting Star International; 51(cl), Kevin Vandiver/HRW Photo; 51(br), Michelle Bridwell/HRW Photo

**CHAPTER 3:** 52(c), Sam Joosten/HBJ Photo; 52(bl), Russell Dian/HRW Photo; 55(cr), Gregg Mancuso/Tony Stone Images; 57(bl), Lee Boltin/HRW Photo; 57(bc), Ken Karp/HRW Photo; 57(br), Russell Dian/HRW Photo; 63(cr), Nathan Benn/Stock Boston; 65(cr), Barbara Davis/University of Texas Speech Dept.; 66(tc), Michael Beasley/Tony Stone Images; 67(bc), Charles Gupton/Stock Boston; 68(bl), /Shooting Star International; 69(c), Gerald Brimacombe/The Image Bank; 73(tl), David Kennedy/TexaStock; 73(tr), Colin Molyneaux/The Image Bank; 73(c), Alvis Upitis/The Image Bank; 74(cr), Michelle Bridwell/HRW; 75(bc), Richard Hutchings/Photo Researchers, Inc.; 77(bl), Daniel Schaefer/HRW Photo; 79(cl), Owen Franken/Stock Boston; 79(br), Michelle Bridwell/HRW Photo

**CHAPTER 4:** 80(tr), William Hubbell/HRW Photo; 80(c), Michael Sullivan/TexaStock; 80(bl), Russell Dian/HRW Photo; 80(br), Michelle Bridwell/HRW Photo; 82(bc), Michael Newman/PhotoEdit; 83(cr), Michael Weisbrot & Family; 86(cr), Loren Santon/Tony Stone Images; 89(tl), Tony Freeman/PhotoEdit; 90(tr), James Sugar/Black Star; 93(tc), Brian Vikander/Westlight; 95(bc), The Bettmann Archive; 97(tl), Jeffry Myers/FPG International; 99(tr), David Kennedy/TexaStock; 100(tr), Michelle Bridwell/HRW Photo; 101 (bc), Ron Sherman/Stock Boston; 105(cl), Bob Daemmrich/Stock Boston; 105(br), Michelle Bridwell/HRW Photo

**UNIT 2 OPENER:** 106(tl), Ulrike Welsch/Ulrike Welsch Photography; 106(tr), B. Hamil/HRW Photo; 106-107(bc), Joseph Nettis/Photo Researchers, Inc.; 106-107(bckgd), Donald C. Johnson/The Stock Market; 107(tr), Tom Campbell/FPG International; 107(br), Bob Daemmrich/The Image Works

**CHAPTER 5:** 108(tr), Michelle Bridwell/HRW Photo; 108(c), Daniel Schaefer/HRW Photo; 108(bl), Rodney Jones/HBJ Photo; 108(bc), George Obremski/The Image Bank; 109(cl), Daniel Schaefer/HRW Photo; 110(c), Richard Hutchings/PhotoEdit; 112(bc), Rhoda Sidney/PhotoEdit; 114(bc), Bob Daemmrich/Stock Boston; 116(tl), Tony Freeman/PhotoEdit; 122(tc), Tony Freeman/PhotoEdit; 125(br), Bob Daemmrich/Tony Stone Images; 128(tc), Matt Meadows/Matt Meadows Photography; 129(br), David Young-Wolff/PhotoEdit; 131(cl), Michael Newman/PhotoEdit; 132(tr), Kip Simons/Imagery; 133(bl), L.O.L. Inc./FPG International; 137(cl), David Koelsch/Outland; 137(cl), Lawrence Migdale; 137(br), R.W. Jones/Westlight

**CHAPTER 6:** 138(c), Richard Hutchings/PhotoEdit; 138(cr), Michelle Bridwell/HRW Photo; 138(bc), Chris Michaels/FPG International; 140(tc), Tony Stone Images; 142(bl), Bob Daemmrich/Stock Boston; 144(br), Michelle Bridwell/HRW Photo; 146(bc), Brent Jones/Stock Boston; 152(tr), Michelle Bridwell/HRW Photo; 153(bl), Mary Kate Denny/PhotoEdit; 155(tr), Richard Hutchings/PhotoEdit; 155(br), Rhoda Sidney/PhotoEdit; 157(cl), Frank Siteman/Stock Boston; 157(br), Michelle Bridwell/HRW Photo

**CHAPTER 7:** 158(tr), Michelle Bridwell/HRW Photo; 158(bl), Eric Beggs/HRW Photo; 158(bc), Dick Luria/FPG International; 161(bl), Mark Antman/The Image Works; 163(br), David Frazier Photolibrary; 165(tl), Mark Antman/The Image Works; 166(tr), Margot Granitsas/The Image Works; 170(bc), John Elk III/Stock Boston; 171(br), Ken Lax/HRW Photo; 173(bl), Comstock; 175(tr), Russell Dian/HRW Photo; 180(tr), Michelle Bridwell/HRW Photo; 181(bl), Jeff Isaac Greenberg/Photo Researchers, Inc.; 184(tl), Doug Wilson/The Stock Solution; 184(bl), Spencer Grant/Photo Researchers, Inc.; 185(cl), Daniel Schaefer/HRW Photo; 185(br), Michelle Bridwell/HRW Photo

**CHAPTER 8:** 186(tl), HRW Photo; 186(c), Michelle Bridwell/HRW Photo; 190(tr), Tony Freeman/PhotoEdit; 191(bl), Richard Pasley/Stock Boston; 192(t), Jeffrey Sylvester/FPG International; 194(cr), Elizabeth Crews/The Image Works; 198(c), P.R. Productions/SuperStock; 200(c), Tony Freeman/PhotoEdit; 205(c), Bonnie Kamin/Comstock; 206(tr), Michelle Bridwell/HRW Photo; 207(bl), Robert Daemmrich/Stock Boston; 207(br), Robert Daemmrich/Tony Stone Images; 209(tr), Bob Daemmrich/Stock Boston; 209(br), Al Satterwhite/The Image Bank; 211(tr), Jim Pickerell/Stock Boston; 211(br), Michelle Bridwell/HRW Photo

**UNIT 3 OPENER:** 212(tc), Richard Hutchings/PhotoEdit; 212(c), Richard Hutchings/PhotoEdit; 212(r), MUG SHOTS/The Stock Market; 213(tr), David R. Frazier Photolibrary; 213(br), Michael Sullivan/TexaStock

**CHAPTER 9:** 214(tl), Lisa Davis/HRW Photo; 214(c), Richard Hutchings/HRW Photo; 214(bl), Telegraph Colour Library/FPG International, Inc.; 216(cl), Rivera Collection/SuperStock; 220(cl), Bill Gallery/Stock Boston; 220(br), Smiley/TexaStock; 220(b), David Young-Wolff/PhotoEdit; 227(bc), Bob Daemmrich/Stock Boston; 228(bl), Kobal Collection/SuperStock; 229(bl), Michelle Bridwell/HRW Photo; 230(bl), Rick Stewart/AllSport USA; 231(tr), Albe Normandin/The Image Bank; 234(tr), Michelle Bridwell/HRW Photo; 235(bc), David R. Frazier Photolibrary; 237(tr), David Young-Wolff/PhotoEdit; 237(cr), Tony Freeman/PhotoEdit; 237(br), Bob Daemmrich/The Image Works; 239(cl), Comstock, Inc.; 239(br), Michelle Bridwell/HRW Photo;

**CHAPTER 10:** 240(cl), Russell Dian/HRW Photo; 240(c), Charles Gupton/Tony Stone Images; 240(bl), Eric Beggs/HRW Photo; 240(br), Rodney Jones/HRW Photo; 241(cr), Russell Dian/HRW Photo; 242(bc), Tony Freeman/PhotoEdit; 246(c), Marc Pokempner/Tony Stone Images; 248(b), Richard Pasley/Stock Boston; 250(tc), Elena Rooraid/PhotoEdit; 252(tc), David Young-Wolff/PhotoEdit; 252(bc), Daniel Schaefer/HRW Photo; 254(c), Derek Smith/The Image Bank; 258(tr), Michelle Bridwell/HRW Photo; 259(bl), Michael Melford/The Image Bank; 263(cl), David R. Frazier Photolibrary; 263(br), Michelle Bridwell/HRW Photo

**CHAPTER 11:** 264(cl), Ken Lax/Ken Lax Photography; 264(br), mga/Photri, Inc.; 270(br), Steve Kirwan/Steve Kirwan Photography; 271(c), Tony Freeman/PhotoEdit; 273(tl), Thomas R. Fletcher/Stock Boston; 273(tc), Daniel Schaefer/HRW; 273(tr), Daniel Schaefer/HRW; 279(br), Rhoda Sidney/Stock Boston; 282(tr), Photo Courtesy of Jim Bearden; 283(bl), Dion Ogust/The Image Works; 283(br), Steve Kirwan/Steve Kirwan Photography; 285(tr), SuperStock; 285(cl), Robert Brenner/PhotoEdit; 285(bl), Jack Fields/Photo Researchers, Inc.; 287(cl), Tony Freeman/PhotoEdit; 287(br), Michelle Bridwell/HRW Photo

**CHAPTER 12:** 288(c), Ken Lax/Ken Lax Photography; 288(tl), Russell Dian/HRW Photo; 288(bl), Cordon Art B.V., M.C. Escher's "METAMORPHOSE III (detail)" © 1997 Cordon Art Baarn-Holland. All rights reserved.; 288(br), Robert Fishman/HRW Photo; 290(bl), PhotoEdit; 297 (c), The Greenwich Workshop, Inc., Eagle's Flight by Bev Doolittle © 1982. The Greenwich Workshop, Inc., 1 Greenwich Place, Shelton, CT 06484.; 298 (bl), David R. Frazier Photolibrary; 302(cr), Dorothy Littell/The Image Works; 304(cl), David Pratt/Positive Images; 304(c), Ellis Herwig/The Picture Cube; 304(cr), Joseph Nettis/Photo Researchers, Inc.; 306(cr), Dennis Purse/Photo Researchers, Inc.; 310(tr), Michelle Bridwell/HRW; 311(bl), Alan Oddie/PhotoEdit; 313(l), HRW Photo; 315(cl), Will McIntyre/Photo Researchers, Inc.; 315(br), Michelle Bridwell/HRW Photo

**CHAPTER 13:** 316(tr), Russell Dian/HRW; 316(c), Michelle Bridwell/HRW Photo; 316(cl), Russell Dian/HRW Photo; 316(bl), Eric Beggs/HRW Photo; 318(br), Larry Kolvoord/TexaStock; 318(cr), Brian Seed/Tony Stone Images; 319(br), Frank Pedrick/The Image Works; 319(cr), Michelle Bridwell/HRW Photo; 325(c), Ron Sherman/Stock Boston; 326(c), Jeff Rowe/HRW Photo; 327(cr), P.R. Productions/SuperStock; 329(c), Skip Barron/Comstock; 332(br), Ron Sherman/Stock Boston; 333(br), Candace Cochrane/Positive Images; 334(tc), Smiley/TexaStock; 334(bc), Robert Dammerich/The Image Works; 336(tl), Yoav Levy/HRW Photo; 336(c), David R. Frazier Photolibrary; 337(c), Sam Dudgeon/HRW; 338, Sam Dudgeon/HRW; 341(cr), Michelle Bridwell/HRW Photo; 342(bc), Jeffry Meyer/FPG International; 343(bl), Culver Pictures, Inc.; 343(br), UPI/Bettmann, Inc.; 346(tr), Michelle Bridwell/HRW Photo; 347(bl), Michelle Bridwell/HRW Photo; 349(tr), Robert Houser/Comstock, Inc.; 349(cr),Terry Farmer/Tony Stone Images; 349(br), Boroff/TexaStock; 351(cl), Robert Daemmrich/Stock Boston; 351(br), Michelle Bridwell/HRW